CALIFORNIA CRIMINAL LAW

CASES, PROBLEMS, AND MATERIALS

Third Edition

■ ■ ■

John E.B. Myers
Visiting Professor of Law, University of California Hastings College of the Law
Professor of Law Emeritus, University of the Pacific-McGeorge School of Law

AMERICAN CASEBOOK SERIES®

444 Cedar Street, Suite 700
St. Paul, MN 55101
1-877-888-1330

Printed in the United States of America

ISBN: 978-1-64242-894-0

For Rowan

PREFACE

Criminal law is a subject that generates strong feelings. The specter of crime is ever-present. Although you don't think about it every day, you realize at some level that you, your loved ones, and you neighbors could be victimized by crime. Society depends on the criminal justice system to deter crime from happening and, when deterrence fails, to punish wrongdoers. Lawyers, judges, and law enforcement officers are the central actors in the effort to keep crime at bay. Perhaps your personal and professional goal is to join the ranks for prosecutors and criminal defense attorneys. If so, you are certain to enjoy the course on criminal law and, I hope, this book. Even if you are not interested in criminal law as a career, you understand the importance of the subject.

This book gives you detailed information on California criminal law. Although a casebook cannot cover every aspect of the subject—that takes volumes—this book provides a foundation. Importantly, the book prepares you for the California Bar Examination, including the Multistate Bar Examination. If you are planning to take the bar in another state, don't worry. California criminal law is sufficiently similar to the law in other states that you will be prepared for bar exam questions elsewhere.

I hope you find the material in this book interesting and provocative. Unfortunately, some of what you read is disturbing. I did not include material for "shock value." The truth is, however, that crime is often horrible, and there is no point sugarcoating it.

For those who want to pursue a career in criminal law, go out there the keep us safe. Protect victims. At the same time, work tirelessly for justice for the accused. Your law degree will give you tools to make a real difference for individuals, your community, and your country.

JOHN E.B. MYERS
Davis, California

July, 2019

Acknowledgments

I gratefully acknowledge receiving permission to reprint the following materials:

ABA Standards for Criminal Justice: Prosecution and Defense Function, 3rd ed. 1993. American Bar Association.

Angela J. Davis, Arbitrary Justice: The Power of the American Prosecutor. 2007. Oxford University Press.

California District Attorneys Association, Uniform Crime Charging Standards. 1996. California District Attorneys Association.

Linda E. Carter, Ellen S. Kreitzberg and Scott W. Howe, Understanding Capital Punishment Law, 4th ed. 2018. Lexis-Nexis.

ACKNOWLEDGMENTS

TRIBUTE

When I started teaching criminal law years ago, I learned from a master, Joshua Dressler. Professor Dressler is one of America's leading scholars on criminal law and criminal procedure. For a time, Joshua was a member of the faculty at Pacific-McGeorge, where I taught for 35 years. Joshua was always happy to guide me along. Until I decided to create a casebook focused on California law, I used Joshua's excellent casebook, Criminal Law (West). Anyone familiar with Joshua's book will quickly see his influence on this book. Indeed, Joshua's fingerprints are all over this book. Thank you Joshua for your inspiration and leadership. To the extent this book has strengths, much of the credit belongs to you.

SUMMARY OF CONTENTS

TABLE OF CONTENTS

TABLE OF CASES

The principal cases are in bold type.

CALIFORNIA CRIMINAL LAW

CASES, PROBLEMS, AND MATERIALS

Third Edition

CHAPTER 1

INTRODUCTION

■ ■ ■

Welcome to criminal law. Criminal law is divisible into three branches. First, the law of crimes and defenses, called substantive criminal law. Second, criminal procedure, covering the law of search and seizure, *Miranda* warnings, arrest, interrogation by police, lineups, and a host of related topics. These two branches—substantive criminal law and criminal procedure—are taught at every American law school, typically as separate courses. The third branch of criminal law is seldom addressed systematically in law school, although it is exceedingly important to prosecutors, defense attorneys, and judges. The third branch consists of the myriad laws, rules of court, and local practices that govern day-to-day practice of criminal law. For example, How do I draft a complaint, information, or indictment? Where do I file it? When is it due? What motions are filed and when? What happens at arraignment, preliminary hearing, trial, and appeal? The details of practicing criminal law are nearly limitless.

When do you learn the third branch of criminal law? Your criminal law and criminal procedure professors will touch on selected aspects of the third branch. If your law school has a criminal law clinic, the clinical experience exposes you to aspects of the third branch. Many second and third year law students work as clerks or interns in local prosecution or defense offices, and these students are immersed in the third branch. In the final analysis, you learn the third branch *after* law school, as part of your "on the job" training as a prosecutor or defense attorney.

The focus of this book is the first branch of criminal law, crimes and defenses. The second branch is your course on criminal procedure. As for the third branch, many students are keen to learn about the practice of criminal law—"the real world." For the most part, the real world will have to await the real world.

NOTE ON THE BAR EXAMINATION

Most readers of this book plan to take the California Bar Examination. Some readers, however, intend to take the bar elsewhere, and may wonder, "Will a book focused primarily on California criminal law prepare me to take the bar in another state?" This book is designed to give students the tools they need to pass criminal law questions on *any* state bar. Bar examinations—

including the California Bar and the Multistate Bar Examination—test general principles of criminal law, and this book covers the necessary general principles.

WHAT IS CRIME?

What is a crime?[1] Basically, a crime is whatever the Legislature says it is! California Penal Code § 15 states: "A crime or public offense is an act committed or omitted in violation of a law forbidding or commanding it, and to which is annexed, upon conviction, either of the following punishments: (1) Death; (2) Imprisonment; (3) Fine; (4) Removal from office; or, (5) Disqualification to hold and enjoy any office of honor, trust, or profit in this State."

In a famous law review article, Henry Hart grappled with the question: "What is a crime?"

HENRY M. HART, JR., THE AIMS OF THE CRIMINAL LAW

23 *Law and Contemporary Problems* 401–441 (1958)

In trying to formulate the aims of the criminal law, it is important to be aware both of the reasons for making the effort and of the nature of the problem it poses.

The statement has been made, as if in complaint, that "there is hardly a penal code that can be said to have a single basic principle running through it." But it needs to be clearly seen that this is simply a fact, and not a misfortune. A penal code that reflected only a single basic principle would be a very bad one. Social purposes can never be single or simple, or held unqualifiedly to the exclusion of all other social purposes; and an effort to make them so can result only in the sacrifice of other values which also are important.

Examination of the purposes commonly suggested for the criminal law will show that each of them is complex and that none may be thought of as wholly excluding the others. Suppose, for example, that the deterrence of offenses is taken to be the chief end. It will still be necessary to recognize that the rehabilitation of offenders, the disablement of offenders, the sharpening of the community's sense of right and wrong, and the satisfaction of the community's sense of just retribution may all serve this end by contributing to an ultimate reduction in the number of crimes. Even socialized vengeance may be accorded a marginal role, if it is understood as the provision of an orderly alternative to mob violence.

---

1 *See* Grant Lamond, What Is a Crime?, 27 *Oxford Journal of Legal Studies* 609 (2007).

The problem, accordingly, is one of the priority and relationship of purposes as well as of their legitimacy—of multivalued rather than of single-valued thinking.

What then are the characteristics of this method?

1. The method operates by means of a series of directions, or commands, formulated in general terms, telling people what they must or must not do. Mostly, the commands of the criminal law are "must-nots," or prohibitions, which can be satisfied by inaction. "Do not murder, rape, or rob." But some of them are "musts," or affirmative requirements, which can be satisfied only by taking a specifically, or relatively specifically, described kind of action. "Support your wife and children," and "File your income tax return."

2. The commands are taken as valid and binding upon all those who fall within their terms when the time comes for complying with them, whether or not they have been formulated in advance in a single authoritative set of words. They speak to members of the community, in other words, in the community's behalf, with all the power and prestige of the community behind them.

3. The commands are subject to one or more sanctions for disobedience which the community is prepared to enforce.

Thus far, it will be noticed, nothing has been said about the criminal law which is not true also of a large part of the noncriminal, or civil, law. The law of torts, the law of contracts, and almost every other branch of private law that can be mentioned operate, too, with general directions prohibiting or requiring described types of conduct, and the community's tribunals enforce these commands. What, then, is distinctive about the method of the criminal law?

Can crimes be distinguished from civil wrongs on the ground that they constitute injuries to society generally which society is interested in preventing? The difficulty is that society is interested also in the due fulfillment of contracts and the avoidance of traffic accidents and most of the other stuff of civil litigation. The civil law is framed and interpreted and enforced with a constant eye to these social interests. Does the distinction lie in the fact that proceedings to enforce the criminal law are instituted by public officials rather than private complaints? The difficulty is that public officers may also bring many kinds of "civil" enforcement actions—for an injunction, for the recovery of a "civil" penalty, or even for the detention of the defendant by public authority. Is the distinction, then, in the peculiar character of what is done to people who are adjudged to be criminals? The difficulty is that, with the possible exception of death, exactly the same kinds of unpleasant consequences, objectively considered, can be and are visited upon unsuccessful defendants in civil proceedings.

What distinguishes a criminal from a civil sanction and all that distinguishes it, it is ventured, is the judgment of community condemnation which accompanies and justifies its imposition. If this is what a "criminal" penalty is, then we can say readily enough what a "crime" is. It is not simply anything which a legislature chooses to call a "crime." It is not simply antisocial conduct which public officers are given a responsibility to suppress. It is not simply any conduct to which a legislature chooses to attach a "criminal" penalty. It is conduct which, if duly shown to have taken place, will incur a formal and solemn pronouncement of the moral condemnation of the community.

At least under existing law, there is a vital difference between the situation of a patient who has been committed to a mental hospital and the situation of an inmate of a state penitentiary. The core of the difference is precisely that the patient has not incurred the moral condemnation of his community, whereas the convict has.

California law recognizes three levels of crime: felonies, misdemeanors, and infractions (Penal Code (PC) § 16). "A felony is a crime which is punishable with death, by imprisonment in the state prison, or [under certain circumstances], by imprisonment in a county jail." (PC § 17(a)).[2] Crimes that are not felonies are misdemeanors or infractions.[3] Some crimes can be charged as felonies or misdemeanors, and are called "wobblers."[4] An infraction cannot be punished by imprisonment.

The State Legislature can enact felonies, misdemeanors, and infractions. Local governments—cities and counties—have authority to enact misdemeanors and infractions, so long as the local laws (called ordinances) are not inconsistent with state law. In *People v. Nguyen* (2014) 222 Cal. App. 4th 1168, 116 Cal. Rptr. 3d 590, the City of Irvine passed an ordinance making it a misdemeanor for a convicted sex offender to enter a city park without permission from the police chief. Nguyen entered a park

---

[2] In 2011, the California Legislature passed the Realignment Act. "As a result of the Realignment Act, numerous offenses previously punishable by specified terms in state prison are now punishable by serving that same term in local custody at the county jail." *People v. Vega* (2014) 222 Cal. App. 4th 1374, 166 Cal. Rptr. 3d 506.

[3] PC § 17(a) defines "felony," and then states, "Every other crime or public offense is a misdemeanor except those offenses that are classified as infractions."

[4] *See Ewing v. California* (2003) 538 U.S. 11, 16, 123 S.Ct. 1179, where the Supreme Court described "wobbler" offenses: "Under California law, certain offenses may be classified as either felonies or misdemeanors. These crimes are known as 'wobblers.' Some crimes that would otherwise be misdemeanors become 'wobblers' because of the defendant's prior record. For example, petty theft, a misdemeanor, becomes a 'wobbler' when the defendant has previously served a prison term for committing specified theft-related crimes. In California, prosecutors may exercise their discretion to charge a 'wobbler' as either a felony or a misdemeanor."

In *People v. Moomey* (2011) 194 Cal.App.4th 850, 123 Cal.Rptr.3d 749, the Court of Appeal stated, "When a defendant is convicted of a wobbler offense, the offense is deemed a felony, unless it is subsequently reduced to a misdemeanor by the sentencing judge."

without the necessary permission, and was charged under the ordinance. Nguyen demurred to the charge, arguing that the *state* statutory scheme imposing restrictions of sex offenders occupied the field and preempted the *local* ordinance. The Court of Appeal agreed, writing, "Under article XI, section 7 of the California Constitution, 'a county or city may make and enforce within its limits all local, police, sanitary, and other ordinances and regulations not in conflict with general [state] laws.' If otherwise valid local legislation conflicts with state law, it is preempted by such law and is void. A conflict exists if the local legislation duplicates, contradicts, or enters an area fully occupied by general law, either expressly or by legislative implication." The Court of Appeal ruled that state laws governing sex offenders occupy the field, preempting the Irvine ordinance.

Some crimes have remained largely unchanged for centuries. Thus, today's definition of murder is very similar to the definition of the 1600s. Other crimes come and go with changes in societal attitudes. For example, the 1873 California Penal Code contained the following provision, called a "blue law": "Every person who keeps open on Sunday any store, workshop, bar, saloon, banking house, or other place of business, for the purpose of transacting business therein, is punishable by fine not less than five nor more than fifty dollars." At an earlier day, adultery—"criminal conversation"—was a crime in California. The law relating to homosexual sexuality has changed dramatically. William Eskridge describes California's changing legal response:[5] "The legislature in 1850 criminalized 'the infamous crime against nature.' The California legislature in 1915 added to the penal code's list of serious felonies 'fellatio' and 'cunnilingus'. In 1952, Governor Warren signed a law eliminating the maximum sentence for consensual sodomy, thereby making it a potential life sentence. The maximum penalty for consensual oral sex was fifteen years in prison. In California, as in nearly all other states, 'gross immorality' was a statutory basis for disciplinary action against a host of licensed professionals, including lawyers. During this period of antihomosexual terror, California law presented homosexuals as presumptive outlaws and enemies of the family. According to the State, these people were depraved subhumans who were incapable of human relationships and ruled by uncontrolled sexual urges and animal desires." Today, the law is dramatically different. In 2003, the U.S. Supreme Court ruled unconstitutional a Texas statute criminalizing consensual sodomy. *Lawrence v. Texas* (2003) 539 U.S. 558, 123 S. Ct. 2472. In 2015, the U.S. Supreme Court, in *Obergefell v. Hodges* (2015) 135 S. Ct. 2584 ruled same-sex marriage legal.

---

[5] William N. Eskridge, The Marriage Cases—Reversing the Burden of Inertia in a Pluralistic Constitutional Democracy, 97 *California Law Review* 1785 (2009).

CALIFORNIA PENAL CODE—NO COMMON LAW CRIMES

American criminal law grew out of English law developed centuries ago. Early English criminal was common law, that is, judge made law. When the United States gained independence from England, states adopted and slowly "Americanized" English common law. In the nineteenth century, there was a movement in the United States toward codification of criminal law. That is, legislatures took over from courts the responsibility for defining crime and punishment. California joined this trend, and California's first penal law—the Crimes and Punishments Act—was enacted in 1850.[6] In 1872, the Legislature adopted the California Penal Code, which went into effect January 1, 1873. The California Penal Code you study in this course, and that you will use in practice, is a direct descendent of the 1873 Code. Indeed, many provisions of today's Penal Code have not changed since 1873.

Today, all crimes in California are legislative. Stated another way, there are no common law crimes in California.[7] Similarly, there are no federal common law crimes.[8] All federal crimes are statutory. Although all crimes—state and federal—are created by the legislature, the courts interpret and apply the substantive criminal law.

LIMITS ON LEGISLATIVE POWER TO DEFINE CRIME AND PUNISHMENT

The power of the California Legislature to define crime and prescribe punishment is broad, emanating from the state's "police power," which is the authority of the state to protect the health, welfare, safety, and morals of the people. Although broad, the power of the Legislature is not unlimited. The U.S. and California Constitutions limit the power of the Legislature to create crimes and punishments. The principle constitutional limitations are explained below.

Ex Post Facto Laws

Article I, Section 9 of the U.S. Constitution provides, "No ex post facto Law shall be passed." The California Constitution is to the same effect (Cal. Const. Art. I, § 9). An ex post facto law is a law that (1) punishes behavior that was not a crime when it was committed; (2) retroactively increases the punishment for a crime; (3) retroactively deprives an accused of a defense

---

[6] Statutes 1850, chapter 99.

[7] *See People v. Sarun Chun* (2009) 45 Cal.4th 1172, 1183, 91 Cal.Rptr.3d 106, 203 P.3d 425, "The power to define crimes and fix penalties is vested exclusively in the legislative branch. There are no nonstatutory crimes in this state."

[8] *Dixon v. United States* (2006) 548 U.S. 1, 12, 126 S.Ct. 2437 ("federal crimes are solely creatures of statute").

that was available under the law when a crime was committed; or (4) retroactively changes the evidence required to convict. *See Beazell v. Ohio* (1924) 269 U.S. 167, 169–170, 46 S.Ct. 68; *Calder v. Bull* (1798) 3 U.S. (Dall.) 386; *John L. v. Superior Court* (2004) 33 Cal.4th 158, 14 Cal.Rptr.3d 261, 91 P.3d 205; *In re Robert M.* (2013), 215 Cal. App. 4th 1178, 155 Cal. Rptr. 3d 795.

Bill of Attainder

A bill of attainder is a law that punishes a person without affording the person a trial. *See United States v. Lovett* (1946) 328 U.S. 303, 66 S.Ct. 1073. The Supreme Court of Nebraska explained in *In re A.M.* (2011) 281 Neb. 482, 797 N.W.2d 233, 253, "The prohibition against bills of attainder prohibits trials by the legislature, and it forbids the imposition of punishment by the legislature on specific persons. A bill of attainder is a legislative act that applies to named individuals or to easily ascertained members of a group in a way that inflicts punishment on them without a judicial trial. [The prohibition against bills of attainder] is an implementation of the separation of powers, a general safeguard against legislative exercise of the judicial function, or more simply—trial by legislature. The prohibition on bills of attainder proscribes legislation that singles out disfavored persons and carries out summary punishment for past conduct. To constitute a bill of attainder, the law must (1) specify the affected persons, (2) inflict punishment, and (3) lack a judicial trial."

Although a Westlaw search for "bill of attainder" yields more than 3,000 hits, a true bill of attainder is rare. Now and again, a misguided lawmaker offers such a bill, but someone in the legislative process spots it for what it is, ensuring that the bill does not become law. Most litigation raising the issue of a claimed bill of attainder is civil rather than criminal, and most such claims fail.[9] For example, the Law School Admission Council (LSAC) is the sponsor of your old friend the LSAT. In *Law School Admission Council, Inc. v. State* (2014) 222 Cal. App. 4th 1265, 166 Cal. Rptr. 3d 647, LSAC sued the State of California over a statute requiring LSAC to make certain accommodations for disabled students taking the LSAT. Among other things, LSAC claimed the statute was a bill of attainder. The Court of Appeal quickly disposed of this claim because the statute did not impose punishment on LSAC. In *Westmoreland v. Chapman* (1968) 268 Cal. App. 3d 1, 5, 74 Cal. Rptr. 363, California Highway Patrol (CHP) officers arrested Westmoreland for drunk driving. A CHP officer

[9] *See Little v. City of North Miami* (1986) 805 F.2d 962 (11th Cir.)(law professor at the University of Florida represented Florida Defenders of the Environment in civil actions against city of North Miami. The professor did not charge for his services. Unhappy with the professor's activity, the City Council passed a resolution censuring the professor and accusing him of improperly using public funds. The resolution was read aloud in a public meeting and sent to the professor's employer and other officials. The professor sued the city, claiming, *inter alia*, that the resolution was a bill of attainder. He lost on that score because the resolution was not a law).

requested that Westmoreland submit to a blood alcohol test, and informed him that if he refused, his driver's license would be suspended. Westmoreland refused the test, and his license was suspended under the so-called "implied consent" law. Westmoreland sued, claiming the implied consent law was a bill of attainder. He lost. The Court of Appeal wrote, "Petitioner's next contention, that section 13353 constitutes a bill of attainder is difficult to comprehend. A bill of attainder is a legislative act which inflicts punishment upon a designated person, or easily ascertainable members of a group, for an alleged crime without a trial. Under the foregoing definition, it is obvious that the implied consent law does not constitute a bill of attainder. The law does not apply to a certain individual nor to a narrowly-defined group, but to all licensed drivers. Secondly, the suspension of a license is civil in nature, and does not constitute punishment for a crime." In *Perez v. County of Monterey* (2019) 32 Cal. App. 5th 257, 243 Cal. Rptr. 3d 683, residents of Monterey County challenged the constitutionality of an ordinance that prohibited most people from keeping more than four roosters on their property. Rejecting the argument that the ordinance was a bill of attainder, the Court of Appeal wrote, "[The ordinance] does not single out a person or group for punishment . . . ."

Constitutional Vagueness

Under the Due Process Clause of the 14th Amendment to the U.S. Constitution, a criminal law must be sufficiently clear that persons of ordinary intelligence can understand what the law prohibits and govern their behavior accordingly.[10] The U.S. Supreme Court wrote in *Connally v. General Construction Co.* (1926) 269 U.S. 385, 391, 46 S.Ct. 126, "That the terms of a penal statute creating a new offense must be sufficiently explicit to inform those who are subject to it what conduct on their part will render them liable to its penalties, is a well-recognized requirement, consonant alike with ordinary notions of fair play and the settled rules of law." In *Kolender v. Lawson* (1983) 461 U.S. 352, 357–358, 103 S.Ct. 1855, the Court explained: "As generally stated, the void-for-vagueness doctrine requires that a penal statute define the criminal offense with sufficient definiteness that ordinary people can understand what conduct is prohibited and in a manner that does not encourage arbitrary and discriminatory enforcement. Although the doctrine focuses both on actual notice to citizens and arbitrary enforcement, we have recognized recently that the more important aspect of vagueness doctrine is not actual notice, but the other principal element of the doctrine—the requirement that a legislature establish minimal guidelines to govern law enforcement. Where the legislature fails to provide such minimal guidelines, a criminal statute

[10] *See People v. Castillolopez,* 225 Cal. App. 4th 638 (2014).

may permit a standardless sweep that allows policemen, prosecutors, and juries to pursue their personal predilections."

The following "vagrancy" statute was part of the 1873 California Penal Code. Is the statute constitutional? Can a person of ordinary intelligence reading the statute tell what conduct is prohibited? Does the statute invite arbitrary and perhaps discriminatory enforcement?

> Every person (except a California Indian) without visible means of living, who has the physical ability to work, and who does not for the space of ten days seek employment, nor labor when employment is offered him; every healthy beggar who solicits alms as a business; every person who roams about from place to place without any lawful business; every idle or dissolute person, or associate of known thieves, who wanders about the streets at late or unusual hours of the night, or who lodges in any barn, shed, shop, out-house, vessel, or place other than such as is kept for lodging purposes, without the permission of the owner or party entitled to the possession thereof; every lewd and dissolute person, who lives in and about houses of ill-fame, and every common prostitute and common drunkard, is a vagrant, and punishable by imprisonment in the County Jail not exceeding ninety days.

Compare the 1873 vagrancy statute with today's Sacramento County loitering ordinance, produced below. Is the Sacramento ordinance an improvement? Does it stand up to constitutional scrutiny?

Sacramento County Code § 9.82.010 defines loitering as "remaining idle in essentially one location or moving about aimlessly." Section 9.82.020 states: "No person shall loiter in such a manner as to: (a) Create or cause to be created a danger of a breach of the peace. (b) Create or cause to be created any disturbance or annoyance to the comfort and repose of any person." Section 9.82.030 provides: "Whenever any peace officer shall, in the exercise of reasonable judgment, decide that the presence of any person in any public or private place is causing or is likely to cause any of the conditions enumerated in Section 9.82.020, he or she may, if he or she deems it necessary for the preservation of the public peace and safety, cite that person for violation of this chapter." Section 9.82.050 states: "The first violation of Section 9.82.020 shall constitute an infraction. Any subsequent violation of Section 9.82.020, or a refusal to leave the premises after having been cited by any peace officer for a violation of Section 9.82.020, shall constitute a misdemeanor."

In *Papachristou v. City of Jacksonville* (1972) 405 U.S. 156, 92 S.Ct. 839, the Supreme Court struck down a Florida vagrancy ordinance quite similar to California's early vagrancy ordinance, quoted earlier. Among other things, the Florida ordinance banned "wandering or strolling around from place to place without any lawful purpose or object." Writing for the Supreme Court, Justice Douglas extolled the virtues of wandering and strolling, citing Walt Whitman's poem, "Song of the Open Road" in which Whitman wrote, "Afoot and light-hearted I take to the open road, Healthy, free, the world before me, The long brown path before me leading wherever I choose. Henceforth I ask not good-fortune, I myself am good-fortune, Henceforth I whimper no more, postpone no more, need nothing, Done with indoor complaints, libraries, querulous criticisms, Strong and content I travel the open road."

Cruel and Unusual Punishments

The Eighth Amendment to the U.S. Constitution provides: "Excessive bail shall not be required, or excessive fines imposed, nor cruel and unusual punishments inflicted." Article I, § 17 of the California Constitution is similar. The prohibition on cruel and unusual punishments is addressed in Chapter 11.

Equal Protection

The Fourteenth Amendment to the U.S. Constitution provides that no state shall "deny to any person within its jurisdiction the equal protection of the laws." In unusual cases, a criminal statute offends principles of equal protection.[11] For example, during the nineteenth century, and for much of the twentieth century, most states, including California, prohibited interracial marriage. These criminal laws were called anti-miscegenation laws. The California Supreme Court struck down California's anti-miscegenation law in *Perez v. Sharp* (1948) 32 Cal.2d 711, 198 P.2d 17. The U.S. Supreme Court followed suit in *Loving v. Virginia* (1967) 388 U.S. 1, 87 S.Ct. 1817. Both courts relied in part on principles of equal protection.

CRIME REPORTS, INVESTIGATION, ARREST, AND BOOKING

Crime is reported through calls to 911, citizens flagging down passing police officers, and police officers observing crimes in progress. When a report is received, law enforcement decides whether to investigate. Some investigations lead nowhere. Others result in the arrest of one or more suspects. When police arrest a person, they typically book the individual into jail. With minor offenses—*e.g.*, infractions—the officer may issue a citation rather than place the suspect under arrest.

[11] *See People v. Tirey* (2014) 225 Cal. App. 4th 1150, 170 Cal. Rptr. 3d 795.

PROFESSIONAL ROLES—PROSECUTION AND DEFENSE

Prosecutors and defense attorneys are key players in the criminal justice system. Like all attorneys, prosecutors and defenders are members of the bar and are subject to the ethical duties of attorneys. In addition, their functions in the criminal justice system impose unique responsibilities on prosecutors and defenders. The American Bar Association (2015) *Standards for Criminal Justice: Prosecution and Defense Function* explain:

Prosecution Function

Standard 3–1.2—The Function of the Prosecutor

(a) The prosecutor is an administrator of justice, a zealous advocate, and an officer of the court. The prosecutor's office should exercise sound discretion and independent performance of the prosecution function.

(b) The primary duty of the prosecutor is to seek justice within the bounds of the law, not merely to convict. The prosecutor serves the public interest and should act with integrity and balanced judgment to increase public safety both by pursuing appropriate criminal charges of appropriate severity, and by exercising discretion to not pursue criminal charges in appropriate circumstances. The prosecutor should seek to protect the innocent and convict the guilty, consider the interests of victims and witnesses, and respect the constitutional and legal rights of all persons, including suspects and defendants.

* * *

(f) The prosecutor is not merely a case-processor but also a problem-solver responsible for considering broad goals of the criminal justice system.

Standard 3–1.3—The Client of the Prosecutor

The prosecutor generally serves the public and not any particular government agency, law enforcement officer or unit, witness or victim.

Defense Function

Standard 4–1.2—Functions and Duties of Defense Counsel

(a) Defense counsel is essential to the administration of criminal justice. A court properly constituted to hear a criminal case should be viewed as an entity consisting of the court (including judge, jury, and other court personnel, where appropriate), counsel for the prosecution, and counsel for the defense.

(b) Defense counsel have the difficult task of serving as officers of the court and as loyal and zealous advocates for their clients. The primary duties that defense counsel owe to their client, to the administration of justice, and as officers of the court, are to serve as their clients' counselor and advocate with courage and devotion; to ensure that constitutional and other legal rights of their clients are protected; and to render effective, high-quality legal representation with integrity.

PROSECUTORIAL DISCRETION

Prosecutors have broad discretion to decide whom to charge with what crime(s). Henry Hart observed, "The breadth of discretion we entrust to the police and prosecuting attorneys in dealing with individuals is far greater than that entrusted to any other kinds of officials and less subject to effective control."[12] In *People v. Valli* (2010) 187 Cal.App.4th 786, 801, 114 Cal.Rptr.3d 335, the Court of Appeal observed, "The decision as to appropriate charges is a matter of prosecutorial discretion. Prosecutorial discretion is basic to the framework of the California criminal justice system. This discretion, though recognized by statute in California, is founded upon constitutional principles of separation of powers and due process of law."

In her book, *Arbitrary Justice: The Power of the American Prosecutor* (2007) (Oxford University Press), Angela Davis analyzes the pros and cons of prosecutorial discretion.

ANGELA DAVIS, ARBITRARY JUSTICE: THE POWER OF THE AMERICAN PROSECUTOR

Delma Banks was convicted of capital murder in Texas and sentenced to death. Just ten minutes before he was scheduled to die, the United States Supreme Court stopped his execution and a year later reversed his sentence. The Court found that the prosecutors in his case withheld crucial exculpatory evidence.

Dwayne Washington was charged with assault with intent to kill and armed burglary in the juvenile court of Washington, D.C. Two adults were arrested with Dwayne and prosecuted in adult court. The prosecutors in the adult cases threatened to charge Dwayne as an adult if he refused to testify against the adults. When Dwayne said he could not testify against them because he didn't know anything about the crime, the prosecutors

---

[12] Henry M. Hart, The Aims of the Criminal Law, 23 *Law and Contemporary Problems* 401–444 (1958).

charged him as an adult, and he faced charges that carried a maximum sentence of life in an adult prison.

Andrew Klepper lived in Montgomery County, a suburb of Washington, D.C. He was arrested for attacking a woman with a baseball bat, sodomizing her at knifepoint with the same bat, and stealing over $2,000 from her. The prosecutors in his case agreed to a plea bargain in which Andrew would plead guilty to reduced charges. As part of the agreement, Andrew would be placed on probation and sent to an out-of-state facility for severely troubled youth, where he would be in a locked facility for six to eight weeks, followed by intensive group therapy in an outdoor setting. Andrew's parents—a lawyer and a school guidance counselor—agreed to foot the bill. Andrew's two accomplices—whose involvement in the crime was much less serious than Andrew's—each served time in jail. . . .

Prosecutorial discretion is essential to the operation of our criminal justice system, despite the potential for abuse. . . .

The lack of enforceable standards and effective accountability to the public has resulted in decision-making that often appears arbitrary, especially during the critical charging and plea bargaining stages of the process. These decisions result in tremendous disparities among similarly situated people, sometimes along race and/or class lines. The rich and white, if they are charged at all, are less likely to go to prison than the poor and black or brown—even when the evidence of criminal behavior is equally present or absent. Although prosecutors certainly are not the only criminal justice officials whose discretionary decisions contribute to unfair disparities, their decisions carry greater consequences and are most difficult to challenge.

VINDICTIVE PROSECUTION

What if a prosecutor increases charges against a defendant, or begins another prosecution against that defendant, in retaliation for the defendant's exercise of a constitutional right? In this circumstance, the defendant can claim "vindictive prosecution." In *People v. Valli* (2010) 187 Cal.App.4th 786, 802, 114 Cal.Rptr.3d 335, the Court of Appeal explained:

> The gravamen of a vindictive prosecution is the increase in charges or a new prosecution brought in retaliation for the exercise of constitutional rights. It is patently unconstitutional to chill the assertion of constitutional rights by penalizing those who choose to exercise them.
>
> Where the defendant shows that the prosecution has increased the charges in apparent response to the defendant's exercise of a procedural right, the defendant has made an initial

> showing of an appearance of vindictiveness. Once the presumption of vindictiveness is raised the prosecution bears a heavy burden of rebutting the presumption with an explanation that adequately eliminates actual vindictiveness. In this regard, the trial court should consider the prosecutor's explanation in light of the total circumstances of the case in deciding whether the presumption has been rebutted.

In *People v. Ledesma* (2006) 39 Cal.4th 641, 47 Cal.Rptr.3d 326, 140 P.3d 657, the Supreme Court wrote that an inference of vindictive prosecution is raised when a convicted defendant exercises the right to appeal the conviction, the conviction is reversed, and, on re-trial, the prosecutor increases the charges, exposing defendant to harsher punishment.

DISCRIMINATORY PROSECUTION

It is unconstitutional for a prosecutor to charge someone on the basis of deliberate invidious discrimination. *People v. Montes* (2014) 58 Cal. 4th 809, 320 P.3d 729, 169 Cal. Rptr. 3d 279. In *Montes,* the Supreme Court wrote, "A prosecutor's discretion to prosecute is constrained by federal principles of equal protection and may not be based on an unjustifiable standard such as race, religion, or other arbitrary classification."

OVERCHARGING

The authority to charge crime is an enormous responsibility that most prosecutors exercise appropriately. Yet, some prosecutors overcharge. In a concurring opinion in *People v. Valli* (2010) 187 Cal.App.4th 786, 806, 114 Cal.Rptr.3d 335, Justice Raye explained:

> It has been a common complaint for many decades that some prosecutors overcharge defendants. One view is that overcharging constitutes harassment designed to make plea proposals coercive by putting undue pressures on defendants to plead guilty to some offense or offenses rather than risk going to trial on numerous charges. Another view is that such overcharging purportedly gives the prosecutor a psychological advantage if a jury is presented with a long list of charges to consider, which makes the defendant look guiltier and provides subconscious pressure on jurors to find the defendant guilty of at least one or two charges.

CHARGING DOCUMENTS IN CRIMINAL CASES

In California there are four accusatory pleadings that commence criminal cases: indictment, complaint, information, and citation. All felonies are prosecuted by indictment or information (PC § 737).

Prosecution by information begins when a prosecutor files a complaint. The complaint is followed by an arraignment (PC § 976(a)). In turn, the arraignment is followed by a preliminary hearing. If the magistrate at the preliminary hearing decides there is enough evidence to require the defendant to stand trial, the complaint is replaced with an information.[13]

Below is a slightly modified version of a complaint filed in Sacramento Superior Court in 2011 against a businessman who was accused of surreptitiously video recording himself having sex with prostitutes.

JAN SCULLY
DISTRICT ATTORNEY
901 G STREET
SACRAMENTO, CA 95814
(916) 874-6218

SUPERIOR COURT OF CALIFORNIA
COUNTY OF SACRAMENTO

THE PEOPLE OF THE STATE OF)
)
vs.)
)
M ___ L ___.,)
)
Defendant.)

The People of the State of California, upon oath of the undersigned, upon information and belief, complain against the defendant above named for the crimes as follows:

COUNT ONE

On or about and between February 01, 2009, and May 01, 2009, at and in the County of Sacramento, State of California, defendant(s) M ___ L ___ did commit a felony namely: a violation of Section 632(a) of the Penal Code of the State of California, in that said defendant did intentionally and without the consent of all parties to a confidential communication, by means of an electronic amplifying and recording device, eavesdrop and record the confidential communication between himself and JANE DOE #1.

[13] When the word "magistrate" appears, the judicial officer involved is a Superior Court judge fulfilling the role of magistrate.

COUNT TWO

For a further and separate cause of action, being a different offense of the same class of crimes and offenses and connected in its commission with the charges set forth in Count One hereof: On or about and between December 01, 2008, and March 01, 2009, at and in the County of Sacramento, State of California, defendant M ___ L ___ did commit a felony namely: a violation of Section 632(a) of the Penal Code of the State of California, in that said defendant did intentionally and without the consent of all parties to a confidential communication, by means of an electronic amplifying and recording device, eavesdrop and record the confidential communication between himself and JANE DOE #2.

COUNT THREE

For a further and separate cause of action, being a different offense of the same class of crimes and offenses and connected in its commission with the charges set forth in Count One hereof: On or about and between December 01, 2008, and March 01, 2009, at and in the County of Sacramento, State of California, defendant M ___ L ___ did commit a felony namely: a violation of Section 632(a) of the Penal Code of the State of California, in that said defendant did intentionally and without the consent of all parties to a confidential communication, by means of an electronic amplifying and recording device, eavesdrop and record the confidential communication between himself and JANE DOE #2.

COUNT FOUR

For a further and separate cause of action, being a different offense of the same class of crimes and offenses and connected in its commission with the charges set forth in Count One hereof: On or about and between August 01, 2008, and December 31, 2008, at and in the County of Sacramento, State of California, defendant M ___ L ___ did commit a felony namely: a violation of Section 632(a) of the Penal Code of the State of California, in that said defendant did intentionally and without the consent of all parties to a confidential communication, by means of an electronic amplifying and recording device, eavesdrop and record the confidential communication between himself and JANE DOE #3.

I declare upon information and belief and under penalty of perjury that the foregoing is true and correct.

Executed at Sacramento County, California, the 8th day of November, 2010.

____

Declarant

As an alternative to an information, a prosecutor may seek an indictment from a grand jury. Prosecutors use the grand jury in complex cases, in cases involving organized crime, and for other reasons.

Misdemeanors and infractions are prosecuted by citation or complaint (PC §§ 740, 853.5–853.6).

ARRAIGNMENT

Arraignment is a defendant's first court appearance. If the defendant is in jail, the arraignment occurs within 48 hours of arrest. If the defendant was arrested without a warrant—a common occurrence—the arraignment also serves as a probable cause hearing to determine whether there is sufficient evidence to hold the accused in jail.

The judge conducting an arraignment is referred to as a magistrate. The arraignment is brief. Defendant has the right to be represented by counsel at the arraignment, and if the defendant cannot afford an attorney, the court appoints the public defender. Defendant is informed of the charge(s) and given an opportunity to enter a plea (PC § 858). In California there are six pleas: (1) guilty; (2) not guilty; (3) nolo contendere;[14] (4) a former judgment of conviction or acquittal of the offense charged; (5) once in jeopardy; and (6) not guilty by reason of insanity. (PC § 1016). The most common pleas are "guilty" and "not guilty."

BAIL

If defendant is eligible for bail, the magistrate conducting the arraignment sets bail. The California Constitution speaks in some detail about bail. Article I, § 12 provides:

> A person shall be released on bail by sufficient sureties, except for (a) Capital crimes when the facts are evident or the presumption great; (b) Felony offenses involving acts of violence on another person, or felony sexual assault offenses on another person, when the facts are evident or the presumption great and the court finds based upon clear and convincing evidence that there is a substantial likelihood the person's release would result in great bodily harm to others; or (c) [felony offenses where the defendant has threatened another with great bodily harm]. Excessive bail may not be required. In fixing the amount of bail, the court shall take into consideration the seriousness of the offense charged, the previous criminal record of the defendant, and the probability of his or her appearing at the trial or hearing of the case. A person may be released on his or her own

[14] A plea of nolo contendere in a case that is punishable as a felony has the same effect as a verdict of guilty.

recognizance in the court's discretion. (*See also* Cal. Const. Art. I, § 28(f)(3)).

Each county has a "Bail Schedule." Some examples from the San Francisco Schedule follow: Bribery—$40,000; Assault with a deadly weapon—$75,000; Lewd act with child—$150,000; Stalking—$75,000; Cause death/mayhem with explosive devise—$2,000,000; Possession of Nunchaku—$40,000; Cane gun—$40,000; Murder—bail set by the judge.

In 2018, the California Legislature ended cash bail, and replaced it with a system of risk-assessment. As this book goes to press, the new law is being challenged in court. You may wish to examine Jodi L. Viljoen, Dana M. Cochrane & Melissa R. Jonnson, Do Risk Assessment Tools Help Manage and Reduce risk of Violence and Reoffending? A Systematic Review, 42 *Law and Human Behavior* 181 (2018) ("Although risk assessment tools are thought to be an important starting point to risk management, it is unclear whether research evidence exists to support this view.").

PRELIMINARY HEARING

When a prosecutor commences a felony prosecution by complaint, a preliminary hearing is required to ensure that there is enough evidence to justify requiring the defendant to stand trial. The defendant can waive the preliminary hearing or "prelim." When a prosecution is commenced by indictment there is no preliminary hearing.

A preliminary hearing is adversarial. The prosecutor offers testimony from witnesses—often a police officer—and the defense attorney can cross-examine the prosecution's witnesses and offer evidence to establish a defense or negate an element of the crime (PC § 866(a)). The defendant has a right to effective assistance of counsel at the preliminary hearing.[15]

At the preliminary hearing, the prosecutor must present enough evidence to persuade the magistrate that there is "sufficient cause"—called probable cause—to believe a crime occurred and that defendant committed it (PC § 872(a)).[16] "Probable cause exists if a person of ordinary caution or prudence would be led to believe and conscientiously entertain a strong suspicion that the defendant committed the crime." *Galindo v. Superior Court* (2010) 50 Cal.4th 1, 5, 112 Cal.Rptr.3d 673, 235 P.3d 1. Probable cause plays an enormously important role in criminal procedure, and you will learn much more about it in that course.

---

[15] *Galindo v. Superior Court* (2010) 50 Cal.4th 1, 235 P.3d 1, 112 Cal.Rptr.3d 673.

[16] The prosecutor's burden of proof at a preliminary hearing is not heavy. In *People v. Chapple* (2006) 138 Cal.App.4th 540, 546, 41 Cal.Rptr.3d 680, the Court of Appeal wrote, "Thus, the prosecution's burden of persuasion at a preliminary hearing is far lower than at trial."

If the magistrate is persuaded by the prosecution's evidence, the magistrate signs an order that the defendant "be held to answer to" the charges. In other words, there is enough evidence to justify putting the defendant on trial. On rare occasions, the magistrate conducting a preliminary hearing dismisses the charges. (*See, e.g., People v. Dawson* in Chapter 4). In most cases, the defendant is held to answer or, as it is sometimes described, bound over for trial.

INDICTMENT BY GRAND JURY

A grand jury is comprised of citizens of the county (PC § 888). The number of grand jurors depends on the population of the county. The grand jury has 23 members if the county has a population greater than 4 million. In counties with a population less than 20,000, the grand jury has 11 members. In all other counties, the grand jury consists of 19 citizens (PC § 888.2).

The grand jury "may inquire into all public offenses committed or triable within the county." (PC § 917). Criminal sessions of the grand jury are closed to the public (PC § 939). The grand jury's civil responsibilities include investigating the functioning of county and city governments.

In criminal matters, a prosecutor presents cases to the grand jury for possible indictment. The prosecutor must present enough evidence to establish probable cause. The grand jury considers testimony from witnesses, documents, real evidence (*e.g.*, a gun, drugs) (PC § 939.6).[17] Unless the suspect is testifying before the grand jury, the suspect has no right to participate in the proceeding personally or by counsel. Nor does the suspect have the right to present evidence to the grand jury. The prosecutor, however, is required to inform the grand jury of evidence that tends to exculpate the suspect (PC § 939.71). "The grand jury shall find an indictment when all the evidence before it, taken together, if unexplained or uncontradicted, would, in its judgment, warrant a conviction by a trial jury" (PC § 939.8). If the grand jury finds an indictment, the jury foreperson signs "A true bill" (PC § 940), and the indictment is filed in court.

JOINDER AND SEVERANCE OF CHARGES

When more than one defendant are charged with a crime, California law favors trying all defendants together. (*People v. Daveggio* (2018) 4 Cal. 5th 790, 415 P.3d 717, 231 Cal. Rptr. 3d 646). PC § 1098 provides in part: "When two or more defendants are jointly charged with any public offense, whether felony or misdemeanor, they must be tried jointly, unless the court

[17] The probable cause sufficient for an indictment is the same as the probable cause required at a preliminary hearing.

order separate trials." The Supreme Court explained in *People v. Letner* (2010) 50 Cal.4th 99, 150, 112 Cal.Rptr.3d 746, 235 P.3d 62:

> Our Legislature has thus expressed a preference for joint trials. But the court may, in its discretion, order separate trials in the face of an incriminating confession [by one joint defendant that is admissible against the confessing defendant but not against other defendant(s)][18], prejudicial association with codefendants, likely confusion resulting from evidence on multiple counts, conflicting defenses, or the possibility that at a separate trial a codefendant would give exonerating testimony.
>
> A joint trial is especially called for when two or more defendants are charged with the same crimes arising out of the same events. The fact that one joint defendant might try to fix blame on another defendant is generally not a sufficient justification for separate trials. Moreover, the fact that defendants have conflicting or antagonistic defenses does not invariably warrant separate trials. A trial court that denies a request for severance abuses its discretion only when the conflict between the defendants *alone* will demonstrate to the jury that they are guilty. If, instead, there exists sufficient independent evidence against the [defendant seeking severance], it is not the conflict alone that demonstrates his or her guilt, and antagonistic defenses do not compel severance. A joint trial is prohibited only where the conflict is so prejudicial that the defenses are irreconcilable, and the jury will unjustifiably infer that this conflict alone demonstrates that both defendants are guilty.

NECESSARILY INCLUDED OFFENSES

Sometimes, when a defendant commits one crime, she necessarily commits another crime that is included within the first. The included offense is typically less serious than the crime committed, and is known as a lesser included offense. For example, a defendant who commits burglary necessarily commits trespass. At trial on the burglary offense, if the jury acquits defendant of burglary, the jury may find the defendant guilty of trespass. PC § 1159 provides that the jury "may find the defendant guilty of any offense, the commission of which is necessarily included in that with which he is charged." The California Supreme Court discussed lesser included offenses in *People v. Reed* (2006) 38 Cal.4th 1224, 1227–1228, 45 Cal.Rptr.3d 353, 137 P.3d 184:

[18] When the Court refers to a confession that is admissible in evidence against the confessing defendant but not against the other defendants on trial, the Court has in mind a legal doctrine called *Aranda-Bruton*, after a California Supreme Court case and a U.S. Supreme Court case. The *Aranda-Bruton* doctrine is generally taught in the evidence course.

> We have applied two tests in determining whether an uncharged offense is necessarily included within a charged offense: the "elements" test and the "accusatory pleading" test. Under the elements test, if the statutory elements of the greater offense include all of the elements of the lesser offense, the latter is necessarily included in the former. Under the accusatory pleading test, if the facts actually alleged in the accusatory pleading include all of the elements of the lesser offense, the latter is necessarily included in the former.[19]

In *People v. Shockley* (2013) 58 Cal. 4th 400, 314 P.3d 798, 165 Cal. Rptr. 3d 497, the Supreme Court decided whether battery is a lesser included offense of lewd and lascivious conduct with a child under 14 years of age. Battery is defined as "any willful and unlawful use of force or violence upon the person of another." (PC § 242). Lewd and lascivious conduct is defined as "any person who willfully and lewdly commits any lewd or lascivious act upon or with the body of a child who is under the age of 14 years, with the intent of arousing, appealing to, or gratifying the lust of that person or the child, is guilty of a felony." (PC § 288(a)). Evidence at Shockley's trial established that the much older Shockley kissed the victim on the lips, stuck his tongue in her mouth, and rubbed her genital area with his hand for five minutes. Shockley was charged with 288(a), and was convicted. On appeal, Shockley argued that the trial judge had a *sua sponte* duty to instruct the jury on battery as a lesser included offense of lewd conduct. The Supreme Court noted, "A trial judge has a *sua sponte* duty to instruct on a lesser offense necessarily included in the charged offense if there is substantial evidence the defendant is guilty only of the lesser. Substantial evidence in this context is evidence from which a reasonable jury could conclude that the defendant committed the lesser, but not the greater, offense." What do you think? Is battery a lesser included offense of 288(a), lewd and lascivious conduct?

MORE THAN ONE CONVICTION CAN ARISE FROM A SINGLE ACT OR COURSE OF CONDUCT

A single act may violate more than one statute. A defendant can be convicted of more than one crime arising from the same act (PC § 954). For example, in *People v. Reed* (2006) 38 Cal.4th 1224, 45 Cal.Rptr.3d 353, 137 P.3d 184, Reed was a convicted felon. San Francisco police officers found him in possession of a loaded and concealed pistol. Reed was convicted of

---

[19] *See* 17 *California Jurisprudence*: *Criminal Law* § 95, p. 173 (3d ed. 2010) (West) ("Where an offense cannot be committed without necessarily committing another, the latter is an offense necessarily included in the former, and a defendant may not be convicted of both. Even absent a request and even over the parties' objections, the trial court must instruct on a lesser offense necessarily included in the charged offense if there is substantial evidence that the defendant is guilty only of the lesser offense.").

three crimes: (1) being a felon in possession of a firearm, (2) carrying a concealed firearm, and (3) carrying a loaded firearm in a public place.

Although a defendant can be convicted of multiple crimes arising from the same act, a convicted defendant cannot be punished multiple times for the same act (PC § 654). The Supreme Court wrote in *People v. Reed*, "When section 954 permits multiple conviction, but section 654 prohibits multiple punishment, the trial court must stay execution of sentence on the convictions for which multiple punishment is prohibited."

There is an exception to the rule that multiple convictions can arise from a single act. In *Reed*, the Supreme Court wrote, "A judicially created exception to the general rule permitting multiple conviction prohibits multiple convictions based on necessarily included offenses." Thus, in the burglary scenario described in the previous subsection, if the jury convicts of burglary, the jury cannot also convict of trespass, a lesser included offense.

DISCOVERY IN CRIMINAL CASES

Pretrial discovery in criminal cases differs significantly from discovery in civil litigation. For example, criminal discovery does not include interrogatories and requests for admission. Depositions, which are common in civil cases, are rare in California criminal practice. An excellent book on discovery is written by Justice Brian M. Hoffstadt, titled *California Criminal Discovery* (5th ed. 2015).

Pretrial discovery is governed by the PC §§ 1054–1054.10 and by the U.S. Constitution. The Penal Code requires the prosecutor to disclose names and addresses of witnesses the prosecutor intends to call at trial, written or recorded statements by witnesses, real evidence (gun, knife), the existence of felony convictions of important prosecution witnesses,[20] and exculpatory evidence (PC § 1054.1). The prosecutor may not disclose the victim's phone number or address to the defendant or a member of the defendant's family. However, the victim's phone number and address may be released to defense counsel (PC § 1054.2).

Discovery in California criminal cases is reciprocal. (*People v. Landers* (2019) 31 Cal. App. 5th 288, 242 Cal. Rptr. 3d 501). Defendant must provide discovery to the prosecution. Thus, the defense must inform the prosecutor of witnesses the defense intends to call at trial, along with written and recorded statements of witnesses. The prosecutor must be informed of real evidence that will be offered at trial (Cal. Const. Art. I, § 30; PC § 1054.3).

---

[20] A witness can be impeached by asking whether the witness has been convicted of a felony that involves dishonesty or moral turpitude (Evid. Code § 788). "Dishonesty" in this context means deceit. Moral turpitude is willingness to do evil to others.

The Penal Code specifies that discovery should be conducted informally and cooperatively by unwritten request. Neither party may obtain access to attorney work product (PC § 1054.6) or to confidential communications protected by the attorney-client privilege.

In addition to discovery mandated by statute, the Due Process Clause of the U.S. Constitution requires the prosecutor to turn over to the defense evidence favorable to the defendant that is relevant to guilt or punishment, including evidence that could be used to impeach government witnesses. *Brady v. Maryland* (1963) 373 U.S. 83, 83 S.Ct. 1194. Evidence is favorable to the defense if it helps the defendant or hurts the prosecution. The prosecutor's duty to disclose applies to information in the control of the prosecutor *and* to information in control of law enforcement—the "prosecution team." The *Brady* duty of disclosure is automatic and does not require a request from the defense attorney. *Brady* is not reciprocal. The defendant has no *Brady* duty to disclose information to the prosecution.

A defendant sometimes claims that an arresting officer used excessive force, fabricated evidence, or committed other misconduct that is relevant to the case. As part of discovery, defendant may seek access to the officer's personnel file to determine if citizens have filed complaints against the officer, or if the officer's employer has imposed discipline. In *Pitchess v. Superior Court* (1974) 11 Cal.3d 531, 113 Cal.Rptr. 897, 522 P.2d 305, the Supreme Court approved such discovery. The Legislature codified *Pitchess* discovery in Evidence Code §§ 1043–1045. In *Galindo v. Superior Court* (2010) 50 Cal.4th 1, 12, 112 Cal.Rptr.3d 673, 235 P.3d 1, the Supreme Court described the procedure when a defendant files a *Pitchess* motion:

> To obtain *Pitchess* discovery of a particular peace officer's personnel records, a criminal defendant must provide not only a written motion and notice to the governmental agency which has custody of the records but also a description of the type of records or information sought as well as affidavits showing good cause for the discovery or disclosure; and the defendant must set forth the materiality of the information sought to the pending litigation. If the defendant shows good cause, the trial court directs the custodian of the records to produce all potentially relevant documents for its examination in chambers, that is, in a nonpublic proceeding designed to protect the officer's privacy.
>
> If, after reviewing the officer's personnel records, the trial court concludes that they do not contain information that is statutorily excluded from disclosure, then disclosure is called for. But the information disclosed to the defense will be limited to names and contact information for persons who have on prior occasions either witnessed or filed complaints of misconduct by the officer who is the subject of the *Pitchess* discovery motion.

PLEA BARGAINING

Plea bargaining plays an important role in criminal litigation. The Supreme Court observed in *People v. Feyrer* (2010) 48 Cal. 4th 426, 527, 106 Cal.Rptr.3d 518, 226 P.3d 998: "Plea negotiations and agreements are an accepted and integral component of the criminal justice system and essential to the expeditious and fair administration of our courts. Plea agreements benefit that system by promoting speed, economy, and the finality of judgments."

Most prosecutions are resolved through a plea bargain in which the defendant agrees to plead guilty in exchange for the prosecutor's agreement to drop some of the charges or recommend a lighter sentence. The judge must approve a plea bargain. In *People v. Cantu* (2010) 183 Cal.App.4th 604, 607, 107 Cal.Rptr.3d 429, the Court of Appeal explained, "Judicial approval is an essential condition precedent to any plea bargain. A plea bargain is ineffective unless and until it is approved by the court."

In 1982, the people of California approved Proposition 8. Among other things, Prop 8 placed limits on plea bargaining. The Legislature codified these limits in Penal Code § 1192.7, which provides in part:

> (a)(2) Plea bargaining in any case in which the indictment or information charges any serious felony, any felony in which it is alleged that a firearm was personally used by the defendant, or any offense of driving under the influence of alcohol, drugs, narcotics, or any other intoxicating substance, or any combination thereof, is prohibited, unless there is insufficient evidence to prove the people's case, or testimony of a material witness cannot be obtained, or a reduction or dismissal would not result in a substantial change in sentence.

In *People v. Barao*, you will see Section 1192.7 at work.

PEOPLE V. BARAO

California Court of Appeal
218 Cal. App. 4th 769, 16 Cal. Rptr. 3d 506 (2013)

NICHOLSON, J.

Defendant Rammel Barao shot and killed Juan Carlos Lorenzo. An information jointly charged defendant and [codefendant Vandell Johnson, Jr.] with murdering Lorenzo in the course of robbing him (Pen.Code, §§ 187; 190.2(a)(17)(A)); and with the robbery of Lorenzo and Lorenzo's companion, Domingo Moyotl (§ 211). Each of these three counts alleged defendant personally used a firearm. (§ 12022.53(d).) Defendant was also charged with possession of a firearm by a previously convicted felon (§ 12021(a)(1)); and unlawful possession of ammunition (§ 12316(b)(1)). The information further alleged defendant had previously been convicted of two serious felonies for purposes of the "Three Strikes" law (§§ 667(a); 1170.12(b)), and that he had served a prior prison term (§ 667.5(b)).

Defendant pleaded not guilty. However, prior to trial, the prosecutor and the defendant sought the court's approval of a plea bargain. Under the proposal, the prosecutor would amend the information by charging defendant with voluntary manslaughter instead of murder, defendant would plead guilty to that charge, and he would admit the gun use, one of the prior strikes, and the prior prison term. In exchange, he would receive a prison term of 41 years. The trial court refused to approve the bargain and denied the request to amend the information.

A jury convicted defendant of second degree murder, and it found the firearm enhancements to be true. The jury also convicted defendant of possession of a firearm and possession of ammunition. It acquitted him of the two robbery counts. The trial court subsequently found the prior strike and prison term allegations to be true, and it sentenced defendant to a state prison term of 75 years to life.

Defendant contends the trial court abused its discretion and violated the constitutional doctrine of separation of powers when it refused to accept the plea bargain and denied the prosecution's motion to amend the information. He claims the prosecutor had determined the evidence was insufficient to prosecute a charge of murder, and the court should have honored that decision. He asserts the plea bargain was not barred by section 1192.7's prohibition of plea bargaining in serious felony cases. He also argues the proposed amendment to the information did not violate any of defendant's substantive rights, and the court denied the amendment based on an improper factor, the disparity in sentencing. We conclude the court did not abuse its discretion in denying the plea bargain and the motion to amend.

The prosecutor and defense counsel believed the proposed plea more correctly conformed to the evidence. The trial court disagreed with that assertion, having been the judge that conducted defendant's preliminary hearing. The prosecutor explained that based on the evidence, it was possible the jury would convict of voluntary manslaughter instead of murder.

This case was prohibited by section 1192.7 from being resolved by plea bargain. That statute, adopted as part of Proposition 8, prohibits plea bargaining in any case in which the information charges a serious felony unless certain exceptions are met. Three of the charges alleged against defendant qualified under the statute as serious felonies: murder, personal use of a firearm, and robbery.

As a result, the case could not be resolved by plea bargain unless one of three exceptions was satisfied: there was "insufficient evidence to prove the people's case, or testimony of a material witness cannot be obtained, or a reduction or dismissal would not result in a substantial change in sentence." The trial court's decision not to approve the plea bargain in effect was a determination that none of these exceptions to the prohibition applied here. The evidence supports the court's determination.

The trial court held there was sufficient evidence to convict defendant of murder. It was intimately familiar with that evidence, as it had heard defendant's preliminary hearing.

The trial court also recognized the plea bargain would result in a substantial change in defendant's likely sentence. In determining whether a plea bargain would result in a substantial change in the sentence, we are to compare the proposed sentence with the sentence the judge would impose without a plea bargain. The actual sentence the court imposed on defendant for second degree murder and his other crimes and enhancements was 75 years to life, a term of imprisonment almost twice as long as the sentence proposed under the plea bargain. The court likely recognized this substantial disparity in the sentence defendant would receive after trial and the one proposed under the plea bargain, and it concluded the plea bargain would result in too drastic a reduction in sentencing.

The prosecution also made no showing that the testimony of a material witness could not be obtained.

Thus, the trial court correctly concluded this case fell within section 1192.7's prohibition of plea bargaining, and it rightly refused to approve the proposed plea. The court did not abuse its discretion to do so.

RIGHT TO TRIAL BY JURY

In criminal prosecutions of felonies and misdemeanors, defendants have the right to trial by jury. The Sixth Amendment to the U.S. Constitution provides, "In all criminal prosecutions, the accused shall enjoy the right to an impartial jury of the State and district wherein the crime shall have been committed." The California Constitution (Art. I, § 16) provides: "Trial by jury is an inviolate right and shall be secured to all."

The importance of trial by jury is deeply ingrained in American law. In *Duncan v. Louisiana* (1968) 391 U.S. 145, 155–156, 88 S.Ct. 1444, the Supreme Court addressed the key role of the jury in American law:

> The guarantees of jury trial in the Federal and State Constitutions reflect a profound judgment about the way in which law should be enforced and justice administered. A right to jury trial is granted to criminal defendants in order to prevent oppression by the Government. Those who wrote our constitutions knew from history and experience that it was necessary to protect against unfounded criminal charges brought to eliminate enemies

> and against judges too responsive to the voice of higher authority. Providing an accused with the right to be tried by a jury of his peers gave him an inestimable safeguard against the corrupt or overzealous prosecutor and against the compliant, biased, or eccentric judge. If the defendant preferred the common-sense judgment of a jury to the more tutored but perhaps less sympathetic reaction of the single judge, he was to have it.

Under the California Constitution, both the defendant *and* the prosecution have the right to trial by jury. The right to trial by jury in a California criminal case "may be waived by the consent of both parties expressed in open court." (Cal. Const. Art. I, § 16). Defense counsel must agree with the defendant's decision to waive a jury.

Question: If you become a defense attorney, can you imagine cases in which you are likely to prefer a bench trial to a jury trial?

In felony cases, "the jury shall consist of 12 persons. In criminal actions in which a misdemeanor is charged, the jury shall consist of 12 persons or a lesser number agreed on by the parties in open court." (Cal. Const. Art. I, § 16). The jury must reach a unanimous verdict.

A jury trial begins with jury selection from a panel of prospective jurors.[21] The judge and the attorneys question prospective jurors, a process called *voir dire*. The prosecutor and defense attorney endeavor to find jurors they believe will be sympathetic to their case.

Attorneys have two types of challenges to prospective jurors: challenges for cause and peremptory challenges. A prospective juror can be challenged for cause if the juror is not qualified to serve (*e.g.*, not a U.S. citizen, does not live in California). A prospective juror may be excused or "struck" for cause because the juror is related to a party, is biased against a party, admits to having already formed an opinion about the case, cannot follow the law or the judge's instructions, and for other reasons indicating inability to be fair and impartial.[22] Attorneys have an unlimited number of challenges for cause.

"Peremptory challenges are designed to be used for any reason, or no reason at all." *People v. Armstrong* (2019) 6 Cal. 5th 735, 433 P.3d 987, 243 Cal. Rptr. 3d 105. Attorneys have a limited number of peremptory challenges by which the attorney may dismiss a prospective juror for any reason except race, ethnicity, gender, religion, or sexual orientation.[23] *See*

---

[21] The statutory law governing juries in criminal and civil cases is found in the Code of Civil Procedure, § 190, et seq.

[22] *See People v. Manibusan* (2013) 58 Cal. 4th 40, 314 P.3d 1, 165 Cal. Rptr. 3d 1 (in a death penalty case, "A trial court may excuse a prospective juror for cause if no reasonable possibility exists the prospective juror could consider imposing the death penalty.").

[23] *See People v. Vines* (2011) 51 Cal.4th 830, 124 Cal.Rptr.3d 830, 251 P.3d 943 ("Both the state and federal Constitutions prohibit the use of preemptory challenges to remove prospective jurors based solely on group bias.").

Batson v. Kentucky (1986) 476 U.S. 79, 106 S.Ct. 1712 and *People v. Wheeler* (1978) 22 Cal.3d 258, 148 Cal.Rptr. 890, 583 P.2d 748. California Code of Civil Procedure § 231.5 codifies the so-called *Batson-Wheeler* rule: "A party shall not use a peremptory challenge to remove a prospective juror on the basis of an assumption that the prospective juror is biased merely because of" his or her race, color, religion, sex, ancestry, national origin, sexual orientation, disability, or similar grounds. The *Batson-Wheeler* rule applies to the defense as well as the prosecution.

A party—usually the defendant—asserting that a prospective juror was excluded on the basis of a prohibited ground makes a *Batson-Wheeler* motion during jury selection. The moving party must establish a *prima facie* case of improper exclusion.[24] A *prima facie* case requires a showing that supports a reasonable inference of systematic exclusion on a prohibited basis. If the moving party meets this burden, the burden shifts to the other side to explain that there was a legitimate, non-discriminatory basis to exclude the juror. The trial court then determines whether intentional discrimination has been shown by a preponderance of the evidence.

The number of preemptory challenges depends on the type of case. If the crime is punishable by death or life in prison, each side has 20 peremptory challenges. For most other offenses, each side has 10 peremptory challenges.

When the jury is selected, the judge administers an oath to the jury and gives the jurors initial instructions.

PROBLEM

You are the public defender for Modoc County, California. Modoc County is located at the northeast corner of the state. The county seat is Alturas. The population of the county is 9,686. The county is overwhelmingly white.

You are assigned to represent James Smith, a 25-year-old Black resident of Modoc County who is charged with burglary, robbery, and murder. The complaint alleges that Mr. Smith broke into the home of an elderly long-time resident of Alturas, robbed her at gunpoint, and shot her.

Can your client get a fair trial in Modoc County? Does the fact that so few Black people live in the county have relevance to this issue? Should you seek to have the case moved to another county? If so, on what basis? With so few Blacks in Modoc County, can your client get an "impartial jury"? Is it fair/correct/wise to assume that Hispanic, American Indian, Asian, or white jurors are incapable of being impartial? Will your client be better off with a bench trial?

---

[24] *See People v. Manibusan* (2013) 58 Cal. 4th 40, 314 P.3d 1, 165 Cal. Rptr. 3d 1.

Assume that during the past five years there have been 50 criminal jury trials in Modoc County.[25] Of the prospective jurors called for jury duty in those five years, only three prospective jurors were Black. Not a single Black juror served on a criminal jury during the five years. Your client has the right to a jury that represents the community. In Modoc County, however, the "community" is Hispanic, American Indian, and white. Almost no one in the "community" is Black. What does "representative" mean in this context?

In *People v. Burney* (2009) 47 Cal.4th 203, 225–226, 97 Cal.Rptr.3d 348, 212 P.3d 639, the Supreme Court discussed the defendant's constitutional right to a representative jury:

> Under the federal and state Constitutions, an accused is entitled to a jury drawn from a representative cross-section of the community. That guarantee mandates that the pools from which juries are drawn must not systematically exclude distinctive groups in the community. In order to establish a *prima facie* violation of the fair-cross-section requirement, the defendant must show: (1) that the group alleged to be excluded is a distinctive group in the community; (2) that the representation of this group in venires from which juries are selected is not fair and reasonable in relation to the number of such persons in the community; and (3) that this underrepresentation is due to systematic exclusion of the group in the jury-selection process. The relevant community for cross-section purposes is the judicial district in which the case is tried. If the defendant establishes a *prima facie* case of systematic underrepresentation, the burden shifts to the prosecution to provide either a more precise statistical showing that no constitutionally significant disparity exists or a compelling justification for the procedure that has resulted in the disparity in the jury venire.
>
> A defendant does not meet the burden of demonstrating that the underrepresentation was due to systematic exclusion, by establishing only statistical evidence of a disparity. A defendant must show, in addition, that the disparity is the result of an improper feature of the jury selection process. When a county's jury selection criteria are neutral with respect to race, ethnicity, sex, and religion, the defendant must identify some aspect of the manner in which those criteria are applied (the probable cause of the disparity) that is constitutionally impermissible.

TRIAL OF A CRIMINAL CASE

Although most criminal cases are settled through plea bargaining, a significant number go to trial. Trials take place in Superior Court. In California there are 58 trial courts, one in each county. The Los Angles trial court has more than 500 judicial officers. A rural county like Colusa has

[25] This number is not accurate.

two judges. You will learn about the trial of criminal cases in courses on evidence and trial advocacy. If you want to be a trial lawyer, there is no better practice than criminal law. Prosecutors and defense counsel are constantly in court or getting ready for court.

In the adversarial system of justice, trials are just that, adversarial. Yet, even in highly contested cases, attorneys are expected to act professionally toward witnesses, the judge, and each other. The Court of Appeal in *In re Marriage of Davenport* (2011) 194 Cal.App.4th 1507, 125 Cal.Rptr.3d 292, ended its opinion "with a reminder to counsel—all counsel, regardless of practice, regardless of age—that zealous advocacy does not equate with 'attack dog' or 'scorched earth'; nor does it mean lack of civility. Zeal and vigor in the representation of clients are commendable. So are civility, courtesy, and cooperation. They are not mutually exclusive." Every lawyer admitted to the California State Bar must take the following oath: "I solemnly swear (or affirm) that I will support the Constitution of the United States and the Constitution of the State of California, and that I will faithfully discharge the duties of an attorney and counselor at law to the best of my knowledge and ability." New admittees to the bar must also swear or affirm: "As an officer of the court, I will strive to conduct myself at all times with dignity, courtesy, and integrity." When you and enter practice, you will develop your unique style as a negotiator and litigator. As you develop your style, keep the Court of Appeals' advice in mind: Zealous advocacy and civility are not mutually exclusive.

Jury Instructions

Jury instructions play a critical role in litigation. Jury instructions for criminal trials are found in two books: *California Jury Instructions: Criminal* (CALJIC) and *Judicial Council of California Criminal Jury Instructions* (CALCRIM). California courts rely on both sets of instructions. CALCRIM is the official instructions approved by the Judicial Council of California.[26]

In criminal trials, the judge instructs the jury at three times during a trial. At the outset of the trial the judge instructs the jurors on how the trial will proceed (CALCRIM 100). The judge informs jurors regarding how they must conduct themselves during the trial. Thus, CALCRIM 101 provides in part: "During the trial, do not talk about the case or about any of the people or any subject involved in the case with anyone, not even your family, friends, spiritual advisors, or therapists." The judge instructs the jury on what constitutes evidence (CALCRIM 104), and informs jurors they are the sole judges of the facts, including the credibility of witnesses (CALCRIM 105).

---

[26] California Rules of Court 2.1050(a) provides: "The California jury instructions approved by the Judicial Council are the official instructions for use in the State of California."

The second time jury instructions are given is in the midst of trial. As a trial unfolds, circumstances arise when the judge, usually at the request of one of the attorneys, gives the jury a limiting instruction. A limiting instruction is called for when a particular item of evidence (*e.g.*, a document) can be considered by the jury for one purpose but not others. The judge "limits" the jury's use of the evidence to the permissible purpose. Another scenario requiring a limiting instruction occurs when a witness says something that is not admissible. The opposing attorney objects to the witness's statement, asks the judge to "strike" the statement from the record, and requests the judge to instruct the jury to disregard the statement.

The third time jury instructions are given is at the end of the trial, when the judge instructs the jury on the law it is to apply to reach a verdict. In simple cases, jury instructions are relatively brief. In complicated cases, jury instructions are lengthy. The prosecutor and defense counsel suggest instructions they would like the judge to give. Sometimes there are pitched battles over what instructions to give. Ultimately, the judge decides the appropriate instructions and reads them aloud to the jury before they retire to deliberate. The jury takes the instructions with them to the jury room and refers to them at their pleasure.

The judge has a *sua sponte* duty to instruct the jury on the general principles of law that are relevant to the case. The judge's duty to instruct *sua sponte* also applies to defenses that are supported by sufficient evidence.

Speedy Trial

Once a defendant is charged, the defendant has the right to a speedy trial. The Sixth Amendment to the U.S. Constitution provides, "In all criminal prosecutions, the accused shall enjoy the right to a speedy and public trial." The California Constitution is to the same effect. (Art. I, § 15. *See also* PC § 1382). In *People v. Williams* (2013) 58 Cal. 4th 197, 315 P.3d 1, 165 Cal. Rptr. 3d 717, the Supreme Court discussed the speedy trial right:

> The Sixth Amendment to the United States Constitution guarantees that "in all criminal prosecutions, the accused shall enjoy the right to a speedy trial." The right to a speedy trial is fundamental and is imposed by the Due Process Clause of the Fourteenth Amendment on the States. The speedy trial guarantee is an important safeguard to prevent undue and oppressive incarceration prior to trial, to minimize anxiety and concern accompanying public accusation and to limit the possibilities that long delay will impair the ability of an accused to defend himself.

The Sixth Amendment right to a speedy trial is generically different from any of the other rights enshrined in the Constitution for the protection of the accused in several important ways. First, there is a societal interest in providing a speedy trial which exists separate from, and at times in opposition to, the interests of the accused. Lengthy pretrial incarceration contributes to the overcrowding and generally deplorable state of local jails, has a destructive effect on human character, and imposes significant costs on society in the form of maintenance expenses and lost wages. Second, unlike other constitutional rights afforded the accused, deprivation of the right to a speedy trial may work to the accused's advantage, as delay is not an uncommon defense tactic. Thus, unlike the right to counsel or the right to be free from compelled self-incrimination, deprivation of the right to speedy trial does not *per se* prejudice the accused's ability to defend himself. Third, the right to speedy trial is a more vague concept than other procedural rights in that it is impossible to definitively say how long is too long in a system where justice is supposed to be swift but deliberate. Accordingly, any inquiry into a speedy trial claim necessitates a functional analysis of the right in the particular context of the case. Finally, the amorphous quality of the right also leads to the unsatisfactorily severe remedy of dismissal of the indictment when the right has been deprived. Such a remedy is more serious than an exclusionary rule or a reversal for a new trial, but it is the only possible remedy.

Because the speedy-trial right is amorphous, slippery, and necessarily relative, the [U.S. Supreme Court] refused to quantify the right into a specified number of days or months or to hinge the right on a defendant's explicit request for a speedy trial. Rather, to determine whether a speedy trial violation has occurred, [the Supreme Court] established a balancing test consisting of four separate enquiries: whether delay before trial was uncommonly long, whether the government or the criminal defendant is more to blame for that delay, whether, in due course, the defendant asserted his right to a speedy trial, and whether he suffered prejudice as the delay's result. None of these four factors is either a necessary or sufficient condition to the finding of a deprivation of the right of speedy trial. Rather, they are related factors and must be considered together with such other circumstances as may be relevant. In sum, these factors have no talismanic qualities; courts must still engage in a difficult and sensitive balancing process. The burden of demonstrating a speedy trial violation lies with the defendant.

Apart from the right to a speedy trial *after* charges are filed, a defendant may argue that the government waited too long to bring charges after the crime occurred. In *People v. Cowan* (2010), 50 Cal.4th 401, 430–431, 113 Cal.Rptr.3d 850, 236 P.3d 1074, the Supreme Court discussed delay in filing charges:

> The due process clauses of the Fifth and Fourteenth Amendments to the United States Constitution and article I, section 15 of the California Constitution protect a defendant from the prejudicial effects of lengthy, unjustified delay between the commission of a crime and the defendant's arrest and charging. Such prearrest or precharging delay does not implicate the defendant's state and federal speedy trial rights, as those rights do not attach until a defendant has been arrested or a charging document has been filed.
>
> When, as here, a defendant does not complain of delay after his arrest and charging, but only of delay between the crimes and his arrest, he is not without recourse if the delay is unjustified and prejudicial. The right of due process protects a criminal defendant's interest in fair adjudication by preventing unjustified delays that weaken the defense through the dimming of memories, the death or disappearance of witnesses, and the loss or destruction of material physical evidence. Accordingly, delay in prosecution that occurs before the accused is arrested or the complaint is filed may constitute a denial of the right to a fair trial and to due process of law under the state and federal Constitutions. A defendant seeking to dismiss a charge on this ground must demonstrate prejudice arising from the delay. The prosecution may offer justification for the delay, and the court considering a motion to dismiss balances the harm to the defendant against the justification for the delay.
>
> Prejudice may be shown by loss of material witnesses due to lapse of time or loss of evidence because of fading memory attributable to the delay.
>
> Under the California standard, negligent, as well as purposeful, delay in bringing charges may, when accompanied by a showing of prejudice, violate due process. This does not mean, however, that whether the delay was purposeful or negligent is irrelevant. Rather, whether the delay was purposeful or negligent is relevant to the balancing process. Purposeful delay to gain advantage is totally unjustified, and a relatively weak showing of prejudice would suffice to tip the scales towards finding a due process violation. If the delay was merely negligent, a greater

showing of prejudice would be required to establish a due process violation.

Proof Beyond a Reasonable Doubt

American law uses three levels, burdens, or standards of proof: beyond a reasonable doubt in criminal cases,[27] preponderance of the evidence in most civil litigation, and clear and convincing evidence in a few civil matters.

Preponderance of the evidence is the least demanding burden of proof—the easiest to meet. The preponderance standard is satisfied when the evidence in favor of a proposition is slightly greater than the evidence against the proposition. Proof beyond a reasonable doubt is the most difficult to achieve. Clear and convincing evidence is somewhere between the other two.

Although percentages do not capture the full flavor of burdens of proof, percents are a useful starting place to think about burdens. Proof beyond a reasonable doubt is similar to 95% certainty. Preponderance of the evidence requires only 51% certainty. Clear and convincing evidence is in the neighborhood of 75% certainty.

As mentioned above, clear and convincing evidence is required in a narrow range of civil litigation. Thus, before a person can be involuntarily committed to a psychiatric hospital for treatment, the government must prove by clear and convincing evidence that the person is mentally ill and a danger to self or others.[28]

In California juvenile court proceedings to protect children from abuse or neglect—called dependency proceedings—the government must prove maltreatment by a preponderance of the evidence.[29] However, if the government seeks to remove a maltreated child from home and place the child in foster care, the government must prove the need for removal by clear and convincing evidence.[30] Also in juvenile court, if the government seeks to permanently sever the parent-child relationship—terminate parental rights—the government must prove parental unfitness by clear and convincing evidence.[31] Under the federal Indian Child Welfare Act, if the government seeks to terminate the parental rights of Indian parents, parental unfitness must be proven beyond a reasonable doubt.[32]

---

[27] *See* PC § 1096.

[28] *Addington v. Texas* (1979) 441 U.S. 418, 99 S.Ct. 1804.

[29] Cal. Welfare & Institutions Code § 355(a).

[30] Cal. Welfare & Institutions Code § 361(c).

[31] *Santosky v. Kramer* (1982) 455 U.S. 745, 102 S.Ct. 1388.

[32] 25 U.S.C. § 1912(f).

In criminal cases, how strong must evidence be to rise to the level of proof beyond a reasonable doubt? The evidence does not have to eliminate *all* doubt of innocence. Yet, the evidence must be so strong that the trier of fact—whether judge or jury—is *nearly certain* the defendant is guilty. In *Jackson v. Virginia* (1979) 443 U.S. 307, 315, 99 S.Ct. 2781, the Supreme Court stated that the beyond a reasonable doubt standard requires the mind of the trier of fact to be in a "subjective state of near certitude" that the defendant is guilty.

In *People v. Daveggio* (2018) 4 Cal. 5th 790, 415 P.3d 717, 231 Cal. Rptr. 3d 646), the Supreme Court wrote, "The federal Constitution's due process guarantee protects the accused against conviction except upon proof beyond a reasonable doubt of every fact necessary to constitute the crime with which he is charged. The Constitution does not require that any particular form of words be used in advising the jury of the government's burden of proof, but it does require that, taken as a whole, the instructions correctly convey the concept of reasonable doubt to the jury. What matters, for federal constitutional purposes, is whether there is a reasonable likelihood that the jury understood the instructions to allow conviction based on insufficient proof." The California jury instruction on reasonable doubt (CALCRIM 220) states:

> A defendant in a criminal case is presumed to be innocent. This presumption requires that the People prove a defendant guilty beyond a reasonable doubt. Whenever I tell you the People must prove something, I mean they must prove it beyond a reasonable doubt.
>
> Proof beyond a reasonable doubt is proof that leaves you with an abiding conviction that the charge is true. The evidence need not eliminate all possible doubt because everything in life is open to some possible or imaginary doubt.
>
> In deciding whether the People proved their case beyond a reasonable doubt, you must impartially compare and consider all the evidence that was received throughout the entire trial. Unless the evidence proves the defendant guilty beyond a reasonable doubt, [the defendant] is entitled to an acquittal and you must find [the defendant] not guilty.

The U.S. Supreme Court discussed the importance of proof beyond a reasonable doubt in *In re Winship* (1970), 397 U.S. 358, 363–364, 90 S.Ct. 1068:

> The reasonable-doubt standard plays a vital role in the American scheme of criminal procedure. It is a prime instrument for reducing the risk of convictions resting on factual error.

> The accused during a criminal prosecution has at stake interests of immense importance, both because of the possibility that he may lose his liberty upon conviction and because of the certainty that he would be stigmatized by the conviction. Accordingly, a society that values the good name and freedom of every individual should not condemn a man for commission of a crime when there is reasonable doubt about his guilt.
>
> Moreover, use of the reasonable-doubt standard is indispensable to command the respect and confidence of the community in applications of the criminal law. It is critical that the moral force of the criminal law not be diluted by a standard of proof that leaves people in doubt whether innocent men are being condemned.

Stages of a Criminal Trial

With the jury selected and sworn, the trial begins with opening statements. The prosecutor goes first, and gives the jury an outline of what the prosecutor believes the evidence will prove. Defense counsel follows with the defense perspective on the case.[33]

The trial is divided into three segments: (1) prosecution case-in-chief, (2) defense case-in-chief, and (3) prosecution case-in-rebuttal. During the prosecution's case-in-chief, the prosecutor offers evidence—witnesses, documents, real evidence (*e.g.*, drugs, a gun). The prosecutor must offer (produce) evidence of every element of the crime, plus evidence identifying defendant as the perpetrator.[34] Defense counsel has the right to cross-examine prosecution witnesses. When the prosecution finishes offering its evidence, the prosecutor rests—"The People rest, your honor." When the prosecution rests, defense counsel typically makes a motion to dismiss part or all of the case, based on the argument that the prosecution's evidence is not sufficient to prove guilt. Assuming the judge denies the motion to dismiss, it is defendant's turn to offer evidence.

The defendant in a criminal case has no obligation to offer evidence—no obligation to put on a case-in-chief. The defendant is entitled to argue that defense evidence is not necessary because the prosecution failed to prove its case.

Assuming the defendant decides to put on a case-in-chief, defense counsel offers testimony from witnesses as well as other evidence. If the

---

[33] If defense counsel wishes, she can postpone her opening statement until the defense case-in-chief.

[34] The burden of producing evidence is discussed in Chapter 9.

defendant decides to testify, the defendant's testimony comes during the defense case-in-chief.[35] At the end of the defense case, the defense rests.

After the defense rests, the prosecutor may offer evidence to rebut evidence raised during the defense case-in-chief. This stage of the trial is the prosecution's case-in-rebuttal.

When all the evidence has been received, the attorneys make closing arguments. Again, the prosecutor goes first. The prosecutor summarizes the evidence and attempts to persuade the jury that the evidence points toward guilt. Defense counsel argues the opposite—the evidence fails to prove defendant's guilt beyond a reasonable doubt.

Throughout trial, prosecution and defense must act professionally. The prosecutor must ensure that the "heat of battle" does not lead to unfair tactics. Defense attorneys sometimes complain of "prosecutorial misconduct." The topic of prosecutorial misconduct is so vast that Bennett Gershman wrote a 600 page book titled *Prosecutorial Misconduct.* The California Supreme Court and Courts of Appeal deal frequently with claims of prosecutorial misconduct. In *People v. Whalen* (2013) 56 Cal. 4th 1, 52, 294 P.3d 915, 152 Cal. Rptr. 3d 673, the Supreme Court wrote, "A prosecutor's conduct violates the federal Constitution when it infects the trial with such unfairness as to make the resulting conviction a denial of due process. Conduct by a prosecutor that does not rise to this level nevertheless violates California law if it involves the use of deceptive or reprehensible methods to attempt to persuade either the court or the jury." Claims of prosecutorial misconduct often arise from the prosecutor's closing argument. In *People v. Edwards* (2013) 57 Cal. 4th 658, 161 Cal. Rptr. 3d 191, the Supreme Court wrote, "A prosecutor's argument may be vigorous as long as it is a fair comment on the evidence, which can include reasonable inferences or deductions to be drawn therefrom. Prosecutors should not purport to rely in jury argument on their outside experience or personal beliefs based on facts not in evidence." The Court of Appeal provides a useful summary of prosecutorial misconduct at trial with the decision in *People v. Caldwell* (2013) 212 Cal. App. 4th 1262, 152 Cal. Rptr. 3d 99:

> Prosecutors are held to an elevated standard of conduct. It is the duty of every member of the bar to maintain the respect due to the courts and to abstain from all offensive personality. A prosecutor is held to a standard higher than that imposed on other attorneys because of the unique function he or she performs in representing the interests, and in exercising the sovereign power, of the state. The prosecutor represents "a sovereignty whose obligation to govern impartially is as compelling as its obligation

[35] The prosecutor cannot call the defendant as a witness during the prosecution's case-in-chief.

to govern at all; and whose interest, therefore, in a criminal prosecution is not that it shall win a case, but that justice shall be done." People v. Hill (1998) 17 Cal. 4th 800, 72 Cal. Rptr. 2d 656.

Prosecutorial misconduct—often occurring during argument—may take a variety of forms. It may include mischaracterizing or misstating the evidence; referring to facts not in evidence; misstating the law, particularly where done in an effort to relieve the People of responsibility for proving all elements of a crime beyond a reasonable doubt; attacking the integrity of, or casting aspersions on defense counsel; intimidating witnesses; referring to a prior conviction of the defendant that was not before the jury; predicting that the defendant, if not found guilty, will commit future crimes; stating a personal opinion, such as an opinion that the defendant is guilty; or appealing to passions or prejudice, such as asking the jury to view the crime through the victim's eyes.

Prosecutors are given wide latitude in trying their cases. The applicable federal and state standards regarding prosecutorial misconduct are well established. Under federal constitutional standards, a prosecutor's intemperate behavior constitutes misconduct if it is so egregious as to render the trial fundamentally unfair under due process principles. Under state law, a prosecutor commits misconduct by engaging in deceptive or reprehensible methods of persuasion.

A prosecutor is prohibited from vouching for the credibility of witnesses or otherwise bolstering the veracity of their testimony by referring to evidence outside the record. Nor is a prosecutor permitted to place the prestige of his or her office behind a witness by offering the impression that he or she has taken steps to assure a witness's truthfulness at trial. However, so long as a prosecutor's assurances regarding the apparent honesty or reliability of prosecution witnesses are based on the facts of the record and the inferences reasonably drawn therefrom, rather than any purported personal knowledge or belief, [his or her] comments cannot be characterized as improper vouching.

Referring to facts not in evidence is clearly misconduct, because such statements tend to make the prosecutor his own witness—offering unsworn testimony not subject to cross-examination. It has been recognized that such testimony, although worthless as a matter of law, can be "dynamite" to the jury because of the special regard the jury has for the prosecutor, thereby effectively circumventing the rules of evidence.

A prosecutor is allowed to make vigorous arguments and may even use such epithets as are warranted by the evidence, as long as these arguments are not inflammatory and principally aimed at arousing the passion or prejudice of the jury. However, a prosecutor commits misconduct if he or she attacks the integrity of defense counsel, or casts aspersions on defense counsel. An attack on the defendant's attorney can be seriously prejudicial as an attack on the defendant himself, and, in view of the accepted doctrines of legal ethics and decorum citation, it is never excusable.

In *Griffin v. California* (1965) 380 U.S. 609, 615, 85 S. Ct. 1229, the United States Supreme Court held that the privilege against self-incrimination of the Fifth Amendment prohibits any comment on a defendant's failure to testify at trial that invites or allows the jury to infer guilt therefrom, whether in the form of an instruction by the court or a remark by the prosecution. It is *Griffin* error for a prosecutor to state that certain evidence is uncontradicted or unrefuted when that evidence could not be contradicted or refuted by anyone other than the defendant testifying on his or her own behalf. It is error for the prosecution to refer to the absence of evidence that only the defendant's testimony could provide.

Griffin error may be committed by either direct or indirect comments on the defendant's failure to testify in his defense. The prohibition, however, does not extend to such comment on the defense's failure at trial to introduce evidence that could reasonably have been expected—save only, of course, the testimony of the defendant himself.

Appeal

If the defendant is acquitted at trial, the prosecution cannot appeal. Thus, nearly all of the cases in this book are appeals by a defendant from a conviction. In all but death penalty cases, the first appeal is to one of the six California Courts of Appeal. The losing party in a Court of Appeal may seek review by the California Supreme Court. Death penalty cases are appealed directly to the California Supreme Court.

If a state court conviction implicates the U.S. Constitution, the losing party in the state appellate court may seek review by the U.S. Supreme Court.

Appellate practice is complex, involving appeals, writs of mandate and prohibition, and the writ of habeas corpus.

NOTE ON THE MODEL PENAL CODE

The American Law Institute began drafting a model penal code in 1952. A decade later, the Model Penal Code (MPC) was published. The MPC has been influential. A Westlaw search for the term "Model Penal Code" disclosed nearly 7,000 hits. A number of states have adopted large portions of the MPC. California is not a MPC state. California has its own Penal Code, dating from 1873. Although the MPC does not apply in California, California courts look to the MPC to inform analysis of certain issues. In *People v. Bipialaka* (2019) 34 Cal. App. 5th 455, 246 Cal. Rptr. 3d 177, the Court of Appeal wrote, "California courts routinely turn to the Model Penal Code for guidance and clarity." A number of MPC sections (*e.g.*, attempt, insanity) are discussed in the text.

CHAPTER 2

ACTUS REUS

■ ■ ■

Crimes have a physical component and a mental component. The physical component is the *actus reus*. The mental component is the *mens rea*, also called criminal intent. The U.S. Supreme Court put it colorfully when it wrote that crime requires an "evil-meaning mind and an evil-doing hand." *Dixon v. United States* (2006) 548 U.S. 1, 5, 126 S.Ct. 2437. The California Penal Code articulates the requirement of *actus reus* and *mens rea* as follows: "In every crime or public offense there must exist a union, or joint operation of act, intent, or criminal negligence."[1] The *actus reus* and *mens rea* requirements are described as follows in CALCRIM 250: "For you to find a person guilty of the crime of _______, that person must not only commit the prohibited act, but must do so with wrongful intent."

All crimes have an *actus reus*. Most, but *not* all, crimes have a *mens rea*. So-called strict liability offenses do not have a *mens rea*. Strict liability offenses do, however, have an *actus reus*. Strict liability offenses are discussed in Chapter 3.

The physical component of crime, the *actus reus*, is an act, a volitional movement of the body. Most of the time the act is obvious. Suppose Beth, who is aware of what she is doing, aims a gun at Paul and volitionally pulls the trigger. Aiming the gun and pulling the trigger are acts.

Suppose Beth aimed the gun at Paul and pulled the trigger because Paul was attacking her with an ax? Does this change the fact that Beth committed a volitional act? What if Beth pulled the trigger because Sally was holding a gun to Beth's head and said, "Unless you shoot Paul, I'll blow your brains out right this instant!" Did Beth commit an act?

Suppose you are standing on top of Half Dome in Yosemite, admiring the view. An unexpected gust of wind knocks you into Bill who is standing next to you, causing Bill to fall to his death. Did you kill Bill? Did you commit a volitional act that killed Bill?

Ralph is driving to the store to buy a candy bar. Suddenly, Ralph has a seizure, during which his car crosses the center line and collides head on with another car, killing the driver. Did Ralph kill the driver? Did Ralph commit a volitional act that killed the driver? Would it make a difference

---

[1] PC § 20.

if Ralph knew, before he started his journey to the store, that he was prone to seizures?

The following two cases—*In re David W.* and *People v. Ross*—grapple with the requirement of a volitional act.

IN RE DAVID W., A PERSON COMING UNDER THE JUVENILE COURT LAW

California Court of Appeal
116 Cal.App.3d 689, 172 Cal.Rptr.2d 266 (1981)

ASHBY, J.

[Editor's note: When a case begins with or contains bracketed material [ ], this indicates that the bracketed material was added by your editor. *In re David W.* is a juvenile court case. In California, the juvenile court is part of the Superior Court. The juvenile court has authority over three groups of children: (1) juvenile delinquents (wards); (2) status offenders;[2] and (3) abused and neglected children (dependents). The statutes governing the juvenile court are in the Welfare and Institutions Code. *In re David W.* is a delinquency case. Section 602 of the California Welfare and Institutions Code defines juvenile delinquency. Basically, a delinquent act is an act committed by a juvenile that would be a crime if committed by an adult.]

Pursuant to Welfare and Institutions Code section 602 the juvenile court found that appellant, a 15 year old, violated Penal Code section 647(f), which provides: "Every person who commits any of the following acts is guilty of disorderly conduct, a misdemeanor: (f) Who is found in any public place under the influence of any drug in such a condition that he is unable to exercise care for his own safety or the safety of others."

On February 6, 1980, Burbank Police Officers Bonnar and Stehr responded to a radio call concerning a juvenile possibly under the influence of a drug creating a disturbance. The call was initiated by appellant's mother who was concerned that appellant could not care for himself and that someone might get hurt. When the officers arrived at her home she directed them to an upstairs bedroom, stating that appellant had become very violent and was causing a disturbance. When the officers got to appellant's bedroom, they observed that appellant was being restrained by his brother and a couple of friends.

Appellant was violently attacking his brother; his speech was extremely slurred; he had trouble keeping balance when standing; his eyes

---

[2] Welfare and Institutions Code § 601(a) defines status offender as: "Any person under the age of 18 years who persistently or habitually refuses to obey the reasonable and proper orders or directions of his or parents, guardian, or custodian, or who is beyond the control of her or parents, guardian, or custodian, or who is under the age of 18 years when he or she violated any ordinance of any city or county of this state establishing a curfew based solely on age is within the jurisdiction of the juvenile court." Section 601 also covers chronic truancy.

were very red; and he had no aroma of alcoholic beverage about him. The officers were trained in the symptoms of persons under the influence of a drug. The officers formed the opinion that appellant was under the influence of a drug, and that he was unable to care for the safety of himself and others.

Appellant could not walk without assistance. The officers handcuffed him and assisted him downstairs by the arms. Appellant's mother had called an ambulance. One of the officers told her, "Cancel the ambulance and we'll take him to the hospital." Appellant was escorted, handcuffed, to the police car, cursing the officers. He was taken to the Burbank Community Hospital. A doctor administered Ipecac to appellant. When that failed to induce vomiting, the doctor prepared to pump appellant's stomach. When the doctor ordered appellant's boots removed for this procedure, a packet containing pills appearing to be Tuinal fell to the floor. Appellant's symptoms were consistent with the influence of Tuinal, and appellant was placed under arrest for possession of a dangerous drug.

Appellant contends the record does not support the trial court's finding that appellant violated Penal Code section 647(f). We agree. When the police found appellant, he was in a bedroom of his own home, which is manifestly not a public place within the meaning of the statute.

Appellant came to be in a public place, to wit, the sidewalk in front of his home and the police vehicle en route to the hospital, only because he was taken there by the police while handcuffed and while apparently resisting at least to the extent of cursing the officers.

While it is also clear that the police officers acted properly in taking custody of appellant and transporting him to the hospital at the request of his mother and for his own benefit by reason of urgent medical necessity, this fact should not justify appellant's prosecution for a crime he did not voluntarily commit. While he was in his home, appellant was not in violation of section 647(f). Although the police had proper grounds and laudable motives to remove appellant for transportation to the hospital, the fact remains that he was compelled by the police officers to go to a public place.

QUESTIONS

1. What did the prosecutor fail to prove? *Actus reus*, *mens rea*, both?

2. Change the facts. Suppose David was not removed from his room by the officers. Rather, the officers stood outside the house and shouted, "David, come out and talk to us." In response, David walked out of the house. Once outside, the officers arrested him for violation of PC § 647(f). Did David violate § 647(f)?

PEOPLE V. ROSS

California Court of Appeal
162 Cal.App.4th 1184, 76 Cal.Rptr.3d 477 (2008)

YEGAN, J.

There are dangerous people in county jail. Statutory and decisional law, founded upon sound public policy and common sense, have as their goal the minimization of violence in jail. As we shall explain, the trial court's order is at variance with this salutary goal. We reverse.

The People appeal from an order setting aside the second count of a two-count information. (Pen. Code § 995.) [Section 995 allows the defense to file a motion to dismiss based on the argument that the defendant was charged without probable cause.] The second count charged respondent with bringing a deadly weapon into a jail in violation of section 4574(a). The issue is whether the statute applies to an arrested person who "involuntarily" enters a jail. We hold that where, as here, the arrestee lies to law enforcement or correctional officials by denying possession of a weapon and enters the jail, the arrestee has violated section 4574. In such instance, the arrestee voluntarily chooses to enter the jail with the weapon.

Respondent was arrested for assault with a knife (Count 1). The police patted her down, but did not find a weapon. They transported her to the Santa Barbara County Jail. Upon arriving at the jail, respondent was asked if she had a weapon on her person. Respondent said "no." During the booking process another officer made a thorough search of respondent and found a knife in the inseam of her undergarments near her left buttocks.

In granting the motion, the trial court said that respondent had not violated section 4574(a), because she had not voluntarily entered the jail. Instead, she had been involuntarily brought into the jail pursuant to her arrest.

Except for strict liability offenses, every crime has two components: (1) an act or omission, sometimes called the *actus reus*; and (2) a necessary mental state, sometimes called the *mens rea*. (Pen. Code § 20) Section 4574(a), provides: "Any person, who knowingly brings or sends into any jail any firearms, deadly weapons, or explosives, and any person who, while lawfully confined in a jail possesses therein any firearm, deadly weapon, explosive, tear gas or tear gas weapon, is guilty of a felony." Here, the *actus reus* of the crime was bringing a deadly weapon into a jail. The *mens rea* was respondent's knowledge that she possessed a deadly weapon and that the location was a jail.

Respondent does not dispute the sufficiency of the evidence to establish the requisite *mens rea*. But she contends that, as a matter of law, the evidence is insufficient to establish the *actus reus*. According to respondent, the *actus reus* must be a voluntary act. Therefore, the statute applies only to persons who "voluntarily" enter a jail, such as inmate visitors. Since she "was brought involuntarily to the jail having been arrested for assault with a deadly weapon," respondent argues that the trial court properly set aside the second count charging a violation of section 4574(a).

The question here is one of statutory interpretation. When construing a statute, a court's goal is to ascertain the intent of the enacting legislative body so that we may adopt the construction that best effectuates the purpose of the law. Generally, the court first examines the statute's words, giving them their ordinary and usual meaning and viewing them in their statutory context, because the statutory language is usually the most reliable indicator of legislative intent. When the statutory language is ambiguous, a court may consider the consequences of each possible construction and will reasonably infer that the enacting legislative body intended an interpretation producing practical and workable results rather than one producing mischief or absurdity.

The plain language of section 4574(a) encompasses respondent's conduct. "Bring" means "to convey, lead, carry, or cause to come along from one place to another" or "to take or carry along with one." (Webster's Third New Internat. Dict. (1981) p. 278). Respondent knowingly took or carried a deadly weapon into the jail after denying that she possessed a weapon. She therefore voluntarily chose to enter the jail with the weapon. The statute requires no more.

Respondent contends that she had a Fifth Amendment right not to disclose her possession of the knife because disclosure would have incriminated her. The knife apparently was the weapon that respondent had used in the commission of the assault (count 1). Since her privilege against self-incrimination protected her from compulsory disclosure of the knife, respondent maintains that she could not have been lawfully convicted of violating section 4574(a).

We disagree. Respondent's Fifth Amendment privilege permitted her to remain silent. It did not protect her from the consequences of lying to a law enforcement officer, who had properly inquired whether she possessed any weapons. While the Fifth Amendment provides suspects with a shield against compelled self-incrimination, it does not provide them with a sword upon which to thrust a lie.

The order setting aside count two of the information is reversed.

QUESTIONS AND NOTES

1. Suppose that upon being escorted into the jail, the intake officer had not asked defendant whether she had any weapons. Would defendant violate § 4574(a) if she deliberately failed to disclose the weapon?

2. Can you reconcile *David W.*, where there was no *actus reus*, with *Ross*, where there was?

3. In 2018, Joseph was captured on the battlefield in Afghanistan and incarcerated at an American base overseas. During confinement, Joseph crafted a knife out of a piece of metal in his cell. In 2020, Joseph was transferred a Federal prison in California. He brought the knife with him, hidden in a pair of pants. In California, a guard discovered Joseph's knife, and Joseph is prosecuted under the following Federal statute: "Any person incarcerated in a Federal prison who possesses any weapon shall be guilty of a felony." Did Joseph violate the statute?

4. The volitional act of the *actus reus* is distinct from the *mens rea* of the crime. Professor Joshua Dressler offers the following useful illustration: "Carl, standing on a target range, aims his gun at the target and pulls the trigger, at which instant Dorothy unforeseeably walks in front of the target and is struck by a bullet from Carl's gun, and dies as a result. On these facts, Carl lacks any blameworthy state of mind (*mens rea*) regarding Dorothy's death. Nonetheless, Carl's act of pulling the trigger was voluntary." Joshua Dressler, *Criminal Law* (4th ed. 2007) (West).

5. The *Ross* court pointed out that judges often find it necessary to interpret statutes in order to determine their meaning. In *People v. Butler* (2011) 195 Cal.App.4th 535, 124 Cal.Rptr.3d 610, Butler filed four false small claims court actions against four different manufacturers of electric razors, alleging that a razor injured his face. The first two manufacturers settled the claims and issued checks to Butler. Eventually, an attorney for one of the manufacturers figured out the scam, and Butler was prosecuted under PC § 550(a)(2), which provides, "It is unlawful to do any of the following: Knowingly present multiple claims for the same loss or injury, including presentation of multiple claims to more than one insurer, with the intent to defraud." Butler argues that he cannot be prosecuted under the statute because he filed his claims with manufacturers, not insurers, thus the statute did not apply to him. Is Butler correct?

UNCONSCIOUSNESS AND *ACTUS REUS*

A person who is unconscious is incapable of acting volitionally. Suppose Sue is asleep in bed with her wife. In her sleep, Sue rolls over and her arm smacks her spouse in the nose. Could Sue be prosecuted for battery, which is "any willful and unlawful use of force or violence upon the person of another"? (PC § 242).

When a person's body moves while the person is somnambulating or convulsing or otherwise unconscious, the person is not "acting" volitionally. Unconsciousness is uncommon, but when it occurs, it is a defense.[3] PC § 26 provides, "All persons are capable of committing crimes except those

[3] You might want to start a list of defenses. Although Chapter 9 goes into detail on defenses, some defenses are discussed elsewhere in the book.

belonging to the following classes: Persons who committed the act charged without being conscious thereof." The CALCRIM jury instruction on unconsciousness is 3425, and provides:

> The defendant is not guilty of ______ if [the defendant] acted while legally unconscious. Someone is legally unconscious when he or she is not conscious of his or her actions. Someone may be unconscious even though able to move.
>
> Unconsciousness may be caused by ______ [insert blackout, epileptic seizure, involuntary intoxication, or sleepwalking].
>
> The defense of unconsciousness may not be based on voluntary intoxication.
>
> The People must prove beyond a reasonable doubt that the defendant was conscious when (he/she) acted. If there is proof beyond a reasonable doubt that the defendant acted as if (he/she) were conscious, you should conclude that (he/she) was conscious. If, however, based on all the evidence, you have a reasonable doubt that (he/she) was conscious, you must find (him/her) not guilty.

Around the United States, there is some disagreement as to whether unconsciousness falls within the insanity defense or whether it is a separate defense. In California, unconsciousness is not part of the insanity defense. Would a defendant who claims she was unconscious care whether unconsciousness is a form of insanity or a separate defense?

With the defense of unconsciousness in mind, consider *People v. Newton.*

PEOPLE V. NEWTON

California Court of Appeal
8 Cal.App.3d 359, 87 Cal.Rptr. 394 (1970)

RATTIGAN, J.

Huey P. Newton appeals from a judgment convicting him of voluntary manslaughter.

Count One of an indictment issued by the Alameda County Grand Jury in November 1967, charged defendant with the murder (Pen. Code § 187) of John Frey; count Two, with assault with a deadly weapon upon the person of Herbert Heanes, knowing or having reasonable cause to know Heanes to be a peace officer engaged in the performance of his duties (Pen. Code § 245b).

The jury acquitted him of the Heanes assault, but found him guilty of the voluntary manslaughter of Frey.

At relevant times, John Frey and Herbert Heanes were officers of the Oakland Police Department. The criminal charges against defendant arose from a street altercation in which Frey was fatally wounded by gunfire, and Heanes and defendant were shot, on October 28, 1967.

Lord was on radio duty in the Oakland Police Administration Building. Officer Frey was also on duty, and alone in a police car, patrolling an assigned beat in Oakland. At about 4:51 a.m., he radioed Lord and requested a check on an automobile which was moving in his vicinity and which bore license number AZM 489. Less than a minute later, Lord told Frey that "we have got some information coming out on that." Frey replied, "Check. It's a known Black Panther vehicle. I am going to stop it at Seventh and Willow. You might send a unit by." Officer Heanes, who was listening to this conversation in his police car on another beat, called in that he was "enroute" to Seventh and Willow Streets.

Officer Heanes testified for the People as follows: He arrived at Seventh and Willow Streets "three to four minutes" after responding by radio to Officer Frey's call. Officer Frey's police car was parked. A beige Volkswagen was parked directly in front of it. Heanes parked his car behind Frey's, alighted and walked to the right rear of the Volkswagen. At this time, two men were seated in the Volkswagen, both in the front seat; Officer Frey was standing near the driver's door of the vehicle, writing a citation.

After a minute or so, Heanes followed Frey to the latter's vehicle, where he heard Frey talk to the police radio dispatcher about an address and a birth date. When Frey finished the radio call, he and Heanes had a conversation in which Frey indicated that defendant, when asked for identification, had produced the Volkswagen registration and given his name as "LaVerne Williams." While Frey remained in his car, Heanes walked forward to the Volkswagen, addressed defendant as "Mr. Williams," and asked if he had any further identification. Defendant, still seated in the vehicle, said "I am Huey Newton." Frey then approached the Volkswagen and conversed with Heanes, who asked defendant to get out of the car. Defendant asked "if there was any particular reason why he should." Heanes asked him "if there was any reason why he didn't want to." Frey then informed defendant that he was under arrest and ordered him out of the car.

Defendant got out of the Volkswagen and walked, "rather briskly" to the rear of the police cars. Frey followed, three or four feet behind defendant and slightly to defendant's right. Heanes followed them, but stopped at the front end of Frey's police car. Defendant walked to the rear part of Heanes's car, Frey still behind him, and turned around. He assumed a stance with his feet apart, knees flexed, both "arms down" at hip level in front of his body.

Heanes heard a gunshot and saw Officer Frey move toward defendant. As he (Heanes) drew and raised his own gun in his right hand, a bullet struck his right forearm.

Heanes returned his attention to Officer Frey and defendant, who were "on the trunk lid of my car tussling." The two were in "actual physical contact" and "seemed to be wrestling all over the trunk area of my car." He next remembered being on his knees at the front door of Frey's car, approximately 30 to 35 feet from the other two men. Defendant was then facing him; Officer Frey was "facing from the side" of defendant, toward the curb, and appeared to be "hanging onto" him. Holding his gun in his left hand, Heanes aimed at defendant and fired "at his midsection." Defendant did not fall. He (Heanes) then heard other gunshots from the area of where Officer Frey and defendant were "tussling on the rear part of my car." Heanes did not see a gun in defendant's hand at any time. He next remembered "laying" in Officer Frey's police car, and calling an "emergency, officer needs assistance, shots fired" on its radio. After that, and through the vehicle's rear window, he saw two men running in a westerly direction toward Seventh and Willow Streets.

Henry Grier, a bus driver employed by AC Transit, gave this testimony for the People: He saw flashing lights on the police cars, and three men in the street. Two of them, a police officer and a "civilian," were walking. The civilian pulled a gun from inside his shirt and "spun around." The first police officer "grabbed him by the arm." The two struggled, and "the gun went off." The officer walking behind them "was hit and he fell"; after he was hit, he drew his gun and fired. Grier stopped the bus immediately and called "central dispatch" on its radio. He saw the civilian, standing "sort of in a crouched position," fire several shots into the first officer as the latter was falling forward. These shots were fired from within a distance of "four or five feet" from the midsection of the officer's body; the last one was fired in the direction of his back as he lay face down on the ground. At the trial, Grier positively identified defendant as the "civilian" mentioned in his account.

Defendant arrived at the emergency desk of Kaiser Hospital at 5:50 a.m. on the same morning. He asked to see a doctor, stating "I have been shot in the stomach." A nurse called the police. Officer Robert Fredericks arrived and placed defendant under arrest. He (defendant) had a bullet wound in his abdomen. The bullet had entered in the front and exited through the back of his body.

Officers Frey and Heanes were taken to Merritt Hospital, where Frey was dead on arrival. He had been shot five times. Officer Heanes had three bullet wounds.

Defendant, testifying in his own behalf, denied killing Officer Frey, shooting Officer Heanes, or carrying a gun on the morning of the shootings.

His account of the episode was as follows: He was driving with Gene McKinney when he noticed a red light through the rear window of the Volkswagen. He pulled over to the curb and stopped. Officer Frey approached the Volkswagen and said "Well, well, well, what do we have? The great, great Huey P. Newton." Frey asked for defendant's driver's license and inquired as to the ownership of the Volkswagen. Defendant handed him his (defendant's) license, and the vehicle registration, and said that the car belonged to LaVerne Williams. Officer Frey returned the license and walked back to his patrol car with the registration.

A few minutes later Officer Heanes arrived, conversed with Frey, then walked up to the Volkswagen and asked, "Mr. Williams, do you have any further identification?" Defendant said, "What do you mean, Mr. Williams? My name is Huey P. Newton." Heanes replied, "Yes, I know who you are." Officer Frey then ordered defendant out of the car. He got out, taking with him a criminal law book in his right hand. He asked if he was under arrest; Officer Frey said no, but ordered defendant to lean against the car. Frey then searched him, placing his hands inside defendant's trousers and touching his genitals. (Officer Heanes had testified that defendant was not searched at any time.) McKinney, who had also alighted from the Volkswagen, was then standing with Officer Heanes on the street side of the Volkswagen.

Seizing defendant's left arm with his right hand, Officer Frey told him to go back to his patrol car. Defendant walked, with the officer "kind of pushing" him, past the first police car to the back door of the second one. Defendant opened his book and said, "You have no reasonable cause to arrest me." The officer said, "You can take that book and stick it up your ass." He then struck defendant in the face, dazing him. Defendant stumbled backwards and fell to one knee. Officer Frey drew a revolver. Defendant felt a "sensation like boiling hot soup had been spilled on my stomach," and heard an "explosion," then a "volley of shots." He remembered "crawling, a moving sensation," but nothing else until he found himself at the entrance of Kaiser Hospital with no knowledge of how he arrived there. He expressly testified that he was "unconscious or semiconscious" during this interval, that he was "still only semiconscious" at the hospital entrance, and that—after recalling some events at Kaiser Hospital—he later "regained consciousness" at another hospital.

The defense called Bernard Diamond, M.D., who testified that defendant's recollections were "compatible" with the gunshot wound he had received; and that "a gunshot wound which penetrates in a body cavity, the abdominal cavity or the thoracic cavity is very likely to produce a profound reflex shock reaction, that is quite different than a gunshot wound which penetrates only skin and muscle and it is not at all uncommon for a person shot in the abdomen to lose consciousness and go into this reflex shock condition for short periods of time up to half an hour or so."

Defendant asserts prejudicial error in the trial court's failure to instruct the jury on the subject of *unconsciousness* as a defense to a charge of criminal homicide. Although the evidence of the fatal affray is both conflicting and confused as to who shot whom and when, some of it supported the inference that defendant had been shot in the abdomen before he fired any shots himself. Given this sequence, defendant's testimony of his sensations when shot—supplemented to a degree, as it was, by Dr. Diamond's opinion based upon the nature of the abdominal wound—supported the further inference that defendant was in a state of unconsciousness when Officer Frey was shot.

Where not self-induced, as by voluntary intoxication or the equivalent, unconsciousness is a complete defense to a charge of criminal homicide. Unconsciousness need not reach the physical dimensions commonly associated with the term (coma, inertia, incapability of locomotion or manual action, and so on); it can exist where the subject physically acts in fact but is not, at the time, conscious of acting.

The judgment of conviction is reversed.

NOTES

1. Huey P. Newton was born in 1942 in Louisiana. Newton's father was a sharecropper and minister. The family moved to Oakland when Newton was three. When he graduated from high school, Newton could not read. He taught himself to read, and paid for college by burglarizing homes in Oakland and Berkeley. While attending Merritt College, Newton studied law and philosophy. He became active in civil rights. In 1966, he co-founded the Black Panther Party for Self Defense. The Black Panther Party grew out of a belief the Oakland Police Department was racist and targeted Blacks unjustly.

Officer Frey was 23 when Newton killed him. Frey left a wife and daughter.

2. Defendant, a 17 year Air Force career officer with a spotless record, was charged with rubbing his finger on his daughter's vagina to satisfy his sexual desire. Defendant claimed that he was innocent because he was asleep when it happened. Defendant had a history of parasomnia, a sleep disorder. Should defendant be permitted to offer expert testimony describing his sleep disorder to prove that he did not commit a volitional act? *United States v. Haravey* (2008) 66 M.J. 585 (Air Force Ct. Crim. App.).

3. A person who drinks so much that the person becomes unconscious is culpable. Acts committed while unconscious due to voluntary intoxication can be prosecuted. For example, an unintentional killing while unconscious due to voluntary intoxication can be involuntary manslaughter.[4]

---

[4] *See People v. Ochoa* (1998) 19 Cal.4th 353, 423–424, 79 Cal.Rptr.2d 408, 966 P.2d 442, where the Supreme Court explained:

CRIMINAL LIABILITY FOR DOING NOTHING—FAILURE TO ACT; OMISSIONS

Normally, the *actus reus* of a crime is an affirmative act—pulling a trigger, taking someone's car. Can a person be guilty of a crime when the person does nothing—no act at all? This issue comes up when someone fails to rescue or provide assistance to someone else. Is it a crime to fail to rescue? In the United States, there generally is no duty to rescue. Because there is no duty to come to someone's aid, there is generally no criminal liability for failing to do so. If an Olympic swimmer is walking past a swimming pool and observes a child drowning in the pool, the swimmer has no duty to rescue the child, and this is so even if the Olympian could rescue the child without risk to the Olympian. Ah, but what if the drowning child is the offspring of the Olympian? Now must the Olympian attempt to rescue her own child? Yes, because a parent has a legal duty to protect the parent's own child. Or, suppose the Olympian was employed at the pool as a lifeguard? If the lifeguard does nothing, is prosecution possible?

A duty to act—and thus liability for failure to act—can arise in the following situations: (1) A statute imposes a duty to act; (2) A relationship such as parent and child imposes a duty to act; (3) There is a contractual relationship that imposes a duty to act; (4) An individual voluntarily assumes the care or protection of another; and (5) An individual creates a risk that threatens another.

Generally, there is no duty to call police if you know a crime has been or is being committed. However, PC § 152.3 states, "Any person who reasonably believes that he or she has observed the commission of any of the following offenses where the victim is a child under the age of 14 years shall notify a peace officer:" murder, rape, and other sex offenses. Failure to report is a misdemeanor. Reporting is not required when the person is related to the victim or the offender. Nor is reporting required if the person fears for her safety or the safety of her family. A person who fails to report may defend on the basis of mistake of fact. "Mistake of fact" is discussed in Chapter 9.

When a person renders himself or herself unconscious through voluntary intoxication and kills in that state, the killing is attributable to his or her negligence in self-intoxicating to that point, and is treated as involuntary manslaughter. Unconsciousness is ordinarily a complete defense to a charge of criminal homicide. If the state of unconsciousness results from intoxication voluntarily induced, however, it is not a complete defense. If the intoxication is voluntarily induced, it can never excuse homicide. Thus, the requisite element of criminal negligence is deemed to exist irrespective of unconsciousness, and a defendant stands guilty of involuntary manslaughter if he voluntarily procured his own intoxication. Unconsciousness for this purpose need not mean that the actor lies still and unresponsive: section 26 describes as incapable of committing crimes person who committed the fact without being conscious thereof. Thus unconsciousness can exist where the subject physically acts in fact but is not, at the time, conscious of acting.

Professionals who work with children, and who suspect a child has been abused or neglected, are required to report their suspicions to law enforcement or child protective services. (PC § 11165 et seq.) Professionals who work with elders must report suspected elder abuse. (Welfare & Institutions Code § 15630 et seq.) Failure to report is a crime.

PC § 152 states, "Every person who, having knowledge of an accidental death, actively conceals or attempts to conceal that death, shall be guilty of a misdemeanor."

PC § 150 states, "Every able-bodied person above 18 years of age who neglects or refuses to join the posse comitatus or power of the county, by neglecting or refusing to aid and assist in taking or arresting any person against whom there may be issued any process" commits an offense.

Vehicle Code § 20001(a) states, "The driver of a vehicle involved in an accident resulting in injury to a person, other than himself or herself, or in the death of a person shall immediately stop the vehicle at the scene of the accident and shall" render necessary aid. Failure to stop and render aid is an offense.

PROBLEM

Sue met Vic at a bar. While at the bar, Sue purchased some jewelry from Vic. As Sue was leaving, Vic asked if he could go with her. Vic appeared extremely drunk. Sue said, "Yes," and the two went to Sue's apartment. While there, Vic asked for a spoon to prepare narcotics for injection. Sue gave Vic a spoon, and Vic injected himself with heroin. Vic passed out, and Sue was unable to rouse him. Sue dragged the unconscious Vic outside and placed him next to trash cans in the alley. It was a warm summer evening. During the night, Vic died from an overdose of narcotics. Can Sue be prosecuted for Vic's death? *People v. Oliver* (1989) 210 Cal.App.3d 138, 258 Cal.Rptr. 138.

CORPUS DELICTI—BODY OF THE CRIME

In every criminal prosecution, the prosecutor must establish the *corpus delicti* or body of the crime. The *corpus delicti* includes: (1) injury, harm, or loss; and (2) criminal agency. For example, in a murder trial, production of a body is not sufficient to establish the *corpus delicti*. The prosecutor must establish that death was due to criminal homicide.

The *corpus delecti* does not include: (1) where the crime occurred; (2) the state of mind of the perpetrator; (3) identity of the perpetrator, or (4) the degree of the crime.

In many criminal prosecutions, the defendant's inculpatory pretrial statements (*e.g.*, confession to police) provide powerful evidence of guilt. Are a defendant's inculpatory pretrial statements sufficient at trial to prove guilt in the absence of any other evidence? That is, are a defendant's pretrial words *alone* sufficient to prove guilt? No. Under the *corpus delicti* rule, a conviction must be supported by some proof in addition to the defendant's pretrial statements.[5] The Supreme Court explained in *People v. Dalton* (2019) 7 Cal. 5th 166:

> To convict an accused of a criminal offense, the prosecution must prove that a crime actually occurred. The *corpus delicti* or body of the crime cannot be proved by *exclusive* reliance on the defendant's extrajudicial statements. The independent proof may be circumstantial and need not be beyond a reasonable doubt, but is sufficient if it permits an inference of criminal conduct, even if a noncriminal explanation is also plausible. There is no requirement of independent evidence of every physical act constituting an element of an offense, so long as there is some slight or prima facie showing of injury, loss, or harm by criminal agency. In every case, once the necessary quantum of independent evidence is present, the defendant's extrajudicial statements may then be considered for their full value to strengthen the case on all issues.

In similar language, the Court of Appeal explained in *People v. Tompkins* (2010) 185 Cal.App.4th 1253, 1259, 110 Cal.Rptr.3d 918: "The *corpus delicti* requirement ensures that a defendant will not be convicted of a crime that never happened. Proof of the *corpus* of a crime may be made by circumstantial evidence and need not amount to proof beyond a reasonable doubt. Rather, the amount of independent proof required is quite small, slight, or minimal, amounting only to a *prima facie* showing permitting a reasonable inference a crime was committed. Once the *corpus delicti* has been established, the defendant's statements may be considered for their full value."

POSSESSION; MOMENTARY POSSESSION; POSSESSION FOR DISPOSAL

Possession of certain items (illegal drugs) is a crime. But what is the meaning of "possession"? Must the defendant be aware of the illegal item to be in possession of the item? Suppose some evil person secretly puts drugs in your backpack. You don't know the drugs are there. Are you in "possession" of the drugs?

Suppose you reach into your backpack and find cocaine planted there by some unknown person. You grab the cocaine and remove it from your bag to figure out what it is. At that moment, you are arrested for possession of cocaine. Are you in "possession" of the cocaine?

---

[5] *See People v. Rosales* (2014) 222 Cal.App.4th 1254, 166 Cal.Rptr.3d 620.

In *People v. Mijares* (1971) 6 Cal.3d 415, 99 Cal.Rptr. 139, 491 P.2d 1115, the Supreme Court discussed the concept of "momentary possession." If a defendant handles an illegal substance for the limited purpose of disposing of it, this is not "possession." In *People v. Cole* (1988) 202 Cal.App.3d 1439, 249 Cal. Rptr. 601, defendant found illegal drugs in his daughter's room. He confiscated the drugs with the intent to destroy them. The next day, before he could get rid of the drugs, the police seized them, and defendant was charged with possession. The *Cole* court ruled that possession for purposes of disposal is not possession. In *People v. Martin* (2001) 25 Cal.4th 1180, 1191, 108 Cal.Rptr.2d 599, 25 P.3d 1081, the Supreme Court disapproved *Cole*. The *Martin* court wrote, "We conclude that the defense of transitory possession applies only to momentary or transitory possession of contraband for the purpose of disposal."

QUESTION

Efrain went to buy methamphetamine from a drug dealer named Jose. While negotiating the sale, Efrain decided to steal the drugs, which he did, and ran away. Jose quickly caught Efrain and put him in a chokehold. About to pass out due to the chokehold, Efrain threw the drugs down in the hope Jose would let him go, which Jose did. The whole episode was observed by a police officer, who arrested Efrain. Efrain is charged with possession of methamphetamine. He wishes to raise the defense of momentary possession. If you are on Efrain's jury, will you "buy" his momentary possession argument? *People v. Paz* (2010) 181 Cal.App.4th 1413, 105 Cal.Rptr.3d 556.

CHAPTER 3

MENS REA

■ ■ ■

Within substantive criminal law, few subjects are more complex than criminal intent—*mens rea*. The mental component of crime has a long and complicated history. *Mens rea* terms include malice, willful, intentional, reckless, and negligent. The same *mens rea* term—*e.g.*, malice—is found in different crimes and has different meanings in each crime. Thus, arson was defined at common law as "the malicious burning of the dwelling house of another." Murder is the "unlawful killing of a human being with malice aforethought." The meaning of "malice" is not the same in arson and murder.

MEANING OF "INTENTIONAL" IN CRIMINAL LAW

The words "intent" and "intentional" are common *mens rea* terms. Outside the law, when we say a person acts "intentionally," we typically mean it is the person's conscious object to act in a certain way or to achieve a certain goal. When you tell your friend, "I intend to go to criminal law today," your friend understands it is your conscious object to go to class. Criminal law uses the word "intentional" this way. Thus, if you decide to kill your professor, and you carry out your plan, you will be charged with intent to kill murder—it was your conscious object to kill; you intended to kill.

Suppose, however, that in your desire to kill your professor, you devise a plan to put a bomb on an airplane that your professor will be on. You design the bomb to explode when the plane is at 35,000 feet. You don't want to kill anyone on the plane but the professor. The bomb goes off as planned, and everyone is killed. Clearly, you killed everyone on the plane. But who did you *intend* to kill? Only the professor, right? It was your conscious object to kill the professor. You did not intend to hurt any of the other passengers or crew. Yet, the law holds that you intended to kill *everyone* on the plane! You can be charged with the intent to kill murder of *all* the people killed. A person is deemed to intend results that the person knows are virtually certain to occur from the person's conduct. This is true even if the person does not want those results to occur. Thus, even if you fervently hoped nobody else on the plane would be hurt, the law says you intended to kill everyone on the plane.

CRIMINAL NEGLIGENCE

In Torts you learn about negligence. The concept of negligence is also used in criminal law, where so-called "criminal negligence" is the *mens rea* for certain crimes (*e.g.*, involuntary manslaughter based on criminal negligence). Although the meaning of negligence is similar in torts and criminal law, there is an important difference. The negligence that will suffice for damages in civil litigation is *not* sufficient for criminal liability.[1] Criminal negligence requires something more—a more serious departure from the conduct of a reasonable person. The Supreme Court described criminal negligence in *People v. Valdez* (2002) 27 Cal.4th 778, 783, 118 Cal.Rptr.2d 3, 42 P.3d 511: "Criminal negligence is aggravated, culpable, or reckless conduct that is such a departure from what would be the conduct of an ordinary prudent or careful person under the same circumstances as to be incompatible with a proper regard for human life. Under the criminal negligence standard, knowledge of the risk is determined by an objective test: If a reasonable person in the defendant's position would have been aware of the risk involved, then defendant is presumed to have had such an awareness."

It is difficult to define the difference between ordinary negligence and criminal negligence. How much more negligent must a defendant be to cross the line separating civil negligence from criminal negligence? It is a matter of degree. Suffice to say that the level of negligence that is sufficient in civil litigation is not sufficient in criminal law. For criminal liability, the defendant's failure to act reasonably must be more than a simple departure from ordinary care, it must be a "gross" departure.[2]

PROBLEM

Isabel is a low income single mother of four children living in Los Angeles. The oldest child is six. The other children are four, three, and one. Isabel has no relatives living nearby to help with childcare, and she cannot afford a babysitter. At 4:00 p.m., Isabel realized she had no food for the baby. Isabel decides to walk four blocks to the grocery store to buy food for the baby. Isabel does not have car. Isabel says to the six-year-old, "Mommy's going to run to the store for food for the baby. Make sure you kids stay inside with the door locked until I get home." While Isabel is at the grocery store, her home catches fire and is quickly engulfed in flame. A neighbor sees the flames, calls the fire

---

[1] *See Sea Horse Ranch, Inc. v. Superior Court of San Mateo County* (1994) 24 Cal.App.4th 446, 454, 30 Cal.Rptr.2d 681 ("Such criminal negligence is of a higher order of culpability than ordinary civil negligence.").

[2] *See Stark v. Superior Court* (2011) 52 Cal.4th 368, 128 Cal.Rptr.3d 611, 257 P.3d 41, the Supreme Court wrote, "Criminal negligence refers to a higher degree of negligence than is required to establish negligent default on a mere civil issue. The negligence must aggravated, culpable, gross, or reckless." *See also*, 17 *California Jurisprudence*: *Criminal Law* § 111, p. 199 (3d ed. 2010) (West) ("Gross negligence has been defined as the want of slight diligence; as an entire failure to exercise care, or the exercise of so slight a degree of care as to justify the belief that there was an indifference to the welfare of others.").

department, and rushes across the street to help. The door is locked. The neighbor sees the three older children standing at the front window crying. The neighbor breaks the front window and pulls the children to safety. The neighbor tries to enter the home after the six-year-old says, "My baby sister is still inside!" but the flames are too intense. Isabel arrives home shortly after the first fire truck pulls up, and has to be restrained by firefighters when she tries to run into the house to save her baby. The baby dies in the fire. Should Isabel be charged with a crime? What offense? Is she guilty of involuntary manslaughter, which requires the killing of a human being with criminal negligence? *People v. Rodriguez* (1960) 186 Cal.App.2d 433, 8 Cal.Rptr. 863.

Would it make a difference if, instead of leaving her children alone for a few minutes to buy baby food, Isabel left them alone the same few minutes to buy beer? Crack cocaine? Would it make a difference if, instead of walking to the store to buy baby food, Isabel left the children unattended for five hours to go to a bar to "party"?

MODEL PENAL CODE APPROACH TO *MENS REA*

Under the Model Penal Code (MPC), there are four mental states: purposely, knowingly, recklessly, and negligently. Although the MPC does not apply in California, the Code's approach to *mens rea* has been influential in the United States, and you should be familiar with the four mental states contained in MPC Section 2.02:

> **Purposely**. A person acts purposely with respect to a material element of an offense when: If the element involves the nature of his conduct or a result thereof, it is his conscious object to engage in conduct of that nature or to cause such a result.
>
> **Knowingly**. A person acts knowingly with respect to a material element of an offense when: If the element involves the nature of his conduct, he is aware that his conduct is of that nature; and if the element involves a result of his conduct, he is aware that it is practically certain that his conduct will cause such a result.
>
> **Recklessly**. A person acts recklessly with respect to a material element of an offense when he consciously disregards a substantial and unjustifiable risk that the material element exists or will result from his conduct. The risk must be of such a nature and degree that, considering the nature and purpose of the actor's conduct and the circumstances known to him, its disregard involves a gross deviation from the standard of conduct that a law-abiding person would observe in the actor's situation.
>
> **Negligently**. A person acts negligently with respect to a material element of an offense when he should be aware of a substantial and unjustifiable risk that the material element exists

> or will result from his conduct. The risk must be of such a nature and degree that the actor's failure to perceive it, considering the nature and purpose of his conduct and the circumstances known to him, involves a gross deviation from the standard of care that a reasonable person would observe in the actor's situation.

The official Comment to MPC § 2.02 is useful in understanding the Code's four mental states. American Law Institute, *Model Penal Code and Commentaries,* Comment to § 2.02 (1985):

> **Purpose and Knowledge**. In defining the kinds of culpability, the Code draws a narrow distinction between acting purposely and knowingly, one of the elements of ambiguity in legal usage of the term "intent." Action is not purposive with respect to the nature or result of the actor's conduct unless it was his conscious object to perform an action of that nature or to cause such a result. It is meaningful to think of the actor's attitude as different if he is simply aware that his conduct is of the required nature or that the prohibited result is practically certain to follow from his conduct.
>
> **Recklessness**. An important discrimination is drawn between acting either purposely or knowingly and acting recklessly. As the Code uses the term, recklessness involves conscious risk creation. It resembles acting knowingly in that a state of awareness is involved, but the awareness is of risk that is of a probability less than substantial certainty; the matter is contingent from the actor's point of view.
>
> The risk of which the actor is aware must of course be substantial in order for the recklessness judgment to be made. The risk must also be unjustifiable. Even substantial risks, it is clear, may be created without recklessness when the actor is seeking to serve a proper purpose, as when a surgeon performs an operation that he knows is very likely to be fatal but reasonably thinks to be necessary because the patient has no other, safer chance. Some principle must, therefore, be articulated to indicate the nature of the final judgment to be made after everything has been weighed: Describing the risk as "substantial" and "unjustifiable" is useful but not sufficient, for these are terms of degree, and the acceptability of a risk in a given case depends on a great, many variables. Some standard is needed for determining how substantial and how unjustifiable the risk must be in order to warrant a finding of culpability. There is no way to state this value judgment that does not beg the question in the last analysis; the point is that the jury must evaluate the actor's conduct and determine whether it should be condemned.
>
> Ultimately, then, the jury is asked to perform two distinct functions. First, it is to examine the risk and the factors that are relevant to how substantial it was and to the justifications for taking it. In each instance, the question is asked from the point of view of the actor's perceptions, *i.e.*, to what extent he was aware: of risk, of factors relating to its substantiality

and of factors relating to its unjustifiability. Second, the jury is to make the culpability judgment in terms of whether the defendant's conscious disregard of the risk justifies condemnation. Considering the nature and purpose of his conduct and the circumstances known to him, the question is whether the defendant's disregard of the risk involved a gross deviation from the standards of conduct that a law-abiding person would have observed in the actor's situation.

Negligence. The fourth kind of culpability is negligence. It is distinguished from purposeful, knowing or reckless action in that it does not involve a state of awareness. A person acts negligently under this subsection when he inadvertently creates a substantial and unjustifiable risk of which he ought to be aware. He is liable if given the nature and degree of the risk, his failure to perceive it is, considering the nature and purpose of the actor's conduct and the circumstances known to him, a gross deviation from the care that would be exercised by a reasonable person in his situation.

QUESTION

Recall the hypothetical in which you intended to kill your professor by putting a bomb on an airplane. The bomb went off and everyone was killed. With what MPC mental state did you kill the professor? With what MPC mental state did you kill the other people on the plane? Under common law principles, with what mental state did you kill the professor? How about the other people on the plane?

MENS REA TERMS IN THE CALIFORNIA PENAL CODE

Section 7 of the Penal Code contains several *mens rea* terms:

1. The word "willfully," when applied to the intent with which an act is done or omitted, implies simply a purpose or willingness to commit the act, or make the omission referred to. It does not require any intent to violate law, or to injure another, or to acquire any advantage.

2. The words "neglect," "negligence," "negligent," and "negligently" import a want of such attention to the nature or probable consequences of the act or omission as a prudent man ordinarily bestows in acting in his own concerns.

3. The word "corruptly" imports a wrongful design to acquire or cause some pecuniary or other advantage to the person guilty of the act or omission referred to, or to some other person.

4. The words "malice" and "maliciously" import a wish to vex, annoy, or injure another person, or an intent to do a wrongful act, established either by proof or presumption of law.

5. The word "knowingly" imports only a knowledge that the facts exist which bring the act or omission within the provisions of this code. It does not require any knowledge of the unlawfulness of such act or omission.

The *mens rea* terms in PC § 7 are only some of the mental states used in California criminal law.

MENTES REAE ARE NOT FUNGIBLE

Mens rea terms have defined meanings. If the accused is charged with a crime that requires one *mens rea,* but the trier of fact concludes she committed the *actus reus* with a different *mens rea,* then she did not commit the charged offense. For example, suppose defendant is charged with false imprisonment under a statute that reads: "A person commits false imprisonment if the person knowingly restrains another unlawfully so as to interfere substantially with the person's liberty." If defendant negligently restrains a person of their liberty, defendant does not commit the charged offense.

SOMETIMES AN ACCIDENT IS JUST AN ACCIDENT

Not every accident involves a tort or a crime. Sometimes an accident is just an accident.[3] PC § 26 recognizes this fact: "All persons are capable of committing crimes except those belonging to the following classes: Persons who committed the act or made the omission charged through misfortune or by accident, when it appears that there was no evil design, intention, or culpable negligence."

PROBLEM

Tim is on trial, charged with infliction of corporal injury on a cohabitant. Tim was living with his girlfriend Michaela, who was pregnant with their child. The prosecution offers evidence that, in the middle of the night, Tim woke Michaela up and told her to get him something to eat. When Michaela declined, Tim poured water over her and punched her in the stomach several times. Michaela ran to the bathroom and locked the door. Tim kicked the door open. When he did so, the door struck Michaela in the head, causing a bump on her head. Tim pulled her hair, punched her in the nose, and hit her head against the wall. Michaela escaped and was taken to hospital where she had a broken nose, black eyes, and bumps on her head. For his part, Tim testifies that he

---

[3] *See* PC § 195, which defines excusable homicide. The statute provides that a homicide is excusable "when committed by accident or misfortune, or in doing any other lawful act by lawful means, with usual and ordinary caution, and without any unlawful intent."

and Michaela had an argument, but that he did not punch her or otherwise assault her. Tim testifies that he did not kick the bathroom door open. Rather, he opened the unlocked bathroom door to talk to Michaela, and the door accidentally hit her in the head. At the end of the trial, Tim's attorney asks the judge to give the jury an instruction on accident. Should the judge give the instruction? *People v. Gonzales* (1999) 74 Cal.App.4th 382, 88 Cal.Rptr.2d 111.

PROVING CRIMINAL INTENT IN COURT

Intent is often challenging to prove in court. Intent is invisible. It is a state of mind. How does a prosecutor prove intent? If the defendant made inculpatory statements before trial, those statements are admissible against the defendant under the hearsay doctrine called "party admissions." (Evidence Code § 1220). The old saying, "Anything you say can be used against you" is pretty much true! (*In re M.S.* (2019) 32 Cal. App. 5th 1177, 244 Cal. Rptr. 3d 580). Deliberately false statements are often admissible as evidence of consciousness of guilt.

In your law school course on Criminal Procedure, you learn about the right of the defendant to remain silent. You also learn—as you have seen on TV—that when the police take someone into custody, and wish to interrogate the person, the police must inform the person of the *Miranda* rights, including the right to an attorney, the right to remain silent, and the fact that anything the person says may be used against the person in court.

In addition to defendant's words—or, instead of defendant's words if defendant clams up—the prosecutor proves criminal intent with circumstantial evidence. In *People v. Manibusan* (2013) 58 Cal. 4th 40, 314 P.3d 1, 165 Cal. Rptr. 3d 1, the Supreme Court observed, "Evidence of a defendant's state of mind is almost inevitably circumstantial, but circumstantial evidence is as sufficient as direct evidence to support a conviction."[4] Often, *mens rea* is evidenced by how the crime was

[4] Direct evidence is defined by Evidence Code § 410 as "evidence that directly proves a fact, without an inference or presumption, and which in itself, if true, conclusively establishes that fact." The testimony of an eyewitness is direct evidence. Circumstantial evidence requires the trier of fact to draw one or more inferences from the evidence to what the evidence is offered to prove. For example, suppose Jane is charged with breaking into the Tiffany & Co. jewelry store in Walnut Creek. Evidence that Jane called in sick from her job at a McDonald's in Walnut Creek on the night of the burglary could be offered as circumstantial evidence that Jane burgled Tiffany's.

CALCRIM 223 states: "Facts may be proved by direct or circumstantial evidence or by a combination of both. Direct evidence can prove a fact by itself. For example, if a witness testifies he saw it raining outside before he came into the courthouse, that testimony is direct evidence that it was raining. Circumstantial evidence may be called indirect evidence. Circumstantial evidence does not directly prove the fact to be decided, but is evidence of another fact or group of facts from which you may logically and reasonably conclude the truth of the fact in question. For example, if a witness testifies that he saw someone come inside wearing a raincoat covered with drops of water, that testimony is circumstantial evidence because it may support a conclusion that it was raining outside. Both direct and circumstantial evidence are acceptable types of evidence to prove or disprove the element of a charge, including intent and mental state and acts necessary to a conviction, and neither is necessarily more reliable than the other."

committed.[5] In many cases, criminal intent flows ineluctably from the way the crime was committed.[6] PC § 21(a) states, "The intent or intention is manifested by the circumstances connected with the offense." In *People v. Avila* (2009) 46 Cal.4th 680, 702, 94 Cal.Rptr.3d 699, 208 P.3d 634, the Supreme Court discussed proof of intent: "Here, defendant repeatedly attempted to stab Montoya, an unarmed and trapped victim, and succeeded in stabbing him in the arm and leg. This evidence alone is substantial evidence of defendant's intent to kill. Defendant asserts that the evidence of intent to kill is not substantial because the injury to Montoya was not serious. Of course, the degree of the resulting injury is not dispositive of defendant's intent. Indeed, a defendant may properly be convicted of attempted murder when no injury results."

Motive is not an element of most crimes. The prosecutor is allowed to prove motive, however, in order to prove the crime was committed by the defendant, and that the defendant had the necessary *mens rea*. The relevant CALCRIM instruction (370) provides: "The People are not required to prove that the defendant had a motive to commit (any of the crimes/the crime) charged. In reaching your verdict you may, however, consider whether the defendant had a motive. Having a motive may be a factor tending to show that the defendant is guilty. Not having a motive may be a factor tending to show the defendant is not guilty."

---

[5] When a defendant is charged with intent to kill murder, the prosecutor has to prove intent to kill. Intent to kill can be inferred from the defendant's statements (party admissions) and the way the crime was committed. Defendant's use of a deadly weapon on the victim can shed light on intent to kill. Professor Dressler describes the so-called deadly weapon rule: "When a person kills another with a deadly weapon, proof of intent-to-kill is buttressed further. The more general proposition that a person intends the natural and probable consequences of her actions is supported by the somewhat more specific proposition that when she intentionally uses a deadly weapon or, more precisely, intentionally used a deadly weapon directed at a vital part of the human anatomy, an intention to kill may properly be inferred." Joshua Dressler, *Understanding Criminal Law* § 31.03[B][1][b], p. 480 (8th ed. 2018). The Pennsylvania Supreme Court wrote in *Commonwealth v. Houser* (2011) 18 A.3d 1128 (Pa.), "To convict a defendant of first degree murder, the Commonwealth must prove: a human being was unlawfully killed; the defendant was responsible for the killing; and the defendant acted with malice and a specific intent to kill. The Commonwealth may use solely circumstantial evidence to prove a killing was intentional, and the fact-finder may infer that the defendant had the specific intent to kill the victim based on the defendant's use of a deadly weapon upon a vital part of the victim's body." The California Court of Appeal wrote in *In re M.S.* (2019) 32 Cal. App. 5th 1177, 244 Cal. Rptr. 3d 580, "Evidence of intent to kill may be satisfied by proof of a single stab wound that penetrates a vital organ. In plunging the knife so deeply into such a vital area of the body of an apparently unsuspecting and defenseless victim, defendant could have had no other intent than to kill."

[6] The California Evidence Code contains two presumptions dealing with intent. Evidence Code § 665 provides: "A person is presumed to intend the ordinary consequences of his voluntary act. This presumption is inapplicable in a criminal action to establish the specific intent of the defendant where specific intent is an element of the crime charged." Evidence Code § 668 provides: "An unlawful intent is presumed from the doing of an unlawful act. This presumption is inapplicable in a criminal action to establish the specific intent of the defendant where specific intent is an element of the crime charged." Sections 665 and 668 make clear that a trier of fact cannot be required to presume *mens rea* from the defendant's conduct. This is true whether the crime is one of specific intent or general intent. However, the trier of fact *may* infer criminal intent—specific or general—from the way the crime was committed.

WHEN "KNOWLEDGE" IS THE *MENS REA*: WILLFUL BLINDNESS AND THE OSTRICH INSTRUCTION

When the *mens rea* for a crime is "knowledge" or "knowingly," the defendant may assert she is not guilty because she did not "know." In *United States v. Garcia* (7th Cir. 2009) 580 F.3d 528, 535–537, the Court of Appeals described the "ostrich instruction" that is given in some cases when the *mens rea* is knowledge:

> The so-called "ostrich instruction" informs the jury that a defendant may not bury her head in the sand to actively avoid the truth; the jury may therefore equate a defendant's deliberate avoidance of knowledge with actual knowledge. The purpose of the ostrich instruction is to inform the jury that a person may not escape criminal liability by pleading ignorance if he knows or strongly suspects he is involved in criminal dealings but deliberately avoids learning more exact information about the nature or extent of those dealings. Deliberate avoidance is not a lesser standard than actual knowledge, it is simply another way to prove such knowledge. An ostrich instruction is appropriate where (1) a defendant claims to lack guilty knowledge, *i.e.*, knowledge of her conduct's illegality, and (2) the government presents evidence from which a jury could conclude that the defendant deliberately avoided the truth. Evidence indicating deliberate indifference may consist of overt, physical acts as well as purely psychological avoidance, a cutting off of one's normal curiosity by an effort of will. The instruction is warranted if the evidence permits an inference that [a defendant] must have forced her suspicions aside and deliberately avoided confirming that she was engaged in criminal activity. On the other hand, we do not infer knowledge from mere negligence; the defendant's avoidance must be active. We have upheld the use of the ostrich instruction many times where a defendant transported under suspicious circumstances packages containing drugs and then claimed ignorance of the packages' contents. We have also held that a scenario in which a defendant admits her association with a group but, despite circumstantial evidence to the contrary, denies knowledge of its illegal activity is a paradigm case for use of the ostrich instruction.

PROBLEMS: SHOULD AN OSTRICH INSTRUCTION BE GIVEN IN THE FOLLOWING CASES?

1. Dell drove to the United States from Mexico in a car in which 110 pounds of marijuana was hidden in a secret compartment between the trunk

and the rear seat. The drugs were seized at the border by officers of U.S. Customs and Border Protection. Dell is charged under a federal statute that prohibits "knowing" possession of drugs. During the prosecution's case-in-chief, a customs agent testifies that he asked Dell if he knew about the secret compartment. Dell responded, "Yeah, but I don't know what's inside it. I thought there was something fishy about the whole thing, but I just wanted the hundred bucks." During the defense case-in-chief, Dell testified that he did not know the marijuana was in the car. Dell testifies that he was in a bar in Tijuana, Mexico, when he was approached by a man named Ray. Ray asked Dell if he would drive a car across the border for $100.00. Ray instructed Dell to drive to a location in Los Angeles and leave the car parked, with the keys in the ashtray. The prosecutor asks the judge to give the ostrich instruction. Dell's attorney disagrees. Should the judge give the instruction? *United States v. Jewell* (1976) 532 F.2d 697 (9th Cir.).

2. Sanchez-Robles, a mother of five, lives in El Centro, California, close to the Mexico/U.S.A. border. She frequently visits friends and relatives in Mexicali, Mexico. She claims that on June 30, four of her daughters, aged 4 to 17, asked her to take them to Mexico for tacos. A friend named Armando Lopez, whom she said she had known for one month, left a van at her apartment, so she borrowed it and left for Mexico with her daughters around 10 p.m. that evening. Sanchez-Robles claims that she did not use her own car that night because her other daughter, Guadalupe, borrowed it to go out on a date. Guadalupe and her boyfriend testified that they went out together that night, taking the Sanchez-Robles car. Sanchez-Robles and the four daughters made the trip to Mexico in the Lopez van. Upon their return to the United States at 11:50 p.m., a customs official at the Calexico port of entry overheard Sanchez-Robles speaking in Spanish to her daughters, all of whom were sitting on the front seat of the van, telling them to be quiet and not say anything. The inspector noticed an odor inside the van, which he recognized as marijuana. When he opened the side door of the van, the odor was stronger. He referred the van to a secondary inspection area, where another officer noticed the odor and took the family inside. The officer at the secondary inspection area characterized the odor from the driver's window of the van as a six on a scale of one to ten, with ten being the strongest, and the odor from the rear of the van as an eight-to-nine. Drug-sniffing dogs alerted customs agents to several areas in the van and, when inspectors took the vehicle apart, they found 43 pounds of cocaine and 417 pounds of marijuana hidden throughout. The dismantling process took an hour and a half, and as the inspectors were removing the contraband, they had to take fresh air breaks because the odor was so strong. Sanchez-Robles is charged with importing marijuana and cocaine and possession of marijuana and cocaine with intent to distribute. Sanchez-Robles testifies that she didn't know what marijuana smelled like and didn't know the vehicle contained drugs. Should the judge give the ostrich instruction? *United States v. Sanchez-Robles* (9th Cir. 1991) 927 F.2d 1070.

NOTE

Your casebook editor can find virtually no mention of willful blindness or the ostrich instruction in California criminal cases or in secondary authorities on California law.

STRICT LIABILITY OFFENSES

All crimes have an *actus reus*. The great majority of crimes have a *mens rea*. A small number of crimes, most of them relatively minor, have no *mens rea*, and are called strict liability offenses. The Court of Appeal explained in *People v. Cole* (2007) 156 Cal.App.4th 452, 475, 67 Cal.Rptr.3d 526, "strict liability is usually reserved for crimes that relate to public health and safety and impose relatively light penalties."

There is one serious felony that by long tradition is a strict liability offense: statutory rape, which is strict liability regarding the minor victim's age. (PC § 261.5).

When a statute does not contain a *mens rea* term, the court must determine whether the crime is strict liability or whether a *mens rea* should be implied, that is, whether a *mens rea* should be read into the statute. The Court of Appeal observed in *People v. Estes* (2013) 218 Cal. App. 4th Supp. 14, 19, 161 Cal. Rptr. 3d 690, "The fact that no mental state is specifically mentioned does not mean that the legislature did not intend to require one." The Supreme Court's decision in *In re Jorge M.* illustrates how a court decides whether a statute that is silent regarding *mens rea* is a strict liability offense or contains an implied *mens rea*.

IN RE JORGE M., A PERSON COMING UNDER THE JUVENILE COURT LAW

California Supreme Court
23 Cal.4th 866, 98 Cal.Rptr.2d 466, 4 P.3d 297 (2000)

WERDEGAR, J.

Jorge M., a minor, was adjudicated a ward of the juvenile court and ordered into a juvenile camp program, in part because he was found to have been in possession of an assault weapon, in violation of Penal Code section 12280(b). Court of Appeal reversed that finding on the ground the record contained insufficient evidence the minor knew the firearm had the characteristics bringing it within the definition of an assault weapon under the Assault Weapons Control Act (§§ 12275–12290 (hereafter the AWCA)), a mental element the Court of Appeal found implicit in section 12280(b) despite the absence of any express scienter language in the statute itself.

We agree with the Court of Appeal that section 12280(b), an alternative felony/misdemeanor punishable by up to three years in state prison (see §§ 17(b), 18), was not intended to define a strict liability offense.

We disagree, however, that actual knowledge regarding the firearm's prohibited characteristics is required. Such a requirement would be inconsistent with the public safety goals of the AWCA. Effective enforcement of that law demands, instead, that a conviction be obtainable upon proof of negligent failure to know, as well as actual knowledge of, the weapon's salient characteristics; the People must prove, that is, that a defendant charged with possessing an unregistered assault weapon knew or reasonably should have known the characteristics of the weapon bringing it within the registration requirements of the AWCA. Because the record of this case contains sufficient evidence to prove the requisite *mens rea*, we reverse the judgment of the Court of Appeal.

On December 5, 1996, while the 16-year-old minor was on in-home probation for possession of a controlled substance, law enforcement officers conducted a probation investigation at the minor's home. The main room of the house had bunk beds in one corner; a door led off this main room to the minor's parents' bedroom. Probation Officer Brian Tsubokawa asked the minor where he kept his personal possessions. The minor pointed to the bunk bed area in the main room. Los Angeles Police Department Officer Manuel Ramirez went to the bunk bed and found three rifles on the top bunk, which the minor told Officer Ramirez was his bed. On a clothes cabinet three feet or less from the minor's bed, Officer Ramirez also found an unregistered SKS-45 semiautomatic rifle with a detachable "banana clip" magazine.

The present petition was then filed against the minor under Welfare and Institutions Code section 602, charging him with possession of an assault weapon (§ 12280(b)) and with firearm possession in violation of the terms and conditions of his probation (§ 12021(d)).

[In juvenile court, a trial is called an adjudication hearing or jurisdictional hearing.] At the adjudication hearing, the officers testified as described above. The minor testified he slept on the floor of his sisters' bedroom and that the weapons belonged to his father. He denied ever "playing" with the weapons. The minor's brother testified that all the rifles belonged to him and his father, not to the minor. He said that he slept on the top bunk bed and that the minor slept in a bedroom used by their sisters. The minor's mother corroborated the brother's account.

The juvenile court found the allegations of the petition true. The minor was adjudged a ward of the court and placed in a camp community placement program for a period not to exceed three years and eight months.

The Court of Appeal reversed the section 12280(b) finding for insufficient evidence. Relying heavily on the persuasive authority of *Staples v. United States* (1994) 511 U.S. 600 (*Staples*), in which the United States Supreme Court held conviction under a federal firearms possession law required proof the defendant knew the features of the gun that brought it within the criminal prohibition, and *People v. Simon* (1995) 9 Cal.4th 493 (*Simon*), in which this court held conviction under a law proscribing the sale or purchase of securities by misrepresentation required proof the defendant knew or should have known the false or misleading nature of the representation, the Court of Appeal held that conviction under section 12280(b) requires proof the defendant "knew that the weapon possessed characteristics which brought it within the statutory definition of an assault weapon." The Court of Appeal, without elaborating the point, further asserted there was "no evidence" of such knowledge in this case.

The AWCA, inter alia, requires registration of assault weapons. At the time of the minor's charged offense, the restricted firearms included only those defined as assault weapons in section 12276 and those declared to be assault weapons pursuant to section 12276.5. The definition in section 12276, subdivisions (a) through (c), consists of a list, one item of which is "SKS with detachable magazine." The question on review, therefore, is whether the Court of Appeal correctly held that the finding the minor possessed an unregistered assault weapon, in violation of section 12280(b), required proof the minor knew the weapon was an SKS with a detachable magazine. To answer that question we must decide whether knowledge of the characteristics bringing a firearm within the AWCA is an element of section 12280(b)'s bar on possession.

Section 12280(b) provides in pertinent part: "Any person who, within this state, possesses any assault weapon, except as provided in this chapter, is guilty of a public offense and upon conviction shall be punished by imprisonment in the state prison, or in a county jail, not exceeding one year."

That the statute contains no reference to knowledge or other language of *mens rea* is not itself dispositive. As we recently explained, the requirement that, for a criminal conviction, the prosecution prove some form of guilty intent, knowledge, or criminal negligence is of such long standing and so fundamental to our criminal law that penal statutes will often be construed to contain such an element despite their failure expressly to state it. Generally, the existence of a *mens rea* is the rule of, rather than the exception to, the principles of Anglo-American criminal jurisprudence. In other words, there must be a union of act and wrongful intent, or criminal negligence. (Pen. Code § 20). So basic is this requirement that it is an invariable element of every crime unless excluded expressly or by necessary implication.

Equally well recognized, however, is that for certain types of penal laws, often referred to as public welfare offenses, the Legislature does not intend that any proof of scienter or wrongful intent be necessary for conviction. Such offenses generally are based upon the violation of statutes which are purely regulatory in nature and involve widespread injury to the public. Under many statutes enacted for the protection of the public health and safety, *e.g.*, traffic and food and drug regulations, criminal sanctions are relied upon even if there is no wrongful intent. These offenses usually involve light penalties and no moral obloquy or damage to reputation. Although criminal sanctions are relied upon, the primary purpose of the statutes is regulation rather than punishment or correction. The offenses are not crimes in the orthodox sense, and wrongful intent is not required in the interest of enforcement.

Whether section 12280(b) can properly be categorized as a public welfare offense, for which the Legislature intended guilt without proof of any scienter, is a question of first impression to which the answer is not obvious. On the one hand, the AWCA, including section 12280, is clearly aimed at protecting public safety by regulating and restricting the possession of assault weapons. On the other hand, the penalties imposed under section 12280(b), an alternative felony/misdemeanor (a "wobbler"), are not "light," and a degree of moral obloquy or damage to reputation necessarily attaches to a felony conviction. In view of the weighty penalty, it is not patently true that the primary purpose of the statute is regulation rather than punishment or correction. As the text and penal nature of section 12280(b) do not provide a clear answer to our question, a fuller examination is required.

A leading criminal law treatise (1 LaFave & Scott, Substantive Criminal Law (1986) § 3.8(a)) lists several considerations courts have commonly taken into account in deciding whether a statute should be construed as a public welfare offense: (1) the legislative history and context; (2) any general provision on *mens rea* or strict liability crimes; (3) the severity of the punishment provided for the crime ("Other things being equal, the greater the possible punishment, the more likely some fault is required"); (4) the seriousness of harm to the public that may be expected to follow from the forbidden conduct; (5) the defendant's opportunity to ascertain the true facts ("The harder to find out the truth, the more likely the legislature meant to require fault in not knowing"); (6) the difficulty prosecutors would have in proving a mental state for the crime ("The greater the difficulty, the more likely it is that the legislature intended to relieve the prosecution of that burden so that the law could be effectively enforced"); (7) the number of prosecutions to be expected under the statute ("The fewer the expected prosecutions, the more likely the legislature meant to require the prosecuting officials to go into the issue of fault"). Finding this framework useful here, where the legislative intent is not readily discerned from the text itself, we consider each factor in turn.

1. The Statute's History and Context

The AWCA was prompted by the belief that assault weapons posed a real, severe and growing threat to public safety, urgently requiring regulation and restriction to reduce the number of such weapons finding their way into the hands of street gangs, drug dealers and the mentally ill. [Note: The Court's lengthy discussion of legislative history is omitted].

2. General Provision on *Mens Rea*

California law contains a generally applicable rule on *mens rea*: section 20, which provides, "In every crime or public offense there must exist a union, or joint operation of act and intent, or criminal negligence." The interpretive rule embodied in this statute is by no means inflexible, public welfare offenses being the chief recognized exception. Nonetheless, at least where the penalties imposed are substantial, section 20 can fairly be said to establish a presumption against criminal liability without mental fault or negligence, rebuttable only by compelling evidence of legislative intent to dispense with *mens rea* entirely.

3. Severity of Punishment

As already noted, possession of an unregistered assault weapon under section 12280(b) is an alternative felony/misdemeanor, also known as a wobbler; that is, the offense is a felony unless charged as a misdemeanor or reduced to a misdemeanor by the sentencing court.

4. Seriousness of Harm to the Public

As already discussed, the Legislature in 1989 regarded the use of assault weapons by criminals and the mentally ill as a grave public safety threat.

The AWCA is a remedial law aimed at protecting the public against a highly serious danger to life and safety. The Legislature presumably intended that the law be effectively enforceable, *i.e.*, that its enforcement would actually result in restricting the number of assault weapons in the hands of criminals and the mentally ill. In interpreting the law to further the legislative intent, therefore, we should strive to avoid any construction that would significantly undermine its enforceability. This is not to suggest this court would or should read any element out of a criminal statute simply to ease the People's burden of proof. But, when a crime's statutory definition does not expressly include any scienter element, the fact the Legislature intended the law to remedy a serious and widespread public safety threat militates against the conclusion it also intended impliedly to include in the definition a scienter element especially burdensome to prove.

5. Difficulty of Ascertaining Facts

Courts have been justifiably reluctant to construe offenses carrying substantial penalties as containing no *mens rea* element where dispensing with *mens rea* would require the defendant to have knowledge only of traditionally lawful conduct. This interpretive guideline holds with particular strength when the characteristics that bring the defendant's conduct within the criminal prohibition may not be obvious to the offender.

The parties debate the application of these principles to construction of section 12280(b). The Attorney General maintains the weapons listed in section 12276 are highly dangerous offensive weapons which are unambiguously hazardous. Assault weapons are typically used by soldiers in a war. The assault weapons listed in section 12276, like the SKS with detachable magazine, are not ambiguous substances such that a person would not be aware of the dangerous character of the weapon after looking at one. The minor, in contrast, again stresses that the AWCA restricts only a subset of semiautomatic firearms, leaving the remainder available for lawful uses such as hunting and target shooting, and that even those semiautomatic firearms classified as assault weapons may, if registered, be lawfully possessed and used for these purposes.

On this point the minor has the better argument. The Attorney General may be correct that anyone who knew the firearm he or she possessed was an "assault weapon" would be likely to know it was potentially regulated or contraband. But this begs the question, for the issue is precisely whether a person violates section 12280(b) if he or she does *not* know the gun has the characteristics making it an assault weapon.

Nor can it be said that all semiautomatic rifles, or even all assault rifles, lack all lawful use, so that anyone in possession of one is overwhelmingly likely to be aware they are restricted or banned firearms.

6. Difficulty of Proving Mental State

We previously noted the seriousness of the public safety threat the Legislature perceived and sought to alleviate by the AWCA and the corresponding unsuitability, to the legislative intent, of any statutory construction that would likely impair the law's effective enforcement. It follows we should not read section 12280(b) as containing any mental state requirement that the prosecution would foreseeably and routinely have special difficulty proving.

An actual knowledge element has significant potential to impair effective enforcement. Although knowledge may be proven circumstantially, in many instances a defendant's direct testimony or prior statement that he or she was actually ignorant of the weapon's salient characteristics will be sufficient to create reasonable doubt. Although the People could rebut a claim of actual ignorance by evidence of the defendant's long and close acquaintance with the particular weapon or familiarity with firearms in general, production of such evidence would predictably constitute a heavy burden for the prosecution.

A scienter requirement satisfied by proof the defendant *should* have known the characteristics of the weapon bringing it within the AWCA, however, would have little or no potential to impede effective enforcement. In most instances the fact a firearm is of a make and model listed in section 12276, or added pursuant to section 12276.5, can be expected to be sufficiently plain on examination of the weapon so that evidence of the markings, together with evidence the accused possessor had sufficient opportunity to examine the firearm, will satisfy a knew-or-should-have-known requirement. Furthermore, because of the general principle that all persons are obligated to learn of and comply with the law, in many circumstances a trier of fact properly could find that a person who knowingly possesses a semiautomatic firearm reasonably should have investigated and determined the gun's characteristics. The exceptional cases in which the salient characteristics of the firearm are extraordinarily obscure, or the defendant's possession of the gun was so fleeting or attenuated as not to afford an opportunity for examination, would appear to be instances of largely innocent possession that, as discussed above, the Legislature presumably did not intend to be subject to felony punishment.

We believe the Legislature intended section 12280(b) to require a degree of scienter regarding the *character* of the firearm; without such a scienter element, the possibility of severely punishing innocent possession is too great.

7. Number of Expected Prosecutions

The Legislature enacted the AWCA in response to what it viewed as a statewide problem of increasing gravity, the rapidly growing use of assault weapons in incidents of criminal violence. Attacking what it perceived to be a widespread threat, the Legislature presumably anticipated a significant number of prosecutions would ensue under the law. Again, our construction should not impose a scienter requirement that would unduly impede the ability to prosecute substantial numbers of violators.

Conclusion

Although the AWCA can be characterized as a remedial law aimed at protecting public welfare, its text, history and surrounding statutory context provide no compelling evidence of legislative intent to exclude all scienter from the offense defined in section 12280(b). Section 20's generally applicable presumption that a penal law requires criminal intent or negligence, the severity of the felony punishment imposed for violation of section 12280(b), and the significant possibility innocent possessors would become subject to that weighty sanction were the statute construed as dispensing entirely with *mens rea*, convince us section 12280(b) was not intended to be a strict liability offense. The gravity of the public safety threat addressed in the AWCA, however, together with the substantial number of prosecutions to be expected under it and the potential difficulty of routinely proving actual knowledge on the part of defendants, convince us section 12280(b) was not intended to contain such an actual knowledge element. Consequently, we construe section 12280(b) as requiring knowledge of, or negligence in regard to, the facts making possession criminal. In a prosecution under section 12280(b), that is to say, the People bear the burden of proving the defendant *knew or reasonably should have known* the firearm possessed the characteristics bringing it within the AWCA.

The judgment of the Court of Appeal is reversed.

PROBLEMS

1. PC § 12370 states: "Any person who has been convicted of a violent felony who purchases, owns, or possesses body armor is guilty of a felony." Defendant, who had been convicted of a violent felony, was arrested wearing a "bullet proof" vest, and charged under Section 12370. The prosecutor argues that Section 12370 creates a strict liability offense. The defense disagrees. Using *In re Jorge M.*, develop arguments for the prosecution and the defense. Who has the stronger argument?

2. Is the following statute a strict liability offense? "Every person who signs the name of another, or of a fictitious person, or falsely makes, alters, forges, utters, publishes, passes, or attempts to pass, as genuine, any prescription for any drug is guilty of forgery and upon conviction thereof shall be punished." The crime is a wobbler. Is it a strict liability statute? Business & Professions Code § 4324.

3. Tim is the captain and owner of the JoAnn, a commercial fishing boat out of San Francisco. Tim and his crew set off to harvest Dungeness crab. As captain, Tim navigates the boat from the wheelhouse, one level up from the deck where the crabs are removed from crab pots and measured by crew members to make sure the crabs are big enough to be legal. Tim can't actually see the crew working with the crabs. Tim trains the crew on how to measure crabs, and informs the crew how big crabs have to be. When the JoAnn docked at Pier 45 in San Francisco, game wardens boarded the boat and measured a sample of the 44,943 pounds of crab. Wardens found that 2.2 percent of the total load was "short," that is too small. Tim was cited with a violation of Fish and Game Code § 8278, which provides: "No Dungeness crab less than six and one-quarter inches in breadth, and no female Dungeness crab, may be taken, except that not more than 1 percent in number of any load of Dungeness crabs may be less than six and one-quarter inches in breadth but not less than five and three-quarters in breath." Is § 8278 a strict liability statute? *People v. Estes* (2013) 218 Cal. App. 4th Supp. 14, 161 Cal. Rptr. 3d 690.

RESPONDEAT SUPERIOR AND CRIMINAL LAW

The doctrine of *respondeat superior*—vicarious liability—plays an important role in tort law. In California criminal law, however, vicarious liability does not apply to crimes that require criminal intent. With strict liability offenses, however, an employer *is* sometimes vicariously criminally liable for an act done by an employee within the scope of the employee's job. Cases imposing vicarious criminal liability are few. *People v. Casey* (1995) 41 Cal. App. 4th Supp. 1, 49 Cal.Rptr.2d 372 is an example. *Casey* involved two California cattle ranch owners who were convicted of misbranding calves that did not belong to them. The Food and Agriculture Code regulates cattle branding. Section 20607 of the Ag Code provides in part, "It is unlawful for any person to use a brand on cattle indicating ownership unless the cattle are owned by him."

When it is time to brand calves, buckaroo crews (cowboys) gather the calves and their mothers from the range. Cattle belonging to different ranchers sometimes intermingle on the range, making it necessary to determine which of two or more ranchers owns particular unbranded calves. Ownership is determined by "mothering up." Calves only suckle from their mother. Since mothers are already branded, it is possible to sort calves by observing "mothering up." In *Casey*, cowboys working for the two ranch owner defendants did not properly "mother up" calves, and, as a result, misbranded calves. The owners did not supervise the branding and were not aware of the mistake. On appeal, the court affirmed the convictions, ruling that Section 20607 is a strict liability offense, and that vicarious liability applied. The court wrote, "That is, the rancher himself is guilty of a violation of the statute if one of his cowboys brands a calf that the rancher does not own. Such a construction will tend to ensure that the branding crews will take the trouble to 'mother up' the calves and to sort out the calves owned by others before proceeding with the branding process."

GENERAL AND SPECIFIC INTENT CRIMES

California distinguishes between general intent and specific intent crimes.

General Intent Crimes

All that is required for guilt of a general intent crime is that the defendant intentionally do the act the law proscribes—the *actus reus*.[7] Said another way, with a general intent crime there is no requirement that the defendant intend to accomplish anything *in addition to* the *actus reus*. Nor is there a requirement that the defendant commit the *actus reus* with any particular motive or desire. Defendant does not have to know the act is illegal. In *People v. Hood* (1969) 1 Cal.3d 444, 456–457, 82 Cal.Rptr. 618, 462 P.2d 370, the Supreme Court explained, "When the definition of a

---

7 *See* 17 *California Jurisprudence*: *Criminal Law* § 103, p. 185 (3d ed. 2010) (West) ("the intention to commit the act constitutes criminal intent.").

crime consists of only the description of a particular act, without reference to intent to do a further act or achieve a future consequence, we ask whether the defendant intended to do the proscribed act. This is deemed to be a general criminal intent."

The *mens rea* for many general intent crimes is "intentional"—did defendant intentionally commit the *actus reus*? The pertinent CALCRIM instruction (250) states: "For you to find a person guilty of [the charged crime], that person must not only commit the prohibited act, but must do so with wrongful intent. A person acts with wrongful intent when he or she intentionally does a prohibited act on purpose, however, it is not required that he or she intend to break the law." Other *mens rea* terms frequently used in general intent crimes are "maliciously," "willfully," and "knowingly."[8]

Battery is a general intent crime. PC § 242 defines battery as "any willful and unlawful use of force or violence upon the person of another." To be guilty of battery, the defendant must willfully (*i.e.*, intentionally) use force on another.[9] It is not necessary that the defendant know her conduct is against the law. Nor is it necessary that the defendant use force for any particular reason or to achieve any particular result.

Specific Intent Crimes

Specific intent crimes fit into two categories: First, the definition of the crime provides that the defendant had a goal of achieving something *in addition to* the *actus reus*. The Supreme Court explained in *Hood*, "When the definition [of a crime] refers to defendant's intent to do some further act or achieve some additional consequence, the crime is deemed to be one of specific intent." 1 Cal.3d at 457.

With the second category of specific intent crimes, the definition of the crime provides that the defendant must commit the *actus reus* with a particular motive or desire. The two categories of specific intent sometimes overlap.

In *People v. Thiel* (2016) 5 Cal. App. 5th 1201, 1209, 210 Cal. Rptr. 3d 744, the Court of Appeal wrote, "Specific intent crimes typically contain

---

[8] *See People v. Rodarte* (2014) 223 Cal. App. 4th 1158, 168 Cal. Rptr. 3d 12 ("Conviction under a statute proscribing conduct done willfully and maliciously does not require proof of a specific intent."); *People v. Cole* (2007) 156 Cal.App.4th 452, 476, 67 Cal.Rptr.3d 526 ("As the cases make clear, a statute proscribing 'willful' behavior typically is a general intent crime, as opposed to a strict liability offense.").

[9] PC § 7(1) states, "The word 'willfully' when applied to the intent with which an act is done or omitted, implies simply a purpose or willingness to commit the act, or make the omission referred to. It does not require any intent to violate law, or to injure another, or to acquire any advantage." *People v. Thiel* (2016) 5 Cal. App. 5th 1201, 1207, 210 Cal. Rptr. 3d 744 (2016)(Someone commits an act willfully when he or she does it willingly or on purpose.").

such phrases as 'with the intent to' achieve or 'for the purpose of' achieving some additional result."

Theft is a specific intent crime. As defined at common law, theft is the trespassory caption and asportation of the personal property of another with the intent to steal. The specific intent is intent to steal. Thus, the defendant must trespassorily take and carry away the personal property of another (*actus reus*), and, *in addition*, must intend to steal the property. If the defendant does not intend to steal the property, the defendant is not guilty of theft.

What difference does it make if a crime is general or specific intent? The distinction is important with issues of mistake of fact (Chapter 9), voluntary intoxication (Chapter 9), and accomplice liability (Chapter 7).

Practice Identifying General and Specific Intent Crimes

To correctly apply the law regarding mistake of fact, voluntary intoxication, and accomplice liability, you must be able to distinguish general intent crimes from specific intent crimes. Distinguishing the two is not always easy. The best way to improve your skill is to practice. With each crime listed below, begin by identifying the *actus reus* and the *mens rea*. Once you have isolated the *actus reus* and the *mens rea,* figure out whether the crime is general intent or specific intent.

Some of the crimes listed below do not contain a *mens rea* term. When a criminal statute is silent regarding *mens rea*, there are two possibilities: First the crime is one of strict liability; *i.e.,* a crime that has no *mens rea*. Second, the crime is not a strict liability offense, and the appropriate *mens rea*—typically "intentional"—is implied, making the crime one of general intent. Earlier in this chapter you read the Supreme Court's decision in *In re Jorge M.* (2000) 23 Cal.4th 866, 872, 98 Cal.Rptr.2d 466, 4 P.3d 297, where the Court wrote, "The requirement that, for a criminal conviction, the prosecution prove some form of guilty intent, knowledge, or criminal negligence is of such long standing and so fundamental to our criminal law that penal statutes will often be construed to contain such an element despite their failure expressly to state it. Generally, the existence of a *mens rea* is the rule of, rather than the exception to, the principles of Anglo-American criminal jurisprudence."

1. Trespassory caption and asportation of the personal property of another with the intent to steal. S

2. Sexual intercourse by a male with a female not his wife, without her consent. G

3. Intentional receipt of stolen property. G

4. Receipt of stolen property with knowledge that it is stolen. S

5. Breaking and entering the dwelling house of another at night with the intent to commit a felony therein.

6. The killing of a human being with malice aforethought.

7. Assault.

8. Assault with intent to commit rape.

9. One who maliciously burns the dwelling house of another is guilty of arson.

10. Kidnapping.

11. Kidnapping for ransom or reward.

12. Mayhem: Every person who unlawfully and maliciously deprives a human being of a member of his body, or disables, disfigures, or renders it useless, or cuts or disables the tongue, or puts out an eye, or slits the nose, ear, or lip, is guilty of mayhem.[10]

13. Aggravated Mayhem: A person is guilty of aggravated mayhem when he or she unlawfully, under circumstances manifesting extreme indifference to the physical or psychological well-being of another person, intentionally causes permanent disability or disfigurement to another human being or deprives a human being of a limb, organ, or member of his or her body.

14. A lawfully married person is guilty of bigamy if the married person marries a second person while the first marriage continues.

15. Every person who knowingly and designedly, by any false or fraudulent representation or pretense, defrauds any other person of money, labor, or property, is guilty of a felony.

16. Every person who, without the express authorization of a duly licensed cable television system knowingly and willfully manufactures, imports into this state, sells, or offers to sell, possesses for sale or advertises for sale, any device designed in whole or in part to decode, descramble, or otherwise make intelligible any encoded, scrambled or other nonstandard signal carried by that cable television system is guilty of a misdemeanor.

17. Every person who, with the intent that the crime be committed, solicits another to commit prostitution shall be punished.

18. Every person who commits prostitution shall be punished.

19. Any person who shall peep secretly into any room occupied by a female person shall be guilty of a misdemeanor.

[10] Mayhem is a very old form of aggravated battery. A Note to the 1873 California Penal Code explains: "Mayhem, at common law, was such a bodily injury as would render a man less able in fighting to defend himself or annoy his adversary."

20. Any person who, while intoxicated or drunk, appears in any public place where one or more persons is present, and manifests a drunken condition by boisterous or indecent conduct, or loud or profane discourse, shall, upon conviction, be fined.

21. Any person who operates a vehicle in a reckless or culpably negligent manner, causing death, shall be guilty of a felony.

22. Whosoever shall unlawfully and maliciously administer to or cause to be administered to or taken by any other person any poison or other destructive or noxious thing, so as thereby to endanger the life of such person, or so as thereby to inflict upon such person any grievous bodily harm shall be guilty of felony.

23. A person who, in committing a battery, intentionally or knowingly causes great bodily harm, or permanent disability or disfigurement commits aggravated battery.

24. Any person who willfully or maliciously constructs or maintains a fire-protection system in any structure with the intent to install a fire protection which is known to be inoperable or to impair the effective operation of a system, so as to threaten the safety of any occupant or user of the structure in the event of a fire, shall be subject to imprisonment.

25. Any person who knowingly has in his or her possession in any jail any controlled substances, without being authorized to so possess the same by the rules of the jail is guilty of a felony.

TRANSFERRED INTENT

The tort doctrine of transferred intent applies in criminal law. For example, Betty intends to kill Rachel. Betty aims at Rachel and fires, but misses and accidentally kills Tammy. Betty's intent to kill Rachel "transfers" to Tammy, and Betty is guilty of murder. Betty committed the *actus reus* of murder; she killed a human being. As well, Betty had the *mens rea* for murder, intent to kill. The fact that Betty killed the "wrong" person does not matter, and certainly is not a defense. Consider the following scenarios:

1. Betty intends to kill Rachel. Betty aims at Rachel and fires. The bullet passes through Rachel and strikes Tammy. Rachel *and* Tammy die. Of what crime(s) is Betty guilty?

2. Betty intends to kill Rachel. Betty aims at Rachel and fires. The bullet passes through Rachel and strikes Tammy. Rachel survives but Tammy dies. Of what crime(s) is Betty guilty?

3. Betty intends to kill Rachel. Betty aims at Rachel and fires. The bullet passes through Rachel and strikes Tammy. Rachel dies but Tammy survives. Of what crime(s) is Betty guilty?

4. Betty intends to kill Rachel. Betty aims at Rachel and fires. The bullet passes through Rachel and strikes Tammy. Rachel and Tammy survive. Of what crime(s) is Betty guilty?

5. Betty intends to kill Rachel. Betty aims at Rachel but misses. The bullet breaks a large department store window, and Betty is charged with: (1) destruction of property, (2) reckless discharge of a firearm, and (3) attempted murder. Is Betty guilty of these offenses?

6. Eric's wife, Dawn, told him to leave the family home after Eric threatened Dawn's father. Eric had been drinking all day—33 beers. Eric took his rifle with him when he left. Eric drove to an AM/PM gas station and convenience store. Because the store employees were counting the day's receipts, the store was closed for a few minutes. The store security guard, Jones, stood outside the store and told customers, including Eric, "The store is closed for ten minutes, please wait outside, and we will get the store open as quick as we can." When Eric tried to enter the store, Jones blocked his way and said, "Sorry sir, we are closed for a few minutes." Eric drove to a nearby field and removed his rifle from the truck, intending to kill Jones. Eric aimed at the man in front of the AM/PM, thinking it was Jones. Eric fired a single bullet, killing Clifford by mistake. Eric is charged with first degree murder of Clifford, and attempted murder of Jones. Is Eric guilty of either or both crimes? *People v. Robbins* (2018) 19 Cal. App. 5th 660, 228 Cal. Rptr. 3d 468.

CONCURRENCE OF *ACTUS REUS* AND *MENS REA*

The *mens rea* must bring about or cause the *actus reus*. PC § 20 provides: "In every crime or public offense there must exist a union, or joint operation of act and intent, or criminal negligence." Consider the following cases:

1. Dell accidently stepped backward into Vic, not realizing Vic was standing behind him. After accidentally bumping into Vic, Dell thought, "I'm glad I did that." Is Dell guilty of battery, defined in PC § 242 as "any willful and unlawful use of force or violence upon the person of another"?

2. Dell broke into Vic's house at night. Dell thought he was entering his own home, and Dell broke in because he forgot his key. Once inside, Dell realized it was not his home. He decided to steal Vic's stereo. Is Dell guilty of burglary, defined at common law as the breaking and entering of the dwelling of another at night with the intent to commit a felony therein?

3. Dell broke into Vic's house at night, knowing it was Vic's house and that he had no right to enter. Dell broke in because it is cold outside, and Dell wanted a warm place to sleep. When he broke in, Dell did not intend to commit a felony inside the house. However, after Dell was inside, he decided to steal Vic's jewelry. Is Dell guilty of burglary?

4. Dell found Vic's wallet lying in the street. Dell picked it up, intending to return it. Later, Dell decided to keep it. Is Dell guilty of theft, defined at common law as the trespassory caption and asportation of the personal property of another with the intent to steal?

5. Dell decided to kill Vic. One day—still intending to kill Vic, and waiting for a good opportunity do so—Dell was driving to the opera when Vic stepped off the curb right in front of Dell's car. Dell did not see Vic before Vic stepped into the path of Dell's car, and Dell was not negligent in any way when his car hit Vic. Is Dell guilty of murder, defined at common law as the killing of a human being with malice aforethought?

CHAPTER 4

CAUSATION

■ ■ ■

To commit a crime, defendant must cause the harm proscribed by statute (*e.g.*, death of a person, loss of property). Criminal law uses "but for" causation and "proximate cause" similar to tort law. The Supreme Court observed in *People v. Jennings* (2010) 50 Cal.4th 616, 644 n.13, 114 Cal.Rptr.3d 133, 237 P.3d 474, "It is well established that the principles of causation, as they apply to tort law, are equally applicable to criminal law." The prosecutor must prove causation beyond a reasonable doubt. Causation issues usually arise in homicide prosecutions.

CAUSE IN FACT—"BUT FOR" CAUSATION

Defendant must be a "but for" cause of harm. Most of the time this is obvious. For example, Dell puts a gun to Vic's head, pulls the trigger and blows Vic's brains out. Clearly, Dell caused Vic's death. Occasionally, "but for" causation is complicated. Consider the following cases:

1. Melinda hits Betty on the head with an ax. Betty will die in 30 minutes from the injury. A minute later, while Betty is dying on the floor, Ruth comes along and kicks Betty in the stomach, causing her to die in 10 minutes rather than 30. Ruth's kick would not have been fatal by itself. However, Ruth shortened Betty's life. Who killed Betty? Clearly, Betty would not have died but for the blow to the head, so Melinda is a "but for" cause of her death. How about Ruth? Is a person who shortens the life of one who is already mortally wounded a "but for" cause of the death? We are all going to die sometime, aren't we?

2. Gary hits Terry in the head with a baseball bat, inflicting a non-fatal wound. At the same time, Larry stabs Terry in the stomach. The stab wound would not by itself be fatal. The combination of the two wounds kills Terry. Are Gary and Larry both "but for" causes of Terry's death?

3. Linda shoots Larry in the head, inflicting an immediately fatal wound. At the same instant, Loopy shoots Larry in the head, inflicting another immediately fatal wound. Assume Linda and Loopy act completely independently of each other. Are Loopy and Linda "but for" causes of Larry's death? To determine causation and liability, it is important that Linda and Loopy act independently of each other. Do you see why?

PROXIMATE CAUSE

The fact that a defendant is a "but for" cause of harm does not mean the defendant is liable. In addition to "but for" causation, defendant must be the proximate cause of harm.[1] In *People v. Roberts* (1992) 2 Cal.4th 271, 302 n.11, 6 Cal.Rptr.2d 276, 826 P.2d 274, the Supreme Court wrote, "There is no bright line demarcating a legally sufficient proximate cause from one that is too remote. Ordinarily the question will be for the jury, though in some instances undisputed evidence may reveal a cause so remote that a court may properly decide that no rational trier of fact could find the needed nexus."

People v. Dawson is a good introduction to proximate cause.

PEOPLE V. DAWSON

California Court of Appeal
172 Cal.App.4th 1073, 91 Cal.Rptr.3d 841 (2009)

RICHMAN, J.

We see, yet again, the tragic consequences that can result from the mixture of boating and alcohol—here, the death of Mark Spier.

Defendant William Dawson was charged with five crimes, two of which were felonies: vessel manslaughter while intoxicated and unlawful operation of a vessel while intoxicated resulting in bodily injury. The charges stemmed from the death of Spier who, himself very intoxicated, jumped off the back of a boat as defendant put the boat in reverse, struck the propeller and died instantly. Following a preliminary hearing, the magistrate declined to hold defendant on the felony charges, finding that he did not cause Spier's death: "What caused the death of this individual was the jumping off while the boat was in reverse." The People appeal, essentially arguing that the magistrate misapplied the law of causation. We agree and we reverse.

It is well established that the principles of causation as they apply to tort law are equally applicable to criminal law. And as in tort law, defendant's act must be the proximate cause of the injury, death, or other harm constituting the crime. We thus turn to the law of proximate cause, well described by our colleagues in *People v. Brady,* 129 Cal.App.4th 1314 (*Brady*). *Brady* involved an appeal by two defendants, Brady and Mortenson, both of whom were convicted of manufacturing, and conspiring to manufacture, methamphetamine. Brady was also convicted of recklessly causing a fire that resulted in the death of two firefighter pilots whose planes collided while they were responding to the fire near the methamphetamine lab. Brady's primary contention on appeal was that the

---

1 *See People v. Holmberg* (2011) 195 Cal.App.4th 1310, 125 Cal.Rptr.3d 878 ("California courts have adopted the substantial factor test in analyzing proximate cause.").

jury instructions and the exclusion of four categories of evidence precluded the jury from properly determining whether his conduct proximately caused the death of the pilots. More specifically, Brady argued that the intervening acts of the pilot Groff and others were superseding causes that absolved him of responsibility for the two deaths. The Court of Appeal rejected these contentions, in a scholarly opinion which began its analysis with an exhaustive exposition of the law of proximate cause:

> The principles of causation apply to crimes as well as torts. Just as in tort law, the defendant's act must be the legally responsible cause (*proximate cause*) of the injury, death or other harm which constitutes the crime. So too, California criminal law relies on civil law formulations of concurrent and superseding cause. The law defines cause in its own particular way. A cause of death is an act or omission that sets in motion a chain of events that produces as a direct, natural and probable consequence of the act or omission the death and without which the death would not occur. In *People v. Roberts,* 2 Cal.4th 271, the Supreme Court emphasized the primary significance of foreseeability to proximate cause.
>
> In general, proximate cause is clearly established where the act is directly connected with the resulting injury, with no intervening force operating. If an intervening act, event or force is present, however, it is necessary to determine whether that act, event or force is sufficient to absolve the defendant of liability because the defendant may also be criminally liable for a result directly caused by his or her act, even though there is another contributing cause.
>
> In law, the term superseding cause means an independent event that intervenes in the chain of causation, producing harm of a kind and degree so far beyond the risk the original wrongdoer should have foreseen that the law deems it unfair to hold him responsible. Where an injury was brought about by a later cause of independent origin the question of proximate cause revolves around a determination of whether the later cause of independent origin, commonly referred to as an intervening cause, was foreseeable by the defendant or, if not foreseeable, whether it caused injury of a type which was foreseeable. If *either* of these questions is answered in the affirmative, then the defendant is not relieved from liability towards the plaintiff. Thus, the defendant remains criminally liable if either the possible consequence might reasonably have been contemplated or the defendant should have foreseen the possibility of harm of the kind that could result from his act.

> [The Court of Appeal] applied that law to Brady's specific contentions, including his claim that the trial court erred in excluding evidence of the blood alcohol level of the pilot Groff. After holding that exclusion of the evidence was not error, the court ended with this: In any event, Brady's attempt to define Groff's intentional misconduct of flying under the influence of alcohol as a superseding cause of the pilots' deaths is unavailing. The issue of proximate causation is increasingly being viewed in terms of the scope of the risk created by the wrongdoer's conduct. Courts usually reduce the tests of proximate cause, both in direct and in intervening cause cases, to a question of foreseeability. To some extent, the language of foreseeability is a short hand expression intended to say that the scope of the defendant's liability is determined by the scope of the risk he negligently created. Consequently, the issue in intervening cause cases, like the issue in others, is whether the general type of harm inflicted was foreseeable and thus within the risk of harm created by the defendant's negligent conduct. It is enough that the defendant should have foreseen the possibility of some harm of the kind which might result from his act. A defendant remains criminally liable if either the possible consequence might reasonably have been contemplated or the defendant should have foreseen the possibility of harm of the kind that could result from his act.

The magistrate held that what caused Spier's death was his jumping off while the boat was in reverse. We interpret this as concluding, in proximate cause terminology, that Spier's act was an unforeseeable intervening cause. Assuming without deciding that the magistrate was correct in this conclusion, this means that the magistrate addressed the first question pertinent to proximate cause as discussed in *Brady*. But he did not discuss the second: whether defendant's conduct caused injury of a type which was foreseeable.

As is clear from the magistrate's ruling, he did not even mention, much less analyze or answer, this second question. In words of *Brady,* if *either* of these questions is answered in the affirmative, then the defendant is not relieved of responsibility. The foreseeability required is of the *risk of harm,* not of the particular intervening act. In other words, the defendant may be liable if his or her conduct was a substantial factor in bringing about the harm, though the defendant neither foresaw nor should have foreseen the extent of the harm or the manner in which it occurred. And the risk that Spier would end up in the water near a churning propeller was foreseeable.

NOTE ON PROXIMATE CAUSE

California courts state that a foreseeable intervening cause is "dependent," and does not supersede or cut off responsibility. When an intervening cause is unforeseeable or remote, the intervening cause is "superseding," and the defendant is not the proximate cause of the harm.

PROBLEMS ON CAUSATION

1. Defendants Kibbe and Krall met the decedent Stafford, at a bar. Stafford had been drinking heavily, and by about 9:00 p.m. he was so intoxicated that the bartender refused to serve him further. Kibbie and Krall saw Stafford offer a one hundred dollar bill for payment, which the bartender refused. At some point during the evening, Stafford began soliciting a ride from the patrons in the bar. Kibbe and Krall, who confessed to having already decided to rob Stafford, offered a ride and the three men left the bar together. As Krall was driving the car, Kibbe demanded Stafford's money and, upon receiving it, forced Stafford to lower his trousers and remove his boots to prove he had no more. At roughly 9:30 p.m., Stafford was abandoned on the side of an unlit, rural two-lane highway. His boots and jacket were placed on the shoulder of the highway; Stafford's eyeglasses, however, remained in the car. It was very cold and strong winds were blowing recently fallen snow across the highway, although the night was clear and the pavement was dry. There was an open and lighted service station no more than one-quarter of a mile away. Stafford crawled to the middle of the northbound lane of traffic and sat down in the road. About half an hour after Kibbe and Krall had abandoned Stafford, Michael Blake, a college student, was driving his pickup truck northbound on the highway at 50 miles an hour, ten miles per hour in excess of the posted speed limit. A car passed Blake in a southbound direction and the driver flashed his headlights at Blake. Immediately thereafter, Blake saw Stafford sitting in the middle of the northbound lane with his hands in the air. Blake testified that he "went into a kind of shock" as soon as he saw Stafford, and that he did not apply his brakes. Blake further testified that he did not attempt to avoid hitting Stafford because he "didn't have time to react." After the collision, Blake stopped his truck and returned to assist Stafford, whereupon he found the decedent's trousers were around his ankles and his shirt was up to his chest. Stafford was wearing neither his jacket nor his boots. Stafford suffered massive head and body injuries as a result of the collision and died shortly thereafter. An autopsy revealed a high alcohol concentration of .25% in his blood. The Medical Examiner testified that the injuries were the direct cause of death. Who caused Stafford's death? *Kibbe v. Henderson* (2d Cir. 1976) 534 F.2d 493.

2. Harry and Mary were married. They lived on a farm far out in the country. Late one cold winter night, Harry beat Mary. Mary left home and walked two miles to her parents' farm. She had on only a nightgown and a thin coat. When she arrived at her parents' home it was 3:00 a.m. Mary was embarrassed about what had happened, and didn't want to wake her parents, so she sat down in a chair on the porch and went to sleep. She froze to death. Is Harry a but for cause of Mary's death? Is he the proximate cause? *State v. Preslar* (1856) 48 N.C. 421.

3. Lydia was driving her Porsche Turbo through a residential district at 50 miles an hour, twice the speed limit of 25 mph. Ten-year-old Marjorie was skateboarding down the street, swerving from one side of the road to the other. Lydia did not see Marjorie and struck her with her car, killing her. Is Lydia the proximate cause of Marjorie's death?

4. Dell was at home. Dell is a good swimmer. He walked to the back yard and noticed his one-year-old daughter drowning in the family swimming pool. Dell called 911 but did not go into the pool to rescue the child. The child drowned. Is Dell the proximate cause of the death?

5. Phyllis was driving under the influence of alcohol. She went through a red light and collided with a car, injuring the driver, Eric. Eric was taken to the hospital emergency department (ED). Unfortunately, the ED doctor negligently gave Eric the wrong medicine, killing Eric. Is Phyllis the proximate cause of Eric's death? Is the doctor liable for Eric's death?

6. Debbie hated Wendy and decided to kill her. Wendy was an avid hot air balloonist. Debbie built a small bomb and hid it in the basket of Wendy's balloon. Wendy took off and was at 500 feet when the bomb caused a fire but failed to explode. With the basket on fire, Wendy descended as quickly as possible. When the balloon was 20 feet above the ground, Wendy jumped out to save herself from being burned. The fall broke her leg. Wendy was miles from help. In great pain and without a cell phone to call for help, Wendy started crawling toward what she thought was a road. Wendy was not paying attention to where she was going, and she fell off a cliff, dying. Is Debbie the proximate cause of Wendy's death?

7. Vickie was a Jehovah's Witness. Members of this faith believe it is a sin to accept a blood transfusion. Bob stabbed Vickie. The knife pierced Vickie's lung. Vickie was rushed to the hospital and required a blood transfusion to save her life. She refused, for religious reasons, to accept the transfusion and died. Is Bob the proximate cause of Vickie's death?

8. A California Highway Patrol trooper tried to pull Dell over for speeding; but rather than stop, Dell sped off and led the officer on a high speed chase. Dell ran a red light. As the CHP trooper entered the intersection, the trooper collided with a car driven by Vic. Vic was killed. Is Dell the proximate cause of Vic's death? What about the CHP officer? Should the officer be charged with anything? *People v. Harris* (1975) 52 Cal.App.3d 419, 125 Cal.Rptr. 40.

9. Dell hit Vic on the head with a lead pipe and stole Vic's wallet. The blow to Vic's head caused severe brain injury. Vic lay in a hospital in a permanent vegetative state, but not brain dead, for six months, with no hope of recovery. Vic's breathing was maintained with a mechanical respirator. Eventually, Vic's family asked the doctor to disconnect the respirator, and Vic died without ever regaining consciousness. Is Dell the proximate cause of Vic's death? *People v. Funes* (1994) 23 Cal.App.4th 1506, 28 Cal.Rptr.2d 758.

CHAPTER 5

CRIMINAL HOMICIDE AND OTHER CRIMES AGAINST THE PERSON

■ ■ ■

This chapter discusses criminal homicide and other crimes against the person, including assault, battery, and kidnapping.

HOMICIDE

Homicide is the killing of a human being by another human being. Not all homicide is criminal.[1] Some homicides are justified. Others are excused. The principles of justification and excuse are explored in Chapter 9.

Suppose Wendy intentionally killed Ted, but Wendy acted in self-defense. Wendy committed homicide because she killed a human being. Self-defense is a justification defense. Other justified homicides are lawful execution, killing in battle, and lethal force used to arrest a fleeing felon. (PC § 196).[2]

Suppose Hank killed Phil because Hank was psychotic and believed Phil was a zombie about to eat Hank's brain. Hank's homicide may be excused because of Hank's mental illness. The insanity defense, which is an excuse defense, is examined in Chapter 9.

Criminal homicide is homicide *without* justification or excuse. Criminal homicide was divided centuries ago into murder and manslaughter.[3] The common law definition of murder was the unlawful killing of a human being by another human being with malice

---

1 *See People v. Elmore* (2014) 59 Cal.4th 121, 172 Cal.Rptr.3d 413, 325 P.3d 951; *People v. Gonzalez* (2012) 54 Cal. 4th 643, 278 P.3d 1242, 142 Cal. Rptr. 3d 893 (I highly recommend the Supreme Court's opinion in *Gonzalez*. Justice Corrigan provides a superb and brief description of the law of homicide).

2 PC § 196 provides: "Homicide is justifiable when committed by public officers and those acting by their command in their aid and assistance, either—(1) In obedience to any judgment of a competent Court; or, (2) When necessarily committed in overcoming actual resistance to the execution of some legal process, or in the discharge of any legal duty; or, (3) When necessarily committed in retaking felons who have been rescued or have escaped, or when necessarily committed in arresting persons charged with felony, and who are fleeing from justice or resisting such arrest." *See also* PC § 197.

3 *See People v. Elmore* (2014) 59 Cal.4th 121, 172 Cal.Rptr.3d 413, 325 P.3d 951.

aforethought.[4] The common law definition of manslaughter was the unlawful killing of a human being by another human being without malice.

Murder requires malice aforethought. At an earlier time, the word "aforethought" had substance. Wayne LaFave describes the original meaning of aforethought, " '[A]forethought' required that the intent to kill be thought out in advance of the killing."[5] Today, the word aforethought has lost nearly all meaning. A killer can formulate the intent to kill—one type of malice aforethought—in an instant. Do not confuse the word "aforethought" in the definition of murder with the concept of "premeditation," which differentiates first degree intent to kill murder from second degree intent to kill murder. (*See* the degrees of murder, *infra*).

In everyday parlance, "malice" means hatred or ill will. No doubt, many murders are committed with such malice. In the crime of murder, however, "malice" has a technical meaning. A person can commit murder—requiring "malice"—without the slightest trace of hatred or ill will. Consider Mary and Paul who were happily married fifty years. Every day of their marriage, they were as much in love as on their wedding day. For the past two years, Mary has suffered from a horribly painful terminal disease. There is no cure, and Mary is in unremitting, devastating pain that takes all the enjoyment out of life. No medications help with the pain. Mary will die from the disease in a matter of weeks. With Paul at her bedside, holding her hand, Mary whispers in his ear, "My love, I can't stand this any more. Please let me die. The pain medicine doesn't help; but you could give me an overdose, and I could just go to sleep and wake up in heaven, where I'll wait for you. Please do this for me, won't you my love?" In his boundless love for his wife, Paul gives Mary the overdose and she passes peacefully away. Paul helped Mary die because he loved her. Yet, Paul acted with "malice" as that word is defined in murder. Indeed, as you will soon learn, Paul probably committed the most serious type of murder: first degree, willful, premeditated, and deliberate murder.

CALIFORNIA STATUTES ON MURDER AND MANSLAUGHTER

The California Penal Code has many sections on criminal homicide. The basic provisions follow:

---

[4] In the early 1600s, Sir Edward Coke defined murder as, "When a man of sound memory and of the age of discretion unlawfully kills any reasonable creature in being, and under the King's peace, with malice aforethought, either express or implied by the law, the death taking place within a year and a day."

[5] Wayne R. LaFave, *Criminal Law* § 14.1 p. 765 (5th ed. 2010) (West).

§ 187. Murder defined; Death of fetus

(a) Murder is the unlawful killing of a human being, or a fetus [except during lawful abortion], with malice aforethought.[6]

§ 188. Malice, express malice, and implied malice defined

(a) For purposes of Section 187, malice may be express or implied.

(1) Malice is express when there is manifested a deliberate intention unlawfully to take away the life of a fellow creature.

(2) Malice is implied when no considerable provocation appears, or when the circumstances attending the killing show an abandoned and malignant heart.

(3) Except as stated in subdivision (e) of Section 189, in order to be convicted of murder, a principal in a crime shall act with malice aforethought. Malice shall not be imputed to a person based solely on his or her participation in a crime.

(b) If it is shown that the killing resulted from an intentional act with express or implied malice, as defined in subdivision (a), no other mental state need be shown to establish the mental state of malice aforethought. Neither an awareness of the obligation to act within the general body of laws regulating society nor acting despite that awareness is included within the definition of malice.

§ 189. Homicide; Degrees

(a) All murder that is perpetrated by means of a destructive device or explosive, a weapon of mass destruction, knowing use of ammunition designed primarily to penetrate metal or armor, poison, lying in wait, torture, or by any other kind of willful, deliberate, and premeditated killing, or that is committed in the perpetration of, or attempt to perpetrate, arson, rape, carjacking, robbery, burglary, mayhem, kidnapping, train wrecking, or any act punishable under [Penal code sections defining various non-rape sex offenses], or murder that is perpetrated by means of discharging a firearm from a motor vehicle, intentionally at another person outside of the vehicle with the intent to inflict death, is murder in the first degree.

(b) All other kinds of murders are of the second degree.

(c) As used in this section the following definitions apply:

(1) "Destructive device" has the same meaning as in Section 16460 [This section describes devices including bombs, grenades, and explosive missiles].

---

[6] At common law, it was not murder to kill an unborn child unless the child was "born alive" and then died from the prenatal injury. The California Legislature added the word "fetus" in 1970.

(2) "Explosive" has the same meaning as in Section 12000 of the Health and Safety Code [anything that explodes: *e.g.*, dynamite nitroglycerine, blasting caps].

(3) "Weapon of mass destruction: means any item defined in Section 11417 [*e.g.*, chemical warfare agents, nuclear agents, vehicle used as a weapon].

(d) To prove the killing was "deliberate and premeditated," it is not necessary to prove the defendant maturely and meaningfully reflected upon the gravity of his or her act.

(e) A participant in the perpetration or attempted perpetration of a felony listed in subdivision (a) in which a death occurs is liable for murder only if one of the following is proven:

(1) The person was the actual killer.

(2) The person was not the actual killer, but, with the intent to kill, aided, abetted, counseled, commanded, induced, solicited, requested, or assisted the actual killer in the commission of murder in the first degree.

(3) The person was a major participant in the underlying felony and acted with reckless indifference to human life, as described in subdivision (d) of Section 190.2.[7]

(f) Subdivision (e) does not apply when the victim is a peace officer who was killed while in the course of his or her duties, where the defendant knew or reasonably should have known that the victim was a peace officer engaged in the performance of his or her duties.

§ 189.1. Killing of peace officer

(a) The Legislature finds and declares that all unlawful killings that are willful, deliberate, and premeditated and in which the victim was a peace officer who was killed while engaged in the performance of his or her duties, where the defendant knew, or reasonably should have known, that the victim was a peace officer engaged in the performance of his or her duties, are considered murder of the first degree for all purposes, including the gravity of the offense and the support of the survivors.

§ 189.5. Mitigation, justification or excuse of homicide

(a) Upon a trial for murder, the commission of the homicide by the defendant being proved, the burden of proving circumstances of mitigation, or that justify or excuse it, devolves upon the defendant, unless the proof on the part of the prosecution tends to show that the

---

[7] *See In re Bennett* (2018) 26 Cal. App. 5th 1002, 237 Cal. Rptr. 3d 610.

crime committed only amounts to manslaughter, or that the defendant was justifiable or excusable.

§ 190. Punishment for murder

(a) Every person guilty of murder in the first degree shall be punished by death, imprisonment in the state prison for life without the possibility of parole, or imprisonment in the state prison for a term of 25 years to life.

Every person guilty of murder in the second degree shall be punished by imprisonment in the state prison for a term of 15 years to life [except those who commit second degree murder of a police officer, or who commit second degree murder by shooting from a car; these murderers serve longer prison sentences].

§ 190.03. Hate crime

(a) A person who commits first-degree murder that is a hate crime shall be punished by imprisonment in the state prison for life without the possibility of parole.

§ 190.05. Previous murder conviction

(a) The penalty for a defendant found guilty of murder in the second degree, who has served a prior prison term for murder in the first or second degree, shall be confinement in the state prison for a term of life without the possibility of parole or confinement in the state prison for a term of 15 years to life.

§ 190.1. Procedure for death penalty trial

A case in which the death penalty may be imposed pursuant to this chapter shall be tried in separate phases as follows:

(a) The question of the defendant's guilt shall be first determined. If the trier of fact finds the defendant guilty of first degree murder, it shall at the same time determine the truth of all special circumstance charged as enumerated in Section 190.2.

[The second phase of a death penalty trial focuses on punishment. The jury hears evidence in aggravation and evidence in mitigation.]

§ 190.2. Punishment for first degree murder; Special circumstances

(a) The penalty for a defendant who is found guilty of murder in the first degree is death or imprisonment in the state prison for life without the possibility of parole if one or more of the following special circumstances has been found to be true:

(1) The murder was intentional and carried out for financial gain.

(2) The defendant was convicted previously of murder in the first or second degree.

(3) The defendant, in this proceeding, has been convicted of more than one offense of murder in the first or second degree.

(4) The murder was committed by means of a destructive device, bomb, or explosive planted, hidden, or concealed in any place, area, dwelling, building, or structure, and the defendant knew, or reasonably should have known, that his or her act or acts would create a great risk of death to one or more human beings.

(5) The murder was committed for the purpose of avoiding or preventing a lawful arrest, or perfecting or attempting to perfect, an escape from lawful custody.

(6) The murder was committed by means of a destructive device, bomb, or explosive that the defendant mailed or delivered, attempted to mail or deliver, or caused to be mailed or delivered, and the defendant knew, or reasonably should have known, that his or her act or acts would create a great risk of death to one or more human beings.

(7) The victim was a peace officer who, while engaged in the course of the performance of his or her duties, was intentionally killed, and the defendant knew, or reasonably should have known, that the victim was a peace officer engaged in the performance of his or her duties; or the victim was a peace officer, or a former peace officer, and was intentionally killed in retaliation for the performance of his or her official duties.

(8) The victim was a federal law enforcement officer [killed under the circumstances described in paragraph (7)].

(9) The victim was a firefighter who, while engaged in the course of the performance of his or her duties, was intentionally killed, and the defendant knew, or reasonably should have known, that the victim was a firefighter engaged in the performance of his or her duties.

(10) The victim was a witness to a crime who was intentionally killed for the purpose of preventing his or her testimony in any criminal or juvenile proceeding.

(11) The victim was a prosecutor or assistant prosecutor or a former prosecutor or assistant prosecutor of any local or state prosecutor's office . . . , and the murder was intentionally carried out in retaliation for, or to prevent the performance of, the victim's official duties.

(12) The victim was a judge . . . .

(13) The victim was an elected official . . . .

(14) The murder was especially heinous, atrocious, or cruel, manifesting exceptional depravity. As used in this section, the phrase "especially heinous, atrocious, or cruel, manifesting exceptional depravity" means a conscienceless or pitiless crime that is unnecessarily torturous to the victim.

(15) The defendant intentionally killed the victim by means of lying in wait.

(16) The victim was intentionally killed because of his or her race, color, religion, nationality, or country of origin.

(17) The murder was committed while the defendant was engaged in, or was an accomplice in, the commission of, or attempted commission of, or the immediate flight after committing, or attempting to commit, the following felonies: (A) Robbery, (B) Kidnapping, (C) Rape, (D) Sodomy, (E) Lewd or lascivious act on a child under age 14, (F) Oral copulation, (G) Burglary, (H) Arson, (I) Train wrecking, (J) Mayhem, (K) Rape by instrument, (L) Carjacking.

(18) The murder was intentional and involved the infliction of torture.

(19) The defendant intentionally killed the victim by the administration of poison.

(20) The victim was juror . . . .

(21) The murder was intentional and perpetrated by means of discharging a firearm from a motor vehicle, intentionally at another person or persons outside the vehicle with intent to inflict death.

(22) The defendant intentionally killed the victim while the defendant was an active participant in a criminal street gang, and the murder was carried out to further the activities of the criminal street gang.

(b) Unless an intent to kill is specifically required under subdivision (a) for a special circumstance enumerated therein, an actual killer, as to whom the special circumstance has been found to be true need not have had any intent to kill at the time of the commission of the offense which is the basis of the special circumstance in order to suffer death or confinement in the state prison for life without the possibility of parole.

(c) Every person, not the actual killer, who, with the intent to kill, aids, abets, counsels, commands, induces, solicits, requests, or assists any actor in the commission of murder in the first degree shall be punished by death or imprisonment in the state prison for life without the possibility of parole if one or more of the special circumstances is subdivision (a) has been found to be true.

(d) Notwithstanding subdivision (c), every person, not the actual killer, who, with reckless indifference to human life and as a major participant, aids, abets, commands, induces, solicits, requests, or assists in the commission of a felony enumerated in paragraph (17) of subdivision (a) which results in the death of some person or persons, and who is found guilty of murder in the first degree therefor, shall be punished by death or imprisonment in the state prison for life without the possibility of parole if a special circumstance enumerated in paragraph (17) of subdivision (a) has been found to be true.

§ 190.3. Punishment for first degree murder

If the defendant has been found guilty of murder in the first degree, and a special circumstance has been charged and found to be true, the trier of fact shall determine whether the penalty shall be death or confinement in state prison for the term of life without the possibility of parole. In the proceedings on the question of penalty, evidence may be presented by both the people and the defendant as to any matter relevant to aggravation, mitigation, and sentence, including, but not limited to, the nature and circumstances of the present offense, any prior felony conviction or convictions whether or not such conviction or convictions involved a crime of violence, the presence or absence of other criminal activity by the defendant which involved the use or attempted use of force or violence or which involved the express or implied threat to use force or violence, and the defendant's character, background, history, mental condition and physical condition.

However, no evidence shall be admitted regarding other criminal activity by the defendant which did not involve the use or attempted use of force or violence or which did not involve the express or implied threat to use force or violence. As used in this section, criminal activity does not require a conviction. . . .

§ 190.5. Death penalty; Age of defendant

(a) Notwithstanding any other provision of law, the death penalty shall not be imposed upon any person who is under the age of 18 at the time of the commission of the crime. The burden of proof as to the age of such person shall be upon the defendant.

(b) The penalty for a defendant found guilty of murder in the first degree, in any case in which one or more special circumstance has been found to be true who was 16 years of age or older and under the age of 18 years at the time of the commission of the crime, shall be confinement in the state prison for life without the possibility of parole or, at the discretion of the court, 25 years to life.

§ 191.5. Gross vehicular manslaughter while intoxicated

(a) Gross vehicular manslaughter while intoxicated is the unlawful killing of a human being without malice aforethought, in the driving of a vehicle, where the driving is in violation of [Vehicle Code sections on driving under the influence], and the killing was either the proximate result of the commission of an unlawful act, not amounting to a felony, and with gross negligence, or the proximate result of the commission of a lawful act that might produce death, in an unlawful manner, and with gross negligence.

(b) Vehicular manslaughter while intoxicated is the unlawful killing of a human being without malice aforethought, in the driving of a vehicle, where the driving is in violation of [Vehicle Code sections on driving under the influence], and the killing was either the proximate result of the commission of an unlawful act, not amounting to a felony, but without gross negligence, or the proximate result of the commission of a lawful act that might produce death, in an unlawful manner, and but without gross negligence.

§ 192. Manslaughter

Manslaughter is the unlawful killing of a human being without malice. It is of three kinds:

(a) Voluntary—upon a sudden quarrel or heat of passion.

(b) Involuntary—in the commission of an unlawful act, not amounting to a felony; or in the commission of a lawful act which might produce death, in an unlawful manner, or without due caution or circumspection. This subdivision shall not apply to acts committed in the driving of a vehicle.[8]

(c) Vehicular—

(1) Except as provided in subdivision (a) of Section 191.5, driving a vehicle in the commission of an unlawful act, not amounting to a felony, and with gross negligence; or driving a vehicle in the commission of a lawful act which might produce death, in an unlawful manner, and with gross negligence.

---

[8] The last sentence of PC § 192(b) states, "This subdivision shall not apply to acts committed in the driving of a vehicle." In *People v. Ferguson* (2011) 194 Cal.App.4th 1070, 124 Cal.Rptr.3d 182, defendant, while driving intoxicated, struck another car, killing one of the occupants of the car. Defendant was charged with depraved heart murder. Defendant acknowledged that "voluntary intoxication cannot be used to negate implied malice in a second degree murder prosecution." Defendant sought a jury instruction that "a person who kills while unconscious due to voluntary intoxication, is guilty of involuntary manslaughter, rather than murder." The trial judge refused the instruction "because although involuntary manslaughter is usually a lesser included offense of murder, in the context of drunk driving it is not." This is so because PC § 192(b) states, "This subdivision shall not apply to acts committed in the driving of a vehicle."

(2) Driving a vehicle in the commission of an unlawful act, not amounting to a felony, but without gross negligence; or driving a vehicle in the commission of a lawful act which might produce death, in an unlawful manner, but without gross negligence.

§ 193. Voluntary manslaughter, involuntary manslaughter and vehicular manslaughter; Punishment

(a) Voluntary manslaughter is punishable by imprisonment in the state prison for 3, 6, or 11 years.

(b) Involuntary manslaughter is punishable by imprisonment for two, three, or four years.

(c) Vehicular manslaughter is punishable [depending on the seriousness of the crime, with imprisonment in state prison or county jail].

§ 194. Murder and manslaughter; Time of death

To make the killing either murder or manslaughter, it is not requisite that the party die within three years and a day after the stroke received or the cause of death administered. If death occurs beyond the time of three years and a day, there shall be a rebuttable presumption that the killing was not criminal.[9]

§ 195. Homicide; Excusable

Homicide is excusable in the following cases:

1. When committed by accident and misfortune, or in doing any other lawful act by lawful means, with usual and ordinary caution, and without any unlawful intent.

2. When committed by accident and misfortune, in the heat of passion, upon any sudden and sufficient provocation, or upon a sudden combat, when no undue advantage is taken, nor any dangerous weapon used, and when the killing is not done in a cruel or unusual manner.

§ 196. Homicide; Justifiable

Homicide is justifiable when committed by public officers and those acting by their command in their aid and assistance, either—

[9] As murder was defined at early common law, one element of the crime was the requirement that the victim die within a year and a day of the wound. In the early 1600s, Sir Edward Coke defined murder as, "When a man of sound memory and of the age of discretion unlawfully kills any reasonable creature in being, and under the King's peace, with malice aforethought, either express or implied by the law, the death taking place within a year and a day." Early in California history, the state had the year and a day rule. After a time, the Legislature changed it to three years and a day. Finally, the current version of the rule was enacted to create a rebuttable presumption that a death is non-criminal if it occurs more than three years and a day after "the stroke received." A prosecutor can rebut the presumption with sufficient evidence that a death more than three years and a day after a "stroke" was caused by the "stroke."

1. In obedience to any judgment of a competent Court; or;

2. When necessarily committed in overcoming actual resistance to the execution of some legal process, or in the discharge of any other legal duty; or,

3. When necessarily committed in retaking felons who have been rescued or have escaped, or when necessarily committed in arresting persons charged with felony, and who are fleeing from justice or resisting such arrest.

§ 197. Homicide; Justifiable

Homicide is also justifiable when committed by any person in any of the following cases:

1. When resisting any attempt to murder any person, or to commit a felony, or to do some great bodily injury upon any person.

2. When committed in defense of habitation, property, or person, against one who manifestly intends or endeavors, by violence or surprise to commit a felony, or against one who manifestly intends and endeavors, in a violent, riotous, or tumultuous manner, to enter the habitation of another for the purpose of offering violence to any person therein.

3. When committed in the lawful defense of such person, or of a spouse, parent, child, master, mistress, or servant of such person, when there is reasonable ground to apprehend a design to commit a felony or to do some great bodily injury, and imminent danger of such design being accomplished; but such person, or the person in whose behalf the defense was made, if he or she was the assailant or engaged in mutual combat, must really and in good faith have endeavored to decline any further struggle before the homicide was committed.

§ 198. Homicide; Justifiable

A bare fear of the commission of any of the offenses mentioned in subdivisions 2 and 3 of Section 197, to prevent which homicide may be lawfully committed, is not sufficient to justify it. But the circumstances must be sufficient to excite the fears of a reasonable person, and the party killing must have acted under the influence of such fears alone.

§ 198.5. Homicide; Use of force presumed reasonable

Any person using force intended or likely to cause death or great bodily injury within is or her residence shall be presumed to have held reasonable fear of imminent peril of death or great bodily injury to self, family, or a member of the household when that force is used against another person, not a member of the family or household, who unlawfully and forcibly enters or has unlawfully and forcibly entered the residence and the person using the force knew or had reason to believe that an unlawful and forcible entry occurred.

MURDER: THE MEANINGS OF MALICE

Over the course of many years, the word "malice" took on the following meanings:

1. Intent to kill. The first meaning of malice is intent to kill. It was defendant's conscious object to kill. PC § 188 defines this type of malice as "a deliberate intention unlawfully to take away the life of a fellow creature." Intent to kill murder is express malice murder.

Example: Dell intended to kill Vic, so Dell walked up to Vic, put a gun to his head and pulled the trigger, intending Vic to die from the bullet. Dell committed intent to kill, express malice murder.

2. Intent to cause grievous bodily injury. Defendant did *not* intend to kill the victim. Rather, defendant intended to inflict a serious non-fatal injury on the victim. The victim died from the injury. This is implied malice because defendant did not intend to kill. California does not have intent to cause grievous bodily injury murder. In California, cases that fit the requirements of intent to cause grievous bodily injury murder are typically prosecuted as depraved heart murder or felony murder.

Example: Dell shot Vic in the leg intending to injure Vic and keep Vic inactive for a few weeks. Dell did not intend to kill Vic, but Vic died from the wound. Dell may be prosecuted for intent to cause grievous bodily injury murder.

3. Depraved heart; also called abandoned and malignant heart. With depraved heart murder, defendant did not intend to kill. Indeed, in most depraved heart murder cases, defendant did not intend to hurt anyone. With depraved heart murder, defendant engaged in conduct that was extremely dangerous to human life. Defendant was aware of the risk to human life but consciously disregarded the risk. In *People v. Bryant* (2013) 56 Cal. 4th 959, 301 P.3d 1136, 157 Cal. Rptr. 3d 522, the Supreme Court wrote, "We have interpreted implied malice as having both a physical and a mental component. The physical component is satisfied by the performance of an act, the natural consequences of which are dangerous to life. The mental component is the requirement that the defendant knows that his conduct endangers the life of another and acts with a conscious disregard for life." With depraved heart murder there typically is no social justification for defendant's conduct.

Depraved heart is implied malice murder.[10] In *People v. Garcia* (2008) 162 Cal.App.4th 18, 26–27, 74 Cal.Rptr.3d 912, the Court of Appeal

[10] PC § 188 provides that malice is implied "when the circumstances attending the killing show an abandoned and malignant heart."

explained: "Express malice is an unlawful intent to kill. Implied malice requires defendant's awareness of engaging in conduct that endangers life."

When a trial judge instructs a jury on the meaning of depraved heart murder, the judge does not use the words "depraved heart" or "abandoned and malignant heart." The jury would not understand these terms. Moreover, the words are pejorative and could unfairly prejudice a jury against a defendant charged with depraved heart murder. The California Supreme Court wrote, "Juries should be instructed that malice is implied when the killing results from an intentional act, the natural consequences of which are dangerous to life, which was deliberately performed by a person who knows that his conduct endangers the life of another and who acts with conscious disregard for life." *People v. Blakeley* (2000) 23 Cal.4th 82, 87, 96 Cal.Rptr.2d 451, 999 P.2d 675.

Drunk driving that causes death is sometimes prosecuted as depraved heart murder. "[A]ppellate courts have upheld numerous murder convictions in cases where defendants have committed homicides while driving under the influence of alcohol." *People v. Wolfe* (2018) 20 Cal. App. 5th 673, 229 Cal. Rptr. 3d 414.

Example: Centuries ago in England, a stone mason was working more than one hundred feet above the ground, helping construct a cathedral. The mason was chipping away at a 60 pound block of stone when his chisel slipped and he ruined the stone. Rather than lower the stone to the ground on the elevator, as he was supposed to do, the mason threw the stone off the front of the cathedral. The mason did not look to see if anyone was passing below, although the mason knew people often walked below. The stone killed a passerby. The stone mason may be charged with depraved heart murder.[11]

4. Felony murder. PC § 189 creates felony murder by providing that a killing "which is committed in the perpetration of, or attempt to perpetrate" certain felonies is murder. In many felony murder cases, defendant does not intend to kill or harm the victim. Indeed, the death may be an accident. In *People v. Bryant* (2013) 56 Cal. 4th 959, 301 P.3d 1136, 157 Cal. Rptr. 3d 522, the Supreme Court wrote, "Felony-murder liability does not require an intent to kill, or even implied malice, but merely an intent to commit the underlying felony."[12]

---

[11] This example is drawn from Wayne R. Lafave, *Criminal Law* (5th ed. 2010) (West).

[12] *People v. Bryant* (2013) 56 Cal. 4th 959, 965, 301 P.3d 1136, 157 Cal. Rptr. 3d 522 ("The felony-murder doctrine, whose ostensible purpose is to deter those engaged in felonies from killing negligently or accidentally, operates to posit that crucial mental state—and thereby to render irrelevant evidence of actual malice or the lack thereof—when the killer is engaged in a felony whose inherent danger to human life renders logical an imputation of malice on the part of all who commit it.")

Example: Dell entered a business to rob it. Dell ordered everyone to the floor, robbed the place, and left. Shortly thereafter, one of the people in the business had a fatal heart attack caused by the fright of the robbery. Robbery is a felony. The death occurred during commission of the robbery, and was causally related to the crime. Dell committed felony murder. *People v. Stamp* (1969) 2 Cal.App.3d 203, 82 Cal.Rptr. 598.

The Legislature was concerned that for some participants in felonies where death occurs, punishment for first degree felony murder is out of proportion to the participant's role in the crime. In 2018, the Legislature amended Section 189 to limit who can be charged with first degree felony murder. Subdivision (e) now provides that a participant in a felony listed in § 189(a) is only liable for felony murder if the participant was the actual killer, was a major participant in the felony who acted with reckless indifference to human life, or who, while acting with intent to kill, aided, abetted, counseled, commanded, induced, solicited, requested, or assisted the actual killer in the killing. The limit on felony murder liability set forth in Subdivision (e) does not apply when the victim is a peace officer.

5. Provocative act murder. This narrow category of murder applies when two or more individuals perpetrate a crime and a police officer or the victim fights back and kills one of the perpetrators. Under provocative act murder, the surviving perpetrators can be held liable for the death of their partner in crime.

Example: A, B, and C enter a convenience store to rob it. A points a gun at the store owner and, chattering insanely, shouts, "Hurry up! Hurry up! Or I'll shoot. Hurry up, this is a robbery. Hurry up or I'll shoot, fool!" Frightened by A's behavior, the owner takes out a gun and shoots B. Under the provocative act murder doctrine, A and C are responsible for the death of B. *People v. Kainzrants* (1996) 45 Cal.App.4th 1068, 53 Cal.Rptr.2d 207.

Summary of the Meaning of Malice. When the average person thinks of murder, the person thinks of intent to kill murder. Intent to kill murder is what we see in the movies and on TV. Under California law, however only one type of murder requires intent to kill. The other types of murder—depraved heart, felony murder, and provocative act—do not require intent to kill. Thus, a person can be a murderer *without* intending to kill.

MALICE AFORETHOUGHT OUTSIDE CALIFORNIA

California's definition of malice aforethought can be traced to English law developed centuries ago. Other states drew on the same common law heritage, and, as a result, malice aforethought is defined similarly across the United States. There are differences here and there, but for the most part, the definition of murder is similar across the country.

DEGREES OF MURDER

Most people understand there are degrees of murder.[13] What people generally do not understand is the complexity of the degrees of murder. In 1794, Pennsylvania was the first state to divide murder into degrees. Under the Pennsylvania approach, first degree murder included: (a) Murder committed in specified ways (*e.g.*, lying in wait); (b) felony murder committed during certain felonies (arson, rape, robbery, burglary); and (c) willful, deliberate, and premeditated murder. Second degree murder included: (a) intent to kill murder that was not first degree murder because it was not carried out in specified ways (*e.g.*, lying in wait) and was not deliberate and premeditated; (b) intent to cause grievous bodily injury murder; and (c) depraved heart murder.

In 1856, the California Legislature followed the Pennsylvania approach, dividing murder into two degrees. PC § 189. Today in California, there are seven types of first degree murder, and four types of second degree murder.

First Degree Murder in California

In California there are seven types of first degree murder.[14]

1. Willful, deliberate, and premeditated killing. "Willful" means intent to kill. Intent to kill murder in which the killer deliberated and premeditated is first degree murder.

2. Felony murder in the first degree. First degree felony murder is a killing that occurs during the commission of a felony listed in PC § 189—arson, rape, carjacking, robbery, burglary, mayhem, kidnapping, train wrecking, and various non-rape sex offenses.

3. Torture murder. Defendant intended to torture, but did not necessarily intend to kill. There must be a causal relationship between the torture and the victim's death. The Supreme Court explained in *People v. Whisenhunt* (2008) 44 Cal.4th 174, 201, 79 Cal.Rptr.3d 125, 186 P.3d 496, "The elements of torture murder are: (1) acts causing death that involve a high degree of probability of the victim's death; and (2) a willful, deliberate, and premeditated intent to cause extreme pain or suffering for the purpose of revenge, extortion, persuasion, or another sadistic purpose." Inflicting pain is not enough for torture murder. There must be evidence that defendant wanted the victim to suffer. It is not necessary that the victim

---

[13] In 1995 there was a movie titled "Murder in the First" starring Christian Slater and Kevin Bacon.

[14] One could argue that there are nine types of first degree murder. The text refers to murder perpetrated by means of (1) a destructive device or explosive, (2) a weapon of mass destruction, or (3) knowing use of ammunition as one type of first degree murder. Arguably, this is three types of murder, not one.

actually experience pain. (*People v. Armstrong* (2019) 6 Cal. 5th 735, 433 P.3d 987, 243 Cal. Rptr. 3d 105).

In *People v. D'Arcy* (2010) 48 Cal.4th 257, 106 Cal.Rptr.3d 459, 226 P.3d 949, defendant was angry with the janitorial firm that gave him contracts for janitorial services. Defendant complained that he was not being paid on time. His anger focused on the company bookkeeper. Defendant purchased a gallon of gasoline, stormed into the bookkeeper's office, poured gas over her, and lit her on fire, killing her. The Supreme Court ruled the evidence was sufficient to prove defendant intended to torture the victim. The Court wrote, "Intent to inflict extreme pain may be inferred from the circumstances of the crime, the nature of the killing, and the condition of the victim's body."

4. Lying in wait. If the prosecutor proves lying in wait, no other evidence of premeditation or intent is necessary. To lie in wait, the perpetrator typically waits in ambush or concealment to take the victim by surprise. A defendant can lie in wait without hiding. For example, a defendant who conceals his purpose from the victim in order to take the victim by surprise, lies in wait. In *People v. Russell* (2010) 50 Cal.4th 1228, 117 Cal.Rptr.3d 615, 242 P.3d 68, the Supreme Court explained the requirements for lying in wait. First, defendant must conceal her purpose. Second, there must be a substantial period of watching and waiting for the opportune moment to attack, although there is no fixed time limit on how long defendant must lie in wait. The time can be quite short, provided the killing is immediately preceded by lying in wait. Defendant does not have to kill at the first opportunity. Third, defendant commits a surprise attack on the unsuspecting victim from a position of advantage.

5. Murder by poison. Murder perpetrated by poison is first degree murder. A defendant who kills by poison does not have to intend to kill to be guilty of first degree murder.

6. Drive by shooting murder. PC § 189 states, "Any murder which is perpetrated by means of discharging a firearm from a motor vehicle, intentionally at another person outside of the vehicle with the intent to inflict death" is first degree murder.

7. Explosives or armor penetrating ammunition. Murder perpetrated "by means of a destructive device or explosive, a weapon of mass destruction, knowing use of ammunition designed primarily to penetrate metal or armor" is first degree murder, whether or not defendant intended to kill.

Second Degree Murder in California

In California there are four kinds of second degree murder.

1. Intent to kill murder without premeditation and deliberation. Sometimes a person strikes out rashly and impulsively, intending to kill, but without premeditating and deliberating. Such killing is typically an immediate reaction to something the victim said or did. An intent to kill murder without premeditation and deliberation is second degree murder.

2. Provocation sufficient to lower first degree intent to kill murder to second degree murder. When a defendant who is charged with first degree intent to kill murder offers evidence that the defendant was adequately provoked by the victim, the defendant may be able to reduce the crime from first degree murder to second degree murder[15] or voluntary heat of passion manslaughter. In *People v. Hernandez* (2010) 183 Cal.App.4th 1327, 1332, 107 Cal.Rptr.3d 915, the Court of Appeal explained: "To reduce a murder to second degree murder, premeditation and deliberation may be negated by heat of passion arising from provocation. If the provocation would not cause an average person to experience deadly passion but it precludes the defendant from subjectively deliberating or premeditating, the crime is second degree murder."[16] If the provocation *would* cause an average person to experience deadly passion, the offense is voluntary manslaughter.

3. Second degree felony murder. When a death occurs during the commission of an inherently dangerous felony that is not listed in PC § 189, the killing is second degree felony murder.[17]

4. Depraved heart murder. Depraved heart murder (PC § 188) is second degree murder.

Note: Provocative act murder can be first or second degree murder.

---

[15] *See* PC § 188, which provides that malice "is implied, when no considerable provocation appears."

[16] In *People v. Hernandez* (2010), 183 Cal.App.4th 1327, 1332, 107 Cal.Rptr.3d 915, the Court of Appeal wrote, "If the provocation would cause a reasonable person to react with deadly passion, the defendant is deemed to have acted without malice so as to further reduce the crime to voluntary manslaughter." *See also, People v. Jones* (2014) 223 Cal. App. 4th 996, 100–101, 167 Cal. Rptr. 3d 659, 663–663.

[17] No statute specifically defines second degree felony murder. The courts interpret Section 188 to create the offense. *People v. Powell* (2018) 5 Cal. 5th 921, 422 P.3d 973, 236 Cal. Rptr. 3d 316.

Premeditation and Deliberation—Dividing Line Between First and Second Degree Intent to Kill Murder

The line separating first degree intent to kill murder from second degree intent to kill murder is premeditation and deliberation.[18] The Supreme Court explained premeditation and deliberation in *People v. Jennings* (2010) 50 Cal.4th 616, 645–646, 114 Cal.Rptr.3d 133, 237 P.3d 474:

> An intentional killing is premeditated and deliberate if it occurred as the result of preexisting thought and reflection rather than unconsidered or rash impulse. In this context, "premeditated" means considered beforehand, and "deliberate" means formed or arrived at or determined upon as a result of careful thought and weighing of considerations for and against the proposed course of action. We normally consider three kinds of evidence to determine whether a finding of premeditation and deliberation is adequately supported—preexisting motive, planning activity, and manner of killing—but these factors need not be present in any particular combination to find substantial evidence of premeditation and deliberation.

It does not take long to premeditate and deliberate. In *People v. Thompson* (2010) 49 Cal.4th 79, 114, 109 Cal.Rptr.3d 549, 231 P.3d 289, the Supreme Court stated: "Premeditation and deliberation can occur in a brief interval. The test is not time, but reflection. Thoughts may follow each other with great rapidity and cold, calculated judgment may be arrived at quickly." In *Thompson*, defendant was just a few feet from victim when he shot him. The Court concluded: "This manner of killing, a close-range shooting without any provocation or evidence of a struggle, reasonably supports an inference of premeditation and deliberation."

In the Following Examples, Did the Defendant Premeditate and Deliberate?

1. The victim was shot "execution style" in the back of the head. *People v. Hawkins* (1995) 10 Cal.4th 920, 42 Cal.Rptr.2d 636, 897 P.2d 574.

2. In a secluded area, defendant shot and killed two victims with a rifle. In order to shoot the victims, defendant had to walk to his car to retrieve the rifle. After killing the first victim, defendant reloaded to kill the second victim. There was evidence that defendant killed the victims to prevent them from testifying against him at his upcoming trial for robbery. *People v. Thomas* (1992) 2 Cal.4th 489, 7 Cal.Rptr.2d 199, 828 P.2d 101.

---

[18] *See People v. Boatman* (2013) 221 Cal. App. 4th 1253, 165 Cal. Rptr. 3d 521 for a thorough discussion of premeditation and deliberation.

3. Dell belonged to a gang known as "211–187." These numbers refer to sections 211 and 187 of the Penal Code. Section 211 is robbery. Section 187 is murder. Defendant entered a convenience store to rob it. The clerk tried to run out the back door, and defendant shot and killed the clerk. Is the name of Dell's gang—211–187—relevant to premeditation and deliberation? *People v. Jones* (2003) 30 Cal.4th 1084, 135 Cal.Rptr.2d 370, 70 P.3d 359.

4. Dell murdered and robbed an elderly couple in their home. The victims were beaten and stabbed multiple times. In *People v. Potts* (2019) 6 Cal. 5th 1012, 436 P.3d 899, 245 Cal. Rptr. 3d 2, the Supreme Court wrote, "The manner of the killings also supports a finding of premeditation and deliberation. The attack—involving multiple weapons, numerous stabs and slashes, and, apparently, a knife-sharpening interlude [during the killings]—was undoubtedly prolonged. In particular, the attacks with the knives suggest deliberation, not only because they came later, but also because plunging a lethal weapon into the chest evidences a deliberate intention to kill. . . . The evidence of premeditation and deliberation was particularly strong with respect to Shirley's murder, because defendant had to travel through the house to reach her after attacking Fred near the front door." After the bloody killings, defendant took time to open a package of cookies, indicating he "was not surprised or dismayed by what he had done."

DEPRAVED HEART MURDER

Depraved heart murder is a killing that shows an "abandoned and malignant heart." PC § 188. This type of murder requires evidence that defendant engaged in extremely reckless behavior carrying a high risk of death. Defendant was aware of the risk and proceeded anyway. The California Supreme Court's decision in *People v. Taylor* discusses depraved heart murder.

PEOPLE V. TAYLOR

California Supreme Court
32 Cal.4th 863, 11 Cal.Rptr.3d 510, 86 P.3d 881 (2004)

BROWN, J.

facts

A defendant shoots a woman, killing her. As a result, her fetus also dies. In the absence of evidence the defendant knew the woman was pregnant, may the defendant be held liable for the second degree implied malice murder of the fetus? We conclude he may, and therefore reverse the judgment of the Court of Appeal.

Defendant Harold Wayne Taylor and the victim, Ms. Patty Fansler, met in the spring of 1997. They dated and then lived together along with

Fansler's three children. In July 1998 Fansler moved out. Defendant was heard threatening to kill Fansler and anyone close to her if she left him. Defendant wanted to "get back" with Fansler, and told one of her friends he could not handle the breakup, and if he could not have her, "nobody else could."

Defendant and Fansler spent New Year's Eve 1998 together. On January 1, 1999, a police officer responded to a call regarding a woman screaming in a motel room. In the room he found defendant and Fansler. Fansler was "upset and crying," and said defendant had raped her. Defendant was arrested, and shortly thereafter Fansler obtained a restraining order against him.

On March 9, 1999, defendant entered Fansler's apartment through a ruse, and after an apparent struggle, shot and killed Fansler. Fansler died of a single gunshot wound to the head. [Defendant fired a second shot in the bedroom that did not hit Fansler.] Fansler also suffered a laceration on the back of her head that penetrated to her skull and chipped the bone, and bruising on her neck, legs, and elbows.

The autopsy revealed that Fansler was pregnant. The fetus was a male between 11 and 13 weeks old who died as a result of his mother's death. The examining pathologist could not discern that Fansler, who weighed approximately 200 pounds, was pregnant just by observing her on the examination table.

The prosecution proceeded on a theory of second degree implied malice murder as to the fetus. The Court of Appeal reversed defendant's second degree murder conviction based on the fetus's death. The court concluded there was evidence to support the physical, but not the mental, component of implied malice murder. "There is not an iota of evidence that defendant knew his conduct endangered fetal life and acted with disregard of that fetal life. It is undisputed that the fetus was 11 to 13 weeks old; the pregnancy was not yet visible and defendant did not know Ms. Fansler was pregnant." In contrast to "the classic example of indiscriminate shooting/implied malice" of a person firing a bullet through a window not knowing or caring if anyone is behind it, "the undetectable early pregnancy here was too latent and remote a risk factor to bear on defendant's liability or the gravity of his offense. The risk to unknown fetal life is latent and indeterminate, something the average person would not be aware of or consciously disregard. Were we to adopt the People's position, we would dispense with the subjective mental component of implied malice. Where is the evidence that defendant acted with knowledge of the danger to, and conscious disregard for, fetal life? There is none. This is dispositive."

Murder is the unlawful killing of a human being, or a fetus, with malice aforethought. Viability is not an element of fetal homicide under section 187(a), but the state must demonstrate that the fetus has progressed beyond the embryonic stage of seven to eight weeks.

Malice may be either express or implied. It is express when the defendant manifests a deliberate intention unlawfully to take away the life of a fellow creature. (§ 188.) It is implied when the killing results from an intentional act, the natural consequences of which are dangerous to life, which act was deliberately performed by a person who knows that his conduct endangers the life of another and who acts with conscious disregard for life. For convenience, we shall refer to this mental state as conscious disregard for life. Implied malice has both a physical and a mental component, the physical component being the performance of an act, the natural consequences of which are dangerous to life, and the mental component being the requirement that the defendant knows that his conduct endangers the life of another and acts with a conscious disregard for life.

It is plain that *implied* malice aforethought does not exist in the perpetrator only in relation to an intended victim. Recklessness need not be cognizant of the identity of a victim or even of his existence. When a defendant commits an act, the natural consequences of which are dangerous to human life, with a conscious disregard for life in general, he acts with implied malice towards those he ends up killing. There is no requirement the defendant specifically know of the existence of each victim.

To illustrate, in *People v. Watson* (1981) 30 Cal.3d 290, the defendant killed a mother and her six-year-old daughter while driving under the influence of alcohol. We found the evidence supported a conclusion that the defendant's conduct was sufficiently wanton to hold him to answer on two charges of second degree murder. Nowhere in our discussion did we indicate the defendant was required to have a subjective awareness of his particular victims, *i.e.*, the mother and daughter killed, for an implied malice murder charge to proceed. Nothing in the language of section 187(a) allows for a different analysis for a fetus. Indeed, had the mother in *Watson* been pregnant, it is difficult to see any logical basis on which to argue the defendant could not have been held to answer for three charges of second degree murder.

Here, as the Attorney General notes, defendant "knowingly put human life at grave risk when he fired his gun twice in an occupied apartment building." As the Attorney General observed during oral argument, if a gunman simply walked down the hall of an apartment building and fired through the closed doors, he would be liable for the murder of all the victims struck by his bullets—including a fetus of one of his anonymous victims who happened to be pregnant. Likewise, defense counsel conceded at oral argument that defendant would be guilty of implied malice murder if one of his bullets had struck an infant concealed by the bed covers. On this point, both counsel are right. Had one of Fansler's other children died during defendant's assault, there would be no inquiry into whether defendant knew the child was present for implied malice murder liability to attach. Similarly, there is no principled basis on which to require defendant to know Fansler was pregnant to justify an implied malice murder conviction as to her fetus.

In battering and shooting Fansler, defendant acted with knowledge of the danger to and conscious disregard for life in general. That is all that is required for implied malice murder. He did not need to be specifically aware how many potential victims his conscious disregard for life endangered.

[Note: In an omitted footnote, the Court stated that the doctrine of transferred intent played no role in its analysis].

FELONY MURDER

Felony murder occurs when a death happens during the perpetration of or attempt to perpetrate certain felonies.[19] The purpose of the felony murder rule is to deter felons from killing accidentally or negligently. The California Supreme Court explained in *People v. Cavitt* (2004) 33 Cal.4th 187, 192, 14 Cal.Rptr.3d 281, 91 P.3d 222, "The purpose of the felony-murder rule is to deter those who commit the enumerated felonies from killing by holding them strictly responsible for any killing committed during the perpetration or attempted perpetration of the felony." Felony murder liability attaches whether the killing is intentional, negligent, or accidental. For felony murder liability, there must be a causal relationship between the felony and the death. The Supreme Court explained in *Cavitt,* "The causal relationship is established by proof of a logical nexus, beyond mere coincidence of time and place, between the homicidal act and the underlying felony."

If the felony is listed in PC § 189, it is first degree felony murder.[20] If the felony is *not* listed in § 189, but the felony *is* inherently dangerous to human life, it is second degree felony murder.[21] If the felony is *not* listed in

[19] The Supreme Court described the purposes of felony murder in *People v. Sarun Chun* (2009) 45 Cal.4th 1172, 1198, 91 Cal.Rptr.3d 106, 203 P.3d 425: "We have identified two [purposes]. The purpose we have most often identified is to deter felons from killing negligently or accidentally by holding them strictly responsible for killings they commit. Another purpose is to deter commission of the inherently dangerous felony itself."

[20] If the felony is listed in PC § 189, it does not matter whether the felony is inherently dangerous to human life.

[21] The crime of second degree felony murder is not mentioned specifically in statute. In *People v. Sarun Chun* (2009) 45 Cal.4th 1172, 1178, 1183, 91 Cal.Rptr.3d 106, 203 P.3d 425, the Supreme Court explained, "We conclude that the rule is based on statute, specifically section 188's definition of implied malice. The second degree felony-murder rule, although derived from the common law, is based on statute."

PC § 189 and is *not* inherently dangerous to human life, then there can be no felony murder prosecution.[22]

Inherently Dangerous to Human Life

What felonies are inherently dangerous to human life? (IDHL) In the United States, there are two approaches to determining whether a felony is IDHL: (1) Facts of the case approach (*i.e.*, how the crime was committed), and (2) Felony in the abstract approach, which ignores how the crime was committed. The felony in the abstract approach looks at the elements of the crime and asks whether the felony is IDHL.

California follows the felony in the abstract approach.[23] In California, ignore the facts of the case and ask, is there a way to violate this statute without it being IDHL? If the answer is "yes," then the felony is *not* IDHL, and the felony will not support a felony murder prosecution. As the Court of Appeal put it in *People v. Garcia* (2008) 162 Cal.App.4th 18, 28 n. 4, 74 Cal.Rptr.3d 912, "An inherently dangerous felony for purposes of second degree felony-murder doctrine is one which, by its very nature, cannot be committed without creating a substantial risk that someone will be killed. In determining whether a felony is inherently dangerous to human life, the court considers the elements of the offense in the abstract, not the defendant's specific conduct."

In *People v. Burroughs* (1984) 35 Cal.3d 824, 201 Cal. Rptr. 319, 678 P.2d 894, the felony was practicing medicine without a license. Section 2052 of the Business and Professions Code states: "Any person who practices [medicine] without having at the time of so doing a valid [license] is guilty of a public offense." In *Burroughs*, a young man—let's call him Bill—was diagnosed with cancer. Bill's doctors said there was little chance of a cure, but they encouraged Bill to undergo chemotherapy. In desperation, Bill consulted defendant, a self-described "healer." Burroughs assured Bill that he could cure him. Burroughs instructed Bill to (1) purchase and read Burroughs' book titled *Healing in the Age of Enlightenment*, (2) stop seeing his regular doctor, (3) drink a special lemonade prepared by defendant, and (4) lie down under colored lights. Bill died. Burroughs did not have a medical license. Could Burroughs be charged with felony murder? Is practicing medicine without a license IDHL?

---

[22] When a death occurs during the commission of a felony that is not dangerous to human life, and that is not listed in § 189, defendant may be convicted of involuntary manslaughter. *See infra* the discussion of involuntary manslaughter.

[23] *See People v. Sarun Chun* (2009) 45 Cal.4th 1172, 1188, 91 Cal.Rptr.3d 106, 203 P.3d 425, "Whether a felony is inherently dangerous is determined from the elements of the felony in the abstract, not the particular facts."

PROBLEM

Are the following felonies IDHL under the California approach? Of course, to determine conclusively whether any of these crimes is IDHL, you would need to read the statute defining the crime: (1) Manufacturing methamphetamine (Health & Safety Code § 11379.6(a)); (2) Shooting a firearm in a grossly negligent manner (PC § 246.3); (3) Extortion (PC §§ 518, 519); (4) Grand theft from a person (PC § 487(c)); (5) Shooting at an unoccupied aircraft (PC § 247(a)); (6) Discharging a laser at an aircraft in flight (PC § 247.5); (7) Arson of a structure (PC § 451); (8) Driving with willful and wanton disregard for public safety while fleeing a police officer (*People v. Howard* (2005) 34 Cal.4th 1129, 23 Cal.Rptr.3d 306, 104 P.3d 107), (9) Kidnapping for ransom or reward (PC § 209(a)).

Merger

As mentioned above, if a felony that is not listed in PC § 189 is not IDHL, it will not support a felony murder prosecution. If the non-listed felony *is* IDHL, there is one more step in the felony murder analysis. The last step asks whether the felony merges into the homicide.[24] If the felony *does* merge, there can be no felony murder prosecution.[25] If the felony does *not* merge, there can be a felony murder prosecution. A felony merges if it is assaultive in nature.[26] The Supreme Court explained in *People v. Sarun Chun* (2009) 45 Cal.4th 1172, 1200, 91 Cal.Rptr.3d 106, 203 P.3d 425: "An 'assaultive' felony is one that involves a threat of immediate violent injury. In determining whether a crime merges, the court looks to its elements and not the facts of the case. Accordingly, if the elements of the crime have an assaultive aspect, the crime merges with the underlying homicide even if the elements also include conduct that is not assaultive."

The merger doctrine does not apply in first degree felony murder. *People v. Powell* (2018) 5 Cal. 5th 921, 422 P.3d 973, 236 Cal. Rptr. 3d 316; *People v. Farley* (2009) 46 Cal.4th 1053, 96 Cal.Rptr.3d 191, 210 P.3d 361.

How Long Does a Felony Continue for Felony Murder Purposes?

In the typical felony murder case, the death occurs during the commission of the felony. What is the outcome if a death occurs while the

---

[24] *See People v. Sarun Chun* (2009) 45 Cal.4th 1172, 1189, 91 Cal.Rptr.3d 106, 203 P.3d 425, "The merger doctrine developed due to the understanding that the underlying felony must be an independent crime and not merely the killing itself. Thus, certain underlying felonies 'merge' with the homicide and cannot be used for purposes of felony murder."

[25] If the felony merges because it is assaultive, this does not mean the defendant gets off scott free. The defendant can be convicted of the felony.

[26] *See People v. Garcia* (2008) 162 Cal.App.4th 18, 29, 74 Cal.Rptr.3d 912, "When, as here, the only underlying, inherently dangerous felony committed by the defendant is an aggravated assault, however, the felony murder does not apply under the merger doctrine."

felon is driving away from the crime scene? It sometimes happens that the police arrive at the crime scene and a chase ensues that ends in the death of an innocent pedestrian or motorist. Is a felon liable for felony murder when a death occurs in the immediate aftermath of the felony? In *People v. Cavitt* (2004) 33 Cal.4th 187, 14 Cal.Rptr.3d 281, 91 P.3d 222, the Supreme Court explained:

> Our case law has consistently rejected a strict construction of the temporal relationship between felony and killing. A killing is committed in the perpetration of an enumerated felony if the killing and the felony are parts of one continuous transaction. We have invoked the continuous-transaction doctrine to make complicit a nonkiller, where the felony and the homicide are parts of one continuous transaction.
>
> Our reliance on the continuous-transaction doctrine is consistent with the purpose of the felony-murder statute, which was adopted for the protection of the community and its residents, not for the benefit of the lawbreaker, and this court has viewed it as obviating the necessity for, rather than requiring, any technical inquiry concerning whether there has been a completion, abandonment, or desistence of the felony before the homicide was completed. In particular, the rule was not intended to relieve the wrongdoer from any possible consequence of his act by placing a limitation upon the *res geste* which is unreasonable or unnatural. The homicide is committed in the perpetration of the felony if the killing and felony are parts of one continuous transaction.
>
> The continuous-transaction doctrine defines the duration of felony-murder liability, which may extend beyond the termination of the felony itself, provided that the felony and the act resulting in death constitute one continuous transaction.

Problems on the Continuous Transaction Doctrine

1. Wilkins builds houses for a living. He was building a house in Palm Springs. At midnight, Wilkins drove his pickup truck to a construction site in Long Beach, which is 113 miles from Palm Springs. Wilkins entered the partially completed home in Long Beach and removed a stove, refrigerator, and dishwasher. He put the appliances in the bed of his truck and set off for Palm Springs, where he intended to install the stolen appliances in the home he was building. Wilkins did not raise the tail gate of the pick up because the appliances occupied the entire bed of the truck as well as three inches of the open tail gate. He did not tie down the appliances. At five in the morning, on the way to Palm Springs on the freeway, the stove worked its way off the back of the pickup and fell onto the freeway. Vic was driving 100 yards behind Wilkins, at the posted speed

limit. Vic swerved to avoid the stove, and collided with a cement bridge abutment, killing him. Is Wilkins liable for Vic's death? *People v. Wilkins* (2013) 56 Cal. 4th 333, 295 P.3d 903, 153 Cal. Rptr. 3d 519.

2. Late one night, Petrilli drove a stolen minivan around San Francisco with his wife and two friends. Several times, Petrilli stopped the van, and his friends got out and robbed someone. After each robbery, the friends returned to the van and Petrilli drove off. The victim of the fourth robbery called 911, and police responded. The victim rode around with the police looking for the van. Eventually, the victim spotted the van in the drive-through lane of a McDonald's restaurant. When Petrilli spotted the police car, he raced out of the drive-through lane. A high speed chase ensued. The chase ended when Petrilli lost control of the van and slammed into a police car, killing the police officer driving the car. Petrilli is charged with four counts of robbery and one count of felony murder. Petrilli argues he had reached a place of safety in the drive through lane at McDonalds. Is he right? *People v. Petrilli* (2014) 226 Cal.App.4th 814, 172 Cal.Rptr.3d 480.

Controversy Surrounding Felony Murder

Felony murder is firmly established in California. You should know, however, that this form of murder is controversial. With felony murder, the prosecutor does not have to prove any *mens rea* for the killing.[27] All that must be proven is that a death occurred during the perpetration of a felony. The prosecutor *does* have to prove that defendant had the *mens rea* for the underlying felony (*e.g.*, robbery, burglary), but there is no *mens rea* for the killing.[28] In many felony murder cases, the defendant did not intend to kill the victim. Yet, despite lack of intent to kill, felony murder imposes very severe sanctions on the defendant—possibly first degree murder. Critics of felony murder argue that it is unjust to impose such serious sanctions on defendants who lack intent to kill or injure. The Model Penal Code rejects felony murder as "indefensible in principle."[29] You read earlier in this chapter that in 2018, the Legislature placed limits on who can be prosecuted for felony murder. Most states have some version of felony murder.

---

[27] *See People v. Sarun Chun* (2009) 45 Cal.4th 1172, 1182, 91 Cal.Rptr.3d 106, 203 P.3d 425, "The felony-murder rule makes a killing while committing certain felonies murder without the necessity of further examining the defendant's mental state."

[28] *See People v. Cavitt* (2004) 33 Cal.4th 187, 197, 14 Cal.Rptr.3d 281, 91 P.3d 222, "The mental state required is simply the specific intent to commit the underlying felony."

[29] *Model Penal Code and Commentaries* §§ 210.0 to 213.6, pp. 38–39 (1980) (American Law Institute).

Felony Murder Liability When an Opponent of the Felony Is the Killer

Consider the following scenario: Able, Baker, and Charlie conspire to rob a bank. They enter the bank with guns drawn and shout, "Nobody move. This is a robbery." An off duty police officer is standing in line, waiting to transact business with a teller. The officer takes out her gun and shouts, "Police! Put down your weapons. You are under arrest." Able shoots at the officer. The officer returns fire and kills Able. Can Baker and Charlie be charged with the death of their co-felon Able? The "killer" is an opponent of the felony, not one of the felons.

STATE V. SOPHOPHONE

Supreme Court of Kansas
270 Kan. 703, 19 P.3d 70 (2001)

LARSON, J.

This is Sanexay Sophophone's direct appeal of his felony-murder conviction for the death of his co-felon during flight from an aggravated burglary in which both men participated. Sophophone and three other individuals conspired to and broke into a house in Emporia. The resident reported the break-in to the police. Police officers responded to the call, saw four individuals leaving the back of the house, shined a light on the suspects, identified themselves as police officers, and ordered them to stop. The individuals, one being Sophophone, started to run away. One officer ran down Sophophone, hand-cuffed him, and placed him in a police car. Other officers arrived to assist in apprehending the other individuals as they were running from the house. An officer chased one of the suspects later identified as Somphone Sysoumphone. Sysoumphone crossed railroad tracks, jumped a fence, and then stopped. The officer approached with his weapon drawn and ordered Sysoumphone to the ground and not to move. Sysoumphone was lying face down but raised up and fired at the officer, who returned fire and killed him. It is not disputed that Sysoumphone was one of the individuals observed by the officers leaving the house that had been burglarized.

Sophophone was charged with conspiracy to commit aggravated burglary, aggravated burglary; obstruction of official duty; and felony murder. Sophophone moved to dismiss the felony-murder charges, contending the complaint was defective because it alleged that he and not the police officer had killed Sysoumphone and further because he was in custody and sitting in the police car when the deceased was killed and therefore not attempting to commit or even fleeing from an inherently dangerous felony. His motion to dismiss was denied by the trial court. Sophophone was convicted by a jury of all counts. He appeals only his conviction of felony murder.

We consider only the question of law—whether Sophophone can be convicted of felony murder for the killing of a co-felon not caused by his acts but by the lawful acts of a police officer acting in self-defense in the course and scope of his duties in apprehending the co-felon fleeing from an aggravated burglary.

The applicable provisions of K.S.A. 21–3401 read as follows: "Murder in the first degree is the killing of a human being committed: . . . (b) in the commission of, attempt to commit, or flight from an inherently dangerous felony."

Sophophone does not dispute that aggravated burglary is an inherently dangerous felony which given the right circumstances would support a felony-murder charge. His principal argument centers on his being in custody at the time his co-felon was killed by the lawful act of the officer which he contends was a "break in circumstances" sufficient to insulate him from further criminal responsibility.

This "intervening cause" or "break in circumstances" argument has no merit under the facts of this case. We have held in numerous cases that time, distance, and the causal relationship between the underlying felony and a killing are factors to be considered in determining whether the killing occurs in the commission of the underlying felony and the defendant is therefore subject to the felony-murder rule. Based on the uncontroverted evidence in this case, the killing took place during flight from the aggravated burglary, and it is only because the act which resulted in the killing was a lawful one by a third party that a question of law exists as to whether Sophophone can be convicted of felony murder.

We have not previously decided a case where the killing was not by the direct acts of the felon but rather where a co-felon was killed during his flight from the scene of the felony by the lawful acts of a third party (in our case, a law enforcement officer).

We look to the prevailing views concerning the applicability of the felony-murder doctrine where the killing has been caused by the acts of a third party. There are two basic approaches to application of the felony-murder doctrine: the agency and proximate cause theories. The agency approach, which is the majority view, limits application of the doctrine to those homicides committed by the felon or an agent of the felon. Under such an approach, the identity of the killer becomes the threshold requirement for finding liability under the felony-murder doctrine. [If the killer is an opponent of the felony (*e.g.*, police officer, victim of the crime), there is no felony murder liability for the surviving felons.] The proximate cause approach provides that liability attaches for *any* death proximately resulting from the unlawful activity—even the death of a co-felon—notwithstanding the killing was by one resisting the crime.

In Dressler, *Understanding Criminal Law*, the question is posed of whether the felony-murder rule should apply when the fatal act is performed by a non-felon. Dressler states:

> This issue has perplexed courts. Two approaches to the question have been considered and applied by the courts. The majority rule [the agency approach] is that the felony-murder doctrine does not apply if the person who directly causes the death is a non-felon. The reasoning of this approach stems from accomplice liability theory. Generally speaking, the acts of the primary party (the person who directly commits the offense) are imputed to an accomplice on the basis of the agency doctrine. It is as if the accomplice says to the primary party: "Your acts are my acts." It follows that a co-felon cannot be convicted of the homicides because the primary party was not the person with whom she was an accomplice. It is not possible to impute the acts of the antagonistic party—the non-felon or the police officer—to a co-felon on the basis of agency.
>
> [The minority approach, called the "Proximate Causation" approach], followed by a few courts for awhile, holds that a felon may be held responsible under the felony-murder rule for a killing committed by a non-felon if the felon set in motion the acts which resulted in the victim's death. Pursuant to this rule, the issue becomes one of proximate causation: if an act by one felon is the proximate cause of the homicidal conduct by the non-felon or the police officer, murder liability is permitted.

The overriding fact which exists in our case is that neither Sophophone nor any of his accomplices "killed" anyone. The law enforcement officer acted lawfully in committing the act which resulted in the death of the co-felon. This does not fall within the language of [Kansas law] since the officer committed no crime. To impute the act of killing to Sophophone when the act was the lawful and courageous one of a law enforcement officer acting in the line of his duties is contrary to the strict construction we are required to give criminal statutes. We hold that under the facts of this case where the killing resulted from the lawful acts of a law enforcement officer in attempting to apprehend a co-felon, Sophophone is not criminally responsible for the resulting death of Somphone Sysoumphone, and his felony-murder conviction must be reversed.

California's Answer When an Opponent of the Felony Kills One of the Felons—Provocative Act Murder

California prosecutors employ the provocative act murder doctrine to impose liability on surviving felons when an opponent of a felony (police officer, victim) kills one or more of the felons.[30] The Supreme Court explained provocative act murder in *People v. Cervantes* (2001) 26 Cal. 4th 860, 867–868, 872, 29 P.3d 225:

> The provocative act murder doctrine has traditionally been invoked in cases in which the perpetrator of the underlying crime instigates a gun battle, either by firing first or by otherwise engaging in severe, life-threatening, and usually gun-wielding conduct, and the police, or a victim of the underlying crime, responds with privileged lethal force by shooting back and killing the perpetrator's accomplice or an innocent bystander.
>
> [Under the provocative act murder doctrine] when the defendant or his accomplice, with a conscious disregard for life, intentionally commits an act that is likely to cause death, and his victim or a police officer kills in reasonable response to such act, the defendant is guilty of murder. In such a case, the killing is attributable, not merely to the commission of a felony, but to the intentional act of the defendant or his accomplice committed with conscious disregard for life.
>
> However, the defendant is liable only for those unlawful killings proximately caused by the acts of the defendant or his accomplice. In all homicide cases in which the conduct of an intermediary is the actual cause of death, the defendant's liability will depend on whether it can be demonstrated that his own conduct proximately caused the victim's death. If the eventual victim's death is not the natural and probable consequence of a defendant's act, then liability cannot attach. Our prior decisions make clear that, where the defendant perpetrates an inherently dangerous felony, the victim's self-defensive killing is a natural and probable response.

In *People v. Gonzalez* (2012) 54 Cal. 4th 643, 278 P.3d 1242, 142 Cal. Rptr. 3d 893, the Supreme Court adds to your understanding of provocative act murder:

---

[30] CALCRIM instruction 560 explains provocative act murder:

The defendant is charged with [robbery]. The defendant is also charged with murder. A person can be guilty of murder under the provocative act doctrine even if someone else did the actual killing.

To prove that the defendant is guilty of murder under the provocative act doctrine, the People must prove that: (1) In committing [robbery], the defendant intentionally did a provocative act; (2) The defendant knew that the natural and probable consequences of the provocative act were dangerous to human life and then acted with conscious disregard for life; (3) In response to the defendant's provocative act [third party, *e.g.*, police officer] killed [the deceased]; and (4) the [deceased's] death was the natural and probable consequence of the defendant's provocative act.

A provocative act is an act: (1) That goes beyond what is necessary to accomplish the [robbery] and (2) Whose natural and probable consequences are dangerous to human life, because there is a high probability that the act will provoke a deadly response.

When someone other than the defendant or an accomplice kills during the commission or attempted commission of a crime, the defendant is not liable under felony murder principles but may nevertheless be prosecuted for murder under the provocative act doctrine. The provocative act doctrine is to be distinguished from the felony murder rule. A provocative act murder case necessarily involves at least three people—in our case, the perpetrator of the underlying offense, an accomplice, and a victim of their crime. A variation on the law of transferred intent, the provocative act doctrine holds the perpetrator of a violent crime vicariously liable for the killing of an accomplice by a third party, usually the intended victim or a police officer. Under the felony murder rule, if an accomplice is killed by a crime victim and not by the defendant, the defendant cannot be held liable for the accomplice's death. The provocative act doctrine is not so limited. Under the provocative act doctrine, when the perpetrator of a crime maliciously commits an act that is likely to result in death, and the victim kills in reasonable response to that act, the perpetrator is guilty of murder. In such a case, the killing is attributable, not merely to the commission of a felony, but to the intentional act of the defendant or his accomplice committed with conscious disregard for life.

A murder conviction under the provocative act doctrine thus requires proof that the defendant personally harbored the mental state of malice, and either the defendant or an accomplice intentionally committed a provocative act that proximately caused an unlawful killing. A provocative act is one that goes beyond what is necessary to accomplish an underlying crime and is dangerous to human life because it is highly probable to provoke a deadly response. Although the doctrine has often been invoked in cases where the defendant initiates or participates in a gun battle, it is not limited to this factual scenario. Malice will be implied if the defendant commits a provocative act knowing that this conduct endangers human life and acts with conscious disregard of the danger.

An important question in a provocative act case is whether the act proximately caused an unlawful death. The defendant is liable only for those unlawful killings proximately caused by the acts of the defendant or his accomplice. In all homicide cases in which the conduct of an intermediary is the actual cause of death, the defendant's liability will depend on whether it can be demonstrated that the defendant's own conduct proximately caused the victim's death. If the eventual victim's death is not the natural and probable consequence of a defendant's act, then liability cannot attach. When the defendant commits an inherently dangerous felony, the victim's self-defensive killing is generally found to be a natural and probable response to the defendant's act, and not an independent intervening cause that relieves the defendant of liability.

PROBLEMS ON THE TYPE AND DEGREE OF MURDER

In the following cases, what crime should be charged? Does malice exist? What type of malice? Express or implied? If murder is the proper charge, what degree of murder?

1. Dell killed the 5-year-old child of his girlfriend. Dell inflicted hundreds of injuries on the child in the 48 hours before death. Dell hit the child with his fists, a belt, and a board. Dell forced the child to eat his own feces. The final beating lasted more than an hour. *People v. Mincey* (1992) 2 Cal.4th 408, 6 Cal.Rptr.2d 822, 827 P.2d 388.

2. Frank tied up his victim so tightly that the ropes cut through her skin. Frank beat the victim's face severely with his fists. Over many hours, Frank used a knife to inflict numerous shallow cuts on the victim's face, breasts, and arms. Eventually, Frank stabbed the victim in the heart, killing her. *People v. Proctor* (1992) 4 Cal.4th 499, 15 Cal.Rptr.2d 340, 842 P.2d 1100.

3. Dell cut the throat of a 12-year-old boy, killing him, after which he chased down the victim's 10-year-old friend, who had begun screaming. The friend ran about 100 yards before Dell caught him and cut his throat, killing him too. *People v. Memro* (1995) 11 Cal.4th 786, 47 Cal.Rptr.2d 219, 905 P.2d 1305.

4. Dorry had dated Vickie, and decided to kill her. Dorry armed herself with a rifle, broke into Vickie's house, and fell asleep on Vickie's bed. Vickie returned home, entered the bedroom, and shook Dorry until she awakened. Dorry pointed the gun at Vickie, who ran outside. Vickie promptly returned and Dorry shot and killed her. *People v. Tuthill* (1947) 31 Cal.2d 92, 187 P.2d 16.

5. Dell is a large man. He inflicted escalating physical abuse on his 2-year-old stepdaughter. The abuse occurred almost every day over a period of 3 months. Among other things, Dell threw the child into her playpen, hit her on the head and face with his hand and fist, poked her in the eye with his finger, and forced her to stand for hours with her hands locked on top of her head. Eventually, the child died of malnutrition and a blow to the abdomen that lacerated her liver. *People v. Mills* (1991) 1 Cal.App.4th 898, 2 Cal.Rptr.2d 614.

6. Will was a prison inmate. He stabbed Bob, another inmate, inflicting a fatal wound. After losing a lot of blood, Bob grabbed a knife and ran up a flight of stairs looking for Will. On the stairs, Bob encountered Vic, a prison guard, who tried to disarm Bob. Bob stabbed and killed Vic. Later that day, Bob died from the wound inflicted by Will. Can Will be prosecuted for the

killing of the prison guard? *People v. Roberts* (1992) 2 Cal.4th 271, 6 Cal.Rptr.2d 276, 826 P.2d 274.

7. Sarah engaged in an illegal street race. Sarah raced her Honda "tuner" through a residential neighborhood at 80 miles an hour and hit and killed a child.

> **Note**: Illegal street racing is obviously dangerous. It may interest you to know that the California Penal Code of 1873 had an early law against "street racing." Section 396 of the 1873 Code read: "Every person driving any conveyance drawn by horses, upon any public road or way, who causes or suffers his horses to run, with intent to pass another conveyance, or to prevent such other from passing his own, is guilty of a misdemeanor."

8. Virginia, while passing a stranger's house in a car, shot into the house "just for fun." Virginia did not know whether anyone was home. The bullet killed a person inside the home. PC § 246 states, "Any person who shall maliciously and willfully discharge a firearm at an inhabited dwelling house is guilty of a felony."

9. Rachel kept a pit bull that was trained to fight other dogs tied up outside her house. Rachel knew a small child lived next door, and that there was no fence separating the properties. When the child approached the dog to pet it, the dog killed the child.

> **Note**: PC § 399(a) provides, "If any person owning or having custody or control of a mischievous animal, knowing its propensities, willfully suffers it to go at large, or keeps it without ordinary care, and the animal, while so at large, or while not kept with ordinary care, kills any human being who has taken all the precautions that the circumstances permitted, or which a reasonable person would ordinarily take in the same situation, is guilty of a felony." PC § 399.5(a) provides, "Any person owning or having custody or control of a dog trained to fight, attack, or kill is guilty of a felony or a misdemeanor if, as a result of that person's failure to exercise ordinary care, the dog bites a human being, on two separate occasions, or on one occasion causing substantial physical injury."

10. Sam was driving on a two lane country road. He had been "stuck" behind a large truck for quite a while. Sam passed the truck on a curve, in an area of road where it was not legal to pass. Sam collided head on with a car approaching from the other direction, killing the driver.

11. Dorothy set fire to her empty store to collect the insurance. A firefighter was killed fighting the blaze. Is Dorothy responsible for the firefighter's death? *State v. Leech* (1990) 114 Wash.2d 700, 790 P.2d 160.

Change the facts. The fire was put out, and the fire truck was headed back to the fire station. The firefighter died when she fell out of the fire truck on the way back to the fire station. Is Dorothy responsible for firefighter's death?

Change the facts again. Dorothy hired an arsonist to burn down Dorothy's building so Dorothy would not have to do the "dirty work" herself. The arsonist started the fire but was trapped in the building and died of smoke inhalation. Is Dorothy liable for the arsonist's death?

12. Terry robs a bank, jumps in her car and speeds away, pursued by police officers. Following a ten minute high speed chase, Terry runs a red light and kills a motorist. Is Terry responsible for the motorist's death?

13. Sophal was planning a one-year birthday party for his child. Sophal borrowed his cousin George's Mitsubishi to drive to the store for party supplies. George is a member of a criminal street gang. While Sophal was stopped at a red light, a Honda driven by members of a gang that was at war with George's gang pulled up next to the Mitsubishi and opened fire, killing Sophal. The shooters thought they were shooting at George. *People v. Sarun Chun* (2009) 45 Cal.4th 1172, 91 Cal.Rptr.3d 106, 203 P.3d 425.

14. Officer Ganz of the Manhattan Beach Police Department was on patrol in a marked police car. Officer Ganz was in uniform. About 11:00 p.m., Office Ganz noticed a car driven by Brady stopped at a traffic light. The front of Brady's car jutted into the intersection. Officer Ganz used his patrol car's loudspeaker to tell Brady to back up. Brady did so, but only a few inches. When the traffic light changed, Brady went through the intersection and turned into a shopping center, where he parked. Officer Ganz activated the flashing lights on top of the police car and parked behind Brady. Officer Ganz got out of his patrol car and walked up to the driver's window of Brady's car. While Ganz was standing next to Brady's car, Brady reached into the glove compartment, pulled out a pistol, and shot Officer Ganz in the chest, striking his bullet proof vest. Officer Ganz leaned back as he was hit. Ganz quickly moved back toward the patrol car in a crouched position. Brady, armed with the pistol, got out of his car and followed Ganz. When Officer Ganz was near the rear of the patrol car, Brady shot him in the back, causing Ganz to fall to the pavement on his stomach. Brady walked to Ganz and, using both hands to steady the gun, shot him in the back of the head, killing him. Brady returned to his car and drove away. When Officer Ganz pulled him over, Brady was on supervised release following a term in federal prison. One condition of his release from prison was that he not possess a firearm. *People v. Brady* (2010) 50 Cal.4th 547, 113 Cal.Rptr.3d 458, 236 P.3d 312.

15. Able and Baker broke into a house to steal whatever they could find. While Baker was downstairs looking for things to steal, Able went upstairs. While upstairs, Able happened to look out the window. To his surprise, Able saw his long time enemy Vic, walking down the street. On the spur of the moment, Able decided to shoot Vic. Able took out his pistol, aimed out the upstairs window, and shot and killed Vic. What should Able be charged with? Is Baker liable for Vic's death? Morris, The Felon's Responsibility for the Lethal Acts of Others, 105 *University of Pennsylvania Law Review* 50 (1956).

16. Perla was upset with Carl because Carl had allegedly harassed her brother Richard. Perla decided to assault Carl. Perla got a .22 rifle loaded with

15 bullets and put it in her car. Perla asked her friend Bill to help with the assault. Perla and Bill drove to the location where they expected to find Carl. Carl was sitting on a park bench. Carl did not know Perla or Bill. When Perla spotted Carl sitting on the bench, she parked behind him and she and Bill got out of the car. Bill walked toward Carl and said, "Hey punk, I'm here to teach you a lesson. Prepare to get your ass whipped." Perla stayed near the car. Bill attacked Carl, and the two started punching each other. Bill pulled a knife and charged at Carl, cutting his cheek. When Bill charged again, Carl ducked, grabbed Bill by the legs, and slammed him to the ground. Bill got up and ran toward the car. Perla quickly retrieved the rifle from the car, cocked it, and pointed it at Carl. She then handed the rifle to Bill. Afraid for his life, Carl charged at Bill. They struggled with the gun, and Carl was shot 3 times. Eventually Carl wrestled the gun away from Bill and Bill started running away. Carl shot and killed Bill as he ran away. Is Perla guilty of any crime(s)? *People v. Gonzalez* (2012) 54 Cal. 4th 643, 278 P.3d 1242, 142 Cal. Rptr. 3d 893.

17. Three felons enter a convenience store to rob it. One of the robbers accidentally shoots and kills the clerk. Who is liable for what?

18. Change the facts in Problem 17. When the felons enter the store, the clerk pulls a gun and kills one of the robbers. Who is liable for what?

19. Three felons enter a store to rob it. The clerk takes out a gun, aims at one of the robbers and fires, accidentally killing an innocent customer in the store. Who is guilty of what?

20. Alice and Beth enter a convenience store to rob it. Charlene waits outside in the getaway car. Once inside the store, Beth pulls a gun and waves it in the face of the store owner, all the while jumping up and down and screaming, "Put the money in the bag. Put the money in the bag. Hurry up. Hurry up or I'll kill you." The store owner's wife takes out a gun and shoots and kills Alice. Who is guilty of what?

21. Norm enters a convenience store to rob it. The clerk activates a silent alarm. While Norm is still inside the store, the police arrive, and a standoff ensues. Eventually, Norm uses the clerk as a human shield and exits the store, holding a gun to the clerk's head. A police sniper aims at Norm's head but accidentally kills the clerk. Is Norm guilty of the clerk's death?

22. April, May, and June agreed to rob a bank. Their plan was to enter the bank with guns drawn, announce "This is a robbery, nobody move," take as much money as possible and escape in a stolen car. On the day of the robbery, April, May, and June drove to the bank. April's role was to be the getaway driver and lookout. April parked in front of the bank with the motor running. May and June put on masks, armed themselves with a pistol and shotgun, entered the bank, and May said, "This is a robbery, nobody move and nobody gets hurt!" A teller triggered a silent alarm, and police officers began arriving within 2 minutes. When April saw police cars arriving, she took off. May and June realized the police had arrived and that April had left. A standoff/hostage situation developed, with May and June threatening to kill customers and

employees of the bank if the police entered. May gave the police an ultimatum, "Either you let us go or I start killing hostages." Within an hour of this ultimatum, May forced a bank customer to the glass doors of the bank, where she and the customer could be seen by police outside. May put a pistol to the customer's head and killed her. At that point, a police SWAT team stormed the bank and exchanged gunfire with May and June. May shot and wounded one SWAT officer. Another SWAT officer aimed at May and fired, but missed and killed a bank employee. May and June were arrested. Following the arrest, a customer said, "I think I'm having a heart attack. I need an ambulance." An ambulance arrived and was speeding to the hospital with the critically ill customer when the ambulance driver lost control of the ambulance and drove off a bridge, killing the ambulance driver, ambulance attendant, and the customer. Of what crimes are April, May, and June guilty?

23. Sheriff's deputies initiated a nighttime vehicle stop for a possible DUI. The driver stopped, but then sped away. The officers pursued the vehicle, which stopped again and sped away again. The car stopped a third time and, as the officers approached the car, the driver reached out the car window and started shooting at the officers. The officers returned fire, attempting to shoot the driver, but accidentally killing the driver's brother, who was sitting in the passenger seat. Of what crimes is the driver guilty? Are the officers guilty of a crime?

24. Fidel Medina worked as an armed security guard at an apartment complex, in a neighborhood claimed by a criminal street gang. One night, Fidel was in the apartment parking lot when he was approached by gang member Cazessus, who was pounding his fist in his palm and saying, "What's up rent-a-cop?" At the same time, Defendant, also a gang member, approached Fidel from a different angle. Cazessus and Defendant approached to within a foot or two of Fidel. Defendant said, "You are not the only one with a gun. I have a gun, too." Defendant displayed a .45 caliber handgun and pulled the slide back to chamber a round. Fidel placed his hand on his own 9 millimeter weapon and said, "Man, put the gun away." Defendant raised his weapon and fired at Fidel, who returned fire, missing Defendant and killing Cazessus. Defendant was shot nine times but survived. Of what crimes is Defendant guilty? Did Fidel commit a crime?

25. Marjorie and her husband Robert lived on the sixth floor of an apartment building in San Francisco. The victim, Diane, lived in the same building. Marjorie and Robert owned two Presa Canario dogs. This breed of dog is large, often weighing over 100 pounds, and standing more than five feet tall when on the hind legs. Presa Canario are often used as guard dogs. A veterinarian warned Marjorie and Robert that the dogs, Bane and Hera, lacked training and discipline, and were dangerous to people. Bane weighed 150 pounds. Hera weighed 130 pounds. The dogs got away from Marjorie, and attacked and killed Diane in the hallway of the apartment building. Before the fatal attack, there were 30 incidents of the dogs being out of control and threatening humans and other animals. When neighbors complained to Marjorie and Robert, they ignored the complaints.

26. Nine-year-old Nadia was walking home from school when Richard approached her in his car. Richard told Nadia he was a teacher, and asked her for help moving some books. Nadia got in the car. Richard drove to a motel where he had earlier rented a room. In the motel room, Richard raped, sodomized, and strangled Nadia. Richard put Nadia's body in a trash can, and put the trash can in the trunk of his car. He drove to a park, waited until it was dark, and then left the trash can in the park. Richard then fled the state.

27. This problem quotes extensively from the California Supreme Court's decision in *People v. Gonzales*, 54 Cal. 4th 1234, 281 P.3d 834, 144 Cal. Rptr. 3d (2012). Genny Rojas was four years old when she died. Genny was removed from her mother's care by child protective services. Genny was living with relatives, Veronica and Ivan Gonzalez when she died.

On the evening of July 21, two neighbors were standing outside a window of the Gonzales apartment. They heard a loud bang, or thud, as if something had hit a wall inside the apartment, immediately followed by the sound of a child crying. Ivan came to the window, looked out, and shut the window forcefully. He emerged from the apartment, slammed the door, and walked off toward a nearby liquor store. He appeared to be angry and in a hurry. Ivan entered the liquor store, where he was a regular customer, at 8:45 p.m. He asked for and received credit, purchased some grocery items, and left after five or 10 minutes.

Around 9:00 that evening another neighbor, Patty Espinoza, heard Veronica Gonzales screaming for help. Veronica said her niece had been burned in the bathtub. Patty came out of her apartment and asked how anyone could be burned in the bathtub. Veronica asked Patty to come with her, and not call the police. In the Gonzales apartment, Patty saw a child lying on the floor. Ivan was nearby. Patty told them she did not know how to perform cardiopulmonary resuscitation (CPR), but that her sister Naomi did. Patty ran to get Naomi, who also lived in the building, and told the Gonzaleses to call 911. Veronica, however, repeatedly said not to call the police.

Naomi Espinoza had heard the commotion, and came out of her apartment upon hearing that a child was not breathing. She saw Ivan carrying a little girl. Naomi, a nurse's assistant, had CPR training. She asked Ivan what happened, and he replied that the child had burned herself in the bathtub. Questioned further by Naomi, Ivan explained that the child did not know how to regulate the water. Naomi told him to take the child into Patty's apartment. Ivan did so, and put her down on the rug.

Naomi testified that she knew the child was dead, "just by looking at her." Nevertheless, she checked for a pulse and attempted CPR. The body was cold, the lips white. Naomi noticed scars on the body and a bald spot on the head. Shortly after the first police officers arrived, Naomi left the apartment.

A 911 call was placed around 9:20 p.m. Sergeant Barry Bennett responded, along with other officers. As he approached the apartment, Veronica met him and directed him inside. Bennett found a little girl lying on the floor. Checking her vital signs, he detected no pulse or breathing. He did not attempt CPR. The body was very cold and felt rigid, indicating to him that the child had been dead for some time. The shirt she was wearing was dry, as were her skin and hair. While he was examining the body, Veronica told Bennett she had put the child in the tub, run the water, and gone to the kitchen to cook dinner. After about 20 minutes, she returned to the bathroom and found the child under the water. Bennett noted that Ivan sat nearby, and described his demeanor as "nonchalant."

Bennett called in homicide and child abuse investigators. It was obvious to him that the death was not accidental and the child had been abused. The entire lower part of her body appeared to have been burned, and there were numerous other injuries.

Fireman John Miller arrived at the apartment at 9:25 p.m. He too assessed the child, and found her cold and without a pulse. He prepared to perform CPR, but found the jaw clenched and difficult to move. Miller concluded that rigor mortis had set in.

A medical examiner came to the scene around 1:00 a.m. He performed a preliminary external examination of the victim. He noted a second- to third-degree burn from her waist to her feet, and other burns on her face, arms, and torso. Rigor mortis, which begins to develop within an hour or two of death, was present. An autopsy was conducted the next morning. Genny was thin and small, but adequately nourished. Her body was covered with injuries.

A large burned area on top of Genny's head had only partially healed. This injury was infected, and at least a week old. It could have been caused by hot liquid, possibly on more than one occasion. The back of the head was also burned. There was hair loss, both in the burned area and elsewhere. A similar burn appeared on the back of the neck and shoulder. The skin on Genny's ears had been eroded, exposing the cartilage. There were also abrasions at the end of her eyebrows and on the bridge of her nose. These injuries could have been caused by rough fabric tightly bound around her head.

There was bruising around both eyes, probably inflicted within a day or two of death. Pinpoint hemorrhages in the right eye were typical of strangulation. The cheekbone, shoulder, and neck were bruised. There were recent burns on both cheeks, in a grid pattern matching the grill on a hairdryer found in the Gonzales apartment. Similar burns appeared on the shoulders and left bicep. Genny's lip was lacerated and torn away from the gum. Numerous small injuries on her face could have been inflicted with a hairbrush. She had suffered a subdural hematoma, the result of a blow or shaking within a day of her death, and an older brain hemorrhage that had been caused by a violent blow.

Genny's neck bore a ligature mark, extending upward behind her left ear. This injury was a week or two old. A similar scar ran from her jawbone to the underside of her chin. There were triangular scars on top of her left shoulder. On her arms were parallel scars typical of the marks left by handcuffs.

Handcuffs matching the marks on Genny's arms were recovered from the Gonzales apartment. Her arms and wrists also had abrasions, which could have been caused by binding with a cord. Bruises on the inside of her thighs suggested she had been grabbed from behind with a great deal of force. Ulcerated areas on both heels in the area of the Achilles tendon were consistent with erosion from binding.

The most significant injury, and the cause of death, was the burn on the lower part of Genny's body. It appeared to be an immersion burn, with spared areas behind the knees, in the groin area, and on the buttocks indicating that Genny had been held down in a fetal position in the tub, with her arms out of the water. Death would have occurred within two to three hours. There was no evidence of drowning. Genny's thymus gland was atrophied, a sign of prolonged stress. It was clear to the examiner that she had been chronically and repeatedly abused.

A pediatric burn expert confirmed that the burn was an immersion injury. He estimated the water temperature at 140 degrees or higher. It would have been seven or eight inches deep, and Genny must have been held down firmly, leaning forward a little. The burn injury could have been inflicted in 10 seconds or less; it could not have occurred gradually. With treatment, the chances of survival would have been around 90 percent. However, within one to four hours of infliction, Genny would have gone into shock. Death could occur quite rapidly thereafter in a child of her age.

The burn on Genny's scalp could have been caused by hot water striking the top of her head and flowing onto her neck and shoulders. The expert did not believe it was accidentally inflicted, or that it could have been caused by Genny tipping over a pot of hot water on the stove.

Officer Bennett went to the Gonzales apartment shortly after he examined Genny's body in Patty Espinoza's apartment. The bathtub in the Gonzales bathroom appeared to be dry, as did the bathroom floor. Human tissue subsequently found in the tub was consistent with Genny's DNA, and not with Ivan's or Veronica's. It took 15 minutes to fill the tub with hot water. When full, the water was eight and a half inches deep, and 140 degrees. At that temperature, it would have taken six to eight seconds to cause the burn on Genny's lower body.

In one bedroom, the area behind the door was cordoned with a string fastened to the doorknob at one end, and to the knob of a nightstand placed against the wall at the other. In this triangular area there was an indentation in the wallboard, 36 inches from the floor. There were bloodstains in the indentation, and on the wall around and below it. A blanket behind the door was stained with matter consistent with Genny's DNA.

The closet in this bedroom yielded a considerable amount of bloodstain evidence. The closet doors were off their tracks, and leaned into the closet. A metal hook was fastened to the closet bar mounting bracket. On the floor beneath the hook was a wooden box, measuring about two feet in all three dimensions. A hole in one of the closet doors afforded a view of the hook. On the wall of the closet, below the hook and above the box, were many bloodstains. Some were created by hair wiping against the wall, others were the result of blood being flung against the wall. There was blood on the closet bar, the hook, and the cloth fastening the hook to the bar. There was a bloody footprint on the wall, but no handprint. There was blood on the edge of the box, and both blood and feces in the box. The interior of the closet door was spattered with blood.

The bloodstains were consistent with a scenario in which a bleeding child Genny's size was suspended from the hook in the closet, rubbing some blood on the surfaces around her and casting some off as she swung back and forth, bracing herself with her feet on the box and the wall. Genny's DNA was consistent with blood samples taken from the closet. What crimes?

What a sad, tragic, horrible case. Poor little Genny! What if Genny survived the torture? She would be severely psychologically damaged. Does society have some obligation to such a child? The government took Genny from a neglectful parent, only for her to end up in a much worse place. Who will take care of her? Where will she live? Who will pay for the years of therapy she will need?

Genny's case is extreme, but cases of neglect and abuse arise every day. California has a complex child protection system, which includes the juvenile court, child protective services, foster care, and adoption. If you are interested in children and families, you may wish to consider working as an attorney in the child protection system. I represent abused and neglect children in juvenile court. I have done many things in my long legal career, but I have never done anything more meaningful than serving as the attorney for children in juvenile court. Some of my law students work in juvenile court. If you ask them, they will tell you, the work is difficult but very satisfying. You won't get rich helping children and families, but you will make a difference. Indeed, there will be times when you save a child's future, and even a child's life.

MANSLAUGHTER

Penal Code § 192 defines manslaughter as "the unlawful killing of a human being without malice." Manslaughter is of three types: voluntary, involuntary, and vehicular.

Voluntary Manslaughter

There are four kinds of voluntary manslaughter in California.

First, intentional killing in the heat of passion on adequate provocation. (PC § 192(a)). In *People v. Soto* (2018) 4 Cal. 5th 968, 974, 415 P.3d 789, 231 Cal. Rptr. 3d 732, the Supreme Court wrote that heat of passion "may preclude the formation of malice and reduce murder to voluntary manslaughter."

Example: Dell shot and killed a man whom Dell believed had stabbed his brother to death two hours earlier. *People v. Brooks* (1986) 185 Cal.App.3d 687, 230 Cal.Rptr. 86.

Voluntary heat of passion manslaughter is discussed in *Girouard v. State* and *People v. Berry, infra.*

Second, unintentional killing with conscious disregard for the danger to human life and knowledge that the conduct endangers the life of another on a sudden quarrel or the heat of passion.[31]

Example: Robert is provoked by Sue while both are standing next to a cliff. Aware of the danger, but not intending to kill, Robert pushes Sue around and she falls to her death.

Third, intentional killing in imperfect self-defense (honest but *un*reasonable belief in the need for self-defense).[32]

Example: Fifteen-year-old Juan shot and killed the unarmed victim. In the past, the victim had threatened Juan. At the time of the shooting, the victim was taunting Juan. *In re Christian S.* (1994) 7 Cal.4th 768, 30 Cal.Rptr.2d 33, 872 P.2d 574.

Fourth, defendant, acting with conscious disregard for human life, unintentionally kills in imperfect self-defense.[33]

Example: Big and Small are drinking. Big and Small get in an argument. Big is 6 feet tall and weighs 300 pounds. Small is 5 feet tall and weighs 100 pounds. Big swings a beer bottle at Small and misses. Small hits Big in the head with a beer bottle. Big charges Small. Small draws a knife. Big and Small struggle, and Big is stabbed. Small did not intend to stab Big. *People v. Blakeley* (2000) 23 Cal.4th 82, 96 Cal.Rptr.2d 451, 999 P.2d 675.

---

[31] *See People v. Lasko* (2000), 23 Cal.4th 101, 104, 96 Cal.Rptr.2d 441, 999 P.2d 666 ("When a killer *intentionally* but unlawfully kills in a sudden quarrel or heat of passion, the killer lacks malice and is guilty only of voluntary manslaughter. We hold here that this is also true of a killer who, acting with conscious disregard for life and knowing that the conduct endangers the life of another, unintentionally but unlawfully kills in a sudden quarrel or heat of passion.")(emphasis in original).

[32] *See People v. Soto* (2018) 4 Cal. 5th 968, 974, 415 P.3d 789, 231 Cal. Rptr. 3d 732 ("Two factors may preclude the formation of malice and reduce murder to voluntary manslaughter: heat of passion and unreasonable self-defense."); *People v. Elmore* (2014) 59 Cal.4th 121, 172 Cal.Rptr.3d 413, 325 P.3d 951 ("A killing committed because of an unreasonable belief in the need for self-defense is voluntary manslaughter, not murder.").

[33] *See People v. Blakeley* (2000) 23 Cal.4th 82, 96 Cal.Rptr.2d 451, 999 P.2d 675.

Involuntary Manslaughter

There are seven kinds of involuntary manslaughter in California.[34]

First, so-called misdemeanor manslaughter. Misdemeanor manslaughter is a killing "in the commission of an unlawful act, not amounting to a felony." (PC § 192(b)). The misdemeanor must be dangerous to human life under the circumstances of its commission.[35] The *mens rea* is criminal negligence.

Example: Dom and Val get into an argument after a game of pool at a bar. Val pushes Dom, and Dom says, "Let's go outside and settle this." Outside, Val takes the first swing and misses. Dom punches Val, who falls, striking his head. Val dies. Fighting in public is a misdemeanor.

Second, a death that occurs "in the commission of a lawful act which might produce death, in an unlawful manner." (PC § 192(b)). Here too the *mens rea* is criminal negligence.

Example: Dufus is cleaning his gun. Dufus believes the gun is empty. Dufus aims the gun at his wife in fun and pulls the trigger, killing his wife.

Third, negligent manslaughter, which is an unintentional killing "without due caution and circumspection." (PC § 192(b)). Obviously, the *mens rea* here is criminal negligence.

Example: *People v. Walker* and *People v. Mehserle, infra*, are examples of negligent manslaughter.

Fourth, a killing during the commission of a felony that is not listed in PC § 189 and that is not inherently dangerous to human life. To continue the drumbeat, the *mens rea* is criminal negligence.

Example: PC § 273a(a) provides: "Any person who, under circumstances or conditions likely to produce great bodily harm or death, willfully causes or permits any child to suffer, or inflicts thereon unjustifiable physical pain or mental suffering, or having the care or custody of any child, willfully causes or permits the person or health of that child to be injured, or willfully causes or permits that child to be placed in a situation where his or her person or health is endangered, shall be punished by imprisonment in a county jail not exceeding one year, or in the state prison for two, four, or six years." Dell uses excessive corporal punishment on his child and unintentionally kills the child.

---

[34] *See People v. Butler* (2010) 187 Cal.App.4th 998, 114 Cal.Rptr.3d 696, discussing involuntary manslaughter.

[35] The misdemeanor does not have to be dangerous to human life in the abstract. It must be dangerous to human life under the circumstances of its commission. *People v. Cox* (2000) 23 Cal.4th 665, 97 Cal.Rptr.2d 647, 2 P.3d 1189.

Fifth, a killing while one is unconscious due to voluntary intoxication.[36]

Example: Sue drinks so much at her graduation party from law school that she renders herself unconscious. While unconscious, Sue accidentally kills someone.

Sixth, defendant, acting without conscious disregard of human life, kills unintentionally in imperfect self-defense.[37]

Example: Mary believes unreasonably that Samantha is about to attack her. To defend herself, Mary kicks Samantha once in the shin. The kick dislodges a blood clot that goes to Samantha's brain, killing her.

Seventh, Vehicular manslaughter.

Heat of Passion Voluntary Manslaughter

California Penal Code § 192(a) defines voluntary manslaughter as a killing "upon a sudden quarrel or heat of passion." In many cases of heat of passion voluntary manslaughter, the defendant intends to kill. However, "intent to kill is not an element of voluntary manslaughter. A defendant commits voluntary manslaughter when a homicide is committed either with intent to kill or with conscious disregard for life."[38]

---

[36] *See People v. Ochoa* (1998) 19 Cal.4th 353, 423–424, 79 Cal.Rptr.2d 408, 966 P.2d 442. The Supreme Court explained:

> When a person renders himself or herself unconscious through voluntary intoxication and kills in that state, the killing is attributable to his or her negligence in self-intoxicating to that point, and is treated as involuntary manslaughter. Unconsciousness is ordinarily a complete defense to a charge of criminal homicide. If the state of unconsciousness results from intoxication voluntarily induced, however, it is not a complete defense. If the intoxication is voluntarily induced, it can never excuse homicide. Thus, the requisite element of criminal negligence is deemed to exist irrespective of unconsciousness, and a defendant stands guilty of involuntary manslaughter if he voluntarily procured his own intoxication. Unconsciousness for this purpose need not mean that the actor lies still and unresponsive: section 26 describes as incapable of committing crimes a person who committed the act without being conscious thereof. Thus unconsciousness can exist where the subject physically acts in fact but is not, at the time, conscious of acting.

[37] *See People v. Butler* (2010) 187 Cal.App.4th 998, 1008–1009, 114 Cal.Rptr.3d 696, where the Court provided a useful description of "disregard for life:"

> Both murder (based on implied malice) and involuntary manslaughter involve a disregard for life; however, for murder the disregard is judged by a subjective standard whereas for involuntary manslaughter the disregard is judged by an objective standard. Implied malice murder requires a defendant's conscious disregard for life, meaning that the defendant subjectively appreciated the risk involved. In contrast, involuntary manslaughter merely requires a showing that a reasonable person would have been aware of the risk. Thus, even if the defendant had a subjective, good faith belief that his or her actions posed no risk, involuntary manslaughter culpability based on criminal negligence is warranted if the defendant's belief was objectively unreasonable. Implied malice also contemplates subjective awareness of a higher degree of risk than does gross negligence, and involves an element of wantonness which is absent from gross negligence.

[38] *People v. Bryant* (2013) 56 Cal. 4th 959, 301 P.3d 1136, 157 Cal. Rptr. 3d 522.

Heat of passion voluntary manslaughter usually comes up when a defendant is charged with intent to kill murder, not manslaughter.[39] The defendant is the one who raises the possibility of heat of passion manslaughter because the defendant wants a jury instruction on manslaughter as an alternative to murder. A defendant who wants a jury instruction on voluntary heat of passion manslaughter must produce evidence of the elements of manslaughter that is sufficient to justify the instruction. In *People v. Avila* (2009) 46 Cal.4th 680, 705, 94 Cal.Rptr.3d 699, 208 P.3d 634, the Supreme Court explained heat of passion manslaughter:

> Manslaughter, an unlawful killing without malice, is a lesser included offense of murder. Although section 192(a) refers to sudden quarrel or heat of passion, the factor which distinguishes the heat of passion form of voluntary manslaughter from murder is provocation. The provocation which incites the defendant to homicidal conduct in the heat of passion must be caused by the victim, or be conduct reasonably believed by the defendant to have been caused by the victim. The victim must taunt the defendant or otherwise initiate the provocation. The heat of passion must be such a passion as would naturally be aroused in the mind of an ordinarily reasonable person under the given facts and circumstances. If sufficient time has elapsed for the passions of an ordinarily reasonable person to cool, the killing is murder, not manslaughter.[40]

As voluntary heat of passion manslaughter evolved at common law, judges approved a small number of provocations that the judges felt were acceptable to mitigate murder to manslaughter. The acceptable provocations were: violent battery, mutual combat, illegal arrest, catching one's spouse in the act of adultery, injury of a close family member, and, according to some courts, assault. Insulting words, no matter how provocative, would not suffice.[41] Common law judges declined to add new provocations. Unless a defendant could fit the facts of his case into one of

---

[39] A prosecutor could charge voluntary heat of passion manslaughter. Most of the time, however, the prosecutor charges intent to kill murder, and it is the defendant who raises the issue of heat of passion in the effort to get a manslaughter jury instruction.

[40] *See People v. Moye* (2009) 47 Cal.4th 537, 550, 98 Cal.Rptr.3d 113, 213 P.3d 652, where the Supreme Court wrote, "Heat of passion arises when at the time of the killing, the reason of the accused was obscured or disturbed by passion to such an extent as would cause the ordinarily reasonable person of average disposition to act rashly and without deliberation and reflection, and from such passion rather than from judgment. However, if sufficient time has elapsed between the provocation and the fatal blow for passion to subside and reason to return, the killing is not voluntary manslaughter."

[41] Originally in California, words would not suffice for adequate provocation. A note to the 1873 Penal Code states, "No words of reproach, however grievous, are sufficient provocation to reduce the offense of an intentional homicide from murder to manslaughter." Today in California, words can suffice for adequate provocation.

the established provocations, he could not get a jury instruction on voluntary heat of passion manslaughter.

The Model Penal Code approach to provocation is found in § 210.3, which provides: "(1) Criminal homicide constitutes manslaughter when: (a) it is committed recklessly; or (b) a homicide which would otherwise be murder is committed under the influence of extreme mental or emotional disturbance for which there is a reasonable explanation."

The following case illustrates the traditional approach to adequate provocation, with its limited number of acceptable provocations.

GIROUARD V. STATE

Court of Appeals of Maryland
321 Md. 532, 583 A.2d 718 (1991)

COLE, JUDGE.

In this case we are asked to reconsider whether the types of provocation sufficient to mitigate the crime of murder to manslaughter should be limited to the categories we have heretofore recognized, or whether the sufficiency of the provocation should be decided by the factfinder on a case-by-case basis. Specifically, we must determine whether words alone are provocation adequate to justify a conviction of manslaughter rather than one of second degree murder.

The Petitioner, Steven S. Girouard, and the deceased, Joyce M. Girouard, had been married for about two months on October 28, 1987, the night of Joyce's death. Both parties, who met while working in the same building, were in the army. They married after having known each other for approximately three months. The evidence at trial indicated that the marriage was often tense and strained, and there was some evidence that after marrying Steven, Joyce had resumed a relationship with her old boyfriend, Wayne.

On the night of Joyce's death, Steven overheard her talking on the telephone to her friend, whereupon she told the friend that she had asked her first sergeant for a hardship discharge because her husband did not love her anymore. Steven went into the living room where Joyce was on the phone and asked her what she meant by her comments; she responded, "nothing." Angered by her lack of response, Steven kicked away the plate of food Joyce had in front of her. He then went to lie down in the bedroom.

Joyce followed him into the bedroom, stepped up onto the bed and onto Steven's back, pulled his hair and said, "What are you going to do, hit me?" She continued to taunt him by saying, "I never did want to marry you and you are a lousy fuck and you remind me of my dad." The barrage of insults continued with her telling Steven that she wanted a divorce, that the marriage had been a mistake and that she had never wanted to marry him.

She also told him she had seen his commanding officer and filed charges against him for abuse. She then asked Steven, "What are you going to do?" Receiving no response, she continued her verbal attack. She added that she had filed charges against him in the Judge Advocate General's Office (JAG) and that he would probably be court martialed.

When she was through, Steven asked her if she had really done all those things, and she responded in the affirmative. He left the bedroom with his pillow in his arms and proceeded to the kitchen where he procured a long handled kitchen knife. He returned to Joyce in the bedroom with the knife behind the pillow. He testified that he was enraged and that he kept waiting for Joyce to say she was kidding, but Joyce continued talking. She said she had learned a lot from the marriage and that it had been a mistake. She also told him she would remain in their apartment after he moved out. When he questioned how she would afford it, she told him she would claim her brain-damaged sister as a dependent and have the sister move in. Joyce reiterated that the marriage was a big mistake, that she did not love him and that the divorce would be better for her.

After pausing for a moment, Joyce asked what Steven was going to do. What he did was lunge at her with the kitchen knife he had hidden behind the pillow and stab her 19 times. Realizing what he had done, he dropped the knife and went to the bathroom to shower off Joyce's blood. Feeling like he wanted to die, Steven went back to the kitchen and found two steak knives with which he slit his own wrists. He lay down on the bed waiting to die, but when he realized that he would not die from his self-inflicted wounds, he got up and called the police, telling the dispatcher that he had just murdered his wife.

When the police arrived they found Steven wandering around outside his apartment building. Steven was despondent and tearful and seemed detached, according to police officers who had been at the scene. He was unconcerned about his own wounds, talking only about how much he loved his wife and how he could not believe what he had done. Joyce Girouard was pronounced dead at the scene.

Steven Girouard was convicted, at a court trial in the Circuit Court for Montgomery County, of second degree murder and was sentenced to 22 years incarceration, 10 of which were suspended. We granted certiorari to determine whether the circumstances of the case presented provocation adequate to mitigate the second degree murder charge to manslaughter.

Petitioner relies primarily on out of state cases to provide support for his argument that the provocation to mitigate murder to manslaughter should not be limited only to the traditional circumstances of: extreme assault or battery upon the defendant; mutual combat; defendant's illegal arrest; injury or serious abuse of a close relative of the defendant's; or the sudden discovery of a spouse's adultery. Those acts mitigate homicide to manslaughter because they create passion in the defendant and are not considered the product of free will.

Petitioner argues that manslaughter is a catchall for homicides which are criminal but that lack the malice essential for a conviction of murder. Steven argues that the trial judge did find provocation (although he held it inadequate to mitigate murder) and that the categories of provocation adequate to mitigate should be broadened to include factual situations such as this one.

The State counters by stating that although there is no finite list of legally adequate provocations, the common law has developed to a point at which it may be said there are some concededly provocative acts that society is not prepared to recognize as reasonable. Words spoken by the victim, no matter how abusive or taunting, fall into a category society should not accept as adequate provocation. According to the State, if abusive words alone could mitigate murder to manslaughter, nearly every domestic argument ending in the death of one party could be mitigated to manslaughter. This, the State avers, is not an acceptable outcome. Thus, the State argues that the taunting words by Joyce Girouard were not provocation adequate to reduce Steven's second degree murder charge to voluntary manslaughter.

Initially, we note that the difference between murder and manslaughter is the presence or absence of malice. Voluntary manslaughter has been defined as an *intentional* homicide, done in a sudden heat of passion, caused by adequate provocation, before there has been a reasonable opportunity for the passion to cool.

In order to determine whether murder should be mitigated to manslaughter we look to the circumstances surrounding the homicide and try to discover if it was provoked by the victim. Over the facts of the case we lay the template of the so-called "Rule of Provocation." The courts of this State have repeatedly set forth the requirements of the Rule of Provocation: (1) There must have been adequate provocation; (2) The killing must have been in the heat of passion; (3) It must have been a sudden heat of passion—that is, the killing must have followed the provocation before there had been a reasonable opportunity for the passion to cool; (4) There must have been a causal connection between the provocation, the passion, and the fatal act.

We shall assume without deciding that the second, third, and fourth of the criteria listed above were met in this case. We focus our attention on an examination of the ultimate issue in this case, that is, whether the provocation of Steven by Joyce was enough in the eyes of the law so that the murder charge against Steven should have been mitigated to voluntary manslaughter. For provocation to be adequate, it must be calculated to inflame the passion of a reasonable man and tend to cause him to act for the moment from passion rather than reason. The issue we must resolve, then, is whether the taunting words uttered by Joyce were enough to inflame the passion of a *reasonable* man so that that man would be sufficiently infuriated so as to strike out in hot-blooded blind passion to kill her. Although we agree with the trial judge that there was needless provocation by Joyce, we also agree with him that the provocation was not adequate to mitigate second degree murder to voluntary manslaughter. Although there are few Maryland cases discussing the issue at bar, those that do hold that words alone are not adequate provocation. Other jurisdictions overwhelmingly agree with our cases and hold that words alone are not adequate provocation. Thus, with no reservation, we hold that the provocation in this case was not enough to cause a reasonable man to stab his provoker 19 times.

The standard is one of reasonableness; it does not and should not focus on the peculiar frailties of mind of the Petitioner. That standard of reasonableness has not been met here. We cannot in good conscience countenance holding that a verbal domestic argument ending in the death of one spouse can result in a conviction of manslaughter. We agree with the trial judge that social necessity dictates our holding. Domestic arguments easily escalate into furious fights. We perceive no reason for a holding in favor of those who find the easiest way to end a domestic dispute is by killing the offending spouse.

Judgment Affirmed.

NOTE ON VOLUNTARY MANSLAUGHTER

In recent decades there has been a move away from the traditional approach to voluntary heat of passion manslaughter, with its limited number of acceptable provocations. Courts increasingly hold that adequacy of provocation should be decided on a case-by-case basis. As you read the California Supreme Court's decision in *People v. Berry*, you will see that California employs the case-by-case approach to provocation.

PEOPLE V. BERRY

California Supreme Court
18 Cal.3d 509, 134 Cal.Rptr. 415, 566 P.2d 777 (1976)

SULLIVAN, J.

Defendant Albert Joseph Berry was charged by indictment with one count of murder (Pen. Code § 187) and one count of assault by means of force likely to produce great bodily injury (Pen. Code § 245(a)). The assault was allegedly committed on July 23, 1974, and the murder on July 26, 1974. In each count, the alleged victim was defendant's wife, Rachel Pessah Berry. A jury found defendant guilty as charged and determined that the murder was of the first degree. (§ 189) Defendant was sentenced to state prison for the term prescribed by law. He appeals from the judgment of conviction.

Defendant contends that there is sufficient evidence in the record to show that he committed the homicide while in a state of uncontrollable rage caused by provocation and therefore that it was error for the trial court to fail to instruct the jury on voluntary manslaughter as indeed he had requested. He claims that he was entitled to an instruction on voluntary manslaughter as defined by statute (§ 192) since the killing was done upon a sudden quarrel or heat of passion. We agree with defendant.

Defendant, a cook, 46 years old, and Rachel Pessah, a 20-year-old girl from Israel, were married on May 27, 1974. Three days later Rachel went to Israel by herself, returning on July 13, 1974. On July 23, 1974, defendant choked Rachel into unconsciousness. She was treated at a hospital where she reported her strangulation by defendant to an officer of the San Francisco Police Department. On July 25, Inspector Sammon, who had been assigned to the case, met with Rachel and as a result of the interview a warrant was issued for defendant's arrest.

While Rachel was at the hospital, defendant removed his clothes from their apartment and stored them in a Greyhound Bus Depot locker. He stayed overnight at the home of a friend, Mrs. Jean Berk, admitting to her that he had choked his wife. On July 26, he telephoned Mrs. Berk and informed her that he had killed Rachel with a telephone cord on that morning at their apartment. The next day Mrs. Berk and two others telephoned the police to report a possible homicide and met Officer Kelleher at defendant's apartment. They gained entry and found Rachel on the bathroom floor. A pathologist from the coroner's office concluded that the cause of Rachel's death was strangulation. Defendant was arrested on August 1, 1974, and confessed to the killing.

At trial defendant did not deny strangling his wife, but claimed through his own testimony and the testimony of a psychiatrist, Dr. Martin Blinder, that he was provoked into killing her because of a sudden and uncontrollable rage so as to reduce the offense to one of voluntary manslaughter. He testified that upon her return from Israel, Rachel announced to him that while there she had fallen in love with another man, one Yako, and had enjoyed his sexual favors, that he was coming to this country to claim her and that she wished a divorce. Thus commenced a tormenting two weeks in which Rachel alternately taunted defendant with her involvement with Yako and at the same time sexually excited defendant, indicating her desire to remain with him. Defendant's detailed testimony, summarized below, chronicles this strange course of events.

After their marriage, Rachel lived with defendant for only three days and then left for Israel. Immediately upon her return to San Francisco she told defendant about her relationship with and love for Yako. This brought about further argument and a brawl that evening in which defendant choked Rachel and she responded by scratching him deeply many times. Nonetheless they continued to live together. Rachel kept taunting defendant with Yako and demanding a divorce. She claimed she thought she might be pregnant by Yako. She showed defendant pictures of herself with Yako. Nevertheless, during a return trip from Santa Rosa, Rachel demanded immediate sexual intercourse with defendant in the car, which was achieved; however upon reaching their apartment, she again stated that she loved Yako and that she would not have intercourse with defendant in the future.

On the evening of July 22nd defendant and Rachel went to a movie where they engaged in heavy petting. When they returned home and got into bed, Rachel announced that she had intended to make love with defendant, "But I am saving myself for this man Yako, so I don't think I will." Defendant got out of bed and prepared to leave the apartment whereupon Rachel screamed and yelled at him. Defendant choked her into unconsciousness.

Two hours later defendant called a taxi for his wife to take her to the hospital. He put his clothes in the Greyhound bus station and went to the home of his friend Mrs. Berk for the night. The next day he went to Reno and returned the day after. Rachel informed him by telephone that there was a warrant for his arrest as a result of her report to the police about the choking incident. On July 25th defendant returned to the apartment to talk to Rachel, but she was out. He slept there overnight. Rachel returned around 11 a.m. the next day. Upon seeing defendant there, she said, "I suppose you have come here to kill me." Defendant responded, "yes," changed his response to "no," and then again to "yes," and finally stated "I have really come to talk to you." Rachel began screaming. Defendant grabbed her by the shoulder and tried to stop her screaming. She continued. They struggled and finally defendant strangled her with a telephone cord.

Dr. Martin Blinder, a physician and psychiatrist, called by the defense, testified that as a result of [the victim's] cumulative series of provocations, defendant at the time he fatally strangled Rachel, was in a state of uncontrollable rage, completely under the sway of passion.

We first take up defendant's claim that on the basis of the foregoing evidence he was entitled to an instruction on voluntary manslaughter as defined by statute which is "the unlawful killing of a human being, without malice upon a sudden quarrel or heat of passion." (§ 192.) It is left to the jurors to say whether or not the facts and circumstances in evidence are sufficient to lead them to believe that the defendant did, or to create a reasonable doubt in their minds as to whether or not he did, commit his offense under a heat of passion. The jury is further to be admonished and advised by the court that this heat of passion must be such a passion as would naturally be aroused in the mind of an ordinarily reasonable person under the given facts and circumstances, and that, consequently, no defendant may set up his own standard of conduct and justify or excuse himself because in fact his passions were aroused, unless further the jury believe that the facts and circumstances were sufficient to arouse the passions of the ordinarily reasonable man. The inquiry is whether or not the defendant's reason was, at the time of his act, so disturbed or obscured by some passion—not necessarily fear and never, of course, the passion for revenge—to such an extent as would render ordinary men of average disposition liable to act rashly or without due deliberation and reflection, and from this passion rather than from judgment.

There is no specific type of provocation required by section 192 and that verbal provocation may be sufficient. The phrase "heat of passion" used in the statute defining manslaughter need not mean "rage" or "anger" but may be any violent, intense, high-wrought or enthusiastic emotion.[42] [A defendant may be] aroused to a heat of passion by a series of events over a considerable period of time.

Defendant's testimony chronicles a two-week period of provocatory conduct by his wife Rachel that could arouse a passion of jealousy, pain and sexual rage in an ordinary man of average disposition such as to cause him to act rashly from this passion. It is significant that both defendant and Dr. Blinder testified that the former was in the heat of passion under an uncontrollable rage when he killed Rachel.

The Attorney General contends that the killing could not have been done in the heat of passion because there was a cooling period, defendant having waited in the apartment for 20 hours. However, the long course of provocatory conduct, which had resulted in intermittent outbreaks of rage under specific provocation in the past, reached its final culmination in the apartment when Rachel began screaming. Both defendant and Dr. Blinder testified that defendant killed in a state of uncontrollable rage, of passion, and there is ample evidence in the record to support the conclusion that this passion was the result of the long course of provocatory conduct by Rachel.

---

[42] In most heat of passion, voluntary manslaughter cases, the dominant emotion is anger. As the Court noted, however, "any violent, intense, high-wrought or enthusiastic emotion" may suffice. *See* Michal Buchhandler-Raphael, Fear-Based Provocation, 67 *American University Law Review* 1719, 1724 (2018)("Courts and commentators sometimes recognize that the concept of 'passion' is sufficiently capacious to encompass any violent, intense, high wrought, or enthusiastic emotion, which allows them to consider a range of emotions, including fear. Yet, this is a minority position, and anger mostly remains the emotion that is typically claimed in provocation cases.").

DOES VOLUNTARY MANSLAUGHTER DISADVANTAGE WOMEN?

As the crime of heat of passion voluntary manslaughter developed at common law, the provocations found adequate to mitigate murder to manslaughter were based on male ideas of pride and affront: catching one's wife *in flagrante delicto*, mutual combat, and violent assault. In the twentieth century, courts expanded the provocations that could suffice for mitigation, and numbers of men who killed wives, ex-wives, or lovers, sought to lower murder to manslaughter based on victim conduct that the men found provocative. Emily Miller commented, "Voluntary manslaughter has never been a female-friendly doctrine. [It] continues to perpetuate a violent form of male subordination of women."[43] In a classic law review article, Victoria Nourse discussed her research on fifteen years of "passion murder cases."[44] Nourse wrote, "Reform [of manslaughter law] has permitted juries to return a manslaughter verdict in cases where the defendant claims passion because the victim left, moved the furniture out, planned a divorce, or sought a protective order." (p. 1332). Nourse, unlike some critics, did not advocate doing away with heat of passion manslaughter. She sought instead to cabin the "defense" to prevent inappropriate use. Two other important critiques of heat of passion manslaughter are Joshua Dressler, Why Keep the Provocation Defense?: Some Reflections on a Difficult Subject, 86 *Minnesota Law Review* 959 (2002), and Aya Gruber, A Provocative Defense, 103 *California Law Review* 273 (2015).

PROBLEMS ON VOLUNTARY MANSLAUGHTER

1. Dell was part of a group of men playing poker at a private home. An argument erupted when Dell accused Bill of cheating. Both men sprang up and started threatening each other. Bill attacked Dell, briefly knocking him out with a punch to the jaw. When Dell regained consciousness, he left the home, saying to Bill, "I'll get you." The next day, seven hours after the argument over cards, Dell walked up to Bill as Bill was eating lunch at a restaurant and shot Bill in the back, killing him. Dell is charged with first degree murder. Dell requests an instruction on voluntary manslaughter. Should the judge give the manslaughter instruction? *State v. Robinson* (1945) 353 Mo. 934, 185 S.W.2d 636.

2. Frank was separated from his wife Sue. Frank believed Sue was dating another man, and this infuriated Frank. Frank placed Sue's home under surveillance nearly every night to see if she was with another man. On several occasions, Frank told Sue, "If I catch you with another man, I'll kill you. If I can't have you, no one can." One night, Frank saw Bill enter Sue's home about 7:30 p.m. No one left the home. At 10:00 p.m. the lights went out. Frank was armed with a pistol. He crossed the street and entered the home by the back door, which was unlocked. He entered Sue's bedroom, turned on the

[43] Emily L. Miller, Comment, (Wo)manslaughter: Voluntary Manslaughter, gender, and the Model Penal Code, 50 *Emory Law Journal* 665, 667, 678 (2001).

[44] Victoria Nourse, Passion's Progress: Modern Law Reform and the Provocation Defense, 106 *Yale Law Journal* 1331 (1997).

light, and saw Sue and Bill in bed together. Bill jumped out of the bed and started toward Frank. Frank pulled out the gun and told Bill to sit down. Frank said, "I want to talk to my wife." Sue screamed at Frank, "Put that gun away and get out of my house. This is none of your business." When Bill again started walking toward Frank, Frank shot and killed Bill. Frank then turned the gun on Sue and killed her. Frank is charged with two counts of first degree murder. Frank requests jury instructions on voluntary manslaughter. Should the judge give the instructions? *People v. Gingell* (1931) 211 Cal. 532, 296 P. 70.

3. Stan was a court reporter. Wanda worked for Stan part time as a transcriber. Wanda was secretly in love with Stan, but Stan was married. One evening, Stan was with some friends at a sports bar watching football on TV. Wanda entered the bar and joined Stan and his friends. Everyone had a good time. When the game was over, Stan got up to leave and Wanda followed him out of the bar. In the parking lot, Wanda said, "Stan, this is difficult for me to say, but I need to say it. I love you. I have loved you for years." Stan replied, "Wanda, that is very flattering, but I'm married. I don't want to hurt your feelings, but I have to get home." Wanda said, "Please stay with me a while." Stan said "no" and entered his car. Wanda said, "If you don't stay with me, I'll follow you home and tell your wife I'm your lover." Stan ignored Wanda and drove out of the parking lot. Wanda got in her car and followed him. Stan tried to lose Wanda, but she stayed behind him. Stan drove all over town in an effort to drive away from Wanda, but she followed him. Finally, when stopped at a traffic light, Stan got out of his car, walked back to Wanda's car, and shouted, "Leave me alone. Stop following me." Wanda replied, "You love me; you know you do. You can't treat me like this." Enraged, Stan reached into Wanda's car and strangled her to death. Stan is charged with first degree murder. Should the judge instruct on voluntary manslaughter? *State v. Harwood* (1974) 110 Ariz. 375, 519 P.2d 177.

4. Zeb provoked Dell in a manner that would justify an instruction on voluntary heat of passion manslaughter. In a rage, Dell aimed his gun at Zeb and fired. Unfortunately, Dell missed and accidently killed Mary, an innocent bystander. May Dell claim voluntary heat of passion manslaughter?

5. Dell intentionally killed Beth. At the time, Dell mistakenly believed that Beth had provoked him. Actually, the provoker was Zeb, and Dell killed the "wrong" person. May Dell nevertheless claim voluntary heat of passion manslaughter?

6. Zeb provoked Dell. Dell pulled a knife and ran toward Zeb intent on killing him. Ruth stepped in front of Dell to stop the attack and Dell fatally stabbed Ruth in order to get to Zeb. May Dell claim voluntary heat of passion manslaughter?

7. Cain was homophobic. He told friends, "I hate gays. They make me sick." Cain was drinking at a bar when he was approached by Vic, a man about his age. Vic struck up a conversation with Cain. The two chatted a while. Vic placed his hand on Cain's thigh and said, "Why don't we go somewhere private." Cain followed Vic outside. In the parking lot, Vic placed his hand on

Cain's groin and said, "I'm want to suck you off." Cain became enraged and beat Vic to death. Cain is charged with first degree intent to kill murder. Did Cain premeditate and deliberate? Should Cain be entitled to a jury instruction on voluntary heat of passion manslaughter? Alexis Kent, A Matter of Law: The Non-Violent Homosexual Advance Defense is Insufficient Evidence of Provocation, 44 *University of San Francisco Law Review* 155 (2009).

8. Chris and Angela lived together for two years. The relationship was rocky, with frequent arguments and yelling. One day, Chris and Angela were arguing. Angela walked out of the house. As she was leaving, she flipped the bird at Chris, so he shot her. Murder or manslaughter? *State v. Thompson* (2013) 836 N.W.2d 470 (Iowa).

9. Robert spent the afternoon at a friend's house, watching football on TV and drinking beer. When Robert got home that evening, his wife, Michelle, confronted him. Michelle expressed frustration with Robert's drinking and chronic unemployment. Michelle then said, "Robert, I'm seeing someone else that I'm in love with. It is not going to work between us because I can't love you no more." Robert opened a drawer, took out a pistol, and shot Michelle in the head at close range. *Ware v. State* (2018) 303 Ga. 847, 815 S.E.2d 837.

10. Claire met Tare, and the two began dating. Soon, Tare moved into Claire's apartment with Claire and her two children. In several incidents, Tare was violent with Claire. He threw her to the ground and dragged her by the hair. Tare locked Claire in a room, and police had to rescue her. Tare once told Claire, "Our relationship will end over your dead body. If I can't have you, no one can." Tare moved out, but kept a key. Claire obtained a Domestic Violence Restraining Order against Tare, requiring that he stay 100 yards away from Claire. Claire started dating Michael. One day, Michael dropped off Claire and the kids at the apartment, after a day of shopping. Not long thereafter, Tare let himself into the apartment. Claire and Tare argued. Tare went to the kitchen and got a long knife. He attacked Claire, stabbing her 17 times and killing her, as the children watched in horror. Tare ran away. Six years later, Tare was caught, and charged with murder. Tare seeks a jury instruction on heat of passion manslaughter. Tare testified in his own behalf that on the fatal day, Claire called him "a nobody." Claire said, "I can do better than you." Claire said, "I was pregnant with your child, but I had an abortion." Tare testified that the next thing he remembered, he was standing in the living room with a bloody knife in his hand. Should the judge give the requested instruction? *People v. Beltran* (2013) 56 Cal. 4th 935, 301 P.3d 1120, 157 Cal. Rptr. 3d 503.

11. Miguel and Omar were in a committed romantic relationship for twenty years. Miguel decided to end the relationship. For several weeks, there was tension between Miguel and Omar about the relationship. Omar heard Miguel talking on the phone to a man Miguel met on line, and with whom Miguel intended to start a relationship. Omar called the "other man" disparaging names. Miguel said, "It is over. I'm leaving." Miguel went to the bedroom and started packing a suitcase to leave. Omar walked to the kitchen and retrieved a long kitchen knife. Omar walked to the bedroom, hiding the

knife behind his back. The two argued. Suddenly Omar removed the knife from behind his back and stabbed Miguel in the chest. Miguel fell the floor. Omar sat on top of him and stabbed him thirteen times. Omar is charged with first degree murder. You are Omar's defense attorney. What will you do? *Commonwealth v. Rivera* (2019) 482 Mass. 259.

Involuntary Manslaughter Based on Criminal Negligence

Involuntary manslaughter based on criminal negligence is addressed in the following two cases: *Walker v. Superior Court* and *People v. Mehserle.*

WALKER V. SUPERIOR COURT

Supreme Court of California
47 Cal.3d 112, 253 Cal.Rptr. 1, 763 P.2d 852 (1988)

MOSK, J.

We consider in this case whether a prosecution for involuntary manslaughter (Pen. Code § 192(b)) and felony child endangerment (§ 273a(1)) can be maintained against the mother of a child who died of meningitis after receiving treatment by prayer in lieu of medical attention. We conclude that the prosecution is permitted by statute as well as the free exercise and due process clauses of the state and federal Constitutions.

Defendant Laurie Grouard Walker is a member of the Church of Christ, Scientist. Her four-year-old daughter, Shauntay, fell ill with flu-like symptoms on February 21, 1984, and four days later developed a stiff neck. Consistent with the tenets of her religion, defendant chose to treat the child's illness with prayer rather than medical care.[1] Defendant contacted an accredited Christian Science prayer practitioner who thereafter prayed for Shauntay and visited the child on two occasions. Defendant also engaged a Christian Science nurse who attended Shauntay on February 27 and again on March 6 and 8.[2] Shauntay nevertheless lost weight, grew disoriented and irritable during the last week of her illness,

[1] "Members of the Church believe that disease is a physical manifestation of errors of the mind. The use of medicine is believed to perpetuate such error and is therefore discouraged. Nonetheless, the Church sets up no abstract criteria for determining what diseases or injuries should be treated by prayer or other methods but, rather, leaves such questions to individual decision in concrete instances. If some turn in what they think is an urgent time of need to medical treatment for themselves or their children, they are *not*—contrary to some recent charges—stigmatized by their church." (Talbot, *The Position of the Christian Science Church* (1983) 26 N.E. Med. J. 1641, 1642, italics in original.)

[2] The Church describes in an amicus curiae brief the role of Christian Science practitioners and nurses: Christian Science practitioners are individuals who devote their full time to healing through prayer, or spiritual treatment. These individuals are approved for listing by the Church in *The Christian Science Journal,* after having given evidence of moral character and healing ability. Practitioners determine their own charges, usually from seven to fifteen dollars per day of treatment, and are paid by their patients. The practitioner's work, however, is a religious vocation, a ministry of spiritual healing in its broadest sense. Christian Scientists may also call upon the services of a Christian Science nurse, who provides such practical care as dressing of wounds for those having spiritual treatment.

and died on March 9 of acute purulent meningitis after a period of heavy and irregular breathing. During the 17 days she lay ill, the child received no medical treatment.

The People charged defendant with involuntary manslaughter and felony child endangerment based on allegations that her criminal negligence proximately caused Shauntay's death. Defendant moved to dismiss the prosecution (Pen. Code § 995).

Defendant's Conduct and the Standard for Criminal Culpability

Defendant contends that she cannot be convicted under either the manslaughter or felony child-endangerment statutes. She rests this contention on a claim that the People will be unable to prove the degree of culpability necessary to convict her under either provision, both of which require criminal negligence in the commission of an offending act. We have defined criminal negligence as aggravated, culpable, gross, or reckless, that is, the conduct of the accused must be such a departure from what would be the conduct of an ordinarily prudent or careful man under the same circumstances as to be incompatible with a proper regard for human life, or, in other words, a disregard of human life or an indifference to consequences. Such negligence is ordinarily to be determined pursuant to the general principles of negligence, the fundamental principle of which is knowledge, actual or imputed, that the act of the slayer tended to endanger life. Defendant [argues] that her conduct cannot, as a matter of law, constitute such negligence.

Defendant contends that her actions are legally insufficient to constitute criminal negligence under the definition of that conduct established in the decisions of this court. Emphasizing her sincere concern and good faith in treating Shauntay with prayer, she claims that her conduct is incompatible with the required degree of culpability. Defendant does not dispute, however, that criminal negligence must be evaluated objectively. The question is whether a reasonable person in defendant's position would have been aware of the risk involved. If so, defendant is presumed to have had such an awareness.

We must reject defendant's assertion that no reasonable jury could characterize her conduct as criminally negligent for purposes of sections 192(b) and 273a(1). As the court in *People v. Atkins* (1975) 53 Cal.App.3d 348, observed in affirming the involuntary manslaughter and felony child-endangerment conviction of a parent whose child died for want of medical care, criminal negligence "could have been found to have consisted of the mother's failure to seek prompt medical attention for her son, rather than waiting several days. There is evidence she knew, or should have known, that her son was seriously injured. Viewing the evidence in the light most favorable to the prosecution, there is substantial evidence here of involuntary manslaughter based on the lack of due caution and circumspection in omitting to take the child to a doctor." When divorced of her subjective intent, the alleged conduct of defendant here is essentially indistinguishable.

In sum, we reject the proposition that the provision of prayer alone to a seriously ill child cannot constitute criminal negligence as a matter of law. Whether this defendant's particular conduct was sufficiently culpable to justify conviction of involuntary manslaughter and felony child endangerment remains a question in the exclusive province of the jury.

Free Exercise Under the First Amendment

Defendant and the Church contend that her conduct is absolutely protected from criminal liability by the First Amendment to the United States Constitution and article I, section 4, of the California Constitution. We do not agree.

The First Amendment bars government from "prohibiting the free exercise" of religion. Although the clause absolutely protects religious belief, religiously motivated conduct "remains subject to regulation for the protection of society." *Cantwell v. Connecticut* (1940) 310 U.S. 296. To determine whether governmental regulation of religious conduct is violative of the First Amendment, the gravity of the state's interest must be balanced against the severity of the religious imposition. If the regulation is justified in view of the balanced interests at stake, the free exercise clause requires that the policy additionally represent the least restrictive alternative available to adequately advance the state's objectives.

Defendant does not dispute the gravity of the governmental interest involved in this case, as well she should not. Imposition of felony liability for endangering or killing an ill child by failing to provide medical care furthers an interest of unparalleled significance: the protection of the very lives of California's children, upon whose "healthy, well-rounded growth into full maturity as citizens" our "democratic society rests, for its continuance." *Prince v. Massachusetts* (1944) 321 U.S. 158. Balanced against this interest is a religious infringement of significant dimensions. Defendant unquestionably relied on prayer treatment as an article of genuine faith, the restriction of which would seriously impinge on the practice of her religion. We note, however, that resort to medicine does not constitute "sin" for a Christian Scientist.

Regardless of the severity of the religious imposition, the governmental interest is plainly adequate to justify its restrictive effect. As the United States Supreme Court stated in *Prince v. Massachusetts*, 321 U.S. at page 170, "Parents may be free to become martyrs themselves. But it does not follow they are free, in identical circumstances, to make martyrs of their children before they have reached the age of full legal discretion when they can make that choice for themselves." The court in *Prince* considered a free-exercise claim asserted by parents whose religious beliefs required that their children sell religious tracts in violation of child labor laws. If parents are not at liberty to "martyr" children by taking their labor, it follows a fortiori that they are not at liberty to martyr children by taking their very lives. As the court explained, "The right to practice religion freely does not include liberty to expose the community or child to communicable disease or the latter to ill health or death."

You may be familiar with the following case, which involved the fatal shooting on New Year's Day 2009 of an unarmed young man by a police officer at the Fruitvale BART station in Oakland. You can search online for "Oscar Grant killing" to find video footage of the shooting. In 2013, a movie called "Fruitvale Station" was released about the shooting.

PEOPLE V. MEHSERLE

California Court of Appeal
206 Cal. App. 4th 1125, 142 Cal. Rptr. 3d 423 (2012)

MARCHIANO, P.J.

Defendant Johannes Mehserle served as a police officer for the Bay Area Rapid Transit District (BART). Shortly after 2:00 a.m. on January 1, 2009, while responding to a report of a fight on a BART train, he shot and killed BART passenger Oscar Grant during a tense confrontation. Defendant was attempting to arrest and handcuff Grant for misdemeanor obstructing a police officer (Pen.Code, § 148), while Grant was lying face down on the BART platform. Defendant shot Grant, who was unarmed, in the back. Defendant contended he meant to pull his taser and shock Grant to subdue him, but accidentally drew his handgun by mistake and fired the fatal shot.

After a trial involving many witnesses, the jury found defendant not guilty of murder or voluntary manslaughter. The jury convicted defendant of involuntary manslaughter (Pen.Code, § 192(b)), thus necessarily finding the shooting was not accidental, but criminally negligent. The trial court sentenced him to two years in prison.

A proper understanding of the events surrounding the shooting requires at the outset a description of the weapons defendant was carrying that night and how they were holstered.

Defendant carried two weapons: a black model 226 40-caliber Sig Sauer handgun and a bright yellow Taser International X26 taser. The handgun weighed more than three times as much as the taser. The handgun had no manual safety switch, while the taser had a safety switch that also functioned as an on/off switch. The taser had a red laser sight; the handgun did not.

Defendant's handgun was holstered on his right side, called the dominant side—presumably because defendant is right-handed. The taser was holstered on defendant's left, or nondominant, side, in a cross-draw configuration for use with the dominant (right) hand. The handgun holster had an automatic locking system, requiring a two-step process to remove the weapon: first, a rotating hood must be pressed down and rotated forward; second, a safety latch must be pushed back to release the weapon from its holster. The taser holster had a safety strap and a safety hood.

In the small hours of the early morning of New Year's Day 2009, Grant boarded a BART train in San Francisco with his fiancée, Sophina Mesa, and several other friends. The group was bound for the Fruitvale BART station. The train was very crowded with New Year's Eve celebrants, and people were standing in the aisles.

As the train approached the Fruitvale BART station in Oakland, Grant began to argue with a fellow passenger and the two men started "tussling around." They attempted to strike each other, but the train was so crowded they were reduced to pushing and shoving. The aggression spread into a large fist fight, involving at least 10 men.

Passengers used the train intercom to report the fight to the operator, who in turn contacted BART central control. Central control apparently contacted BART police, whose dispatcher contacted officers in the field with a report of a fight at the Fruitvale BART station in the train's "lead car, no weapons, all black clothing, large group of Black Males."

The train reached the Fruitvale station and stopped at the platform. The train doors opened. The fight stopped. BART Police officers Anthony Pirone and Marysol Domenici were on the street level of the station. Pirone went up to the platform and saw five African-American men, including Grant and Michael Greer, and one woman standing on the platform by the lead car and talking. As Pirone approached, Grant and Greer got back on the train. According to a bystander, Pirone appeared to be agitated and said, "This train isn't fucking going anywhere, I'm not stupid, I see you guys."

Pirone ordered the three men who remained on the platform, who apparently were Jackie Bryson, Nigel Bryson and Carlos Reyes, to stand against the platform wall and keep their hands visible. He pulled his taser and pointed it at the men as he ordered them to the wall. Pirone called Domenici and told her to come up to the platform, where he instructed her to watch the detained men against the wall.

Pirone ordered Grant off the train. By one account he said, "Get off the fucking train, otherwise I'm going to pull you out." By another account he said, "Get off the train motherfuckers." By his own account, Pirone said, "Get the fuck off the train." Grant got off the train. Pirone took Grant over to the three detainees and shoved him against the wall. The men sat down after being ordered to do so by Domenici.

Pirone went back to the train for Greer and ordered him out, saying "Get the fuck off my train." Pirone denied using profanity when he ordered Greer off the train, because of the presence of female passengers. Greer did not comply. Pirone said, "I've asked you politely. I'm going to have to remove you in front of all these people now." Pirone grabbed Greer by his hair and the scruff of his neck and forced him off the train. Train passengers described Pirone as hostile, angry, mean, and aggressive. One passenger said Pirone acted "like a punk." Defendant concedes Pirone was "verbally and physically abusive in his attempt to remove both Greer and Grant from the train."

According to Pirone, Greer struggled to break free once the two were on the platform. Pirone, therefore, pushed Greer and knocked him off balance. Pirone said Greer spun around and raised his fists, so Pirone used a takedown maneuver and swept Greer's legs out from under him, knocking him to the ground. Pirone handcuffed Greer. Several passengers testified that in their opinion Pirone used excessive or unnecessary force, or that his behavior was excessive.

Grant, Jackie Bryson, and Reyes jumped to their feet and shouted, "This is fucked up, this is fucked up." Domenici told them to "stay out of it." The three continued to yell at Pirone to stop what he was doing. Pirone approached Reyes and told him to "shut the fuck up." A cell phone video taken by a passenger shows Pirone striking Grant with his fist. There was testimony that Pirone shoved Grant against the wall. Pirone forced Grant to his knees. A passenger's video shows Pirone drawing his taser and pointing it at the detainees. Grant pleaded with Pirone not to tase him because "I have a daughter." Domenici drew her taser and pointed it at the seated detainees, who kept their hands up and kept saying "don't tase me."

According to a BART surveillance video, defendant and his partner, Officer Woffinden, arrived on the platform at 2:08:27 a.m. Defendant ordered the men who were approaching Domenici to "get back." Defendant drew his taser and pointed it at the detainees, including Grant. The taser's red laser sight was trained on Grant's chest and groin.

Referring to Grant, Pirone said, "that motherfucker is going to jail" for "148," a reference to Penal Code section 148, resisting a police officer. Pirone testified he gave the order to arrest Grant and Greer. Defendant thought Pirone told him to arrest Grant and Jackie Bryson. Pursuant to BART policy, Officers Pirone and Domenici were the officers in charge because they had been the first on the scene.

Grant was kneeling on the ground. Pirone was yelling in Grant's face, "Bitch-ass nigger, right. Bitch-ass nigger, right. Yeah." Defendant stepped behind Grant and grabbed his hands. Grant fell forward onto the ground. Pirone thought defendant had forced Grant to the platform, but defendant denied this.

Pirone and defendant placed Grant on his stomach. Pirone used his knees to pin Grant's neck to the ground. Grant protested, "I can't breathe. Just get off of me. I can't breathe. I quit. I surrender. I quit." Defendant ordered Grant to give up his arms, presumably so he could handcuff him. Grant responded that he couldn't move. Defendant repeatedly pulled at Grant's right arm, which apparently was under Grant's body.

Meanwhile, defendant was heard to exclaim, "fuck this." He told Pirone, "I can't get his hands, his hands are in his waistband, I'm going to tase him, . . . get back."

A cell phone video shows defendant tugging three separate times on his handgun, unsuccessfully trying to remove it from his holster. On the fourth try, defendant was able to remove his handgun. He stood up, held the weapon apparently with both hands, and fired a bullet into Grant's back. The time was 2:11:04.

Several witnesses said that defendant appeared surprised and dumbfounded after the shooting. One witness heard defendant say, "Oh, shit!" or "Oh, my God." Another heard defendant say, "Oh, shit, I shot him," or, "Oh God, oh shit, I shot him." Defendant holstered his handgun and put his hands to his head, then bent over and put his hands on his knees. Grant was still conscious and exclaimed, "Oh, you shot me, you shot me." Defendant handcuffed Grant and searched him for weapons. Grant was unarmed.

Shortly after the shooting, defendant talked to Pirone on the platform and said, "I thought he was going for a gun." In the minutes after the shooting he had several conversations on the platform with Pirone and three other officers, and said nothing about mistaking his handgun for his taser. Later, at the station, he cried and told a support person, Officer Foreman, that he thought Grant was going for a gun. He did not say he mistook his handgun for his taser.

Grant was taken to Highland Hospital. He had a single gunshot wound that penetrated his right lung and caused excessive blood loss. He died about three or four hours after having surgery.

Defendant testified as follows: He did not intend to shoot Grant, but only to tase him. He mistakenly drew and fired his handgun. As defendant approached Grant to arrest him, Grant was on his knees with both hands behind his back. Grant fell to the ground; defendant did not push him. Grant ended up on his stomach with his right hand underneath his body.

Defendant focused on getting control of Grant's right arm, which was tense. Defendant could not free it by pulling it out or by ordering Grant to give up his arm. Defendant did not hear Grant complain that he could not breathe. Defendant did not notice that Pirone had restrained Grant by placing his knee on Grant's neck.

Defendant saw Grant's right hand go into his pocket as if he were grabbing for something. Although he did not see a weapon, he thought Grant might be reaching for one. He decided to tase Grant. He stood up to get sufficient distance to properly deploy the taser, and announced, "I'm going to tase him. I'm going to tase him."

Defendant was not aware he had mistakenly drawn his handgun until he heard the shot. He looked down and saw he was holding his handgun. He testified, "There were no flags that popped up, there were no red flags." He was unaware he had to tug at his handgun three times before freeing it from its holster, and did not notice the lack of a red laser sight which would have emanated from his taser.

Defendant denied losing control of his emotions and judgment during the attempt to arrest Grant, and believed tasing Grant would have been consistent with BART policy. Defendant voluntarily resigned from the BART police force.

BART Police Sergeant Stewart Lehman testified that he trained defendant on the use of the taser. The training was the minimum six and one-half hours. Lehman believed the training period was "a minimum," but admitted the training was up to industry standards and the standards set by POST and the taser manufacturer. He testified that defendant did not have his own taser and holster issued to him, which would have enabled him to practice at home.

Greg Meyer, a consultant in police tactics, testified as an expert in the "use and deployment of tasers, taser training methods and procedures, laws of arrest, arrest procedures, and the use of lethal and non-lethal force." In his opinion, Grant's re-entering the BART train upon seeing Pirone and his standing up after being told to sit against the wall were sufficient to violate section 148—and thus, Grant was being lawfully arrested for resisting a police officer.

It was also Meyer's opinion defendant was entitled to rely, without question, on Pirone's order to arrest Grant. Meyer did acknowledge that Pirone's conduct was "loud and aggressive," and his calling Grant a "bitch-ass nigger" was aggressive behavior. He did opine, however, the use of a taser on Grant would have been appropriate because Grant was physically, as opposed to passively, resisting arrest.

Several BART officers testified that defendant was dependable and even-tempered, and did not show a tendency to use inappropriate aggression toward suspects.

Defendant contends there is insufficient evidence of the requisite criminal negligence to sustain his conviction of involuntary manslaughter. Specifically, he contends he "accidentally fired his gun" and Grant's death was "a tragic error."

We first address defendant's contention that Grant's killing was an "accident." In the context of the law of homicide, a killing through accident or misfortune is excusable and is not a crime. For a killing to be "accidental," a defendant must act without negligence. Here, the jury was so instructed. Nevertheless, the jury found defendant guilty of a criminally negligent killing. The guilty verdict of involuntary manslaughter, which we conclude is supported by substantial evidence, is simply inconsistent with the characterization of the killing as "accidental."

Section 192 defines manslaughter as "the unlawful killing of a human being without malice." Section 192(b) defines involuntary manslaughter in two ways: as a killing in "the commission of an unlawful act, not amounting to felony" or a killing "in the commission of a lawful act which might produce death, in an unlawful manner, or without due caution and circumspection."

The jury was properly instructed on both theories of involuntary manslaughter, with section 149 (police officer unnecessarily assaulting any person) the misdemeanor in support of the first theory. The governing *mens rea* for both theories of involuntary manslaughter is criminal negligence.

We need only briefly discuss the first prong of manslaughter liability, *i.e.*, misdemeanor manslaughter. The jury was instructed that they could find defendant guilty of manslaughter if they found he violated section 149, which provides that a peace officer may not, "under color of authority and without lawful necessity, assault or beat any person." Specifically, the trial court instructed the jury that they could find defendant guilty of violating section 149 if, while arresting Grant, he used "more force than was necessary under the circumstances." There is evidence that Grant was on the ground, being pinned by Pirone, and complaining that he could not breathe. Grant verbally surrendered. The jury could have concluded he was not a threat and defendant did not have to tase him. And, since Grant was unarmed; no other officer had drawn his or her weapon; and the dispatch specifically said that no weapons were involved in the fight on the train, defendant did not have to use deadly force.

But we believe the controlling issue is not whether defendant violated section 149 while he was arresting Grant. We find sufficient evidence that his conduct of mistakenly drawing and firing his handgun instead of his taser constitutes criminal negligence under the second prong of manslaughter liability: that defendant committed a lawful act in an unlawful manner, or without due caution and circumspection—*i.e.*, he believed he was tasing an arrestee, but mistakenly, and criminally negligently, drew and fired his handgun with lethal results.

The definition of criminal negligence in California has been settled since 1955, when the California Supreme Court adopted the definition set forth in American Jurisprudence: "There must be a higher degree of negligence than is required to establish negligent default on a mere civil issue. The negligence must be aggravated, culpable, gross, or reckless, that is, the conduct of the accused must be such a departure from what would be the conduct of an ordinary prudent or careful person under the same circumstances as to be incompatible with a proper regard for human life, or, in other words, a disregard of human life or an indifference to the consequences." (*People v. Penny* (1955) 44 Cal.2d 861, 879, 285 P.2d 926).

It is important to distinguish between the mental states for involuntary manslaughter on the one hand, and implied-malice murder, on which the jury found defendant not guilty, on the other. Implied malice contemplates a subjective awareness of a higher degree of risk than does gross *i.e.*, criminal negligence, and involves an element of wantonness which is absent in gross negligence. A finding of gross negligence is made by applying an objective test: if a reasonable person in defendant's position would have been aware of the risk involved, then defendant is presumed to have had such an awareness. However, a finding of implied malice depends upon a determination that the defendant actually appreciated the risk involved, *i.e.*, a subjective standard.

We know of no California case in which a police officer was convicted of involuntary manslaughter due to handgun/taser confusion. But we believe this record demonstrates substantial evidence that defendant's conduct was criminally negligent due to the following evidence.

First, the jury could have reasonably found defendant did not need to use a taser at all. Regardless of the question whether Grant initially resisted arrest, at the time defendant decided to use his taser, the jury could have reasonably found that Grant was immobilized—being pinned by Pirone—and compliant. Grant said, "I can't breathe," "I quit," and "I surrender." Although defendant was having difficulty obtaining control of Grant's hand, the jury could have found in view of Grant's position and demeanor that this did not present a proper situation for the use of a taser.

Second, the jury could have reasonably found that when defendant did decide to use his taser he was criminally negligent in mistaking his handgun for his taser. Defendant's handgun was peculiarly distinguishable from his taser for a number of reasons. Defendant had drawn his taser earlier. The handgun weighed more than three times as much as the taser. The taser was bright yellow. The handgun was black. The taser had an on/off safety switch. The handgun did not. The taser had a red laser sight. The handgun did not. The handgun was holstered on defendant's right, or dominant side, with a two-step release mechanism requiring defendant to push down and forward and then back on a separate safety switch. The taser, in contrast, was holstered on defendant's left, or nondominant side, for a cross-draw by defendant's right hand and had only a safety strap and safety hood. A reasonable jury could conclude that a reasonably prudent person could distinguish between the two weapons, and drawing the deadly weapon—heavier, of a different color, and on the dominant side of the body with a complicated release mechanism under the circumstances—amounted to criminal negligence. Thus, the jury could have reasonably found defendant's conduct rose to the level of conscious indifference to the consequences of his acts, and was not a mere mistake.

This conclusion is supported by two additional facts. First, defendant twice drew his taser on the platform shortly before the shooting, strongly suggesting he was familiar with the weapon and its location on his body. Second, a cell phone video shows him struggling to remove his handgun from his holster three times immediately prior to freeing the weapon and shooting Grant. A reasonable jury could conclude a reasonably prudent person would have known he was holding his deadly handgun and not his nonlethal taser.

The jury also heard evidence that in the past 10 or 11 years, several hundred thousand, if not a million, tasers had been deployed by 13,000 police agencies across the United States. In all that time, with all those deployments, the jury was told there were only six documented instances of taser/handgun confusion in the United States and Canada.

Finally, the jury could reasonably have concluded the situation on the platform was not an extreme high-stress situation at the time of the shooting itself. There were seven officers on the platform, the detainees were under control, and the crowd from the train was being held back. Apparently, no other officer drew a firearm. The officers were shocked when defendant fired on Grant. Also, defendant's use of the phrase "fuck this" just before he shot Grant could, in the minds of the jury, bespeak a tone of recklessness about subduing the suspect.

We conclude there is sufficient evidence from which the jury could legitimately have found that defendant acted with the requisite criminal negligence to support his conviction for involuntary manslaughter.

PROBLEMS

1. Dorothy and her boyfriend Phil live together in a small town in California. Dorothy is the mother of a 17-month-old baby. Phil is not the father, but he acted as the child's parent. Dorothy and Phil loved the child. They are quite poor and have little formal education. The baby became ill, but Dorothy

and Phil did not know how ill. They noticed the baby's cheek was swollen, and they thought the baby was teething. The swelling remained for two weeks. The baby was fussy and could not keep food down. Eventually, the baby's cheek turned a bluish color. Dorothy and Phil did not seek medical care for the baby because they could not afford it, and they thought the baby would get better. Tragically, the baby died. The baby had an abscessed tooth that became gangrenous. What, if anything, should Dorothy and Phil be charged with? *State v. Williams* (1971) 4 Wash.App. 908, 484 P.2d 1167.

2. Dell and his wife Sue argued. Sue said, "I should kill you." Dell replied, "I'll make it easy for you." Dell went to his workshop and got a gun. Standing in front of Sue, Dell loaded the gun and handed it to Sue muzzle first. When Sue grabbed the barrel, the gun accidentally discharged, killing Sue. *People v. Freudenberg* (1953) 121 Cal.App.2d 564, 263 P.2d 875.

3. Paul was practicing his quick draw with his pistol. Paul thought the gun was unloaded. Paul drew the gun and playfully pointed it at his 4-year-old child. Paul pulled the trigger. The "unloaded" gun fired, killing the child. *People v. Walls* (1966) 239 Cal.App.2d 543, 49 Cal.Rptr. 82.

4. Mary had a loaded gun in her bedside table for protection. Mary's 7-year-old son went into Mary's room, removed the gun and was playing with it with his little sister when the gun went off killing the sister.

5. Rob came home one night to find his wife in bed with Rob's best friend. Outraged, Rob jumped in his car and sped away from home, reaching speeds in excess of 100 miles per hour on the freeway. Within minutes of leaving home, Rob collided with a car travelling much slower, killing the driver.

6. Tom got in a fight with his neighbor Paul. Paul punched Tom in the nose, breaking Tom's nose. Tom went to the hospital to have his nose fixed. The next morning, Tom went to Paul's house to, in Tom's words, "return the favor." Tom rang the doorbell, and when Paul opened the door, Tom punched Paul in the nose. Paul fell backward and struck his head on the floor. Unfortunately, the impact caused bleeding inside Paul's head that led to his death.

7. Sea Horse Ranch is located on Highway 1 in Half Moon Bay. For readers unfamiliar with Highway 1, this two lane highway stretches south to north along the coast, and has many exquisitely beautiful views of the ocean. The Ranch kept horses on its property. The corral for the horses was in disrepair, and one dark night a horse escaped from the corral and walked onto Highway 1, where it was hit by a car, killing the passenger in the car. There was a history of horses escaping from the run down corral. There was no lighting on the highway, and it was virtually impossible to see the horse walking down the road until it was too late. The prosecutor intends to file charges against Sea Horse Ranch, which is a California corporation, and the president of the corporation. What charges, if any, are appropriate? A corporation can be criminally liable for the conduct of its officers. As well, an

officer of a corporation can be criminally liable for acts of the corporation if the officer is a participant in the acts or is aware of their commission and is in control of the illegal behavior. *Sea Horse Ranch, Inc. v. Superior Court of San Mateo County* (1994) 24 Cal.App.4th 446, 30 Cal.Rptr.2d 681.

HOMICIDE ON THE BAR EXAMINATION

You have seen the complexity of murder and manslaughter in California law. The California Bar Examination—including the essay portion and the Multistate Bar Examination—does not test the full range of California homicide law. The bar tests general principles of criminal law. On the bar, you are likely to encounter murder, with the four traditional meanings of "malice"—intent to kill, intent to cause grievous bodily injury, depraved heart, and felony murder. As for manslaughter, you may encounter (1) voluntary heat of passion manslaughter on adequate provocation, and (2) involuntary manslaughter of the criminal negligence and misdemeanor manslaughter varieties.

ASSAULT AND BATTERY

You learn about assault and battery in your torts class, as well as in criminal law. Assault is a general intent offense, punished as a misdemeanor. PC § 240 defines assault as "an unlawful attempt, coupled with a present ability, to commit a violent injury on the person of another." Basically, an assault is an attempt to commit a battery. Assault is a lesser included offense of battery. There is no crime of attempted assault.

The Penal Code defines several types of assault, which carry increased penalties. Examples include assault of a police officer, firefighter, paramedic, process server, animal control officer, and others.

It is a felony to commit assault with a deadly weapon. (Penal Code § 245(a)(1)). A deadly weapon is an object, instrument, or weapon used in a way that is capable of producing, or likely to produce, death or great bodily injury, or likely to produce death or great bodily injury. A gun is a deadly weapon, as is a dirk and a blackjack. It would seem a knife should qualify, but not all knives in all circumstances—*e.g.*, long bladed knife vs. butter knife. (*In re B.M.* (2018) 6 Cal. 5th 528, 431 P.3d 1180, 241 Cal. Rptr. 3d 543). To determine whether an object, including a knife, is a deadly weapon, consider the nature of the object, how the object was used, and any other relevant facts. It is not enough that the object is capable of producing death or great bodily injury. The way the object was used must make it likely to cause such results. A mere possibility of serious injury is not enough. On the other hand, it is not necessary that the victim suffer injury.

The following objects can be deadly weapons: a straight pin hidden in an apple, a fence post, a BB or pellet gun, a tire iron, a beer bottle, a knife, a pencil, a dog, a car, pepper spray.

You remember Bruce Lee and Jackie Chan, the famous movie star martial artists. What you may not know is that when it comes to martial arts, Bruce and Jackie were the real thing—they possessed formidable, real-world martial arts skills. If Bruce or Jackie attacked you with his fists or feet, would that be an assault with a "deadly weapon"? Bare feet or fists are not deadly weapons. However, a beating with feet or fists can result in liability for assault likely to cause great bodily injury.

In *In re Gavin T.* (1998) 66 Cal. App. 4th 238, 77 Cal. Rptr. 2d 717, fifteen year old Gavin was outside his school, eating lunch with friends. After taking a bite of an apple, Gavin decided to throw the apple against a brick wall. The wall was the outside of a classroom. Somehow, the apple missed the wall and sailed through a narrow opening of the classroom door, hitting a teacher in the head. Unfortunately, the teacher lost her balance, fell to the floor, and was knocked out. Gavin was charged in juvenile court with assault with a deadly weapon—a partially eaten apple. Is a partially eaten apple a deadly weapon?

In *People v. Russell* (2005) 129 Cal. App. 4th 776, 28 Cal. Rptr. 3d 862, Russell pushed the victim into the path of an oncoming car. Did Russell commit assault with a deadly weapon?

In California criminal law, a battery is defined by PC § 242 as "any willful and unlawful use of force or violence upon the person of another." Simple battery is a general intent crime, punished as a misdemeanor. A brief touch of a person can be a battery. The victim need suffer no injury. The batterer can hit the victim's body, their clothes, or an item closely associated with the person. It is a battery to force the victim to jump out a window.

California law enhances the punishment for certain batteries, including sexual battery, battery causing serious bodily injury, battery on school property, and battery against teachers, police, elders, and children.

CRIMINAL THREATS

Criminal threats, also called terroristic threats, are punished as a felony. Penal Code § 422(a) provides:

> Any person who willfully threatens to commit a crime which will result in death or great bodily injury to another person, with the specific intent that the statement, made verbally, in writing, or by means of an electronic communication device, is to be taken as a threat, even if there is no intent of actually carrying it out, which on its face and under the circumstances in which it is made, is so unequivocal, unconditional, immediate, and specific as to convey to the person threatened, a gravity of purpose and an immediate prospect of execution of the threat, and thereby causes

that person reasonably to be in sustained fear for his or her safety or for his or her immediate family's safety, shall be punished . . . .

In *In re Ryan D.* (2002) 100 Cal. App. 4th 854, 123 Cal. Rptr. 2d 193, a female high school resource officer cited Ryan—a 15-year-old student at the school—for possession of marijuana. A month later, in Ryan's art class at school, he turned in a drawing of a youth firing a handgun at the back of the head of a female police officer. The officer had blood in her hair, and pieces of her face were being blown away. The art teacher found the drawing very disturbing, and turned it over to the vice principal. The vice principal confronted Ryan, who admitted the picture depicted him—Ryan—shooting the school resource officer who cited him. Ryan said he disliked police in general, and was angry at the resource officer for citing him. When the officer saw the picture, she found it "pretty shocking." Ryan is charged in juvenile court with criminal threats. Is he guilty?

Another high school kid shared the following poem with a friend, Wendy, at school: "I am Dark, Destructive, and Dangerous. I slap on my face of happiness, but inside I am evil!! For I can be the next kid to bring guns to kill students at school. So parents watch your children cuz I'm BACK!!" Wendy was terrified. She told her teacher, who notified police. *In re George T.* (2004) 33 Cal. 4th 620, 93 P.3d 1007, 16 Cal. Rptr. 3d 61. Is George's poem a terroristic threat?

Lipsett had a long history of physically abusing his former girlfriend. One day, at the woman's home, two young men, who were her friends, were present with her. Defendant entered the home and assaulted the woman multiple times. She called 911. When police arrived, an officer interviewed the two young men, who were sitting on a couch. As the police officer questioned the men, Lipsett appeared behind the officer. Looking directly at the men, Lipsett put his index finger to his mouth, indicating "be quite." Then, Lipsett, moved his finger across his throat, indicating, it would seem, "If you talk, you die." Criminal threat? *People v. Lipsett* (2001) 223 Cal. App. 4th 1060, 167 Cal. Rptr. 3d 797.

KIDNAPPING

Kidnapping is "simple" or "aggravated." Simple kidnapping is defined in PC § 207(a): "Every person who forcibly, or by any other means of instilling fear, steals or takes, or holds, detains, or arrests any person in this state, and carries the person into another country, state, or county, or into another part of the same county, is guilty of kidnapping," a felony. The words "carries the person" are the asportation element of kidnapping. "Asportation" means movement or carrying away. A person who detains someone without asportation may be guilty of false imprisonment.[45] Simple kidnapping is a general intent offense. Consent is a defense to kidnapping.

For simple kidnapping, asportation must be substantial, that is, more than trivial movement. Two or more trivial movements cannot be combined to achieve the necessary substantial carrying away. The court considers how far the victim was moved, and where.

Aggravated kidnapping includes kidnapping for ransom. Aggravated kidnaping is a specific intent crime. PC § 209(a) punishes "any person who seizes, confines, . . . [or] kidnaps another person . . . for ransom." Some forms of kidnapping for ransom do not require asportation.

Aggravated kidnapping also includes kidnapping to commit robbery, rape, or other sex offense (PC § 209(b)). For this form of aggravated kidnapping, "the movement [asportation] of the victim [must be] beyond that merely incidental to the commission of, and increases the risk of harm to the victim over and above that necessarily present in, the intended underlying offense." (PC § 209(b)(2)). The punishment is life with the possibility of parole.

In *People v. Russell* (2019) 2019 WL 636240 (not reported), the Court of Appeal explained:

> Section 209, subdivision (b)(1) provides that any person who kidnaps or carries away any individual to commit robbery, rape [or other sex crime] . . . shall be punished by imprisonment in the state prison for life with the possibility of parole. Aggravated kidnapping is committed only if the movement of the victim is (1) beyond that merely incidental to the commission of, and (2) increases the risk of harm to the victim over and above that necessarily present in, the intended underlying offense.
>
> With respect to the first element (whether the movement was more than merely incidental to the commission of the intended crime), the jury considers the scope and nature of the movement, which includes the actual distance a victim is moved. There is, however, no minimum distance a defendant must move a victim to satisfy this element. "Incidental" means that the asportation plays no significant or substantial part in the planned offense, or that it be to a more or less trivial change of location having no bearing on the evil at hand.
>
> For the second element (whether the movement increased a victim's risk of harm), the jury considers such factors as the decreased likelihood of detection, the danger inherent in a victim's foreseeable attempts to escape, and the attacker's enhanced

---

[45] False imprisonment is the unlawful violation of the personal liberty of another. PC § 236. False imprisonment is a lesser included offense of kidnapping.

> opportunity to commit additional crimes. The fact that these dangers do not in fact materialize does not, of course, mean that the risk of harm was not increased. The increased harm may be physical or psychological.
>
> These two elements are not mutually exclusive, but interrelated.

The Supreme Court adds to your understanding of aggravated kidnapping with its decision in *People v. Dominguez* (2006) 39 Cal. 4th 1141, 140 P.3d 866, 47 Cal. Rptr. 3d 575:

> The essence of aggravated kidnapping is the increase in the risk of harm to the victim caused by the forced movement. We have articulated various circumstances the jury should consider, such as whether the movement decreases the likelihood of detection, increases the danger inherent in a victim's foreseeable attempts to escape, or enhances the attacker's opportunity to commit additional crimes. . . . We have repeatedly stated no minimum distance is required to satisfy the asportation requirement, so long as the movement is substantial.
>
> Measured distance, therefore, is a relevant factor, but one that must be considered in context, including the nature of the crime and its environment. In some cases a shorter distance may suffice in the presence of other factors, while in others a longer distance, in the absence of other circumstances, may be found insufficient. For example, moving robbery victims between six and 30 feet within their home or apartment or 15 feet from the teller area of a bank to its vault may be viewed as merely incidental to the commission of the robbery and thus insufficient to satisfy the asportation requirement of aggravated kidnapping. Yet, dragging a store clerk nine feet from the front counter of a store to a small back room for the purpose of raping her or forcibly moving a robbery victim 40 feet within a parking lot into a car might, under the circumstances, substantially increase the risk of harm to the victim and thus satisfy the asportation requirement.

Aggravated kidnapping includes kidnapping to commit carjacking (PC § 209.5(a)). The victim must be moved a substantial distance from the place of the carjacking.

KIDNAPPING QUESTIONS

1. In *People v. Stinson* (2019) 31 Cal. App. 5th 464, 242 Cal. Rptr. 3d 606, victim drove his car to a friend's home. While sitting in the car, victim noticed two men next to the car. One man opened the passenger side door, sat in the passenger seat, pointed a gun at victim, and said, "Don't move, or I'll shoot." The men stole victim's wallet and phone. The men ordered victim out

of the car, and forced him into the trunk of the car. Victim was moved 6 to 8 feet from the driver's seat to the trunk, with a gun pointed at his head. With victim in the trunk, the robbers went through victim's car. Victim thought he would be killed. The robbers left, and victim pulled the emergency release in the trunk to free himself. He called 911. Did the robbers kidnap the victim?

2. Defendant and two other men approached a bank to rob it. When the robbers were a few feet from the entrance, a customer walked out the door, leaving the bank. One of the robbers grabbed the customer and forced her back into the bank. Inside the bank, one robber held a gun over his head, and said, "This is a robbery. Everybody get down on the floor." Everyone complied, including the customer forced back into the bank. The man with the gun stood watch in the bank lobby, while the other man went behind the "bandit barrier" that separates tellers from customers. This man scooped money into a bag. The robbers ran out of the bank and into a waiting stolen car. Did the robbers kidnap the people in the bank? What about the customer who was grabbed and returned to the bank? *People v. Briggs* (2018) 2018 WL 4611367 (not published).

3. The murder victim was found buried in a shallow grave in an orchard next to a rural road. The victim had been walking along the road when two men dragged her off the road, down a 12 foot embankment, and into the orchard. Once down the embankment, the victim could not be seen by a motorist passing on the road. Defendant is charged with strangling and raping the victim. Defendant admits he had sex with the victim in the orchard, but denies killing her. *People v. Dominguez* (2006) 39 Cal. 4th 1141, 140 P.3d 866, 47 Cal. Rptr. 3d 575.

CHAPTER 6

RAPE AND OTHER SEX OFFENSES

■ ■ ■

Rape and other sex offenses are common. Approximately one in five women is a victim of attempted or completed sexual violence while in college.

Rape and sexual abuse have adverse short- and long-term consequences. Many victims experience some or all of the symptoms of Posttraumatic Stress Disorder (PTSD). Frazier writes, "Studies that have assessed the prevalence of PTSD among recent victims report that the vast majority meet the criteria for PTSD immediately post-rape and that approximately 50% continue to meet the criteria at one year post-rape."[1] Many survivors experience depression, fear, anxiety, health problems, difficulty with interpersonal relationships, and substance abuse.

ELEMENTS OF RAPE

Blackstone defined rape as "carnal knowledge of a woman forcibly and against her will."[2] For much of the twentieth century, rape was defined as sexual intercourse by a man with a woman not his wife, without her consent, effectuated by force or threat of force. A married man was legally incapable of raping his wife. Today, the "marital exception" to rape has disappeared. As well, statutes are being amended to make rape gender neutral.

Lack of consent is an element of rape. Consent is an act of free will. California Penal Code § 261.6 defines consent as "positive cooperation in act or attitude to an exercise of free will." A woman who "consents" out of fear that the defendant will hurt her does not consent freely.

The fact that a woman conversed with a man followed forced sex does not mean she consented. Nor does the fact that she asked the man to use a condom. (PC § 261.7) A person may be too intoxicated or intellectually disabled to consent.

Traditionally, when a woman consented to penetration, she could not change her mind following penetration. It was too late. This rule is

---

[1] Patricia A. Frazier, The Scientific Status of Research on Rape Trauma Syndrome. In 2 David L. Faigman, David H. Kaye, Michael J. Saks & Joseph Sanders, *Modern Scientific Evidence: The Law and Science of Expert Testimony* § 13–2.2.1[3], p. 125 (2002) (St. Paul: West).

[2] 4 William Blackstone, Commentaries *210.

changing.[3] The California Court of Appeal wrote in *People v. Ireland* (2010) 188 Cal.App.4th 328, 336, 114 Cal.Rptr.3d 915, "Withdrawal of consent can occur at any time." If the woman conveys her change of heart to the man and he persists with force, rape occurs.[4] As the Maryland Court of Appeal put it in *State v. Baby* (2008) 404 Md. 220, 946 A.3d 463, "We hold that a woman may withdraw consent for vaginal intercourse after penetration has occurred and that, after consent has been withdrawn, the continuation of vaginal intercourse by force or the threat of force may constitute rape."

Force is an element of rape.[5] Force can be actual or threatened. Force can be established by testimony from the victim. Force can be inferred from how the crime was committed. Thus, force can be inferred from injuries, size difference between victim and defendant, restraint of the victim, degree of violence, or the position or condition of a murder victim's body. The requirement of force may be less when the victim is a child or a frail elder.

The degree of force required for rape is evolving.[6] Bennett Capers writes, "Since the 1980s, the trend has been to de-emphasize the presence of force and to instead emphasize the absence of consent."[7] The CALCRIM jury instruction on rape provides, "Intercourse is accomplished by force if a person uses enough physical force to overcome the woman's will." (CALCRIM 1000).[8]

CALIFORNIA STATUTES ON RAPE

California law has numerous sex offenses.[9] This chapter focuses on rape. Relevant California Penal Code sections follow:

§ 261. Rape defined

(a) Rape is an act of sexual intercourse accomplished with a person not the spouse of the perpetrator, under any of the following circumstances:

---

[3] The California Supreme Court ruled that a victim can withdraw consent following penetration. *In re John Z.* (2003) 29 Cal.4th 756, 128 Cal.Rptr.2d 783, 60 P.3d 183.

[4] *State v. Bunyard* (2006) 281 Kan. 392, 133 P.3d 14 (rape can occur when victim withdraws consent following penetration).

[5] Defendant must accomplish penetration by force, violence, menace, or fear of immediate and unlawful bodily injury to the victim or someone else.

[6] Bennett Capers, The Unintentional Rapist, 87 *Washington University Law Review* 1345–1395, 1354 (2010).

[7] Bennett Capers, The Unintentional Rapist, 87 *Washington University Law Review* 1345–1395, 1354 (2010).

[8] *People v. Griffin* (2004) 33 Cal. 4th 1015, 1023-1024, 94 P.3d 1089, 16 Cal. Rptr. 3d 891, "the prosecution need only show the defendant used physical force to a degree sufficient to support a finding that the act of sexual intercourse was against the will of the [victim]."

[9] *See, e.g.*, Penal Code § 285 (incest); § 286 (forcible sodomy); § 288 (lewd and lascivious acts).

(1) Where a person is incapable, because of a mental disorder or developmental or physical disability, of giving legal consent, and this is known or reasonably should be known to the person committing the act.[10]

(2) Where it is accomplished against a person's will by means of force, violence, duress, or menace, or fear of immediate and unlawful bodily injury on the person or another.

(3) Where a person is prevented from resisting by any intoxicating or anesthetic substance, or any controlled substance, and this condition was known, or reasonably should have been known by the accused.[11]

(4) Where a person is at the time unconscious of the nature of the act, and this is known to the accused. As used in this paragraph, "unconscious of the nature of the act" means incapable of resisting because the victim meets one of the following conditions:

(A) Was unconscious or asleep.[12]

(B) Was not aware, knowing, perceiving, or cognizant that the act occurred.

(C) Was not aware, knowing, perceiving, or cognizant of the essential characteristics of the act due to the perpetrator's fraud in fact.

(D) Was not aware, knowing, perceiving, or cognizant of the essential characteristics of the act due to the perpetrator's fraudulent representation that the sexual penetration served a professional purpose when it served no professional purpose.

(5) Where a person submits under the belief that the person committing the act is the victim's spouse, and this belief is induced by

---

[10] *See People v. Giardino* (2000) 82 Cal.App.4th 454, 460, 98 Cal.Rptr.2d 315, "By itself, the existence of actual consent is not sufficient to establish a defense to a charge of rape. That the supposed victim actually consented to sexual intercourse disproves rape only if he or she had sufficient capacity to give that consent. For example, if the victim is so unsound of mind that he or she is incapable of giving legal consent, the fact that he or she may have given actual consent does not prevent a conviction of rape. Hence, the consent defense fails if the victim either did not actually consent or lacked the capacity to give legally cognizable consent."

[11] *See People v. Giardino* (2000) 82 Cal.App.4th 454, 462, 98 Cal.Rptr.2d 315, "We conclude that, just as subdivision (a)(1) of section 261 proscribes sexual intercourse with a person who is not capable of giving legal consent because of a mental disorder or physical disability, section 261(a)(3) proscribes sexual intercourse with a person who is not capable of giving legal consent because of intoxication. In both cases, the issue is not whether the victim actually consented to sexual intercourse, but whether he or she was capable of exercising the degree of judgment a person must have in order to give legally cognizable consent."

[12] *See People v. Giardino* (2000) 82 Cal.App.4th 454, 461 n.4, 98 Cal.Rptr.2d 315, A person with the capacity to consent may withhold consent. Some people are legally incapable on consenting to sex. "Both types of consent are lacking in the case of an unconscious or sleeping victim. While in that state, the victim not only lacks the capacity to give legal consent, he or she cannot possibly give actual consent."

an artifice, pretense, or concealment practiced by the accused, with intent to induce the belief.[13]

(6) Where the act is accomplished against the victim's will by threatening to retaliate in the future against the victim or any other person, and there is a reasonable possibility that the perpetrator will execute the threat. As used in this paragraph, "threaten to retaliate" means a threat to kidnap or falsely imprison, or to inflict extreme pain, serious bodily injury, or death.

(7) Where the act is accomplished against the victim's will by threatening to use the authority of a public official to incarcerate, arrest, or deport the victim or another, and the victim has a reasonable belief that the perpetrator is a public official.

§ 261.5. Unlawful sexual intercourse with person under 18

(a) Unlawful sexual intercourse is an act of sexual intercourse accomplished with a person who is not the spouse of the perpetrator, if the person is a minor. [The age difference between the victim and the perpetrator determines the seriousness of the offense.]

§ 261.6. Consent defined

In a prosecution under Section 261 [and other sections], in which consent is at issue, "consent" shall be defined to mean positive cooperation in act or attitude pursuant to an exercise of free will. The person must act freely and voluntarily and have knowledge of the nature of the act or transaction involved. A current or previous dating or marital relationship shall not be sufficient to constitute consent where consent is at issue.

§ 261.7. Evidence that victim requested that defendant use condom or other birth control device

In prosecution under Section 261 [and other sections], in which consent is at issue, evidence that the victim suggested, requested, or otherwise communicated to the defendant that the defendant use a condom or other birth control device, without additional evidence of consent, is not sufficient to constitute consent.

§ 262. Rape of spouse

(a) Rape of a person who is the spouse of the perpetrator is an act of sexual intercourse accomplished under any of the following circumstances:

---

13 *See People v. Leal* (2009) 180 Cal.App.4th 782, 103 Cal.Rptr.3d 351. Defendant entered victim's home through an open window; defendant digitally penetrated victim as she lay sleeping with her husband; the victim thought her husband committed the act; defendant's conviction affirmed.

(1) Where it is accomplished against a person's will by means of force, violence, duress, menace, or fear of immediate and unlawful bodily injury on the person or another.

§ 263. Rape; essentials

The essential guilt of rape is the outrage to the person and feelings of the victim of the rape. Any sexual penetration, however slight, is sufficient to complete the crime.

§ 264. Rape; punishment

(a) Except as provided in subdivision (c), rape as defined in Section 261 or 262, is punishable by imprisonment in the state prison for three, six, or eight years.

(b) [Defendant may be ordered to pay a fine.]

(c)(1) Any person who commits [forcible] rape upon a child who is under 14 years of age shall be punished by imprisonment in the state prison for 9, 11, or 13 years.

CONSENT IN RAPE PROSECUTIONS

Lack of consent is an element of rape. The Court of Appeal explored "consent" in *People v. Ireland.*

PEOPLE V. IRELAND

Court of Appeal
188 Cal.App.4th 328, 114 Cal.Rptr.3d 915 (2010)

DAWSON, J.

Following a jury trial, Anthony Ireland (appellant) was convicted of four counts of forcible rape (Pen.Code, § 261(a)(2)). As to each count, the jury found true the allegations that appellant used a deadly weapon and that he committed the crimes against multiple victims and with a deadly weapon. The trial court sentenced appellant to a total term of 100 years in state prison, consisting of four consecutive 25-year-to-life terms.

On appeal, appellant contends there is insufficient evidence to sustain his forcible rape convictions. We find no prejudicial error and affirm.

Facts

Each of appellant's four convictions of forcible rape involved a different victim but a similar scenario.

Count 1: V.B.

In late October of 2007, V.B. was working as a prostitute on Motel Drive when appellant, in a four-door burgundy car, approached and asked her for a "date," which she described as an agreement to have sex for an agreed-upon amount of money. The two agreed on a price of $40. V.B. suggested they go to her motel room but appellant declined, saying he had once been robbed in a motel room. He suggested they drive down the street and park, and V.B. agreed. They parked in a driveway near railroad tracks.

Appellant told V.B. to get into the back seat of the car, which she did. When appellant entered the back seat, V.B. felt a metal knife against her neck. V.B. began to cry and begged appellant "please don't hurt me." V.B. testified she was afraid and did not want to die. Appellant told her to be quiet and that he would not hurt her if she cooperated. V.B. was afraid that, if she resisted, appellant would cut or stab her.

Appellant then had vaginal intercourse with V.B., while holding the knife to her throat. V.B. described the knife as a big butcher knife with a seven-to nine-inch blade and a wooden handle. Appellant told her to make noises like she enjoyed the sex act, but instead she cried "loudly" the entire time. After appellant ejaculated, he exited the car and threw the condom he was wearing into the bushes. When V.B. asked if she could leave, appellant said yes. V.B. then exited the car and ran. Appellant did not pay her.

V.B. had never met appellant prior to the incident. She did not consent to the sexual act as it happened, and she did not agree to the use of the knife when she got into the car. V.B. did not report the incident to the police at first, because she was a prostitute.

Count 2: J.W.

In late September or early October of 2007, J.W. was working as a prostitute when appellant, in a four-door burgundy car, pulled up next to her and asked for a "date." J.W. was tired and ready to go home, so she quoted him a $100 price, thinking he would not agree to it. But appellant agreed to the price, and J.W. got into the car. J.W. told appellant she had a motel room, but he said he had a bad experience in a motel room, and they instead drove to a location five minutes away and parked.

The two agreed to have sex in the car, so J.W. climbed into the back seat. Appellant got out of the driver's seat and walked to the back. When he opened the back door, J.W. asked him for her money. Appellant said, "oh, oh, yeah," reached toward the waist of his pants, and pulled out a large knife with a 10-inch blade.

Appellant got into the back seat and on top of J.W. and held the knife to the side of her neck. When J.W. asked appellant what he was doing, he told her to "shut up." J.W. felt that appellant had an erection and asked him to put on a condom. He told her to put it on him. J.W. was afraid appellant might "slice [her] neck off." She asked appellant not to hurt her. She cooperated because she was fearful she might die.

Appellant held the knife to J.W.'s throat the entire time. She was very frightened and asked appellant to remove the knife from her neck. But appellant said "no" because "you might scream." He told her not to scream or make any sudden movements or he would use the knife. J.W. did not scream, because she was afraid appellant might stab her in the neck.

Appellant had sex with her. After he ejaculated, he got out of the car and threw the condom on the ground. He did not pay her. J.W. never agreed to have sexual intercourse with appellant while he held a knife to her throat.

J.W. did not report the incident to the police, but she did tell others on the street about the incident. After the incident, she saw appellant in his car at a liquor store. She yelled at him to leave and told other women in the area, "that's him, don't get in his car."

J.W. was later contacted by the police and asked if she knew anyone bothering the women in the area. She related to them what had happened to her.

Count 3: A.H.

In October of 2007, A.H. was working as a prostitute when appellant, in a red four-door car, pulled up and asked her for a "date." They agreed on $60. A.H. got into appellant's car and they drove to a cemetery and parked.

Once there, they both got out of the car and A.H. got into the back seat. A.H. told appellant she needed her money. He told her she would get it but, when he got into the back seat, he put a big kitchen knife to her throat. A.H. said "no," but appellant held the knife to A.H.'s throat, told her to put a condom on him, and then told her to remove her pants and get on her knees. She complied because she was afraid he was going to kill her. She didn't say anything else because she was too afraid. Appellant then had vaginal intercourse with her, after which she got out of the car and left. Appellant did not pay her.

A.H. had never met appellant before the incident and did not agree to the use of the knife. She did not report the incident because she had been "hurt" when she was younger and the police had done nothing about it. Here, she was later contacted by police and told them what had happened.

Count 4: C.S.

In November of 2007, C.S. (sometimes known as Baby), who was 15 years old at the time, was working as a prostitute when appellant, in a four-door burgundy car, asked her for a "car date." They agreed on $80. C.S. suggested they go to a hotel, but appellant suggested they drive to a cemetery, and C.S. agreed.

Once there, C.S. got out of the car, got into the back seat, and asked appellant for her money. Appellant acted as if he were going to get the money from his pocket but, instead, pulled out a large knife with an eight- to 10-inch blade from the front of his pants. Appellant put the blade to C.S.'s neck and said, "do what I say and you won't get hurt." She was "shocked" and "scared" that she might die. She requested that he use a condom, and appellant complied. Appellant then had vaginal intercourse with her. He held the knife to her throat the entire time. C.S. did not agree to the use of the knife, but she thought appellant would cut her if she did not comply. After the incident, C.S. asked appellant for a ride back and he agreed. Appellant did not pay her.

About a week later, C.S. was on the street when she was contacted by police because it was late and she looked young. One of the officers mentioned there had been rapes in the area. C.S. described what had happened to her and gave the officer a description of appellant, his vehicle, and the assault.

Police Investigation

In November of 2007, Detective Neal Cooney, a sexual assault investigator, received information from another officer informing him of sexual assaults on female prostitutes. The description of the assailant, his vehicle, and his modus operandi were similar. On November 6, 2007, while conducting surveillance, Detective Cooney struck-up a conversation with J.W., who was walking the street. She explained she had been raped at knifepoint a few weeks earlier. Her description of the suspect was similar to that already received. Later that evening, Detective Cooney observed a vehicle that fit the suspect's vehicle description. Detective Cooney initiated a traffic stop. Appellant was the only occupant of the vehicle. Appellant consented to a search, but told Detective Cooney that he had a knife on his right side. Cooney removed the knife from appellant's waistband and arrested appellant. V.B., J.W., and A.H. subsequently identified appellant in a photographic lineup as the man who raped them. Detective Cooney and another officer interviewed appellant at the police station. The interview, which was recorded, was subsequently played for the jury during trial. Appellant told the officers he carried a butcher knife for protection. He also said he had had sex with three or four prostitutes, whom he subsequently described as one blonde, one Asian, and two Black females. Appellant initially claimed all of the women consented to sex and that he used the knife with one, the blonde, because it turned her on. He denied putting it to her neck to hurt her but said he rubbed it on her body. After further questioning, appellant admitted he used the knife on "Baby." Appellant told her he was going to use the knife, but she did not want him to do so. He then told her, "Well I'm going to do it. I was just like let me do it." After he promised he wouldn't kill her, she agreed. He claimed to put the knife to her breasts and her lower neck area. Appellant then admitted he also used the knife on one of the Black women but said he quit when she became scared. When she said she did not want to do "it," he told her, "you already said you were going to do it." After they had sex, she jumped out of the car without taking any money. Appellant then said he had had sex with another "black girl." He initially gave her money for sex. About half way through the sexual act, appellant pulled out a knife. After they had sex, he took the money back from her.

Discussion

1. Sufficiency of the Evidence

Appellant argues there is insufficient evidence to convict him of any of the forcible rapes. He specifically contends that each woman consented to engage in sex acts in return for money and, although each woman objected to the use of the knife, the use of the knife did not automatically terminate the consent. He claims there was insufficient evidence to establish that each woman withdrew her consent and communicated that withdrawal of consent to appellant. We disagree.

Withdrawal of consent can occur at any time. Here the trial court gave the standard instruction on withdrawal of consent: "A woman who initially consents to an act of intercourse may change her mind during the act. If she does so, under the law, the act of intercourse is then committed without her consent if: (1) she communicated to [appellant] that she objected to the act of intercourse and attempted to stop the act; (2) she communicated her objection through words or acts that a reasonable person would have understood as showing her lack of consent; and (3) [appellant] forcibly continued the act of intercourse despite her objection."

Appellant's argument is that each victim gave her consent to the sex act that was committed, that his use of the knife during the act did not automatically negate that consent, and that there was insufficient evidence that any of the victims communicated a withdrawal of consent to him. Respondent, on the other hand, contends the determinative question is not whether the victims communicated a withdrawal of consent. Instead, according to respondent, appellant's use of the knife, along with his express or implied threat to harm his victims if they did not cooperate, did automatically negate their previously given consent.

We agree with respondent's analysis. There is no doubt that, at the beginning of each encounter, each victim freely consented to intercourse. But as to each of the victims, appellant communicated the express or implied threat that, if they did not continue to cooperate even after he produced the knife and held it to their throats, he would do them harm.

It is not appellant's position that there is insufficient evidence to show a lack of consent, from each of the victims, after appellant displayed his knife and threatened them. There is more than substantial evidence that each victim's continued participation in the sexual encounter with appellant was in fact nonconsensual after that point. Instead, appellant's position is that because, as to each victim, consent had once been given, each victim was required not only to withdraw that consent but also to communicate that withdrawal to him—to communicate it, if not expressly, at least by implication. We disagree.

The essence of consent is that it is given out of free will. That is why it can be withdrawn. While there exists a defense to rape based on the defendant's actual and reasonable belief that the victim does consent, we do not require that victims communicate their lack of consent. Lack of consent need not be proven by direct testimony but may be inferred from use of force or duress. We certainly do not require that victims resist. Yet this is what appellant proposes here. At the time of the offenses, appellant told his victims to cooperate or be hurt. Now he contends they were required to express to him their lack of cooperation. That cannot be the law. When appellant used the knife and expressly or impliedly threatened his victims, and in the absence of any conduct by the victims indicating that they continued to consent, the previously given consent no longer existed, either in fact or in law. Consent induced by fear is no consent at all.

From all of this evidence, it is clear that these victims did not continue to consent when appellant put the knife to their throats and that appellant knew they did not continue to consent. Thus, if they were required to communicate a withdrawal of consent, they adequately did so.

Substantial evidence supports each of the convictions of forcible rape, and we reject appellant's claim to the contrary. The judgment is affirmed.

SHOULD LACK OF CONSENT BE ELIMINATED AS AN ELEMENT OF RAPE?

In California, lack of consent is an element of the crime of rape. Thus, the prosecutor must prove lack of consent beyond a reasonable doubt. Should lack of consent be eliminated as an element of the crime, making rape forcible sexual intercourse? There is a move in this direction. The Model Penal Code (§ 213.1) defines rape as "A male who has sexual intercourse with a female not his wife is guilty of rape if he compels her to submit by force or by threat of imminent death, serious bodily injury, extreme pain or kidnapping." Note that absence of consent is not an element. The Uniform Code of Military Justice defines rape as follows: "Any person subject to this chapter who causes another person of any age to engage in a sexual act by using force against that other person is guilty of rape." As with the Model Penal Code, consent is not an element of the crime. When consent is eliminated as an element, it becomes an affirmative defense, and the burden of proving consent can be placed on defendant.

Do you favor amending California law to remove "against a person's will" as an element of rape?

MUST VICTIM RESIST?

Until 1980, California law required a victim of rape to resist the attack unless the capacity to resist was overcome by force or threat.[14] In *People v. Barnes*, the Supreme Court discusses the "resistance requirement" and other aspects of rape law. The decision, issued in 1986, gives you insights into important changes in rape law that were underway in the later twentieth century.

PEOPLE V. BARNES

California Supreme Court
42 Cal.3d 284, 228 Cal.Rptr. 228, 721 P.2d 110 (1986)

BIRD, C. J.

Was the Court of Appeal correct in relying on a rape complainant's lack of "measurable resistance" to overturn convictions of rape and false imprisonment as unsupported by sufficient evidence?

Marsha M. had known appellant about four years as of May of 1982. They were neighbors and acquaintances. She had been to his house briefly once before to buy some marijuana. A couple of weeks before the present incident, they had drunk wine together at her house.

Around 10 p.m. on May 27, 1982, appellant called Marsha and invited her over for some drinks to celebrate his parents' having come into a sum of money. Marsha was undecided and told appellant to call back or she would call him.

Over the next two hours, appellant called twice to see what Marsha had decided to do. She finally told him she would come over and that she wanted to buy a little marijuana from him. She asked him to meet her outside his house.

Marsha arrived at appellant's house around 1 a.m. Appellant was waiting for her outside the front gate. It was cold. Appellant suggested they go inside and smoke some marijuana. At first Marsha refused. She told appellant she had to get up early and wanted to buy the marijuana and go home. However, after a couple of minutes, appellant persuaded her to come inside.

Marsha followed appellant through the house to a room off the garage. At first, they carried on a conversation which Marsha described as "normal chatter." Appellant provided some marijuana and they both smoked it.

---

[14] The Penal Code of 1873 defined rape: "Rape is an act of sexual intercourse accomplished with a female, not the wife of the perpetrator, under either of the following circumstances: . . . 3. Where she resists, but her resistance is overcome by force or violence. 4. Where she is prevented from resisting by threats of immediate and great bodily harm, accompanied by apparent power of execution."

Appellant offered some cocaine, but she refused. She kept telling appellant she wanted to hurry up and leave.

After 10 or 15 minutes, appellant began to hug Marsha. She pushed him away and told him to stop. She did not take him seriously as he was "just coming on."

Appellant continued his advances despite Marsha's insistence that she only wanted to buy marijuana and leave. When appellant asked her why she was in such a hurry, she reiterated she just wanted him to give her the marijuana and let her go since she had to get up early in the morning. Appellant told her he did not want her to leave. Marsha finally said goodbye and walked out of the room. Until this point, things between them had been "decent and friendly."

As Marsha approached the front gate, appellant, who was behind her and appeared angry, stated, "No, you don't go leaving. You don't just jump up and leave my goddamn house." He began "ranting and raving" and arguing with her. He wanted to know why she was "trying to leave." He told her that she made him feel as if she had stolen something; that she was acting like he was "a rapist or something." Marsha characterized appellant's behavior as "psychotic."

When she reached the front gate, Marsha did not try to open it because she did not know how. She asked appellant to open it, but he just stood looking at her. This behavior made her nervous. When she asked appellant what was wrong, he "reared back" as if he were going to hit her.

They argued at the gate for about 20 minutes. Marsha told appellant she did not understand what he was arguing with her about and that he seemed to be trying to find a reason to be angry with her. She told him, "I came to your house to get some grass. Now, I want to leave. You won't let me leave."

Appellant replied that he was going to let her leave but needed to put his shoes on first. He then returned to the room and Marsha followed. She said she returned to the room because she felt she could not get out the front gate by herself.

As she was following appellant, the door leading to the stairs closed behind her, prompting him to shout that she was "slamming the goddamn door" in his house. After they entered the room, appellant closed the door behind them. He was "fussing" at Marsha, talking and "carrying on" the whole time he was putting on his shoes. He stated, "I don't know what the hell you bitches think you want to do." Marsha was confused and concerned about what was happening and about what appellant was going to do. Several times, appellant stopped talking and looked at her "funny."

Appellant then stood up and began to "lecture" Marsha. He was angry. He began to threaten her, telling her he was a man and displaying the muscles in his arms. He grabbed her by her sweater collar and told her he could pick her up with one hand and throw her out. Flexing his muscles, he stated, "You see this? I am a man. You respect me like a man. I am no kid."

Appellant also told Marsha of his past sexual exploits. He stated: "I had bitches do anything I want. I have had bitches suck me. I have had them do that. I can make you do anything I want. You understand me?" Occasionally, appellant would stop talking, "rear back," look at her and tell her how much she upset him.

At one point appellant said, "You're so used to seeing the good side of me. Now you get to see the bad." Then he became quiet and stared at her. This statement again made Marsha believe he was going to hit her.

Marsha asked appellant whether he wanted to hit her. She told him she could not fight him. Appellant responded by lecturing her. Marsha began to move toward the door. When appellant noticed her, he said, "I don't know why you're standing by the door. What are you looking at the door for?" Marsha thought appellant pushed the door closed a little tighter.

Appellant continued talking but then suddenly turned and started hugging Marsha "affectionately." He told her he did not mean to "fuss" at her. By now, Marsha felt she was in the room with a "psychotic person" who had again changed personalities. Approximately 40 minutes had elapsed since they entered the room a second time. It was at this juncture that Marsha began to "play along" and feign compliance with appellant's desires.

In an effort to get out of appellant's house, Marsha suggested they go to her house where they could be alone. Appellant told her not to worry about his parents coming home. He continued to hug and talk to her. After a few minutes, appellant stated, "I have to have some of this right now," and told Marsha to remove her clothes. Marsha refused. Appellant reacted by telling her she was going to upset him and by making some type of gesture. In response, Marsha removed her clothes. An act of sexual intercourse ensued which lasted about one hour and included the exchange of kisses. Afterward, both appellant and Marsha fell asleep.

Marsha testified she engaged in sexual intercourse with appellant because she felt if she refused, he would become physically violent. She based this assessment on appellant's actions and words, including his statements that she was about to "see the bad side" of him and that he could throw her out if he wanted.

Marsha awoke around 4 a.m. She cajoled appellant into walking her to the front gate and opening it so she could leave. She returned home and immediately called Kaiser Hospital to request an examination. She was eventually referred to the sexual trauma center and examined for venereal disease.

Marsha did not report the incident to the police that day because she was confused and felt "it was my word against his." She had been told at the sexual trauma center that she had three days within which to make a report. After discussing the incident with a coworker, she reported it to the police the following day.

Appellant telephoned Marsha the morning of the incident and a couple of days later. On both occasions she hung up on him.

The defense was consent. Appellant's testimony was substantially similar to Marsha's regarding the events prior to her arrival at his house. However, the versions differed markedly as to the subsequent events.

Appellant testified that the first time they were in the room together he gave Marsha some marijuana and refused payment for it. They smoked some marijuana. Appellant told Marsha he had "feelings for her," he was sexually attracted to her and did not want her to leave so quickly. According to appellant, they did not argue over anything. He was surprised that she was in such a rush to leave.

At the front gate, they continued to talk. He again expressed feelings of sexual attraction for her. According to appellant, it was Marsha who first returned to the room. There, she told him she would stay a little while longer. Then, without being asked, she started removing her clothes. Consensual sexual intercourse ensued during which Marsha returned appellant's hugs and kisses. Appellant testified he did not threaten Marsha in any way, make gestures toward her, display his muscles or force her to stay. He confirmed the fact that he had telephoned Marsha twice afterwards. However, he testified they talked briefly each time.

Appellant was convicted after a jury trial of one count each of rape and false imprisonment (Pen. Code §§ 261(2), 236) as to Marsha M. The Court of Appeal reversed these convictions as unsupported by substantial evidence. This court granted the Attorney General's petition for review in order to clarify the requirements for conviction under section 261(2) as amended by the Legislature in 1980.

Until its amendment in 1980, former section 261, subdivisions 2 and 3 defined rape as an act of sexual intercourse under circumstances where the person resists, but where "resistance is overcome by force or violence" or where "a person is prevented from resisting by threats of great and immediate bodily harm, accompanied by apparent power of execution."

The Legislature amended section 261 in 1980 to delete most references to resistance.

The events in this case occurred on May 28, 1982. Therefore, appellant was charged, tried and convicted under section 261(2) as amended in 1980. In the Court of Appeal, appellant argued that the evidence was insufficient to sustain his conviction of rape under that statute. Inexplicably, the Court of Appeal quoted and relied upon the language from *People v. Nash* (1968) 261 Cal.App.2d 216, which reiterated the requirements of rape prior to the 1980 amendment to section 261: "The offense of rape is committed when the victim resists the act, but her resistance is overcome by force or violence. Although she must resist in fact, an extraordinary resistance is not required. The amount of resistance need only be such as to manifest her refusal to consent to the act."

Using the defunct *Nash* formula as its analytical foundation, the Court of Appeal proceeded to review the evidence in light of certain facts which bore mainly on the existence *vel non* of resistance by Marsha and of threats by appellant. It concluded that (1) "at no time did appellant specifically threaten physical harm to Marsha unless she consented to an act of intercourse"; (2) "Marsha removed her clothes and acceded to his demands without any explicit protestation or measurable resistance to appellant's advances"; (3) the record does not contain "credible evidence of solid value from which an inference can be made beyond a reasonable doubt that appellant intended to have intercourse with Marsha irrespective of her protestations or passive resistance"; and (4) the record shows only "Marsha's bare assertion of an uncommunicated resistance to the act in question." On this basis, the Court of Appeal reversed appellant's conviction of rape.

It is undisputed that the Court of Appeal erred in applying the requirements of former section 261 to the facts of this case. Section 261(2) contains no reference to resistance by the prosecuting witness or to threats by the accused.

The importance of resistance lay in its relationship to the issues of force and consent. The accused's conduct became criminal only if the complainant failed to consent, exhibited resistance, and was overcome in this will by the accused's use of force or violence. By establishing resistance, the state was able to prove the key elements of the crime: the accused's intent to use force in order to accomplish an act of sexual intercourse, and the woman's nonconsent.

Appellant's minimization of the 1980 amendment also ignores the crucial role the resistance requirement has played in the history of rape laws. That the Legislature's elimination of resistance represents a profound change in the law is evident from a review of its historical evolution. At common law, the crime of rape was defined as "the carnal knowledge of a woman forcibly and against her will." (4 Blackstone, Commentaries 201.) Historically, it was considered inconceivable that a woman who truly did not consent to sexual intercourse would not meet force with force. The law originally demanded "utmost resistance" from the woman to ensure she had submitted rather than consented. Not only must she have resisted to the "utmost" of her physical capacity, the resistance must not have ceased throughout the assault.

California long ago rejected this "primitive rule" of utmost resistance. "A woman who is assaulted need not resist to the point of risking being beaten into insensibility. If she resists to the point where further resistance would be useless or, until her resistance is overcome by force or violence, submission thereafter is not consent." In our state, it had long been the rule that the resistance required by former section 261(2), was only that which would reasonably manifest refusal to consent to the act of sexual intercourse.

Nevertheless, courts refused to uphold a conviction of rape by force where the complainant had exhibited little or no resistance. The law demanded some measure of resistance, for it remained a tenet that a virtuous woman would by nature resist a sexual attack.

The requirement that a woman resist her attacker appears to have been grounded in the basic distrust with which courts and commentators traditionally viewed a woman's testimony regarding sexual assault. According to the 17th century writings of Lord Matthew Hale, in order to be deemed a credible witness, a woman had to be of good fame, disclose the injury immediately, suffer signs of injury and cry out for help. (1 Hale, History of the Pleas of the Crown (1st Am. ed. 1847) p. 633.)

This distrust was formalized in the law in several areas. For example, juries were traditionally advised to be suspect and cautious in evaluating a rape complainant's testimony, particularly where she was "unchaste."

In most jurisdictions, corroboration of the complaining witness was necessary for a conviction of rape.

Skeptical of female accusers, the majority of courts and commentators considered it appropriate that the "prosecutrix" in all sexual assault cases undergo psychiatric examination before trial.

Recently, however, the entire concept of resistance to sexual assault has been called into question. It has been suggested that while the presence of resistance may well be probative on the issue of force or nonconsent, its absence may not.

For example, some studies have demonstrated that while some women respond to sexual assault with active resistance, others "freeze." The "frozen fright" response resembles cooperative behavior. These findings belie the traditional notion that a woman who does not resist has consented. They suggest that lack of physical resistance may reflect a "profound primal terror" rather than consent.

Additionally, a growing body of authority holds that to resist in the face of sexual assault is to risk further injury. On the other hand, other findings indicate that resistance has a direct correlation with *deterring* sexual assault.

In sum, it is not altogether clear what the absence of resistance indicates in relation to the issue of consent. Nor is it *necessarily* advisable for one who is assaulted to resist the attack. It is at least arguable that if it fails to deter, resistance may well increase the risk of bodily injury to the victim. This possibility, as well as the evolution in societal expectations as to the level of danger a woman should risk when faced with sexual assault, are reflected in the Legislature's elimination of the resistance requirement. In so amending section 261(2), the Legislature has demonstrated its unwillingness to dictate a prescribed response to sexual assault. For the first time, the Legislature has assigned the decision as to whether a sexual assault should be resisted to the realm of personal choice.

The elimination of the resistance requirement is also consistent with the modern trend of removing evidentiary obstacles unique to the prosecution of sexual assault cases. For example, in enacting section 1112 in 1980, the Legislature barred psychiatric examinations of rape complainants. In recent years, the Legislature has also prohibited the instructional admonition that an "unchaste woman" is more likely to consent than her chaste counterpart; and has largely precluded the use of evidence of a complaining witness's sexual conduct to prove consent.

This court has made similar strides. Over a decade ago, the use of CALJIC No. 10.22, embodying the deprecatory "Hale instruction,"[18] was disapproved. That holding laid to juridical rest the notion that those who claim to be victims of sexual offenses are presumptively entitled to less credence than those who testify as the alleged victims of other crimes.

Moreover, consistent with the principle of *equalizing* the position of rape complainants before the fact-finder, this court recently disallowed expert testimony on the issue of "rape trauma syndrome" for the purpose of proving nonconsent and as a means of bolstering the prosecuting witness's testimony.

By removing resistance as a prerequisite to a rape conviction, the Legislature has brought the law of rape into conformity with other crimes such as robbery, kidnapping and assault, which require force, fear, and nonconsent to convict. In these crimes, the law does not expect falsity from

[18] Former CALJIC No. 10.22 read: A charge such as that made against the defendant in this case is one which is easily made and, once made, difficult to defend against, even if the person accused is innocent. Therefore, the law requires that you examine the testimony of the female person named in the information with caution. The instruction was based on Sir Matthew Hale's well-worn 17th century admonition that the testimony of "sometimes malicious and false" rape complainants must be cautiously scrutinized since rape "is an accusation easily to be made and hard to be proved, and harder to be defended by the party accused, tho never so innocent."

the complainant who alleges their commission and thus demand resistance as a corroboration and predicate to conviction. Nor does the law expect that in defending oneself or one's property from these crimes, a person must risk injury or death by displaying resistance in the face of attack. The amendment of section 261(2), acknowledges that previous expectational disparities, which singled out the credibility of rape complainants as suspect, have no place in a modern system of jurisprudence.

For these reasons, the Court of Appeal's reliance upon any absence of resistance by Marsha was improper.

The question remains whether proper application of amended section 261 to the instant facts compels reversal of appellant's convictions of rape by means of force or fear of unlawful bodily injury and false imprisonment.

The proper test to determine a claim of insufficient evidence in a criminal case is whether, on the entire record, a rational trier of fact could find appellant guilty beyond a reasonable doubt. In making this determination, the appellate court must view the evidence in a light most favorable to respondent and presume in support of the judgment the existence of every fact the trier could reasonably deduce from the evidence.

Marsha's testimony constitutes substantial evidence of rape by means of force or fear of immediate and unlawful bodily injury under the provisions of section 261, subdivision (2). From the moment she arrived at appellant's house, she communicated to him that she did not want to stay and intended to leave after purchasing marijuana. She initially refused appellant's suggestion that they go inside, but ultimately agreed so that she could obtain the marijuana. Once inside, she repeated her desire to proceed with the drug transaction so she could leave. She rebuffed the first round of appellant's physical advances by pushing him away and telling him to stop. When appellant disregarded this rebuff and continued his advances, Marsha left the room and went to the front gate. At this point, appellant's demeanor changed markedly. He cursed and berated Marsha for leaving, apparently in an effort to intimidate her.

At the front gate, Marsha repeatedly requested that appellant "let me leave," a plea which fell on deaf ears. Significantly, on at least one such occasion, appellant "reared back"—a gesture which made Marsha believe he was going to hit her. Appellant created the impression, even if it were untrue, that the outside gate was locked and that Marsha would not be able to open it. He reinforced this impression by telling her he would *let* her leave after he returned to the room for his shoes.

Back in the room, appellant shouted at Marsha, cursing the fact she had caused the door to slam. He interrupted his angry, verbal onslaught only to stop all activity and look at Marsha in a "funny" manner. He threatened her by displaying his muscles, grabbing her by the collar, and claiming he could pick her up with one hand and throw her out.

Most importantly, he ominously informed her he could make her do "anything he wanted" and that she was about to see the "bad side" of him. These statements were made in conjunction with his boasting of having had other women perform sex acts upon him and with Marsha's statement to him that she could not fight him. Appellant's response of pressing the door closed when he saw Marsha's movement toward it also suggested coercion. Finally, when Marsha initially refused to remove her clothes, appellant warned her—both physically and verbally—that her refusal "was going to make him angry."

In light of the totality of these circumstances, the jury, having observed the witnesses and their demeanor, could reasonably have concluded that Marsha's fear of physical violence from appellant if she did not submit to sexual intercourse was genuine and reasonable. Under these facts, a reasonable juror could have found that Marsha's subsequent compliance with appellant's urgent insistence on coitus was induced either by force, fear, or both, and, in any case, fell short of a consensual act.

RAPE SHIELD STATUTES

In many rape cases the defendant admits sex but claims the victim consented. Prior to the 1970s, courts generally allowed defense counsel to attempt to prove consent by offering evidence that the victim had consented to sex with other men. The idea was that an "unchaste" woman was more likely to have consented to sex with the defendant than a "virtuous" or "pure" woman. Evidence of "unchaste character" took three forms. First, if the victim testified, defense counsel could cross-examine the victim and ask her about the details of any previous sexual relationships with men other than defendant. Second, defense counsel was permitted to offer witnesses to testify that the victim had a bad reputation in the community for chastity. Third, defense counsel could call the victim's past lovers to the witness stand and have them describe their sexual relations with the victim. Thus, in many rape cases the defendant effectively put the victim "on trial."

In the 1970s, as part of the feminist movement, advocates sought reforms of rape law. Among other things, reform advocates sought to eliminate the use at trial of evidence of a woman's prior sexual relations with other men. Advocates argued that the fact that a woman had consensual sex with other men was not relevant to whether she consented to sex with defendant. This argument carried the day, and states enacted laws called "rape shield statutes" to limit evidence of the victim's prior sexual conduct with others. California's rape shield statutes are found in the Evidence Code.[15]

---

[15] California's rape shield statute is found at Evidence Code §§ 782; 1103(c). In addition to the rape shield found in the Evidence Code, the Penal Code provides:

CAN THE WAY A PERSON DRESSED BE RELEVANT IN A RAPE PROSECUTION?

Is the way a victim dressed ever relevant to a charge of forcible rape? Michael Kuzmich wrote:

> A Florida jury acquitted an alleged knife-wielding rapist because, as one juror put it, "The victim was dressed with that skirt, you could see everything she had. She was advertising for sex." The victim was wearing a short lace skirt, a brief top, and did not have any underwear on. Although the victim's clothing was admittedly less-than-modest, and there were stories that reported the victim to be a prostitute, it was the jurors' statements in justification of the acquittal that are so troubling. Said one female juror, "She was obviously dressed for a good time, but we felt she may have bit off more than she could chew."[16]

California Evidence Code § 1103(c)(2) provides: "Evidence of the manner in which the victim was dressed at the time of the commission of the offense shall not be admissible when offered by either party on the issue of consent in any prosecution for [rape], unless the evidence is determined by the court to be relevant and admissible in the interests of justice." The Uniform Code of Military Justice, 10 U.S.C. § 920(14) states, "The manner of dress of the person involved in the sexual conduct at issue shall not constitute consent."

PROBLEMS ON RAPE

1. Jane worked for a San Rafael accounting firm. Defendant was a customer of the firm. Defendant stopped by the accounting firm to sign his tax return. Jane walked from behind her desk to where Defendant was sitting to

---

§ 1127d. **Instruction on prior sexual conduct of victim in rape case**

(a) In any criminal prosecution for the crime of rape the jury shall not be instructed that it may be inferred that a person who has previously consented to sexual intercourse with persons other that the defendant or with the defendant would be therefore more likely to consent to sexual intercourse again. However, if evidence was received that the victim consented to and did engage in sexual intercourse with the defendant on one or more occasions prior to that charged against the defendant in this case, the jury shall be instructed that this evidence may be considered only as it relates to the question of whether the victim consented to the act of intercourse charged against the defendant in the case, or whether the defendant had a good faith reasonable belief that the victim consented to the act of sexual intercourse. The jury shall be instructed that it shall not consider this evidence for any other purpose.

(b) A jury shall not be instructed that the prior sexual conduct in and of itself of the complaining witness may be considered in determining the credibility of the witness.

§ 1127e. **Unchaste character; use of term prohibited**

The term "unchaste character" shall not be used by any court in any criminal case in which the defendant is charged with [rape].

[16] Michael John James Kuzmich, Chapter 127 Prevents Evidence of Victim's Manner of Dress in Rape Cases to Prove Consent, 30 *McGeorge Law Review* 637 (1999).

show him where to sign. Defendant stood up and grabbed Jane from behind, pinning her arms to her body. Defendant then tried to place his hand in her pants, but the pants were too tight. Defendant started to loosen Jane's pants zipper. Jane said, "Stop it. What do you think you are doing?" Jane tried to push Defendant away, but he became angry. Defendant said, "My penis is hard. Touch it." When Jane refused, Defendant grabbed Jane's hand and held it against his groin. Defendant pulled down Jane's pants and forced her to lie on the floor. Defendant unzipped his pants and pulled out his erect penis. At that moment, Jane's boss returned from lunch and walked in. Jane said, "Help," and her boss told Defendant to leave Jane alone and never return. Should Defendant be charged with a crime? Could Defendant claim the victim consented? *People v. Boo* (Cal. Ct. App. 2008) 2008 WL 2898661 (Nonpublished).

2. Mary is the branch manager at an Avis car rental office in Sacramento. Defendant called the office and lied to Mary, saying he was her boss's boss. Defendant told Mary, "I've heard good things about you. I think you are in line for a promotion. Listen, there is a potential client in town today who could bring several million dollars in business to us. His name is Michael Day, and he is going home to Texas this evening. I'd like you to take Mr. Day to lunch and sell our company to him. Get his account and you will have that promotion. Meet Mr. Day in front of the Hyatt Hotel where he is staying." Mary drove to the Hyatt, where Defendant was standing out front posing as the non-existent Mr. Day. As Mary drove out of the parking lot, she asked, "Where would you like to eat?" Defendant said, "I'm not really hungry." Defendant directed Mary to drive to a park and park the car in a secluded area. Defendant stroked Mary's shoulder and said, "You are very attractive." Mary became frightened and said, "What are you doing?" Defendant replied, "Well, how are you going to sell the company to me? I'd hate to have to tell your boss you proved him wrong." Defendant touched Mary's thigh. She pushed his hand away. Defendant said, "Your boss assured me that you would take care of me." Mary said, "Listen, I'm not comfortable with this. I'm taking you back to the hotel." Defendant removed his penis from his pants and started masturbating. Mary said, "Put your dick back in your pants." Defendant grabbed Mary's hand and placed it on his penis. Mary yanked her hand away. Defendant then forced Mary's head toward his penis, causing his penis to briefly enter her mouth. Mary pulled her head away. Defendant masturbated until he ejaculated. He said, "I'll tell your boss you took care of me." Should Defendant be charged with a crime? *People v. Adams* (Cal. Ct. App. 2008) 2008 WL 4226866 (Nonpublished).

3. Sue had previously dated Defendant, and they had engaged in consensual sex. Long after they broke up, Defendant dropped by Sue's apartment to visit. They started drinking. With her consent, Defendant gave Sue a back massage. Sue went into her bedroom to retrieve something, and Defendant followed her. Defendant lay down on the bed and motioned Sue to lie down with him, which she did. Defendant started rubbing Sue's back, and Sue said, "I don't want to do anything tonight." Defendant became angry and

told Sue she was a bitch. They argued about Sue's refusal to have sex. The argument turned physical, with Sue hitting Defendant and Defendant hitting Sue. Sue started to cry, and Defendant said, "Your tears are not going to help you." Defendant removed his pants and said, "Take off your clothes." When Sue refused, Defendant removed her clothes. Defendant lay Sue on the bed and had intercourse with her. Sue did not resist. She simply lay on the bed motionless and crying until Defendant ejaculated. Should Defendant be charged with a crime? *People v. Newman* (Cal. Ct. App. 2008) 2008 WL 4817017 (Nonpublished).

4. Beth is 28 years of age. She was born deaf and mute. Beth has cerebral palsy, a seizure disorder, and is developmentally delayed, functioning at the level of a 12-year-old child. Beth is paralyzed on her right side. Beth can walk, but slowly and with a pronounced limp. Although Beth cannot talk, she can use sign language to communicate. Beth worked part time at a restaurant folding napkins. Defendant is a taxi driver. He drives a taxi van, and he regularly took Beth to work and then drove her home after work. One day, Defendant picked Beth up at her mother's home where she lived. Rather than drive to the restaurant, Defendant drove to a secluded area and parked. Defendant entered the passenger area of the van via the side door. Defendant and Beth gave very different versions of what happened next. According to Beth, Defendant removed his pants, removed her pants, placed a condom on his penis, and penetrated her vagina, all without saying a word. Beth did not consent. After he ejaculated, he dressed Beth and himself and drove her to work. According to Defendant, he parked the van because he was concerned that Beth's seat belt was not properly attached. When he climbed into the back of the van he noticed that Beth was "playing with herself." Beth unzipped his pants and tried to pull out his penis. Defendant resisted Beth's advances. Beth signed, "Make love to me." Defendant put on a condom and had consensual sex with Beth. He then drove Beth to work. Should Defendant be charged with a crime? *People v. De La Cruz* (Cal. Ct. App. 2008) 2008 WL 5401639 (Nonpublished).

5. Sojka met the victim at a bar. They drank, played pool, and talked for several hours, enjoying each other's company. Over the course of the evening, Sojka and the victim were mildly amorous with one another. Sojka offered the victim a ride home. Upon arriving at the victim's apartment, they kissed in the car, and the victim invited Sojka to come in. Once inside the victim's apartment, their accounts of what happened differed. According to the victim, she went to the bathroom, and when she came out, Sojka was standing there completely naked. Sojka forced himself on her. She was shocked and said "Stop it." Sojka persisted and removed the victim's clothes, kissed her all over, digitally penetrated her vagina, performed oral sex on her, and asked her to orally copulate him, which she refused to do. The victim did not scream. The victim objected the entire time. When Sojka climbed on top of the victim and attempted intercourse, he finally began to heed the victim's pleas to stop. Sojka got dressed and left. Sojka, on the other hand, stated that after the victim came out of the bathroom, the two started kissing, removed each other's clothes, and

dropped to the floor. He fondled the victim and performed oral sex on her. The victim seemed excited and was moaning with pleasure. The victim did not complain, resist, or act like she wanted him to stop. When Sojka climbed on top of the victim to initiate sexual intercourse, she pushed him away and yelled at him to stop. He got up, put his clothes on, and left. Attempted rape? *People v. Sojka* (2011) 196 Cal.App.4th 733, 126 Cal.Rptr.3d 400.

6. Prado threatened a woman with violence unless she put her finger in her own vagina. Rape? *Commonwealth v. Prado* (2018) 94 Mass. App. Ct. 253, 113 N.E.3d 365.

OTHER SEX OFFENSES IN CALIFORNIA LAW

The Penal Code contains numerous sex crimes in addition to rape. Thus, it is a crime to inveigle or entice a minor into prostitution (PC § 266). It is a felony to "purchase" an individual to place the person into prostitution (PC § 266e). Pimping and pandering are against the law (PC §§ 266h, 266i). It is a wobbler to induce another to engage in sexual intercourse, sexual penetration, oral copulation, or sodomy when the victim's consent is procured by fraud or false statement that is intended to create fear in the victim (PC § 266c). Bigamy is a crime (PC § 281). Sodomy is "sexual conduct consisting of contact between the penis of one person and the anus of another person" (PC § 286). Sodomy with a minor is a crime, as is forcible sodomy against a victim of any age. Oral copulation of a child is a crime, as is forcible oral copulation against a victim of any age (PC § 288a). Sexual assault on an animal is a misdemeanor (PC § 286.5). Lewd or lascivious acts upon children are punishable (PC § 288). Incest (PC § 285) is defined as "Persons being within the degrees of consanguinity within which marriages are declared by law to be incestuous and void, who intermarry with each other, or who being 14 years of age or older, commit fornication or adultery with each other, are punishable by imprisonment." In *People v. McEvoy* (2013) 215 Cal. App. 4th 431, 154 Cal. Rptr. 3d 914, McEvoy was two years older than his sister. Both were adults. One night, the victim awoke to find McEvoy licking her vagina. McEvoy said, "We were meant to be. We are soulmates. We will always be together." Frightened, the victim "froze." McEvoy pulled down the victim's underwear and penetrated her vagina with his penis. The victim pretended to be asleep. Charged with incest, McEvoy argued "that section 285 violates the right to liberty under the due process clause of the Fourteenth amendment by criminalizing consensual sexual activity between adults. His argument was based on *Lawrence v. Texas* (2003) 539 U.S. 558, 123 S. Ct. 2472, 156 L. Ed. 2d 508, which found unconstitutional a Texas statute prohibiting 'deviate sexual intercourse with another individual of the same sex.'" Should McEvoy's argument carry the day?

CHILD SEXUAL ABUSE

Child sexual abuse is common. The true prevalence of sexual abuse of children is unknown because the crime occurs in secret. It is estimated that approximately 20 percent of girls experience some form of sexually inappropriate experience during childhood, from minor touching to brutal rape. The rate of abuse among boys appears to be lower than among girls. Five to fifteen percent of boys are sexually abused. Sexual abuse occurs at all ages, from infancy through adolescence.

Most child sexual abuse victims know the perpetrator. Finkelhor writes, "Sexual abuse is committed primarily by individuals known to the child, unlike the child molester stereotype that prevailed until the 1970s. In adult retrospective surveys, victims of abuse indicate that no more than 10% to 30% of offenders were strangers, with the remainder being either family members or acquaintances."[17] Because the perpetrator often has continuing access to the victim, multiple episodes of sexual abuse are common.

Sexual abuse has short- and long-term effects. Berliner writes, "Research conducted over the past 3 decades indicates that a wide range of psychological, health, and interpersonal problems are more prevalent among those who have been sexually abused in childhood compared to those who have not."[18] It is important to understand that not all sexually abused children exhibit manifestations of harm or stress. For children who are symptomatic, symptoms vary from child to child. With the exception of Posttraumatic Stress Disorder, aspects of which are seen in approximately half of abused children, there is no symptom or group of symptoms that is observed in a majority of sexually abused children. Generally, the more severe the abuse, the more likely the child will be symptomatic.

Sexual abuse is often difficult to prove in court. In *Pennsylvania v. Ritchie* (1987) 480 U.S. 39, 60, 107 S.Ct. 989, the Supreme Court wrote, "Child abuse is one of the most difficult crimes to detect and prosecute, in large part because there often are no witnesses except the victim."[19] In the same vein, the New York Court of Appeals wrote in *In re Nicole V.* (1987) 71 N.Y.2d 112, 117, 524 N.Y.S.2d 19, 518 N.E.2d 914, "Abuse is difficult to detect because the acts are predominantly nonviolent and usually occur in secret rendering the child the only witness."

Unlike physical child abuse, where the child's injuries often provide powerful evidence, medical evidence is lacking in most sexual abuse

---

[17] David Finkelhor, Current Information on the Scope and Nature of Child Sexual Abuse, 4 *The Future of Children* 31–53, at 45 (1994).

[18] Lucy Berliner, Child Sexual Abuse: Definitions, Prevalence, and Consequences. In John E.B. Myers (Ed.), *The APSAC Handbook on Child Maltreatment* 215–232, at 221 (3d ed. 2011) (Sage).

[19] 480 U.S. at 60.

cases.[20] Typically, the child's testimony is the most important evidence. When children are prepared for the courtroom and provided emotional support through the process, most testify effectively. Yet, testifying is not easy. The Washington Supreme Court observed in *State v. Jones* (1989) 112 Wash.2d 488, 772 P.2d 496, 499, "Feeling intimidated and confused by courtroom processes, embarrassed at having to describe sexual matters, and uncomfortable in their role as accuser of a defendant who may be a parent, other relative or friend, children often are unable or unwilling to recount the abuses committed on them."[21] Some children are too young, too traumatized, or too frightened to testify effectively or at all.

SEXUAL PSYCHOPATH LAWS AND THEIR MODERN-DAY DESCENDANTS

The brutal rape or sexual assault of a child by a stranger outrages the public, frightens parents, generates media coverage, and activates politicians.[22] The reaction is particularly intense when a sex offender murders a child. In a newspaper article in 1937, F.B.I. director J. Edgar Hoover warned, "The sex fiend, most loathsome of all the vast army of crime, has become a sinister threat to the safety of American childhood and womanhood."[23] During the 1940s and 1950s popular magazines discussed the danger of sex offenders and offered advice to protect children.[24] In 1946, *Coronet* magazine published a widely read article stating, "The sexual

[20] For in-depth analysis of proof of child abuse *see* John E.B. Myers, *Myers on Evidence of Interpersonal Violence: Child Maltreatment, Intimate Partner Violence, Rape, Stalking, and Elder Abuse* (6th ed. 2016).

[21] *State v. Jones* (1989) 112 Wash.2d 488, 772 P.2d 496, 499.

[22] *See* Philip Jenkins, *Moral Panic: Changing Concepts of the Child Molester in Modern America* (1998) (Yale University Press); Benjamin Apfelberg, Carl Sugar & Arnold Z. Pheffer, A Psychiatric Study of 250 Sex Offenders, 100 *American Journal of Psychiatry* 762–770 (1944) ("Because children have often been the sexual objects of perverts, the community has demanded swift and severe punishment for such offenders."); Crime: Horror Week, *Newsweek* p. 19 (Nov. 28, 1949) ("Either there was an unusual spate of ghastly sex crimes against children last week or some quirk in the week's news reporting made it seem so. In Los Angeles, headlines told of the discovery of the body of 6-year-old Linda Joyce Glucoft, stabbed with an ice pick and strangled with a necktie about the neck. The body was found in a rubbish heap in the yard of Fred Stroble, 67-year-old baker already wanted on a child-molestation charge." The story contains pictures of Stroble in his jail cell, the victim while she was alive, and her distraught parents); Ralph Brancale & F. Lovell Bixby, How to Treat Sex Offenders, 184 *The Nation* 293–295 (April 6, 1957) ("spectacular and brutal sex crimes have a special power to inflame public sentiment which quickly embraces all sex offenders, the harmless as well as the dangerous."); Crime: The Sex Rampage, *Newsweek*, p. 22 (Feb. 13, 1950) ("A sex crime against a child is so horrible that it arouses the wrath of the community in which it occurs like no other event. Several of them arouse the whole nation and, if spread over the front pages of newspapers, become a 'sex crime wave.' ").

[23] J. Edgar Hoover, War on the Sex Criminal, *New York Herald Tribune* (Sept. 26, 1937).

[24] *See, e.g.,* Irma W. Hewlett, What Shall We Do About Sex Offenders?, 25 *Parents Magazine* 36, 38, 67–68, 70–71 (August, 1950) ("A great number of such crimes occur all over the country."); Medicine: Sex Psychopaths, *Newsweek*, p. 50 (March 9, 1953) (stressing the danger of sex offenders); Edith M. Stern, The Facts on Sex Offenders, 29 *Parents Magazine* 42–43, 137–138, 140 (1954) ("When such a sexual offense against a child is reported, our habitual feeling of safety is blown to bits. Sickened, frightened, appalled, we feel that something, anything must be done to protect our children from such experiences.").

pervert is lurking right now in the community where you live."[25] *Coronet* offered eight recommendations. First, "vice squads should operate constantly in every community, tirelessly tracking down every instance of perversion, however slight." Second, communities should keep track of sex offenders and should supply the data to the F.B.I. Third, citizens should be on the watch for perverts, and should turn them in. Fourth, many sex offenders are not only criminals, they are crazy and should be locked up. Fifth, states should provide indeterminate commitment for insane sex criminals. Sixth, plea bargaining with sex offenders should be "outlawed immediately." Seventh, research into sex offenders should be funded. Eighth, parents and teachers should provide sex education to children, including information on the dangers of sex offenders.

Beginning in Michigan in 1937, many states—including California—enacted special laws dealing with sex offenders. The laws were called "Sexual Psychopath Acts" or "Mentally Disordered Sex Offender Laws." Among other things, the laws authorized involuntary psychiatric hospitalization of certain dangerous sex offenders. Psychiatrist Karl Bowman described the laws, "In California and in a considerable number of other states the traditional body of sex crime law has been supplemented by legislation providing specialized procedures for detaining and treating dangerous sex deviates. The basic idea of these new types of law is that numerous sex offenders who are neither insane nor mentally deficient are characterized by personality disorders which predispose them, without regard to consequences, to the commission of sex acts considered dangerous to society. It is felt that imprisonment and other traditional legal penalties will neither deter them or have any rehabilitative effects on them. As an alternative or addition, provisions for treatment and prevention are authorized."[26]

Sexual psychopath laws were little used in most states, and by the 1970s they were largely a dead letter. In the 1990s, however, sexual psychopath laws were resurrected. At the beginning of the twenty-first century, all states have one or more of the following: sex offender registration laws, public notification laws, or involuntary civil commitment laws.

Sex Offender Registration

All states have laws requiring convicted sex offenders to register with designated law enforcement authorities. (PC § 290 et seq.). Failure to register is a crime. Police agencies use registry information to generate

[25] Charles Harris, Sex Crimes: Their Cause and Cure, 20 *Coronet* 3–9 (August, 1946).

[26] Karl M. Bowman, *California Sexual Deviation Research* p. 34 (January, 1953) (California Department of Mental Hygiene).

lists of suspects in investigations. Many states allow certain employers to inquire whether job applicants are registered sex offenders.

Public Notification of Sex Offenders Living in the Community

Under registration laws, the police know the whereabouts of sex offenders. The public, however, is generally not privy to registry information. Is it wise to provide information on sex offenders to the public, or, more narrowly, to families living near offenders? On the one hand, parents are in the best position to protect their children from a sex offender living nearby. On the other hand, disclosure of information to the public is a major invasion of privacy, leading to stigma, ostracism, and even vigilantism. The specter of vigilantism is not just theoretical. Washington was the first state to enact a community notification statute. Not long thereafter, a convicted child rapist was about to be released from prison. Five days prior to release, the local sheriff distributed fliers containing his picture, a description of his crime, and a statement that he received no treatment while in prison. A crowd gathered where the offender planned to live, and a short time later the house burned to the ground.

The Washington community notification statute started a cascade of similar laws, usually called Megan's laws to honor seven-year-old Megan Kanka, who was murdered by a twice-convicted sex offender living across the street from Megan's family. In 1994, the offender lured Megan into his house, where he brutally raped her and strangled her with a belt. If Megan's parents had known a dangerous sex offender lived across the street, perhaps they could have protected her. Megan's tragic death spurred states and the federal government to action, and all states now have some form of Megan's law (PC § 290.45).

Public notification laws were challenged in court. The Megan's law in New Jersey was attacked as a violation of the constitution. In 1995, the New Jersey Supreme Court rejected the challenge, writing, "The Constitution does not prevent society from attempting to protect itself from convicted sex offenders. To rule otherwise is to find that society is unable to protect itself from sexual predators by adopting the simple remedy of informing the public of their presence."[27]

Involuntary Civil Commitment of Violent Sexual Predators

Some particularly dangerous convicted sex offenders are not safe at large. Yet, when their prison term expires, they are entitled to release. Most such offenders cannot be committed for psychiatric treatment because they do not have the kind of mental illness required for involuntary psychiatric hospitalization. In 1990, Washington State passed a law

[27] *Doe v. Poritz* (1995) 142 N.J. 1, 662 A.2d 367, 422.

permitting involuntary civil commitment of "sexually violent predators." Other states, including California, followed suit (California Welfare and Institutions Code § 6600 et seq.). In 1997, the U.S. Supreme Court upheld the constitutionality of civil commitment laws.[28]

[28] *Kansas v. Hendricks* (1997) 521 U.S. 346, 117 S.Ct. 2072.

CHAPTER 7

ACCOMPLICE LIABILITY

■ ■ ■

The person who commits a crime is the perpetrator. In California, the perpetrator is called a principal. An accomplice is someone who assists the principal, and who intends that the crime be committed.[1] In California, an accomplice is also a principal. (PC § 31). In *People v. Thompson* (2010) 49 Cal.4th 79, 116–118, 109 Cal.Rptr.3d 549, 231 P.3d 289, the Supreme Court provided a concise description of accomplice liability:

> Principals include those who aid and abet in the commission of a crime. Aider and abettor liability is premised on the combined acts of all the principals, but on the aider and abettor's own *mens rea*. We have defined the required mental states and acts for aiding and abetting as: (a) the direct perpetrator's *actus reus*—a crime committed by the direct perpetrator, (b) the aider and abettor's *mens rea*—knowledge of the direct perpetrator's unlawful intent and an intent to assist in achieving those unlawful ends, and (c) the aider and abettor's *actus reus*—conduct by the aider and abettor that in fact assists the achievement of the crime. A sharp line does not always exist between the direct perpetrator and the aider and abettor: It is often an oversimplification to describe one person as the actual perpetrator and the other as the aider and abettor. When two or more persons commit a crime together, both may act in part as the actual perpetrator *and* in part as the aider and abettor of the other, who also acts in part as an actual perpetrator. One person might lure the victim into a trap while another fires the gun; in a stabbing case, one person might restrain the victim while the other does the stabbing. In either case, both participants would be direct perpetrators as well as aiders and abettors of the other. The aider and abettor doctrine merely makes aiders and abettors liable for their accomplices' actions as well as their own. It obviates the

---

[1] *See Rosemond v. United States* (2014) 572 U.S. 65, 134 S. Ct. 1240 ("a person may be responsible for a crime he has not personally carried out if he helps another to complete its commission.").

An accomplice does not have to participate in every aspect of the crime. In *Rosemond v. United States* (2014) 572 U.S. 65, 134 S. Ct. 1240, 1246, the Supreme Court wrote, "The common law imposed aiding and abetting liability on a person (possessing the requisite intent) who facilitated any part—even though not every part—of a criminal venture."

necessity to decide who was the aider and abettor and who the direct perpetrator or to what extent each played which role.

Everyday examples of accomplices are the getaway driver who sits in the car while the robbers rob the bank, and the lookout who stands a block away from the bank watching for police. In *Thompson*, the Supreme Court referred to an accomplice as an aider and abettor. The word "aider" refers to the conduct of an accomplice. The word "abettor" refers to the accomplice's mental state.

Mere presence at the scene of a crime does not make one an accomplice. In the bank robbery described above, the customers and bank employees are not accomplices—they are victims. There is generally no duty to stop or prevent crime, so bank customers and employees who comply with the robbers' demand, "Don't move," do not become accomplices by complying, and "allowing" the crime to continue.

An accomplice is guilty of the crime committed by the perpetrator. CALCRIM 400 states: "A person may be guilty of a crime in two ways. One, he or she may have directly committed the crime. I will call that person the perpetrator. Two, he or she may have aided and abetted a perpetrator, who directly committed the crime. A person is equally guilty of the crime whether he or she committed it personally or aided and abetted the perpetrator who committed it."

In the bank robbery mentioned above, the getaway driver and the lookout are guilty of bank robbery. The getaway driver will not be heard to say, "But I didn't rob the bank. I was sitting outside in a car." The lookout cannot defend by saying, "You can't convict me. I was a block away. I never got close to the bank." Again, an accomplice is guilty of the crime committed by the perpetrator.

It is important to understand that an accomplice is not charged with or convicted of the "crime" of accomplice. There is no such crime. An accomplice derives liability from the perpetrator who commits the crime. Accomplice liability grows out of the relationship between the person who commits a crime and the accomplice(s). Thus, if the perpetrator committed robbery, the accomplice is guilty of robbery.

At common law, four terms were used to describe the parties to crime: (1) principal in the first degree; (2) principal in the second degree; (3) accessory before the fact; (4) and accessory after the fact.

A principal in the first degree is the perpetrator of the crime—the person who personally commits the *actus reus* with the necessary *mens rea*. A principal in the second degree (accomplice) aids, assists, or encourages the crime and is actually or constructively present at the scene of the crime. In the bank robbery described above, the getaway driver and the lookout are principals in the second degree. An accessory before the fact (also an accomplice) aids, assists, or encourages the crime but is not actually or constructively present at the scene of the crime. An example of an accessory before the fact is the person who knew about the bank robbery and obtained the guns used for the robbery, but was miles away when the bank was robbed.

An accessory after the fact was defined at common law as a person who did not take part in the planning or perpetration of the crime, but who, after the crime was committed, sheltered, hid, or otherwise assisted the parties to avoid arrest or prosecution. At early common law, an accessory after the fact could be convicted of the crime committed by the principal in the first degree. Thus, in the bank robbery described above, an accessory after the fact could be convicted of the bank robbery even though the accessory played no role in the planning or perpetration of the robbery. Today, an accessory after the fact is not convicted of the crime committed by the principal in the first degree. Today, someone who helps a criminal avoid arrest or prosecution may be convicted of some variety of obstruction of justice.

California law does not use the terms principal in the first degree, principal in the second degree, and accessory before the fact.[2] PC § 30 states, "The parties to crimes are classified as: (1) Principals; and (2) Accessories." PC § 31 provides, "All persons concerned in the commission of a crime, whether it be felony or misdemeanor, and whether they directly commit the act constituting the offense, or aid and abet in its commission, or, not being present, have advised and encouraged its commission are principals in any crime so committed."

Section 31 provides that a person is a principal who uses an "innocent instrumentality" such as a child or a person with intellectual disability to commit the *actus reus*.

Section 32 defines accessory as follows: "Every person who, after a felony has been committed, harbors, conceals, or aids a principal in such felony, with the intent that said principal may avoid or escape from arrest, trial, conviction or punishment, having knowledge that said principal has committed such felony or has been charged with such felony or convicted thereof, is an accessory to such felony." Section 33 provides the punishment for an accessory—a fine not exceeding $5,000 or imprisonment in state prison, or imprisonment in county jail up to one year.

In *People v. Plengsangtip* (2007) 148 Cal.App.4th 825, 836, 56 Cal.Rptr.3d 165, the Court of Appeal stated the elements of accessory liability: "(1) someone other than the accused, that is, a principal, must have committed a specific, completed felony; (2) the accused must have

[2] The Penal Code of 1873 stated in a note that in California the word "principal" includes what at common law would be "the principal of the first and second degree, and the accessory before the fact." p. 34.

harbored, concealed, or aided the principal; (3) with knowledge that the principal committed the felony; and (4) with the intent that the principal avoid or escape from arrest, trial, conviction, or punishment." In *People v. Moomey* (2011) 194 Cal.App.4th 850, 123 Cal.Rptr.3d 749, the Court of Appeal described the "knowledge" requirement of accessory liability: "Knowledge that the principal committed a felony or has been charged with the commission of one is an essential element of accessory liability. In determining whether the alleged accessory has such knowledge, the jury may consider such factors has his possible presence at the crime or other means of knowledge of its commission, as well as his companionship and relationship with the principal before and after the offense."

The Supreme Court's decision in *People v. Beeman* provides a helpful analysis of accomplice liability.

PEOPLE V. BEEMAN

California Supreme Court
35 Cal.3d 547, 199 Cal.Rptr. 60, 674 P.2d 1318 (1984)

REYNOSO, J.

Timothy Mark Beeman appeals from a judgment of conviction of robbery, burglary, false imprisonment, destruction of telephone equipment and assault with intent to commit a felony (Pen. Code §§ 211, 459, 236, 591, 221). Appellant was not present during commission of the offenses. His conviction rested on the theory that he aided and abetted his acquaintances James Gray and Michael Burk.

The primary issue before us is whether the standard California Jury Instructions (CALJIC Nos. 3.00 and 3.01) adequately inform the jury of the criminal intent required to convict a defendant as an aider and abettor of the crime.

We hold that instruction No. 3.01 is erroneous. Sound law, embodied in a long line of California decisions, requires proof that an aider and abettor rendered aid with an intent or purpose of either committing, or of encouraging or facilitating commission of, the target offense. It was, therefore, error for the trial court to refuse the modified instruction requested by appellant. Our examination of the record convinces us that the error in this case was prejudicial and we therefore reverse appellant's convictions.

James Gray and Michael Burk drove from Oakland to Redding for the purpose of robbing appellant's sister-in-law, Mrs. Marjorie Beeman, of valuable jewelry, including a 3.5 carat diamond ring. They telephoned the residence to determine that she was home. Soon thereafter Burk knocked at the door of the victim's house, presented himself as a poll taker, and asked to be let in. When Mrs. Beeman asked for identification, he forced her into the hallway and entered. Gray, disguised in a ski mask, followed. The two subdued the victim, placed tape over her mouth and eyes and tied her to a bathroom fixture. Then they ransacked the house, taking numerous pieces of jewelry and a set of silverware. The jewelry included a 3.5 carat, heart-shaped diamond ring and a blue sapphire ring. The total value of these two rings was over $100,000. In the course of the robbery, telephone wires inside the house were cut.

Appellant was arrested six days later in Emeryville. He had in his possession several of the less valuable of the stolen rings. He supplied the police with information that led to the arrests of Burk and Gray. With Gray's cooperation appellant assisted police in recovering most of the stolen property.

Burk, Gray and appellant were jointly charged. After the trial court severed the trials, Burk and Gray pled guilty to robbery. At appellant's trial they testified that he had been extensively involved in planning the crime.

Burk testified that he had known appellant for two and one-half years. He had lived in appellant's apartment several times. Appellant had talked to him about rich relatives in Redding and had described a diamond ring worth $50,000. According to Burk the feasibility of robbing appellant's relatives was first mentioned two and one-half months before the incident occurred. About one week before the robbery, the discussions became more specific. Appellant gave Burk the address and discussed the ruse of posing as a poll taker. It was decided that Gray and Burk would go to Redding because appellant wanted nothing to do with the actual robbery and because he feared being recognized. On the night before the offense appellant drew a floor plan of the victim's house and told Burk where the diamond ring was likely to be found. Appellant agreed to sell the jewelry for 20 percent of the proceeds.

Two days before the offense, appellant told Gray that he wanted nothing to do with the robbery of his relatives. On the day preceding the incident appellant and Gray spoke on the telephone. At that time appellant repeated he wanted nothing to do with the robbery, but confirmed that he had told Burk that he would not say anything if the others went ahead.

Appellant Beeman's testimony contradicted that of Burk and Gray as to nearly every material element of his own involvement. Appellant testified that he did not participate in the robbery or its planning. He confirmed that Burk had lived with him on several occasions, and that he had told Burk about Mrs. Beeman's jewelry, the valuable diamond ring, and the Beeman ranch, in the course of day-to-day conversations. He claimed that he had sketched a floor plan of the house some nine months prior to the robbery, only for the purpose of comparing it with the layout of a house belonging to another brother. He at first denied and then admitted describing the Beeman family cars, but insisted this never occurred in the context of planning a robbery.

Appellant stated that Burk first suggested that robbing Mrs. Beeman would be easy some five months before the incident. At that time, and on the five or six subsequent occasions when Burk raised the subject, appellant told Burk that his friends could do what they wanted but that he wanted no part of such a scheme.

Appellant agreed that he had talked with Gray on the phone two days before the robbery, and said he had then repeated he did not want to be involved. He claimed that Burk called him on the way back from Redding because he feared appellant would report him to the police, but knew appellant would want to protect Gray, who was his closer friend.

Appellant requested that the jury be instructed that aiding and abetting liability requires proof of intent to aid. The request was denied.

After three hours of deliberation, the jury submitted two written questions to the court: "We would like to hear again how one is determined to be an accessory and by what actions can he absolve himself"; and "Does inaction mean the party is guilty?" The jury was reinstructed in accord with the standard instructions, CALJIC Nos. 3.00 and 3.01. The court denied appellant's renewed request that the instructions be modified, explaining that giving another, slightly different instruction at this point would further complicate matters. The jury returned its verdicts of guilty on all counts two hours later.

Penal Code section 31 provides in pertinent part: "All persons concerned in the commission of a crime, whether they directly commit the act constituting the offense, or aid and abet in its commission, or, not being present, have advised and encouraged its commission, are principals in any crime so committed." Thus, those persons who at common law would have been termed accessories before the fact and principals in the second degree as well as those who actually perpetrate the offense, are to be prosecuted, tried and punished as principals in California. The term "aider and abettor" is now often used to refer to principals other than the perpetrator, whether or not they are present at the commission of the offense.

CALJIC No. 3.00 defines principals to a crime to include "Those who, with knowledge of the unlawful purpose of the one who does directly and actively commit or attempt to commit the crime, aid and abet in its commission, or those who, whether present or not at the commission or attempted commission of the crime, advise and encourage its commission." CALJIC No. 3.01 defines aiding and abetting as follows: "A person aids and abets the commission of a crime if, with knowledge of the unlawful purpose of the perpetrator of the crime, he aids, promotes, encourages or instigates by act or advice the commission of such crime."

Appellant asserts that the current instructions, in particular CALJIC No. 3.01, substitute an element of knowledge of the perpetrator's intent for the element of criminal intent of the accomplice, in contravention of common law principles and California case law. He argues that the instruction given permitted the jury to convict him of the same offenses as the perpetrators without finding that he harbored either the same criminal intent as they, or the specific intent to assist them, thus depriving him of his constitutional rights to due process and equal protection of the law. Appellant further urges that the error requires reversal because it removed a material issue from the jury and on this record it is impossible to conclude that the jury necessarily resolved the same factual question that would have been presented by the missing instruction.

The People argue that the standard instruction properly reflects California law, which requires no more than that the aider and abettor have knowledge of the perpetrator's criminal purpose and do a voluntary act which in fact aids the perpetrator.

There is no question that an aider and abettor must have criminal intent in order to be convicted of a criminal offense. The essential conflict in current appellate opinions is between those cases which state that an aider and abettor must have an intent or purpose to commit or assist in the commission of the criminal offenses, and those finding it sufficient that the aider and abettor engage in the required acts with knowledge of the perpetrator's criminal purpose.

We conclude that the weight of authority and sound law require proof that an aider and abettor act with knowledge of the criminal purpose of the perpetrator *and* with an intent or purpose either of committing, or of encouraging or facilitating commission of, the offense.

When the definition of the offense includes the intent to do some act or achieve some consequence beyond the *actus reus* of the crime, the aider and abettor must share the specific intent of the perpetrator. By "share" we mean neither that the aider and abettor must be prepared to commit the offense by his or her own act should the perpetrator fail to do so, nor that the aider and abettor must seek to share the fruits of the crime. Rather, an aider and abettor will "share" the perpetrator's specific intent when he or she knows the full extent of the perpetrator's criminal purpose and gives aid or encouragement with the intent or purpose of facilitating the perpetrator's commission of the crime.

CALJIC No. 3.01 inadequately defines aiding and abetting because it fails to insure that an aider and abettor will be found to have the required mental state with regard to his or her own act. While the instruction does include the word "abet," which encompasses the intent required by law, the word is arcane and its full import unlikely to be recognized by modern jurors. Moreover, even if jurors were made aware that "abet" means to encourage or facilitate, and implicitly to harbor an intent to further the crime encouraged, the instruction does not *require* them to find that intent because it defines an aider and abettor as one who "aids, promotes, encourages *or* instigates." Thus, the instruction would technically allow a conviction if the defendant knowing of the perpetrator's unlawful purpose, negligently or accidentally aided the commission of the crime.

We suggest that an appropriate instruction should inform the jury that a person aids and abets the commission of a crime when he or she, acting with (1) knowledge of the unlawful purpose of the perpetrator; and (2) the intent or purpose of committing, encouraging, or facilitating the commission of the offense, (3) by act or advice aids, promotes, encourages or instigates, the commission of the crime.

Following the Supreme Court's *Beeman* decision, the jury instruction on aiding and abetting was changed. The instruction is now found at CALCRIM 401, providing:

> To prove that the defendant is guilty of a crime based on aiding and abetting that crime, the People must prove that:
>
> 1. The perpetrator committed the crime;
>
> 2. The defendant knew that the perpetrator intended to commit the crime;
>
> 3. Before or during the commission of the crime, the defendant intended to aid and abet the perpetrator in committing the crime;
>
> AND
>
> 4. The defendant's words or conduct did in fact aid and abet the perpetrator's commission of the crime.
>
> Someone aids and abets a crime if he or she knows of the perpetrator's unlawful purpose and he or she specifically intends to, and does in fact, aid, facilitate, promote, encourage, or instigate the perpetrator's commission of that crime.
>
> If all of these requirements are provided, the defendant does not need to actually have been present when the crime was committed to be guilty as an aider and abettor.

During jury deliberations in *Beeman,* jurors asked the judge "by what actions can [a defendant] absolve himself" of accomplice liability. CALCRIM 401 provides the answer:

A person who aids and abets a crime is not guilty of that crime if he or she withdraws before the crime is committed. To withdraw, a person must do two things:

1. He or she must notify everyone else he or she knows is involved in the commission of the crime that he or she is no longer participating. The notification must be made early enough to prevent the commission of the crime.

AND

2. He or she must do everything reasonably within his or her power to prevent the crime from being committed. He or she does not have to actually prevent the crime.

The People have the burden of proving beyond a reasonable doubt that the defendant did not withdraw. If the People have not met this burden, you may not find the defendant guilty under an aiding and abetting theory.

Do you agree that defendant Timothy Beeman's efforts to withdraw fell short of the requirements of CALCRIM 401?

The Supreme Court's decision in *People v. McCoy* clarifies the relationship between perpetrator and accomplice.

PEOPLE V. MCCOY

California Supreme Court
25 Cal.4th 1111, 108 Cal.Rptr.2d 188, 24 P.3d 1210 (2001)

CHIN, J.

We granted review to decide whether an aider and abettor may be guilty of greater homicide-related offenses than those the actual perpetrator committed. Because defenses or extenuating circumstances may exist that are personal to the actual perpetrator and do not apply to the aider and abettor, the answer, sometimes, is yes. We reverse the judgment of the Court of Appeal, which concluded otherwise.

Codefendants Ejaan Dupree McCoy and Derrick Lakey were tried together and convicted of crimes arising out of a drive-by shooting in Stockton in 1995. McCoy drove the car and Lakey was in the front passenger seat, with others in the back. The car approached four people standing on a street corner. McCoy leaned out of the window and shouted something. A flurry of shots was fired from the car toward the group. Witnesses saw both McCoy and Lakey shooting handguns. Two of the group were shot, one fatally. The other two escaped injury. Someone from outside the car returned fire, wounding Lakey. The evidence showed that McCoy fired the fatal bullets.

At trial, McCoy but not Lakey testified. McCoy admitted shooting but claimed he did so because he believed he would be shot himself.

A jury found McCoy and Lakey guilty of various crimes, including first degree murder and two counts of attempted murder. The Court of Appeal unanimously reversed McCoy's murder and attempted murder convictions, finding that the trial court prejudicially misinstructed the jury on McCoy's theory of unreasonable self-defense, a theory that, if the jury had accepted it, would have reduced the crimes to voluntary manslaughter and attempted voluntary manslaughter.

The Court of Appeal also reversed Lakey's murder and attempted murder convictions "for two independent reasons: (1) under California law, a defendant who is tried as an aider and abettor cannot be convicted of an offense greater than that of which the actual perpetrator is convicted, where the aider and abettor and the perpetrator are tried in the same trial upon the same evidence, and (2) on this record, we cannot conclude with reasonable certainty that any participant acted with malice in connection with the murder and attempted murder counts, so we cannot say that the crimes of murder or attempted murder have been committed." Justice Hull dissented as to Lakey and would have affirmed his conviction.

We granted the Attorney General's petition for review limited to whether the Court of Appeal correctly reversed Lakey's murder and attempted murder convictions.

The question before us is whether reversal of McCoy's convictions also requires reversal of Lakey's. The Court of Appeal divided on the question. The majority found that McCoy, whose gun fired the fatal bullets, was guilty as the direct perpetrator and Lakey as an aider and abettor. It interpreted certain cases to mean that an aider and abettor may not be guilty of a greater offense than the direct perpetrator and concluded therefore that if McCoy was guilty of crimes less than murder or attempted murder, then Lakey also could only be guilty of those lesser crimes. Accordingly, it concluded that reversal of McCoy's convictions compelled reversal of Lakey's convictions. Justice Hull disagreed. He argued that "neither law nor logic requires that an aider and abettor be afforded the benefit of a mitigating factor applicable only to the actual perpetrator to reduce a homicide from murder to manslaughter."

Resolution of this question requires a close examination of the nature of aiding and abetting liability. "All persons concerned in the commission of a crime, whether they directly commit the act constituting the offense, or aid and abet in its commission, are principals in any crime so committed." (Pen. Code § 31). Thus, a person who aids and abets a crime is guilty of that crime even if someone else committed some or all of the criminal acts. Because aiders and abettors may be criminally liable for acts not their own, cases have described their liability as "vicarious." This description is accurate as far as it goes. But, as we explain, the aider and abettor's guilt for the intended crime is not entirely vicarious. Rather, that guilt is based on a combination of the direct perpetrator's acts and the aider and abettor's *own* acts and *own* mental state.

Except for strict liability offenses, every crime has two components: (1) an act or omission, sometimes called the *actus reus*; and (2) a necessary mental state, sometimes called the *mens rea*. (Pen. Code § 20). This principle applies to aiding and abetting liability as well as direct liability. An aider and abettor must do something *and* have a certain mental state.

We have described the mental state required of an aider and abettor as different from the mental state necessary for conviction as the actual perpetrator. The difference, however, does not mean that the mental state of an aider and abettor is less culpable than that of the actual perpetrator. An aider and abettor's mental state must be at least that required of the direct perpetrator. To prove that a defendant is an accomplice the prosecution must show that the defendant acted with knowledge of the criminal purpose of the perpetrator *and* with an intent or purpose either of committing, or of encouraging or facilitating commission of, the offense. When the offense charged is a specific intent crime, the accomplice must share the specific intent of the perpetrator;[3] this occurs when the accomplice knows the full extent of the perpetrator's criminal purpose and gives aid or encouragement with the intent or purpose of facilitating the perpetrator's commission of the crime. What this means here, when the charged offense and the intended offense—murder or attempted murder—are the same, *i.e.*, when guilt does not depend on the natural and probable consequences doctrine, is that the aider and abettor must know and share the murderous intent of the actual perpetrator.

Aider and abettor liability is thus vicarious only in the sense that the aider and abettor is liable for another's actions as well as that person's own actions. When a person chooses to become a part of the criminal activity of another, she says in essence, "your acts are my acts." But that person's *own* acts are also her acts for which she is also liable. Moreover, that person's mental state is her own; she is liable for her *mens rea*, not the other person's.

As stated by Professor Dressler, "many commentators have concluded that there is no conceptual obstacle to convicting a secondary party of a more serious offense than is proved against the primary party. As they reason, once it is proved that the principal has caused an *actus reus*, the

[3] If the offense charged is a general intent crime, the aider and abettor must knowingly and intentionally facilitate the perpetrator's commission of the crime, but does not have to have some additional intent or purpose.

liability of each of the secondary parties should be assessed according to his own *mens rea*. That is, although joint participants in a crime are tied to a single and common *actus reus*, the individual *mentes reae* or levels of guilt of the joint participants are permitted to float free and are not tied to each other in any way. If their *mentes reae* are different, their independent levels of guilt will necessarily be different as well." (Dressler, Understanding Criminal Law (2d ed. 1995) § 30.06[C], p. 450).

Professor Dressler explained how this concept operates with homicide. "An accomplice may be convicted of first-degree murder, even though the primary party is convicted of second-degree murder or of voluntary manslaughter. This outcome follows, for example, if the secondary party, premeditatedly, soberly and calmly, assists in a homicide, while the primary party kills unpremeditatedly, drunkenly, or in provocation. Likewise, it is possible for a primary party negligently to kill another (and, thus, be guilty of involuntary manslaughter), while the secondary party is guilty of murder, because he encouraged the primary actor's negligent conduct, with the intent that it result in the victim's death."

The statement that an aider and abettor may not be guilty of a greater offense than the direct perpetrator, although sometimes true in individual cases, is not universally correct. Aider and abettor liability is premised on the combined acts of all the principals, but on the aider and abettor's own *mens rea*. If the *mens rea* of the aider and abettor is more culpable than the actual perpetrator's, the aider and abettor may be guilty of a more serious crime than the actual perpetrator.

Moreover, the dividing line between the actual perpetrator and the aider and abettor is often blurred. It is often an oversimplification to describe one person as the actual perpetrator and the other as the aider and abettor. Although Lakey was liable for McCoy's actions, he was an actor too. He was in the car and shooting his own gun, although it so happened that McCoy fired the fatal shots. Moreover, Lakey's guilt for *attempted* murder might be based entirely on his own actions in shooting at the attempted murder victims.

As another example, assume someone, let us call him Iago, falsely tells another person, whom we will call Othello, that Othello's wife, Desdemona, was having an affair, hoping that Othello would kill her in a fit of jealousy. Othello does so without Iago's further involvement. In that case, depending on the exact circumstances of the killing, Othello might be guilty of manslaughter, rather than murder, on a heat of passion theory. Othello's guilt of manslaughter, however, should not limit Iago's guilt if his own culpability were greater. Iago should be liable for his own acts as well as Othello's, which he induced and encouraged. But Iago's criminal liability, as Othello's, would be based on his own personal *mens rea*. If, as our hypothetical suggests, Iago acted with malice, he would be guilty of murder even if Othello, who did the actual killing, was not.

We thus conclude that when a person, with the mental state necessary for an aider and abettor, helps or induces another to kill, that person's guilt is determined by the combined acts of all the participants as well as that person's own *mens rea*. If that person's *mens rea* is more culpable than another's, that person's guilt may be greater even if the other might be deemed the actual perpetrator.

As applied here, Lakey and McCoy were to some extent both actual perpetrators and aiders and abettors. Both fired their handguns, although McCoy's gun inflicted the fatal wounds. Once the jury found, as it clearly did, that Lakey acted with the necessary mental state of an aider and abettor, it could find him liable for both his and McCoy's acts, without having to distinguish between them. But Lakey's guilt was also based on his own mental state, not McCoy's. McCoy's unreasonable self-defense theory was personal to him. A jury could reasonably have found that Lakey did not act under unreasonable self-defense even if McCoy did. Thus, his conviction of murder and attempted murder can stand, notwithstanding that on retrial McCoy might be convicted of a lesser crime or even acquitted.

We reverse the judgment of the Court of Appeal and remand the matter for further proceedings consistent with our opinion.

PROBLEM

People v. McCoy discussed whether an accomplice can be liable for a more serious offense than the actual perpetrator. What about the opposite situation? Can an accomplice be liable for a less serious offense than the actual perpetrator? Bennie Nero stabbed and killed the victim. Bennie's sister, Lisa Brown, aided and abetted Bennie by handing him the knife. If Bennie is found guilty of murder, and the jury concludes Lisa was an accomplice to the murder, must the jury convict Lisa of murder? Or may the jury convict Lisa of a less serious offense? *People v. Amezcua* (2019) 6 Cal. 5th 886, 434 P.3d 1121, 243 Cal. Rptr. 3d 842; *People v. Daveggio* (2018) 4 Cal. 5th 790, 415 P.3d 717, 231 Cal. Rptr. 3d 646); *People v. Nero* (2010) 181 Cal.App.4th 504, 104 Cal.Rptr.3d 616.

PROBLEMS ON ACCOMPLICE LIABILITY

1. Hopkins and the victim were friends living in San Francisco. They decided to "get high" so they purchased some heroin. While sitting in Hopkins' car, they "cooked" the heroin. Hopkins injected himself with a dose of heroin. Victim had difficulty injecting himself because he could not find a vein to insert the needle into his arm. To help, Hopkins tied a cloth tightly around victim's arm to bring out a vein. The technique worked, and victim injected himself with heroin. Victim overdosed and passed out. Hopkins drove victim to the

hospital, but victim died from the overdose. Is Hopkins liable for the death? *People v. Hopkins* (1951) 101 Cal.App.2d 704, 226 P.2d 74.

2. Lewis, age thirty, drove a 16-year-old female and an 18-year-old male to a secluded location for the purpose of videotaping them engage in consensual sexual intercourse. Lewis is charged with statutory rape, defined in PC § 261.5 as "sexual intercourse accomplished with a person who is not the spouse of the perpetrator, if the person is a minor. For the purposes of this section, a 'minor' is a person under the age of 18 years and an 'adult' is a person who is at least 18 years of age." Is Lewis guilty? *People v. Lewis* (1952) 113 Cal.App.2d 468, 248 P.2d 461.

3. Do you remember the following problem from Chapter 4 on causation? Linda shoots Larry in the head, inflicting an immediately fatal wound. At the same instant, Loopy shoots Larry in the head, inflicting another immediately fatal wound. Assume Linda and Loopy act completely independently of each other. Are Loopy and Linda "but for" causes of Larry's death? Do you now have a better understanding of why it is important for this question that Linda and Loopy acted independently of each other?

At some point a crime ends. It is finished. Once the crime is over, an accomplice to the crime is not responsible for future wrongdoing committed by the perpetrator of the completed crime. When a crime ends depends on the crime. In *People v. Fleming* (2018) 27 Cal. App. 5th 754, 238 Cal. Rptr. 3d 429, the Court of Appeal noted, "[A]n assault is complete once the violence that would complete the battery is commenced. An assault is an incipient or inchoate battery; a battery is a consummated assault. A battery is complete when the willful and unlawful use of force or violence occurs." The Court also observed that "a murder ends with the death of the victim."

The First Circuit Court of Appeals' decision in *Figueroa-Cartagena* provides insight into when a crime is over for purposes of accomplice liability.

UNITED STATES V. FIGUEROA-CARTAGENA

United States Court of Appeals, First Circuit
612 F.3d 69 (2010)

LIPEZ, CIRCUIT JUDGE.

Appellant Neliza Figueroa-Cartagena ("Neliza") was found guilty of aiding and abetting a carjacking that resulted in death. She and two co-defendants, Félix Gabriel Castro-Davis ("Gabriel") and Félix Alberto Castro-Davis ("Alberto"), appealed their convictions. We affirm Neliza's carjacking conviction.

The jury could have found from the evidence presented at trial that Gabriel and Alberto carjacked Héctor Pérez-Torres on the afternoon of July 15, 2006 in Caguas, Puerto Rico. There was no evidence presented regarding what happened in the immediate aftermath of the carjacking. Later that evening, Gabriel and Alberto arrived at Neliza's parents' house in Cayey with Pérez handcuffed inside his own car. Gabriel had been living at the house with Neliza, whom he was dating at the time. Although Neliza did not arrive with Gabriel and Alberto, she placed a phone call at that time to her brother José, who was inside the house, and asked him to step outside to speak with Gabriel. When José went outside, Gabriel offered him money to guard Pérez for a while. José agreed, and Gabriel and Alberto left to withdraw money using Pérez's ATM card.

While watching Pérez, José grew nervous and called Gabriel to urge him to hurry. Neliza answered the phone and assured him they were nearby. Just after the conversation ended, however, Pérez jumped from the car and attempted to escape. José unsuccessfully tried to force him back into the car, and a struggle ensued until Gabriel, Alberto, and Neliza arrived and subdued Pérez. In the meantime, several neighbors approached the house to inquire about the noise. Neliza told them not to get involved, and she and Gabriel closed a gate to prevent them from approaching.

José went to a gas station after the fight to wash his car and drink a beer. Gabriel, Alberto, and Neliza followed to check on him. Neliza was driving her own car, Gabriel was driving Pérez's car, and Alberto was sitting in Pérez's car holding Pérez in a headlock. The three spoke briefly with José and then drove off in the same direction.

The next day, Neliza and Gabriel met José at the house. Gabriel explained that he and Alberto had killed Pérez the night before by asphyxiating him with duct tape.[3] Gabriel and Neliza instructed José to threaten the neighbors and tell them to remain silent about the previous day's events.

Neliza's challenge to her carjacking conviction focuses on the temporal limits of the crime. She claims that her involvement, if any, with Alberto and Gabriel's criminal scheme began long after those two had seized Pérez's car. In her view, there was no basis for the jury to conclude that she aided and abetted the carjacking because it is not possible to aid and abet a crime that has already been committed.

The basic legal premise of her argument—that she cannot be convicted of aiding and abetting a completed crime—is sound. A person cannot be found guilty of aiding and abetting a crime that already has been committed.

This point has important implications for Neliza's liability. To fully understand those implications, we must draw a careful distinction between the "offense" of carjacking and the offense conduct. For purposes of aiding and abetting liability, it is the duration of the *offense conduct* that matters,

[3] The government has not alleged that Neliza was directly involved in the killing of Pérez.

since the aiding and abetting statute states a rule of criminal responsibility for *acts* which one assists another in performing.

The factual premise of Neliza's argument—that she did not become involved until after Gabriel and Alberto seized the car—is also sound. The first sign of Neliza's involvement in the criminal episode was a phone call she made to her brother José on the evening of July 15, 2006, asking him to step outside the house to speak with Gabriel. But the seizure of the vehicle occurred several hours earlier, in the mid-to late-afternoon. There was no evidence suggesting what Neliza might have been doing at the time of the seizure or when she became entangled in the carjacking scheme. The government attempted to fill this gap at trial by arguing that "somebody" must have driven Alberto and Gabriel from Cayey to the scene of the carjacking in Caguas: "They didn't walk from Cayey to Salchichón in Caguas. Somebody took them there, and that someone is Neliza Figueroa-Cartagena." But the government presented no evidence to support that theory. Needless to say, Alberto and Gabriel could have arrived in Caguas in any number of ways, and they may have sought Neliza's aid after they seized the car. The government's theory is pure conjecture, which cannot form the basis for a criminal conviction.

It would seem to follow that Neliza's conviction cannot stand because there is insufficient evidence that she participated in the carjacking offense conduct. But that conclusion rests on a third, unstated assumption: that the offense conduct for carjacking begins and ends when the vehicle is first seized. In our circuit, at least, that is not the law. We have held that when a carjacking victim is taken hostage, the commission of the carjacking continues at least while the carjacker maintains control over the victim and his or her car.

That gloss on the carjacking statute casts Neliza's argument in a different light. As we have said, an individual who arrives on the scene after the offense conduct has ended cannot be held liable as an aider and abettor. But when the criminal conduct extends over a period of time, a latecomer may be convicted of aiding and abetting even if she did not learn of the crime at its inception but knowingly assisted at a later stage.

Neliza's participation fits within the latter category. Under our precedent, the carjacking offense conduct remained ongoing while Pérez was a hostage in the car for many hours after Neliza became involved. During that time, Neliza lent significant aid to Alberto and Gabriel: she allowed them to hold Pérez at her parents' house, she helped recruit her brother as a guard, and she warded off curious neighbors. She was not "merely present" at the scene of the crime; her aid was essential to the success of the scheme, and she may therefore be held liable as an aider and abettor.

Affirmed.

THE NATURAL AND PROBABLE CONSEQUENCES DOCTRINE: SCOPE OF ACCOMPLICE LIABILITY

An accomplice is liable for the crime committed by the perpetrator. For example, Zeb drives Bob to a jewelry store late at night so Bob can break in and steal jewels. Zeb parks behind the store and Bob breaks in, cracks the safe, and steals jewelry. Bob emerges from the store and Zeb and Bob drive away. Zeb is liable for burglary and theft even though he never set foot in the store.

In addition to liability for the crime the accomplice intended to aid and abet, an accomplice can be liable for crimes the accomplice did *not* intend to aid and abet, and did not know were going to occur. An accomplice is liable for crimes committed by the perpetrator that are a natural and probable consequence of the intended or target crime.[4] The Court of Appeal explained in *In re Loza* (2018) 27 Cal. App. 5th 797, 238 Cal. Rpt. 3d 516, "Generally, a defendant may be convicted of a crime either as a perpetrator or as an aider and abettor. An aider and abettor can be held liable for crimes that were intentionally aided and abetted (target offenses); an aider and abettor can also be held liable for any crimes that were not intended, but were reasonably foreseeable (nontarget offenses). Liability for intentional, target offenses is known as 'direct' aider and abettor liability; liability for unintentional, nontarget offenses is known as the natural and probable consequences doctrine." In *People v. Chiu* (2014) 59 Cal.4th 155, 172 Cal.Rptr.3d 438, 325 P.3d 972, the Supreme Court explained, "A nontarget offense is a natural and probable consequence of the target offense if, judged objectively, the additional offense was reasonably foreseeable. The inquiry does not depend on whether the aider and abettor actually foresaw the nontarget offense. Rather, liability is measured by whether a reasonable person in the defendant's position would have or should have known that the charged offense was a reasonably foreseeable consequence of the act aided and abetted." Consider Zeb, Bob, and the heist at the jewelry store. When Bob entered the store he unexpectedly encountered a security guard. The security guard tried to capture Bob, and Bob killed her. Bob completed the theft, rushed out, jumped in the car, and Zeb sped away. Is Zeb liable for murder? Zeb will argue that he intended to help Bob commit burglary and theft, but he had no intent to hurt anyone.

Change the facts further. When Bob entered the store and unexpectedly encountered the security guard, he raped her. After raping the guard, Bob left the store. Zeb and Bob drove away. Is Zeb liable for rape?

---

[4] *See People v. Chiu* (2014) 59 Cal.4th 155, 172 Cal.Rptr.3d 438, 325 P.3d 972; *People v. Lisea* (2013) 213 Cal. App. 4th 408, 414, 152 Cal. Rptr. 3d 557 ("the natural and probable consequences doctrine constitutes a type of aiding and abetting.").

To determine whether an accomplice is liable for a crime that the accomplice did *not* intend to aid and abet, answer the following questions: (1) Did the perpetrator commit or attempt to commit a crime *in addition to* the target crime? (2) Was the additional crime, although not planned at the outset, a reasonably foreseeable consequence of the target crime, or, in other words, was the additional crime a natural and probable consequence of the target crime?

Apply this two part framework to the break in at the jewelry store. In the first variant, Bob unexpectedly encountered a security guard in the store and killed her. (1) Bob committed the additional crime of murder. (2) Is it foreseeable that when a burglar enters a jewelry store in the middle of the night, the burglar might unexpectedly encounter a security guard and kill the guard? Stated another way, is the death of a security guard in such circumstances a natural and probable consequence of burglary and theft? This question is for the jury. What do you think? Add that in 2014, the Supreme Court held that the natural and probable consequences doctrine cannot support a premeditated murder conviction for an accomplice. *People v. Chiu* (2014) 59 Cal. 4th 155, 325 P.3d 972, 172 Cal. Rptr. 3d 438; *See also, In re Loza* (2018) 27 Cal. App. 5th 797, 238 Cal. Rptr. 3d 516.

As for the second variant, when Bob unexpectedly encountered the security guard, he didn't kill her, he raped her. Is it foreseeable that when a burglar enters a jewelry store in the middle of the night to steal jewelry, the thief will rape a woman he unexpectedly encounters in the store? Is rape a natural and probable consequence of burglary and theft of a business?

In *People v. Medina,* the Supreme Court discusses the liability of an accomplice for a crime the accomplice did not intend to aid and abet.

PEOPLE V. MEDINA

California Supreme Court
46 Cal.4th 913, 95 Cal.Rptr.3d 202, 209 P.3d 105 (2009)

CHIN, J.

In this case, a verbal challenge by defendants (members of a street gang) resulted in a fistfight between defendants and the victim (a member of another street gang). After the fistfight ended, one of the defendants shot and killed the victim as he was driving away from the scene of the fight with his friend. The jury found the gunman guilty of murder and attempted murder of the friend, as the actual perpetrator, and two other participants in the fistfight guilty of those offenses as aiders and abettors. The Court of Appeal affirmed the gunman's convictions, but reversed the participants' convictions. It held there was insufficient evidence that the nontarget offenses of murder and attempted murder were a natural and probable consequence of the target offense of simple assault which they had aided and abetted.

Because a rational trier of fact could have concluded that the shooting death of the victim was a reasonably foreseeable consequence of the assault, on the facts of this case, we reverse the judgment of the Court of Appeal relating to the nonshooting defendants.

A person who knowingly aids and abets criminal conduct is guilty of not only the intended crime but also of any other crime the perpetrator actually commits that is a natural and probable consequence of the intended crime. The latter question is not whether the aider and abettor *actually* foresaw the additional crime, but whether, judged objectively, it was *reasonably* foreseeable. Liability under the natural and probable consequences doctrine is measured by whether a reasonable person in the defendant's position would have or should have known that the charged offense was a reasonably foreseeable consequence of the act aided and abetted.

Although variations in phrasing are found in decisions addressing the doctrine—"probable and natural," "natural and reasonable," and "reasonably foreseeable"—the ultimate factual question is one of foreseeability. Thus, a natural and probable consequence is a foreseeable consequence. But to be reasonably foreseeable the consequence need not have been a strong probability; a possible consequence which might reasonably have been contemplated is enough. A reasonably foreseeable consequence is to be evaluated under all the factual circumstances of the individual case and is a factual issue to be resolved by the jury.

In examining the whole record in the light most favorable to the prosecution, we conclude that a rational trier of fact could have found that the shooting of the victim was a reasonably foreseeable consequence of the gang assault in this case.

PROBLEMS ON THE NATURAL AND PROBABLE CONSEQUENCES DOCTRINE OF ACCOMPLICE LIABILITY

1. On December 12, the defendant and two other men—the defendant's step-brother, Phillip Willey, and Jeffrey Colby—drove from defendant's trailer to the house of a friend, Joel Fuller. Fuller, with a sawed-off shotgun in his possession, joined the others. Later that evening, Fuller suggested that the four men drive to the house of a reputed cocaine dealer, Norman Grenier, take Grenier by surprise, and rob him. Defendant agreed to the plan, reasoning that Grenier, being a drug dealer, would not call the police to report the robbery. The four drove to Grenier's house, which was situated in a heavily wooded rural area. Defendant and Fuller left the car and approached the house. Defendant carried a hunting knife, and Fuller was armed with the shotgun. Willey and Colby drove off in defendant's car and returned later for defendant

and Fuller. Defendant and Fuller walked to the back of Grenier's house. At that time, Grenier and his girlfriend were watching television in their living room. Defendant and Fuller intended to break in the back door in order to place themselves between Grenier and the bedroom, where they believed Grenier kept a loaded shotgun. Because the back door was blocked by snow, the two men walked around to the front of the house. Under their revised plan, defendant was to break the living room picture window whereupon Fuller would show his shotgun to Grenier, who presumably would be dissuaded from offering any resistance. Defendant broke the living room window. Fuller immediately fired a blast from the shotgun through the broken window, hitting Grenier in the chest and killing him. Fuller entered through the broken window and took $1,300 from Grenier's pocket. The two men returned to the road and waited behind a bush for the return of the car. Assume defendant had no intent to hurt Grenier. Of what crimes is defendant guilty? *State v. Linscott* (Me. 1987) 520 A.2d 1067.

2. Dopy was a long time employee of Safeway. Dopy devised a plan to rob the Safeway where he worked. Dopy asked his friends Idiot and Stupid to rob the store, and they agreed. Dopy gave Idiot and Stupid the combination of the safe. Dopy told Idiot and Stupid how many employees would be at the store when it opened at 7:00 a.m. Dopy was at home on the day of the robbery because he was not scheduled to work that day. Idiot and Stupid waited at the store, and when the manager arrived at 6:00 a.m., they took him prisoner and put him in the meat locker. As additional employees arrived, they were placed in the meat locker. When a female employee arrived, Idiot took her to secluded part of the store and raped her. Stupid opened the safe, and Idiot and Stupid made off with $50,000. Who is guilty of what crimes?

3. Dickey and Cullumber were unemployed drug addicts living in Fresno. Cullumber's 76-year-old grandmother, Mrs. Caton, lived nearby. Mr. Freiri, aged 67, paid rent to live in Mrs. Caton's home. Cullumber told Dickey that his grandmother kept large amounts of cash hidden in her home. Cullumber proposed that they steal the money to buy drugs. Cullumber told Dickey, "Granny's old, and so is the guy who lives with her. There won't be no problem getting the money, and we won't hurt nobody." Cullumber and Dickey went to Mrs. Caton's house and stole the money as planned. While in the house, Cullumber "went nuts," attacking his grandmother and Mr. Freiri. As soon as Cullumber "went nuts," Dickey ran away. He took no part in the beating. When Mrs. Caton's daughter did not hear from her, the daughter went to Mrs. Caton's home, where she found her mother on the floor of her bedroom covered in blood. Mrs. Caton had been beaten so savagely that her eyes bulged out of the sockets like golf balls. She had multiple stab wounds. Mrs. Caton died several days later. Mr. Freiri was found dead in the dining room. He died from multiple stab wounds to the chest, armpit, and forearm. He also had a bone-deep cut on his head. He was stabbed so ferociously that his ribs were broken by the knife. Suspicion soon turned to Cullumber. When the police came looking for him, Cullumber killed himself. What charges can be brought

against Dickey? *People v. Dickey* (2005) 35 Cal.4th 884, 28 Cal.Rptr.3d 647, 111 P.3d 921.

4. Nancy B owned a tanning salon in Sacramento. One evening, after Nancy had closed for the day and locked the door, eight young men burst in. Seven of the men had guns. Defendant was one of the men. The men demanded money. Nancy was threatened, beaten, and tied up. One of the men—not Defendant—pulled down Nancy's pants, pushed a gun into her vagina, and threatened to fire it unless she told them where she kept her money and valuables. The men ransacked the business, stole money and jewelry, and left. Of what crimes is Defendant guilty? *People v. Nguyen* (1993) 21 Cal.App.4th 518, 26 Cal.Rptr.2d 323.

5. Eduardo and his friend Juan, members of the Sureno criminal street gang, encountered Pascual, a member of the Nortenos criminal street gang, in the parking lot of a grocery store. The Surenos exchanged insults and gang signs with the Norteno. The three shoved shopping carts at each other. Eduardo ran to his car, got a gun, and fired three shots at Pascual, missing. Unfortunately, one of the bullets hit a child playing nearby, seriously injuring the child. Is Juan liable for the injury to the child? *People v. Lisea* (2013) 213 Cal. App. 4th 408, 152 Cal. Rptr. 3d 557.

NOTE ON THE NATURAL AND PROBABLE CONSEQUENCES DOCTRINE AND FIRST DEGREE PREMEDITATED MURDER

In *People v. Chiu* (2014) 59 Cal.4th 155, 172 Cal.Rptr.3d 438, 325 P.3d 972, the Supreme Court ruled that an accomplice may not be convicted of first degree premeditated murder under the natural and probable consequences doctrine. Liability for second degree murder is possible under the doctrine. An accomplice can be convicted of first degree premeditated murder when evidence establishes that the accomplice intended to aid and abet that crime.

FAILURE TO PROTECT ONE'S CHILD AS A BASIS FOR ACCOMPLICE LIABILITY

Parents have a legal as well as a moral duty to protect their child from harm. It sometimes happens that a parent—nearly always a mother—fails to protect her child from a spouse or partner who abuses the child. Can the parent who failed to protect the child be prosecuted? Consider two sad cases, *People v. Ogg* and *People v. Rolon.*

PEOPLE V. OGG

California Court of Appeal
219 Cal. App. 4th 173, 161 Cal. Rptr. 3d 584 (2013)

GILBERT, P.J.

A parent has an exceptional and unique relationship with his or her children; this principle needs no citation.

A mother knows her child is continuously sexually molested by mother's boyfriend. She can act to protect her child from this crime, but chooses not to do so. We conclude that the mother's failure to protect her child from continuous sexual abuse supports her conviction as an aider and abettor of the crime.

Lynda Gabriella Ogg appeals from a judgment after conviction of aiding and abetting the continuous sexual abuse of her daughter A.R. by Daniel Ogg. The trial court sentenced Ogg to the upper term of 16 years in prison.

In 1993, A.R. was born. When she was about 6 years old, Ogg began dating Daniel and he moved into her home. During the following 10 years, Daniel sexually abused A.R. Ogg was not present during the abuse. At trial, A.R. testified that Daniel performed oral sex on her more than three times when she was between the ages of 6 and 10, more than three times when she was between the ages of 10 and 12, and more than three times when she was between the ages of 12 and 14.

A.R. testified that the abuse began as a "food game" when she was 6 years old. Daniel told A.R. to close her eyes and he put food in her mouth, asking her to guess what it was. Then he placed his penis in her mouth and told her that it was a hot dog. Later, he placed his penis in her mouth without the "food game" pretense. A.R. believed this happened about seven times.

When A.R. was 6 years old, she informed her mother that Daniel had placed his penis in her mouth. In a later police interview, Ogg denied that this conversation occurred. Thereafter, Daniel's sexual abuse of A.R. ceased for approximately a year. A.R. testified that when she was about 8 years old, he forced her to orally copulate him once a month. When she was 10 years old, Daniel performed oral sex on her. A.R. did not remember the frequency of the abuse.

Daniel's biological daughter P., who was 4 years younger than A.R., also lived in the Ogg home. Ogg worked outside the home, but Daniel did not.

When A.R. was 10 years old, she again informed her mother that Daniel placed his penis in her mouth. Ogg asked "if [she] liked it." A.R. replied, "No." Ogg responded that A.R. could either call the police or give Daniel another chance. Ogg said to A.R. that if A.R. "gave him another chance, [A.R.] couldn't tell anyone because they would go to jail and [A.R. would] go to foster care." A.R. decided to give Daniel another chance. She "was scared to go to the police." A.R. feared that if she told the police about her abuse, her little brother would be placed in foster care. Ogg told her that foster care "was really bad and [Ogg] used to get raped and molested in foster care."

In 2004, Ogg married Daniel; A.R. was then 11 years old. Daniel continued to orally copulate A.R. When she was 12, he began kissing her on her mouth and digitally penetrating her. Before she was 14, he tried to have sexual intercourse with her but she "squirmed away" and complained of pain. When she was 14, he had sexual intercourse with her every two weeks. When she was 15, he stopped for five months, but then began again. The abuse stopped at age 16 when A.R. told a friend who reported it.

Police officers arrested Daniel. When interviewed by the police, Ogg denied knowing "anything" regarding the sexual abuse. Eventually, she admitted to an investigator that Daniel had mentioned it when A.R. was 10 years old. Ogg stated that Daniel awoke from sleep and said that "he had been having impure thoughts, and that he had had [A.R.] take off her clothes, sit next to him and touch his penis." Daniel added that he "would have [A.R.] get undressed and sit next to him, and he would put her hand on his penis and she'd take it off and he'd put it back, and then he'd take it off and then that was it." Ogg stated that she was upset and did not go to work the following day. Instead, she took A.R. to breakfast and spent the day with her discussing Daniel's acts. A.R. "confirmed" the abuse. Ogg did not express disbelief about the abuse to the investigator.

Ogg said she did not know how many times it happened. She said, "It probably happened a few times but I don't know. Nobody gave me a number." The investigator asked, "But you inferred from the one time that it happened several times?" Ogg answered, "It kind of seemed like it." Ogg said she asked Daniel "if anything else happened" and he said "No." Ogg claimed no knowledge of sexual touching, oral sex, or sexual intercourse between Daniel and A. R.

Ogg admitted that she had no "good reason" for not calling the police. She "asked [A.R.] what she wanted [Ogg] to do" and "[A.R.] didn't know." Ogg "didn't know what to do either." Ogg thought Daniel's behavior was inappropriate, but he "said he wouldn't do it again and [she] believed him." She "kept checking with [A. R.]" whether anything else happened and A.R. said "No." Ogg did not question Daniel again. She expressed fear that she would lose her children.

For several months afterward, Ogg did not leave A.R. alone with Daniel. She occasionally asked A. R., "Has anything happened?" and A.R. would respond, "No." Ogg "figured everything's okay" because when the family watched television A.R. would "lay down behind Daniel and play with his hair."

Jan Schulman, Ogg's mother, testified that after Daniel's arrest, she asked Ogg why she did not protect A.R. Ogg replied that "the kids would come and go, but Daniel would be in her life forever."

Ogg concedes that she failed to protect A. R., but contends that the evidence is insufficient to establish that she acted with the intent or purpose of committing, encouraging, or facilitating commission of the crime of continuous sexual abuse of a child to support her conviction as an aider and abettor.

All persons involved in the commission of a crime, whether acting directly or aiding and abetting, are principals in the crime committed. A principal commits continuous sexual abuse of a child under the age of 14 years if the person has recurring access to the child over a period of at least three months and "engages in three or more acts of substantial sexual conduct" or "three or more acts of lewd or lascivious conduct" with the child. (§ 288.5.) Lewd and lascivious conduct requires proof of specific intent to arouse, appeal to, or gratify the sexual desires of either party. Substantial sexual conduct does not require proof of specific intent. It requires proof only of "penetration of the vagina or rectum of either the victim or the offender by the penis of the other or by any foreign object, oral copulation, or masturbation of either the victim or the offender." (§ 1203.066(b))

An aider and abettor must share the specific intent of the perpetrator. He or she shares the specific intent of the perpetrator if he or she knows the full extent of the perpetrator's criminal purpose and gives aid or encouragement with the intent or purpose of facilitating the perpetrator's commission of the crime. It is not necessary that the aider and abettor be prepared to commit the offense by his or her own act should the perpetrator fail to do so, nor that the aider and abettor seek to share the fruits of the crime.

Generally, failure to prevent a crime is insufficient to establish aiding and abetting liability. But aiding and abetting liability can be premised on a parent's failure to fulfill his or her common law duty to protect his or her child from attack. (People v. Rolon (2008) 160 Cal. App. 4th 1206). Thus, in *People v. Swanson-Birabent* (2003) 114 Cal. App. 4th 733, 744, 7 Cal. Rptr. 3d 744, the court found sufficient evidence to hold a mother to answer for two counts of committing lewd and lascivious acts upon her child, as an aider and abettor, because she watched and did nothing to intervene while her boyfriend twice performed oral sex on the child in their bed.

Sufficient evidence and reasonable inferences therefrom establish that Ogg knew the full extent of Daniel's criminal purpose and, by her inaction, intended to facilitate his sexual abuse. It is a reasonable inference that Ogg, the mother and caretaker of her minor daughter, knew Daniel had molested A.R. and would continue to molest her without intervention. A.R. told Ogg twice that Daniel was molesting her and Ogg believed her. Daniel also admitted to Ogg that he molested A.R. Ogg facilitated the continuing sexual abuse when she kept Daniel in the home, married him, and discouraged A.R. from reporting the abuse. She warned A.R. that if A.R. reported the abuse to the police, she would be placed in foster care and implied that she could be raped, and that Ogg would be incarcerated. This is substantial evidence to support the reasonable inference that Ogg's warnings were motivated by her selfish desire to continue her relationship with Daniel, and that she had no concern for A. R.'s protection. Ogg said as much when she explained to her mother that children "come and go, but Daniel and I are forever." Ogg also expressed no concern for A.R.'s welfare in her police interview.

It matters not that Ogg did not intend to gratify her own sexual desires. Her conviction requires proof that she failed to protect her daughter when she knew of Daniel's criminal purpose. She both acted and failed to act with the intent to facilitate his abuse. Substantial evidence supports the inference that Ogg chose to facilitate the abuse rather than sever her relationship with Daniel. Moreover, Ogg concealed the abuse by dissuading A.R. from reporting it. The culpability of a person who, in essence, condones such abusive behavior and then attempts to hide it, thereby compounding the psychological harm to the child, must be as great as that of the perpetrator.

We reject the argument that Ogg cannot be guilty of aiding and abetting because she was not present when Daniel committed his crimes against A.R. That, up to now, there have been no reported California decisions directly on point does not persuade us otherwise.

The judgment is affirmed.

QUESTION

Would Ogg be an accomplice if she didn't know about the sexual abuse, but suspected it?

PEOPLE V. ROLON

California Court of Appeal
160 Cal.App.4th 1206, 73 Cal.Rptr.3d 358 (2008)

EPSTEIN, P.J.

We hold that a parent has a duty to protect his or her young child and may be criminally culpable on an aider and abettor theory for an assault causing death and on an implied malice theory for murder where the parent fails to take reasonably necessary steps for the child's protection, so long as the parent, with ability to do so, fails to take those steps with the intent of facilitating the perpetrator's assaultive offense. We hold that the evidence in this case was sufficient to support guilt for the child's death on either theory. We affirm.

Anthony Bill Lopez was the father of six of appellant's seven children, including her one-year-old son Isaac. Although a court order prohibited appellant from allowing Lopez to visit or stay at her apartment, he had stayed there for about a week before the homicide in this case. The court order also forbade any unmonitored contact between Lopez and appellant's children, and appellant was not permitted to act as the monitor.

On April 19, 2003, a social worker made an unannounced visit to the apartment. Lopez hid in a bedroom closet, and appellant told the social worker that he was not in the home. The social worker did not notice any injuries on Isaac during the visit.

On April 20, 2003, at about 6:00 or 7:00 p.m., Lopez immersed Isaac in a tub of water and unspecified chemicals. Lopez then threw him against a wall, in appellant's presence. Isaac had been crying, but stopped after he hit the wall. Lopez went to sleep at about midnight that night, while appellant stayed up to watch Isaac.

At about 2:00 a.m. on April 21, Lopez woke to the sound of Isaac crying. Lopez said Isaac might be hungry and asked appellant's son Christian to heat some food for him. Isaac continued to cry after being fed. Lopez punched Isaac in the chest. Appellant told Lopez to leave Isaac alone, and Lopez told her to shut up and not get involved.

Appellant's neighbor Kristal Cardenas shared a wall with appellant. In the early morning hours of April 21, she heard a screaming child in appellant's apartment and a series of thumps against the wall that lasted for three minutes. The thumps and the screams ceased simultaneously.

At about 6:00 a.m. that morning, Lopez said he would take care of Isaac and told appellant to go to bed, which she did. Isaac was strapped into a car seat at that point. An hour later, Lopez woke appellant and told her Isaac was not breathing. She got up and saw Lopez administering cardiopulmonary resuscitation to Isaac, who was lying on a towel. Lopez told her he had wrapped a stuffed toy and a jacket around Isaac because he would not stop crying. He told her not to use the phone and asked her to help him revive Isaac, because otherwise, "they're going to take all the kids away." Appellant and Lopez immersed Isaac in a bathtub filled with water. When that failed to wake Isaac, Lopez attempted cardiopulmonary resuscitation again. Isaac did not respond. Lopez then poured rubbing alcohol on Isaac's body. He then wrapped Isaac in a blanket and put him in a crib.

That day, appellant and Lopez kept the other children in the apartment, telling them that Isaac was at the hospital. At about 11:00 p.m. that night, Lopez left the apartment to purchase gasoline. When Lopez returned, he instructed appellant and the children to go to bed. Appellant rose around 2:00 a.m. the following morning and saw Lopez in the kitchen. Lopez said he was going to erase Isaac's identifying features, and he took Isaac into the bathroom with the gasoline, a chair and a bucket. Appellant stood outside the bathroom while Lopez burned Isaac's body in the bucket. Lopez brought the body out of the bathroom and began wrapping it in plastic, instructing appellant not to look. At around 7:00 a.m., he left the house with the plastic-wrapped body, the bucket and the chair. Police officers subsequently arrested Lopez and discovered Isaac's body in his van.

An autopsy revealed that Isaac suffered 24 blunt force injuries before he died, four of which were inflicted near the time of death and the remainder of which were inflicted no more than one day before death. The tissue connecting his upper lip to his gum was torn, and one of his teeth was chipped. The pathologist who conducted the autopsy concluded that all of the injuries, with the possible exception of one bruise on Isaac's back, were nonaccidental.

Isaac's lungs were blotchy and blood had pooled in them, indicating that he suffocated. His blood and stomach contained ethanol (drinking alcohol), isopropanol (rubbing alcohol), brompheniramine (an antihistamine), and pseudoephedrine (a decongestant). The pseudoephedrine was present in levels indicating that Isaac had been fed between 80 to 90 milligrams of children's medicine, which was between five to twenty-five times the normal dosage for a child. In the opinion of the pathologist who conducted the autopsy, Isaac had a lethal amount of pseudoephedrine in his system when he died. The pathologist concluded that Isaac's death was probably caused by a combination of suffocation, the pseudoephedrine overdose and his injuries.

At trial, the People's theory was that Lopez killed Isaac and that appellant aided and abetted Lopez by failing to perform her parental duty to protect Isaac. Over appellant's objection, the court instructed the jury that appellant had a duty to take all steps reasonably necessary under the circumstances to protect Isaac from harm. Also over objection, the court gave modified versions of [California jury instructions] to the effect that appellant's failure to perform her duty would be the equivalent of an affirmative act for the purposes of finding aiding and abetting, implied malice and second degree murder. Appellant requested that the court instruct the jury according to the defense of duress, but the court refused. On January 31, 2007, the jury convicted appellant on all counts. This is a timely appeal from the judgment.

Appellant argues that the trial court incorrectly instructed the jury that a parent may be liable for aiding and abetting a crime and for second degree murder on an implied malice theory by intentionally failing to act to protect his or her child from harm.

A person who aids and abets the commission of a crime is a principal to that crime. (§ 31.) Proof of aider and abettor liability requires proof in three distinct areas: (a) the direct perpetrator's *actus reus*—a crime committed by the direct perpetrator, (b) the aider and abettor's *mens rea*—knowledge of the direct perpetrator's unlawful intent and an intent to assist in achieving those unlawful ends, and (c) the aider and abettor's *actus reus*—conduct by the aider and abettor that in fact assists the achievement of the crime. A person who aids and abets a crime may be liable for any other offense that was a natural and probable consequence of the crime aided and abetted. When an individual's criminal liability is based on the *failure* to act, it is well established that he or she must first be under an existing legal duty to take positive action.

In *People v. Swanson-Birabent* (2003) 114 Cal.App.4th 733, the defendant was charged with committing a lewd or lascivious act on a child under 14. On two occasions, she stood by and said nothing while her boyfriend sexually fondled her daughter. The court extensively quoted *State v. Walden*, 293 S.E.2d 780 (N.C. 1982), in which the Supreme Court of North Carolina held that a parent who is present while his or her child is being attacked, and who fails to take all steps reasonably possible to protect the child, commits an act of omission showing the parent's consent and contribution to the crime being committed. In California, parents have a duty to exercise reasonable care, supervision, protection, and control over their minor children. The court concluded that there was probable cause for the charges against the defendant because her failure to perform that duty aided the crime by encouraging its commission.

Based on *Swanson,* the trial court gave the following special instruction to the jury: "The word 'act' as used in these instructions includes an omission or failure to act in those situations where a person is under a legal duty to act. A parent has a legal duty to his or her minor child to take every step reasonably necessary under the circumstances in a given situation to exercise reasonable care for the child, to protect the child from harm, and to obtain reasonable medical attention for the child."

Our research has disclosed no California case other than *Swanson* that addresses whether a parent can aid and abet a crime victimizing his or her child by failing to intervene. Most other jurisdictions that have considered the issue have decided it in the affirmative. We are satisfied that the better rule is that parents have a common law duty to protect their children and may be held criminally liable for failing to do so: a parent who knowingly fails to take reasonable steps to stop an attack on his or her child may be criminally liable for the attack if the purpose of nonintervention is to aid and abet the attack. For these reasons, we agree with the *Swanson* court in its conclusion that aiding and abetting liability can be premised on a parent's failure to fulfill his or her common law duty to protect his or her child from attack.

We emphasize, however, that liability as an aider and abettor requires that the parent, by his or her inaction, intend to aid the perpetrator in commission of the crime, or a crime of which the offense committed is a reasonable and probable outcome. In this case, the modified instructions correctly required the jury to find appellant's intent and conduct separately. Under these instructions, the jury could reasonably infer appellant's intent to aid Lopez from her presence at the scene of the crime, her duty to protect her child and her failure to do so.

Appellant argues that her actions were reasonable under the circumstances because she did take every step reasonably necessary under the circumstances. In this case, appellant attempted to strike Lopez at least once during the week before the homicide. According to her statement to the interrogating officers, she reprimanded Lopez when he punched her son, and after he told her to "shut up" and not involve herself, she continued "fighting" with him. She did not explain what she meant by "fighting." She made no effort to aid her son: she did not scream, call 911, ask a neighbor to help or call for help, or do anything else. Instead, she went to sleep and left her son alone with Lopez although she knew Lopez had recently punched him and thrown him against a wall. From this evidence, a reasonable jury could infer that appellant was capable of taking some action to protect her child and that she chose not to do so, but to go to sleep and leave her son alone with Lopez. These inferences support the conclusion that appellant did not take every step reasonably necessary under the circumstances to protect her son.

The judgment is affirmed.

QUESTION

Do you agree with the decisions in both cases? Are both mothers culpable?

NOTE—ACCOMPLICE TO SUICIDE

Committing suicide is not a crime in California. However, one can be an accomplice to suicide by helping someone commit suicide, and the crime is a felony. PC § 401.

CONVICTION CANNOT BE BASED ON THE UNCORROBORATED TESTIMONY OF AN ACCOMPLICE

A criminal conviction cannot be predicated entirely on the uncorroborated testimony of an accomplice. PC § 1111 provides: "A conviction cannot be had upon the testimony of an accomplice unless it is corroborated by such other evidence as shall tend to connect the defendant with the commission of the offense; and the corroboration is not sufficient if it merely shows the commission of the offense or the circumstances thereof."

Corroborative evidence is evidence that tends to make a proposition more probable. In *People v. Thompson* (2010) 49 Cal.4th 79, 123, 109 Cal.Rptr.3d 549, 231 P.3d 289, the Supreme Court discussed the corroboration requirement for accomplice testimony: "The corroborating evidence may be circumstantial or slight and entitled to little consideration when standing alone, and it must tend to implicate the defendant by relating to an act that is an element of the crime. The corroborating evidence need not by itself establish every element of the crime, but it must, without aid from an accomplice's testimony, tend to connect the defendant with the crime."[5]

Don't be confused by the rule that a conviction cannot be predicated on the uncorroborated testimony of an accomplice. The testimony of an accomplice *is* admissible, and can be considered by the jury along with other evidence in the case. The limitation is that the testimony of an accomplice, *standing alone*, and without any other evidence of guilt, is not sufficient to support a conviction.

One accomplice cannot corroborate another. However, a defendant's out-of-court statements can corroborate an accomplice. (*See People v. Diaz* (2015) 60 Cal. 4th 1176, 345 P.3d 62, 185 Cal. Rptr. 3d 431). Consider *State v. Helmenstein*. Where did the prosecution's evidence fall short?

STATE V. HELMENSTEIN

Supreme Court of North Dakota
163 N.W.2d 85 (1968)

STRUTZ, JUDGE.

This is an appeal from the district court of Oliver County. The defendant was informed against on a charge of burglary of a grocery store in Hannover. After trial, the court found the defendant guilty of the offense as charged. This appeal is from the judgment of conviction and from an order denying the defendant's motion for new trial.

[Defendant] contends that there was no corroboration of testimony of witnesses for the State who were accomplices of the defendant in the commission of the offense; that, as a consequence, the evidence against the defendant was insufficient under the law to convict him of the offense charged.

The record discloses that, on the night of the alleged burglary, two groups of young people had been driving around in the vicinity of Center, North Dakota. During the evening, these two groups met at the park in Center. Someone in one of the groups had obtained some beer, and this was passed around and all of them drank some of it. After a while, they all

[5] *See also People v. Whalen* (2013) 56 Cal. 4th 1, 55, 294 P.3d 915, 152 Cal. Rptr. 3d 673 ("The testimony of accomplices must be corroborated by such other evidence as shall tend to connect the defendant with the commission of the offense. Such evidence may not come from, or require aid or assistance from the testimony of other accomplices or the accomplice himself. The evidence, however, need not corroborate every fact to which the accomplice testifies. Corroborating evidence may be slight, may be entirely circumstantial, and need not be sufficient to establish every element of the charged crime.").

decided to get into one of the automobiles and ride around. They got into the defendant's car. A short time later, someone suggested that they drive to Hannover, about six miles west of Center, and break into the store at that place. When this suggestion was made, one person in the party said she wanted some bananas. Someone else expressed a desire for other articles which could be secured at the store. They drove over to Hannover and parked the car some distance from the store, and three of the party, including the defendant, went to the store, broke in, and returned with beer, cigarettes, candy, and bananas. They then drove back toward Center. On the way, the parties all agreed on what story they would tell the officers of the law if any of them should be questioned. At Center, they divided the loot and separated.

At the trial, five of the young people who had been in this party testified for the State against the defendant. The only witness other than those who were in the party on the night of the burglary was Harold Henke, the owner of the store that had been burglarized. His testimony established that he owned the store, that on the morning following the burglary he found that the store had been entered during the night, and that approximately $130 worth of merchandise had been taken. His testimony in no way connected the defendant with the offense, but merely established the fact that a crime had been committed.

The trial court found the defendant guilty. It found that Glen Zahn, who was one of the group of young people who had been in the party, was not an accomplice because he had taken no active part in the commission of the burglary and that he had fallen asleep after the party had reached Hannover and while the actual burglary was being committed. The trial court further found that the witness Zahn had had too much beer and was, in fact, pretty well under the influence at the time of the commission of the crime.

The first question for us to consider is whether there was competent evidence against the defendant sufficient to sustain the judgment of conviction. Our statute provides that a conviction may not be had upon the testimony of an accomplice unless his testimony is corroborated by such other evidence as tends to connect the defendant with the commission of the offense, and the corroboration is not sufficient if it merely shows the commission of the offense or the circumstances thereof. Every material fact testified to by an accomplice need not be corroborated. All that is necessary is that the corroboration tend to connect the defendant with the commission of the offense.

The first issue facing us is the determination of the status of those persons who were members of the party of young people on the night of the alleged burglary who were called as witnesses by the State. If all of them were accomplices, then clearly the evidence against the defendant in this case is insufficient to support his conviction, for there is no evidence tending to connect him with the offense.

Let us examine the record before us to determine the status of the witnesses who testified for the State and who were members of the party of young people on the night of the burglary. Carol Weiss contends that she was against the burglary, but she kept her feelings to herself and did not express them. The record discloses that when the burglary was planned she expressed a desire for some bananas. She would not admit at the trial that she had asked for bananas to be secured for her in the burglary, but neither did she deny it. She merely says that she does not remember whether or not she asked for bananas. Most of the other witnesses, however, stated definitely that she did say that she wanted them to get some bananas for her. This clearly would make her an accomplice, even though she now insists that she had misgivings about the burglary and that she especially didn't want to have her brother become involved in it.

Janice Zahn also was called as a witness by the State. She testified that when someone suggested that they break into the store at Hannover, everybody agreed. Thus she admitted that she herself agreed to the burglary when it was suggested, and we believe this makes her, as well as every other person in the party, an accomplice.

Another witness called by the State, who was in the party on the night of the burglary, was Kenneth Cahoon. He admitted that he took part in the actual burglary of the store with the defendant and with one Clem Rohrich. So his status clearly is that of an accomplice. He further stated that after the burglary had been suggested, the parties drove to Hannover and parked their car. Before the three who committed the actual burglary went to the store, it was agreed by all of the parties that if anyone should be caught, each girl would wait for her boyfriend, and that if any of the girls should be caught and punished, each boyfriend would wait for his girl. This witness further testified, in response to a question as to whether anyone protested the plan to burglarize the store, that everyone was agreeable and that, after they had parked the car in Hannover, they stopped to make plans before three of them went to the store and broke in.

As has already been pointed out, the owner of the store, the only witness for the State other than members of the party, could testify only that his store had been burglarized and that some merchandise had been taken. His testimony in no way connected the defendant with the offense, but merely established the fact that an offense had been committed. The only testimony, therefore, which could possibly have corroborated the testimony of the above-named persons—all of whom have clearly been shown to be accomplices—would be the testimony of the witness Glen Zahn. The decision in this case therefore depends entirely upon whether Glen Zahn was an accomplice. If he was not, he furnishes the necessary corroboration of the testimony of the accomplices which is required to connect the defendant with the commission of the crime. However, if he, too, was an accomplice, then there is no testimony except that of accomplices which in any way connects the defendant with the offense and, under our law, the defendant cannot be convicted upon the testimony of accomplices alone, unless such testimony is corroborated by other evidence which tends to connect the defendant with the commission of the offense.

Let us therefore examine the testimony of Glen Zahn to see what he himself said. He contends that he had secret objections to the burglary which he did not express to anyone. He further testified that he was asleep when the burglary was committed and that he did not take part in the actual burglary of the store. The trial court found that Glen had had too much to drink and that he was asleep during the time of the burglary and in no way aided or abetted or encouraged the crime. Zahn's own testimony, however, discloses that he does not claim to have fallen asleep until the three members of the party left the parked car for the store, for he remembers their leaving. After the burglary had been accomplished, all of them together made up a story to tell to investigating officers in case any of them should be questioned. Zahn admits that he helped make up the story to mislead the officers of the law, and he says, "Well, we all made a story together." Why would Zahn feel it necessary to make up a story to mislead the officers if he had no part in the offense? We believe that the record clearly shows that the burglary in this case was the result of a plan in which each of the parties had a part, and that each of these young people encouraged and countenanced the offense and that each of them thus was concerned in its commission.

We believe that all of the persons who were in this group of young people were thus involved in the burglary, and each of them—including Glen Zahn—was an accomplice of the defendant who is being tried for the burglary. Certainly, from all of the facts in this case, the witness Zahn was concerned in the commission of the burglary. Since we hold Zahn to be an accomplice, there is no evidence in this case, other than that of persons who also are accomplices, connecting the defendant with the commission of the offense with which he is charged. Therefore, the evidence against him is insufficient to sustain the judgment of conviction.

For reasons stated herein, the judgment and sentence of the trial court is reversed and the complaint against the defendant is dismissed.

MODEL PENAL CODE APPROACH TO ACCOMPLICE LIABILITY

Section 2.06 of the Model Penal Code is titled "Complicity." The section provides, in part:

(1) A person is guilty of an offense if it is committed by how own conduct, or by the conduct of another person for which it is legally accountable, or both.

(2) A person is legally accountable for the conduct of another when:

(a) acting with the kind of culpability that is sufficient for the commission of the offense, he causes an innocent or irresponsible person to engage in such conduct; or

(b) he is made accountable for the conduct of such other person by the Code or by the law defining the offense; or

(c) he is an accomplice of another person in the commission of the offense

(3) A person is an accomplice of another person in the commission of an offense if:

(a) with the purpose of promoting or facilitating the commission of the offense, he

(i) solicits such other person to commit it, or

(ii) aids or agrees or attempts to aid such other person in planning or committing it, or

(iii) having a legal duty to prevent the commission of the offense, fails to make proper effort so to do; or

(b) his conduct is expressly declared by law to establish his complicity.

The MPC rejects liability based on the natural and probable consequences doctrine, as do approximately ten states.

CHAPTER 8

INCHOATE CRIMES: SOLICITATION, CONSPIRACY, AND ATTEMPT

■ ■ ■

This chapter addresses the three inchoate crimes: solicitation, conspiracy, and attempt. The word "inchoate" means partly in existence or imperfectly formed. Solicitation, conspiracy, and attempt are inchoate because they are steps toward the completion of an intended target crime.

SOLICITATION

Solicitation is the offense of asking someone else to commit or join in a crime. California Penal Code § 653f(a) states: "Every person who, with the intent that the crime be committed, solicits another to [commit any of a long list of crimes] shall be punished by imprisonment in a county jail for not more than one year or in the state prison, or by a fine."[1] The *actus reus* of solicitation is requesting another person to commit or join in a specified crime. The *mens rea* is the intent that the crime be committed. In *People v. Superior Court* (2007) 41 Cal.4th 1, 11, 58 Cal.Rptr.3d 421, 157 P.3d 1017, the Supreme Court explained, "A solicitation requires only that a person invite another to commit or join in an enumerated crime (including murder) with the intent that the crime be committed. The solicitation is complete once the request is made and is punishable irrespective of the reaction of the person solicited." Solicitation is a specific intent crime.

If the solicitee agrees to commit the crime, a conspiracy is formed and the solicitation merges into the conspiracy. The word "merge" in this context means the defendant cannot be convicted of both the solicitation and the conspiracy. The solicitation merges into the conspiracy and disappears. If the solicitee commit the crime, the solicitor is liable as a principal.

Can a solicitation constitute an attempt? Generally, no. However, a solicitation can ripen into an attempt if the solicitor takes further steps toward the intended crime.[2]

---

[1] Solicitation to commit certain crimes requires the testimony of two witnesses or one witness and corroborative evidence. PC § 653f(f).

[2] *See People v. York* (1998) 60 Cal.App.4th 1499, 71 Cal.Rptr.2d 303.

PROBLEM

Dell had consensual sex with Beth, and Beth became pregnant. Later Dell was incarcerated. While in prison, Dell wrote the following letter to a fellow gang member: "By the way loc, could you & the homies do me a big favor & take care that white bitch, Beth for me. Ha, ha, ha!! Cuzz, it's too late to have abortion so I think a miss carrage would do just fine. I aint fista pay child support for this bull-shit loc. You think you can get the homies or home girls to do that for me before she have the baby." Can Dell be prosecuted for solicitation? Solicitation of what crime? Would it make a difference if the letter was not received by the fellow gang member because it was intercepted by prison authorities? *People v. Saephanh* (2000) 80 Cal.App.4th 451, 94 Cal.Rptr.2d 910.

CONSPIRACY

A conspiracy is an agreement between two or more persons to commit a crime (PC § 182).[3] The *actus reus* of conspiracy is the agreement to commit a crime. The agreement can be verbal. No writing is required. Indeed, the agreement can be inferred from the conduct of the parties. In *People v. Herrera* (2000) 83 Cal.App.4th 46, 64, 98 Cal.Rptr.2d 911, the Court of Appeal wrote that the agreement, "may be inferred from the conduct, relationship, interests, and activities of the alleged conspirators before and during the alleged conspiracy."

The *mens rea* of conspiracy is twofold: (1) intent to agree, and (2) intent to commit the target offense. Conspiracy is a specific intent crime. Conspiracy is not divided into degrees.

In addition to agreement and intent, many states, including California, require an overt act in furtherance of the conspiracy. The overt act is an element of the crime. PC § 184 provides, "No agreement amounts to a conspiracy, unless some act, besides such agreement, be done within this state to effect the object thereof, by one or more of the parties to such agreement." At least one overt act must occur in California. Only one of the conspirators need commit an overt act. The overt act does not have to be criminal. For example, if Beth and Betty agree to rob a bank, and Betty goes online to find the nearest Wells Fargo Bank, going online is an overt act. If a person agrees to commit a crime, but withdraws before an overt act is committed, the person is not guilty of conspiracy.

Why punish conspiracy? Group criminal activity is thought to be particularly dangerous. The Court of Appeal put it this way in *People v. Williams* (1980) 101 Cal.App.3d 711, 721, 161 Cal.Rptr. 830:

> To unite, back of a criminal purpose, the strength, opportunities and resources of many is obviously more dangerous

---

[3] *See People v. Powers-Monachello* (2010) 189 Cal.App.4th 400, 116 Cal.Rptr.3d 899.

and more difficult to police than the efforts of a lone wrongdoer. Collaboration magnifies the risk to society both by increasing the likelihood that a given quantum of harm will be successfully produced and by increasing the amount of harm that can be inflicted. As the Unites States Supreme Court wrote in *Callanan v. United States* (1961), 364, U.S. 587, "Concerted action both increases the likelihood that the criminal object will be successfully attempted and decreases the probability that the individuals will depart from their path of criminality. Group association for criminal purposes often, if not normally, makes possible the attainment of ends more complex than those which one criminal could accomplish. Nor is the danger of a conspiratorial group limited to the particular end toward which it has embarked. Combination in crime makes more likely the commission of crimes unrelated to the original purpose for which the group was formed. In sum, the danger which a conspiracy generates is not confined to the substantive offense which is the immediate aim of the enterprise."

The danger of group criminal activity is exemplified by the September 11, 2001 attack on the World Trade Center in New York City. Could one person acting alone have committed that horrible crime?

Conspiracy is a separate crime from the target offense. Thus, a defendant may be convicted of both the conspiracy and the target offense. The conspiracy does not merge into the target offense.[4] If the target offense is not completed or attempted, the conspiracy remains.

A charge of conspiracy has substantive and procedural advantages for the prosecution. First, anything any of the conspirators say during the course of and in furtherance of the conspiracy is admissible in court against *all* the conspirators under a hearsay exception called the co-conspirator exception.[5] Second, all the conspirators can be tried together. Third, venue is proper in any jurisdiction where the conspiracy was formed or any conduct in furtherance of the conspiracy took place. Fourth, so-called *Pinkerton* liability applies (*Pinkerton* is discussed later.)

A person can join an ongoing conspiracy. The late joiner is not responsible for acts that were done before the person joined the conspiracy.

A person can withdraw from a conspiracy by affirmatively rejecting the conspiracy and communicating that rejection to the other members of the conspiracy known to the person. A mere change of heart is not enough to withdraw from a conspiracy. The would-be-withdrawer must let the other conspirators know "I want nothing further to do with this. I'm out."

4 In a few states and under the Model Penal Code the conspiracy does merge into the target offense, which means the conspiracy cannot be charged.

5 Evidence Code § 1223. Federal Rules of Evidence 801(d)(2)(E).

Once a conspirator withdraws, the ex-conspirator is not guilty of post-withdrawal crimes committed by the remaining conspirators.

It is important to understand the relationship between conspiracy and accomplice liability. If you join a conspiracy, you are an accomplice to the offenses contemplated by the conspiracy. In rare instances, however, it is possible to be an accomplice without being a conspirator. Suppose you are standing in line at the bank, waiting to speak to a teller. You notice that the "customer" speaking to the teller has a gun and is quietly robbing the bank. Apparently, the teller activated a silent alarm because you observe the first police car pull into the parking lot. To be helpful you say, "Excuse me there Mr. bank robber, but I thought you'd like to know the cops are here. You had better hurry up and finish your robbery." You are not in a conspiracy to rob the bank, but you may be an accomplice. It is also possible to be a conspirator without being an accomplice. For example, large narcotics distribution conspiracies have many members. Often, members of the conspiracy are in different cities or countries, and do not know each other. Suppose a member of the conspiracy in Los Angeles makes a drug sale. A member of the same conspiracy in Mexico knows nothing of the sale, and does not aid or abet it in any way. The conspirator in Mexico is not an accomplice to the LA drug sale, but is a member of the conspiracy.

When conspirators commit more than one offense, how many conspiracies are there? One conspiracy to commit multiple crimes? Or separate conspiracies for each offense? It depends on the conspiratorial agreement(s). The U.S. Supreme Court explained in *Braverman v. United States* (1942) 317 U.S. 49, 53, 63 S.Ct. 99, "The precise nature and extent of the conspiracy must be determined by reference to the agreement which embraces and defines its objects. Whether the object of a single agreement is to commit one or many crimes, it is in either case that agreement which constitutes the conspiracy which the statute punishes." The California Court of Appeal wrote in *People v. Meneses* (2008) 165 Cal.App.4th 1648, 1669, 82 Cal.Rptr.3d 100, "It is well-settled that the essence of the crime of conspiracy is the agreement, and thus it is the number of agreements (not the number of the victims or number of statutes violated) that determine the number of conspiracies."

In California, a conspiracy requires agreement between two or more persons.[6] It takes two to tango, so to speak. Thus, if a would-be conspirator "agrees" with an undercover police officer to commit a crime that the officer has no intention of committing, there is no conspiracy. As Justice Cardozo

---

[6] Conspiracy at common law required the agreement of two or more persons to commit a crime. Professor Dressler calls this the "plurality" requirement. Joshua Dressler, *Understanding Criminal Law* § 29.06[A], p. 446 (5th ed. 2009). California follows the common law approach. The Model Penal Code rejects the common law plurality approach, and allows conspiracy where one person "agrees" with an undercover police officer.

wrote, "It is impossible for a man to conspire with himself."[7] On the other hand, if three people agree to commit a crime and, unbeknownst to two of them, the third is a police officer, there is a conspiracy.

When does a conspiracy end? In many cases, a conspiracy ends when the conspirators are arrested. Sometimes, conspirators commit the contemplated crime and avoid detection. In such cases, the conspiracy ends when the crime is complete and the successful ex-conspirators go their separate ways. In many conspiracies, the conspiratorial plan includes not only the target crime, but also steps to get away, conceal the offense, or mislead police. In *People v. Gann* (2011) 193 Cal.App.4th 994, 123 Cal.Rptr.3d 208, for example, a brother and sister conspired to murder their stepfather. Their plan was to shoot the victim and make it look as though there had been a home invasion robbery. The Court of Appeal wrote: "While a conspiracy is usually deemed to have ended when the substantive crime for which the conspirators are being tried is either attained or defeated, it is for the trial court to determine precisely when the conspiracy has ended. A conspiracy is not necessarily a single event which unalterably takes place at a particular point in time when the participants reach a formal agreement; it may be flexible, occurring over a period of time and changing in response to changed circumstances. Further, there may be a situation where a conspiracy will be deemed to have extended beyond the substantive crime to activities contemplated and undertaken by the conspirators in pursuance of the objectives of the conspiracy." The *Gann* Court ruled that the siblings' murderous conspiracy extended beyond the killing, and included their scheme to mislead police with the staged home invasion.

Proving the Agreement in Conspiracy

Because conspirators agree in secret, it can be difficult to prove the conspiratorial agreement. Consider *Commonwealth v. Azim*.

COMMONWEALTH V. AZIM

Superior Court of Pennsylvania
313 Pa.Super. 310, 459 A.2d 1244 (1983)

PER CURIAM:

Appellant was arrested, along with Mylice James and Thomas Robinson, on September 18, 1977 for simple assault, robbery, and conspiracy. The victim of the robbery was Jerry Tennenbaum, a Temple University student. Appellant drove a car in which the other two men were passengers. Appellant stopped the car, Robinson called Tennenbaum over to the curb, the two passengers got out of the car, inflicted bodily injury on

---

7 *Morrison v. California* (1934) 291 U.S. 82, 92, 54 S.Ct. 281.

Tennenbaum, took his wallet which had fallen to the ground, and immediately left the scene in the same car driven by appellant. Robinson and appellant were tried to a jury and convicted as co-defendants in April 1978.

At trial, the prosecution presented evidence that established that appellant was the driver of the car in which James and Robinson (the men who demanded money from Tennenbaum and beat and choked him) rode. Robinson was seated on the front seat, next to appellant. Robinson rolled down the car window, twice beckoned to the victim to come close to the car, and when Tennenbaum refused, the two passengers got out, assaulted Tennenbaum, and took his wallet. Appellant sat at the wheel, with the engine running and lights on, and the car doors open, while the acts were committed in the vicinity of the car. He then drove James and Robinson from the scene.

Among those circumstances relevant to proving conspiracy are association with alleged conspirators, knowledge of the commission of the crime, presence at the scene of the crime, and, at times, participation in the object of the conspiracy. Conspiracy to commit burglary has been found where the defendant drove codefendants to the scene of a crime and then later picked them up. We find no merit in appellant's claim that he was merely a hired driver, with no knowledge of his passengers' criminal activity.

We hold that a rational factfinder could find, beyond a reasonable doubt, that appellant conspired with James and Robinson to commit assault and robbery. Once conspiracy is established and upheld, a member of the conspiracy is also guilty of the criminal acts of his co-conspirators, even if he is not present at the time the acts are committed.

Conspiracy to Commit Murder

In *People v. Swain*, the Supreme Court analyzed conspiracy to commit murder.

PEOPLE V. SWAIN

Supreme Court of California
12 Cal.4th 593, 49 Cal.Rptr.2d 390, 909 P.2d 994 (1996)

BAXTER, J.

Defendants Jamal K. Swain and David Chatman were each convicted of conspiracy to commit murder and other crimes, stemming from the drive-by shooting death of a 15-year-old boy. As we shall explain, we hold that intent to kill is a required element of the crime of conspiracy to commit murder. In light of the jury instructions given, and general verdicts returned, we cannot determine beyond a reasonable doubt whether the jury found that the defendants conspired with an intent to kill. That conclusion requires us to reverse defendants' conspiracy convictions.

Prosecution evidence established that a brown van passed through the Hunter's Point neighborhood of San Francisco about 2 a.m. on January 13, 1991. It slowed down near the spot where the young victim, who was of Samoan descent, and his friends were listening to music on the street.

A young Black male who appeared to have no hair was driving the van. Suddenly several shots were fired from the front of the van. Defendant Chatman and another young man also fired guns from the rear of the van. One of the intended victims had yelled out "drive-by" as a warning of the impending shooting, so most of the people on the street ducked down. The 15-year-old victim, Hagbom Saileele, who was holding the radio from which music was playing, was shot twice from behind. He later died in surgery.

The jury first returned a verdict finding defendant Chatman guilty of second degree murder and conspiracy. As instructed, the jury also made a finding that the target offense of the conspiracy was murder in the second degree. Several days later, the jury returned verdicts against defendant Swain, finding him not guilty of murder or its lesser included offenses, but guilty of conspiracy. Once again, the jury made a finding under the conspiracy count that the target offense of the conspiracy was murder in the second degree.

Defendants contend the jury should have been instructed that proof of intent to kill is required to support a conviction of conspiracy to commit murder, whether the target offense of the conspiracy—murder—is determined to be in the first or second degree. More particularly, defendants assert it was error to instruct the jury on the principles of implied malice second degree murder in connection with the determination of whether they could be found guilty of conspiracy to commit murder, since implied malice does not require a finding of intent to kill. We agree.

We commence our analysis with a brief review of the elements of the crime of conspiracy, and of murder, the target offense of the conspiracy here in issue.

Conspiracy is an inchoate crime. It does not require the commission of the substantive offense that is the object of the conspiracy. As an inchoate crime, conspiracy fixes the point of legal intervention at the time of agreement to commit a crime, and thus reaches further back into preparatory conduct than attempt.

The crime of conspiracy is defined in the Penal Code as "two or more persons conspiring to commit any crime," together with proof of the commission of an overt act "by one or more of the parties to such agreement" in furtherance thereof. (Pen. Code, §§ 182(a)(1), 184.) Conspiracy is a specific intent crime. The specific intent required divides logically into two elements: (a) the intent to agree, or conspire, and (b) the intent to commit the offense which is the object of the conspiracy. To sustain a conviction for conspiracy to commit a particular offense, the prosecution must show not only that the conspirators intended to agree *but also that they intended to commit the elements of that offense.*

Turning next to the elements of the target offense of the conspiracy here in issue, Penal Code section 187 defines the crime of murder as the "unlawful killing of a human being with malice aforethought." (Pen. Code, § 187(a).) Malice aforethought may be express or implied. It is express when there is manifested a deliberate intention unlawfully to take away the life of a fellow creature. It is implied, when no considerable provocation appears, or when the circumstances attending the killing show an abandoned and malignant heart. Proof of unlawful "intent to kill" is the functional equivalent of express malice.

Penal Code section 189 distinguishes between murders in the first degree and murders in the second degree. "All murder which is perpetrated by means of a destructive device or explosive, poison, lying in wait, torture, or by any other kind of willful, deliberate, and premeditated killing, or which is committed in the perpetration of, or attempt to perpetrate, [certain enumerated felonies], or any murder which is perpetrated by means of discharging a firearm from a motor vehicle, intentionally at another person outside of the vehicle with the intent to inflict death, is murder of the first degree. All other kinds of murders are of the second degree."

California law, in turn, recognizes three theories of second degree murder. The first is unpremeditated murder with express malice. The second, of particular concern here, is implied malice murder. The third theory is second degree felony murder.

As noted, the jury in this case was instructed on the elements of murder, including principles of implied malice second degree murder. Under the instructions given, the jury could have based its verdicts finding defendants guilty of conspiracy to commit murder in the second degree on a theory of implied malice murder.

We have noted that conspiracy is a specific intent crime requiring an intent to agree or conspire, and a further intent to commit the target crime, here murder, the object of the conspiracy. Since murder committed with intent to kill is the functional equivalent of express malice murder, conceptually speaking, no conflict arises between the specific intent element of conspiracy and the specific intent requirement for such category of murders. Simply put, where the conspirators agree or conspire with specific intent to kill and commit an overt act in furtherance of such agreement, they are guilty of conspiracy to commit express malice murder.

The conceptual difficulty arises when the target offense of murder is founded on a theory of implied malice, which requires no intent to kill.

Implied malice murder, in contrast to express malice, requires instead an intent to do some act, the natural consequences of which are dangerous to human life. When the killing is the direct result of such an act, the requisite mental state for murder—malice aforethought—is implied. In such circumstances, it is not necessary to establish that the defendant intended that his act would result in the death of a human being. Hence, under an implied malice theory of second degree murder, the requisite mental state for murder—malice aforethought—is by definition implied, as a matter of law, from the specific intent to do some act dangerous to human life together with the circumstance that a killing has resulted from the doing of such act.

Stated otherwise, all murders require, at the core of the *corpus delicti* of the offense, a killing. Murder is the unlawful killing of a human being with malice aforethought. (Pen. Code, § 187(a).) But only in the case of implied malice murder is the requisite mental state—malice aforethought—implied from the specific intent to do some act other than an intentional killing and the resulting circumstance: a killing that has in fact occurred as the direct result of such an act.

The element of malice aforethought in implied malice murder cases is therefore derived or implied, in part through hindsight so to speak, from (i) proof of the specific intent to do some act dangerous to human life and (ii) the circumstance that a killing has resulted therefrom. It is precisely due to this nature of implied malice murder that it would be illogical to conclude one can be found guilty of conspiring to commit murder where the requisite element of malice is implied. Such a construction would be at odds with the very nature of the crime of conspiracy—an inchoate crime that fixes the point of legal intervention at the time of agreement to commit a crime, and indeed reaches further back into preparatory conduct than the crime of attempt—precisely because commission of the crime could never be established, or be deemed complete, unless and until a killing actually occurred.

We conclude that a conviction of conspiracy to commit murder requires a finding of intent to kill, and cannot be based on a theory of implied malice.

Complex Conspiracies—Chains, Wheels, and Related Works of Art

It is useful to differentiate simple from complex conspiracies. If three people agree to rob a bank, this is a simple conspiracy. Indeed, if fifteen people agree to rob a bank, it is a simple conspiracy, and this is so even though each of the fifteen has a different job (*e.g.,* lookout, getaway driver, robber, safe-cracker, etc.).

A large scale drug distribution operation is a classic example of a complex conspiracy. The drug—let's say heroin—is produced outside the United States. The foreign manufacturer sells the drug to individuals who smuggle the drug into our country. The smuggler sells the drug to high level drug dealers in various cities. Each high level drug dealer has a network of employees who distribute the drug, ending with small time drug dealers standing on street corners selling small quantities of heroin. When we look at the conspiracy as a whole, it stretches from the fields where the poppies are grown all the way to the small time criminal on the street corner. How many people are involved? It may be twenty. It may be hundreds. How many conspiracies are there? Obviously, there is a conspiracy between the manufacturers and the smugglers. They met face-to-face in some smoky bar in some far away place and agreed to the sale—a conspiracy. Equally obviously, there is a conspiracy between each small time drug dealer and their employer—they too met face-to-face and agreed to break the law. But is the smuggler across the ocean in a conspiracy with the small time drug dealer standing on a corner in America? These two don't know each other. They have never met or communicated. At the same time, the manufacturer knows that the drug will eventually be sold by someone *like* the corner drug dealer. For his part, the corner drug dealer knows the heroin came from *somewhere*—it doesn't grow on trees. As long as each player in this scheme knows others are involved, *all* the players are members of *one* conspiracy. Each person in the distribution scheme is a link in a conspiratorial chain, and all are tied together for purposes of conspiracy liability. Conspiracies that involve distribution of illegal drugs or stolen property are often called chain conspiracies or vertical conspiracies.

Before we leave the complex drug distribution conspiracy, ask yourself, is a customer who buys drugs for personal use a member of the conspiracy? The Connecticut Supreme Court discussed this issue in *State v. Allan* (2014) 311 Conn. 1, 83 A.3d 326:

> The Circuit Courts of Appeals uniformly acknowledge that evidence of a mere buyer-seller relationship, without more, does not constitute a conspiracy to distribute drugs. Two lines of reasoning have emerged for this conclusion. One group of federal Circuit Courts of Appeals have reasoned that, in a buyer-seller relationship, there is no singularity of purpose and thus no meeting of the minds. Mere proof of a buyer-seller agreement without any prior or contemporaneous understanding does not support a conspiracy conviction because there is no common illegal purpose: In such circumstances, the buyer's purpose is to buy; the seller's purpose is to sell. Accordingly, a mere buyer-seller relationship lacks an essential element necessary to form a conspiracy. Another group of federal Circuit Courts of Appeals

have reasoned that, under the common-law definition of conspiracy, when a buyer purchases illegal drugs from a seller, two persons have agreed to a concerted effort to achieve the unlawful transfer of the drugs from the seller to the buyer. This would constitute a conspiracy with the alleged objective of a transfer of drugs. Nonetheless, these courts further reason that Congress did not intend to subject buyers, particularly addicts, who purchase drugs for personal use, to the severe liabilities intended for distributors. Accordingly, this latter group has deemed a mere buyer-seller relationship to fall within a narrow exception to the general conspiracy rule for such transactions.

We view the first group's characterization to be the correct view of the law. Nonetheless, regardless of whether a court characterizes this issue as a proper application of conspiracy law or an exception to a literal application of that law in furtherance of legislative intent, a survey of federal case law indicates that the principle that conspiracy to sell narcotics cannot be found on the mere basis of a buyer-seller relationship universally stems from two tenets of common-law conspiracy. First, mere association with a member of a conspiracy or acquiescence in the object or purpose of a conspiracy is not sufficient to satisfy the intent elements of conspiracy. Second, conspiracy is a separate and distinct offense from the underlying crime that is the object of the agreement. Accordingly, in the context of a drug sale between two alleged coconspirators, the federal courts have held that there must be evidence of an agreement to distribute drugs and that such an agreement must be in addition to the purchase and sale between the two parties. Liability will arise as a coconspirator, therefore, when the buyer and seller shared a conspiratorial purpose to advance other transfers, whether by the seller or by the buyer. By contrast, when the government's proof shows no more than a simple sales transaction between alleged coconspirators, its case for conspiracy will fail.

In addition to a chain conspiracy, another complex conspiracy is a wheel conspiracy. In a wheel conspiracy (also called a hub and spoke conspiracy), a single individual or small group of individuals—the hub—transacts some type of illegal business with separate individuals—spokes—who may or may not know each other. Clearly, there is a conspiracy between the hub and each spoke. The hub and spoke *agree* to break the law. Let's suppose there are 25 spokes. How many conspiracies are there? Twenty-five if the individual spokes know nothing of each other and are not somehow mutually dependent on the continuing success of the hub. On the other hand, if the spokes *are* to some degree mutually dependent on the continuing success of the hub—perhaps spokes benefit financially from the continued success of the hub—then there may be one conspiracy involving the hub and *all* or *some* of the spokes. A prosecutor seeking to connect the hub and spokes into one conspiracy is said to construct a "rim" of mutual interest around the spokes: a rim that connects the spokes together to form one wheel conspiracy.

With the principles of complex conspiracies in mind, consider the following cases. What does the conspiracy in each case look like? A chain? A wheel? Some combination of the two? On a separate piece of paper (or on your computer), *draw a picture* of each conspiracy—that's right, draw a picture. Physically drawing a picture helps you analyze a complex conspiracy. If the conspiracy is a hub and spoke conspiracy, is there a rim connecting the various spokes?

1. Several individuals working together smuggle narcotics into San Francisco from Asia. Half the drugs are sold to a major drug dealer in Las Vegas, and the other half to a major drug dealer in Sacramento. The Las Vegas "king pin" employs mid-level drug dealers, each of whom is responsible for selling drugs in part of Las Vegas. Each mid-level dealer employs numerous street-level drug dealers to sell the drugs in the mid-level dealer's sector of the city. In Sacramento, the "king pin" directly employs street-level dealers (cutting out the middle man). The Las Vegas and Sacramento king pins know each other and do not consider themselves in competition. *United States v. Bruno* (2d Cir. 1939) 105 F.2d 921.

2. This case arose in California in the 1940s, when abortion was illegal in California and nearly all other states. Stern performed illegal abortions. Women desiring to end a pregnancy would ask a doctor, nurse, pastor, pharmacist, or other individual, "Who can I turn to for an abortion?" If the professional was sympathetic, the professional told the woman about Stern. Stern paid a small referral fee to each professional who referred a woman for his services. Stern performed 37 abortions on referral from professionals. Some professionals referred only one woman. Others referred multiple women over time. *Anderson v. Superior Court* (1947) 78 Cal. App. 2d 22, 177 P.2d 315.

3. Brown was a mortgage broker. He devised a scheme to obtain fraudulent home loans for customers. Brown advertised "home loans at such low rates they should be illegal." When a customer went to Brown's office, the customer learned that the loan was indeed illegal. Some customers walked out. Thirty-seven, individuals, however, agreed with Brown to obtain fraudulent loans with which to purchase homes. Most of the customers who got fraudulent loans did not know any of the other customers. Six of the customers, however, were members of one family, and they agreed together that each would use Brown's services to obtain

fraudulent loans. *Kotteakos v. United States* (1946) 328 U.S. 750, 66 S. Ct. 1239.

4. The Rosales family of El Paso, Texas operated a drug ring. The family's primary contact in Oklahoma was Williams, who distributed marijuana to several mid-level drug dealers in Oklahoma. The mid-level dealers distributed the marijuana to street-level drug dealers. Herrera was one of the mid-level drug dealers in Oklahoma. Herrera sold quantities of marijuana to Caldwell. Anderson was a long time friend of Caldwell. Caldwell introduced Anderson to Herrera. Herrera hired Anderson to be another one of Herrera's dealers. The Drug Enforcement Administration (DEA) intercepted incriminating phone calls regarding distribution of marijuana between Herrera and Caldwell, and a number of similar calls between Herrera and Anderson. The DEA did not intercept any calls between Caldwell and Anderson. A grand jury indicted Caldwell for conspiracy to distributed marijuana. The indictment listed Caldwell, Herrera, and Anderson as members of the same conspiracy. Is Caldwell in a conspiracy with Anderson? *United States v. Caldwell* (10th Cir. 2009) 589 F.3d 1323.

5. Haynes, Black, Terry, Johnson, and Jones were indicted for conspiracy involving corrupt police officers and drug dealers in Chicago. The drug dealers in the enterprise provided the corrupt cops with information about the location of drugs and money held by other drug dealers. The bad cops used the information to conduct traffic stops and home invasions to seize drugs and money, which they kept for themselves, giving part of the loot to the drug dealers in on the scheme. The leader of the conspiracy was Jones, a Chicago police officer. In May, Jones called his former partner, Johnson, and asked for his assistance in ripping off a drug dealer. At the time, Johnson was on duty with his partner, Black. Johnson and Black agreed to help Jones rip off the drug dealer. Johnson, Black, and Jones waited in an unmarked police car near an intersection where the drug dealer was supposed to park to make a delivery. When they spotted the dealer's car, Johnson activated the lights on the police car and stopped the drug dealer. Jones took a large quantity of drugs from the dealer's car, and the dealer was released. Jones sold the drugs and paid Johnson, Black, and the drug dealer who had informed him of the whereabouts of the dealer who was ripped off. In August, Jones was informed by a drug dealer that a drug dealer named Montgomery had a large quantity of drugs and money in his home. Jones contacted another of his former partners, Haynes, and asked Haynes if he would like to rip off a drug dealer. Haynes talked it over with his partner Terry, and the two agreed to carry out the plot. Haynes and Terry went to Montgomery's house, announced themselves as police officers, and seized a large quantity of drugs and more than $150,000 is cash. The proceeds were divided between Jones, Haynes, Terry, and the drug dealer in on the plot. What does this conspiracy—or these

conspiracies—look like? *United States v. Haynes* (7th Cir. 2009) 582 F.3d 686.

When Is a Provider of Lawful Goods or Services in a Conspiracy with a Customer Whom the Provider Knows or Suspects Is Putting the Goods or Services to Unlawful Ends?

A merchant who provides lawful goods or services is not in a conspiracy with a customer simply because the merchant knows or suspects that the customer intends to put the goods or services to unlawful ends. *People v. Lauria* discusses the circumstances in which a provider of lawful goods or services can be found to be in a conspiracy with a customer.

PEOPLE V. LAURIA

Court of Appeal
251 Cal.App.2d 471, 59 Cal.Rptr. 628 (1967)

FLEMING, J.

In an investigation of call-girl activity the police focused their attention on three prostitutes actively plying their trade on call, each of whom was using Lauria's telephone answering service, presumably for business purposes.

On January 8, 1965, Stella Weeks, a policewoman, signed up for telephone service with Lauria's answering service. Mrs. Weeks, in the course of her conversation with Lauria's office manager, hinted broadly that she was a prostitute concerned with the secrecy of her activities and their concealment from the police. She was assured that the operation of the service was discreet and "about as safe as you can get." It was arranged that Mrs. Weeks need not leave her address with the answering service, but could pick up her calls and pay her bills in person.

On February 11, Mrs. Weeks talked to Lauria on the telephone and told him her business was modelling and she had been referred to the answering service by Terry, one of the three prostitutes under investigation. She complained that because of the operation of the service she had lost two valuable customers, referred to as tricks. Lauria defended his service and said that her friends had probably lied to her about having left calls for her. But he did not respond to Mrs. Weeks' hints that she needed customers in order to make money, other than to invite her to his house for a personal visit in order to get better acquainted. In the course of his talk he said "his business was taking messages."

On April 1, Lauria and the three prostitutes were arrested. Lauria complained to the police that this attention was undeserved, stating that Hollywood Call Board had 60 to 70 prostitutes on its board while his own service had only 9 or 10, that he kept separate records for known or suspected prostitutes for the convenience of himself and the police. When asked if his records were available to police who might come to the office to investigate call girls, Lauria replied that they were whenever the police had a specific name. However, his service didn't "arbitrarily tell the police about prostitutes on our board. As long as they pay their bills we tolerate them." In a subsequent voluntary appearance before the grand jury Lauria testified he had always cooperated with the police. But he admitted he knew some of his customers were prostitutes, and he knew Terry was a prostitute because he had personally used her services, and he knew she was paying for 500 calls a month.

Lauria and the three prostitutes were indicted for conspiracy to commit prostitution, and nine overt acts were specified. Subsequently the trial court set aside the indictment as having been brought without reasonable or probable cause. (Pen. Code, § 995.) The People have appealed, claiming that a sufficient showing of an unlawful agreement to further prostitution was made.

To establish agreement, the People need show no more than a tacit, mutual understanding between coconspirators to accomplish an unlawful act. Here the People attempted to establish a conspiracy by showing that Lauria, well aware that his codefendants were prostitutes who received business calls from customers through his telephone answering service, continued to furnish them with such service. This approach attempts to equate knowledge of another's criminal activity with conspiracy to further such criminal activity, and poses the question of the criminal responsibility of a furnisher of goods or services who knows his product is being used to assist the operation of an illegal business. Under what circumstances does a supplier become a part of a conspiracy to further an illegal enterprise by furnishing goods or services which he knows are to be used by the buyer for criminal purposes?

The two leading cases on this point face in opposite directions. In *United States v. Falcone,* 311 U.S. 205, the sellers of large quantities of sugar, yeast, and cans were absolved from participation in a moonshining conspiracy among distillers who bought from them, while in *Direct Sales Co. v. United States,* 319 U.S. 703, a wholesaler of drugs was convicted of conspiracy to violate the federal narcotic laws by selling drugs in quantity to a codefendant physician who was supplying them to addicts. The distinction between these two cases appears primarily based on the proposition that distributors of such dangerous products as drugs are required to exercise greater discrimination in the conduct of their business than are distributors of innocuous substances like sugar and yeast.

In the earlier case, *Falcone,* the sellers' knowledge of the illegal use of the goods was insufficient by itself to make the sellers participants in a conspiracy with the distillers who bought from them. Such knowledge fell short of proof of a conspiracy, and evidence on the volume of sales was too vague to support a jury finding that respondents knew of the conspiracy from the size of the sales alone.

In the later case of *Direct Sales,* the conviction of a drug wholesaler for conspiracy to violate federal narcotic laws was affirmed on a showing that it had actively promoted the sale of morphine sulphate in quantity and had sold codefendant physician, who practiced in a small town in South Carolina, more than 300 times his normal requirements of the drug, even though it had been repeatedly warned of the dangers of unrestricted sales of the drug. The court contrasted the restricted goods involved in *Direct Sales* with the articles of free commerce involved in *Falcone*: "All articles of commerce may be put to illegal ends," said the court. "But all do not have inherently the same susceptibility to harmful and illegal use. This difference is important for two purposes. One is for making certain that the seller knows the buyer's intended illegal use. The other is to show that by the sale he intends to further, promote, and cooperate in it. This intent, when given effect by overt act, is the gist of conspiracy. While it is not identical with mere knowledge that another purposes unlawful action it is not unrelated to such knowledge. The step from knowledge to intent and agreement may be taken. There is more than suspicion, more than knowledge, acquiescence, carelessness, indifference, lack of concern. There is informed and interested cooperation, stimulation, instigation. And there is also a 'stake in the venture' which, even if it may not be essential, is not irrelevant to the question of conspiracy."

While *Falcone* and *Direct Sales* may not be entirely consistent with each other in their full implications, they do provide us with a framework for the criminal liability of a supplier of lawful goods or services put to unlawful use. Both the element of *knowledge* of the illegal use of the goods or services and the element of *intent* to further that use must be present in order to make the supplier a participant in a criminal conspiracy.

Proof of *knowledge* is ordinarily a question of fact and requires no extended discussion in the present case. The knowledge of the supplier was sufficiently established when Lauria admitted he knew some of his customers were prostitutes and admitted he knew that Terry, an active subscriber to his service, was a prostitute. In the face of these admissions he could scarcely claim to have relied on the normal assumption an operator of a business or service is entitled to make, that his customers are behaving themselves in the eyes of the law. Because Lauria knew in fact that some of his customers were prostitutes, it is a legitimate inference he knew they were subscribing to his answering service for illegal business purposes and were using his service to make assignations for prostitution. On this record we think the prosecution is entitled to claim positive knowledge by Lauria of the use of his service to facilitate the business of prostitution.

The more perplexing issue in the case is the sufficiency of proof of *intent* to further the criminal enterprise. The element of intent may be proved either by direct evidence, or by evidence of circumstances from which an intent to further a criminal enterprise by supplying lawful goods or services may be inferred. Direct evidence of participation, such as advice from the supplier of legal goods or services to the user of those goods or services on their use for illegal purposes, provides the simplest case. When the intent to further and promote the criminal enterprise comes from the lips of the supplier himself, ambiguities of inference from circumstance need not trouble us. But in cases where direct proof of complicity is lacking, intent to further the conspiracy must be derived from the sale itself and its surrounding circumstances in order to establish the supplier's express or tacit agreement to join the conspiracy.

In the case at bench the prosecution argues that since Lauria knew his customers were using his service for illegal purposes but nevertheless continued to furnish it to them, he must have intended to assist them in carrying out their illegal activities. Thus through a union of knowledge and intent he became a participant in a criminal conspiracy. Essentially, the People argue that knowledge alone of the continuing use of his telephone facilities for criminal purposes provided a sufficient basis from which his intent to participate in those criminal activities could be inferred.

In examining precedents in this field we find that sometimes, but not always, the criminal intent of the supplier may be inferred from his knowledge of the unlawful use made of the product he supplies. Some consideration of characteristic patterns may be helpful.

1. Intent may be inferred from knowledge, when the purveyor of legal goods for illegal use has acquired a stake in the venture. In the present case, no proof was offered of inflated charges for the telephone answering services furnished the codefendants.

2. Intent may be inferred from knowledge, when no legitimate use for the goods or services exists.

3. Intent may be inferred from knowledge, when the volume of business with the buyer is grossly disproportionate to any legitimate demand, or when sales for illegal use amount to a high proportion of the seller's total business. In such cases an intent to participate in the illegal enterprise may be inferred from the quantity of the business done. For example, in *Direct Sales,* the sale of narcotics to a rural physician in quantities 300 times greater than he would have normal use for provided potent evidence of an intent to further the illegal activity. No evidence of any unusual volume of business with prostitutes was presented by the prosecution against Lauria.

Inflated charges, the sale of goods with no legitimate use, sales in inflated amounts, each may provide a fact of sufficient moment from which the intent of the seller to participate in the criminal enterprise may be inferred. In such instances participation by the supplier of legal goods to the illegal enterprise may be inferred because in one way or another the supplier has acquired a special interest in the operation of the illegal enterprise. His intent to participate in the crime of which he has knowledge may be inferred from the existence of his special interest.

When we review Lauria's activities in the light of this analysis, we find no proof that Lauria took any direct action to further, encourage, or direct the call-girl activities of his codefendants and we find an absence of circumstance from which his special interest in their activities could be inferred. Neither excessive charges for standardized services, nor the furnishing of services without a legitimate use, nor an unusual quantity of business with call girls, are present. The offense which he is charged with furthering is a misdemeanor, a category of crime which has never been made a required subject of positive disclosure to public authority. Under these circumstances, although proof of Lauria's knowledge of the criminal activities of his patrons was sufficient to charge him with that fact, there was insufficient evidence that he intended to further their criminal activities, and hence insufficient proof of his participation in a criminal conspiracy with his codefendants to further prostitution. Since the conspiracy centered around the activities of Lauria's telephone answering service, the charges against his codefendants likewise fail for want of proof.

The order is affirmed.

Pinkerton Liability—When Is a Member of a Conspiracy Liable for a Crime Committed by a Fellow Conspirator That Was Not Contemplated by the Conspiracy?

A conspirator is liable when another member of a conspiracy commits the very crime contemplated by the conspiracy. But what if a member of the conspiracy commits a crime that was *not* contemplated by the conspiracy? Obviously, the perpetrator is guilty. But are the other members of the conspiracy responsible for this crime—a crime they did not agree to and did not personally commit? We have already seen that accomplices can be liable for crimes they did not intend to aid and abet. A similar kind of liability applies to conspirators.[8] A conspirator is liable for a crime committed by a co-conspirator if the crime was a natural and probable consequence of the conspiracy.

[8] *See People v. Delgado* (2013) 56 Cal. 4th 480, 486 n. 2, 297 P.3d 859, 154 Cal. Rptr. 3d 621 ("Conspirators bear a similar derivative liability for the criminal acts of their conspirators."); *People v. Maciel* (2013) 57 Cal. 4th 482, 160 Cal. Rptr. 3d 305, 304 P.3d 983 ("One who conspires with others to commit a felony is guilty as a principal. Each member of the conspiracy is liable for the acts of any of the others in carrying out the common purpose, *i.e.*, all acts within the reasonable and probable consequences of the common unlawful design.").

Consider Barry, Larry, Terry, and Mary. The four agree to rob a bank. Barry, Larry, and Terry burst into the bank with guns drawn and shout, "Nobody move, this here is a big time robbery!" Mary is the get away driver and is outside in the getaway car. Barry holds everyone at gunpoint. Terry goes into the safe and scoops up money. Larry decides to steal a Rolex watch from a customer in the bank. While in the safe, Terry decides to beat up the bank employee he took with him to the safe. Of what crimes are Berry, Terry, Larry, and Mary guilty? To help you answer this question, consider *Pinkerton v. United States* and *People v. Zielesch*.

The Model Penal Code rejects *Pinkerton* liability. A number of states that adopted the MPC engrafted *Pinkerton* onto their version of the law.[9]

PINKERTON V. UNITED STATES

United States Supreme Court
328 U.S. 640, 66 S.Ct. 1180 (1946)

MR. JUSTICE DOUGLAS delivered the opinion of the Court.

Walter and Daniel Pinkerton are brothers who live a short distance from each other on Daniel's farm. They were indicted for violations of the Internal Revenue Code. The indictment contained ten substantive counts and one conspiracy count. The jury found Walter guilty on nine of the substantive counts and on the conspiracy count. It found Daniel guilty on six of the substantive counts and on the conspiracy count. [Note: The indictment did not charge Daniel as an accomplice to the substantive offenses.]

It has been long and consistently recognized by the Court that the commission of the substantive offense and a conspiracy to commit it are separate and distinct offenses. A conviction for the conspiracy may be had though the substantive offense was completed. A conspiracy is a partnership in crime. It has ingredients, as well as implications, distinct from the completion of the unlawful project. For two or more to confederate and combine together to commit or cause to be committed a breach of the criminal laws is an offense of the gravest character, sometimes quite outweighing, in injury to the public, the mere commission of the contemplated crime. It involves deliberate plotting to subvert the laws, educating and preparing the conspirators for further and habitual criminal practices. And it is characterized by secrecy, rendering it difficult of detection, requiring more time for its discovery, and adding to the importance of punishing it when discovered.

It is contended that there was insufficient evidence to implicate Daniel in the conspiracy. But we think there was enough evidence for submission

---

[9] *See* Andrew Ingram, Pinkerton Short-Circuits the Model Penal Code, 64 *Villanova Law Review* 71 (2019).

of the issue to the jury. There is, however, no evidence to show that Daniel participated directly in the commission of the substantive offenses on which his conviction has been sustained, although there was evidence to show that these substantive offenses were in fact committed by Walter in furtherance of the unlawful agreement or conspiracy existing between the brothers. The question was submitted to the jury on the theory that each petitioner could be found guilty of the substantive offenses, if it was found at the time those offenses were committed petitioners were parties to an unlawful conspiracy and the substantive offenses charged were in fact committed in furtherance of it.

We have here a continuous conspiracy. There is here no evidence of the affirmative action on the part of Daniel which is necessary to establish his withdrawal from it. And so long as the partnership in crime continues, the partners act for each other in carrying it forward.

A different case would arise if the substantive offense committed by one of the conspirators was not in fact done in furtherance of the conspiracy, did not fall within the scope of the unlawful project, or was merely a part of the ramifications of the plan which could not be reasonably foreseen as a necessary or natural consequence of the unlawful agreement. But as we read this record, that is not this case.

Affirmed.

MR. JUSTICE RUTLEDGE, dissenting in part.

The judgment concerning Daniel Pinkerton should be reversed. In my opinion it is without precedent here and is a dangerous precedent to establish.

Daniel and Walter, who were brothers living near each other, were charged in several counts with substantive offenses, and then a conspiracy count was added naming those offenses as overt acts. The proof showed that Walter alone committed the substantive crimes. There was none to establish that Daniel participated in them, aided and abetted Walter in committing them, or knew that he had done so. Daniel in fact was in the penitentiary, under sentence for other crimes, when some of Walter's crimes were done.

The court's theory seems to be that Daniel and Walter became general partners in crime by virtue of their agreement and because of that agreement without more on his part Daniel became criminally responsible as a principal for everything Walter did thereafter in the nature of a criminal offense of the general sort the agreement contemplated, so long as there was not clear evidence that Daniel had withdrawn from or revoked the agreement.

Guilt [in criminal law] remains personal, not vicarious. It should be kept so.

PEOPLE V. ZIELESCH

California Court of Appeal
179 Cal.App.4th 731, 101 Cal.Rptr.3d 628 (2009)

SCOTLAND, P.J.

The tragic loss of life in this case illustrates the danger that faces law enforcement officers every day, even during what on the surface appear to be routine encounters.

Defendant Gregory Fred Zielesch bailed Brendt Volarvich out of jail and asked that, in return, Volarvich kill Doug Shamberger, who had been sleeping with defendant's wife. Volarvich agreed but needed a "piece" to carry out the hit. Defendant provided Volarvich with a .357 magnum revolver and $400 to purchase some methamphetamine. The next day, while driving back to defendant's house, Volarvich was stopped by California Highway Patrol Officer Andrew Stevens for a traffic violation. High on methamphetamine and afraid of being sent back to jail, Volarvich shot and killed Officer Stevens with defendant's gun when the officer walked up to the driver's window and greeted Volarvich with a friendly, "How are you doing today?"

We reject defendant's contentions that his murder conviction must be reversed because the shooting of Officer Stevens was not in furtherance of the conspiracy to kill Shamberger and "was both unforeseen and unforeseeable."

As we will explain, when defendant bargained for the assassin's services and armed him with a gun and money to buy methamphetamine, defendant knew that the assassin had an unstable personality, with the "mentality" to kill someone other than the intended victim of the assassination. Defendant also knew that the assassin had just been released from jail, was on searchable probation, and would not want to be returned to custody if a law enforcement officer found the assassin in possession of methamphetamine and defendant's gun. From these facts, jurors reasonably could conclude the cold-blooded murder of Officer Stevens was a natural and probable consequence of the conspiracy to kill Shamberger because a reasonable person, knowing what defendant knew, would recognize that if the unstable, methamphetamine using, and armed assassin were detained by a law enforcement officer before the assassination was completed, it is likely that he would kill the officer to avoid arrest and complete his mission.

The law has been settled for more than a century that each member of a conspiracy is criminally responsible for the acts of fellow conspirators committed in furtherance of, and which follow as a natural and probable consequence of, the conspiracy, even though such acts were not intended by the conspirators as a part of their common unlawful design.

Recognizing that criminal agency poses a greater threat to society than that posed by an independent criminal actor, the law seeks to deter criminal combination by recognizing the act of one as the act of all. Conspiracy to commit a target offense makes it more likely that additional crimes related to the target offense will be committed. In combining to plan a crime, each conspirator risks liability for conspiracy as well as the substantive offense; in planning poorly, each risks additional liability for the unanticipated, yet reasonably foreseeable consequences of the conspiratorial acts, liability which is avoidable by disavowing or abandoning the conspiracy.

The question whether an unplanned crime is a natural and probable consequence of a conspiracy to commit the intended crime is not whether the aider and abettor *actually* foresaw the additional crime, but whether, judged objectively, the unplanned crime was *reasonably* foreseeable. To be reasonably foreseeable, the consequence need not have been a strong probability; a possible consequence which might reasonably have been contemplated is enough. Whether the unplanned act was a reasonably foreseeable consequence of the conspiracy must be evaluated under all the factual circumstances of the individual case and is a factual issue to be resolved by the jury, whose determination is conclusive if supported by substantial evidence.

The People argued the murder furthered the goals of the conspiracy because, in order to successfully murder Shamberger, one of the goals of the conspiracy had to be to avoid detection; and the murder was a natural and probable consequence of the conspiracy because "a reasonable person would foresee that there would be police intervention" at some point during the execution of the plot to kill Shamberger, and defendant, with actual knowledge of Volarvich's "volatile and unstable" nature, gave him the gun to carry out the murder. Defendant's attorney argued no conspiracy existed between defendant and Volarvich; being pulled over by an officer on a country road in Woodland constituted an "extremely unusual" event, the intervention of which rendered Officer Steven's death not a natural and probable consequence of the alleged conspiracy; and Volarvich killed Officer Stevens because "he did not want to go to jail," not because of a conspiracy to kill Shamberger.

The jury found defendant guilty of both the conspiracy and murder charges, implicitly finding the murder of Officer Stevens was committed in furtherance of, and followed as a natural and probable consequence of, the conspiracy. We conclude the jury's finding is supported by substantial evidence. The object of the conspiracy between defendant and Volarvich was to end the life of defendant's nemesis with the .357 magnum revolver supplied by defendant for that purpose. Defendant knew Volarvich had a proclivity for using methamphetamine, having used the drug with Volarvich the night before he gave him the gun to carry out the hit, and having given Volarvich $400 to purchase more methamphetamine. Defendant admitted knowing Volarvich had an unstable personality; after receiving news of Officer Stevens' murder, defendant told Pina that Volarvich's "mentality was there." Defendant also had reason to know that Volarvich, who was on searchable probation, would be taken into custody if a law enforcement officer detained him and found the gun. From these facts, the jury could find that a natural and probable consequence, i.e., a reasonably foreseeable "possible consequence" of the defendant's conspiracy with assassin Volarvich to murder Shamberger was that, if Volarvich were detained by a law enforcement officer before completing the job, Volarvich would kill the officer to avoid arrest and complete his mission to assassinate Shamberger.

The judgment is affirmed.

NOTE

The CALCRIM 417 jury instruction on *Pinkerton* liability states:

> A member of a conspiracy is criminally responsible for the crimes that he or she conspires to commit, no matter which member of the conspiracy commits the crime.
>
> A member of a conspiracy is also criminally responsible for any act of any member of the conspiracy if that act is done to further the conspiracy and that act is a natural and probable consequence of the common plan or design of the conspiracy. This rule applies even if the act was not intended as part of the original plan. Under this rule, a defendant who is a member of the conspiracy does not need to be present at the time of the act.
>
> A natural and probable consequence is one that a reasonable person would know is likely to happen if nothing unusual intervenes. In deciding whether a consequence is natural and probable, consider all of the circumstances established by the evidence.
>
> A member of a conspiracy is not criminally responsible for the act of another member if that act does not further the common plan or is not a natural and probable consequence of the common plan.
>
> The defendant is not responsible for the acts of another person who was not a member of the conspiracy even if the acts of the other person helped accomplish the goal of the conspiracy.
>
> A conspiracy member is not responsible for the acts of other conspiracy members that are done after the goal of the conspiracy had been accomplished.

PROBLEMS

1. Recall the problems earlier in this chapter for which you drew pictures of conspiracies? Return to those problems and consider the implications of *Pinkerton* liability.

2. Davis grew marijuana in his backyard in Los Osos. Johnson decided to steal Davis's crop. Rather than commit the crime himself, Johnson recruited Alvarez and Baker. Davis heard a knock on his front door. When he opened the door, Alvarez and Baker forced their way in. Baker had a gun. Baker told Davis, "Sit down or I'll shoot you." Davis did as ordered. Alvarez scooped dried marijuana into bags while Baker kept guard over Davis. Baker forced Davis to look at the gun. Over the course of five minutes, Baker yelled at Davis, saying, "I'll kill you if you try anything." "I'm quick on the trigger, homie." "I'm a fucking thug." "You don't want to fuck with me, homie." "You ever seen Pulp Fiction, homie?" All the while, Baker kept the gun aimed at Davis's head. Davis's own gun was under the cushion of the couch where he was sitting. When Baker momentarily looked toward Alvarez, Davis grabbed his gun and started firing wildly, killing Alvarez. Baker ran away. Is Johnson liable for the death of Alvarez? *People v. Johnson* (2013) 221 Cal. App. 4th 623, 164 Cal. Rptr. 3d 505.

Wharton's "Rule"

The general rule is that a conspiracy to commit a crime is itself a crime, and is punishable in addition to the target offense—there is no merger. For example, if Sue and Betty conspire to rob a bank and actually rob the bank, they can be prosecuted for conspiracy *and* bank robbery. Wharton's Rule is an exception to the general rule. If Wharton's Rule applies, only the target offense can be prosecuted, not the conspiracy to commit the target offense—the conspiracy merges.

Francis Wharton (1820–1889) wrote an influential nineteenth century treatise on criminal law. In his book, Wharton articulated the rule that bears his name—Wharton's Rule. The modern version of the rule provides: "An agreement by two persons to commit a particular crime cannot be prosecuted as a conspiracy when the crime is of such a nature as to necessarily require the participation of two persons for its commission." R. Anderson, *Wharton's Criminal Law and Procedure* (1957).

Wharton's rule only applies when the crime requires two people for its commission. If the crime can be committed by one person acting alone, Wharton's Rule does not apply. The U.S. Supreme Court wrote that the "classic Wharton's Rule offenses" are "adultery, incest, bigamy, [and] dueling." *Iannelli v. United States* (1975) 420 U.S. 770, 95 S.Ct. 1284. Can you have a duel with yourself? Can one person commit adultery? These crimes require two people. In the bank robbery prosecution of Sue and

Betty, mentioned above, Wharton's Rule does not apply because it *is* possible for one person, acting alone, to rob a bank.

Even if a crime requires two people, Wharton's Rule does not apply if more than the minimum number of people required to commit the crime actually participate in the offense. Wharton's rule does not apply when the consequences of the crime impact more than the participants. Finally, Wharton's Rule is no longer a "rule." In *Iannelli*, the U.S. Supreme Court stated, "Wharton's Rule has current vitality only as a judicial presumption, to be applied in the absence of legislative intent to the contrary." If legislative history indicates the legislature intended punishment of *both* the conspiracy and the target offense, Wharton's Rule is inapplicable.

In California there is little case law on Wharton's Rule. In *People v. Lee* (2006) 136 Cal.App.4th 522, 529, 38 Cal.Rptr.3d 927, the Court of Appeal wrote, "The rule is considered in modern legal thinking as an aid in construction of statutes, a presumption that the Legislature intended the general conspiracy section be merged with the specific substantive offense. It applies only where it is impossible to have the substantive offense without concerted efforts amounting to conspiracy."

Does Wharton's Rule apply to the following case? PC § 4573.9 provides: "Notwithstanding any other provision of law, any person, other than a person held in custody, who sells, furnishes, administers, or gives away to any person held in custody in any state prison any controlled substance, the possession of which is prohibited is guilty of a felony." Dell, a prison inmate, asked his wife Rachel to deliver illegal drugs to him during a visit to the prison. Rachel was searched when she entered the prison and drugs were found on her person. Dell is prosecuted for conspiracy to violate the target offense. *People v. Lee* (2006) 136 Cal.App.4th 522, 38 Cal.Rptr.3d 927.

ATTEMPT

The law does not punish criminal intent alone. Crime consists of *mens rea and actus reus.* Short of completion of a crime, however, the law punishes attempts to commit crime. But why punish attempt? After all, nothing happened. The law of attempt allows police to *prevent* crime by arresting individuals who have demonstrated their dangerousness *before* they complete their intended crime. Someone who has tried and failed to commit a crime is probably motivated to mount another attempt. As the saying goes, "If at first you don't succeed, try try again."

The *mens rea* for attempt is the intent to commit a target crime (*e.g.*, murder, robbery, arson). Every attempt is a specific intent crime. This is true even if the target crime is a general intent crime. PC § 21a provides, "An attempt to commit a crime consists of two elements: a specific intent to commit the crime, and a direct but ineffectual act done toward its commission."

There are two types of attempt: complete and incomplete. With a complete attempt, defendant took every step she intended to take to commit the crime, but for some reason the crime was not committed. For example, Dorothy decided to kill Frank. Dorothy went to Frank's house. When Frank opened the door, Dorothy took careful aim at Frank's head and pulled the trigger, but missed. This is attempted murder, and is a complete attempt. Dorothy took every step she intended to take. Nothing remained to be done.

With an incomplete attempt, steps remain to be taken before the crime can occur. For some reason the defendant stops or is stopped. Perhaps the police arrest the defendant. Perhaps the defendant has a change of heart and decides not to commit the crime. If the defendant crossed the line of attempt—the line that separates preparation from attempt—a crime occurred, and abandonment is not a defense.

The *actus reus* of an incomplete attempt is an act that is a substantial step toward completion of the target crime, or, in the words of PC § 21a, "a direct but ineffectual act done toward its commission." As stated above, mere preparation to commit a crime is not an attempt. On the other hand, an offender does not have to take the last step proximate to completing a crime in order to cross the line separating preparation from attempt.[10] In many cases the attempt is obvious. Thus, a would-be bank robber who bursts into a bank with guns drawn but who is arrested before uttering the words "Nobody move this is a bank robbery" commits attempted robbery. In other cases, it is difficult to determine whether a defendant crossed the sometimes blurry line separating preparation from attempt. Courts describe the line with phrases like "the commencement of the consummation,"[11] "some appreciable fragment of the crime,"[12] and "the line separating preparation from perpetration." These phrases are colorful but not very helpful. In the final analysis, each case of incomplete attempt is decided on its own facts. Returning to the would-be bank robber, suppose she never made it to the bank. She obtained the gun she intended to use in the robbery and stole a car to serve as the getaway vehicle. While driving to the bank to commit the crime, and still ten miles away, she had a change of heart and drove to church. Attempted bank robbery?

In analyzing incomplete attempts, many courts around the country employ the so-called "proximity approach." Under the proximity approach, the primary question is: How close did the defendant get to completing the offense? The closer the defendant got, the more likely the line was crossed.

---

[10] *See People v. Hajek,* 58 Cal. 4th 1144 (2014).

[11] *State v. Bereman* (1954) 177 Kan. 141, 276 P.2d 364.

[12] *People v. Buffum* (1953) 40 Cal.2d 709, 256 P.2d 317.

In assessing proximity, courts consider (1) the number of acts remaining before the crime could occur, (2) the distance to be covered before the crime could occur, and (3) how close in time the offender got to completing the crime.

Courts sometimes state that when proof of the offender's intent is clear, the line is crossed earlier.

An occasional court employs the so-called equivocality test, in which we pretend the defendant's conduct from the beginning was video recorded. To determine whether an attempt occurred, watch the video with the sound turned off. Without audio, the viewer has no access to defendant's words. If defendant said, "I'm going to rob a bank today," the viewer is oblivious. If defendant's conduct—sans words shedding light on intent—points unequivocally to attempt, defendant is guilty. If defendant's conduct was equivocal, no attempt.

The Model Penal Code approach to incomplete attempts asks whether defendant committed an act that constitutes a "substantial step in a course of conduct planned to culminate in the commission of the crime."[13] Unlike the proximity approach, which asks, "How close did the defendant get to completing the crime?" the Model Penal Code asks, "How far did the defendant go toward completing the crime?" Most of the time the result is the same under the Model Penal Code and the proximity approach. In close cases, however, conduct that does not get close enough under the proximity approach goes far enough to cross the line in the Model Penal Code. Indeed, the drafters of the Model Penal Code intended to broaden attempt liability.

The Model Penal Code describes behaviors that can corroborate a defendant's intent to commit a crime, helping determine whether an incomplete attempt occurred. The behaviors are: (1) lying in wait for the victim, (2) searching for the victim, (3) convincing the victim to go to the place where the crime will be perpetrated, (4) reconnoitering the location where the crime will be committed (*e.g.*, casing a bank), and (5) possession of burglar's tools or other instruments for use in the crime.[14] These factors are equally useful with the proximity approach to incomplete attempts.

Within every completed crime there is an attempt. When a defendant is charged with a completed crime, and convicted of the same, the attempt merges into the conviction. Thus, a defendant cannot be convicted of both a completed crime and an attempt to commit the crime. However, if the jury acquits the defendant of the completed crime, the jury can convict of the attempt to commit the crime.

People v. Staples is a good introduction to California attempt law.

---

[13] Model Penal Code § 5.01.

[14] Model Penal Code § 5.01(2).

PEOPLE V. STAPLES

California Court of Appeal
6 Cal.App.3d 61, 85 Cal.Rptr. 589 (1970)

REPPY, J.

Facts

Defendant was charged in an information with attempted burglary (Pen. Code, §§ 664, 459). In October 1967, while his wife was away on a trip, defendant, a mathematician, under an assumed name, rented an office on the second floor of a building in Hollywood which was over the mezzanine of a bank. Directly below the mezzanine was the vault of the bank. Defendant was aware of the layout of the building, specifically of the relation of the office he rented to the bank vault. Defendant paid rent for the period from October 23 to November 23. The landlord had 10 days before commencement of the rental period within which to finish some interior repairs and painting. During this prerental period defendant brought into the office certain equipment. This included drilling tools, two acetylene gas tanks, a blow torch, a blanket, and a linoleum rug. The landlord observed these items when he came in from time to time to see how the repair work was progressing. Defendant learned from a custodian that no one was in the building on Saturdays. On Saturday, October 14, defendant drilled two groups of holes into the floor of the office above the mezzanine room. He stopped drilling before the holes went through the floor. He came back to the office several times thinking he might slowly drill down, covering the holes with the linoleum rug. At some point in time he installed a hasp lock on a closet, and planned to, or did, place his tools in it. However, he left the closet keys on the premises. Around the end of November, apparently after November 23, the landlord notified the police and turned the tools and equipment over to them. Defendant did not pay any more rent. It is not clear when he last entered the office, but it could have been after November 23, and even after the landlord had removed the equipment. On February 22, 1968, the police arrested defendant. After receiving advice as to his constitutional rights, defendant voluntarily made an oral statement which he reduced to writing.

Among other things which defendant wrote down were these: "Saturday, the 14th. I drilled some small holes in the floor of the room. Because of tiredness, fear, and the implications of what I was doing, I stopped and went to sleep. At this point I think my motives began to change. The actual commencement of my plan made me begin to realize that even if I were to succeed, a fugitive life of living off of stolen money would not give the enjoyment of the life of a mathematician however humble a job I might have. I still had not given up my plan however. I felt I had made a certain investment of time, money, effort and a certain psychological commitment to the concept. I came back several times thinking I might store the tools in the closet and slowly drill down (covering the hole with a rug of linoleum square). As time went on (after two weeks or so), my wife came back and my life as bank robber seemed more and more absurd."

Defendant's position in this appeal is that, as a matter of law, there was insufficient evidence upon which to convict him of a criminal attempt under Penal Code section 664. Defendant claims that his actions were all preparatory in nature and never reached a stage of advancement in relation to the substantive crime which he concededly intended to commit (burglary of the bank vault) so that criminal responsibility might attach.

In order for the prosecution to prove that defendant committed an attempt to burglarize as proscribed by Penal Code section 664, it was required to establish that he had the specific intent to commit a burglary of the bank and that his acts toward that goal went beyond mere preparation. The required specific intent was clearly established in the instant case. Defendant admitted in his written confession that he rented the office fully intending to burglarize the bank, that he brought in tools and equipment to accomplish this purpose, and that he began drilling into the floor with the intent of making an entry into the bank.

The question of whether defendant's conduct went beyond "mere preparation" raises some provocative problems. The briefs and the oral argument of counsel in this case point up a degree of ambiguity and uncertainty that permeates the law of attempts in this state. Each side has cited us to a different so-called "test" to determine whether this defendant's conduct went beyond the preparatory stage. Predictably each respective test in the eyes of its proponents yielded an opposite result.

Defendant relies heavily on the following language: "Preparation alone is not enough to convict for an attempt, there must be some appreciable fragment of the crime committed, it must be in such progress that it will be consummated unless interrupted by circumstances independent of the will of the attempter, and the act must not be equivocal in nature." (*People v. Buffum*, 40 Cal.2d 709). Defendant argues that while the facts show that he did do a series of acts directed at the commission of a burglary—renting the office, bringing in elaborate equipment and actually starting drilling—the facts do not show that he was interrupted by any outside circumstances. Without such interruption and a voluntary desistence on his part, defendant concludes that under the above stated test, he has not legally committed an attempt. The Attorney General has replied that even if the above test is appropriate, the trial judge, obviously drawing reasonable inferences, found that defendant was interrupted by outside circumstances—the landlord's acts of discovering the burglary equipment, resuming control over the premises, and calling the police.

However, the Attorney General suggests that another test is more appropriate: Whenever the design of a person to commit crime is clearly shown, slight acts in furtherance of the design will constitute an attempt.

The People argue that defendant's felonious intent was clearly set out in his written confession; that the proven overt acts in furtherance of the design, although only needing to be slight, were, in fact, substantial; that this combination warrants the affirmance of the attempt conviction.

We suggest that the confusion in this area is a result of the broad statutory language of section 664, which reads in part: "Any person who attempts to commit any crime, but fails, or is prevented or intercepted in the perpetration thereof, is punishable." This is a very general proscription against all attempts not specifically made a crime. The statute does not differentiate between the various types of attempts which may be considered culpable. Reference must be made to case law in order to determine precisely what conduct constitutes an attempt. However, the statute does point out by the words "fails," "prevented," and "intercepted," those *conditions* which separate an attempt from the substantive crime.

An examination of the decisional law reveals *at least two* general categories of attempts, both of which have been held to fall within the ambit of the statute. In the first category are those situations where the actor does all acts necessary (including the last proximate act) to commit the substantive crime, but nonetheless he somehow is unsuccessful. This lack of success is either a "failure" or a "prevention" brought about because of some extraneous circumstances, *e.g.*, a malfunction of equipment, a miscalculation of operations by the actor or a situation wherein circumstances were at variance with what the actor believed them to be. Certain convictions for attempted murder illustrate the first category. Some turn on situations wherein the actor fires a weapon at a person but misses, takes aim at an intended victim and pulls the trigger, but the firing mechanism malfunctions, plants on an aircraft a homemade bomb which sputters but does not explode. After a defendant has done all acts necessary under normal conditions to commit crime, he is culpable for an attempt if he is unsuccessful *because* of an extraneous or fortuitous circumstance.

However, it is quite clear that under California law an overt act, which, when added to the requisite intent, is sufficient to bring about a criminal attempt, need not be the last proximate or ultimate step towards commission of the substantive crime. It is not necessary that the overt act proved should have been the ultimate step toward the consummation of the design. It is sufficient if it was the first or some subsequent step in a direct movement towards the commission of the offense after the preparations are made. Police officers need not wait until a suspect, who aims a gun at his intended victim, actually pulls the trigger before they arrest him; nor do these officers need to wait until a suspect, who is forcing the lock of a bank door, actually breaks in before they arrest him for attempted burglary.

Applying criminal culpability to acts directly moving toward commission of crime (but short of the last proximate act necessary to consummate the criminal design) under section 664 is an obvious safeguard to society because it makes it unnecessary for police to wait before intervening until the actor has done the substantive evil sought to be prevented. It allows such criminal conduct to be stopped or intercepted when it becomes clear what the actor's intention is and when the acts done show that the perpetrator is actually putting his plan into action. Discovering precisely what conduct falls within this latter category, however, often becomes a difficult problem. Because of the lack of specificity of section 664, police, trial judges, jurors, and in the last analysis, appellate courts, face the dilemma of trying to identify that point beyond which conduct passes from innocent to criminal absent a specific event such as the commission of a prohibited substantive crime.

Our courts have come up with a variety of tests which try to distinguish acts of preparation from completed attempts. The preparation consists in devising or arranging the means or measures necessary for the commission of the offense; the attempt is the direct movement toward the commission after the preparations are made. The act must reach far enough towards the accomplishment of the desired result to amount to the commencement of the consummation. Where the intent to commit the substantive offense is clearly established, acts done toward the commission of the crime may constitute an attempt, where the same acts would be held insufficient to constitute an attempt if the intent with which they were done is equivocal and not clearly proved.

None of the above statements of the law applicable to this category of attempts provide a litmus-like test, and perhaps no such test is achievable. Such precision is not required in this case, however. There was definitely substantial evidence entitling the trial judge to find that defendant's acts had gone beyond the preparation stage. Without specifically deciding where defendant's preparations left off and where his activities became a completed criminal attempt, we can say that his drilling activity clearly was an unequivocal and direct step toward the completion of the burglary. It was a fragment of the substantive crime contemplated, i.e., the beginning of the "breaking" element. Further, defendant himself characterized his activity as the *actual commencement of his plan*. The drilling by defendant was obviously one of a series of acts which logic and ordinary experience indicate would result in the proscribed act of burglary.

Affirmed.

In *People v. Decker,* the Supreme Court explored attempt law in the context of a defendant who hired a "hit" man to kill his sister.

PEOPLE V. DECKER

California Supreme Court
41 Cal.4th 1, 58 Cal.Rptr.3d 421, 157 P.3d 1017 (2007)

BAXTER, J.

Defendant and real party in interest Ronald Decker has been charged with the attempted willful, deliberate, and premeditated murder of his sister, Donna Decker, and her friend, Hermine Riley Bafiera. (Pen.Code § 664, subd. (a).) According to the evidence offered at the preliminary hearing, Decker did not want to kill these women himself—as he explained, "he would be the prime suspect" and "would probably make a mistake somehow or another"—so he sought the services of a hired assassin.

Decker located such a person (or thought he did). He furnished the hired assassin with a description of his sister, her home, her car, and her workplace, as well as specific information concerning her daily habits. He also advised the assassin to kill Hermine if necessary to avoid leaving a witness behind. Decker and the hired assassin agreed on the means to commit the murder, the method of payment, and the price. The parties also agreed that Decker would pay $5,000 in cash as a downpayment. Before Decker handed over the money, the assassin asked whether Decker was "sure" he wanted to go through with the murders. Decker replied, "I am absolutely, positively, 100 percent sure, that I want to go through with it. I've never been so sure of anything in my entire life." All of these conversations were recorded and videotaped because, unknown to Decker, he was talking with an undercover police detective posing as a hired assassin.

Decker does not dispute that the foregoing evidence was sufficient to hold him to answer to the charge of solicitation of the murder of Donna and Hermine but argues that this evidence was insufficient to support a charge of their attempted murder.

On August 20, 2003, Ronald Decker (identifying himself only as "Ron") placed a telephone call to Russell Wafer, a gunsmith at Lock, Stock and Barrel in Temple City (Los Angeles County). Decker said he was looking for someone to do some "work" for him and arranged to meet privately with Wafer the following week. During that meeting, Decker explained that he had been in contact with Soldier of Fortune magazine, had done some research, and came up with Wafer's name as a possible "contractor" for a local "job"—"basically it was that he wanted someone taken care of." Decker added that he could not kill the victim himself because he would be a prime suspect. Wafer advised that while he could not handle the job, his friend "John" from Detroit might be interested. After Decker offered to pay the killer $35,000 and an additional $3,000 to Wafer as a finder's fee, Wafer said he would try to contact John. He instructed Decker to call him back the following week.

In reality, however, Wafer did not know a "John" in Detroit who would be interested in a contract murder. Wafer instead called the Los Angeles County Sheriff's Department, spoke to Detective Wayne Holston, and agreed to assist in a sting operation. When Decker called Wafer on September 2, Wafer claimed he had been in contact with "John," who was coming to town shortly. Wafer asked Decker for his phone number and promised to arrange a meeting with "John." Based on the physical description Wafer had provided and on the phone number Decker had supplied, Holston located a photograph of Decker. Wafer immediately recognized Decker as "Ron," the man he had met the previous week. At Holston's request, Wafer arranged a meeting with Decker for the evening of September 5 at a golf course parking lot in Arcadia. Holston accompanied Wafer to the meeting and was introduced as "John" from Detroit. Holston was wearing a "wire," and the encounter was both videotaped and recorded.

After Wafer left the two men alone, Decker explained that a "lady" owed him a lot of money and that the only way for him to get it back was "to take her out." Decker subsequently identified the target as his sister, Donna Decker, and provided descriptions of her person, her mode of dress, her residence, her office, her car, and her daily habits. Decker offered Holston $25,000 to perform the execution, with a $10,000 bonus if it were a "nice, neat, clean job." Decker reiterated that he could not do it himself, as "he would be the prime suspect," and might "slip up" somewhere. When Decker proposed that Holston kill Donna in an automobile accident, Holston warned him that she might survive such an accident. Decker agreed that this might not be the best method, since he wanted her "totally expired," and said he appreciated Holston's advice: "I want a professional—someone that's gonna do the job, and do it right—and do it right." When Holston then proposed killing Donna during a staged robbery or carjacking, Decker said that would be "great" and urged Holston to "shoot her in the heart and head both, just to make sure." Decker added that Donna spent a lot of time with her friend and coworker, Hermine Riley Bafiera, and that Holston might need to "take out" Hermine as well to avoid having a witness. Decker did not care for Hermine, either.

When Holston said he could complete the job within a week, Decker replied, "Marvelous. The sooner the better." Holston also asked for some money up front, and Decker said he could supply him with $5,000 in cash as a downpayment in a couple of days "so you can start right away." The downpayment was also designed to prove Decker's sincerity, since "once this goes into effect—she's gonna be killed." Decker could barely contain his eagerness: "Well that's what I want. I don't want go to the hospital then come home. I want absolutely positively expired. Totally expired."

Decker and Holston met again at the golf course on September 7. This meeting was also videotaped and recorded. Decker gave Holston $5,000 in cash, wrapped in two plastic bundles. He reiterated that Holston, after

Donna had been murdered, should use a pay phone to leave him a voicemail message—Holston was to say that "the paint job has been completed"—and that Holston would get the rest of the money about a month later. Decker also reiterated that "if Hermine is in the car, with her, you cannot, I understand if I were in your business, I would never leave a witness. You have to take her out too. Whoever's with her you gotta take the other person out too. But don't charge me double."

Holston told Decker that he had already performed some intelligence work, that he was "convinced" he would see the victim the next day, and that he could get this "job" done quickly—eliciting another "marvelous" from Decker—and explained that "once I leave here, it's done. So, you sure you want to go through with it?" Decker replied, "I am absolutely, positively, 100 percent sure, that I want to go through with it. I've never been so sure of anything in my entire life. Do it very fast, as fast as you can." At the end of the conversation, Decker seemed "very pleased" and thanked Holston and Wafer. A short time after Holston and Wafer drove off, Decker was arrested.

The superior court's dismissal of the attempted murder charges, which was based on undisputed facts, constitutes a legal conclusion subject to independent review on appeal. The question for us is whether it appears from the preliminary examination that a public offense has been committed, and there is sufficient cause to believe the defendant guilty thereof. Sufficient cause means such a state of facts as would lead a man of ordinary caution or prudence to believe and conscientiously entertain a strong suspicion of the guilt of the accused. Evidence which will justify prosecution under the above test need not be sufficient to support a conviction.

Attempted murder requires the specific intent to kill and the commission of a direct but ineffectual act toward accomplishing the intended killing. (Pen.Code § 21a). The uncontradicted evidence that Decker harbored the specific intent to kill his sister (and, if necessary, her friend Hermine) was overwhelming. Decker expressed to both Wafer and Holston his desire to have Donna killed. He researched how to find a hired assassin. He spent months accumulating cash in small denominations to provide the hired assassin with a downpayment and had also worked out a method by which to pay the balance. He knew the layout of his sister's condominium and how one might enter it surreptitiously. He had tested the level of surveillance in the vicinity of her home and determined it was "not really that sharp." He chronicled his sister's daily routine at both her home and her office. He offered Holston recommendations on how his sister should be killed and what materials would be necessary. And, at both meetings with Holston, he insisted that Hermine, if she were present, be killed as well, so as to prevent her from being a witness.

The controversy in this case, as the parties readily concede, is whether there was also a direct but ineffectual act toward accomplishing the intended killings. For an attempt, the overt act must go beyond mere preparation and show that the killer is putting his or her plan into action; it need not be the last proximate or ultimate step toward commission of the crime or crimes. Nor need it satisfy any element of the crime. However, between preparation for the attempt and the attempt itself, there is a wide difference. The preparation consists in devising or arranging the means or measures necessary for the commission of the offense; the attempt is the direct movement toward the commission after the preparations are made. It is sufficient if it is the first or some subsequent act directed towards that end after the preparations are made.

As simple as it is to state the terminology for the law of attempt, it is not always clear in practice how to apply it. As other courts have observed, "much ink has been spilt in an attempt to arrive at a satisfactory standard for telling where preparation ends and attempt begins." Indeed, we have ourselves observed that none of the various tests used by the courts can possibly distinguish all preparations from all attempts.

Although a definitive test has proved elusive, we have long recognized that whenever the design of a person to commit crime is clearly shown, slight acts in furtherance of the design will constitute an attempt. Viewing the entirety of Decker's conduct in light of his clearly expressed intent, we find sufficient evidence under the slight-acts rule to hold him to answer to the charges of attempted murder.

The judgment of the Court of Appeal is affirmed.

Dissenting Opinion by WERDEGAR, J.

My colleagues hold that defendant's conduct in soliciting the murder of his sister, reaching an agreement with a hired assassin to do the killing, and making a downpayment under the agreement establishes probable cause to believe defendant himself attempted the murder. I respectfully dissent. An attempt to commit a crime consists of two elements: a specific intent to commit the crime, and a direct but ineffectual act done toward its commission. (Pen. Code § 21a.) Defendant's conduct in this case does not include "a direct but ineffectual act" done toward the murder's commission. Accordingly, he cannot be guilty of attempted murder.

PROBLEMS

1. In this question, decide when D crosses the line and commits attempted murder. D decided to kill his enemy V, who lived 5 miles away. The inspiration for this question comes from Joshua Dressler's *Cases and Materials on Criminal Law.*

a. D purchased a pistol and ammunition from a sports store.

b. D took lessons on proper use of the pistol.

c. The day before he planned to kill V, D put the unloaded gun and a box of ammunition in the glove compartment of his car.

d. On the day of the planned killing, D Mapquested directions to V's house.

e. D got in his car and started the motor with the intent to drive to V's home and shoot him.

f. D knew that V worked until 5:00 p.m. At 4:00 p.m., D drove the 5 miles to V's house and parked in front of V's house.

g. While sitting in his car in front of V's house, D loaded the gun and placed in on his lap.

h. At 5:30 p.m., V arrived home and parked his car in his driveway. As V was walking toward his front door, D placed his hand on the gun.

i. D raised the gun and aimed it at V. At that moment a police car happened to drive down the street. D saw the police car and placed the gun back on his lap. D drove home without firing at V.

j. The next day, at 4:30 p.m., D again drove to V's house and parked across the street. When V got home and exited his car, D aimed and prepared to fire. At that moment, V's young daughter ran out of the house to greet her father, and D decided not to kill V. D drove home and abandoned his plan to kill V.

2. In 1955, when abortion was a crime, Adrienne Scheuplein, an investigator for the district attorney, went to the office of appellant, a licensed physician. She introduced herself as Kathryn Phillips and told appellant that she was pregnant and that she had come to him for the same reason as the young woman who had referred her to him. He directed her to go to a laboratory for a test to establish pregnancy. She was later informed by telephone that the test was positive and requested to call again at appellant's office. When she went to his office the second time, the co-defendant Inez Burns was there. Appellant told Mrs. Scheuplein that it was difficult to do anything about her problem and asked if the operation could be performed at the place she was staying. It was subsequently arranged that the operation would be performed at Mrs. Scheuplein's home. Appellant told Mrs. Scheuplein that a suitcase would be delivered at her home and that the person who would perform the operation would get in touch with her and he gave her specific instructions on preparing herself for surgery. The suitcase was delivered that night and the following morning Inez Burns arrived. Mrs. Burns went to the kitchen and began making arrangements for the operation. The suitcase containing the surgical instruments was brought into the kitchen, the instruments were wrapped in towels and placed on the stove in pans of water to boil. A sheet was placed over the window to conceal it from the view of any person outside. Mrs. Burns placed cotton, jars of Pitocin, Ergotrate, Metsol and ammonia and a

large roll of gauze on a side table. Mrs. Scheuplein paid Mrs. Burns $525 in marked money. These activities occupied about 45 minutes during which Mrs. Burns talked of her past activities and reassured Mrs. Scheuplein about the pending operation. When the water in the pans containing the instruments was starting to boil, Mrs. Scheuplein went upstairs, supposedly to disrobe, and the police arrived and arrested Mrs. Burns. Mrs. Burns admitted that she was there for the purpose of performing an abortion. *People v. Berger* (1955) 131 Cal.App.2d 127, 280 P.2d 136.

3. Dell decided to kill his wife by putting a bomb at her office. Dell hired someone else to make the bomb. Dell accompanied the bomb maker to the office to install the bomb, but was arrested in the office building before the bomb was installed. *People v. Lanzit* (1924) 70 Cal.App. 498, 233 P. 816.

4. Linda decided to blow up a government building. Linda manufactured a bomb. She drove to the building and parked two blocks away. Linda exited her car with the bomb. When she was a block from the building, she was arrested. *People v. Stites* (1888) 75 Cal. 570, 17 P. 693.

5. Margaret went to Paul's house at night to commit burglary. Margaret entered Paul's property. She was apprehended below a bedroom window with her arms extended upward to the window. *People v. Davis* (1938) 24 Cal.App.2d 408, 75 P.2d 80.

6. On the evening of January 5, Tracie Reeves and Molly Coffman, both twelve years of age and students in middle school, spoke on the telephone and decided to kill their homeroom teacher, Janice Geiger. The girls agreed that Coffman would bring rat poison to school the following day so that it could be placed in Geiger's coffee. The girls also agreed that they would thereafter steal Geiger's car and drive to the mountains. Reeves then contacted Dean Foutch, a local high school student, informed him of the plan, and asked him to drive Geiger's car. Foutch refused this request. On the morning of January 6, Coffman placed a packet of rat poison in her purse and boarded the school bus. During the bus ride Coffman told another student, Christy Hernandez, of the plan. Coffman also showed Hernandez the packet of rat poison. Upon their arrival at school, Hernandez informed her homeroom teacher, Sherry Cockrill, of the plan. Cockrill then relayed this information to the principal of the school, Claudia Argo. When Geiger entered her classroom that morning she observed Reeves and Coffman leaning over her desk; and when the girls noticed her, they giggled and ran back to their seats. At that time Geiger saw a purse lying next to her coffee cup on top of the desk. Shortly thereafter Argo called Coffman to the principal's office. Rat poison was found in Coffman's purse. *State v. Reeves* (Tenn. 1996) 916 S.W.2d 909.

Attempted Murder

To commit attempted murder, defendant must intend to kill. Consider three defendants, Ann, Betty, and Charlene.[15] Each defendant kills a victim. Ann intended to kill. Betty acted with a depraved heart. Charlene accidentally killed her victim during the commission of a felony. Ann, Betty, and Charlene are all guilty of murder. Now change the facts: None of the victims died. Who is guilty of attempted murder?

Attempted murder is not divided into degrees. There is no crime of second degree attempted murder. Nor is there a crime of attempted felony murder or attempted depraved heart murder.

The cases in this section explore attempted murder.

PEOPLE V. SMITH

California Supreme Court
37 Cal.4th 733, 37 Cal.Rptr.3d 163, 124 P.3d 730 (2005)

BAXTER, J.

The defendant in this case challenges the sufficiency of the evidence to support his conviction of two counts of attempted murder where he fired a single bullet into a slowly moving vehicle, narrowly missing a mother and her infant son. The evidence showed that the mother, who was known to defendant and was driving, and her baby, who was secured in a car seat directly behind her, were each in defendant's line of fire when he fired a single .38-caliber round at them from behind the car as it pulled away from the curb. The bullet shattered the rear windshield, narrowly missed both the mother and baby, passed through the mother's headrest, and lodged in the driver's side door.

On appeal, defendant contends his conviction of the attempted murder of the baby must be reversed for lack of substantial evidence that he harbored the requisite specific intent to kill the child. We disagree. Under the applicable deferential standard of review, we conclude the evidence is sufficient to support the jury's verdict finding defendant acted with intent to kill the baby as well as the mother. The fact that only a single bullet was fired into the vehicle does not, as a matter of law, compel a different conclusion. Accordingly, the judgment of the Court of Appeal shall be affirmed.

On the afternoon of February 18, 2000, Karen A. drove her boyfriend, Renell T., Sr. (Renell), to a friend's house on Greenholme Lane in Sacramento. She was driving her four-door Chevy Lumina, with Renell seated in the front passenger seat and their three-month-old baby, Renell

[15] This example is drawn from Wayne R. LaFave, *Criminal Law* § 11.3(a), p. 617 (5th ed. 2010) (West).

T., Jr., secured in a rear-facing infant car seat in the backseat directly behind her. She parked alongside the curb on the street in front of the house, and Renell got out of the car. As Karen waited in the car to make sure Renell's friend was home, she saw defendant approaching from behind. Karen recognized defendant as a former friend. She had last spoken to him during a telephone conversation eight to nine months earlier during which he had told her the next time he saw her he would "slap the shit out of her."

Defendant walked up to the open front passenger window of Karen's car, looked inside and said, "Don't I know you, bitch?" Overhearing the statement, Renell turned around from the walkway leading to the house and said, "Well, you don't know me." As Renell walked back toward the car, defendant lifted his shirt to display a handgun tucked in his waistband. Renell said, "It is cool," and backed away from defendant. According to Karen, a group of men on the street corner began approaching the car, and as Renell was entering the vehicle through the front passenger door, defendant and the other men began hitting him.

As soon as Renell was securely inside the car, Karen started to pull away from the curb. After driving about one car length, she looked in her rearview mirror and saw defendant standing "straight behind" her holding a gun. She heard a single gunshot, and although she did not see defendant pull the trigger, he was the only person she had seen with a gun. The bullet shattered the rear windshield, narrowly missed both Karen and the baby, passed through the driver's headrest, and lodged in the driver's side door. As soon as Karen reached a place of safety, she stopped to check the baby for injuries. He was screaming, his face covered with pieces of broken glass.

Renell's testimony generally corroborated Karen's testimony. He declined to identify defendant as the assailant because he did not want to be a snitch, but identified the assailant's gun as a .38-caliber revolver. After the shooting, a Sacramento County deputy sheriff searched defendant's room at his mother's home and recovered two .38-caliber shell casings.

Defendant testified he was unarmed on the day of the shooting, and that it was Renell who had displayed a gun during the confrontation. He claimed that Karen was his ex-girlfriend and that he had spoken to her over the telephone the day before the shooting. During this conversation, defendant told Karen the next time he saw her he would "slap the shit out of her." Karen hung up, and then Renell called back and threatened to "smoke" defendant. Defendant suggested he and Renell meet on Greenholme Lane the next day. When Renell arrived at the agreed location with Karen and the baby, defendant approached the car, saw Karen and the baby inside, and said, "What are you doing here, bitch?" Renell got out of the car, and defendant challenged him to a fistfight. Renell responded by pulling a semiautomatic handgun from his waistband. Although Renell did not fire, defendant heard a shot, hit the ground, heard several more shots and heard glass shattering. Defendant saw two .38-caliber casings lying on the ground, picked them up, put them in his pocket and brought them to his mother's house.

Defendant was charged by information with the attempted murder of Karen A. (Pen.Code §§ 664, 187) [and] the attempted murder of the baby (§§ 664, 187). [The jury found defendant guilty of all charges].

The Court of Appeal rejected defendant's claim that the evidence was insufficient to support his conviction of the attempted murder of the baby. We granted defendant's petition for review.

Defendant does not challenge his conviction of the attempted murder of Karen. A. But he argues his conviction of the attempted murder of the baby must be reversed because, as stated in his opening brief, "only a single attempted murder conviction was possible on the facts here." Specifically, defendant asserts that the fact that he fired only one bullet into the vehicle reflects his intent to kill only one victim—Karen A. He urges that "there was no proof of animus toward the baby," and argues his conviction of the attempted murder of that victim must be reversed for lack of substantial evidence that he harbored specific intent to kill the child.

We first consider the mental state required for conviction of attempted murder. The mental state required for attempted murder has long differed from that required for murder itself. Murder does not require the intent to kill. Implied malice—a conscious disregard for life—suffices. In contrast, attempted murder requires the specific intent to kill and the commission of a direct but ineffectual act toward accomplishing the intended killing. Hence, in order for defendant to be convicted of the attempted murder of the baby, the prosecution had to prove he acted with specific intent to kill that victim.

Intent to unlawfully kill and express malice are, in essence, one and the same. To be guilty of attempted murder of the baby, defendant had to harbor express malice toward that victim. Express malice requires a showing that the assailant either desires the result, i.e., death, or knows, to a substantial certainty, that the result will occur.

The mental state required for attempted murder is further distinguished from the mental state required for murder in that the doctrine of transferred intent applies to murder but not attempted murder. In its classic form, the doctrine of transferred intent applies when the defendant intends to kill one person but mistakenly kills another. The intent to kill the intended target is deemed to transfer to the unintended victim so that the defendant is guilty of murder. In contrast, the doctrine of transferred intent does not apply to attempted murder: To be guilty of attempted murder, the defendant must intend to kill the alleged victim, not someone else. Whether the defendant acted with specific intent to kill must be judged separately as to each alleged victim.

The prosecution had only to prove that defendant purposefully shot at the baby with express malice in order to establish the requisite state of mind for conviction of attempted murder.

Two important principles of law will further serve to inform the inquiry whether defendant could properly be convicted of two counts of attempted murder on the evidence introduced below, notwithstanding that he fired only one shot into the vehicle.

First, with few exceptions, motive itself is not an element of a criminal offense. The jury below was properly so instructed. The crimes of murder and attempted murder are no exception. True, evidence of motive is often probative of intent to kill. Here, defendant was formerly acquainted with the mother, exchanged words with her, and called her a "bitch" moments before the shooting. These circumstances suggested a motive for defendant's wanting to shoot at the mother, which in turn was probative of whether he shot at her with intent to kill. But evidence of motive is not required to establish intent to kill, and evidence of motive alone may not always fully explain the shooter's determination to shoot at a fellow human being with lethal force.

The second principle often furnishes the evidentiary ground for an inference that a shooter acted with intent to kill. Evidence of motive aside, it is well settled that intent to kill or express malice, the mental state required to convict a defendant of attempted murder, may in many cases be inferred from the defendant's acts and the circumstances of the crime. There is rarely direct evidence of a defendant's intent. Such intent must usually be derived from all the circumstances of the attempt, including the defendant's actions. The act of firing toward a victim at a close, but not point blank, range in a manner that could have inflicted a mortal wound had the bullet been on target is sufficient to support an inference of intent to kill. The fact that the shooter may have fired only once and then abandoned his efforts out of necessity or fear does not compel the conclusion that he lacked the animus to kill in the first instance. Nor does the fact that the victim may have escaped death because of the shooter's poor marksmanship necessarily establish a less culpable state of mind.

These principles, taken together, reflect that the act of purposefully firing a lethal weapon at another human being at close range, without legal excuse, generally gives rise to an inference that the shooter acted with express malice. That the shooter had no particular motive for shooting the victim is not dispositive, although again, where motive is shown, such evidence will usually be probative of proof of intent to kill. Nor is the circumstance that the bullet misses its mark or fails to prove lethal dispositive—the very act of firing a weapon in a manner that could have inflicted a mortal wound had the bullet been on target is sufficient to support an inference of intent to kill. Where attempted murder is the charged crime because the victim has survived the shooting, this principle takes on added significance. Finally, even if the shooting was not premeditated, with the shooter merely perceiving the victim as a momentary obstacle or annoyance, the shooter's purposeful use of a lethal weapon with lethal force against the victim, if otherwise legally unexcused, will itself give rise to an inference of intent to kill.

Applying these principles to the facts at hand, and viewing the evidence in the light most favorable to the People, presuming the existence of every fact the jury could reasonably deduce from the evidence in support of the judgment, we conclude the evidence is sufficient to support defendant's conviction of the attempted murder of the baby.

Evidence that defendant purposefully discharged a lethal firearm at the victims, both of whom were seated in the vehicle, one behind the other, with each directly in his line of fire, can support an inference that he acted with intent to kill both.

Dissenting Opinion by WERDEGAR, J.

I respectfully dissent. In my view, defendant's conviction for the attempted murder of Renell T., Jr., is unsupported by substantial evidence.

Defendant fired a single bullet into a moving car, narrowly missing the driver and her infant son, after quarreling with the driver and the driver's boyfriend. There was ample evidence to support the jury's finding defendant was trying to kill the driver. The evidence was ample also that he acted recklessly, or even with conscious disregard for life, as to the baby. The evidence was insufficient, however, to permit the jury to infer beyond a reasonable doubt that defendant intended to kill the baby, with whom, as far as the evidence showed, defendant had no quarrel at all. The majority struggles to articulate grounds for upholding the second attempted murder conviction. In the course of that struggle, the majority loses sight of the crucial difference between implied malice, or conscious disregard for life, and express malice, which is the specific intent to kill a person.

PEOPLE V. STONE

California Supreme Court
46 Cal.4th 131, 92 Cal.Rptr.3d 362, 205 P.3d 272 (2009)

CHIN, J.

Can a person who shoots into a group of people, intending to kill one of the group, but not knowing or caring which one, be convicted of attempted murder? Yes. The mental state required for attempted murder is the intent to kill *a* human being, not a *particular* human being.

Around 8:30 p.m. on the evening of October 21, 2005, Officer Mark Pescatore was on duty with two other police officers at a parking lot carnival in Lemoore. Officer Pescatore observed a group of 10 to 25 youths blocking the pathways and moving about the carnival area. About half of those in the group were wearing red, a color associated with Norteno street gangs. One of the officers believed the group was "looking for trouble." The group included 16-year-old Joel F. as well as "Jamal," a Norteno gang member. Sixteen-year-old Camilo M., a member of a Sureno street gang, and his friend Abel Rincon were also at the carnival.

Several members of the Norteno gang called Camilo "scrapa," a derogatory term for a Sureno, and challenged him and Rincon to fight. Camilo and Rincon decided not to fight and left the carnival. A group of Nortenos followed them, and Jamal kicked Rincon's truck as Rincon and Camilo drove away. Camilo and Rincon returned home and told several people, including defendant, what had happened at the carnival. A short time later, Camilo and Rincon and others, including defendant, returned to the carnival in Rincon's truck. Rincon drove. Defendant sat on the passenger side of the truck.

Meanwhile, at the carnival, the police directed the Norteno group to leave, and about 10 of them went to a grassy area in the parking lot. When Rincon and his companions returned to the carnival, Rincon drove his truck past the group of Nortenos twice. On the third pass, he stopped the truck 10 to 15 feet from the group and held up three fingers, denoting a gang sign. Defendant rolled down his passenger window, pulled out a gun, and fired it. The truck then left the scene.

Defendant was charged with and convicted of a single count of attempted murder for firing a single shot at a group of 10 people. Attempted murder requires the specific intent to kill and the commission of a direct but ineffectual act toward accomplishing the intended killing. The main issue before us on review concerns the nature of the intent-to-kill requirement. Specifically, the question is whether the intent must be to kill a particular person, or whether a generalized intent to kill someone, but not necessarily a specific target, is sufficient.

If a person targets one particular person, under some facts a jury could find the person *also,* concurrently, intended to kill—and thus was guilty of the attempted murder of—other, nontargeted, persons. The fact the person desires to kill a particular target does not preclude finding that the person also, concurrently, intended to kill others within the "kill zone." For example, if a person placed a bomb on a commercial airplane intending to kill a primary target, but also ensuring the death of all the passengers, the person could be convicted of the attempted murder of all the passengers, and not only the primary target.

We conclude that a person who intends to kill can be guilty of attempted murder even if the person has no specific target in mind. An indiscriminate would-be killer is just as culpable as one who targets a specific person.

One difference regarding intent to kill does exist between murder and attempted murder. A person who intends to kill can be guilty of the murder of each person actually killed, even if the person intended to kill only one. The same is not necessarily true regarding attempted murder. Rather, guilt of attempted murder must be judged separately as to each alleged victim. But this is true whether the alleged victim was particularly targeted or randomly chosen. As the district attorney aptly summarizes in this case, "A defendant who intends to kill one person will be liable for multiple counts of murder where multiple victims die, but only one count of attempted murder where no one dies." But when no one dies that person *will* be guilty of attempted murder even if he or she intended to kill a random person rather than a specific one.

We reverse the judgment of the Court of Appeal and remand the matter to that court for further proceedings consistent with our opinion.

NOTE ON THE "KILL ZONE" THEORY OF ATTEMPTED MURDER

In *Stone*, the Supreme Court mentioned the "kill zone" theory. The Court of Appeal in *People v. Bragg* (2008) 161 Cal.App.4th 1385, 1393–1394, 75 Cal.Rptr.3d 200 explained the kill zone theory of attempted murder:

> To be guilty of attempted murder, a defendant must intend to kill the victim of the attempt and not some other person. Someone who in truth does not intend to kill a person is not guilty of that person's attempted murder even if the crime would have been murder—due to transferred intent—if the person were killed. To be guilty of attempted murder, the defendant must intend to kill the alleged victim, not someone else. The defendant's mental state must be examined as to each alleged attempted murder victim. Someone who intends to kill only one person and attempts unsuccessfully to do so, is guilty of the attempted murder of the intended victim, but not of others.
>
> But the intent to kill necessary to a charge of attempted murder of a victim other than the primary victim may, in an appropriate case, be established by proving that defendant acted with concurrent intent as to the other victim. The fact the person desires to kill a particular target does not preclude finding that the person also, concurrently, intended to kill others within the kill zone. The intent is concurrent when the nature and scope of the attack, while directed at a primary victim, are such that we can conclude the perpetrator intended to ensure harm to the primary victim by harming everyone in that victim's vicinity. The kill zone concept applies when, for

instance, someone puts a bomb on an aircraft intended to kill one of the many passengers on the airplane or fires on a crowd in a manner devastating enough to kill everyone in the group that includes the primary victim. If the defendant is unsuccessful in killing his primary target, he is deemed to have concurrently intended to kill the others and may be found guilty of the attempted murder of everyone in the kill zone.

The next case, *People v. Pham*, deepens your understanding of relationship between attempted murder and the "kill zone" and "transferred intent" theories. The *Pham* court also discusses so-called "impossible attempts." Impossible attempts are discussed later in this chapter.

PEOPLE V. PHAM

California Court of Appeal
192 Cal.App.4th 552, 121 Cal.Rptr.3d 458 (2011)

ROBIE, J.

Convicted of second degree murder, two counts of attempted murder, and discharging a firearm at an inhabited dwelling, and sentenced to 79 years to life in prison, defendant Anh-Tuan Dao Pham appeals.

We reject defendant's argument that there was insufficient evidence to support his convictions for attempted murder. Defendant implicitly admits there was sufficient evidence that he was the person who fired a gun a number of times into a group of people, and he expressly admits that "the evidence adduced at trial showed that he had the specific intent to kill two African-American males" when he fired the gun. Defendant's complaint about his convictions is that the evidence showed the two African-American males he intended to kill "were not present in the group" when he committed the shooting, wounding two different people instead. According to defendant, under these facts he was wrongfully convicted of attempted murder based on the doctrine of transferred intent because "if he intended to kill two specific people and in doing so wounded two unintended targets, he is not guilty of the attempted murders of the two unintended targets."

For their part, the People contend defendant's attempted murder convictions were not wrongly based on transferred intent, but correctly based on concurrent intent, also known as the "kill zone" theory of attempted murder, which our Supreme Court explained in *People v. Bland* (2002) 28 Cal. 4th 313, 48 P.3d 1107. According to the People, "it was enough that defendant had a generalized intent to kill people standing in the group," and "the fact that he may have been mistaken in his belief that the African-American males were part of the group does not change the analysis."

We conclude that neither side has it right. As we will explain, defendant's convictions were not based on the jury's improper application of transferred intent to the crime of attempted murder, as defendant contends. At the same time, however, this was not a case in which defendant created a "kill zone," and thus the jury could not have convicted him of the attempted murder charges based on concurrent intent, as the People argue. Instead, defendant's attempted murder convictions are supported by substantial evidence that he specifically tried to murder two people by shooting into a group of people where he thought they were, although it turned out he was mistaken. Under well-established California law, the fact that his targets were not present at the scene of the shooting does not excuse him from criminal liability for attempted murder because factual impossibility is not a defense to a charge of attempt. Accordingly, we will affirm the attempted murder convictions.

At approximately 11:30 p.m. on February 22, 2007, an African-American teenager named Dominique Hickman was walking home from a friend's house in South Sacramento when he was struck in the back by a bullet that had first ricocheted off a hard surface. The bullet wound killed him; his body was found there the next morning.

Seven .45-caliber shell casings were found at the scene. A defect in a sound wall that appeared to have been made by a bullet was also found nearby.

A little over an hour later, it was discovered that someone had just crashed a stolen car into the garage of a house on Caymus Drive, about four miles away from where Hickman was shot. About 10 to 15 minutes later, as a group of people were gathered in the front yard of the Caymus Drive residence, a white car drove past and the passenger—a young, Asian male—fired a gun at the crowd numerous times. Two people were injured in the shooting. Six .45-caliber shell casings were found at the scene.

Just before the shooting, the white car had driven past the residence followed by a van that one of the residents and a friend of his recognized from an incident a week earlier. In that incident, someone threw a rock at the van.

In a statement to sheriff's deputies a week after the shootings, defendant admitted he was the shooter in the Caymus Drive incident. He said that when he was with his 14-year-old friend, Thomas Tran, and another friend, he got into an altercation with two Black teenagers, and one of them threw a rock and dented his mother's van. He committed the Caymus Drive shooting because he was mad about the dent. Defendant also admitted to the deputies that he told Tran, "I shot at the people who threw the rock at the car."

Defendant denied any knowledge of the Hickman shooting, ballistics testing revealed, however, that the cartridge casings found at the scenes of both shootings were fired from the same gun. Tests also showed gunshot residue on the passenger side of the stolen car that crashed into the Caymus Drive residence.

Defendant was charged with the murder of Hickman, two counts of attempted murder for shooting the two bullets that caused injuries in the Caymus Drive shooting, and one count of discharging a firearm at an inhabited dwelling, along with various firearm enhancement allegations.

At trial in the fall of 2009, defendant testified that on February 22, 2007, he was at his house with his 19-year-old friend, Hung Nguyen, and several others, when Hung's brother, Davis Nguyen, who was 22 or 23 years old, called and asked defendant and Hung to steal a car for him. According to defendant, they went out and stole a Honda Accord and left it where Davis could pick it up, then went back to defendant's house. Later, Davis came over and said he had just shot at someone. Davis left the gun with defendant, then asked defendant and Hung to take him home and to get rid of the stolen car. After dropping Davis off, they retrieved the stolen car, then came up with the idea of driving it into the house where they thought the problem had started with the two African-American teenagers the week before. Defendant claimed he drove the stolen car into the garage. He also claimed that later, on the way to get something to eat, they drove back past the Caymus Drive residence to see what was going on, then shortly thereafter Hung said he wanted to go back and scare the people there. Defendant claimed he drove their friend's white car on the way back, and Hung was in the passenger seat. As he drove slowly past the residence, Hung shot several times. Defendant claimed he originally admitted to being the shooter because he was scared Davis might do something to him or his family if he "told on" Hung.

The jury did not believe defendant's story and convicted him of all four charges, fixing the murder at second degree.

On appeal, defendant contends there was insufficient evidence to support the attempted murder convictions because "the evidence adduced showed that he had the specific intent to kill two African-American males who were not present in the group" on Caymus Drive. Specifically, defendant contends the evidence showed that his intent was "to kill the two African-American males with whom he had an altercation the week prior," but neither of them was present in front of the Caymus Drive house when the drive-by shooting occurred. In his view, because "there was no evidence adduced at trial that he intended to kill anyone who was in the group of people standing outside the house on Caymus Drive, the prosecution clearly advocated his guilt under a theory of transferred intent that was disallowed as to attempted murder in" *Bland.*

In *Bland,* the Supreme Court explained that while, in the context of the crime of murder, intent to kill is deemed transferred or extended to every person actually killed when the defendant tries to kill a particular person but ends up killing others as well, this concept of transferred intent does not apply to the inchoate crime of attempted murder. According to the Supreme Court, "Someone who in truth does not intend to kill a person is not guilty of that person's attempted murder even if the crime would have been murder—due to transferred intent—if the person were killed. To be guilty of attempted murder, the defendant must intend to kill the alleged victim, not someone else. The defendant's mental state must be examined as to each alleged attempted murder victim. Someone who intends to kill only one person and attempts unsuccessfully to do so, is guilty of the attempted murder of the intended victim, but not of others."

In defendant's view, because the evidence showed he was trying to kill two people who were not present at the scene of the shooting, the jury could not have found he intended to kill anyone who actually was present, and therefore the evidence was insufficient to support the charges of attempted murder. In other words, defendant's argument is that he could not be convicted of attempted murder because, while he harbored the intent to kill, the two people he intended to kill were not in the group at which he shot, even though he "mistakenly believed" they were, and his intent to kill them could not be "transferred" to the two people he ended up wounding.

The People argue that defendant's attempted murder convictions were "based on the legally correct doctrine of concurrent intent," not "the legally impermissible doctrine of transferred intent." Describing what also has been called the "kill zone" theory, the People contend that "concurrent intent applies when a defendant intends to kill a particular target, and uses a mode of attack that, by its nature and scope, shows a concurrent intent to kill persons in the vicinity of the intended target." According to the People, "the fact that defendant may have been mistaken in his belief that the African-American males he intended to shoot were part of the group he shot at does not change the analysis." In the People's view, the evidence that defendant "repeatedly fired a .45 caliber gun into the midst of a group" was sufficient to support his two attempted murder convictions. Indeed, the People contend they "could have charged defendant with several additional counts of attempted murder, up to at least the number of shots fired into the group."

We begin our analysis by rejecting the People's reliance on concurrent intent. As even the People admit in their brief, the concept of concurrent intent applies when a defendant intends to kill a particular target, and uses a mode of attack that, by its nature and scope, shows a concurrent intent to kill persons in the vicinity of the intended target. Here, the evidence—consisting primarily of defendant's own admissions to sheriff's deputies—showed that defendant's intended targets were the two African-American teenagers he held responsible for damaging his mother's van. But the fact that defendant fired a gun at a group of people he thought included those teenagers, by itself, does not demonstrate that he had a generalized intent to kill people standing in the group, as the People argue. Just because a defendant fires a gun repeatedly at a group of people does not necessarily mean the defendant can be convicted of as many counts of attempted murder as the number of bullets he fired. The question—which is a factual one for the jury to decide—is whether, based on the particular evidence in the case, it can be inferred that defendant had the concurrent intent to kill not only his intended target but others in the target's vicinity.

Here, we need not resort to the kill zone theory to uphold defendant's two convictions for attempted murder, and thus we need not determine whether there was sufficient evidence for the jury to find, based on the nature of the shooting, that defendant intended to kill more people than just the two African-American teenagers he believed had damaged his mother's van. Instead, as we will explain, it was enough that he intended to kill those two persons, and it did not matter that they were not at the scene of the shooting.

As we have previously suggested, defendant finds the absence of his intended targets to be the critical factor in the analysis of whether his attempted murder convictions are supported by substantial evidence. Specifically, he believes the absence of his intended targets is what makes the convictions unsupportable, because, as the Supreme Court explained in *Bland*, his intent to kill them cannot be transferred to the two people he actually ended up shooting.

What both defendant and the People have missed, however, is a basic concept of criminal law that supports defendant's convictions for attempted murder without resort to either the discredited theory of transferred intent or the overused theory of concurrent intent/kill zone. That concept is that an attempt to commit a crime is a crime even if it would have been impossible for the defendant to complete the commission of the offense. If there is an apparent ability to commit the crime in the way attempted, the attempt is indictable, although, unknown to the person making the attempt, the crime cannot be committed, because the means employed are in fact unsuitable, or because of extrinsic facts, such as the nonexistence of some essential object, or an obstruction by the intended victim, or by a third person. Our courts have repeatedly ruled that persons who are charged with attempting to commit a crime cannot escape liability because the criminal act they attempted was not completed due to an impossibility which they did not foresee: factual impossibility is not a defense to a charge of attempt.

Here, as even defendant himself admits, the evidence supported the conclusion that defendant attempted to kill two African-American males he believed were in the group gathered outside the house on Caymus Drive. Unbeknownst to him, the two individuals he intended to kill were not there. Under the foregoing authorities, however, defendant cannot escape liability for his attempt to kill them just because, contrary to his belief, it turned out his intended victims were not where he thought they were. His crimes were complete when, with the intent to kill the two teenagers, he fired shots into a group in which he thought they were. Under these circumstances, the evidence was sufficient to support defendant's two convictions for attempted murder.

PROBLEMS ON ATTEMPTED MURDER

1. Late at night, Dell fired a single bullet from a distance of 60 feet at a group of seven men standing on a sidewalk. Defendant thought he was shooting at members of a rival gang. As it turned out, the seven men were police officers. The bullet struck one of the officers in the finger. None of the officers was killed. How many counts of attempted murder should Dell be charged with? What if Dell had used a machine gun and fired 50 bullets in a few seconds, missing everyone? *People v. Perez* (2010) 50 Cal.4th 222, 112 Cal.Rptr.3d 310, 234 P.3d 557.

2. D was a member of a gang that was at war with a rival gang. D drove his truck into the territory of the rival gang and parked a quarter of a block from a group of 15 to 20 children and adults who were outside on a dead end street. The children were playing in the street. The adults were gathered in small groups talking. Two men standing on the street noticed D's truck and walked toward it. The men flashed gang signs at the truck. D flashed the sign of his gang and then picked up the semi-automatic pistol lying in his lap. D fired 5 times in the direction of the men approaching his truck. One of the bullets struck and killed a child playing in the street. No one else was injured. What should D be charged with?

3. Six people, including Vic, drove to a market on Fruitridge Road in Sacramento. The area around the market was claimed by a gang known as the Fruitridge Bloods. When the six individuals arrived at the market, Dell and his friends were standing near the entrance. Dell and his friends were members of the Fruitridge Bloods. Vic and Dell grew up together, but had not seen each other in quite a while. Vic walked up to Dell and said, "What's up dog?" Dell replied, "Nothing, just kicking back, being bool." Vic said, "I'm a Crip, cuz" and Dell replied, "Fuck you then." When Dell said "being bool" he meant "being cool." Members of the Bloods sometimes change the letter "c" to a "b". It would be appropriate for one Blood to say to another Blood "being bool," but saying this to a Crip would be an insult. Vic and his friends entered the store. Outside, Dell yelled at Vic, "Bring your bitch ass outside." Vic thought that Dell wanted to fight, so Vic started to exit the store, followed by his five friends. As Vic emerged from the store, Dell drew a gun from his belt and fired seven times in Vic's direction. Vic was not hit, but two of his friends were wounded. What crimes should Dell be charged with? *People v. Bragg* (2008) 161 Cal.App.4th 1385, 75 Cal.Rptr.3d 200.

4. Dell was upset with his girlfriend. Dell threatened the girlfriend, who left their apartment out of fear. Dell proceeded to get drunk. Dell called his girlfriend's father's home and asked if she was there. The father, Vic, said "No, she is not here." Dell responded, "I should kill you man" and hung up. A few hours later, Dell drove to Vic's home and parked in an alley behind the home. Dell knew that Vic, his wife, and three children lived in the home, but Dell did not know who, if anyone, was at home. It was late at night, and Dell could see a light on in one room. The TV was on in the room, and Dell could see the flickering of the TV through the window shades, which were closed. Dell fired two shots through the window of the room with the TV. No one was hit. What crime(s) did Dell commit? *People v. Felix* (2009) 172 Cal.App.4th 1618, 92 Cal.Rptr.3d 239.

5. Rivera 13 and Pico Nuevo are rival gangs in the city of Pico Rivera. Bray and Leon are members of Rivera 13. Bray was driving his truck with Leon in the passenger seat. Bray stopped at a traffic light and a Toyota stopped next to the truck. There were three men in the Toyota, with one in the back seat behind the front passenger seat. Leon recognized the man sitting in the front passenger seat as a member of the Pico Nuevo gang. When the light changed, the Toyota accelerated away and Bray followed close behind. Intending to shoot the man in the front passenger seat of the Toyota, Leon leaned out the window of the truck and fired one shot. The bullet hit the right rear brake light, travelled through the trunk, and struck and killed the man riding in the rear seat. Of what crimes are Leon and Bray guilty? *People v. Leon* (2010) 181 Cal.App.4th 452, 104 Cal.Rptr.3d 601.

6. Police officers Scott and Peterson responded to a dispatch that shots had been fired near a market. The officers arrived at the same time and saw Dell standing in the store parking lot with a gun in his hand. The officers exited their patrol cars. Officer Scott yelled at Dell to drop the gun. Dell ran behind the store. Other police officers arrived. Officers Scott and Peterson walked to a corner of the store, peeked around the corner, but did not see Dell. The officers rounded the corner and walked along the back of the store single file. They heard a noise. Officer Scott, who was in front, crouched down, with Officer Peterson standing behind him and just off his shoulder. Dell emerged from a recess in the building and fired one shot toward the officers, hitting neither of them. Of what crime(s) is Dell guilty? *People v. Chinchilla* (1997) 52 Cal.App.4th 683, 60 Cal.Rptr.2d 761.

7. Elanor stopped at the Anderson Lounge in Anderson, California. She parked behind the bar and entered by the back door. When she entered the bar, she was confronted by Lenart, who had a bundle under his arm and a gun in his hand. Lenart ordered Elanor to "get down on the floor." Elanor started to comply, then suddenly turned and grabbed the gun with both hands in an effort to take it away from Lenart. A struggle ensued, and Elanor pulled the gun away from Lenart and ran out of the bar with it. Lenart pursued her, but soon turned around, got in his truck, and sped away. When police arrived, they discovered the body of the bartender, face down on the floor of the bar with a bullet wound to the back of the head. The bartender had been killed "execution

style." Lenart is charged with attempted murder of Elanor. Is he guilty? *People v. Lenart* (2004) 32 Cal.4th 1107, 12 Cal.Rptr.3d 592, 88 P.3d 498.

8. David was a parolee at large. There were outstanding warrants for David's arrest, and the police were looking for him. Among other crimes, David had assaulted a man, breaking his nose. David was a member of the Hell's Angles motorcycle gang. He was known to be violent and unpredictable. Police learned David was in a house. The 15 member SWAT team surrounded the house, took cover, and called out for David to come out with his hands up. Five police officers were stationed in front of the house. Three were at the back, three on the right side, and the remaining four on the left side. David yelled, "Back up. I have a bomb. I'll blow up the house." The police fired tear gas into the house. From within, David fired many rounds out the front, back, and right side of the house. He fired no rounds out of the left side of the house. Officers returned fire. Eventually, David surrendered. What should David be charged with? *People v. Virgo* (2013) 222 Cal. App. 4th 788, 166 Cal. Rptr. 3d 384.

9. Andrew belonged to a criminal street gang. Andrew and another gang member drove to a pool hall, where they encountered members of a rival gang. Insults were traded. Andrew and his friend went to their car, while the rival gang members went back inside the pool hall. Andrew parked his car near the exit of the pool hall parking lot so he could see into any vehicles leaving the lot. An hour later, six members of the rival gang exited the pool hall, got into an SUV, and headed toward the exit of the parking lot. When the SUV was alongside Andrew's car, Andrew said to his friend, "That's them." Andrew took out his semiautomatic pistol and opened fire on the SUV, instantly killing the driver, wounding a passenger, and missing others in the vehicle. What crimes did Andrew commit? Is Andrew's friend guilty too? *People v. Tran* (2018) 20 Cal. App. 5th 561, 229 Cal. Rptr. 3d 152.

Attempting the Impossible

Poaching deer out of deer hunting season was a continuing problem in a rural county. Poachers would drive slowly along rural roads at night and use spotlights to locate deer near the road. With the deer in the spotlight, the poacher would shoot the deer. Game wardens determined to catch the poachers. The wardens took a deer hide from a deer recently hit by a car and had a taxidermist stuff the deer so it looked remarkably lifelike. The wardens took the stuffed deer to a likely place and put the deer about 50 yards from the road. The wardens hid on the other side of the road. Around 1:30 a.m., a four wheel drive pickup drove slowly down the road scanning the area with a spotlight. The spotlight illuminated the stuffed deer and an occupant of the truck said, "Stop, I see one." The truck stopped and a shot rang out. The bullet found its mark in the stuffed deer. The wardens rushed the truck and arrested the two occupants who, it must be said, were astonished by the sudden appearance of "the law." The two were charged with attempted poaching. They pleaded not guilty and proceeded to trial. Their defense was that it was impossible for them to commit the crime of attempted poaching because the deer they shot was stuffed. And here is the amazing thing: They won! In *State v. Guffey* (1953) 262 S.W.2d 152, 156, the Missouri Court of Appeals ruled it is not "a crime to attempt to do that which it is legally impossible to do"—take a stuffed deer out of season.

Guffy is representative of a small body of cases on the so-called impossibility defense. The theory is this: A person cannot be guilty of attempting to commit a crime when, under the circumstances, it was impossible to commit the crime. Some states recognized the defense.[16] Today, most states, including California, and the Model Penal Code, reject the idea that one cannot be guilty of attempting to commit a crime that it would be impossible to commit.

PROBLEMS

1. Dell went to a bar. He danced with a young woman. Soon after they started dancing, the woman collapsed in Dell's arms, apparently unconscious. Dell told the woman's friends he would take her to her home and put her to bed to "sleep it off." Dell placed the woman in his car and drove to her home, where he put her in bed. Dell decided to have sex with the unconscious women, which he did. As it turned out, the woman was not unconscious. She was dead! She died the moment she fell into Dell's arms at the bar. Dell is charged with attempted rape. Does he have a defense? Why attempted rape rather than rape? *United States v. Thomas* (1962) 32 Court of Military Appeals 278.

2. Bobby asked Gary to steal herbicide for him for use on his farm. Gary burglarized the County Farmer's Co-Op and stole the requested herbicide. As Gary left the Co-Op, he was arrested and the police recovered the herbicide. Gary told the police he was working for Bobby. Gary agreed to cooperate with the police by delivering the herbicide to Bobby and telling Bobby it was stolen. After Bobby received the herbicide, he was arrested and charged with attempted receipt of stolen property knowing it is stolen. Is Bobby guilty? *Bandy v. State* (Tenn. 1979) 575 S.W.2d 278.

3. Twenty-five-year-old Chris wanted to have sex with a minor. He went online and entered a chat room for teens. Chris said online that he was 16. Chris mentioned the high school he attended and his hobbies. Before long, Chris got a message from Becca, who said she was fourteen. In reality, Becca was a police officer posing as a teenager for the express purpose of catching online sexual predators. Becca and Chris struck up an online friendship, and before long the conversation turned to sex. Chris invited Becca to meet him so they could "hook up." They agreed they wanted to have sexual intercourse. They agreed to meet at a park. At the appointed hour, Chris drove to the park, parked his car, and walked to the place he expected to meet Becca. Chris was arrested and charged with attempted child sexual abuse. Is Chris guilty? *People v. Thousand* (2001) 465 Mich. 149, 631 N.W.2d 694.

---

[16] For a thorough analysis of the impossible attempt doctrine *see People v. Thousand* (2001) 465 Mich. 149, 631 N.W.2d 694.

4. Moser is a pickpocket. It was the annual Frontier Day in Bakersfield, and the parade had just started. Moser spotted his victim, an elderly man named Hitchcock, who was watching the parade. Moser moved directly behind Hitchcock and had his fingers in Hitchcock's back pocket when he was arrested by Officer Jones, who had watched the whole thing. As it turns out, Mr. Hitchcock's pocket was empty. Moser is charged with attempted theft. Is he guilty? *People v. Fiegelman* (1939) 33 Cal.App.2d 100, 91 P.2d 156.

MERGER OF INCHOATE OFFENSES

When does an inchoate offense merge into the completed or attempted crime?[17] Consider the following scenarios.

1. Dell asked Tom to commit a robbery, but Tom refused. What can Dell and Tom be charged with?

2. Dell asked Tom to commit a robbery and Tom agreed, but for reasons beyond their control, the crime was neither completed nor attempted. What can Dell and Tom be charged with?

3. Dell asked Tom to commit a robbery and Tom agreed. The robbery occurred. What can Dell and Tom be charged with?

4. Dell asked Tom to commit a robbery and Tom agreed. Tom attempted the robbery but failed. What can Dell and Tom be charged with?

5. Ann hated Vickie and wanted her killed. Lacking the courage to kill Vickie herself, Ann asked Beth to kill Vickie, which Beth did. Of what are Ann and Beth guilty?

6. Suppose Beth tried but failed to kill Vickie. Of what are Ann and Beth guilty?

7. Suppose Beth agreed to kill Vickie, but the killing was not accomplished or attempted. Of what are Ann and Beth guilty?

8. Suppose that when Ann asked Beth to kill Vickie, Beth said, "Are you nuts? I want nothing to do with you." Beth left. Of what are Ann and Beth guilty?

---

[17] The inspiration for this exercise is drawn from Wayne R. LaFave, *Criminal Law* (5th ed. 2010) (West).

CHAPTER 9

DEFENSES

■ ■ ■

According to *California Jurisprudence*, "A 'defense' is any set of identifiable conditions or circumstances that may prevent conviction for an offense. The defendant is entitled to utilize any and all defenses in his or her behalf and may present inconsistent defenses."[1]

This chapter discusses the following defenses: failure of elements defenses, mistake of fact, mistake and ignorance of law, self-defense, defense of others, defense of property, necessity, duress, intoxication, insanity, infancy, entrapment, statute of limitations, and the so-called cultural defense.

A number of legal doctrines that partake of a defense are addressed in other chapters. For example, the chapter on murder discusses heat of passion voluntary manslaughter, which can mitigate murder to manslaughter.

FRAMEWORK OF DEFENSES

Before delving into specific defenses, this section provides a framework to understand defenses. It is useful to divide defenses into three categories: (1) Failure of elements defenses, (2) affirmative defenses, and (3) public policy defenses.

Failure of Elements Defenses (FED)

The prosecutor must prove every element of the charged crime beyond a reasonable doubt. As well, the prosecutor must prove defendant was the perpetrator (or an accomplice or conspirator). One way to defend a case is to attack the prosecution's evidence in an effort to raise a reasonable doubt that the government met its burden of proving guilt. As explained by the Court of Appeal in *People v. Gonzales* (1999) 74 Cal.App.4th 382, 390, 88 Cal.Rptr.2d 111, "When a defense is one that negates proof of an element of the charged offense, the defendant need only raise a reasonable doubt of the existence of that fact. This is so because the defense goes directly to guilt or innocence." In this casebook, the term "failure of elements defense" (FED) is used to describe defenses that seek to raise a reasonable doubt

---

[1] *California Jurisprudence*, vol. 19, § 1, p. 435 (2009) (West).

that the prosecution proved one or more element of the crime or defendant's identity.[2]

Mistake of fact, discussed below, is a FED. If the jury believes defendant's evidence of mistake, then defendant lacked the *mens rea* required for guilt. Accident is another FED. In *People v. Gonzales, supra*, the Court of Appeal wrote, "The accident defense is a claim that the defendant acted without forming the mental state necessary to make his actions a crime."[3] Alibi is a FED. If, at the moment the bank was robbed in San Diego, defendant was in the swimming pool at the Emirate Palace Hotel in Abu Dhabi, defendant has an alibi. The idea with FEDs is that the prosecution failed to prove one or more elements of its case.

Affirmative Defenses

An affirmative defense asserts facts that are separate from the elements of the charged crime and that, if true, create a defense. In *People v. Noble* (2002) 100 Cal.App.4th 184, 189, 121 Cal.Rptr.2d 918, the Court of Appeal explained, "An affirmative defense is one which does not negate an essential element of a cause of action or charged crime, but instead presents new matter to excuse or justify conduct that would otherwise lead to liability."

Self-defense is an affirmative defense. The elements of self-defense are separate from the elements of murder or assault. Self-defense is a complete defense. A defendant who acted in self-defense is acquitted.[4] Other affirmative defenses include necessity, duress, and insanity.

Public Policy Defenses

In a few situations, the legislature decides individuals should not be prosecuted even though they may be guilty! The statute of limitations is such a defense, based on the public policy that it is unfair to prosecute individuals if so much time has elapsed since the offense that it will be difficult for the defendant to mount an effective defense. Evidence may be hard to find. Witnesses may have forgotten what happened, moved away, or died. California law on statutes of limitations is complex, and is not addressed in this book.[5] One aspect of the statute of limitations requires mention, however. There is no statute of limitation on prosecution of "an

---

[2] Professor Paul Robinson uses the term "failure of proof defense" in his law review article on defenses. Paul H. Robinson, Criminal Law Defenses: A Systematic Analysis, 82 *Columbia Law Review* 199 (1982). In his book, *Understanding Criminal Law*, Professor Joshua Dressler also uses the term failure of proof.

[3] 74 Cal.App.4th at 390.

[4] In addition to "perfect" self-defense, which is a complete defense, California recognizes "imperfect" self-defense, which is a partial defense. Perfect and imperfect self-defense are discussed later in this chapter.

[5] The limitations period generally depends upon the punishment prescribed for the offense.

offense punishable by death or by imprisonment in the state prison for life or for life without the possibility of parole, or for the embezzlement of public money." (PC § 799). Because there is no statute of limitations on murder, it is not unusual to see prosecution of "cold case" murders years—even decades—after the killing.

Certain diplomats have immunity from prosecution—diplomatic immunity. *See Silva v. Superior Court* (1975) 52 Cal.App.3d 269, 125 Cal.Rptr. 78.

JUSTIFICATION OR EXCUSE?—DOES IT MATTER?

By long tradition, affirmative defenses are justifications or excuses.[6] With a justification defense, defendant's conduct under the circumstances was morally correct. Self-defense is a justification defense. A person who kills in self-defense takes a life, but only because the person who died was attacking the defender. It is unfortunate a life was lost, but under the circumstances, the defender did the morally correct thing. Society makes the value judgment that it can be justifiable to kill in self-defense.

The necessity defense is a justification. The classic example of necessity is the person who sees a lightning-ignited forest fire raging toward a small town. It is the middle of the night, and the sleeping townsfolk are unaware they are about to be engulfed in flame. To save the lives of the villagers, our person makes a firebreak by burning a farmer's corn field. Everyone in the village is saved. You would think our person would be hailed as a hero, but no, the local prosecutor charges our person with arson of the corn field! It may occur to you to ask, why would the prosecutor charge our person with arson? It is true that our person deliberately burned the field (arson), but given our person's conduct under the circumstances, and the prosecutor's broad discretion, the prosecutor is not compelled to file charges. Indeed, if our person really did burn the field to save the village, it is extremely unlikely a prosecutor will file charges. So, why *did* the prosecutor charge? Putting that interesting question aside without an answer (What do you think?), and returning to the defense of necessity, society makes the value judgment that in extreme circumstances, it is better for a person to commit one evil—break the law, in this case arson—in order to prevent a greater evil—death of one or more people. Our person selected the lesser of two evils—violate the law by burning the field rather than allow lives to be lost. Under the circumstances, burning the field was the morally defensible thing to do.

An excuse defense differs from a justification as follows: With a justification such as self-defense, defendant did the right thing under the circumstances. By contrast, with an excuse defense, defendant did the

---

[6] *See* H.L.A. Hart, *Punishment and Responsibility: Essays in the Philosophy of Law* pp. 13–14 (1968) (Oxford University Press).

wrong thing; defendant's act was not morally defensible. Yet, despite the fact that what the defendant did was wrong, we afford the defendant a defense because there is something wrong with the defendant; some defect that renders the defendant morally blameless. The insanity defense is an excuse. When an insane person kills an innocent victim because the insane person thinks the victim is from Mars and is about to vaporize him with a ray gun, we do not say the insane person did the right thing. It was wrong. Yet, because the insane person's mental illness renders the person morally blameless, it is wrong to punish the person.

Duress is also an excuse. I put a gun to your head and say, "Unless you go into that convenience store, point this knife at the clerk, and demand the money, I'll blow your brains out *right now*!" There is no way to escape, get help, or take the gun away, so you enter the store, threaten the clerk with the knife, and run out with money. If you are charged with robbery,[7] you can successfully raise the duress defense. You did what most people would do under the circumstances. Society makes the judgment that what you did was wrong, but under the circumstances of such extreme pressure, you are not blameworthy. It does not feel right to punish you.

Although it does not feel right to punish *you*, what about *me*, the one who put the gun to your head and threatened you? Should I be prosecuted? What crimes did I commit?

There was a time in early law when the consequences for a defendant differed depending on whether a defense was a justification or an excuse. No more. Today, justifications and excuses are complete defenses. If the jury accepts the defense, the defendant is acquitted.[8] The defendant doesn't care whether the defense is a justification or an excuse, as long as it *works*. Today, courts often use the terms justification and excuse interchangeably. Yet, because it is the tradition to distinguish excuse from justification, and because the moral baggage attached to each is different, this book maintains the distinction.

BURDENS OF PROOF AND PRODUCING EVIDENCE REGARDING DEFENSES

The prosecution must prove every element of the crime, plus identity, beyond a reasonable doubt. What about defenses? Who has the burden of proving defenses such as self-defense, duress, insanity, mistake of fact, etc.? Does the defendant have the burden of proving defenses? Or does the prosecution have the burden of *dis*proving defenses?

---

[7] If the facts are as suggested in the text, you probably won't be charged.

[8] This is not always true. If a defendant is acquitted based on the insanity defense, the defendant does not walk out of the courthouse a free person. Instead, the defendant will likely be committed to an institution.

Before you can answer these questions, you need to understand two important principles of evidence law: (1) the burden of producing evidence, also called the burden of going forward with evidence, and (2) the burden of proof.

The burden of producing evidence is the obligation, at the appropriate stage of a trial, to produce evidence on a particular point.[9] The evidence might be the testimony of a witness, a document, or a gun or drugs (called "real evidence"). In a criminal case, during the prosecution's case-in-chief, the prosecutor has the burden to produce (*i.e.*, offer) admissible evidence of every element of the crime, plus evidence that the defendant was the perpetrator. What happens if the prosecutor fails to meet the burden of producing evidence? In that event, at the end of the prosecution's case-in-chief, the judge dismisses the case because the prosecutor failed to meet the burden of production; failed to offer evidence of every element of the crime plus identity. The case will *not* go to the jury for decision because the prosecution failed to meet its burden of producing evidence.

Thus, the effect of the burden of producing evidence is that if the party with the burden fails to carry the burden, the party loses! The party loses the entire case or the portion of the case on which the party failed to carry the burden of production. California Evidence Code § 550(a) articulates this rule as follows, "The burden of producing evidence as to a particular fact is on the party against whom a finding on that fact would be required in the absence of further evidence."

The party with the burden of proof on an issue also has the burden of producing evidence on that issue.[10] Evidence Code § 550(b) provides, "The burden of producing evidence as to a particular fact is initially on the party with the burden of proof as to that fact."

---

[9] How much evidence is needed to satisfy the burden of producing evidence? Evidence Code § 110 states, " 'Burden of producing evidence' means the obligation of a party to introduce evidence sufficient to avoid a ruling against him on the issue." This is not very enlightening. Section 110 does not state how much evidence is enough to avoid an adverse ruling. Insight is provided by Roger C. Park, David P. Leonard & Steven H. Goldberg in their book *Evidence Law: A Student's Guide to the Law of Evidence as Applied in American Trials* (2d ed. 2004), where the authors write:

> What does it take to "meet" a burden of producing evidence? For obvious reasons, this question has no quantifiable answer. To satisfy the burden of production does not mean a party must offer enough to *require* the jury to render a verdict in its favor on the issue. The party must merely offer evidence sufficient to *justify* a reasonable jury in rendering a verdict in its favor. Thus, if a directed verdict or similar motion is made against a party who has the burden of production, the court may grant the motion only if it finds that it would be unreasonable for the jury to decide in favor of the party with the burden. If a verdict in favor of the party with the burden would be reasonable, it must deny the motion. (p. 100).

[10] In civil litigation, the burden of producing evidence, *and* even the burden of proof, can be shifted from the party that started with the burden(s) to the opponent by operation of a presumption. Presumptions play an important role in civil litigation, and you may learn presumption law in the course on evidence. In criminal law, however, presumptions play almost no role. In particular, it would be unconstitutional to shift the burden of proof on any element of the crime from the prosecution to the defense by operation of a presumption or other means.

Which party has the burden of proof, and the accompanying burden of producing evidence? Allocation of the burden of proof is governed by the substantive law that applies to the case. As mentioned previously, in criminal cases the prosecution has the burden of proof (and production) of every element of the crime plus identity.[11] In a civil tort action based on negligence, the plaintiff has the burden of proof (and production) of every element of a cause of action for negligence.[12]

Now that you know something about the burden of producing evidence and the burden of proof, you are equipped to answer the questions posed above. In a criminal case, who has the burden of proof regarding defenses? There are several possibilities. Perhaps the prosecutor should be required to disprove every possible defense, whether or not the defendant relies on a defense. This approach makes little sense, would be enormously burdensome, and is not the law in California or elsewhere. Only defenses that are actually raised in a case are subject to burdens of proof and production. Suppose, for example, that Jane is on trial for committing murder in Modesto. Jane does not deny that the victim was murdered. Her defense is that she was in Russia when the crime occurred. Jane does not rely on self-defense, and neither she nor the prosecution will offer evidence of self-defense. Self-defense in not in the case.

Change the facts, Jane admits she killed the victim, but claims she acted in self-defense. We must decide two questions: (1) Who has the burden of producing evidence of self-defense? and (2) Who has the burden of proof regarding self-defense? As for the first question—the burden of producing evidence—California and other states impose the burden of production on the party raising the defense. Jane must produce evidence of each element of self-defense. In the typical trial, the defense meets its burden of production by offering evidence during the defense case-in-chief.[13] Thus, Jane might testify in her own behalf during the defense case-in-chief and describe how she acted in self-defense.

If a defendant with the burden of producing evidence of a defense fails to meet the burden, then the defense is not in the case. At the end of the trial, the judge will not instruct the jury on the defense, and the jury will not be allowed to consider the defense. In Jane's case, if Jane's attorney fails to meet the burden of producing evidence of self-defense, then the judge will not instruct the jury on self-defense. As you can see, it is

---

[11] Evidence Code § 520 provides: "The party claiming that a person is guilty of crime or wrongdoing has the burden of proof on that issue."

[12] Evidence Code § 521 provides: "The party claiming that a person did not exercise the requisite degree of care has the burden of proof on that issue."

[13] Defense counsel may be able to obtain evidence pertinent to a defense through cross-examination of the prosecution's witnesses during the prosecution case-in-chief. In Jane's case, for example, the defense attorney cross-examining a prosecution witness might get the witness to testify to facts that favor Jane's claim of self-defense. Answers during cross-examination are evidence, and, when favorable, may be used to meet the defense's burden of producing evidence.

extremely important for defense counsel to understand the circumstances under which the defense has a burden of producing evidence, what evidence must be produced to meet the burden, and how to effectively offer the evidence at trial. Failure in Jane's case to meet the burden of production means no jury instruction on self-defense will be given.

Recall from earlier in this chapter that defenses fall into three categories: (1) failure of elements defenses (FED) (*e.g.*, mistake of fact), (2) affirmative defenses (*e.g.*, self-defense, insanity) and (3) public policy defenses (*e.g.*, statute of limitations). The law regarding burdens of production and proof differ with the category of defense.

A FED is based on the argument that the prosecutor failed to prove one or more elements of the crime. Mistake of fact is a FED. With mistake of fact, defendant argues that because of a mistake, she lacked the *mens rea* for the crime. In order to get a jury instruction on mistake of fact, defendant has the burden of producing evidence of mistake—defendant has the burden of production. Defendant does not have the burden of proof regarding *mens rea*. The burden of proof of *all* elements of the crime remains on the prosecution.[14] If the defendant meets the burden of production by offering evidence of mistake, the judge will give the appropriate jury instruction at the end of the case, and the jury will be authorized to consider defendant's claim of lack of *mens rea* due to mistake. What if the defendant fails to meet the burden of producing evidence of mistake of fact? In that case, the judge will not give a mistake of fact instruction to the jury.

Shift gears from FEDs to affirmative defenses like self-defense and duress. With affirmative defenses, the defendant has the burden of producing evidence of the defense. If the defendant fails to meet this burden, the judge will not instruct the jury on the defense. Thus, in Jane's murder trial, described above, if Jane wants a jury instruction on self-defense, the defense attorney must offer evidence of every element of self-defense. If defense counsel meets the burden of producing evidence of self-defense, the jury will be instructed on self-defense.

The remaining question pertains to the burden of proof. With affirmative defenses like self-defense, who has the burden of proof? Must defendant prove the defense? Or must the prosecution *dis*prove the defense? With affirmative defenses, the legislature is free to allocate the burden of proof as it deems appropriate. The legislature may conclude that the defendant should shoulder not only the burden of producing evidence, but *also* the burden of proving the defense—the burden of proof. Alternatively, the legislature may decide that once the defendant meets the

[14] *See People v. Noble* (2002) 100 Cal.App.4th 184, 189, 121 Cal.Rptr.2d 918, "Where a 'defense' negates an essential element of the crime charged rather than introducing new matter, however, the state may not constitutionally place the burden of persuasion on that issue upon the defendant."

burden of producing evidence of the defense, the prosecution should have the burden to disprove the defense. Returning to self-defense, the legislature may decide that the defendant should have the burden of proving self-defense. Alternatively, the legislature may decide that once the defendant raises self-defense, the prosecutor should have the burden to prove that the defendant did not act in self-defense.

Generally, when a legislature imposes the burden to disprove an affirmative defense on the prosecution, the legislature requires the prosecution to disprove the defense beyond a reasonable doubt. By contrast, when a legislature imposes the burden of proof of an affirmative defense on the defendant, the burden is usually a preponderance of the evidence or clear and convincing evidence.

You may be wondering, is it constitutional to impose on the defendant the burden of proving an affirmative defense? Doesn't the Constitution require the burden of proof to remain on the prosecution? The answer is: The Constitution requires the prosecution to bear the burden of proving the elements of the crime plus identity. The elements of affirmative defenses, however, are separate from the elements of the crime. Imposing on the defendant the burden of proving the elements of an affirmative defense does not diminish the prosecution's burden of proving the elements of the crime plus identity. Consider Jane's claim of self-defense. Jane's claim rests on elements that are separate from the elements of murder. The burden of proving murder remains on the prosecution. Thus, it is constitutional for a legislature to impose the burden of proving affirmative defenses on the defendant because doing so does not relieve the prosecution of the burden of proving the elements of the crime.[15]

Now that you understand the nature of defenses and the burdens of production and proof, observe how the U.S. Supreme Court addressed these issues in *Dixon v. United States.*

DIXON V. UNITED STATES

United States Supreme Court
548 U.S. 1, 126 S.Ct. 2437 (2006)

JUSTICE STEVENS delivered the opinion of the Court.

facts

In January 2003, petitioner Keshia Dixon purchased multiple firearms at two gun shows, during the course of which she provided an incorrect address and falsely stated that she was not under indictment for a felony. As a result of these illegal acts, petitioner was indicted and convicted on one count of receiving a firearm while under indictment in violation of 18 U.S.C. § 922(n) and eight counts of making false statements in connection

[15] *See People v. Noble* (2002) 100 Cal.App.4th 184, 189, 121 Cal.Rptr.2d 918, "The burden to prove an affirmative defense may be imposed on the defendant in a criminal matter without violating his or her right to due process."

with the acquisition of a firearm in violation of § 922(a)(6). At trial, petitioner admitted that she knew she was under indictment when she made the purchases and that she knew doing so was a crime; her defense was that she acted under duress because her boyfriend threatened to kill her or hurt her daughters if she did not buy the guns for him.

Petitioner contends that the trial judge's instructions to the jury erroneously required her to prove duress by a preponderance of the evidence instead of requiring the Government to prove beyond a reasonable doubt that she did not act under duress.

The crimes for which petitioner was convicted require that she have acted "knowingly," § 922(a)(6), or "willfully," § 924(a)(1)(D). Unless the text of the statute dictates a different result, the term "knowingly" merely requires proof of knowledge of the facts that constitute the offense. And the term "willfully" in § 924(a)(1)(D) requires a defendant to have acted with knowledge that his conduct was unlawful. In this case, then, the Government bore the burden of proving beyond a reasonable doubt that petitioner knew she was making false statements in connection with the acquisition of firearms and that she knew she was breaking the law when she acquired a firearm while under indictment. Although the Government may have proved these elements in other ways, it clearly met its burden when petitioner testified that she knowingly committed certain acts—she put a false address on the forms she completed to purchase the firearms, falsely claimed that she was the actual buyer of the firearms, and falsely stated that she was not under indictment at the time of the purchase—and when she testified that she knew she was breaking the law when, as an individual under indictment at the time, she purchased a firearm.

Petitioner contends, however, that she cannot have formed the necessary *mens rea* for these crimes because she did not freely choose to commit the acts in question. But even if we assume that petitioner's will was overborne by the threats made against her and her daughters, she still *knew* that she was making false statements and *knew* that she was breaking the law by buying a firearm. The duress defense, like the defense of necessity may excuse conduct that would otherwise be punishable, but the existence of duress normally does not controvert any of the elements of the offense itself. Criminal liability is normally based upon the concurrence of two factors, an evil-meaning mind and an evil-doing hand. Like the defense of necessity, the defense of duress does not negate a defendant's criminal state of mind when the applicable offense requires a defendant to have acted knowingly or willfully; instead, it allows the defendant to avoid liability because coercive conditions or necessity negates a conclusion of guilt even though the necessary *mens rea* was present.

The jury instructions in this case were consistent with this requirement and, as such, did not run afoul of the Due Process Clause when they placed the burden on petitioner to establish the existence of duress by a preponderance of the evidence.

Having found no constitutional basis for placing upon the Government the burden of disproving petitioner's duress defense beyond a reasonable doubt, we next address petitioner's argument that the modern common law requires the Government to bear that burden. In making this argument, petitioner recognizes that, until the end of the 19th century, common-law courts generally adhered to the rule that the proponent of an issue bears the burden of persuasion on the factual premises for applying the rule.

It bears repeating that, at common law, the burden of proving affirmative defenses—indeed, all circumstances of justification, excuse or alleviation—rested on the defendant. This common-law rule accords with the general evidentiary rule that the burdens of producing evidence and of persuasion with regard to any given issue are both generally allocated to the same party. And, in the context of the defense of duress, it accords with the doctrine that where the facts with regard to an issue lie peculiarly in the knowledge of a party, that party has the burden of proving the issue. The long-established common-law rule is that the burden of proving duress rests on the defendant.

Congress can, if it chooses, enact a duress defense that places the burden on the Government to disprove duress beyond a reasonable doubt. In the context of the firearms offenses at issue—as will usually be the case, given the long-established common-law rule—we presume that Congress intended the petitioner to bear the burden of proving the defense of duress by a preponderance of the evidence.

MISTAKE OF FACT

The prosecution must prove every element of the crime beyond a reasonable doubt, including *mens rea*. If the prosecution fails to prove *mens rea*, then the defendant must be acquitted. There are cases in which the defendant made a mistake that negates *mens rea*. In other words, because of a mistake, defendant lacked the *mens rea* of the crime. PC § 26 provides, "All persons are capable of committing crimes except those belonging to the following classes: Persons who committed the act or made the omission charged under an ignorance or mistake of fact, which disproves any criminal intent."

The Court of Appeal summarized mistake of fact in *People v. Meneses* (2008) 165 Cal.App.4th 1648, 1661, 82 Cal.Rptr.3d 100:

> For criminal liability to attach to an action, the standard rule is that there must exist a union, or joint operation of act and intent, or criminal negligence. Generally, the prosecution must prove some form of guilty mental state. A defendant may refute

> guilt by showing a mistake of fact disproving criminal intent. A person is usually considered incapable of committing a crime if he or she committed the act or made the omission charged under an ignorance or mistake of fact, which disproves any criminal intent. As examples, a reasonable yet mistaken belief that the victim consented to sex is a defense to forcible rape; a good faith and reasonable belief that the complaining witness was at least 18 years old is a defense to statutory rape; and a defendant's bona fide and reasonable belief that he was divorced is a defense to bigamy.

Consider Sue, who goes to a restaurant to have dinner with friends. When she arrives, she hands her white wool coat to the attendant in the cloak room. Sue enjoys dinner with her friends, after which she returns to the cloak room and is handed a white wool coat. Sue puts the coat on and leaves. Unfortunately, the coat was not Sue's, and Sue is prosecuted for theft, the trespassory caption and asportation of the personal property of another with the intent to steal. Did Sue steal the coat? She *did* trespassorily take and carry away the personal property of another, but did she steal it? Your instincts say "no," and you are right. Sue is not guilty of theft. Her mistake about the coat—she thought it was hers—negates the *mens rea* of intent to steal.

When the facts suggest that the defendant may have made a mistake that negates *mens rea*, defense counsel asks herself, "Is this a general intent crime or a specific intent crime?" If it is a strict liability offense, mistake of fact does not help the defendant because there is no *mens rea* for a mistake to negate (mistake of fact eliminates *mens rea*). If the crime is one of general criminal intent or specific intent, a mistake that negates *mens rea* is a possible defense—a FED.

With a general intent crime, the defendant's mistake must have been honest (*i.e.*, Sue must honestly have believed the coat was hers), *and* the mistake must have been reasonable under the circumstances. With a specific intent crime, the defendant's mistake must have been honest, but it does *not* have to be reasonable. If Sue honestly believed the coat was hers then she didn't indent to steal it, and this is true even if her mistake was unreasonable. You intend to steal or you don't. There is no middle ground.

With these principles in mind, consider *People v. Navarro.*

PEOPLE V. NAVARRO

California Superior Court, Appellate Division
99 Cal. App. 3d Supp. 1, 160 Cal.Rptr. 692 (1979)

DOWDS, JUDGE.

Defendant, charged with grand theft, appeals his conviction after a jury trial of petty theft. His contention on appeal is that the jury was improperly instructed. Defendant was charged with stealing four wooden beams from a construction site. The state of the evidence was such that the jury could have found that the defendant believed either (1) that the beams had been abandoned as worthless and the owner had no objection to his taking them or (2) that they had substantial value, had not been abandoned and he had no right to take them.

The court refused two jury instructions proposed by defendant reading as follows:

Defendant's A

If one takes personal property with the good faith belief that the property has been abandoned or discarded by the true owner, he is not guilty of theft. This is the case even if such good faith belief is unreasonable.

Defendant's B

If one takes personal property with the good faith belief that he has permission to take the property, he is not guilty of theft. This is the case even if such good faith belief is unreasonable.

Instead, the court instructed the jury in the words of the following modified instructions:

Modified Defendant's A

If one takes personal property in the reasonable and good faith belief that the property has been abandoned or discarded by the true owner, he is not guilty of theft.

Modified Defendant's B

If one takes personal property in the reasonable and good faith belief that he has the consent or permission of the owner to take the property, he is not guilty of theft.

The question for determination on appeal is whether the defendant should be acquitted if there is a reasonable doubt that he had a good faith belief that the property had been abandoned or that he had the permission of the owner to take the property or whether that belief must be a reasonable one as well as being held in good faith.

Evidence was presented from which the jury could have concluded that defendant believed that the wooden beams had been abandoned and that the owner had no objection to his taking them, i.e., that he lacked the specific criminal intent required to commit the crime of theft (intent permanently to deprive an owner of his property).

The trial court in effect instructed the jury that even though defendant in good faith believed he had the right to take the beams, and thus lacked the specific intent required for the crime of theft, he should be convicted unless such belief was reasonable. In doing so it erred. It is true that if the jury thought the defendant's belief to be unreasonable, it might infer that he did not in good faith hold such belief. If, however, it concluded that defendant in good faith believed that he had the right to take the beams, even though such belief was unreasonable as measured by the objective standard of a hypothetical reasonable man, defendant was entitled to an acquittal since the specific intent required to be proved as an element of the offense had not been established.

The judgment is reversed.

People v. Navarro is straight forward—it makes sense. Compare *Navarro* to *People v. Lawson*. Does *Lawson* make sense?

PEOPLE V. LAWSON

California Court of Appeal
215 Cal. App. 4th 108, 155 Cal. Rptr. 3d 236 (2013)

KING, J.

On October 28, 2010, William Gibson was working as a loss prevention agent at the Walmart store in Rancho Cucamonga. Around 10:00 a.m., Gibson was doing paperwork and watching video surveillance of the store from inside his office next to the customer service registers. Around 10:10 a.m., defendant walked into the store and proceeded directly to the customer service area, where he returned some items and was issued a gift card.

After he received a call from the customer service desk that defendant was leaving the area, Gibson left his office and began following defendant inside the store. Gibson observed defendant as he went to the jewelry department, returned a pair of earrings, and received another gift card. The two gift cards defendant received were for approximately $104 and $124.

Defendant then proceeded to the menswear department where he selected a purple sweater with a hoodie. After defendant selected the hoodie, he walked to the "middle action alley" of the store, an empty space in the center of the store that customers walk through. There, defendant took the hoodie off its hanger, put the sales tag inside the hoodie, threw the hoodie over his shoulder, and walked to the cash registers. The price of the hoodie was $20, and its sales tag had a bar code that is scanned at the register.

Defendant first walked to the area of register No. 15. He then proceeded to register No. 11 where he selected a pack of gum, and returned to register No. 15. At register No. 15, he had the cashier select some cigars or cigarettes for him. The cashier scanned the gum and cigarettes and defendant paid for them. Defendant did not take the hoodie off his shoulder or present it to the cashier. Five or six minutes passed between the time defendant selected the hoodie in the menswear department and the time he purchased the other items at the register.

After paying for the gum and cigarettes, defendant walked out of the store. As soon as he was outside the store, Gibson stopped him. The hoodie was still on defendant's left shoulder. Gibson identified himself and asked defendant to come back inside the store. Defendant cooperated. He walked back into the store with Gibson and did not try to run away. The jury was shown surveillance videotapes and still photographs of defendant's movements inside the store.

During closing argument, defendant's trial counsel maintained that the prosecution failed to prove that defendant intended to steal the hoodie when he walked out of the store with it on his shoulder. As submitted: "Did Mr. Gibson jump to the conclusion that defendant was stealing? Did the People prove this case beyond a reasonable doubt that defendant had the intent to deprive Walmart of their property? And the answer is no. Because defendant merely forgot. And that's a reasonable interpretation of what occurred." "How do we know that defendant didn't just forget?"

On appeal, defendant contends the trial court erroneously failed to instruct the jury, *sua sponte*, on the defense of ignorance or mistake of fact. He argues: "Because there was sufficient evidence from which a reasonable jury could have found that defendant did not intend to steal the sweatshirt, and because the defense's theory of the case was that defendant had committed nothing more than an absent-minded mistake (analogous to inadvertently pocketing a borrowed pen), the superior court had a sua sponte duty to instruct the jury on the defense of mistake of fact—which is a complete defense to a charge of petty theft."

Defendant's claim that he simply forgot that the hoodie was on his shoulder as he went through the checkout line and walked out of the store does not square with the requirements for the defense of ignorance or mistake of fact. As we explain, the defense of mistake of fact is simply inapplicable to these facts.

Defendant was charged with petty theft, specifically theft by larceny. (§ 484.) The elements of theft by larceny are well settled: the offense is committed by every person who (1) takes possession (2) of personal property (3) owned or possessed by another, (4) by means of trespass and (5) with intent to steal the property, and (6) carries the property away. The act of taking personal property from the possession of another is always a trespass unless the owner consents to the taking freely and unconditionally or the taker has a legal right to take the property. The fifth element of the crime states the specific intent or mental state element, while other elements identify the requisite criminal conduct.

Section 26 lists classes of persons deemed incapable of committing crimes, and includes "persons who committed the act charged under an ignorance or mistake of fact, which disproves any criminal intent" "without being conscious thereof" or "through misfortune or by accident, when it appears that there was no evil design, intention, or culpable negligence." Section 26 thus describes a range of circumstances or "defenses" which, the Legislature has recognized, operate to negate the mental state element of crimes and show there is no union of act and criminal intent or mental state.

Notwithstanding the myriad circumstances or "defenses" that may operate to negate the mental state element of a given crime, the particular "defense" of mistake of fact requires, at a minimum, an actual belief "in the existence of circumstances, which, if true, would make the act with which the person is charged an innocent act. For general intent crimes, the defendant's mistaken belief must be both actual and reasonable, but if the mental state of the crime is a specific intent or knowledge, then the mistaken belief must only be actual. In all cases, however, the defendant's mistaken belief must relate to a set of circumstances which, if existent or true, would make the act charged an innocent act.

Here, defendant's alleged mistake of fact was that he forgot the hoodie was on his shoulder when he walked out of the store without paying for it. The act of forgetting about the hoodie does not amount to a mistaken belief in a set of circumstances which, if true, would have made defendant's act of walking out of the store with the hoodie lawful.

We observe that the mistake-of-fact defense would apply if defendant had been in the store earlier during the day, left his hoodie there, returned to get it, and, believing that someone had hung it up, took it off the hanger and walked out with it over his shoulder. The act of walking out of the store with the hoodie and without paying for it would be innocent because in this hypothetical defendant would have believed, although mistakenly, that the hoodie he had left in the store earlier, and the one he had on his shoulder when he walked out of the store, was rightfully his.

Defendant did not have a mistaken belief in a set of facts which, if true, would have rendered his act of walking out of the store with the hoodie innocent. In sum, the defense of mistake of fact is inapplicable to the present facts.

PROBLEMS ON MISTAKE OF FACT

1. Dell went to a sports bar after work to watch a football game with friends. After spending several hours with his friends, Dell picked up his computer bag and left the bar. Unfortunately, Dell picked up the wrong bag, and Dell is charged with theft of someone else's computer. At trial, Dell testifies in his own behalf that he thought the bag he took was his. The bag he took was the same color and size as his bag. When he got home, he put the bag in a closet without looking inside the bag. Dell's attorney requests the following jury instruction: "If one takes personal property with the good faith belief that the property is his, he is not guilty of theft. This is the case even if such good faith belief is unreasonable." The prosecutor objects to this instruction. Should the judge give the requested instruction?

2. Defendant is charged with rape, defined as "sexual intercourse against the victim's will by force or the threat of force." At trial, defendant testifies in his own defense and says, "I thought she consented." Defense counsel requests the following jury instruction: "If defendant had sexual intercourse with the victim in the good faith belief that the victim consented, he is not guilty of rape. This is the case whether the defendant's good faith belief is reasonable or unreasonable." The prosecutor objects to this instruction. Should the judge give the instruction?

3. Remember Sue, who went to the restaurant and checked her white wool coat at the cloak room? When she left she was given a white wool coat. Change the facts. Sue checked her white wool coat when she arrived at the restaurant. When she left, however, she was handed a black mink coat! Sue put on the mink and left. Sue is charged with theft. Sue testifies at trial that she thought the coat was hers, and defense counsel requests the following instruction: "If one takes personal property with the good faith belief that the property is hers, she is not guilty of theft. This is the case even if such good faith belief is unreasonable." The prosecutor objects. Should the judge give the instruction?

4. Pete worked at Wal-Mart. James Mayfield was a manager at Wal-Mart. At his trial for robbery and kidnapping, Pete testified that Mayfield convinced him that Mayfield was working for the Central Intelligence Agency (CIA). Mayfield told Pete that the CIA was interested in recruiting Pete as an agent. Pete testified that he believed he was involved in a complicated CIA operation called "Double White" which required Pete to stage a robbery in order to establish his outlaw status so that he could more easily infiltrate a drug cartel. Pete testified that Mayfield told him that the sheriff's department was involved with the drug cartel, and the staged robbery must look real so that the sheriff's department would report the robbery back to the cartel.

Pete testified that the plan was to seek out Roger, another employee of the Wal-Mart, who knew of the plan, and that Roger would lead Pete to the "cash room." Pete testified that Mayfield told him not to wear a mask or gloves, and to make sure the cameras in the store recorded the robbery so the drug cartel would know that he robbed the store. Pete testified that he believed the money taken from Wal-Mart would be recovered and returned immediately to the store. He testified, "It wasn't a robbery. I never believed it was a robbery. If I would have believed it was a robbery I wouldn't have went in there. It was just to appear to be a robbery, but they weren't going to let me keep the money."

Pete testified that he went into the Wal-Mart armed with a handgun. Roger, his contact, was not working that day, so Pete met Brandon, another manager, whom Mayfield said also knew about the plan. Pete testified he pointed the gun at Brandon and ordered him into the cash room, making sure the cameras could see the gun. Once Pete entered the cash room, he took more than $100,000 in cash.

Pete ordered Brandon to walk outside the store and into the parking lot after the money was taken. Pete testified, "Brandon was supposed to come with me, to walk outside the store. This was part of the plan because they have a girl that stands there. When you walk out of Wal-Mart she checks your bags. I had a big bag of money. If I'm not walking with the manager out the door, she's going to check the bag, and it's going to create confusion."

Once out of the store, Pete testified he believed someone from the CIA was going to pick him up, because he did not have a car. A white Mercedes pulled up and parked right next to Pete, and Pete testified "I thought the Benz was my ride." A woman got out of the car, began screaming, threw her purse and keys at Pete, and ran away. Pete testified, "I figured it was for show."

Pete took the car, and proceeded to evade the police. Pete testified that Mayfield told him a CIA agent would intercept the local police so that Pete would not get caught.

Pete maintained he thought he was working for the CIA, and therefore did not have the requisite *mens rea* to commit any crime. How should the judge instruct the jury? *State v. Blurton* (2002) 352 S.C. 203, 573 S.E.2d 802.

NOTE

Observe that in each of the problems above, defendant testified and described the alleged mistake. In order to get a mistake of fact instruction, the defense must present evidence that a mistake was indeed made. The defense must shoulder the burden of producing evidence of mistake. If there is no evidence defendant made a mistake, then the judge will not give a mistake of fact instruction to the jury at the end of the trial.

Mistake of Fact in Rape Prosecutions

In rape prosecutions, four defenses predominate: (1) nothing happened—the woman is lying; (2) there was rape, but someone else did it—mistaken identity; (3) the woman consented—there was sex but no rape; or (4) sex occurred and the woman did *not* consent, but the defendant mistakenly believed she consented—mistake of fact. With mistake of fact, defendant argues his mistake about consent negates *mens rea*, that is, he lacked intent to commit rape. If defendant was honestly mistaken about consent, then "both the victim and the accused are telling the truth."[16] Catherine MacKinnon remarked, "A woman is raped but not by a rapist."[17] In *People v. Mayberry*, the Supreme Court analyzed mistake of fact regarding consent.

PEOPLE V. MAYBERRY

California Supreme Court
15 Cal.3d 143, 125 Cal.Rptr. 745, 542 P.2d 1337 (1975)

RICHARDSON, J.

An information was filed charging Franklin Mayberry with [rape] against the prosecutrix (Miss Nancy B.). Following a trial, a jury found [defendant] guilty as charged.

[Defendant appeals from the judgment], contending that the prosecutrix' testimony is inherently improbable and that inadequate instructions require reversal of the judgments. We have concluded that the court erred in refusing to give instructions concerning mistake of fact and that the error requires reversal.

Miss B., the prosecutrix, testified to the following effect: About 4 p.m. on July 8, 1971, she left her apartment in Oakland to walk to a nearby grocery store. As she passed a liquor store, she heard "catcalls" from some men, and Franklin, whom she had never seen before, grabbed her arm. She dug her fingernails into his wrist, and he released her. After she turned to leave, he kicked her, threw a bottle which struck her, and shouted obscenities at her. She remonstrated and continued on her way.

After she entered the grocery store, Franklin suddenly appeared beside her and said something to the effect that she was going to go outside with him and if she did not cooperate she would "pay for it." She replied she did not want to accompany him and looked for a store security guard but saw none. The only store personnel she observed were busy with customers and were too far away for her to gain their attention. Because of her own confusion and fear of Franklin, she accompanied him outside the

---

[16] *People v. Romero* (1985) 171 Cal.App.3d 1149, 1155, 215 Cal.Rptr. 634.

[17] Catherine A. Mackinnon, Feminism, Marxism, Method and the State: Toward Feminist Jurisprudence, 8 *Signs* 635, 654 (1983).

store, where they remained for approximately 20 minutes. During this time Miss B. observed no one available to assist her although two women left the store in her vicinity.

Franklin, in a threatening manner, mentioned to Miss B. having sex. She rejected this, but Franklin told her she "was going to have to go with him," and, when she refused, struck her in the chest with his fist, knocking her down. Franklin directed obscenities at her, held his fist up to her face, and told her "you are going to come with me" and added that if she did not do so he would "knock every tooth out of her mouth." She asked him to leave her alone, but Franklin seized her wrist and said "come on." In an attempt "to buy time," she told Franklin she wanted to purchase some cigarettes, and he agreed. Placing his hand beneath her elbow, he accompanied her to a store, approximately 100 feet away, where she purchased cigarettes for herself and Franklin. She did not explain to the clerk her predicament because she was feeling "completely beaten" and did not think the clerk would help her.

After completing the purchase, she sat on a curb, attempted to engage Franklin in conversation and smoked a cigarette. During this period, in her words, she "put on an act" and tried "to fool" Franklin, thinking that she might be able to escape. He eventually said, "we are leaving." She "tried to talk him out of it," and he became angry and, uttering an obscenity, ordered her to "get up." She complied, and he again seized her elbow and started to guide her. While walking several blocks, they passed some business establishments, but Miss B. noticed no one on the street. She did not want to accompany him but, because of fear, did not resist.

Franklin led her to an apartment house and entered ahead of her. After they entered his apartment, he barricaded the door behind them. She did not attempt to flee because, having a leg that was stiff from an arthritic condition, she could not run fast. Approximately 15 minutes of further conversation ensued during which she unsuccessfully attempted to persuade Franklin "to change his mind." Without her consent, he then engaged in several acts of sexual intercourse and oral copulation with her. During the sexual assault he struck her, and because of fear she did not physically resist his advances.

Franklin took the stand in his own behalf and testified as follows: he saw Miss B. about 4 p.m. on July 8, 1971, and engaged her in conversation, after which he accompanied her to the grocery and the store where she purchased cigarettes. They then walked to his home. He did not threaten her, nor did she protest but accompanied him willingly and agreed to, and did engage in, intercourse.

Defendant's Claim that the Prosecutrix' Testimony is Inherently Improbable

In arguing that the prosecutrix' testimony is inherently improbable, [defendant points] to the facts that the prosecutrix did not report the assault in front of the liquor store to the police from a telephone that was available near the grocery store; that she did not physically resist Franklin after the initial encounter; that she failed to attempt to flee or obtain help even though there were opportunities for her to do so; that there was no evidence Franklin was armed; and that she had "a lighted cigarette just prior to the time that she left defendants' apartment," suggesting thereby, in some way, a friendly parting.

To be improbable on its face the evidence must assert that something has occurred that it does not seem possible could have occurred under the circumstances disclosed. Viewed in the light of the foregoing expressions, it cannot be said that the prosecutrix' testimony is inherently improbable. She testified that, although she was aware of the telephone by the grocery store, she did not think of it and planned to call the police from her home. She explained that she did not physically resist Franklin after the initial encounter because she was afraid of him. Although they were about the same size and there is no evidence he was armed, she had been threatened, struck, and knocked down and the jury, which had an opportunity to observe them and hear their testimony, could well have concluded that her fear was not unreasonable. She explained her failure to flee on the ground she could not run fast due to her stiff leg. Her failure to elicit help from others (*e.g.*, persons at the grocery store) might have been deemed suspicious, but it was also susceptible to a conclusion that she was too frightened to think clearly. Her testimony that "she did have a lighted cigarette just prior to the time that she left defendants' apartment" which testimony is not amplified, is not significant and discloses at most an unusual circumstance.

Franklin's Claim that Court Erred in Refusing to Give Requested Instructions

The court refused to give requested instructions that directed the jury to acquit Franklin of the rape if the jury had a reasonable doubt as to whether Franklin reasonably and genuinely believed that Miss B. freely consented to sexual intercourse with him. Franklin contends that the court thereby erred. The Attorney General argues that the court properly refused to give the instructions because "mistake of fact instructions as to consent should be rejected as against the law and public policy."

Penal Code section 261 provides, "Rape is an act of sexual intercourse, accomplished with a female not the wife of the perpetrator, under either of the following circumstances: 2. Where she resists, but her resistance is overcome by force or violence; 3. Where she is prevented from resisting by threats of great and immediate bodily harm, accompanied by apparent power of execution." There is, of course, no rape if a female of sufficient capacity consents to sexual intercourse.

Penal Code section 26 recites, generally, that one is incapable of committing a crime who commits an act under a mistake of fact disproving any criminal intent.

In *People v. Hernandez,* 61 Cal.2d 529, we considered the matter of intent within a context similar to that presented in the instant case. The defendant in *Hernandez* was convicted of statutory rape under former subdivision 1 of Penal Code section 261, which provided "Rape is an act of sexual intercourse, accomplished with a female not the wife of the perpetrator. 1. Where the female is under the age of eighteen years." On appeal the defendant contended that the court erred in excluding evidence that he had in good faith a reasonable belief that the prosecutrix was 18 years or more in age, and in *Hernandez* we upheld the contention.

Although *Hernandez* dealt solely with statutory rape, its rationale applies equally to rape by means of force or threat and kidnapping. Those statutory provisions, like that involved in *Hernandez,* neither expressly nor by necessary implication negate the continuing requirement that there be a union of act and wrongful intent. The severe penalties imposed for those offenses and the serious loss of reputation following conviction make it extremely unlikely that the Legislature intended to exclude as to those offenses the element of wrongful intent. If a defendant entertains a reasonable and bona fide belief that a prosecutrix voluntarily consented to accompany him and to engage in sexual intercourse, it is apparent he does not possess the wrongful intent that is a prerequisite under Penal Code section 20 to a conviction of either kidnapping (§ 207) or rape by means of force or threat (§ 261, subds. 2 & 3).

Reversed.

When Is a *Mayberry* Instruction Required?

A trial judge does not give a *Mayberry* mistake of fact instruction every time defense counsel requests one. In *People v. Williams* (1992) 4 Cal. 4th 354, 360–361, 841 P.2d 961, the Supreme Court explained that mistake of fact has both subjective and objective components. The court wrote: "The subjective component asks whether the defendant honestly and in good faith, albeit mistakenly, believed that the victim consented to sexual intercourse. To satisfy this requirement there must be evidence of substantial equivocal behavior by the woman that led the defendant to erroneously conclude she consented." If there is no equivocal conduct by the victim, then a mistake of fact instruction is not warranted. If there was substantial equivocal conduct by the victim, then the objective component asks whether defendant's mistake was reasonable under the circumstances. If the woman's account of what happened is consistent only with rape and the defendant argues actual consent, then there is no middle ground from which the defendant can argue he reasonably misinterpreted the victim's conduct, and a mistake of fact instruction in not warranted.

In *People v. Dominguez* (2006) 39 Cal. 4th 1141, 1148–1149, 140 P.3d 866, defendant was charged with raping and murdering a woman. The victim was strangled to death in an orchard. She had serious genital injuries consistent with forcible rape. Defendant denied killing the victim, but admitted having sex with her in the orchard. Defendant claimed the sex was consensual. The Supreme Court wrote: "Defendant presented no evidence he *mistakenly* believed [the victim] consented to have sex. Instead, he testified she had *in fact* consented. [The victim] of course could not testify, but the evidence she was killed after engaging in sexual intercourse and that she was beaten and strangled and suffered severe trauma to her vagina and cervix suggests she resisted rather than consented. These contrasting scenarios create no middle ground from which defendant could argue he reasonably misinterpreted the victim's conduct."

In *Dominguez* there was no equivocal victim conduct that defendant could mistake for consent. Are the facts different in *People v. May* (1989) 213 Cal. App. 3d 118, 261 Cal. Rptr. 502? Is there enough evidence in *May* of equivocal victim conduct to justify a *Mayberry* instruction?

> Maria testified she and her friend Tim went to Joe Frogger's bar in Santa Rosa. Maria had two Bloody Marys and was finishing some soup when defendant May walked in. He came up and sat next to her and they engaged in pleasant conversation. He gave her his business card and bought drinks for her. At one point Maria told May she was going to the bathroom to "powder her nose" which, she explained, meant that she was going to snort cocaine. May then told her that he could obtain more cocaine for her. Maria accepted the offer. Without notifying Tim, she left the bar with May, to whom she admitted she felt an attraction. After drinking at two other bars, they drove to May's apartment.
>
> Maria testified that upon entering, May told Maria that the bedroom light was on and that she should go in there and take her clothes off. He then went into the kitchen and starting cooking something on the stove. She followed him into the kitchen, told him "no" and grabbed a steak knife. May took the knife out of her hand and slapped her face. He grabbed her arm, led her to the bedroom and again told her to disrobe. This time she did not refuse, but stood there for awhile. Finally, because she was afraid, she took her clothes off and got on the bed.

May removed his clothes and got on the bed with her. She then tried to roll off the bed, but he slapped her again. He positioned himself so that his penis was in her mouth and his mouth was on her vagina. He told her to get his penis "nice and hard," and she began to suck on it because she felt she had no choice. While they were on the bed, May struck her a number of times with his open hand and closed fist and licked and bit her vagina. At some point while she was orally copulating him, she felt sick and vomited over the side of the bed. Just then the phone rang and May got up and left the bedroom. Maria took advantage of this opportunity to get dressed and left the apartment.

May took the stand in his own defense. He testified that at Joe Frogger's, Maria looked over at him and smiled and he smiled back. He introduced himself and bought drinks for her and her friends. After "powdering her nose" in the bathroom, Maria returned and asked him if he wanted to "buy some pussy" for $50. He agreed, and they left the bar together.

According to May, after visiting several bars, drinking beer and flirting with each other, he drove Maria to his apartment. She followed him into the kitchen where they were giggling fondling, playing around. She visited the bathroom for a few minutes and then invited him into the bedroom. She offered him cocaine, but he declined because he didn't use hard drugs. She ingested the cocaine herself, and they embraced on the bed. She took off all her clothes, unzipped his fly and orally copulated him. He told her to stop because he had too much to drink and couldn't get an erection. Maria got dressed and told him not to worry because "it could happen to anybody."

They went outside his apartment and she asked for $20 "for the blow job." When he declined to pay because he had not achieved erection, she threatened to have him killed and slapped him. Instinctively, he slapped her back and told her to get lost.

In *People v. Hernandez*, the Court of Appeal grappled with mistake of fact.

PEOPLE V. HERNANDEZ

California Court of Appeal
180 Cal.App.4th 337, 103 Cal.Rptr.3d 101 (2009)

MCINTYRE, J.

A jury convicted 21-year-old Carlos Morales Hernandez of sodomy and rape.

Hernandez argues that he is entitled to a new trial because the court erred in failing to instruct the jury on his theory of the defense, specifically, his reasonable but mistaken belief that the victim consented. We affirm the judgment.

The victim was the main witness for the prosecution. She lived in a one-bedroom cottage with her two-year-old daughter. The victim had seen Hernandez two or three times at church where he was introduced as "Carlos." She had also seen Hernandez in her neighborhood, but had no direct contact with him.

On August 4, 2007, the victim returned home from work around 7:00 p.m. and began cooking dinner for her daughter's father, Rufino Perez. After dinner, Perez stayed to talk. The victim fell asleep on the bed with her daughter. She testified that Perez always locked the outside door when he left.

A noise awakened the victim early the following morning. She saw a shadow and demanded, "Who's there?" A person moved toward her saying, "Be quiet. I'm Carlos." She recognized the voice and face as belonging to Hernandez. The victim reached for her cellular and land-line phones which were on a table next to the bed. Hernandez grabbed the phones and threw them aside saying, "Don't try it."

Hernandez told the victim "that he had killed and he was fleeing from the police because he had killed a policeman." Thinking that Hernandez wanted help, the victim indicated that he could stay on the sofa in the living room. However, Hernandez said that he "wanted to be with" her. The victim was unsure what Hernandez wanted until he started to touch her feet and legs. At that point, she realized that Hernandez was trying to talk her into having sex with him. Hernandez was carrying a two-foot-long metal object later described by Hernandez as an exercise bar. She also testified that Hernandez stunk of alcohol. The victim was afraid for herself and her daughter.

Hernandez repeated his demand that the victim let him be with her "just once," and she asked him to respect her. She attempted to cover herself with the blankets and cross her feet, which angered Hernandez. He gave her ten minutes to give in and let him have sex with her or "something bad was going to happen." Hernandez held the metal object near his chest.

Meanwhile, the victim's daughter woke up and moved toward the victim to nurse. She covered her daughter so she could not see Hernandez.

The victim's daughter began to cry. Hernandez initially refused to let the victim prepare a bottle for the child, then grabbed the victim and took her to the kitchen. Hernandez repeatedly told the victim to keep her daughter quiet. Finally the victim said, "Let me give her a bottle and then do whatever you want with me." The victim thought that Hernandez was going to hurt her or her daughter and therefore believed she had no choice.

They returned to the bedroom and the victim gave her daughter the bottle. Hernandez would not leave her alone, played with her body and took off her panties. While the victim tried to quiet the child, Hernandez sodomized her.

Hernandez turned the victim on her back, but she got on the floor so her daughter could not see what was happening. The victim felt the metal rod on the floor and pushed it farther under the bed. Hernandez lost his erection and was unable to penetrate the victim's vagina. In frustration, he hit the floor next to the victim's face. Hernandez tried to suck the victim's breasts, but she asked him not to do it because her daughter was still breastfeeding. At trial, the victim had trouble remembering whether Hernandez was able to penetrate her vagina or ejaculated in her genital area, but testified that "yes, he did put it in."

After ejaculating, Hernandez got off the victim and said, "Forgive me. Forgive me. I don't know why I came here to do that." He also told her that something bad would happen if she called the police. Hernandez took the metal bar and left.

The victim called Perez for help, and he called the police. The investigating officer found the victim on the bed in the fetal position crying. She cried throughout the interview, making it difficult for the officer to get a statement. The victim agreed to undergo a sexual assault examination. Results of DNA analysis showed that Hernandez was the likely contributor of the semen taken from the victim's genital area. The police investigation revealed pry marks around the door frame of the victim's house.

Police arrested Hernandez at work. Detective Steve Bernier interviewed him with the help of an interpreter. The prosecution played a video of the interview at trial. When told he would be tested for drugs, Hernandez stated that the test would likely show the presence of crystal, marijuana, and beer. He also admitted using $20 worth of "crystal" and told Bernier that he was "crazy" on beer and crystal when he went to the victim's apartment. He also stated he went there because he "wanted her" and had desired her for about six months. Throughout the interview Hernandez maintained that the victim consented to having sex with him, acknowledging that he threatened to hurt her "just once." He told Bernier that he lied about killing someone to scare the victim into submission. He also acknowledged carrying the metal exercise bar and agreed to accompany police to his residence to retrieve it. Hernandez admitted sodomizing the victim but said that she told him to "do it" to her.

Hernandez argues that the court violated his constitutional right to present a defense by denying his request to include [a] mistake of fact [instruction.] We conclude that the court properly denied Hernandez's request.

The Supreme Court explained that "the *Mayberry* defense has two components, one subjective, and one objective. The subjective component asks whether the defendant honestly and in good faith, albeit mistakenly, believed that the victim consented. In order to satisfy this component, a defendant must adduce evidence of the victim's equivocal conduct on the basis of which he erroneously believed there was consent. In addition, the defendant must satisfy the objective component, which asks whether the defendant's mistake regarding consent was reasonable under the circumstances. Thus, regardless of how strongly a defendant may subjectively believe a person has consented to sexual intercourse, that belief must be formed under circumstances society will tolerate as reasonable in order for the defendant to have adduced substantial evidence giving rise to a *Mayberry* instruction."

Hernandez maintains the following facts were sufficient to entitle him to the *Mayberry* instruction: (1) the victim knew him from church; (2) he made clear his desires by caressing her, saying he wanted to be with her, and trying to persuade her to have sex with him; (3) he smelled of alcohol and appeared to be drunk and excited; (4) he never swung or otherwise threatened the victim with the metal bar and eventually put it on the floor; (5) the victim told him that if he let her give her baby a bottle, he could do whatever he wanted with her; and (6) she acquiesced to his repeated requests for sexual activity.

Although these facts may support an argument that Hernandez *subjectively* believed the victim consented to sexual intercourse, they do not satisfy the *objective* component of the analysis. The conduct Hernandez now argues was equivocal must be viewed in the context of the circumstances surrounding the conduct he described. The record shows that Hernandez broke into the home that the victim shared with her two-year-old daughter in the early hours of the morning carrying a two-foot long metal bar. He said that he wanted to be with her. Hernandez threw the victim's phones out of reach, told her he had killed a policeman, held the metal rod near his chest, and gave her ten minutes to give in to his demands for sex or "something bad was going to happen." The victim attempted to cover herself and her daughter with the blankets and crossed her feet after he began touching her feet and legs. She feared for herself and her daughter and repeatedly attempted to protect the child. On this record, the trial court properly ruled that viewed objectively, it was unreasonable as a matter of law for Hernandez to believe the victim consented to sexual intercourse. Accordingly, the court did not err in refusing to instruct the jury.

In *People v. Hanna*, defendant was charged with attempting to have sex with a child under fourteen. Defendant argued that he mistakenly thought the woman was over eighteen.

PEOPLE V. HANNA

California Court of Appeal
218 Cal.App.4th 455, 160 Cal. Rptr. 3d 210 (2013)

NICHOLSON, ACTING P.J.

Defendant George Hanna appeals from his convictions of several crimes. The jury concluded he arranged a meeting with a minor in order to engage in lewd and lascivious behavior (Pen. Code, § 288.4(b)), attempted lewd and lascivious conduct with a child under the age of 14 years (§§ 288(a); 664), and attempted to use harmful material to seduce a minor (§§ 288.2(b); 664).

He claims the court erred as to the charge of attempted lewd conduct with a child under the age of 14 years by not instructing the jury on the defense of mistake of fact regarding the victim's true age. We disagree with each of his contentions and affirm the judgment.

A 13-year-old minor lived with her father, D.R. (hereafter father). Acting against her father's rule, the minor maintained an Internet MySpace social network account. After learning of this, father viewed the minor's MySpace page. The minor's profile name or moniker was "Brebre," which was not her actual first name. She falsely stated on her MySpace profile that she was 18 years old. She also had posted a picture of herself wearing a top with spaghetti straps pulled down below her shoulders which her father would not allow.

While father was viewing the MySpace page, at around midnight, the page indicated the minor had just received an e-mail from someone named "King Jorge" (hereafter King). King asked the minor if she wanted to have oral sex. To dissuade King from any further sexual communications with his daughter, father responded to the message by writing, "I'm 13, is that okay with you?"

King wrote back by instant messaging instead of e-mail. He wrote, "Are you a cop?" Father responded, "LOL," meaning "laughing out loud." Father was continuing to play the role of a 13-year-old to identify King and possibly arrange a meeting with him. Father then wrote, "Are you a weirdo?"

To father's last question, King wrote, "No. Do you live in Sacramento?" Father responded, "Well, why the fuck wud nbe a pig [sic]," referring to King's earlier question about being a cop. Answering King's next question about where the minor lived, father wrote, "Well, yeh, my profile says that."

King typed back, "This might be a set up." Father, responded, "Not very smart," referring to King's question of where the minor lived. Answering the assertion of a setup, father wrote, "Then bye King, if you don't want to chat. L8R."

King responded, "I do. Tell me about yourself." Father wrote, "I go to South Park Middle School. H8TIN life there." South Park Middle School was a fictional name based on the South Park television show. Father also asked King to tell about himself.

King wrote, "I'm a bouncer at a Latin night club." Father asked him, "What [do you] bounce LOL." King responded he was a security guard at a club. He also mentioned the MySpace profile said Brebre was 18. Still acting the part of his daughter, father wrote, "I know but I can't see the hot older guys if I don't lie. Foo, get with it."

The dialogue continued, with father trying to keep King communicating with him by making King think he was a real 13-year-old girl who was interested in older men.

At 12:22 a.m., father wrote: "You have a girlfriend? I don't need another dude with a chica."

King: "I don't have a chica."

Father: "Na, you don't want to fuck with a 13 year old. You're playing with me. My last man fucked me a few time but started to get weird on me and stop [sic]. Older guys always do."

King: "No way. I'm totally interested in you."

At 12:28 a.m., father wrote: "I can't drive yet. God you're fine. I saw your pics."

At 12:30 a.m., father wrote: "Um, once but my last man kept trying to fuc in the azz. I didn't like it. It hurt so bad never been eaten out." (Sic.) At about the same time, King wrote: "No my dick is too fat. I wouldn't try doing that to you." (Sic.) Father responded, "Really. No way. How fat?"

Believing he might be able to get King into more trouble, father asked to see a picture of his penis. King wrote back, "If you want to see my dick go to PhoneShag.com and search for "mother_fucker." Wanting to receive the actual picture, father wrote that his phone would not pull up the Web site.

At about 12:36 a.m., King wrote, "I know, I really want to suck some pussy." Father responded, "Want mine hotty?"

Ultimately, father scheduled a place and time to meet King. The two were to meet at a nearby convenience store as soon as possible that morning after the chat ended. King wrote he would be in a white truck that had a broken radiator.

Father wrote, "Hey, you have condoms? I ran out." King wrote, "In a half hour go outside." Father responded, "I can't get preg again," meaning "she" could not get pregnant again. King then wrote, "No, I don't."

Father wrote back, "They sell them in the store where I'm about to meet you." Father testified he told King to go inside the store and buy condoms with the hope of getting him recorded on the store's video cameras.

King wrote back, "I'm eating your pussy, right?" Father responded, "Can you get them first, but I want to fuck you."

Father went directly to the convenience store and waited. He also took along his own camera. After waiting a while, he went inside to buy a drink. Walking away from the counter, he looked outside and saw a white truck drive in pretty fast. It had water spilling out underneath it.

Father got his camera ready and walked out of the store. A man exited the truck and began walking towards the store. As father walked up to the man, he raised his camera to take a picture of him. The man asked, "Do I know you?" Father replied, "Yeah, you want to fuck my 13 year old," and then he started taking pictures. The man walked away. As he did, he made a gesture of turning around to get into his truck. Father said, "Don't do it. I'll kill you." The man ran down the street, leaving his truck in the parking lot. In court, father identified defendant as the man he met at the convenience store.

Later that morning, defendant admitted to an investigating police officer that he had been browsing MySpace earlier when someone with the moniker of "Brebre" contacted him. Brebre said she thought he "was fine and wanted to fuck." Defendant said he did not know Brebre was 13. When the officer reminded him he had been told by Brebre she was 13, he said he must not have read that part of their messages. She had told him she was 18 and he thought she looked 18.

He said that after he and Brebre were to meet at the convenience store, they were to go back to her house "to check things out and if it happened, it happened." They never met, he said, because a male approached him and threatened to kill him.

Detectives inspecting defendant's personal computer found that the text of instant messages between "King Jorge" and "Brebre" had been deleted and moved into "unallocated space" on the hard drive. They saved the text of the messages and printed them out as part of their report. In addition, detectives found a digital image of a penis in the hard drive's unallocated space.

Defendant asked the court to instruct the jury on good faith mistake of fact regarding Brebre's age as a defense to the charges, including the charge of attempted lewd conduct with a person under the age of 14 years. The trial court denied the request. It apparently believed the mistake-of-fact defense did not apply to a claim of attempted lewd conduct with a child under the age of 14 years. It also denied the request as to the other charged offenses because it determined there was insufficient evidence to support the defense. It held there was insufficient evidence that defendant reasonably and actually believed Brebre was 18 years old so as to justify instructing on the mistake-of-fact defense.

Defendant claims the court erred by not instructing the jury on his mistake-of-fact defense. He argues the defense applies to an attempt to commit a lewd act on a minor under 14 years of age, that sufficient evidence justified giving an instruction on the defense here, and that the court's failure to give the instruction was prejudicial. Neither defendant nor the Attorney General has cited a published opinion addressing whether the mistake-of-fact defense applies to an attempt to commit a lewd act on a child under 14 years of age, and we have found none.

We conclude the mistake-of-fact defense applies to an attempt to commit a lewd act on a child under 14 years of age, and there was sufficient evidence here to justify instructing on the defense. However, we conclude the court's omission of the instruction was not prejudicial error.

The mistake-of-fact defense, as a matter of public policy, does not apply to the commission of a lewd act on a child under the age of 14 years. Defendant, however, was not charged with committing a lewd act. He was charged with attempting to commit a lewd act.

An attempt to commit any crime requires a specific intent to commit that particular offense. In this case, to sustain a conviction of attempted violation of section 288(a), the prosecution had the burden of demonstrating (1) the defendant intended to commit a lewd and lascivious act with a child under 14 years of age, and (2) the defendant took a direct but ineffectual step toward committing a lewd and lascivious act with a child under 14 years of age. To attempt a violation of section 288(a), the defendant must have specifically intended to commit a lewd act on a child under 14 years of age. If defendant's intent was to commit a lewd act on an 18-year-old, he cannot by definition be guilty of an attempt to commit a lewd act on a 13-year-old. If the facts were as he allegedly believed, the commission of the acts he attempted would not have violated section 288(a). He would have lacked the specific intent required to commit the attempt crime. Thus, we conclude a mistake-of-fact defense may apply to the crime of attempting to commit a lewd act on a child under 14 years of age.

The defense of mistake of fact was not only available to defendant, but there was sufficient evidence during trial to instruct on it. The trial court had a duty sua sponte to instruct on the defense because defendant was relying on it, substantial evidence supported it, and the defense was not inconsistent with the defendant's theory of the case. Evidence of a defense is sufficiently substantial to trigger a trial court's duty to instruct on it sua sponte if it is sufficient for a reasonable jury to find in favor of the defense.

There was substantial evidence on which a jury could believe defendant intended to have sexual relations with an 18-year-old. Brebre's MySpace profile listed her age as 18. Although father, pretending to be Brebre, digitally "told" defendant "she" was 13 and lied on her profile page, father also depicted Brebre as sexually experienced beyond her years. In father's explicit, masked words, Brebre had already had sex with other older men, run out of her supply of condoms, and had even been pregnant. Defendant told the investigating officer that Brebre said she was 18. This was sufficient evidence to justify giving the mistake-of-fact instruction.

MISTAKE OR IGNORANCE OF LAW

Mistake of *fact* that negates *mens rea* is a defense. Generally, however, ignorance of or a mistake about the *law* is not a defense. The old shibboleth *ignorantia juris non excusat*—"ignorance of the law is no excuse"—is really true (most of the time). In *People v. Meneses* (2008) 165 Cal.App.4th 1648, 1661–1662, 82 Cal.Rptr.3d 100, the Court of Appeal explained:

> The courts have drawn a distinction between mistakes of fact and mistakes of law. While a mistake of fact usually is a defense, a mistake of law usually is not. It is commonly said that ignorance of the law is no excuse. In the absence of specific language to the contrary, ignorance of a law is not a defense to a charge of its violation. If the act itself is punishable when knowingly done, it is immaterial that the defendant thought it was lawful. As an illustration: a defendant's ignorance of a girl's age may be a defense to statutory rape, but a defendant's ignorance of the law prohibiting sex with underage girls is no defense.

The law presumes citizens know the law. This is rubbish, of course. Apart from *malum in se* crimes like murder, rape, robbery, and burglary—crimes that are inherently evil—the more realistic presumption is that *no one* knows the law! There are hundreds of crimes scattered through the Penal and other California codes. Many of these crimes are not inherently evil; they are not obviously criminal. They are *malum prohibitum*, criminal only because the Legislature says so. No one knows all the law. Be that as it may, the fact that a person does not know the existence of a crime—including one that is *malum prohibitum*—is not generally a defense. As the Supreme Court put it in *Stark v. Superior Court* (2011) 52 Cal.4th 368, 128 Cal.Rptr.3d 611, 257 P.3d 41, "A defendant may not escape criminal liability by asserting that he did not know the criminal law." This is nearly always so when the crime is one of general intent. The fact that defendant did not know her conduct violated a general intent offense is not a defense.

With specific intent crimes requiring a specified state of knowledge or belief, a mistake about the law is sometimes a defense. In *Meneses*, the Court of Appeal explained:

> There are a number of circumstances in which violation of a penal statute is premised on the violator's harboring a particular mental state with respect to the nonpenal legal status of a person, thing, or action. In such cases, the principle is firmly established that defendant is not guilty if the offense charged requires any special mental element, such as that the prohibited act be committed knowingly, fraudulently, corruptly, maliciously, or wilfully, and this element of the crime was lacking because of some mistake of nonpenal law. The mistake must be one of *nonpenal* law. Thus, a taxpayer may defend against a felony tax fraud charge on the basis, for example, that he mistakenly believed certain deductions were proper under the tax laws, but not on the basis that he was unaware it was a crime to lie on one's tax return.

In *People v. Noori* (2006) 136 Cal.App.4th 964, 39 Cal.Rptr.3d 153, defendants were in the business of receiving money for transmission to Iran. People with relatives in Iran would go to defendants' business to send money "home" to the family. Absent a license, it is a crime to receive money for the purpose of transmitting it to a foreign country. Defendants did not have the required license, and were charged under the law. The prosecutor argued that the crime is one of general criminal intent, and that all the prosecutor had to prove was: (1) defendants lacked the required license, and (2) defendants received money for transfer to a foreign country. Defendants argued that the statute should be interpreted to require knowledge of the license requirement. Under the defendants' view, the statute creates a specific intent crime, requiring the prosecution to prove: (1) defendants lacked the required license, (2) defendants received money for transfer to a foreign country, *and* (3) defendants were aware of the licensing requirement. Defendants asserted that they were unaware of the license requirement, and therefore not guilty. The trial court ruled that the statute created a general intent crime, and that defendants' lack of knowledge of the license requirement was not a defense. Defendants were convicted, and the Court of Appeal affirmed. The appellate court wrote:

As Justice Story explained nearly two centuries ago, "it is a common maxim, familiar to all minds, that ignorance of the law will not excuse any person, either civilly or criminally." Our courts have consistently endorsed that principle. It is an emphatic postulate of both civil and penal law that ignorance of a law is no excuse for a violation thereof. Of course it is based on a fiction, because no man can know all the law, but it is a maxim which the law itself does not permit any one to gainsay. It is expected that the jury and the court, where it is shown that in fact the defendant was ignorant of the law, and innocent of any intention to violate the same, will give the defendant the benefit of the fact, and impose only a light penalty. The rule rests on public necessity; the welfare of society and the safety of the state depend upon its enforcement. If a person accused of crime could shield himself behind the defense that he was ignorant of the law which he violated, immunity from punishment would in most cases result. No system of criminal justice could be sustained with such an element in it to obstruct the course of its administration. The denser the ignorance the greater would be the exemption from liability.

Knowledge of the unlawfulness of an act or omission is not required *unless* the Legislature has specifically decreed otherwise. California case law has long held that the requirement of "knowingly" is satisfied where the person involved has knowledge of the facts, though not of the law.

A mistake of law is not a defense to a general intent crime, but in some circumstances it may be a defense to a specific intent crime.

PROBLEM

You are a business person and you plan to open a new plant. You hire an attorney to make sure all laws are complied with. The attorney does extensive research and assures you that what you are doing is legal. You proceed with construction of the new plant, but midway through construction you are charged with a crime because you did not get a required permit. As it turns out, your attorney was wrong! At trial, can you defend the charge with the argument that you relied on the advice of the attorney?

Suppose the attorney who advised you your conduct was lawful was a government lawyer? Again, the lawyer was wrong. If you are prosecuted, can you argue, "I relied on the opinion of a government attorney that my conduct was lawful"? Consider the Supreme Court's opinion in *People v. Chacon.*

PEOPLE V. CHACON

California Supreme Court
40 Cal.4th 558, 53 Cal.Rptr.3d 876, 150 P.3d 755 (2007)

CORRIGAN, J.

Maria Chacon was charged with violating Government Code section 1090 by holding a financial interest in a contract made by the public agency of which she was a member. [Section 1090 states in pertinent part: "Members of the Legislature, state, county, district, judicial district, and city officers or employees shall not be financially interested in any contract made by them in their official capacity, or by any body or board of which they are members."] The trial court ruled *in limine* that defendant could assert the defense of entrapment by estoppel. As a result, the People announced they could not proceed and the court dismissed the case. We conclude that an entrapment by estoppel defense is not available in this case.

Defendant, while a member of the Bell Gardens City Council, sought and obtained appointment as city manager. Her conduct in securing that position resulted in criminal charges under Government Code section 1090.

Defendant solicited the support of fellow councilmember Rogelio Rodriguez, advising him of her desired salary and terms. However, the Bell Gardens Municipal Code provided that a councilmember was ineligible for appointment for one year following his or her departure from the council. City Attorney Arnoldo Beltran drafted an ordinance eliminating the waiting period, and Councilmember Pedro Aceituno placed it on the council agenda. Defendant joined the other councilmembers in voting unanimously for the ordinance.

The council met in a special closed session to choose a city manager. Defendant excused herself from this session, but remained in a nearby office. During a break, City Attorney Beltran asked Councilmember Aceituno to meet with defendant and the mayor to discuss defendant's appointment and contract terms. After Aceituno returned to the session, the council approved defendant's appointment, but modified her requested terms. The council then announced its decision in a public session. Defendant accepted the appointment, resigned from the council and signed an employment contract, approved by Beltran.

Defendant was charged with violating Government code section 1090 because, as a city councilmember, she had "participated in making or causing to be made for the Bell Gardens City Council an employment contract in which she was financially interested or had the expectation of financial interest." By pretrial motion, defendant informed the court she sought to call Beltran as a witness. She represented that Beltran advised her on the legality of her efforts to become city manager and was actively involved in the appointment process. Concerned that Beltran might invoke his Fifth Amendment privilege not to testify, defendant asked the court to grant him use immunity. By separate motion, the prosecutor sought to exclude evidence of Beltran's advice as irrelevant, arguing that because defendant was charged with a general intent crime, advice of counsel was not a defense.

On the eve of trial, defendant advised the court that she intended to assert the defense of "entrapment by estoppel." She contended that the defense, based on federal due process, applied because she relied on advice from a government official that her conduct was legal. The court declined to confer immunity on the city attorney, and took the novel question of the defense under submission.

The court ultimately denied the motion to exclude evidence of Beltran's advice and ruled that defendant could present evidence of entrapment by estoppel. The court expressed doubt that a city official's advice could bind the state, but felt compelled to follow *Cox v. Louisiana*, 379 U.S. 559 (1965). In *Cox*, the United States Supreme Court reversed a conviction because the defendant had acted at the direction of the local police chief. Applying *Cox*, the court ruled that it would "permit" the defense, noting the jury must determine whether defendant reasonably relied on Beltran's advice.

In a pretrial memorandum, defendant argued, "As demonstrated at the preliminary hearing, Mrs. Chacon relied upon the legal advice and actions of the Bell Gardens City Attorney when she entered into that employment contract as city manager."

At oral argument, defense counsel requested immunity for City Attorney Beltran by making an offer of proof as to what Beltran "could say" at trial. Defense counsel recounted Beltran's anticipated testimony as follows: "I was asked whether this waiting period was essential under state law, or whether we could adopt the ordinance that we finally adopted. I ordered my subordinate to do a memo on that. I took that memo and drafted a statute. I put that statute on the agenda. I had the council vote on it. I was there to explain anything they wanted. As I drafted the statute and as I said in the statute, the waiting period was not required by state law. And if we got rid of the waiting period, we would be in accordance with state law. I spoke to Mrs. Chacon about whether or not this statute was a legal statute, and her actions, if she became city manager or any council member became city manager, whether that would be legal. I authorized that as yes, it would be in compliance with state law. And actions were taken with regard to my advice. I, then, on December 7th, I placed on the agenda the appointment of Mrs. Chacon to be City Manager. I always do that. I asked Mr. Aceituno to see what she wanted as far as salary. I was in a closed session with the rest of the council members talking about the legality of a city councilman becoming city manager, about the terms and contracts of employment, about what the requirements were for city manager. I urged Mrs. Chacon to become city manager. I thought she would be a good city manager. I thought it would be good for the city of Bell Gardens, and I prevailed upon her to sign the contract and give it a try. I told her that if she became city manager, that was an automatic resignation from the city council, and I never gave any indication that there was anything improper about this entire situation." Defense counsel advised the trial court that witnesses other than Beltran could provide some, but not all of this information.

Entrapment by estoppel, based on principles of federal due process, has been recognized by the federal courts and in some sister states. The defense evolved from three United States Supreme Court opinions, although none used the term "entrapment by estoppel." The concept was first applied in *Raley v. Ohio*, 360 U.S. 423 (1959). Defendants there were convicted of contempt for refusing to answer questions before Ohio's Un-American Activities Commission. The defendants had invoked their privilege against self-incrimination after being advised of their right to do so by the commission chairman. The advice, however, was contrary to the Ohio immunity statute, which eliminated the availability of the privilege for persons testifying before legislative committees. The United States Supreme Court held that the contempt convictions violated due process: "After the Commission, speaking for the State, acted as it did, to sustain the Ohio Supreme Court's judgment would be to sanction an indefensible sort of entrapment by the State—convicting a citizen for exercising a privilege which the State had clearly told him was available to him."

In *Cox v. Louisiana*, the Supreme Court applied *Raley* to reverse the convictions of protestors arrested for picketing across the street from a courthouse. The leader of the demonstration had been given permission by the police chief to demonstrate at the location. The demonstrators were nevertheless arrested and convicted under a state statute barring certain demonstrations "near" any courthouse. In reversing the convictions, the Supreme Court observed: "The highest police officials of the city, in the presence of the Sheriff and Mayor, in effect, told the demonstrators that they could meet where they did. In effect, appellant was advised that a demonstration at the place it was held would not be one 'near' the courthouse within the terms of the statute. The Due Process Clause does not permit convictions to be obtained under such circumstances."

In *United States v. Pennsylvania Chemical Corp.*, 411 U.S. 655 (1973), the court considered the defense in a regulatory setting involving a corporate defendant found to have discharged refuse into navigable waters. The Supreme Court, relying on *Raley* and *Cox*, held the defendant should have been allowed to present a defense that it had been mislead by administrative regulations which appeared to permit the defendant's actions.

Federal cases applying the entrapment by estoppel defense, while varying slightly in their formulation, rest on the premise that the government may not actively provide assurances that conduct is lawful, then prosecute those who act in reasonable reliance on those assurances. Under these limited circumstances, fundamental fairness supports the defense, even when the prosecution can prove each element of the crime. Courts have cautioned that the defense is narrowly circumscribed. The defense is a narrow exception to the general rule that ignorance of the law is no excuse.

We assume, as do the parties, that defendant would have produced evidence consistent with the offer of proof described above. Under these facts, the defense of entrapment by estoppel is not available as a matter of law.

We also assume, but do not decide, that defendant's conduct would fall within the proscription of Government code section 1090. A contract made in violation of that section may be voided by any party except the financially interested official. To incur criminal liability, an official must act both willfully and knowingly. An official who purposefully makes the prohibited contract acts "wilfully." To act "knowingly" the official must be aware there is a reasonable likelihood that the contract may result in a personal financial benefit to him. An official is *not* required to know that his conduct is unlawful. Therefore, reliance on advice of counsel as to the lawfulness of the conduct is irrelevant.

Nevertheless, defendant argues that she is entitled to assert the defense of entrapment by estoppel because City Attorney Beltran is a government lawyer, authorized to advise the city council on legal matters. Defendant's attempt to rely on existing authority fails. Unlike those charged in *Cox* and *Raley*, defendant was not an ordinary citizen confronting the power of the state. Defendant was a member of the executive branch of government. A public office is a position held for the benefit of the people; defendant was obligated to discharge her responsibilities with integrity and fidelity. The law in question regulates the very manner in which defendant was empowered to exercise her governmental authority. For over a hundred years our courts have consistently held that that our conflict-of-interest statute, now embodied in Government code section 1090, is intended to enforce the government's right to the absolute, undivided, uncompromised allegiance of public officials by proscribing any personal interest. In our society, people of ordinary sensibility should recognize, without the intervention of a criminal proscription, that a public official is a trustee and that it is wrong for such a trustee to engage in self-dealing, including the contingent feathering of one's own nest.

For these reasons, we are reluctant to extend the defense to public officials who seek to defend conflict of interest accusations by claiming reliance on the advice of public attorneys charged with counseling them and advocating on their behalf. Recognizing entrapment by estoppel in such circumstances is antithetical to the strong public policy of strict enforcement of conflict of interest statutes and the attendant personal responsibility demanded of our officials.

The city attorney offering an interpretation of Government code section 1090 to council members in the course of his daily responsibilities acts simply as a lawyer advising a client. Government Code section 1090 applies statewide to members of the Legislature, state, county, district, judicial district, and city officers or employees. City Attorney Beltran's clients are the officials of Bell Gardens. Section 1090 is one of the myriad of state statutes he and other city attorneys must advise upon in the course of their daily responsibilities. Beltran is not authorized to criminally enforce or administer this law.

Private attorneys interpret and advise their clients on the application of statutes under all kinds of circumstances. Yet the average citizen cannot rely on a private lawyer's erroneous advice as a defense to a general intent crime. The defense of action taken in good faith, in reliance upon the advice of a reputable attorney that it was lawful, has long been rejected. The theory is that this would place the advice of counsel above the law and would place a premium on counsel's ignorance or indifference to the law. Defendant cannot evade that rule by asserting the attorney who mistakenly advised her happened to hold a governmental position.

We express no view as to whether defendant's conduct violated Government Code section 1090. We hold only that the defense of entrapment by estoppel is not available under the offer of proof contained in this record.

NOTE ON IMMUNITY FROM PROSECUTION

In *Chacon*, the Supreme Court mentioned immunity from prosecution. Individuals have a right not to incriminate themselves—a right to remain silent. The Fifth Amendment to the U.S. Constitution states in part, "No person shall be compelled in any criminal case to be a witness against himself." The California Constitution is identical (Cal. Const. Art. I, § 15). Although the Fifth Amendment refers only to criminal cases, the right against self-incrimination applies in civil as well as criminal proceedings.

If the prosecution wants to compel a person's testimony, the prosecution can ask a judge to grant the person immunity from prosecution (PC § 1324). If the judge grants immunity, the person must testify even though the testimony might be incriminating. In addition to asking a judge to grant immunity, the prosecution, on its own, can extend immunity to individuals.

There are two kinds of immunity: (1) use immunity, and (2) transactional immunity. Use immunity prevents the use against a person of their immunized testimony. Use immunity also extends to information derived from the testimony. A person who receives use immunity has no right to refuse to testify. A person who has been granted use immunity can be prosecuted, but the prosecutor cannot use the compelled testimony (or information derived from the testimony).

If a person is given transactional immunity, the person cannot be prosecuted for any transaction described in the person's testimony. Transactional immunity is broader than use immunity.

The defendant in a criminal case cannot compel the prosecutor to grant immunity to a person the defense would like to call as a witness.

SELF-DEFENSE

Self-defense is a justification defense. The elements are: (1) the defender honestly believed the defender was in imminent danger of being killed or suffering great bodily injury or was in imminent danger of being raped, maimed or robbed; (2) the defender honestly believed that the immediate use of deadly force was necessary to defend against the imminent danger; (3) the defender's beliefs in (1) and (2) were reasonable in the circumstances as they were known to and appeared to the defender[18]; (4) the defender used no more force that reasonably necessary to defend against the imminent danger; (5) the defender was not the initial aggressor.[19]

A threat to harm or attack someone in the future—"I'm going to stab you next week"—does not justify killing in self-defense. There is time to turn for help to the police or the courts.

A defender can be reasonable but wrong. For example, Sue is walking down the street late at night. Suddenly a large man runs at her menacingly and yelling, "I'm going to get you." When the man is a few feet away from Sue, he reaches into his pocket and pulls out what Sue believes to be a knife. Feeling she is about to be killed, Sue shoots and kills the man. As it turns out, the object in the man's hand was a cell phone. The man did not intend to harm Sue. Sue was wrong about the need to defend herself. Yet, if Sue is charged with killing the man, she may succeed in raising self-defense. Sue was wrong but reasonable.

---

[18] *See* PC § 198, which provides: "A bare fear [of attack] is not sufficient to justify it. But the circumstances must be sufficient to excite the fears of a reasonable person, and the party killing must have acted under the influence of such fears alone."

[19] Self-defense may not be claimed by someone "who, through his own wrongful conduct (*e.g.*, the initiation of a physical assault or the commission of a felony), has created circumstances under which his adversaries' attack." *People v. Frandsen* (2011) 196 Cal.App.4th 266, 126 Cal.Rptr.3d 640. The *Frandsen* court went on to write, "It follows, a fortiori, that the imperfect self-defense doctrine cannot be invoked in such circumstances."

A defendant claiming self-defense has the burden of presenting evidence of each element of self-defense. This done, the prosecutor must disprove self-defense beyond a reasonable doubt.[20]

Self-defense is a complete defense. PC § 199 provides that when a homicide is justified, "the person indicted must, upon his trial, be fully acquitted and discharged."

The decision in *United States v. Peterson* is a good place to start your study of self-defense. Why did Mr. Peterson's claim of self-defense fail?

UNITED STATES V. PETERSON

United States Court of Appeals for the District of Columbia
483 F.2d 1222 (1973)

SPOTTSWOOD W. ROBINSON, III, CIRCUIT JUDGE:

Indicted for second-degree murder, and convicted by a jury of manslaughter as a lesser included offense, Bennie L. Peterson urges reversal. He asserts that the judge twice erred in the instructions given the jury in relation to his claim that the homicide was committed in self-defense. One error alleged was an instruction that the jury might consider whether Peterson was the aggressor in the altercation that immediately foreran the homicide. The other was an instruction that a failure by Peterson to retreat, if he could have done so without jeopardizing his safety, might be considered as a circumstance bearing on the question whether he was justified in using the amount of force which he did. After careful study of these arguments in light of the trial record, we affirm Peterson's conviction.

The events immediately preceding the homicide are not seriously in dispute. The version presented by the Government's evidence follows. Charles Keitt, the deceased, and two friends drove in Keitt's car to the alley in the rear of Peterson's house to remove the windshield wipers from the latter's wrecked car. While Keitt was doing so, Peterson came out of the house into the back yard to protest. After a verbal exchange, Peterson went back into the house, obtained a pistol, and returned to the yard. In the meantime, Keitt had reseated himself in his car, and he and his companions were about to leave. Upon his reappearance in the yard, Peterson paused briefly to load the pistol. "If you move," he shouted to Keitt, "I will shoot." He walked to a point in the yard slightly inside a gate in the rear fence and, pistol in hand, said, "If you come in here I will kill you." Keitt alighted from his car, took a few steps toward Peterson and exclaimed, "What the hell do you think you are going to do with that?" Keitt then made an about-face, walked back to his car and got a lug wrench. With the wrench in a raised position, Keitt advanced toward Peterson, who stood

[20] Some states place the burden of proof on the defendant claiming self-defense.

with the pistol pointed toward him. Peterson warned Keitt not to "take another step" and, when Keitt continued onward shot him in the face from a distance of about ten feet. Death was apparently instantaneous. Shortly thereafter, Peterson left home and was apprehended 20-odd blocks away.

More than two centuries ago, Blackstone, best known of the expositors of the English common law, taught that "all homicide is malicious, and of course, amounts to murder, unless *justified* by the command or permission of the law; *excused* on the account of accident or self-preservation; or *alleviated* into manslaughter, by being either the involuntary consequence of some act not strictly lawful, or (if voluntary) occasioned by some sudden and sufficiently violent provocation." Tucked within this greatly capsulized schema of the common law of homicide is the branch of law we are called upon to administer today. No issue of justifiable homicide, within Blackstone's definition is involved. But Peterson's consistent position is that as a matter of law his conviction of manslaughter—alleviated homicide—was wrong, and that his act was one of self-preservation—excused homicide. The Government, on the other hand, has contended from the beginning that Keitt's slaying fell outside the bounds of lawful self-defense. The questions remaining for our decision inevitably track back to this basic dispute.

By the early common law, justification for homicide extended only to acts done in execution of the law, such as homicides in effecting arrests and preventing forcible felonies, and homicides committed in self-defense were only excusable. The distinction between justifiable and excusable homicide was important because in the latter case the slayer, considered to be not wholly free from blame, suffered a forfeiture of his goods. However, the distinction has largely disappeared. More usually the terms are used interchangeably, each denoting a legally non-punishable act, entitling the accused to an acquittal.

Self-defense, as a doctrine legally exonerating the taking of human life, is as viable now as it was in Blackstone's time, and in the case before us the doctrine is invoked in its purest form. But the law of self-defense is a law of necessity; the right of self-defense arises only when the necessity begins, and equally ends with the necessity; and never must the necessity be greater than when the force employed defensively is deadly. The necessity must bear all semblance of reality, and appear to admit of no other alternative, before taking life will be justifiable as excusable. Hinged on the exigencies of self-preservation, the doctrine of homicidal self-defense emerges from the body of the criminal law as a limited though important exception to legal outlawry of the arena of self-help in the settlement of potentially fatal personal conflicts.

So it is that necessity is the pervasive theme of the well defined conditions which the law imposes on the right to kill or maim in self-defense. There must have been a threat, actual or apparent, of the use of deadly force against the defender. The threat must have been unlawful and immediate. The defender must have believed that he was in imminent peril of death or serious bodily harm, and that his response was necessary to save himself therefrom. These beliefs must not only have been honestly entertained, but also objectively reasonable in light of the surrounding circumstances. It is clear that no less than a concurrence of these elements will suffice.

Here the parties' opposing contentions focus on the roles of two further considerations. One is the provoking of the confrontation by the defender. The other is the defendant's failure to utilize a safe route for retreat from the confrontation. The essential inquiry, in final analysis, is whether and to what extent the rule of necessity may translate these considerations into additional factors in the equation. To these questions, in the context of the specific issues raised, we now proceed.

[Peterson objected to two aspects of the jury instructions.] The first of Peterson's complaints centers upon an instruction that the right to use deadly force in self-defense is not ordinarily available to one who provokes a conflict or is the aggressor in it. Mere words, the judge explained, do not constitute provocation or aggression; and if Peterson precipitated the altercation but thereafter withdrew from it in good faith and so informed Keitt by words or acts, he was justified in using deadly force to save himself from imminent danger or death or grave bodily harm. And, the judge added, even if Keitt was the aggressor and Peterson was justified in defending himself, he was not entitled to use any greater force than he had reasonable ground to believe and actually believed to be necessary for that purpose. Peterson contends that there was no evidence that he either caused or contributed to the conflict, and that the instructions on that topic could only misled the jury.

It has long been accepted that one cannot support a claim of self-defense by a self-generated necessity to kill. The right of homicidal self-defense is granted only to those free from fault in the difficulty; it is denied to slayers who incite the fatal attack, encourage the fatal quarrel or otherwise promote the necessitous occasion for taking life. The fact that the deceased struck the first blow, fired the first shot or made the first menacing gesture does not legalize the self-defense claim if in fact the claimant was the actual provoker. In sum, one who is the aggressor in a conflict culminating in death cannot invoke the necessities of self-preservation. Only in the event that he communicates to his adversary his intent to withdraw and in good faith attempts to do so is he restored to his right of self-defense. This body of doctrine traces its origin to the fundamental principle that a killing in self-defense is excusable only as a matter of genuine necessity. Quite obviously, a defensive killing is unnecessary if the occasion for it could have been averted, and the roots of that consideration run deep with us.

In the case at bar, the trial judge's charge fully comported with these governing principles. The remaining question, then, is whether there was evidence to make them applicable to the case. A recapitulation of the proofs shows beyond peradventure that there was.

It was not until Peterson fetched his pistol and returned to his back yard that his confrontation with Keitt took on a deadly cast. Prior to his trip into the house for the gun, there was, by the Government's evidence, no threat, no display of weapons, no combat. There was an exchange of verbal aspersions and a misdemeanor against Peterson's property was in progress but, at this juncture, nothing more. The evidence is uncontradicted that when Peterson reappeared in the yard with his pistol, Keitt was about to depart the scene. The uncontroverted fact that Keitt was leaving shows plainly that so far as he was concerned the confrontation was ended. It demonstrates just as plainly that even if he had previously been the aggressor, he no longer was.

Not so with Peterson, however, as the undisputed evidence made clear. Emerging from the house with the pistol, he paused in the yard to load it, and to command Keitt not to move. He then walked through the yard to the rear gate and, displaying his pistol, dared Keitt to come in, and threatened to kill him if he did. While there appears to be no fixed rule on the subject, the cases hold, and we agree, that an affirmative unlawful act reasonably calculated to produce an affray foreboding injurious or fatal consequences is an aggression which, unless renounced, nullifies the right of homicidal self-defense. We cannot escape the abiding conviction that the jury could readily find Peterson's challenge to be a transgression of that character.

The situation at bar is not unlike that presented in *Laney v. United States*, 294 F. 412 (D.C. Cir. 1923). There the accused, chased along the street by a mob threatening his life, managed to escape through an areaway between two houses. In the back yard of one of the houses, he checked a gun he was carrying and then returned to the areaway. The mob beset him again, and during an exchange of shots one of its members was killed by a bullet from the accused's gun. In affirming a conviction of manslaughter, the court reasoned: "It is clearly apparent that, when defendant escaped from the mob into the back yard he was in a place of comparative safety, from which, if he desired to go home, he could have gone by the back way, as he subsequently did. The mob had turned its attention to a house on the opposite side of the street. According to Laney's testimony, there was shooting going on in the street. His appearance on the street at that juncture could mean nothing but trouble for him. Hence, when he adjusted his gun and stepped out into the areaway, he had every reason to believe that his presence there would provoke trouble. We think his conduct in adjusting his revolver and going into the areaway was such as to deprive him of any right to invoke the plea of self-defense."

Similarly, in *Rowe v. United States*, 370 F.2d 240 (D.C. Cir. 1966), the accused was in the home of friends when an argument, to which the friends became participants, developed in the street in front. He left, went to his nearby apartment for a loaded pistol and returned. There was testimony that he then made an insulting comment, drew the pistol and fired a shot into the ground. In any event, when a group of five men began to move toward him, he began to shoot at them, killing two, and wounding a third. We observed that the accused left an apparently safe haven to arm himself and return to the scene, and that he inflamed the situation with his words to the men gathered there, even though he could have returned silently to the safety of the friends' porch. We held that these facts could have led the jury to conclude that the accused returned to the scene to stir up further trouble, if not actually to kill anyone, and that his actions instigated the men into rushing him. Self-defense may not be claimed by one who deliberately places himself in a position where he has reason to believe his presence would provoke trouble.

We noted the argument that a defendant may claim self-defense if he arms himself in order to proceed upon his normal activities, even if he realizes that danger may await him; we responded by pointing out that the jury could have found that the course of action defendant here followed was for an unlawful purpose. We accordingly affirmed his conviction of manslaughter over his objection that an acquittal should have been directed.

We are brought much the readier to the same conclusion here. We think the evidence plainly presented an issue of fact as to whether Peterson's conduct was an invitation to and provocation of the encounter which ended in the fatal shot. We sustain the trial judge's action in remitting that issue for the jury's determination.

The second aspect of the trial judge's charge as to which Peterson asserts error concerned the undisputed fact that at no time did Peterson endeavor to retreat from Keitt's approach with the lug wrench. The judge instructed the jury that if Peterson had reasonable grounds to believe and did believe that he was in imminent danger of death or serious injury, and that deadly force was necessary to repel the danger, he was required neither to retreat nor to consider whether he could safely retreat. Rather, said the judge, Peterson was entitled to stand his ground and use such force as was reasonably necessary under the circumstances to save his life and his person from pernicious bodily harm. But, the judge continued, if Peterson could have safely retreated but did not do so, that failure was a circumstance which the jury might consider, together with all others, in determining whether he went further in repelling the danger, real or apparent, than he was justified in going.

Peterson contends that this imputation of an obligation to retreat was error, even if he could safely have done so. He points out that at the time of the shooting he was standing in his own yard, and argues he was under no duty to move. We are persuaded to the conclusion that in the circumstances presented here, the trial judge did not err in giving the instruction challenged.

Within the common law of self-defense there developed the rule of "retreat to the wall," which ordinarily forbade the use of deadly force by one to whom an avenue for safe retreat was open. This doctrine was but an application of the requirement of strict necessity to excuse the taking of human life, and was designed to insure the existence of that necessity. Even the innocent victim of a vicious assault had to elect a safe retreat if available, rather than resort to defensive force which might kill or seriously injure.

In a majority of American jurisdictions, contrarily to the common law rule, one may stand his ground and use deadly force whenever it seems reasonably necessary to save himself. While the law of the District of Columbia on this point is not entirely clear, it seems allied with the strong minority adhering to the common law.

That is not to say that the retreat rule is without exceptions. Even at common law it was recognized that it was not completely suited to all situations. Today it is the more so that its precept must be adjusted to modern conditions nonexistent during the early development of the common law of self-defense. One restriction on its operation comes to the fore when the circumstances apparently foreclose a withdrawal with safety. The doctrine of retreat was never intended to enhance the risk to the innocent; its proper application has never required a faultless victim to increase his assailant's safety at the expense of his own. On the contrary, he could stand his ground and use deadly force otherwise appropriate if the alternative were perilous, or if to him it reasonably appeared to be.

The trial judge's charge to the jury incorporated each of these limitations on the retreat rule. Peterson, however, invokes another—the so-called "castle" doctrine. It is well settled that one who through no fault of his own is attacked in his home is under no duty to retreat therefrom. The oft-repeated expression that "a man's home is his castle" reflected the belief in olden days that there were few if any safer sanctuaries than the home. The "castle" exception, moreover, has been extended by some courts to encompass the occupant's presence within the curtilage outside his dwelling. Peterson reminds us that when he shot to halt Keitt's advance, he was standing in his yard and so, he argues, he had no duty to endeavor to retreat.

Despite the practically universal acceptance of the "castle" doctrine in American jurisdictions wherein the point has been raised, its status in the District of Columbia has never been squarely decided. But whatever the fate of the doctrine in the District law of the future, it is clear that in absolute form it was inapplicable here. The right of self-defense, we have said, cannot be claimed by the aggressor in an affray so long as he retains that unmitigated role. It logically follows that any rule of no-retreat which may protect an innocent victim of the affray would, like other incidents of a forfeited right of self-defense, be unavailable to the party who provokes or stimulates the conflict. Accordingly, the law is well settled that the "castle" doctrine can be invoked only by one who is without fault in bringing the conflict on. That, we think, is the critical consideration here.

We need not repeat our previous discussion of Peterson's contribution to the altercation which culminated in Keitt's death. It suffices to point out that by no interpretation of the evidence could it be said that Peterson was blameless in the affair. And while, of course, it was for the jury to assess the degree of fault the evidence well nigh dictated the conclusion that it was substantial.

The only reference in the trial judge's charge intimating an affirmative duty to retreat was the instruction that a failure to do so, when it could have been done safely, was a factor in the totality of the circumstances which the jury might consider in determining whether the force which he employed was excessive. We cannot believe that any jury was at all likely to view Peterson's conduct as irreproachable. We conclude that for one who, like Peterson, was hardly entitled to fall back on the "castle" doctrine of no retreat, that instruction cannot be just cause for complaint.

The judgment of conviction appealed from is accordingly affirmed.

NOTE ON CONSCIOUSNESS OF GUILT

In *Peterson,* Judge Robinson mentioned that "shortly [after the shooting], Peterson left home and was apprehended 20-odd blocks away." Why did the judge mention this fact? Precipitously leaving the scene of a crime can be evidence that the individual had a reason to flee—namely, the individual is guilty and is fleeing to avoid capture. Evidence of flight—also called evidence of consciousness of guilt—is routinely admitted at trial. If the person leaving the scene wishes to offer an innocent explanation for their sudden departure, they are free to do so.

DUTY TO RETREAT?

If the elements of self-defense are present, may a defender stand her ground and defend herself? Or must the defender run away—retreat—if running away is safe? Professor Dressler puts it this way: "If an innocent person is attacked, and if he has only two realistic options—use deadly force or retreat to a place of safety—must he choose the latter option?"[21] The Model Penal Code requires retreat. MPC § 3.04(b)(ii) states that a person cannot use force in self-defense if the person "knows that he can avoid the necessity of using such force with complete safety by retreating." In California and the majority of other states, there is no duty to retreat.[22] The California Court of Appeal wrote in *People v. Clark* (2011) 201 Cal. App. 4th 235, 250, 136 Cal. Rptr. 3d 10, "A defendant is not required to retreat and may in fact pursue the assailant until the danger of injury or unlawful touching has passed, but a defendant may use force only as long as the danger exists or reasonably appears to exist." Do you believe a defender should be required to retreat if safe retreat is available? Or should a defender be allowed to stand her ground and defend herself?

CASTLE DOCTRINE

In a jurisdiction that requires retreat, a defender has never been required to retreat within her own home from an assault by an intruder. A person's home is her castle. There is no safe retreat from one's castle. The Model Penal Code embraces the castle doctrine as follows: "The actor is not obliged to retreat from his dwelling unless he was the initial aggressor."

In a no duty to retreat state like California, the castle doctrine is unnecessary. In California, there is no duty to retreat *anywhere*.

Intimate Partner Violence and Self-Defense

Intimate partner violence (IPV) is as old as humanity. During much of Western history, society not only turned a blind eye toward most IPV, the law actually approved moderate physical chastisement of a wife by her husband. In early Roman law "the husband had the power to chastise, sell or even kill the wife, having the same authority over her as over his child."[23] In England, a husband had authority to employ "moderate" physical chastisement of his wife. In 1765, Blackstone wrote in his *Commentaries on the Laws of England* that a "husband also (by the old law) might give his wife moderate correction."[24]

In America, a husband's right of chastisement took shallow root, and soon withered on the vine.[25] The Puritans of Massachusetts had laws

---

[21] Joshua Dressler, *Understanding Criminal Law* § 1802[C][1], p. 226 (5th ed. 2012).

[22] In *People v. Flannelly* (1900) 128 Cal. 83, 60 P. 670, the California Supreme Court ruled that if X is the first aggressor with non-deadly force, and the victim of the non-deadly attack responds with deadly force, then X has a duty to retreat before he can defend.

[23] William L. Burdick, *The Principles of Roman Law and Their Relation to Modern Law* p. 225 (1938, Reprint 1989) (Holmes Beach, Florida: Wm. W. Gaunt & Sons).

[24] 1 William Blackstone, *Commentaries on the Laws of England in Four Books* p. 444 (1765) (Re-Printed from the British Copy, Page for Page with the Last Edition 1771).

[25] *Brown v. Brown* (1914) 88 Conn. 42, 89 A. 889; State v. Buckley, 2 Del. Rep. 552, 552 (Harrington) (1838); *Abbott v. Abbott* (1877) 67 Me. 304, 307; *Commonwealth v. McAfee* (1871) 108 Mass. 458, 461; *Poor v. Poor* (1836) 8 N.H. 307, 313.

against intimate partner violence as early as 1640.[26] In 1824, the Mississippi Supreme Court acknowledged the utility of chastisement, but ruled that a husband could be prosecuted for excessive force.[27] Although the Mississippi court stated that prosecution was possible, the court felt domestic squabbles should generally not be litigated in public. The court wrote, "Family broils and dissentions cannot be investigated before the tribunals of the country, without casting a shade over the character of those who are unfortunately engaged in the controversy. To screen from public reproach those who may be thus unhappily situated, let the husband be permitted to exercise the right of moderate chastisement, in cases of great emergency, and use salutary restraints in every case of misbehavior, without being subjected to vexatious prosecutions, resulting in the mutual discredit and shame of all parties concerned."[28]

In 1873, the North Carolina Supreme Court ruled that a husband had no right of physical chastisement.[29] The Court wrote, "We may assume that the old doctrine, that a husband had a right to whip his wife, provided he used a switch no larger than his thumb, is not the law in North Carolina. Indeed, the Courts have advanced from that barbarism until they have reached the position, that the husband has no right to chastise his wife, under any circumstances."[30]

Cases of serious spousal abuse were prosecuted in North Carolina. Like their colleagues in Mississippi, however, the justices of the North Carolina Supreme Court felt it was unseemly for family matters to be aired in public courtrooms. In 1868, the North Carolina court wrote, "The courts have been loath to take cognizance of trivial complaints arising out of the domestic relations—such as master and apprentice, teacher and pupil, parent and child, husband and wife. Not because those relations are not subject to the law, but because the evil of publicity would be greater than the evil involved in the trifles complained of; and because they ought to be left to family government."[31]

By 1890, the North Carolina court had changed its mind about the propriety of litigating domestic assaults in public. In *State v. Dowell*,[32] the Court wrote, "It was at one time held in our state that the relation of husband and wife gave the former immunity to the extent that the court would not go behind the domestic curtain, and scrutinize too nicely every family disturbance, even though amounting to an assault. But since *State*

---

[26] Elizabeth Pleck, *Domestic Tyranny: The Making of Social Policy Against Family Violence from Colonial Times to the Present* 13 (1987).

[27] *Bradley v. State* (1824) 2 Miss. 73 (Walker 158).

[28] *Bradley v. State* (1824) 2 Miss. 73, at 74 (Walker 158).

[29] *State v. Oliver* (1874) 70 N.C. 60.

[30] *State v. Oliver* (1874) 70 N.C. 60, at 70.

[31] *State v. Rhodes* (1868) 61 N.C. 453, at 454.

[32] (1890) 106 N.C. 722, 11 S.E. 525.

v. Oliver [1874], we have refused 'the blanket of the dark' to these outrages on female weakness and defenselessness. So it is now settled that, technically, a husband cannot commit even a slight assault upon his wife, and that her person is as sacred from his violence as from that of any other person."[33]

Joel Bishop was one of the nineteenth century's leading commentators on the law of domestic relations and the law of crimes. In 1877, Bishop wrote, "The right of chastisement does not pertain to [husbands] in this country. Therefore, [a husband] may be indicted for assault and battery committed on [his wife]."[34] The Connecticut Supreme Court wrote to similar effect in 1914, "It is now as unlawful for him to beat or falsely imprison his wife as for another to do so, and he is amenable to the criminal law for such an offense."[35]

Today's wide-ranging laws and social policies on IPV find their roots in the 1960s and 1970s. The women's movement of that period focused national attention on violence against women. Shelters for battered women sprang up around the country. Legislatures passed laws authorizing civil protection orders for battered women. Police departments rethought their approach to IPV. Prosecutors took IPV cases more seriously.

Intimate Partner Violence (IPV) is common.[36] The U.S. Justice Department reports that in 2008, females above age twelve experienced over half a million nonfatal violent victimizations by intimate partners.[37]

---

[33] 11 S.E. at 525.

[34] 1 Joel Prentiss Bishop, *Commentaries on the Criminal Law* §§ 891–892, pp. 497–498 (6th ed. 1877) (Boston: Little, Brown).

[35] *Brown v. Brown* (1914) 88 Conn. 42, 89 A. 889, 890.

[36] Sandra A. Graham-Bermann, Shannon Lynch, Victoria Banyard, Ellen R. DeVoe, & Hilda Halabu, Community-Based Intervention for Children Exposed to Intimate Partner Violence: An Efficacy Trial, 75 *Journal of Consulting and Clinical Psychology* 199–209, 199 (2007); Bonnie S. Fisher & Saundra L. Regan, The Extent and Frequency of Abuse in the Lives of Older Women and Their Relationship with Health Outcomes, 46 *Gerontologist* 200–209, at 200 (2006); B.B. Robbie Rossman, Jacqueline G. Rea, Sandra A. Graham-Bermann, & Perry M. Butterfield, Young Children Exposed to Domestic Violence. In Peter G. Jaffe, Linda L. Baker, & Alison J. Cunningham, *Protecting Children from Domestic Violence: Strategies for Community Intervention*, pp. 30–48, at 31 (2004) (New York: Guilford); Murray A. Straus & Richard J. Gelles, How Violent Are American Families? Estimates from the National Family Violence Resurvey and Other Studies. In Murray A. Straus & Richard J. Gelles (Eds.), *Physical Violence in American Families: Risk Factors and Adaptations to Violence in 8,145 Families*, pp. 95–112 (1990) (New Brunswick: Transaction); Patricia Tjaden & Nancy Thoennes, *Full Report of the Prevalence, Incidence, and Consequences of Violence Against Women: Findings from the National Violence Against Women Survey*. U.S. Department of Justice, Office of Justice Programs, National Institute of Justice (2000); Carol Zlotnick, Dawn M. Johnson, & Robert Kohn, Intimate Partner Violence and Long-Term Psychosocial Functioning in a National Sample of American Women, 21 *Journal of Interpersonal Violence* 262–275, 262 (2006).

See People v. Brown (2004) 33 Cal.4th 892, 898, 16 Cal.Rptr.3d 447, 94 P.3d 574, "Domestic violence is a serious social and legal problem in the United States, occurring in every economic, racial, and ethnic group."

[37] Shannan Catalano, Erica Smith, Howard Snyder & Michael Rand, Female Victims of Violence. U.S. Department of Justice, Office of Justice Programs, Bureau of Justice Statistics (Sept. 2009).

During the same year, men experienced just over 100,000 nonfatal victimizations by partners. It is estimated that 17% to 28% of married or cohabiting couples experience IPV each year.[38] IPV is underreported.[39]

In 2007, intimate partners were responsible for 14% of all homicides. Some 1,640 women and 700 men died at the hands of intimates.[40] Straus and Gelles write, "Women are seldom murder victims outside the family."[41]

In 2000, Tjaden and Thoennes issued an important report for the U.S. Department of Justice on the prevalence of IPV.[42] The key findings of Tjaden and Thoennes's *National Violence Against Women Survey* are discussed below, interlaced with findings from other research. Tjaden and Thoennes found that in the United States, one of every five women is assaulted at some point in her life by an intimate partner. Approximately 1.3 million women are physically assaulted every year by a spouse, former spouse, or boyfriend. "Violence against women is primarily intimate partner violence: 64.0 percent of the women who reported being raped, physically assaulted, and/or stalked since age 18 were victimized by a current or former husband, cohabiting partner, boyfriend, or date."[43]

Battered women who are pregnant report being hit in the stomach. Boyle and colleagues write, "The severity of domestic violence seems to escalate during pregnancy."[44]

---

[38] Kathryn H. Howell, Sandra A. Graham-Bermann, Ewa Czyz & Michelle Lilly, Assessing Resilience in Preschool Children Exposed to Intimate Partner Violence, 25 *Violence and Victims* 150–164 (2010).

[39] *People v. Brown* (2004) 33 Cal.4th 892, 898, 16 Cal.Rptr.3d 447, 94 P.3d 574, "As compared to other crimes, domestic violence is vastly underreported, and until the last 20 to 30 years was largely hidden from public examination."

[40] Shannan Catalano, Erica Smith, Howard Snyder & Michael Rand, Female Victims of Violence. U.S. Department of Justice, Office of Justice Programs, Bureau of Justice Statistics (Sept. 2009).

[41] Murray A. Straus & Richard J. Gelles, How Violent are American Families? Estimates from the National Family Violence Resurvey and Other Studies. In Murray A. Straus & Richard J. Gelles (Eds.), *Physical Violence in American Families: Risk Factors and Adaptations to Violence in 8,145 Families*, pp. 95–112, at 98 (1990) (New Brunswick: Transaction).

[42] Patricia Tjaden & Nancy Thoennes, *Full Report of the Prevalence, Incidence, and Consequences of Violence Against Women: Findings from the National Violence Against Women Survey*. U.S. Department of Justice, Office of Justice Programs, National Institute of Justice (2000) (Tjaden and Thoennes's research was supported by the National Institute of Justice and the Centers for Disease Control and Prevention. Tjaden and Thoennes conducted a national telephone survey of women's experiences with domestic violence. The survey was conducted between November 1995 and May 1996).

[43] Patricia Tjaden & Nancy Thoennes, *Full Report of the Prevalence, Incidence, and Consequences of Violence Against Women: Findings from the National Violence Against Women Survey*. U.S. Department of Justice, Office of Justice Programs, National Institute of Justice (2000).

[44] A. Boyle, S. Robinson, & P. Atkinson, Domestic Violence in Emergency Medicine Patients, 21 *Emergency Medicine Journal* 9–13 (2004).

Women commit IPV against men.[45] Straus writes, "In contrast to their behavior outside the family, within the family women are about as violent as men."[46] Yet, "women are significantly more likely than men to be injured during an assault."[47] Straus and Gelles point out the danger *to* women of IPV *by* women. "Let us assume that most of the assaults by women are of the 'slap the cad' genre and are not intended to and do not physically injure the husband. [The] danger to a woman of such behavior is that it sets the stage for the husband to assault her. Sometimes this is immediate and severe retaliation. But regardless of whether that occurs, the fact that she slapped him provides a precedent and justification for him to hit her when *she* is being obstinate, 'bitchy,' or 'not listening to reason' as he sees it."[48]

Many women victimized by intimate partner violence live in households with children. It is estimated that as many as 15.5 million children are exposed to IPV every year in the United States.[49] Young children are more likely than older children to be exposed to IPV.[50]

Many parents in violent relationships believe their children are unaware of the violence, but this is usually wishful thinking. Kitzmann and colleagues write, "Although many parents report trying to shelter their children from marital violence, research suggests that children in violent homes commonly see, hear, and intervene in episodes of marital violence."[51] Graham-Bermann and Howell write, "When IPV occurs, children are

---

[45] Murray A. Straus & Richard J. Gelles, How Violent Are American Families? Estimates from the National Family Violence Resurvey and Other Studies. In Murray A. Straus & Richard J. Gelles (Eds.), *Physical Violence in American Families: Risk Factors and Adaptations to Violence in 8,145 Families*, pp. 95–112 (1990) (New Brunswick: Transaction) Patricia Tjaden & Nancy Thoennes, *Full Report of the Prevalence, Incidence, and Consequences of Violence Against Women: Findings from the National Violence Against Women Survey*. U.S. Department of Justice, Office of Justice Programs, National Institute of Justice (2000).

[46] Murray A. Straus, The National Family Violence Surveys. In Murray A. Straus & Richard J. Gelles (Eds.), *Physical Violence in American Families: Risk Factors and Adaptations to Violence in 8,145 Families*, pp. 3–16 (1990) (New Brunswick: Transaction).

[47] Patricia Tjaden & Nancy Thoennes, *Full Report of the Prevalence, Incidence, and Consequences of Violence Against Women: Findings from the National Violence Against Women Survey*, p. iv. U.S. Department of Justice, Office of Justice Programs, National Institute of Justice (2000).

[48] Murray A. Straus & Richard J. Gelles, How Violent Are American Families? Estimates from the National Family Violence Resurvey and Other Studies. In Murray A. Straus & Richard J. Gelles (Eds.), *Physical Violence in American Families: Risk Factors and Adaptations to Violence in 8,145 Families*, pp. 95–112, at 105 (1990) (New Brunswick: Transaction).

[49] Sandra A. Graham-Berman & Kathryn H. Howell, Child Maltreatment in the Context of Intimate Partner Violence. In John E.B. Myers (Ed.), *The APSAC Handbook on Child Maltreatment* 167–180 (2011) (Sage).

[50] Linda L. Baker, Peter G. Jaffe, Steven J. Berkowitz, & Miriam Berkman, *Children Exposed to Violence: A Handbook for Police Trainers to Increase Understanding and Improve Community Response*, p. 1 (2002) (London, Ontario, Canada: Centre for Children and Families in the Justice System); Sandra A. Graham-Bermann & Suzanne Perkins, Effects of Early Exposure and Lifetime Exposure to Intimate Partner Violence (IPV) on Child Adjustment, 25 *Violence and Victims* 427–439, at 427 (2010).

[51] Katherine M. Kitzmann, Noni K. Gaylord, Aimee R. Holt, & Erin D. Kenny, Child Witnesses to Domestic Violence: A Meta-Analytic Review, 71 *Journal of Consulting and Clinical Psychology* 339–352, at 339 (2003).

eyewitnesses to most of it. Several studies documented that children were at home and present during IPV assaults 75% of the time. In one study of children exposed to IPV, mothers reported that their children witnessed all of the incidents of threats and mild violence. The children witnessed 78% of incidents of severe violence."[52]

A man who beats his wife or girlfriend is apt to beat his child.[53] Bancroft and Silverman write, "Children exposed to batterers are themselves at high risk to become direct targets of physical abuse and of sexual abuse."[54] Graham-Bermann and Howell write, "Children who witness IPV in the home are 15 times more likely to be abused as compared to the national average."[55] Studies of the co-occurrence of IPV and child abuse indicate a co-occurrence rate of 30 percent to 60 percent.[56] Children are sometimes injured when they try to protect their mother.[57] Even when they do not intervene, children are injured accidentally during episodes of IPV.[58]

Witnessing IPV isn't good for anyone. Research on the psychological impact on children of exposure to IPV documents the association between exposure to IPV and short-and long-term harmful consequences. Baker and colleagues observe, "Watching, hearing, or later learning of a parent being harmed threatens the sense of stability and security typically provided by

---

[52] Sandra A. Graham-Berman & Kathryn H. Howell, Child Maltreatment in the Context of Intimate Partner Violence. In John E.B. Myers (Ed.), *The APSAC Handbook on Child Maltreatment* 167–180, at 169 (2011) (Sage).

[53] Nadine J. Kaslow & Martie P. Thompson, Associations of Child Maltreatment and Intimate Partner Violence with Psychological Adjustment Among Low SES, African American Children, 32 *Child Abuse & Neglect* 888–896 (2008); Jeffrey L. Edleson, Amanda L. Ellerton, Ellen A. Seagren, Staci L. Kirchberg, Sarah O. Schmidt & Amirthini T. Ambrose, Assessing Child Exposure to Adult Domestic Violence, 29 *Children and Youth Services Review* 961–971 (2007); Jeffrey L. Edleson, Should Childhood Exposure to Adult Domestic Violence Be Defined as Child Maltreatment Under the Law?, In Peter G. Jaffe, Linda L. Baker, & Alison J. Cunningham, *Protecting Children from Domestic Violence: Strategies for Community Intervention*, pp. 8–29, at 17 (2004) (New York: Guilford).

[54] Lundy Bancroft & Jay G. Silverman, *The Batterer as Parent: Addressing the Impact of Domestic Violence on Family Dynamics* p. 1 (2002) (Thousand Oaks, Cal.: Sage).

[55] Sandra A. Graham-Berman & Kathryn H. Howell, Child Maltreatment in the Context of Intimate Partner Violence. In John E.B. Myers (Ed.), *The APSAC Handbook on Child Maltreatment* 167–180, at 169 (2011) (Sage).

[56] Jeffrey L. Edleson, Lyungai F. Mbilinyi, Sandra K. Beeman, & Annelies K. Hagemeister, How Children Are Involved in Adult Domestic Violence: Results from a Four-City Telephone Survey, 18(1) *Journal of Interpersonal Violence* 18–32 (2003); Sandra A. Graham-Berman & Kathryn H. Howell, Child Maltreatment in the Context of Intimate Partner Violence. In John E.B. Myers (Ed.), *The APSAC Handbook on Child Maltreatment* 167–180 (2011) (Sage).

[57] Linda L. Baker, Peter G. Jaffe, Steven J. Berkowitz, & Miriam Berkman, *Children Exposed to Violence: A Handbook for Police Trainers to Increase Understanding and Improve Community Response*, p. 17 (2002) (London, Ontario, Canada: Centre for Children and Families in the Justice System).

[58] Sandra A. Graham-Berman & Kathryn H. Howell, Child Maltreatment in the Context of Intimate Partner Violence. In John E.B. Myers (Ed.), *The APSAC Handbook on Child Maltreatment* 167–180 (2011) (Sage).

family."[59] Rossman and colleagues write, "Exposure to repetitive adult domestic violence may be just as traumatic for many young children as personal experience of maltreatment."[60] Exposure during childhood to IPV is a risk factor in adults for depression, low self-esteem, and other trauma-related symptoms.[61]

Watching repeated violent attacks on one's mother, or between one's parents, is intrinsically damaging. Children exposed to such violence fear for their mother and for themselves. Living in constant apprehension of the next outburst of violence takes a toll. Abusive men often isolate their wife or girlfriend, and the isolation imposed on the woman extends to the children, cutting them off from sources of positive feedback and constructive adult role models.[62] Children who grow up in violent, socially isolated homes may come to view violence as normal.[63]

In rare cases the victim of domestic violence kills the batterer. In *People v. Humphrey*, the Supreme Court addressed this issue.

PEOPLE V. HUMPHREY

California Supreme Court
13 Cal.4th 1073, 56 Cal.Rptr.2d 142, 921 P.2d 1 (1996)

CHIN, J.

The Legislature has decreed that, when relevant, expert testimony regarding "battered women's syndrome" is generally admissible in a criminal action. (Evid. Code, § 1107.) We must determine the purposes for which a jury may consider this evidence when offered to support a claim of self-defense to a murder charge.

The trial court instructed that the jury could consider the evidence in deciding whether the defendant actually believed it was necessary to kill in self-defense, but not in deciding whether that belief was reasonable. The instruction was erroneous. Because evidence of battered women's syndrome may help the jury understand the circumstances in which the

---

[59] Linda L. Baker, Peter G. Jaffe, Steven J. Berkowitz, & Miriam Berkman, *Children Exposed to Violence: A Handbook for Police Trainers to Increase Understanding and Improve Community Response*, p. 16 (2002) (London, Ontario, Canada: Centre for Children and Families in the Justice System).

[60] B.B. Robbie Rossman, Jacqueline G. Rea, Sandra A Graham-Bermann, & Perry M. Butterfield, Young Children Exposed to Adult Domestic Violence. In Peter G. Jaffe, Linda L. Baker, & Alison J. Cunningham, *Protecting Children from Domestic Violence: Strategies for Community Intervention*, pp. 30–48, at 30 (2004) (New York: Guilford).

[61] Jeffrey L. Edleson, Lyungai F. Mbilinyi, Sandra K. Beeman, & Annelies K. Hagemeister, How Children Are Involved in Adult Domestic Violence: Results from a Four-City Telephone Survey, 18 *Journal of Interpersonal Violence* 18–32, 19 (2003).

[62] National Resource Center on Domestic Violence, *Children Exposed to Intimate Partner Violence*. (2002) (Harrisburg, Pa.: Author).

[63] Lundy Bancroft & Jay G. Silverman, *The Batterer as Parent: Addressing the Impact of Domestic Violence on Family Dynamics* (2002) (Thousand Oaks, Cal.: Sage).

defendant found herself at the time of the killing, it is relevant to the reasonableness of her belief. Moreover, because defendant testified, the evidence was relevant to her credibility. The trial court should have allowed the jury to consider this testimony in deciding the reasonableness as well as the existence of defendant's belief that killing was necessary. Finding the error prejudicial, we reverse the judgment of the Court of Appeal.

During the evening of March 28, 1992, defendant shot and killed Albert Hampton in their Fresno home. Officer Reagan was the first on the scene. A neighbor told Reagan that the couple in the house had been arguing all day. Defendant soon came outside appearing upset and with her hands raised as if surrendering. She told Officer Reagan, "I shot him. That's right, I shot him. I just couldn't take him beating on me no more." She led the officer into the house, showed him a .357 magnum revolver on a table, and said, "There's the gun." Hampton was on the kitchen floor, wounded but alive.

A short time later, defendant told Officer Reagan, "He deserved it. I just couldn't take it anymore. I told him to stop beating on me." "He was beating on me, so I shot him. I told him I'd shoot him if he ever beat on me again." A paramedic heard her say that she wanted to teach Hampton "a lesson." Defendant told another officer at the scene, Officer Terry, "I'm fed up. Yeah, I shot him. I'm just tired of him hitting me. He said, 'You're not going to do nothing about it.' I showed him, didn't I? I shot him good. He won't hit anybody else again. Hit me again; I shoot him again. I don't care if I go to jail. Push comes to shove, I guess people gave it to him, and, kept hitting me. I warned him. I warned him not to hit me. He wouldn't listen."

Officer Terry took defendant to the police station, where she told the following story. The day before the shooting, Hampton had been drinking. He hit defendant while they were driving home in their truck and continued hitting her when they arrived. He told her, "I'll kill you," and shot at her. The bullet went through a bedroom window and struck a tree outside. The day of the shooting, Hampton "got drunk," swore at her, and started hitting her again. He walked into the kitchen. Defendant saw the gun in the living room and picked it up. Her jaw hurt, and she was in pain. She pointed the gun at Hampton and said, "You're not going to hit me anymore." Hampton said, "What are you doing?" Believing that Hampton was about to pick something up to hit her with, she shot him. She then put the gun down and went outside to wait for the police.

Hampton later died of a gunshot wound to his chest. The neighbor who spoke with Officer Reagan testified that shortly before the shooting, she heard defendant, but not Hampton, shouting. The evening before, the neighbor had heard a gunshot. Defendant's blood contained no drugs but had a blood-alcohol level of .17 percent. Hampton's blood contained no drugs or alcohol.

Defendant claimed she shot Hampton in self-defense. To support the claim, the defense presented first expert testimony and then nonexpert testimony, including that of defendant herself.

Dr. Lee Bowker testified as an expert on battered women's syndrome. The syndrome, he testified, "is not just a psychological construction, but it's a term for a wide variety of controlling mechanisms that the man or it can be a woman, but in general for this syndrome it's a man, uses against the woman, and for the effect that those control mechanisms have."

Dr. Bowker had studied about 1,000 battered women and found them often inaccurately portrayed "as cardboard figures, paper-thin punching bags who merely absorb the violence but didn't do anything about it." He found that battered women often employ strategies to stop the beatings, including hiding, running away, counterviolence, seeking the help of friends and family, going to a shelter, and contacting police. Nevertheless, many battered women remain in the relationship because of lack of money, social isolation, lack of self-confidence, inadequate police response, and a fear (often justified) of reprisals by the batterer. "The battering man will make the battered woman depend on him and generally succeed at least for a time." A battered woman often feels responsible for the abusive relationship, and "she just can't figure out a way to please him better so he'll stop beating her." In sum, "It really is the physical control of the woman through economics and through relative social isolation combined with the psychological techniques that make her so dependent."

The violence can gradually escalate, as the batterer keeps control using ever more severe actions, including rape, torture, violence against the woman's loved ones or pets, and death threats. Battered women sense this escalation. In Dr. Bowker's "experience with battered women who kill in self-defense their abusers, it's always related to their perceived change of what's going on in a relationship. They become very sensitive to what sets off batterers. They watch for this stuff very carefully. Anybody who is abused over a period of time becomes sensitive to the abuser's behavior and when she sees a change acceleration begin in that behavior, it tells them something is going to happen."

Dr. Bowker described defendant's relationship with Hampton. Hampton was a 49-year-old man who weighed almost twice as much as defendant. The two had a battering relationship that Dr. Bowker characterized as a "traditional cycle of violence." The cycle included phases of tension building, violence, and then forgiveness-seeking in which Hampton would promise not to batter defendant any more and she would believe him. During this period, there would be occasional good times. For example, defendant told Dr. Bowker that Hampton would give her a rose.

"That's one of the things that hooks people in. Intermittent reinforcement is the key." But after a while, the violence would begin again. The violence would recur because "basically the woman doesn't perfectly obey. That's the bottom line." For example, defendant would talk to another man, or fail to clean house "just so."

The situation worsened over time, especially when Hampton got off parole shortly before his death. He became more physically and emotionally abusive, repeatedly threatened defendant's life, and even shot at her the night before his death. Hampton often allowed defendant to go out, but she was afraid to flee because she felt he would find her as he had in the past. "He enforced her belief that she can never escape him." Dr. Bowker testified that unless her injuries were so severe that "something absolutely had to be treated," he would not expect her to seek medical treatment. "That's the pattern of her life."

Dr. Bowker believed defendant's description of her experiences. In his opinion, she suffered from battered women's syndrome in "about as extreme a pattern as you could find."

Defendant confirmed many of the details of her life and relationship with Hampton underlying Dr. Bowker's opinion. She testified that her father forcefully molested her from the time she was seven years old until she was fifteen. She described her relationship with another abusive man as being like "Nightmare on Elm Street." Regarding Hampton, she testified that they often argued and that he beat her regularly. Both were heavy drinkers. Hampton once threw a can of beer at her face, breaking her nose. Her dental plates hurt because Hampton hit her so often. He often kicked her, but usually hit her in the back of the head because, he told her, it "won't leave bruises." Hampton sometimes threatened to kill her, and often said she "would live to regret it." Matters got worse towards the end.

The evening before the shooting, March 27, 1992, Hampton arrived home "very drunk." He yelled at her and called her names. At one point when she was standing by the bedroom window, he fired his .357 magnum revolver at her. She testified, "He didn't miss me by much either." She was "real scared."

The next day, the two drove into the mountains. They argued, and Hampton continually hit her. While returning, he said that their location would be a good place to kill her because "they wouldn't find her for a while." She took it as a joke, although she feared him. When they returned, the arguing continued. He hit her again, then entered the kitchen. He threatened, "This time, bitch, when I shoot at you, I won't miss." He came from the kitchen and reached for the gun on the living room table. She grabbed it first, pointed it at him, and told him "that he wasn't going to hit her." She backed Hampton into the kitchen. He was saying something, but she did not know what. He reached for her hand and she shot him. She believed he was reaching for the gun and was going to shoot her.

Several other witnesses testified about defendant's relationship with Hampton, his abusive conduct in general, and his physical abuse of, and threats to, defendant in particular. This testimony generally corroborated defendant's. A neighbor testified that the night before the shooting, she heard a gunshot. The next morning, defendant told the neighbor that Hampton had shot at her, and that she was afraid of him. After the shooting, investigators found a bullet hole through the frame of the bedroom window and a bullet embedded in a tree in line with the window. Another neighbor testified that shortly before hearing the shot that killed Hampton, she heard defendant say, "Stop it, Albert. Stop it."

Defendant was charged with murder with personal use of a firearm. At the end of the prosecution's case-in-chief, the court granted defendant's motion under Penal Code section 1118.1 for acquittal of first degree murder.

The court instructed the jury on second degree murder and both voluntary and involuntary manslaughter. It also instructed on self-defense, explaining that an actual and reasonable belief that the killing was necessary was a complete defense; an actual but unreasonable belief was a defense to murder, but not to voluntary manslaughter. In determining reasonableness, the jury was to consider what "would appear to be necessary to a reasonable person in a similar situation and with similar knowledge."

The court also instructed: "Evidence regarding Battered Women's Syndrome has been introduced in this case. Such evidence, if believed, may be considered by you only for the purpose of determining whether or not the defendant held the necessary subjective honest belief which is a requirement for both perfect and imperfect self-defense. However, that same evidence regarding Battered Women's Syndrome may not be considered or used by you in evaluating the objective reasonableness requirement for perfect self-defense."

With an exception not relevant here, Evidence Code section 1107(a), makes admissible in a criminal action expert testimony regarding "battered women's syndrome, including the physical, emotional, or mental effects upon the beliefs, perceptions, or behavior of victims of domestic violence."

For killing to be in self-defense, the defendant must actually and reasonably believe in the need to defend. If the belief subjectively exists but is objectively unreasonable, there is imperfect self-defense, i.e., the defendant is deemed to have acted without malice and cannot be convicted of murder, but can be convicted of manslaughter. To constitute perfect self-defense, i.e., to exonerate the person completely, the belief must also be objectively reasonable. As the Legislature has stated, "The circumstances must be sufficient to excite the fears of a reasonable person." (Pen. Code, § 198; see also § 197, subds. 2, 3.) Moreover, for either perfect or imperfect self-defense, the fear must be of imminent harm. Fear of future harm—no matter how great the fear and no matter how great the likelihood of the harm—will not suffice. The defendant's fear must be of *imminent* danger to life or great bodily injury.

Although the belief in the need to defend must be objectively reasonable, a jury must consider what would appear to be necessary to a reasonable person in a similar situation and with similar knowledge. It judges reasonableness from the point of view of a reasonable person in the position of defendant. To do this, it must consider all the facts and circumstances in determining whether the defendant acted in a manner in which a reasonable man would act in protecting his own life or bodily safety. A defendant is entitled to have a jury take into consideration all the elements in the case which might be expected to operate on his mind.

Battered women's syndrome has been defined as a series of common characteristics that appear in women who are abused physically and psychologically over an extended period of time by the dominant male figure in their lives.

The trial court allowed the jury to consider the battered women's syndrome evidence in deciding whether defendant actually believed she needed to kill in self-defense. The question here is whether the evidence was also relevant on the reasonableness of that belief.

The Attorney General concedes that Hampton's behavior towards defendant, including prior threats and violence, was relevant to reasonableness, but distinguishes between evidence of this behavior—which the trial court fully admitted—and expert testimony about its effects on defendant. The distinction is untenable. To effectively present the situation as perceived by the defendant, and the reasonableness of her fear, the defense has the option to explain her feelings to enable the jury to overcome stereotyped impressions about women who remain in abusive relationships. It is appropriate that the jury be given a professional explanation of the battering syndrome and its effects on the woman through the use of expert testimony.

Contrary to the Attorney General's argument, we are not changing the standard from objective to subjective, or replacing the reasonable "person" standard with a reasonable "battered woman" standard. Evidence Code section 1107 states "a rule of evidence only" and makes "no substantive change." The jury must consider defendant's situation and knowledge, which makes the evidence relevant, but the ultimate question is whether a reasonable person, not a reasonable battered woman, would believe in the need to kill to prevent imminent harm. Moreover, it is the jury, not the expert, that determines whether defendant's belief and, ultimately, her actions, were objectively reasonable.

Battered women's syndrome evidence was also relevant to defendant's credibility. It would have assisted the jury in objectively analyzing defendant's claim of self-defense by dispelling many of the commonly held misconceptions about battered women. For example, in urging the jury not to believe defendant's testimony that Hampton shot at her the night before the killing, the prosecutor argued that "if this defendant truly believed that Hampton had shot at her, on that night, I mean she would have left. If she really believed that he had tried to shoot her, she would not have stayed." Dr. Bowker's testimony would help dispel the ordinary lay person's perception that a woman in a battering relationship is free to leave at any time. The expert evidence would counter any common sense conclusions by the jury that if the beatings were really that bad the woman would have left her husband much earlier. Popular misconceptions about battered women would be put to rest. If the jury had understood defendant's conduct in light of battered women's syndrome evidence, then the jury may well have concluded her version of the events was sufficiently credible to warrant an acquittal on the facts as she related them.

The judgment of the Court of Appeal is reversed.

NOTE ON BATTERED VICTIMS WHO KILL THEIR BATTERER

Cases in which battered victims kill (or attempt to kill) the batterer and seek to raise a claim of self-defense fall into three categories: (1) cases like *Humphrey* that are similar to a traditional self-defense scenario; (2) cases in which the battered person kills the batterer while the batterer sleeps; and (3) cases in which the battered person hires a "hit" man to kill the batterers. Courts do not approve claims of self-defense in scenarios (2) and (3).

Self-Defense Against Home Invaders and Burglars

When someone breaks into a home and attacks the occupants with deadly force, the occupants can defend themselves. Two sections of the Penal Code focus on self-defense in the home, adding to basic self-defense principles. PC § 197(2) states in part: "Homicide is also justifiable when committed in defense of habitation against one who manifestly intends and endeavors, in a violent, riotous or tumultuous manner, to enter the habitation of another for the purpose of offering violence to any person therein." PC § 198.5 states: "Any person using force intended or likely to cause death or great bodily injury within his or her residence shall be presumed to have held a reasonable fear of imminent peril of death or great bodily injury to self, family, or a member of the household when that force is used against another person, not a member the family or household, who unlawfully and forcibly enters or has unlawfully and forcibly entered the residence and the person using the force knew or had reason to believe that an unlawful and forcible entry occurred."

PROBLEMS ON SELF-DEFENSE

1. Vic and Dell did not know each other. On the fatal night, Vic and Dell were in a bar. Vic took a couple of steps toward Dell. Dell felt threatened, pulled out a gun and killed Vic. Self-defense? *People v. Wong* (1947) 83 Cal.App.2d 60, 187 P.2d 828.

2. Vinny attacked Tom by punching him in the nose and threatening to kill him. Tom fought back and managed to knock Vinny out with an uppercut. As Vinny lay unconscious on the floor, Tom continued hitting him, eventually killing him. Can Tom claim self-defense? *People v. Shade* (1986) 185 Cal.App.3d 711, 230 Cal.Rptr. 70.

3. Ruth attacked Desiree with her fists. Desiree responded by stabbing Ruth in the chest, killing her. Self-defense?

4. Bill took out his pistol and started firing at Ed in an effort to kill him. Ed grabbed a rifle and fired at Bill but missed, killing a child who was playing nearby. Can Ed rely on self-defense? Should Bill be responsible for the child's death?

5. Ralph is a bully. One day, Ralph encountered Nancy walking her dog on a public sidewalk near the ocean. Ralph said, "Hey lady, this is my sidewalk. Go walk your ugly dog somewhere else. If I see you here again with that mutt, I'll throw both of you in the ocean and watch you drown. Get lost." Nancy left. She wondered what to do. She decided not to call the police. She armed herself with a legal pistol and walked her dog down the same beachfront sidewalk. Ralph saw her and said, "I thought I told you to keep away from here. Now you're gonna get it." Ralph took a step toward Nancy. Nancy took out the pistol and shot and killed Ralph. If Nancy is prosecuted for murder, can she claim self-defense? This problem is based on Joshua Dressler, *Cases and Materials on Criminal Law* (5th ed. 2009) (West).

6. Billy Burglar broke into Sue's seaside shack at six a.m. Shocked, Sue slung a semiautomatic to her shoulder and blasted Billy. Can Sue be prosecuted criminally? If Billy survived, could he sue Sue? *Goldfuss v. Davidson* (1997) 79 Ohio St.3d 116, 679 N.E.2d 1099.

7. Dill was sitting in his parked car in a parking lot. Victor was parked nearby. Victor's car would not start because the battery was dead. Victor approached Dill's car and said, "Sorry to bother you, but could you give me a jump to get my car started? I've got a dead battery." Dill, said, "Yeah, for five bucks." The request to be paid made Victor angry and he said, "Five bucks! You want me to pay you for a lousy jump? Screw you man." Being sworn at made Dill mad and the two men started yelling at each other. Enraged, Victor took a knife out of his pocket and lunged at Dill through the open car window. Dill moved his body quickly so Victor could not stab him. Dill reached under the seat and grabbed a gun, opened the car door, quickly jumped out of the car,

and fired one shot at Victor, killing him. If Dill is charged with murder, can he successfully claim self-defense? Are there any additional facts about what happened you would like to know? *State v. Dill* (La. Ct. App. 1984) 461 So.2d 1130.

8. Jim was visiting his sister Sue in her two bedroom apartment. Gerry arrived, knocked, and was allowed into the apartment. Gerry and Sue had dated, but Sue recently broke off the relationship. Gerry was a large man, and he was very intoxicated. Gerry and Sue argued about their relationship, and Jim tried to calm things down. Eventually, Sue went into her bedroom and locked the door. Gerry then shifted his wrath to Jim, yelling about how unfairly he was treated by Sue. Jim urged Gerry to leave. Jim noticed that Gerry had a gun in his waistband. Jim disarmed Gerry by grabbing the pistol out of Gerry's waistband. This made Gerry madder, and he pulled a knife out of his pocket and advanced toward Jim with the knife held over his head. Jim backed up near the door to the second bedroom. From there he fired a shot, hitting Gerry in the ankle. The ankle injury did not stop Gerry, who continued his advance on Jim. Jim fired a second time, killing Gerry. Jim is charged with murder. Can Jim successfully claim self-defense? *State v. Garrison* (1987) 203 Conn. 466, 525 A.2d 498.

9. While driving on Lincoln Boulevard toward the Santa Monica freeway with his wife, John saw Charles, whom he knew. Charles motioned for John to stop. John pulled into the parking lot where Charles was standing and got out of his car to talk to Charles. Charles accused John of having an affair with his wife and threatened to kill him. John returned to his car and drove off. As John was about to drive onto the freeway on-ramp, his car stalled. John looked in his rear view mirror and saw Charles jogging up to his car from behind. John pulled out a gun and fired, killing Charles. Self-defense? *People v. Johnson* (2002) 98 Cal.App.4th 566, 119 Cal.Rptr.2d 802.

DEFENSE OF OTHERS

A person may come to the assistance of another who is being attacked or threatened with imminent attack. If the victim is being attacked or threatened with deadly force, the rescuer may use deadly force to protect the victim. In *People v. Garcia*, 2010 WL 2062201 (Nonpublished), the Court of Appeal explained: "The belief in the need to defend another person, whether reasonable or unreasonable, requires that the defendant believe that the other person is in imminent danger of serious bodily injury and that lethal force is necessary to prevent death or great bodily injury. Fear of future harm—no matter how great the fear and no matter how great the likelihood of the harm—will not suffice. The defendant's fear must be of imminent danger to life or great bodily injury."

People v. Randle addresses defense of others and imperfect self-defense.[64]

PEOPLE V. RANDLE

California Supreme Court
35 Cal.4th 987, 28 Cal.Rptr.3d 725, 111 P.3d 987 (2005)

BROWN, J.

The central question presented by this case is whether one who kills in the actual but unreasonable belief he must protect another person from imminent danger of death or great bodily injury is guilty of voluntary manslaughter, and not murder, because he lacks the malice required for murder. In other words, should California recognize the doctrine of imperfect defense of others? We conclude the answer is, yes.

The homicide victim Brian Robinson lived with his parents and his cousin, Charles Lambert. Late one evening, as Robinson drove up to their home, he saw defendant getting out of Lambert's car, holding a large stereo speaker he had just stolen from it.

Robinson confronted defendant, saying he was going to "beat your ass." Defendant pulled a .25-caliber pistol from his pocket and fired it several times. Defendant and his cousin Byron W., who had helped him break into Lambert's car, then fled on foot. Byron retained a backpack full of Lambert's stereo equipment.

Defendant claimed he fired after Robinson "reached for his hip." However, he did not claim he thought Robinson was reaching for a gun or other deadly weapon. Moreover, Byron testified Robinson approached them with a cup or bottle in his hand. Defendant and Byron agreed it was some sort of object made of glass that Robinson threw at them after defendant fired the pistol.

Defendant gave conflicting accounts as to his aim. On the one hand, he claimed he "fired the gun in the air." On the other hand, he earlier testified, "I shot at him."

Defendant testified he heard Robinson say something about getting a gun himself, and that he heard two loud bangs behind them as they fled. Byron testified he also heard gunshots as they ran. There was no evidence to corroborate these claims.

Robinson went into his house and roused Lambert. The two men got into a truck and pursued defendant and Byron. Defendant eluded them,

---

64 Self-defense may not be claimed by someone "who, through his own wrongful conduct (*e.g.*, the initiation of a physical assault or the commission of a felony), has created circumstances under which his adversaries' attack." *People v. Frandsen* (2011) 196 Cal.App.4th 266, 126 Cal.Rptr.3d 640. The *Frandsen* court went on to write, "It follows, a fortiori, that the imperfect self-defense doctrine cannot be invoked in such circumstances."

but they caught Byron. According to Lambert's testimony, he and Robinson took turns beating Byron with their fists. After Byron fell to the ground, Robinson kicked him. Lambert pulled Robinson off Byron. Having recovered the stolen stereo equipment, they returned to the truck. However, Robinson jumped out of the truck and began beating Byron again. As he did, Robinson yelled at Lambert to "get pops," meaning Robinson's father; Lambert drove off to do so. While Lambert was present, the beating of Byron lasted "probably five, ten minutes."

Byron testified his assailants hit and kicked him. One of them stomped on his chest, stepped on his head, and kicked him in the mouth. The beating continued for five minutes. One of the men spoke of putting Byron in the truck and taking him into the hills. Byron was bleeding from the mouth; his nose was broken. He was hollering his lungs out. He thought he was going to die. He was being beaten when defendant cried out, "Get off my cousin." Byron's assailant continued beating him, and then defendant opened fire. Defendant, Byron believed, saved his life.

Defendant testified he ran away, but then backtracked in search of Byron. Defendant saw someone beating Byron. Defendant shouted, "Stop. Get off my cousin." Byron's assailant glanced at defendant, but then resumed beating Byron. Defendant testified he fired his gun to make the man stop beating Byron.

Two prior statements defendant had made, one to the police and the other to a deputy district attorney, were played for the jury. According to defendant's statement to the police, Robinson was beating Byron when defendant first shot at him. Defendant was, he said, "mainly thinking about getting him off my little cousin." However, defendant admitted shooting at Robinson after Robinson started running away. In his statement to the deputy district attorney, defendant said he warned Robinson to get off Byron, shot once in the air, and then when Robinson did not respond, shot at him. Again, defendant admitted shooting at Robinson while he was running away. Defendant added he ceased firing because he ran out of ammunition.

As previously stated, although defendant and Byron testified Robinson was still beating Byron when defendant fired the shots, defendant, in his statements to the police and the deputy district attorney, said he fired one shot at Robinson while Robinson was running away.

The cause of Robinson's death was a bullet wound in the abdomen. The bullet was a .25 caliber. It entered Robinson's lower right chest or upper abdomen and lodged in the left side of his abdomen. Robinson was not wounded in the back.

At trial, defendant asked for an instruction on imperfect defense of another. The trial court denied the request. After deliberating five days, the jury convicted defendant of second degree murder (Pen.Code §§ 187,

189) and automobile burglary (§ 459). The jury also sustained firearm use allegations on both the murder count (§ 12022.53(d)) and the automobile burglary count (§ 12022.5(a)). Defendant was sentenced to a term of 40 years to life imprisonment. This timely appeal followed.

Holding the trial court erred in refusing to instruct on imperfect defense of another, the Court of Appeal reversed the judgment convicting defendant of second degree murder.

We conclude the trial court prejudicially erred in refusing to instruct the jury on the doctrine of imperfect defense of others. Accordingly, we affirm the judgment of the Court of Appeal, reversing the trial court judgment insofar as it convicted defendant of second degree murder, and we remand the cause for further proceedings consistent with the views expressed herein.

Again, the central question presented by this case is whether one who kills in the actual but unreasonable belief he must protect another person from imminent danger of death or great bodily injury is guilty of voluntary manslaughter, and not murder, because he lacks the malice required for murder.

Defendant contends such a person is guilty, under the doctrine of imperfect defense of others, of only voluntary manslaughter, and that the trial court prejudicially erred in refusing his request to instruct the jury on the doctrine.

The Attorney General contends (1) California has not recognized the doctrine of imperfect defense of others; (2) even assuming California does recognize the doctrine, defendant was not entitled to invoke it because he created the circumstances leading to the killing; and (3) in any event, any error in refusing to give the requested instruction was harmless here.

We begin by reviewing the related concepts of self-defense and defense of others. Self-defense is perfect or imperfect. For perfect self-defense, one must actually *and* reasonably believe in the necessity of defending oneself from imminent danger of death or great bodily injury. A killing committed in perfect self-defense is neither murder nor manslaughter; it is justifiable homicide.

One acting in imperfect self-defense also actually believes he must defend himself from imminent danger of death or great bodily injury; however, his belief is unreasonable. Imperfect self-defense mitigates, rather than justifies, homicide; it does so by negating the element of malice.

Under the doctrine of imperfect self-defense, when the trier of fact finds that a defendant killed another person because the defendant *actually*, but unreasonably, believed he was in imminent danger of death or great bodily injury, the defendant is deemed to have acted without malice and thus can be convicted of no crime greater than voluntary manslaughter. Imperfect self-defense obviates malice because that most culpable of mental states cannot coexist with an actual belief that the lethal act was necessary to avoid one's own death or serious injury at the victim's hand.

Defendant contends defense of others, like self-defense, has an imperfect form. That is, defendant contends, if a killing is committed by someone who actually but unreasonably believes he is acting under the necessity of defending another person from imminent danger of death or great bodily injury, then the killing is voluntary manslaughter, not murder, because the killer is not acting with malice.

[The Court analyzes the defendant and the Attorney General's argument for and against adoption of imperfect self-defense of other, and decides the doctrine does apply in California.]

The Attorney General contends defendant is not entitled to invoke the doctrine of imperfect defense of others because he created the circumstances leading to the killing. It is well established that the ordinary self-defense doctrine—applicable when a defendant reasonably believes that his safety is endangered—may not be invoked by a defendant who, through his own wrongful conduct (*e.g.*, the initiation of a physical assault or the commission of a felony), has created the circumstances under which his adversary's attack or pursuit is legally justified. It follows, a fortiori, that the imperfect self-defense doctrine cannot be invoked in such circumstances. For example, the imperfect self-defense doctrine would not permit a fleeing felon who shoots a pursuing police officer to escape a murder conviction even if the felon killed his pursuer with an actual belief in the need for self-defense.

The Attorney General's argument fails because although defendant's criminal conduct certainly set in motion the series of events that led to the fatal shooting of Robinson, the retreat of defendant and Byron and the subsequent recovery of the stolen equipment from Byron extinguished the legal justification for Robinson's attack on Byron. The record supports the conclusion that Robinson was taking the law into his own hands, meting out the punishment he thought Byron deserved, and not making a citizen's arrest as the Attorney General claims. While Robinson may well have had a right to pursue Byron for the purpose of recovering Lambert's stolen property, and to use reasonable force to retrieve it, the beating of Byron by Robinson and Lambert went well beyond any force they were entitled to use. Moreover, after they recovered the stolen stereo equipment and returned to their truck, Robinson jumped out of the truck and began beating Byron again. At that point Robinson's use of force was completely unjustified, and it was at that point, or shortly thereafter, that defendant shot Robinson.

While we hold defendant's conduct did not create circumstances legally justifying Robinson's attack on Byron, we should not be understood as condoning it in any respect.

PROBLEM

Should the trial court instruct on defense of others based on the following facts: Sue lived with Bob. Bob routinely beat Sue with his fists and threatened to kill her. One day, Sue called her brother Dell to come pick her up because Bob was drunk and hitting her. Dell drove to his sister's house and knocked on the front door. He could hear Sue and Bob yelling at each other, and he heard Bob say, "I'm gonna cut your throat, bitch." Dell entered the home and saw Bob walking into the garage. Dell followed Bob to try to get him to calm down. In the garage, Bob said, "What the are you doing here? Get out of my house." Dell said, "Cool down man, you're drunk. Chill." Bob picked up a knife from the work bench and said, "I should cut you, punk." Dell picked up another knife. Bob lunged drunkenly at Dell and Dell jumped aside to avoid being stabbed. Bob turned around and headed back into the house with the knife in his hand. Dell followed. Bob yelled, "Where are you woman?" At that point, Dell stabbed Bob in the back, killing him. Dell told the police, "I thought he was going after my sister."

NOTE ON IMPERFECT SELF-DEFENSE

In *People v. Elmore* (2014) 59 Cal.4th 121, 172 Cal.Rptr.3d 413, 325 P.3d 951, the California Supreme Court asked "whether the doctrine of unreasonable self-defense is available when belief in the need to defend oneself is entirely delusional." The court concluded that the answer is no.

DEFENSE OF PROPERTY

A person is justified in using reasonable non-deadly force to protect property. Use of a spring gun is prohibited. *People v. Ceballos* (1974) 12 Cal.3d 470, 116 Cal.Rptr. 233, 526 P.2d 241.

NECESSITY

Necessity is a justification defense, often called the choice of evils defense. California has the necessity defense, although there is no statute creating the defense. The elements of necessity are: (1) defendant acted in an emergency to prevent a significant imminent harm or evil to defendant or others; (2) there was no adequate legal alternative; (3) the harm caused by violating the law was less than the harm to be prevented (the choice of evils); (4) defendant subjectively believed she/he was choosing the lesser evil; (5) defendant's belief was reasonable under the circumstances as they appeared to defendant; and (6) defendant did not contribute substantially to the emergency.[65]

A defendant wishing a jury instruction on necessity has the burden of producing evidence of each element of the defense. As well, defendant has the burden of proving the defense by a preponderance of the evidence.

In *Nelson v. State* the Alaska Supreme court grappled with a claim of necessity. Where did Nelson's necessity claim get stuck?

NELSON V. STATE

Alaska Supreme Court
597 P.2d 977 (1979)

MATTHEWS, JUSTICE.

Shortly after midnight on May 22, 1976, Dale Nelson drove his four-wheel drive truck onto a side road off the Steese Highway near mile 68. His truck became bogged down in a marshy area about 250 feet off the highway. Nelson testified that he was afraid the truck might tip over in the soft ground. He and his two companions, Lynnette Stinson and Carl Thompson, spent an hour unsuccessfully trying to free the vehicle. At about 1:00, Nelson began walking with Stinson down the highway. An acquaintance drove by and offered to help, but was unable to render much assistance. He then drove Nelson and Stinson to a Highway Department Yard where heavy equipment was parked. The yard was marked with "no-trespassing" signs. After waiting several hours for someone to come by, they decided to take a dump truck and use it to pull out Nelson's vehicle. The dump truck also became stuck.

At approximately 10:00 that morning a man identified only as "Curly" appeared. His vehicle was also stuck further down the highway. Curly offered to assist Nelson. They returned to the heavy equipment yard and took a front-end loader, which they used to free the dump truck. They then used the dump truck to free Curly's car. The dump truck was returned to the equipment yard, but when Nelson attempted to use the front-end loader to free his own truck the front-end loader also became bogged down.

Frustrated and tired after twelve hours of attempting to free his vehicle, Nelson and his companions quit and went to sleep. Two of them slept in a tent. One of them went to sleep in the truck. They were awakened by a Highway Department employee, who placed them under citizen's arrest.

Considerable damage was done to both the front-end loader and the dump truck as a result of Nelson's attempt to free his truck. Ultimately,

[65] *See People v. Maclin* (2014) 2014 WL 2091368 ("Illinois courts have repeatedly held that a necessity instruction is properly denied when the defendant was not without blame in causing or developing the situation at issue.").

the truck was pulled from the mud three days later. Nelson was convicted in district court of reckless destruction of personal property and joyriding.

The sole question presented is whether the jury was properly instructed on the defense of necessity. Nelson requested an instruction which read: "You are instructed that the defendant is allowed to use a motor vehicle of another person without permission if the use is for an emergency in the case of immediate and dire need. You are further instructed that once the defendant has raised the issue of emergency or necessity, the state must prove the lack of emergency or necessity beyond a reasonable doubt."

Over Nelson's objection, the court gave an instruction on the necessity defense which read as follows: "You are instructed that it is a defense to a crime such as joyriding or taking someone else's motor vehicle without his permission that the person acted out of necessity in a case of immediate and dire need. However, such a defense exists only when natural forces create a situation wherein it becomes necessary for a person to violate the law in order to avoid a greater evil to himself or his property. The harm which is to be avoided must be the greater harm and it must be immediate and dire. Where a reasonable alternative other than violating the law is available in order to avoid the harm the defense of necessity is not applicable."

Nelson argues that the jury instruction was erroneous because it allowed the jury to apply what he calls an objective, after-the-fact test of need and emergency, rather than a subjective, reasonable man test. By this we assume Nelson means that he was entitled to have explained to the jury that they must view the question of necessity from the standpoint of a reasonable person knowing all that the defendant did at the time he acted.

The defense of necessity may be raised if the defendant's actions, although violative of the law, were necessary to prevent an even greater harm from occurring. "The rationale of the necessity defense is not that a person, when faced with the pressure of circumstances of nature, lacks the mental element which the crime in question requires. Rather, it is this reason of public policy: the law ought to promote the achievement of higher values at the expense of lesser values, and sometimes the greater good for society will be accomplished by violating the literal language of the criminal law." W. LaFave & A. Scott, Criminal Law § 50 at 382 (1972).

Commentators generally agree that there are three essential elements to the defense: (1) the act charged must have been done to prevent a significant evil; (2) there must have been no adequate alternative; (3) the harm caused must not have been disproportionate to the harm avoided.

The instruction given adequately describes these requirements for the jury. Nelson argues that he was entitled to wording which would explicitly allow the jury to find a necessity defense if a reasonable person at the time of acting would have believed that the necessary elements were present. Nelson is correct in stating that the necessity defense is available if a person acted in the reasonable belief that an emergency existed and there were no alternatives available even if that belief was mistaken. Moreover, the person's actions should be weighed against the harm reasonably foreseeable at the time, rather than the harm that actually occurs.

Assuming that the instruction given was not worded adequately to convey these concepts to the jury, we would find the error harmless, for Nelson failed to make out a case for the necessity defense. The "emergency" situation claimed by Nelson to justify his appropriation of the construction equipment was the alleged danger that his truck, stuck in the mud, might tip over, perhaps damaging the truck top. However by the time Nelson decided to use the equipment the truck had already been stuck for several hours. The dire nature of the emergency may be judged by the fact that some twelve hours later, having unsuccessfully attempted to remove the vehicle from the mud, one of Nelson's companions fell asleep in the truck, which had still not tipped over.

Nor can it be said that Nelson had no lawful alternatives in his situation. The record shows that during the time Nelson was trying to free the vehicle people stopped on several different occasions and offered their services in the form of physical assistance, rides, or offers to telephone state troopers or a tow truck.

Finally, it cannot be said that the harm sought to be avoided in this case potential damage to Nelson's truck was greater than the harm caused by Nelson's illegal actions. Even disregarding the actual damage to the equipment caused by Nelson's use, the seriousness of the offenses committed by Nelson were disproportionate to the situation he faced. The legislature has made this clear by making reckless destruction of personal property a crime punishable by imprisonment for up to one year and a $5,000 fine, and joyriding punishable by imprisonment for up to one year and a $1,000 fine. The equipment taken by Nelson was marked with no trespassing signs. Nelson's fears about damage to his truck roof were no justification for his appropriation of sophisticated and expensive equipment.

Affirmed.

In *People v. Lovercamp*, the Court of Appeal analyzed allowing prisoners to claim the necessity defense to justify escape.

PEOPLE V. LOVERCAMP

California Court of Appeal
43 Cal.App.3d 823, 118 Cal.Rptr. 110 (1974)

GARDNER, P. J.

Defendant and her codefendant, Ms. Wynashe, were convicted by a jury of escape from the California Rehabilitation Center (Welf. & Inst. Code § 3002).

Defendant and Ms. Wynashe were inmates of the California Rehabilitation Center. They departed from that institution and were promptly captured in a hayfield a few yards away. At trial, they made the following offer of proof:

They had been in the institution about two and one-half months and during that time they had been threatened continuously by a group of lesbian inmates who told them they were to perform lesbian acts—the exact expression was "fuck or fight." They complained to the authorities several times but nothing was done about their complaints. On the day of the escape, 10 or 15 of these lesbian inmates approached them and again offered them the alternative—"fuck or fight." This time there was a fight, the results of which were not outlined in the offer of proof. After the fight, Ms. Wynashe and defendant were told by this group of lesbians that they "would see the group again." At this point, both defendant and Ms. Wynashe feared for their lives. Ms. Wynashe was additionally motivated by a protective attitude toward defendant Lovercamp who had the intelligence of a 12-year-old. It was represented that a psychiatrist would testify as to defendant's mental capacity. On the basis of what had occurred, the threats made, the fact that officials had not done anything for their protection, Ms. Wynashe and defendant felt they had no choice but to leave the institution in order to save themselves.

The court rejected the offer of proof. The defendants then offered no evidence. The case was submitted to the jury and to the surprise of no one the jury found both defendants guilty.

While defendant makes several contentions on appeal, one is dispositive—the offer of proof.

Some preliminary observations are in order. When our culture abandoned such unpleasantries as torture, dismemberment, maiming and flogging as punishment for antisocial behavior and substituted in their place loss of liberty, certain problems immediately presented themselves. As a "civilized" people, we demanded that incarceration be under reasonably safe and humane conditions. On the other hand, we recognized that the institutional authorities must be afforded a certain firmness of program by which the malefactors be kept where sentenced for the allotted period of time. Realizing that a certain percentage of penal inmates are going to be uncooperative, disruptive and, in some cases, downright dangerous, we invested our institutional officials with disciplinary powers over inmates far above any such powers granted to governmental authorities outside prison walls. It is hardly earth shattering to observe that prisons are not Brownie Camps and that within the inmate population are those who, if given the opportunity, will depart without due process of law. Therefore, as an aid to prison authorities and to discourage self-help release from incarceration, the offense of escape was born. Simply stated, if an inmate intentionally leaves lawful custody, he commits a new crime.

However, rather early in the legal history of the offense of escape, it became clear that all departures from lawful custody were not necessarily escapes or, to put it more accurately, there was a possible defense to an escape charge, to wit, necessity. In 1 Hale P.C. 611 (1736), it was written that if a prison caught fire and a prisoner departed to save his life, the necessity to save his life "excuseth the felony." So, too, we may assume that a prisoner with his back to the wall, facing a gang of fellow inmates approaching him with drawn knives, who are making it very clear that they intend to kill him, might be expected to go over the wall rather than remain and be a martyr to the principle of prison discipline.

However, the doctrine of necessity to "excuseth the felony" carried with it the seeds of mischief. It takes little imagination to conjure stories which could be used to indicate that to the subjective belief of the prisoner conditions in prison are such that escape becomes a necessity. Inevitably, severe limitations were affixed to this defense and the general rule evolved that intolerable living conditions in prison afforded no justification for escape. A reading of the cases invoking this rule presents a harsh commentary on prison life in these United States of America, revealing (with proper consideration of the sources of the complaints), prison life which is harsh, brutal, filthy, unwholesome and inhumane. A fair sampling of the authorities indicate that the defense has been rejected in cases involving unsanitary conditions in jail—"a filthy, unwholesome and loathsome place, full of vermin and uncleanliness;" unmerited punishment at the hands of the custodian; or escape from solitary confinement when the cell was infested with bugs, worms and vermin and when the toilet was flushed the contents ran out on the floor; extremely bad food, guard brutality, inadequate medical treatment and inadequate recreational and educational programs. Under the above general rule, none of these situations excused the felony.

Traditionally, the courts have balanced the interests of society against the immediate problems of the escaping defendant. This has tended to focus attention away from the immediate choices available to the defendant and the propriety of his cause of action. Thus, reprehensible conditions have been found to be insufficient to justify the escape, the public interest outweighing the defendant's interest.

We conclude that the defense of necessity to an escape charge is a viable defense. However, before *Lovercamp* becomes a household word in prison circles and we are exposed to the spectacle of hordes of prisoners leaping over the walls screaming "rape," we hasten to add that the defense of necessity to an escape charge is extremely limited in its application. This is because of the rule that upon attaining a position of safety from the immediate threat, the prisoner must promptly report to the proper authorities.

From all of the above, we hold that the proper rule is that a limited defense of necessity is available if the following conditions exist: (1) The prisoner is faced with a specific threat of death, forcible sexual attack or substantial bodily injury in the immediate future; (2) There is no time for a complaint to the authorities or there exists a history of futile complaints which make any result from such complaints illusory; (3) There is no time or opportunity to resort to the courts; (4) There is no evidence of force or violence used towards prison personnel or other "innocent" persons in the escape; and (5) The prisoner immediately reports to the proper authorities when he has attained a position of safety from the immediate threat.

Applying the above rules to the offer of proof in the instant case, we find the following: (1) The prisoners were faced with a specific threat of forcible sexual attack in the immediate future. While we must confess a certain naivete as to just what kind of exotic erotica is involved in the gang rape of the victim by a group of lesbians and a total ignorance of just who is forced to do what to whom, we deem it a reasonable assumption that it entails as much physical and psychological insult to and degradation of a fellow human being as does forcible sodomy. (2) There existed a history of futile complaints to the authorities which made the results of any belated complaint illusory. (3) Between the time of the fight and the time the ladies went over the wall, there obviously existed no time for resort to the courts by the filing of a petition for an extraordinary writ. (4) No force was involved in the escape. (5) Because the defendants were apprehended so promptly and in such close proximity to the institution, we do not know whether they intended to immediately report to the proper authorities at the first available opportunity. Obviously, even though the defendant may have the mentality of a 12-year-old, on retrial it must be anticipated that she will so testify. Whether that testimony is believable under the facts and circumstances of this case, will be a question of fact addressed to the jury.

Whether any of the conditions requisite to this defense exist is a question of fact to be decided by the trier of fact after taking into consideration all the surrounding circumstances. The offer of proof in the instant case was sufficient to require the submission of this defense to the jury in an appropriate manner. The trial court erred in not submitting this matter to the jury.

PROBLEMS ON NECESSITY

1. Tom has glaucoma, which will eventually lead to blindness. Marijuana is a treatment for glaucoma, but marijuana is illegal without a prescription. Tom does not have a prescription. Tom grows marijuana for his personal medicinal use and is arrested. Can Tom prevail on a defense of necessity?

2. June is a convicted felon. While June was in a bar, minding her own business, Bob sat down next to June and tried to convince June to go out with him. June declined. Bob became obnoxious and threatened June with harm if she refused his advances. June left to get away from Bob. Bob followed her. In the parking lot, Bob threatened to kill June. Bob removed a gun from his pocket and waived it in the air. June grabbed the gun and ran away, only to be stopped a block away by a police officer. June is charged with the crime of being a felon in possession of a firearm. Can June claim necessity?

3. Anne and Cindy are mountain climbers. They are half way up a vertical climb. It is more than 1000 feet straight down. They are connected by a rope. Anne is in the lead. Suddenly, Cindy slips, hits her head, and is knocked unconscious. Cindy is dangling from the rope. Anne is hanging on with her hands, but can only hang on a little while longer. Anne cannot secure the rope. Either Anne cuts the rope and allows Cindy to fall to her death, or Anne *and* Cindy fall to their deaths together. What should Anne do?

4. Jennifer was married to Jason. The relationship was stormy, and the couple often argued. On several occasions when he was drunk, Jason hit Jennifer with his fists, causing bruises. On Memorial Day, Jennifer and Jason went to a remote lake in the mountains, fifty miles east of their Sacramento home. They had a picknick and too much to drink. They started arguing, and Jason threatened, "I should just leave you here. Find your own ride home." The argument escalated, and Jason picked up a rock and threw it a Jennifer, narrowly missing her head. Jennifer was frightened Jason would hurt her. While Jason was off in the bushes going to the bathroom, Jennifer jumped in the car and drove away. She drove a mile to a ranger station to ask for help. On the way to the station, she was stopped by a sheriff's deputy, and charged with driving under the influence. May Jennifer employ the necessity defense? *Axelberg v. Commissioner of Public Safety*, 848 N.W.2d 206 (Minn. 2014).

Civil Disobedience and the Necessity Defense

Bob opposes abortion. Abortion is legal under certain circumstances. Bob firmly believes all abortion is murder. To protest abortion and save the lives of innocent children, Bob blocks the entrance to an abortion clinic. Bob is prosecuted for criminal trespass. At trial, Bob wishes to take the stand to inform the jury of the reasons for his actions. In other words, Bob wants to raise the necessity defense. The prosecutor argues that the reasons for Bob's conduct are irrelevant. What should the judge do? Consider *People v. Weber*.

PEOPLE V. WEBER

California Court of Appeal
162 Cal. App. 3d Supp. 1, 208 Cal.Rptr. 719 (1984)

MILKES, J.

We have consolidated for decision convictions for trespass, obstruction of a street and/or sidewalk during demonstrations by nuclear protesters at General Dynamics and the United States Navy Submarine Base at Ballast Point.

All of the defendants raise a similar contention on appeal: The trial court's refusal to allow the defense of necessity. Appellants contend that they were thwarted in presenting evidence to the jury that their actions were motivated by a sincere belief in discussing and publicizing the dangers of nuclear weapons.

Peaceful demonstrations, protests and dissent need no defense; they are the cornerstone of a society based on the rule of law. As suggested by Justice William O. Douglas, the right to dissent "is the only thing that makes life tolerable for a judge on the appellate level." All thoughtful persons remember the horror and sorrow of Hiroshima and Nagasaki. But we are confronted with a more complex resolution than may be determined by raising a single moral issue. We must respect, above all, the pluralism that simply does not see nuclear disarmament and other emotional issues from the same single perspective. Our concern cannot be a single dimension. We must be equally concerned with the protection of rights, including property rights of others. We do not see all things or all issues from the same angle; nor do we all march to the same drummer.

In *People v. Patrick*, 126 Cal. App. 3d 952 (1981), which involved the issue of deprogramming a suspected "cult" member, the Court of Appeal, in rejecting a defense of necessity, exposited: "First, although the exact confines of the necessity defense remain clouded, a well-established central element involves the emergency nature of the situation, i.e., the imminence of the greater harm which the illegal act seeks to prevent. The commission of a crime cannot be countenanced where there exists the possibility of some alternate means to alleviate the threatened greater harm."

There must be a showing of imminence of peril before the defense of necessity is applicable. A defendant is not entitled to a claim of duress or necessity unless and until he demonstrates that, given the imminence of the threat, violation of the law was the only reasonable alternative. The uniform requirement of California authority discussing the necessity defense is that the situation presented to the defendant be of an emergency nature, that there be threatened physical harm, and that there was no legal alternative course of action available.

There were other forms of protest available to the defendants which disembowel the defense of necessity.

DURESS

Duress is an excuse defense.[66] The elements of duress are: (1) Defendant was threatened that if defendant refused to commit a crime, the life of defendant or someone else would be in immediate danger; (2) Defendant believed the threat; (3) Defendant's belief was reasonable in light of the circumstances known to the defendant.[67]

Defendant has the burden of producing evidence of each element of the defense. This done, the prosecutor has the burden to disprove duress beyond a reasonable doubt.

Duress is not a defense to the charge of a capital crime.[68] (*People v. Daveggio* (2018) 4 Cal. 5th 790, 415 P.3d 717, 231 Cal. Rptr. 3d 646).

The Ninth Circuit's decision in *United States v. Contento-Pachon* is a good illustration of duress.

UNITED STATES V. CONTENTO-PACHON

United States Court of Appeals, Ninth Circuit
723 F.2d 691 (1984)

BOOCHEVER, CIRCUIT JUDGE.

This case presents an appeal from a conviction for unlawful possession with intent to distribute a narcotic controlled substance. At trial, the defendant attempted to offer evidence of duress and necessity defenses. The district court excluded this evidence on the ground that it was insufficient to support the defenses. We reverse because there was sufficient evidence of duress to present a triable issue of fact.

The defendant-appellant, Juan Manuel Contento-Pachon, is a native of Bogota, Colombia and was employed there as a taxicab driver. He asserts that one of his passengers, Jorge, offered him a job as the driver of a

---

[66] PC § 26 provides: "All persons are capable of committing crimes except those belonging to the following classes: Persons (unless the crime is punishable with death) who committed the act or made the omission charged under threats or menaces sufficient to show that they had reasonable cause to and did believe their lives would be endangered if they refused."

[67] *See United States v. Diaz-Castro* (C.A. 1st Cir. 2014) 752 F.3d 101.

[68] *See People v. Powell* (2018) 6 Cal. 5th 136, 425 P.3d 1006, 237 Cal. Rptr. 3d 793, where the Supreme Court wrote: "The defense of duress is available to defendants who commit crimes, except murder, under threats or menaces sufficient to show that they had reasonable cause to and did believe their lives would be endangered if they refused. Although duress is not a defense to any form of murder, duress can, in effect, provide a defense to murder on a felony-murder theory by negating the underlying felony. If one is not guilty of the felony due to duress, once cannot be guilty of felony murder based on that felony."

privately-owned car. Contento-Pachon expressed an interest in the job and agreed to meet Jorge and the owner of the car the next day.

Instead of a driving job, Jorge proposed that Contento-Pachon swallow cocaine-filled balloons and transport them to the United States. Contento-Pachon agreed to consider the proposition. He was told not to mention the proposition to anyone, otherwise he would "get into serious trouble." Contento-Pachon testified that he did not contact the police because he believes that the Bogota police are corrupt and that they are paid off by drug traffickers.

Approximately one week later, Contento-Pachon told Jorge that he would not carry the cocaine. In response, Jorge mentioned facts about Contento-Pachon's personal life, including private details which Contento-Pachon had never mentioned to Jorge. Jorge told Contento-Pachon that his failure to cooperate would result in the death of his wife and three year-old child.

The following day the pair met again. Contento-Pachon's life and the lives of his family were again threatened. At this point, Contento-Pachon agreed to take the cocaine into the United States.

The pair met two more times. At the last meeting, Contento-Pachon swallowed 129 balloons of cocaine. He was informed that he would be watched at all times during the trip, and that if he failed to follow Jorge's instruction he and his family would be killed.

After leaving Bogota, Contento-Pachon's plane landed in Panama. Contento-Pachon asserts that he did not notify the authorities there because he felt that the Panamanian police were as corrupt as those in Bogota. Also, he felt that any such action on his part would place his family in jeopardy.

When he arrived at the customs inspection point in Los Angeles, Contento-Pachon consented to have his stomach x-rayed. The x-rays revealed a foreign substance which was later determined to be cocaine.

At Contento-Pachon's trial, the government moved to exclude the defenses of duress and necessity. The motion was granted. We reverse.

Duress

There are three elements of the duress defense: (1) an immediate threat of death or serious bodily injury, (2) a well-grounded fear that the threat will be carried out, and (3) no reasonable opportunity to escape the threatened harm. Sometimes a fourth element is required: the defendant must submit to proper authorities after attaining a position of safety.

Factfinding is usually a function of the jury, and the trial court rarely rules on a defense as a matter of law. If the evidence is insufficient as a matter of law to support a duress defense, however, the trial court should exclude that evidence.

The trial court found Contento-Pachon's offer of proof insufficient to support a duress defense because he failed to offer proof of two elements: immediacy and inescapability. We examine the elements of duress.

Immediacy: The element of immediacy requires that there be some evidence that the threat of injury was present, immediate, or impending. A veiled threat of future unspecified harm will not satisfy this requirement. The district court found that the initial threats were not immediate because "they were conditioned on defendant's failure to cooperate in the future and did not place defendant and his family in immediate danger."

Evidence presented on this issue indicated that the defendant was dealing with a man who was deeply involved in the exportation of illegal substances. Large sums of money were at stake and, consequently, Contento-Pachon had reason to believe that Jorge would carry out his threats. Jorge had gone to the trouble to discover that Contento-Pachon was married, that he had a child, the names of his wife and child, and the location of his residence. These were not vague threats of possible future harm. According to the defendant, if he had refused to cooperate, the consequences would have been immediate and harsh.

Contento-Pachon contends that he was being watched by one of Jorge's accomplices at all times during the airplane trip. As a consequence, the force of the threats continued to restrain him. Contento-Pachon's contention that he was operating under the threat of immediate harm was supported by sufficient evidence to present a triable issue of fact.

Escapability: The defendant must show that he had no reasonable opportunity to escape. The district court found that because Contento-Pachon was not physically restrained prior to the time he swallowed the balloons, he could have sought help from the police or fled. Contento-Pachon explained that he did not report the threats because he feared that the police were corrupt. The trier of fact should decide whether one in Contento-Pachon's position might believe that some of the Bogota police were paid informants for drug traffickers and that reporting the matter to the police did not represent a reasonable opportunity of escape.

If he chose not to go to the police, Contento-Pachon's alternative was to flee. We reiterate that the opportunity to escape must be reasonable. To flee, Contento-Pachon, along with his wife and three year-old child, would have been forced to pack his possessions, leave his job, and travel to a place beyond the reaches of the drug traffickers. A juror might find that this was not a reasonable avenue of escape. Thus, Contento-Pachon presented a triable issue on the element of escapability.

Surrender to Authorities: As noted above, the duress defense is composed of at least three elements. The government argues that the defense also requires that a defendant offer evidence that he intended to turn himself in to the authorities upon reaching a position of safety. Although it has not been expressly limited, this fourth element seems to be required only in prison escape cases. In cases not involving escape from prison there seems little difference between the third basic requirement that there be no reasonable opportunity to escape the threatened harm and the obligation to turn oneself in to authorities on reaching a point of safety. Once a defendant has reached a position where he can safely turn himself in to the authorities he will likewise have a reasonable opportunity to escape the threatened harm.

That is true in this case. Contento-Pachon claims that he was being watched at all times. According to him, at the first opportunity to cooperate with authorities without alerting the observer, he consented to the x-ray. We hold that a defendant who has acted under a well-grounded fear of immediate harm with no opportunity to escape may assert the duress defense, if there is a triable issue of fact whether he took the opportunity to escape the threatened harm by submitting to authorities at the first reasonable opportunity.

Necessity

The defense of necessity is available when a person is faced with a choice of two evils and must then decide whether to commit a crime or an alternative act that constitutes a greater evil. Contento-Pachon has attempted to justify his violation of [the federal statute] by showing that the alternative, the death of his family, was a greater evil.

Traditionally, in order for the necessity defense to apply, the coercion must have had its source in the physical forces of nature. The duress defense was applicable when the defendant's acts were coerced by a human force. This distinction served to separate the two similar defenses. But modern courts have tended to blur the distinction between duress and necessity.

Contento-Pachon's acts were allegedly coerced by human, not physical forces. Therefore, the necessity defense was not available to him. The district court correctly disallowed his use of the necessity defense.

Contento-Pachon presented credible evidence that he acted under an immediate and well-grounded threat of serious bodily injury, with no opportunity to escape. Because the trier of fact should have been allowed to consider the credibility of the proffered evidence, we reverse.

PROBLEMS ON DURESS

1. Jill participated in four robberies. She was the getaway driver in each. In her prosecution for robbery, Jill requests a jury instruction on duress. Jill claims that in each robbery she was told she would be killed if she did not cooperate. Should the judge instruct on duress? *People v. Kearns* (1997) 55 Cal.App.4th 1128, 64 Cal.Rptr.2d 654.

2. Pete is in prison. He is charged with possession of a knife while in prison. A search of Pete's cell disclosed a knife hidden in Pete's mattress. Pete requests a duress instruction. Pete testifies that the inmate in the next cell stuck a knife to Pete's throat and said, "Unless to hide my knife in your cell, this is just a taste of what you'll get." Should the judge give the requested instruction? *People v. Otis* (1959) 174 Cal.App.2d 119, 344 P.2d 342.

3. Raquel is charged with intent to kill murder. Raquel does not deny that she placed poison in the victim's beer, but Raquel requests a jury instruction on duress. Raquel wishes to testify that the only reason she poisoned the victim was that she was told that unless she did so, she and her two young children would be killed. Should the judge give the requested instruction?

4. One morning, two sisters, ages 12 and 13, escaped from their home and ran to a neighbor's house, shouting that their step-father threatened them with a knife. The neighbors had never seen the girls before, even though they lived nearby. The neighbors called 911. The girls were dirty, with matted hair. They had not bathed in weeks, and smelled bad. The girls described horrible living conditions. They were always confined to their rooms, and were constantly monitored by video camera. They had to ask permission to use the bathroom. Their only food was pasta, which they ate in their room. They rarely brushed their teeth or bathed. The step-father and the girls' mother beat them with objects as a form of discipline. They had not been to school in years. Step-father and Mother are charged with child cruelty. Mother raises a duress defense. Mother wants to offer evidence that step-father regularly beat Mother, and, on several occasions, cut Mother with a knife. Mother argues she was compelled by step-father's violence and threats of violence against her and the children to participate in step-father's cruelty toward the children. Does Mother have a viable duress defense? *State v. Richter* (2018) 245 Ariz. 1, 424 P.3d 402.

VOLUNTARY INTOXICATION

Voluntary intoxication is an excuse defense to certain crimes. PC § 29.4 provides:

> (a) No act committed by a person while in a state of voluntary intoxication is less criminal by reason of his or her having been in that condition. Evidence of voluntary intoxication shall not be admitted to negate the capacity to form any mental states for the crimes charged, including, but not limited to,

purpose, intent, knowledge, premeditation, deliberation, or malice aforethought, with which the accused committed the act.

(b) Evidence of voluntary intoxication is admissible solely on the issue of whether or not the defendant actually formed a required specific intent, or, when charged with murder, whether the defendant premeditated, deliberated, or harbored express malice aforethought.

(c) Voluntary intoxication includes the voluntary ingestion, injection, or taking by any other means of any intoxicating liquor, drug, or other substance.

Voluntary intoxication is not a defense to a general intent crime. The Supreme Court wrote in *People v. Atkins* (2001) 25 Cal.4th 76, 81, 104 Cal.Rptr.2d 738, 18 P.3d 660, "Evidence of voluntary intoxication is inadmissible to negate the existence of general criminal intent."

In the context of homicide, evidence of voluntary intoxication is admissible on the issues of premeditation, deliberation, and express malice. Voluntary intoxication is not admissible on the question of implied malice.[69] Nor is voluntary intoxication admissible to prove defendant believed it was necessary to act in self-defense.

Voluntary intoxication can be a defense to a specific intent offense. In *People v. Soto* (2018) 4 Cal. 5th 968, 976–977, 415 P.3d 789, 231 Cal. Rptr. 3d 732, the Supreme Court remarked, "Evidence of voluntary intoxication may be introduced to negate an element requiring relatively complex cognition—a mental function integral to many crimes that contain a definition that refers to defendant's intent to do some further act or achieve some additional consequence—because alcohol can interfere with such intent.

Voluntary intoxication can impact accomplice liability. In *People v. Mendoza* (1998) 18 Cal.4th 1114, 1132, 77 Cal.Rptr.2d 428, 959 P.2d 735, the Supreme Court ruled that voluntary intoxication can be relevant to whether or not a defendant formed the intent necessary to aid and abet. The Court wrote, "The aider and abettor must specifically intend to aid the perpetrator, whether the intended crime itself requires a general or a specific intent on the part of the perpetrator."

Early in the development of the law, intoxication was an aggravating factor, not a defense. That is, a drunk defendant was *more* culpable than a sober defendant, and deserved harsher punishment! A number of states have abolished the defense of voluntary intoxication (Florida; Utah). The

---

[69] *See People v. Soto* (2018) 4 Cal. 5th 968, 977, 415 P.3d 789, 231 Cal. Rptr. 3d 732, where the Supreme Court wrote: "By prohibiting evidence of voluntary intoxication to negate *implied* malice, the Legislature . . . agreed . . . that a defendant who acts with conscious disregard for life should be punished for murder regardless of whether voluntary intoxication impaired his or her judgment."

U.S. Supreme Court upheld a Montana statute abolishing the defense. *Montana v. Egelhoff* (1996) 518 U.S. 37, 116 S.Ct. 2013. Should voluntary intoxication be abolished as a defense?

PROBLEMS ON INTOXICATION

1. Dell planned to rob a grocery store. Dell hid in the bushes outside the store in the early morning, waiting for the first employee to arrive. The manager arrived, and Dell took her prisoner, using a gun. As more employees arrived, Dell took them prisoner. All the employees were tied up. Dell took money from the safe and fled. Shortly after Dell left, the store manager died of a heart attack caused by the stress of the robbery. If you are the prosecutor, what will you charge Dell with? As defense counsel, your client tells you he was high on drugs and alcohol at the time of the crime. What, if any, impact will Dell's voluntary intoxication have?

2. Tom and John are Navy sailors. Their ship is in port in San Francisco, and Tom and John are on liberty in the city. They spend all their money getting drunk at a bar. To get more money they decide to rob a cab driver. They hail a cab driven by a woman. Tom and John tell the driver to drive to a remote location. Once there, John hits the driver on the head, knocking her out. They take the driver's money. They also have sex with the driver while she is unconscious. Tom and John are charged with rape and robbery. They wish to claim voluntary intoxication. The prosecutor objects to any evidence of voluntary intoxication. What should the trial judge do?

INVOLUNTARY INTOXICATION

Involuntary intoxication is a defense in all jurisdictions. There are four types of involuntary intoxication: (1) Coerced intoxication; (2) Innocent or mistaken intoxication (spiked punch at the senior prom); (3) An unanticipated reaction to a drug taken on medical advice; and (4) pathological intoxication—defendant knew she was taking a drug, but the reaction was highly excessive. Involuntary intoxication is a defense to specific as well as general intent crimes.

Consider the sad story of Walter Scott, described by the Court of Appeal in *People v. Scott* (1983) 146 Cal.App.3d 823, 194 Cal.Rptr. 633:

> On the evening of August 1, 1981, Walter, accompanied by his brother Charles Scott, attended a family reunion-type party. The brother noticed a large punch bowl filled with red punch and saw the punch bowl refilled several times during the course of the party. He also observed defendant drinking some of the punch.
>
> At some point in the evening the supply of ice ran low and the brother volunteered to go to the store to get more. When he left, everyone, including defendant, appeared to be behaving normally. However, when he returned the brother noticed that the behavior

of the party guests had changed dramatically. He began looking for defendant and while doing so he noticed a number of guests holding cups of punch behaving strangely and in some cases bizarrely. One man, pointing to the floor, stated there was a dog in the room. Several people holding glasses of punch in their hands were vomiting. When the brother finally located defendant, he noticed that defendant's eyes were unusually large and dilated, and that defendant appeared uncoordinated. Defendant also appeared not to recognize his brother. Feeling that something was wrong, the brother took defendant by the hand and led him out of the house and into his car.

On the way home defendant told his brother he could see a big fireball in the sky and that he could see the brother and his in-laws in the flames. Defendant described it as "Hell" and he stated either that they were trying to pull him in there or he was trying to pull them out. At some point during the ride home, defendant stuck his head out of the car window and stated that he felt "good enough to fly home." The brother, who had received some instruction on drug intoxication and had also previously seen people who were on PCP (phencyclidine), believed defendant might be on PCP.

The morning after the party the brother called defendant; defendant sounded as if he were back to normal. Defendant indicated he did not remember what he had done the evening before.

Eleanor Michele Sutton was also present at the party. She noticed defendant, whom she had never met before, with a cup of punch in his hand, talking about the Bible and stating that the world was coming to an end. Sutton herself did not drink anything at the party.

During an interview with Dr. Robert Summerour, a forensic psychiatrist, defendant stated that at some point during the party he began to see intense colors and heard helicopters and loud sirens. He stated that his body was clumsy, he was sweating, had difficulty talking, and felt as if his heart was beating rapidly. Defendant remembered being led away from the party and into a car by his brother and also his attempt to jump out of the car window during the ride home. Defendant could not remember what occurred after he arrived home, although he did remember preaching about the Bible and the world coming to an end.

Defendant further told Dr. Summerour that the next day he felt a little more hyperactive than usual but attended church with his family and proceeded through the day without incident.

However, when he awakened on Monday morning, August 3, 1981, he felt queasy and decided not to go to work. After taking his children to school, defendant took his mother-in-law, Frances Nichols, with him to purchase some glass to replace broken windows at his house. While inside the store, defendant began to feel the same feelings he had at the party. The clerk "spooked" him because he (the clerk) "looked like he was from Mars." Defendant ran out of the store and into his car, and then imagined he observed a long funeral go by in which he sensed that he was the deceased. Defendant began to drive on the freeway at a high speed.

On the return glass-purchase trip defendant drove past her house without stopping, stating that he was driving to Bakersfield to talk with his mother. Ms. Nichols observed defendant looking over his shoulder frequently, driving fast and making rapid lane changes. While on the freeway defendant stated to Ms. Nichols the CIA was after him and was following him in an airplane because he was a secret agent. He said he had to get to the police for help. He started calling Ms. Nichols "Baby," an affectionate term that he usually addressed to his wife. Defendant was sweating profusely and repeatedly stated that he was thirsty. Ms. Nichols observed that defendant's eyes were "glassy and weird," that he was talking fast and that he did not seem to be making sense. Finally, when the car overheated and stopped running, defendant jumped out of the car and ran up the offramp. Ms. Nichols eventually lost sight of him.

About this time, 13-year-old Robert Briggs was sitting on his motor bike in the driveway of a gas station in Riverside County. Defendant approached him, stated he was a secret agent and demanded the boy give him the motor bike. When Robert refused, defendant hit him on the helmet, knocking him off the bike, and then proceeded to mount the bike. Defendant attempted to kick-start the cycle, but was unsuccessful.

Douglas Bushlen was driving his pickup truck toward the highway 91 onramp when he observed a man knock a kid off a motor bike at a Shell service station. He then observed other people trying to get the man off the bike and decided to drive into the service station and offer assistance. The man, defendant, then ran toward Bushlen's stopped truck and jumped on the back of it. Defendant told Bushlen to drive on, that he was from the FBI and the CIA. Bushlen then drove to and parked at the Magnolia Lumber Yard; a few minutes later defendant got off the truck.

Bushlen testified that defendant seemed "kind of crazy" and appeared restless and hyperactive. He also appeared frightened and stated in a loud voice that the President of the United States and he had fallen out of an airplane. He appeared to be under the influence of something and did not seem to know who or where he was.

Christopher Bell was operating a forklift at the Magnolia Lumber Yard when defendant arrived in the back of Bushlen's pickup truck. Bell observed defendant banging on the side of the truck stating that he was with the secret police and that he wanted to get inside the truck. At some point defendant got off the truck, walked toward Bell and pointed toward the freeway, stating that the President was going by. Bell stopped the forklift and got off. Defendant then jumped on top of the forklift and tried to start it, declaring that he needed the forklift for police business. Bell removed the key from the ignition and told defendant he could use the telephone inside the store to call the police. According to Bell defendant was speaking in a loud voice and was perspiring profusely.

Once inside the building, defendant called Information in an attempt to get in touch with Washington, D.C., stating that he was "John Shaft" and that he was from the CIA. When the call failed to go through, defendant hung up and re-dialed the operator. This time he asked for the police and stated that "they" were trying to "kill the President." He stated either that he or the President had fallen out of an airplane.

Defendant then hung up the phone, ran out of the building, jumped into a nearby truck and tried to start it. The truck's owner, Cecil Endeman, followed close behind. Endeman's stepson was sitting in the passenger seat when defendant jumped inside, closed the door and asked, "How do you start this vehicle?" Defendant then announced in a loud voice, "I'm with the CIA and I need to use the car." Endeman demanded that defendant get out of the car, at which point defendant ran back inside the building.

Defendant then telephoned his mother, stating: "I don't know where I'm at but tell somebody to come get me." He then asked the owner of the lumber yard to call the police. Defendant asked for everyone's names and addresses, indicating that he needed them for his "report." He appeared restless and frightened to those who were present.

Defendant was charged with attempted unlawful driving or taking of a vehicle (PC § 664, Veh. Code § 10851). Involuntary intoxication that eliminates *mens rea* is a potential defense to general and specific intent crimes. Does defendant have a defense?

MENTAL ILLNESS—INSANITY

A person's mental condition can be relevant for four purposes in a criminal proceeding: (1) Defendant's mental illness *at the time of the offense* may meet the requirements of the insanity defense; (2) Defendant's mental illness *at the time of the offense* may suggest that defendant lacked the *mens rea* for the crime; (3) Defendant's mental illness *at the time of trial* may render the defendant incompetent to stand trial; and (4) A seriously mentally ill prisoner cannot be executed (PC § 3704).

Mental Illness and *Mens Rea*

A person's mental illness may rob the person of the capacity to have the *mens rea* for the charged offense (PC § 28).[70] Used for this purpose, mental illness is a FED. Mental illness can be a defense when defendant is charged with a specific intent offense. Mental illness cannot eliminate general intent, unless the offense requires "knowledge."[71] In *People v. Mills*, the Supreme Court discusses the roles mental illness play in criminal law.

PEOPLE V. MILLS

California Supreme Court

55 Cal.4th 663, 147 Cal. Rptr. 3d 833 (2012)

My case

CORRIGAN, J.

rule

"When a defendant pleads not guilty by reason of insanity, and also joins with it another plea or pleas, the defendant shall first be tried as if only such other plea or pleas had been entered, and in that trial the defendant shall be conclusively presumed to have been sane at the time the offense is alleged to have been committed." (Pen. Code, § 1026(a).) In this case defendant was charged with murder, pled not guilty, and also raised

[70] PC § 28 states: "(a) Evidence of mental disease, mental defect, or mental disorder shall not be admitted to show or negate the capability to form any mental state, including, but not limited to, purpose, intent, knowledge, premeditation, deliberation, or malice aforethought, with which the accused committed the act. Evidence of mental disease, mental defect, or mental disorder is admissible solely on the issue of whether or not the accused actually formed a required specific intent, premeditated, deliberated, or harbored malice aforethought, when a specific intent crime is charged. (b) As a matter of public policy there shall be no defense of diminished capacity, diminished responsibility, or irresistible impulse in a criminal action or juvenile adjudication hearing. (c) This section shall not be applicable to an insanity hearing pursuant to Section 1026." PC § 25(a) states, "The defense of diminished capacity is hereby abolished."

[71] *See People v. Thiel* (2016) 5 Cal. App. 5th 1201, 1209, 210 Cal. Rptr. 3d 744 ("Accordingly, the rule has developed that evidence of mental illness may be offered to show the absence of specific intent but not to prove the absence of general intent."); *People v. Bejarano* (2009) 180 Cal.App.4th 583, 103 Cal.Rptr.3d 190.

an insanity defense. At the guilt phase trial, the prosecutor requested a jury instruction that defendant was conclusively presumed to have been sane at the time of the offense. Defendant objected that the instruction might lead the jury to disregard the evidence of his mental illness and its effect on the intent required for murder. The court overruled the objection, gave the instruction on the presumption of sanity, and refused defendant's request for an instruction on the legal definition of sanity.

The jury convicted defendant of first degree murder. In the subsequent sanity trial it found that he was sane at the time of the offense. The court sentenced him to a term of 50 years to life in prison. On appeal below, defendant contended the guilt phase instruction on the conclusive presumption of sanity was improper because (1) it told the jury to presume the existence of a mental state critical to the state's burden of proof, violating due process, and (2) it had no application to any issue before the jury, violating state law. The Court of Appeal affirmed the judgment.

The question of a defendant's sanity is entirely irrelevant at the guilt phase of a bifurcated trial under section 1026. Therefore, no instruction on the subject should be given. However, the error was harmless in this case.

Shortly before 5:00 on the afternoon of April 21, 2005, Jason Jackson-Andrade entered the Amtrak station in Emeryville. Eyewitness testimony established the ensuing events. As Jackson-Andrade sat on a bench on the platform, defendant approached him and launched a tirade of insults. He told Jackson-Andrade, "You ain't getting on that train." Jackson-Andrade went into the station, sat down, and asked a woman if she knew the man outside. She said she did not. Jackson-Andrade told her he had not done anything, but the man was "cussing" at him and acting as though he wanted to kill him.

Defendant walked around on the platform for several minutes, bouncing on his toes, humming, and talking to himself. He then began walking toward the station in a determined manner, saying, "You got a gun, nigger? You got a gun? You got a gun?" He entered the station, approached Jackson-Andrade, and twice said, "Motherfucker, you want to kill me?" He also asked, "You got a gun?" As Jackson-Andrade looked up at him, defendant said, "Well, if you ain't got no motherfucking gun, I do," and produced a revolver from his pocket. Defendant shot Jackson-Andrade, who held up his hands and said, "Please, don't shoot me again, don't shoot." Jackson-Andrade fell from his seat and began crawling away. Defendant shot him five more times in the back and once in the back of the thigh.

When the police arrived, defendant lay on the ground, sliding his gun forward and assuming a prone position. He told them he was the only shooter. Jackson-Andrade died at the scene.

Defendant testified in his own defense. He claimed that because of death threats from various individuals, he and his wife had left their home in Merced to live with his cousin Telitha in Rodeo. He had been visiting another cousin in Sacramento in the days before the murder. As he walked around Sacramento, he began to suspect that he was being followed. On the morning of the murder, he stole a car at gunpoint and drove from Sacramento to Rodeo. He had Telitha take him to the Amtrak station because he did not want the people following him to find her or his wife. As he approached the station, he heard someone say, "You're going to feel it today," which he took to mean that he was going to be shot.

On the platform, defendant became suspicious of two men, one of whom looked at him and said into his cell phone, "He looks scared." Defendant claimed that after these men left, Jackson-Andrade beckoned to him. As defendant approached, Jackson-Andrade became angry and threatened to kill him. Jackson-Andrade then got up and went into the station, pausing at the door to make a hand gesture indicating that he had a gun. Defendant was nervous, and had to go to the bathroom, so he entered the station. When he saw Jackson-Andrade sitting inside talking to a lady, defendant "jumped" and the contents of his backpack spilled onto the floor. Jackson-Andrade got up and put his hand into his pocket. Defendant thought he was reaching for a gun, so he shot him. As Jackson-Andrade lay on the ground, defendant again thought he was reaching for a weapon, so defendant shot him again. Defendant testified that he shot only twice, but on cross-examination admitted he had reloaded his gun and continued firing.

Defendant's wife and cousin testified that he told them people were after him. His wife said he thought radio commercials were speaking to him, that the FBI was in a FedEx truck, and that cars were following him. A psychologist testified for the defense. After interviewing defendant, reviewing the police reports and witness statements, and giving defendant several psychological tests, he concluded that in April 2005 defendant suffered from a delusional disorder in the paranoid spectrum. The expert carefully focused his testimony. In his opinion, defendant did not suffer from a severe mental illness like schizophrenia or bipolar disease, nor were his delusions utterly beyond the realm of possibility. They concerned events that might actually happen, but defendant's belief in them was a function of his paranoid personality style. He tended to be hypervigilant, interpreting events in a personalized and threatening way. Stress exacerbated his symptoms.

The theory of the defense was good faith but unreasonable self-defense, also known as "imperfect" self-defense. Defense counsel urged the jury to find defendant guilty only of manslaughter, because he actually but unreasonably believed the victim posed an imminent threat when he shot him. However, counsel also argued that defendant's fear was not purely delusional. Noting the jury would be instructed that the fear giving rise to unreasonable self-defense may not derive from delusion alone, counsel contended defendant's fears were based on actual facts and experiences that he misinterpreted due to his paranoia.

The prosecutor requested a special instruction based on section 1026: "For purposes of reaching your verdict during this guilt phase of the proceedings, the defendant is conclusively presumed to have been sane at the time of the offense." Defendant filed a written objection, arguing that "giving this instruction would violate Defendant's rights to due process and a fair trial because it might tend to confuse the jury and would have the effect of lowering the prosecution's burden of proving intent. Specifically, the Defense submits this instruction might be misinterpreted by the jury as directing them to disregard Defendant's evidence regarding mental illness, and that the jury may misinterpret this instruction as directing them to presume a mental condition which has not been adequately defined or distinguished from Defendant's evidence regarding mental illness." If the instruction were to be given, defendant asked the court to instruct the jury on the legal definition of insanity, and advise it that "The presumption of sanity does not mean you are to disregard evidence of mental illness. You may consider such evidence as directed by other instructions I have given you."

The court gave the special instruction on the presumption of sanity, immediately following an instruction on unreasonable self-defense. It refused to give defendant's proposed additional language, stating: "I don't want to get into what the definition of sanity is in this phase of the proceedings and I don't think that you can be wrong by correctly stating the law."

While sanity is conclusively presumed at the guilt phase of a bifurcated trial, the mens rea element of a crime is not presumed, conclusively or otherwise. Whenever a particular mental state, such as a specific intent, is by statute made an essential element of a crime, that specific state must be proved like any other fact. Evidence of mental disease, mental defect, or mental disorder is admissible solely on the issue of whether or not the accused actually formed a required specific intent, premeditated, deliberated, or harbored malice aforethought, when a specific intent crime is charged." (§ 28(a)) Therefore, competent evidence that the defendant did or did not possess the required mental state is admissible, whereas evidence tending to show legal sanity or insanity is not.

Thus, while the evidence of a defendant's mental state at the guilt and sanity phases may be overlapping, the defendant's sanity is irrelevant at the guilt phase and evidence tending to prove insanity, as opposed to the absence of a particular mental element of the offense, is inadmissible (§ 28(a)).

Notably, a defendant may suffer from a diagnosable mental illness without being legally insane under the M'Naghten standard. A defendant who elects to plead both not guilty and not guilty by reason of insanity may have the opportunity to employ mental state evidence in two different ways. At the guilt phase, the People must prove all elements of the charged offense, including mens rea. The defense may not claim insanity. It may, however, produce lay or expert testimony to rebut the prosecution's showing of the required mental state. If found guilty, at the next phase of trial the defendant bears the burden of proving, by a preponderance of the evidence, that he was legally insane when he committed the crime. (Evid. Code, §§ 115, 522).

Defendant points out that defense counsel objected to the instruction on the presumption of sanity and proposed a clarification. He urges us to hold that the instruction violated his federal constitutional right to due process. The instruction on the presumption of sanity had no bearing on any issue before the jury at the guilt phase of defendant's trial. Nevertheless, defendant fails to establish that he was deprived of due process. Because of the facts and the way this case was tried, the jury was unlikely to have applied the presumption of sanity in a way that unconstitutionally affected the burden of proof.

The jury was instructed on mental illness and its effect on defendant's actual formation of the intent required for murder. The instruction on the conclusive presumption of sanity could be understood to conflict with that instruction. However, defendant did not claim that his mental illness resulted in a general absence of the requisite mental state. His claim was narrower and less directly related to considerations of sanity. He admitted that he intentionally shot the victim, and did not dispute the intent to kill. His argument was that he unreasonably believed in the need to defend himself, and therefore acted without malice and was guilty only of manslaughter.

Presumed sanity is consistent with unreasonable self-defense. A person may be entirely free of any mental disease but actually, although unreasonably, believe in the need for self-defense. Indeed, defendant could not claim unreasonable self-defense based entirely on delusion. His expert was careful to explain that defendant's paranoia was not entirely delusional. In this respect, the presumption of sanity did no harm to the theory of the defense.

Competence to Stand Trial

PC § 1367(a) provides: "A person cannot be tried or adjudged to punishment while that person is mentally incompetent. A defendant is mentally incompetent for purposes of this chapter if, as a result of mental disorder or developmental disability, the defendant is unable to understand the nature of the criminal proceedings or to assist counsel in the conduct of a defense in a rational manner."

If a judge has doubts about a defendant's competence to stand trial, the judge orders a psychological evaluation of the defendant.[72] The criminal proceeding is suspended during the evaluation. A trial may be held to adjudicate competence. At the trial, the defendant is presumed competent, and incompetence must be established by a preponderance of the evidence.[73] If defendant is incompetent to stand trial, defendant is committed to an institution for treatment. If the defendant becomes competent to stand trial, the prosecution resumes.

The Insanity Defense

Insanity is an excuse defense. In the United States, there are four approaches to the insanity defense: (1) M'Naghten; (2) M'Naghten plus irresistible impulse; (3) the Model Penal Code, and (4) the "product rule." The Rhode Island Supreme Court's decision in *State v. Johnson* describes the insanity defense.

STATE V. JOHNSON

Rhode Island Supreme Court
121 R.I. 254, 399 A.2d 469 (1979)

DORIS, JUSTICE.

The sole issue presented by this appeal is whether this court should abandon the M'Naghten test in favor of a new standard for determining the criminal responsibility of those who claim they are blameless by reason of mental illness. For the reasons stated herein, we have concluded that the time has arrived to modernize our rule governing this subject.

Before punishing one who has invaded a protected interest, the criminal law generally requires some showing of culpability in the offender. The requirement of a *mens rea*, or guilty mind, is the most notable example of the concept that before punishment may be exacted, blameworthiness must be demonstrated. That some deterrent, restraint, or rehabilitative purpose may be served is alone insufficient. It has been stated that the criminal law reflects the moral sense of the community. The fact that the law has, for centuries, regarded certain wrongdoers as improper subjects for punishment is a testament to the extent to which that moral sense has developed. Thus, society has recognized over the years that none of the three asserted purposes of the criminal law rehabilitation, deterrence and

[72] *See* California Criminal Rules of Court 4.130(b)(1), "The court must initiate mental competency proceedings if the judge has a reasonable doubt, based on substantial evidence, about the defendant's competence to stand trial."

[73] *See* California Criminal Rules of Court 4.130(e)(2).

retribution is satisfied when the truly irresponsible, those who lack substantial capacity to control their actions, are punished. The law appreciates that those who are substantially unable to restrain their conduct are, by definition, incapable of being deterred and their punishment in a correctional institution provides no example for others.

The law of criminal responsibility has its roots in the concept of free will. As Mr. Justice Jackson stated: "How far one by an exercise of free will may determine his general destiny or his course in a particular matter and how far he is the toy of circumstance has been debated through the ages by theologians, philosophers, and scientists. Whatever doubts they have entertained as to the matter, the practical business of government and administration of the law is obliged to proceed on more or less rough and ready judgments based on the assumption that mature and rational persons are in control of their own conduct." Gregg Cartage & Storage Co. v. United States, 316 U.S. 74, 79–80 (1942).

Our law proceeds from this postulate and seeks to fashion a standard by which criminal offenders whose free will has been sufficiently impaired can be identified and treated in a manner that is both humane and beneficial to society at large. The problem has been aptly described as distinguishing between those cases for which a correctional-punitive disposition is appropriate and those in which a medical-custodial disposition is the only kind that is legally permissible.

Daniel M'Naghten attempted to assassinate Sir Robert Peel, Prime Minister of England, but mistakenly shot Peel's private secretary instead. This assassination had been preceded by several attempts on the lives of members of the English Royal House, including Queen Victoria herself. After the jury acquitted M'Naghten the public indignation, spearheaded by the Queen, was so pronounced that the Judges of England were summoned before the House of Lords to justify their actions. In an extraordinary advisory opinion, issued in a pressure-charged atmosphere, Lord Chief Justice Tindal, speaking for all but one of the 15 judges articulated what has become known as the M'Naghten rules: "To establish a defense on the ground of insanity it must be clearly proved that, at the time of committing the act, the party accused was laboring under such a defect of reason, from disease of the mind, as not to know the nature and quality of the act he was doing, or if he did know it, that he did not know that what he was doing was wrong." This dual-pronged test, issued in response to the outrage of a frightened Queen, rapidly became the predominant rule in the United States.

The M'Naghten rule has been the subject of considerable criticism and controversy for over a century. The test's emphasis upon knowledge of right or wrong abstracts a single element of personality as the sole symptom or manifestation of mental illness. M'Naghten refuses to recognize volitional or emotional impairments, viewing the cognitive element as the singular cause of conduct.

M'Naghten has been further criticized for being predicated upon an outmoded psychological concept because modern science recognizes that "insanity" affects the whole personality of the defendant, including the will and emotions. One of the most frequent criticisms of M'Naghten has been directed at its all-or-nothing approach, requiring total incapacity of cognition. We agree that nothing makes the inquiry into responsibility more unreal for the psychiatrist than limitation of the issue to some ultimate extreme of total incapacity, when clinical experience reveals only a graded scale with marks along the way. The law must recognize that when there is no black and white it must content itself with different shades of gray.

Responding to criticism of M'Naghten as a narrow and harsh rule, several courts supplemented it with the "irresistible impulse" test. With this combined approach, courts inquire into both the cognitive and volitional components of the defendant's behavior. Although a theoretical advance over the stringent right and wrong test, the irresistible impulse doctrine has also been the subject of widespread criticism. Similar to M'Naghten's absolutist view of capacity to know, the irresistible impulse is considered in terms of a complete destruction of the governing power of the mind. A more fundamental objection is that the test produces the misleading notion that a crime impulsively committed must have been perpetrated in a sudden and explosive fit. Thus, the irresistible impulse test excludes those far more numerous instances of crimes committed after excessive brooding and melancholy by one who is unable to resist sustained psychic compulsion or to make any real attempt to control his conduct.

The most significant break in the century-old stranglehold of M'Naghten came in 1954 when the Court of Appeals for the District of Columbia declared that, an accused is not criminally responsible if his unlawful act was the product of mental disease or mental defect. Durham v. United States, 214 F.2d 862 (D.C. Cir. 1954). Durham generated voluminous commentary and made a major contribution in recasting the law of criminal responsibility. In application, however, the test was plagued by significant deficiencies. The elusive, undefined concept of productivity posed serious problems of causation and gave the jury inadequate guidance. Most troublesome was the test's tendency to result in expert witnesses' usurpation of the jury function. As a result, in Washington v. United States, 390 F.2d 444 (D.C. Cir. 1967), the court took the extreme step of proscribing experts from testifying concerning productivity altogether. Finally, in United States v. Brawner, 471 F.2d 969 (D.C. Cir. 1972), the court abandoned Durham, decrying the "trial by label" that had resulted.

Responding to the criticism of the M'Naghten and irresistible impulse rules, the American Law Institute incorporated a new test of criminal responsibility into its Model Penal Code.[74] The Model Penal Code test has received widespread and evergrowing acceptance. It has been adopted with varying degrees of modification in 26 states and by every federal court of appeals that has addressed the issue. Although no definition can be accurately described as the perfect or ultimate pronouncement, we believe that the Model Penal Code standard represents a significant, positive improvement over our existing rule. Most importantly, it acknowledges that volitional as well as cognitive impairments must be considered by the jury in its resolution of the responsibility issue. The test replaces M'Naghten's unrealistic all-or-nothing approach with the concept of "substantial" capacity. Additionally, the test employs vocabulary sufficiently in the common ken that its use at trial will permit a reasonable three-way dialogue between the law-trained judges and lawyers, the medical-trained experts, and the jury.

We today adopt the Model Penal Code test.

California Statutes on the Insanity Defense

California uses M'Naghten, but not irresistible impulse.[75] PC § 25(b) states: "In any criminal proceeding, including any juvenile court proceeding, in which a plea of not guilty by reason of insanity is entered, this defense shall be found by the trier of fact only when the accused person proves by a preponderance of the evidence that he or she was incapable of knowing or understanding the nature and quality of his or her act and of distinguishing right from wrong at the time of the commission of the offense."

Notice an important difference between M'Naghten and Section 25(b). M'Naghten provides: "the party accused was laboring under such a defect of reason, from disease of the mind, as not to know the nature and quality of the act he was doing, *or* if he did know it, that he did not know that what he was doing was wrong." Section 25(b), by contrast, states, "he or she was incapable of knowing or understanding the nature and quality of his or her act *and* of distinguishing right from wrong at the time of the commission of the offense." M'Naghten uses the word "or." Section 25(b) uses the word "and." In *People v. Skinner* (1985) 39 Cal. 3d 765, 704 P.2d 752, the Supreme Court ruled that use of the word "and" in Section 25(b) was a

[74] "(1) A person is not responsible for criminal conduct if at the time of such conduct, as a result of mental disease or defect, he lacks substantial capacity either to appreciate the criminality (wrongfulness) of his conduct or to conform his conduct to the requirements of law.

"(2) As used in this article, the terms 'mental disease or defect' do not include an abnormality manifested only by repeated criminal or otherwise antisocial conduct." Model Penal Code.

[75] For the history of the insanity defense in California *see People v. Skinner* (1985) 39 Cal. 3d 765, 704 P.2d 752.

result of careless drafting. The Court interpreted Section 25(b) so that "and" means "or." The Court's interpretation makes California law consistent with M'Naghten.

PC § 25.5 states, "In any criminal proceeding in which a plea of not guilty by reason of insanity is entered, this defense shall not be found by the trier of fact solely on the basis of a personality or adjustment disorder, a seizure disorder, or an addiction to, or abuse of, intoxicating substances."

Penal Code § 1026(a) provides, "When a defendant pleads not guilty by reason of insanity, and also joins with it another plea or pleas, the defendant shall first be tried as if only such other plea or pleas had been entered, and in that trial the defendant shall be conclusively presumed to have been sane at the time the offense is alleged to have been committed. If the jury shall find the defendant guilty, or if the defendant pleads only not guilty by reason of insanity, then the question whether the defendant was sane or insane at the time the offense was committed shall be promptly tried, either before the same jury or before a new jury in the discretion of the court. In that trial, the jury shall return a verdict either that the defendant was sane at the time the offense was committed or was insane at the time the offense was committed." If the jury finds the defendant was sane, then the judge imposes sentence. If the jury finds the defendant was insane, then the judge determines whether the defendant has regained sanity. If the defendant is still insane, then the defendant is committed to an institution.

The CALCRIM instruction (3450) on insanity provides in part:

> You have found the defendant guilty of _______. Now you must decide whether (he/she) was legally insane when (he/she) committed the crime[s]. The defendant must prove that it is more likely than not that (he/she) was legally insane when (he/she) committed the crime[s]. The defendant was legally insane if: (1) When (he/she) committed the crime[s], (he/she) had a mental disease or defect; and (2) Because of that disease or defect, (he/she) was incapable of knowing or understanding the nature and quality of (his/her) act or was incapable of knowing or understanding that (his/her) act was morally or legally wrong.
>
> None of the following qualify as a mental disease or defect for purposes of an insanity defense: personality disorder, adjustment disorder; seizure disorder, or an abnormality of personality or character made apparent only by a series of criminal or antisocial acts.
>
> Special rules apply to an insanity defense involving drugs or alcohol. Addiction to or abuse of drugs or intoxicants, by itself, does not qualify as legal insanity. This is true even if the intoxicants cause organic brain damage or a settled mental

disease or defect that lasts after the immediate effects of the intoxicants have worn off. Likewise, a temporary mental condition caused by the recent use of drugs or intoxicants is not legal insanity. If the defendant suffered from a settled mental disease or defect caused by long-term use of drugs or intoxicants, that settled mental disease or defect combined with another mental disease or defect may qualify as legal insanity. A settled mental disease or defect is one that remains after the effect of the drugs or intoxicants has worn off.

PROBLEM ON INSANITY

Dell finished a marathon ten hour session playing the video game Grand Theft Auto: San Andreas. The game engages players in missions to commit murder, drive-by shootings, burglary, theft, and other crimes. Dell had been awake for days due to his use of crystal methamphetamine. Every day for the preceding week, Dell used some combination of methamphetamine, alcohol, ecstasy, crack cocaine, and hallucinogenic mushrooms. Dell was hallucinating during and after completing the video game. Dell heard a little green person telling him, "It's time to do this. You can do this." Dell got in his car and drove to a randomly chosen store. Dell walked into the store wearing a ski mask and carrying a sawed-off shotgun. He demanded money. While waiting for the store clerk to empty the cash register, Dell noticed his car slowly rolling away because he forgot to put it in park. Dell ran after the car without taking any money from the store. Still wearing the ski mask and carrying the shotgun, Dell jumped in the car, which was stopped in the middle of a busy street right in front of a sheriff deputy. Dell took off, followed by the deputy. Dell was arrested following a high speed pursuit. The prosecutor charged Dell with attempted robbery, evading a police officer, and possession of a sawed-off shotgun. Defendant entered a plea of not guilty by reason of insanity. Will the defense work? *People v. Henning* (2009) 178 Cal.App.4th 388, 100 Cal.Rptr.3d 419.

In *Clark v. Arizona*, the U.S. Supreme Court analyzed the constitutionality of an Arizona statute that limited the use at trial of evidence of mental illness.

CLARK V. ARIZONA

Supreme Court of the United States
548 U.S. 735, 126 S.Ct. 2709 (2006)

JUSTICE SOUTER delivered the opinion of the Court.

The case presents two questions: whether due process prohibits Arizona's use of an insanity test stated solely in terms of the capacity to tell whether an act charged as a crime was right or wrong; and whether Arizona violates due process in restricting consideration of defense evidence of mental illness and incapacity to its bearing on a claim of insanity, thus eliminating its significance directly on the issue of the mental element of the crime charged (known in legal shorthand as the *mens rea,* or guilty mind). We hold that there is no violation of due process in either instance.

I

In the early hours of June 21, 2000, Officer Jeffrey Moritz of the Flagstaff Police responded in uniform to complaints that a pickup truck with loud music blaring was circling a residential block. When he located the truck, the officer turned on the emergency lights and siren of his marked patrol car, which prompted petitioner Eric Clark, the truck's driver (then 17), to pull over. Officer Moritz got out of the patrol car and told Clark to stay where he was. Less than a minute later, Clark shot the officer, who died soon after but not before calling the police dispatcher for help. Clark ran away on foot but was arrested later that day with gunpowder residue on his hands; the gun that killed the officer was found nearby, stuffed into a knit cap.

Clark was charged with first-degree murder for intentionally or knowingly killing a law enforcement officer in the line of duty. In March 2001, Clark was found incompetent to stand trial and was committed to a state hospital for treatment, but two years later the same trial court found his competence restored and ordered him to be tried. Clark waived his right to a jury, and the case was heard by the court.

At trial, Clark did not contest the shooting and death, but relied on his undisputed paranoid schizophrenia at the time of the incident in denying that he had the specific intent to shoot a law enforcement officer or knowledge that he was doing so, as required by the statute. Accordingly, the prosecutor offered circumstantial evidence that Clark knew Officer Moritz was a law enforcement officer. The evidence showed that the officer was in uniform at the time, that he caught up with Clark in a marked police car with emergency lights and siren going, and that Clark acknowledged the symbols of police authority and stopped. The testimony for the prosecution indicated that Clark had intentionally lured an officer to the scene to kill him, having told some people a few weeks before the incident that he wanted to shoot police officers. At the close of the State's evidence, the trial court denied Clark's motion for judgment of acquittal for failure to prove intent to kill a law enforcement officer or knowledge that Officer Moritz was a law enforcement officer.

In presenting the defense case, Clark claimed mental illness, which he sought to introduce for two purposes. First, he raised the affirmative defense of insanity, putting the burden on himself to prove by clear and convincing evidence that at the time of the commission of the criminal act he was afflicted with a mental disease or defect of such severity that he did not know the criminal act was wrong. Second, he aimed to rebut the prosecution's evidence of the requisite *mens rea,* that he had acted intentionally or knowingly to kill a law enforcement officer.

The trial court ruled that Clark could not rely on evidence bearing on insanity to dispute the *mens rea.* The court cited *State v. Mott,* 187 Ariz. 536, 931 P.2d 1046, which refused to allow psychiatric testimony to negate specific intent, and held that Arizona does not allow evidence of a defendant's mental disorder short of insanity to negate the *mens rea* element of a crime.

As to his insanity, then, Clark presented testimony from classmates, school officials, and his family describing his increasingly bizarre behavior over the year before the shooting. Witnesses testified, for example, that paranoid delusions led Clark to rig a fishing line with beads and wind chimes at home to alert him to intrusion by invaders, and to keep a bird in his automobile to warn of airborne poison. There was lay and expert testimony that Clark thought Flagstaff was populated with "aliens" (some impersonating government agents), the "aliens" were trying to kill him, and bullets were the only way to stop them. A psychiatrist testified that Clark was suffering from paranoid schizophrenia with delusions about "aliens" when he killed Officer Moritz, and he concluded that Clark was incapable of luring the officer or understanding right from wrong and that he was thus insane at the time of the killing. In rebuttal, a psychiatrist for the State gave his opinion that Clark's paranoid schizophrenia did not keep him from appreciating the wrongfulness of his conduct, as shown by his actions before and after the shooting (such as circling the residential block with music blaring as if to lure the police to intervene, evading the police after the shooting, and hiding the gun).

The judge then issued a special verdict of first-degree murder, expressly finding that Clark shot and caused the death of Officer Moritz beyond a reasonable doubt and that Clark had not shown that he was insane at the time. The judge noted that though Clark was indisputably afflicted with paranoid schizophrenia at the time of the shooting, the mental illness "did not distort his perception of reality so severely that he did not know his actions were wrong."

Clark moved to vacate the judgment and sentence, arguing, among other things, that Arizona's insanity test and its *Mott* rule each violate due process. As to the insanity standard, Clark claimed (as he had argued earlier) that the Arizona Legislature had impermissibly narrowed its standard in 1993 when it eliminated the first part of the two-part insanity test announced in *M'Naghten's Case.* The court denied the motion.

We granted certiorari to decide whether due process prohibits Arizona from thus narrowing its insanity test or from excluding evidence of mental illness and incapacity due to mental illness to rebut evidence of the requisite criminal intent. We now affirm.

II

Clark first says that Arizona's definition of insanity, being only a fragment of the Victorian standard from which it derives, violates due process. The landmark English rule in *M'Naghten's Case, supra,* states that "the jurors ought to be told that to establish a defence on the ground of insanity, it must be clearly proved that, at the time of the committing of the act, the party accused was laboring under such a defect of reason, from disease of the mind, as not to know the nature and quality of the act he was doing; or, if he did know it, that he did not know he was doing what was wrong."

The first part asks about cognitive capacity: whether a mental defect leaves a defendant unable to understand what he is doing. The second part presents an ostensibly alternative basis for recognizing a defense of insanity understood as a lack of moral capacity: whether a mental disease or defect leaves a defendant unable to understand that his action is wrong.

When the Arizona Legislature first codified an insanity rule, it adopted the full *M'Naghten* statement. In 1993, the legislature dropped the cognitive incapacity part, leaving only moral incapacity as the nub of the stated definition. Under current Arizona law, a defendant will not be adjudged insane unless he demonstrates that "at the time of the commission of the criminal act he was afflicted with a mental disease or defect of such severity that he did not know the criminal act was wrong,"

Clark challenges the 1993 amendment excising the express reference to the cognitive incapacity element. He insists that the side-by-side *M'Naghten* test represents the minimum that a government must provide in recognizing an alternative to criminal responsibility on grounds of mental illness or defect, and he argues that elimination of the *M'Naghten* reference to nature and quality offends a principle of justice so rooted in the traditions and conscience of our people as to be ranked as fundamental.

History shows no deference to *M'Naghten* that could elevate its formula to the level of fundamental principle, so as to limit the traditional recognition of a State's capacity to define crimes and defenses.

Even a cursory examination of the traditional Anglo-American approaches to insanity reveals significant differences among them, with four traditional strains variously combined to yield a diversity of American standards. The main variants are the cognitive incapacity, the moral incapacity, the volitional incapacity, and the product-of-mental-illness tests. The first two emanate from the alternatives stated in the *M'Naghten* rule. The volitional incapacity or irresistible-impulse test, which surfaced over two centuries ago (first in England, then in this country), asks whether a person was so lacking in volition due to a mental defect or illness that he could not have controlled his actions. And the product-of-mental-illness test was used as early as 1870, and simply asks whether a person's action was a product of a mental disease or defect. Fourteen jurisdictions, inspired by the Model Penal Code, have in place an amalgam of the volitional incapacity test and some variant of the moral incapacity test, satisfaction of either (generally by showing a defendant's substantial lack of capacity) being enough to excuse. The alternatives are multiplied further by variations in the prescribed insanity verdict: a significant number of these jurisdictions supplement the traditional "not guilty by reason of insanity" verdict with an alternative of "guilty but mentally ill." Four States have no affirmative insanity defense, though one provides for a "guilty and mentally ill" verdict. These four, like a number of others that recognize an affirmative insanity defense, allow consideration of evidence of mental illness directly on the element of *mens rea* defining the offense.

With this varied background, it is clear that no particular formulation has evolved into a baseline for due process, and that the insanity rule, like the conceptualization of criminal offenses, is substantially open to state choice.

We are satisfied that neither in theory nor in practice did Arizona's 1993 abridgment of the insanity formulation deprive Clark of due process.

III

Clark's second claim of a due process violation challenges the rule adopted by the Supreme Court of Arizona in *State v. Mott.* This case ruled on the admissibility of testimony from a psychologist offered to show that the defendant suffered from battered women's syndrome and therefore lacked the capacity to form the *mens rea* of the crime charged against her. The opinion variously referred to the testimony in issue as "psychological testimony," and "expert testimony," The state court held that testimony of a professional psychologist or psychiatrist about a defendant's mental incapacity owing to mental disease or defect was admissible, and could be considered, only for its bearing on an insanity defense; such evidence could not be considered on the element of *mens rea,* that is, what the State must show about a defendant's mental state (such as intent or understanding) when he performed the act charged against him.

Understanding Clark's claim requires attention to the categories of evidence with a potential bearing on *mens rea*. First, there is "observation evidence" in the everyday sense, testimony from those who observed what Clark did and heard what he said; this category would also include testimony that an expert witness might give about Clark's tendency to think in a certain way and his behavioral characteristics. This evidence may support a professional diagnosis of mental disease and in any event is the kind of evidence that can be relevant to show what in fact was on Clark's mind when he fired the gun. Observation evidence in the record covers Clark's behavior at home and with friends, his expressions of belief around the time of the killing that "aliens" were inhabiting the bodies of local people (including government agents), his driving around the neighborhood before the police arrived, and so on. Observation evidence can be presented by either lay or expert witnesses.

Second, there is "mental-disease evidence" in the form of opinion testimony that Clark suffered from a mental disease with features described by the witness. As was true here, this evidence characteristically but not always comes from professional psychologists or psychiatrists who testify as expert witnesses and base their opinions in part on examination of a defendant, usually conducted after the events in question. The thrust of this evidence was that, based on factual reports, professional observations, and tests, Clark was psychotic at the time in question, with a condition that fell within the category of schizophrenia.

Third, there is evidence we will refer to as "capacity evidence" about a defendant's capacity for cognition and moral judgment (and ultimately also his capacity to form *mens rea*). This, too, is opinion evidence. Here, as it usually does, this testimony came from the same experts and concentrated on those specific details of the mental condition that make the difference between sanity and insanity under the Arizona definition. In their respective testimony on these details the experts disagreed: the defense expert gave his opinion that the symptoms or effects of the disease in Clark's case included inability to appreciate the nature of his action and to tell that it was wrong, whereas the State's psychiatrist was of the view that Clark was a schizophrenic who was still sufficiently able to appreciate the reality of shooting the officer and to know that it was wrong to do that.

It is clear that *Mott* itself imposed no restriction on considering evidence of the first sort, the observation evidence. We read the *Mott* restriction to apply, rather, to evidence addressing the two issues in testimony that characteristically comes only from psychologists or psychiatrists qualified to give opinions as expert witnesses: mental-disease evidence (whether at the time of the crime a defendant suffered from a mental disease or defect, such as schizophrenia) and capacity evidence (whether the disease or defect left him incapable of performing or experiencing a mental process defined as necessary for sanity such as appreciating the nature and quality of his act and knowing that it was wrong).

Mott was careful to distinguish this kind of opinion evidence from observation evidence generally and even from observation evidence that an expert witness might offer, such as descriptions of a defendant's tendency to think in a certain way or his behavioral characteristics; the Arizona court made it clear that this sort of testimony was perfectly admissible to rebut the prosecution's evidence of *mens rea,* Thus, only opinion testimony going to mental defect or disease, and its effect on the cognitive or moral capacities on which sanity depends under the Arizona rule, is restricted.

In this case, the trial court seems to have applied the *Mott* restriction to all evidence offered by Clark for the purpose of showing what he called his inability to form the required *mens rea,* (that is, an intent to kill a police officer on duty, or an understanding that he was engaging in the act of killing such an officer). Thus, the trial court's restriction may have covered not only mental-disease and capacity evidence as just defined, but also observation evidence offered by lay (and expert) witnesses who described Clark's unusual behavior.

Clark's argument that the *Mott* rule violates the Fourteenth Amendment guarantee of due process turns on the application of the presumption of innocence in criminal cases, the presumption of sanity, and the principle that a criminal defendant is entitled to present relevant and favorable evidence on an element of the offense charged against him.

The first presumption is that a defendant is innocent unless and until the government proves beyond a reasonable doubt each element of the offense charged, including the mental element or *mens rea.* As applied to *mens rea* (and every other element), the force of the presumption of innocence is measured by the force of the showing needed to overcome it, which is proof beyond a reasonable doubt that a defendant's state of mind was in fact what the charge states.

The presumption of sanity is equally universal in some variety or other, being (at least) a presumption that a defendant has the capacity to form the *mens rea* necessary for a verdict of guilt and the consequent criminal responsibility. This presumption dispenses with a requirement on the government's part to include as an element of every criminal charge an allegation that the defendant had such a capacity. The force of this presumption, like the presumption of innocence, is measured by the quantum of evidence necessary to overcome it; unlike the presumption of innocence, however, the force of the presumption of sanity varies across the many state and federal jurisdictions, and prior law has recognized considerable leeway on the part of the legislative branch in defining the presumption's strength through the kind of evidence and degree of persuasiveness necessary to overcome it.

There are two points where the sanity or capacity presumption may be placed in issue. First, a State may allow a defendant to introduce (and a factfinder to consider) evidence of mental disease or incapacity for the bearing it can have on the government's burden to show *mens rea.* In such States the evidence showing incapacity to form the guilty state of mind, for example, qualifies the probative force of other evidence, which considered alone indicates that the defendant actually formed the guilty state of mind. If it is shown that a defendant with mental disease thinks all blond people are robots, he could not have intended to kill a person when he shot a man with blond hair, even though he seemed to act like a man shooting another man. In jurisdictions that allow mental-disease and capacity evidence to be considered on par with any other relevant evidence when deciding whether the prosecution has proven *mens rea* beyond a reasonable doubt, the evidence of mental disease or incapacity need only support what the factfinder regards as a reasonable doubt about the capacity to form (or the actual formation of) the *mens rea,* in order to require acquittal of the charge. Thus, in these States the strength of the presumption of sanity is no greater than the strength of the evidence of abnormal mental state that the factfinder thinks is enough to raise a reasonable doubt.

The second point where the force of the presumption of sanity may be tested is in the consideration of a defense of insanity raised by a defendant. Insanity rules like *M'Naghten* and the variants discussed in Part II, *supra,* are attempts to define, or at least to indicate, the kinds of mental differences that overcome the presumption of sanity or capacity and therefore excuse a defendant from customary criminal responsibility, even if the prosecution has otherwise overcome the presumption of innocence by convincing the factfinder of all the elements charged beyond a reasonable doubt. The burden that must be carried by a defendant who raises the insanity issue, again, defines the strength of the sanity presumption. A State may provide, for example, that whenever the defendant raises a claim of insanity by some quantum of credible evidence, the presumption disappears and the government must prove sanity to a specified degree of certainty. Or a jurisdiction may place the burden of persuasion on a defendant to prove insanity as the applicable law defines it, whether by a preponderance of the evidence or to some more convincing degree.

The third principle implicated by Clark's argument is a defendant's right as a matter of simple due process to present evidence favorable to himself on an element that must be proven to convict him. As already noted, evidence tending to show that a defendant suffers from mental disease and lacks capacity to form *mens rea* is relevant to rebut evidence that he did in fact form the required *mens rea* at the time in question; this is the reason that Clark claims a right to require the factfinder in this case to consider testimony about his mental illness and his incapacity directly, when weighing the persuasiveness of other evidence tending to show *mens rea,* which the prosecution has the burden to prove.

As Clark recognizes, however, the right to introduce relevant evidence can be curtailed if there is a good reason for doing that. While the Constitution prohibits the exclusion of defense evidence under rules that serve no legitimate purpose or that are disproportionate to the ends that they are asserted to promote, well-established rules of evidence permit trial judges to exclude evidence if its probative value is outweighed by certain other factors such as unfair prejudice, confusion of the issues, or potential to mislead the jury. And if evidence may be kept out entirely, its consideration may be subject to limitation, which Arizona claims the power to impose here. State law says that evidence of mental disease and incapacity may be introduced and considered, and if sufficiently forceful to satisfy the defendant's burden of proof under the insanity rule it will displace the presumption of sanity and excuse from criminal responsibility. But mental-disease and capacity evidence may be considered only for its bearing on the insanity defense, and it will avail a defendant only if it is persuasive enough to satisfy the defendant's burden as defined by the terms of that defense. The mental-disease and capacity evidence is thus being channeled or restricted to one issue and given effect only if the defendant carries the burden to convince the factfinder of insanity; the evidence is not being excluded entirely, and the question is whether reasons for requiring it to be channeled and restricted are good enough to satisfy the standard of fundamental fairness that due process requires. We think they are.

The first reason supporting the *Mott* rule is Arizona's authority to define its presumption of sanity (or capacity or responsibility) by choosing an insanity definition, as discussed in Part II, *supra,* and by placing the burden of persuasion on defendants who claim incapacity as an excuse from customary criminal responsibility. No one, certainly not Clark here, denies that a State may place a burden of persuasion on a defendant claiming insanity. And Clark presses no objection to Arizona's decision to require persuasion to a clear and convincing degree before the presumption of sanity and normal responsibility is overcome.

But if a State is to have this authority in practice as well as in theory, it must be able to deny a defendant the opportunity to displace the presumption of sanity more easily when addressing a different issue in the course of the criminal trial. Yet, as we have explained, just such an opportunity would be available if expert testimony of mental disease and incapacity could be considered for whatever a factfinder might think it was worth on the issue of *mens rea*. As we mentioned, the presumption of sanity would then be only as strong as the evidence a factfinder would accept as enough to raise a reasonable doubt about *mens rea* for the crime charged; once reasonable doubt was found, acquittal would be required, and the standards established for the defense of insanity would go by the boards.

Are there, characteristics of mental-disease and capacity evidence giving rise to risks that may reasonably be hedged by channeling the consideration of such evidence to the insanity issue on which, in States like Arizona, a defendant has the burden of persuasion? We think there are: in the controversial character of some categories of mental disease, in the potential of mental-disease evidence to mislead, and in the danger of according greater certainty to capacity evidence than experts claim for it.

Arizona's rule serves to preserve the State's chosen standard for recognizing insanity as a defense and to avoid confusion and misunderstanding on the part of jurors. For these reasons, there is no violation of due process.

JUSTICE KENNEDY, dissenting.

In my submission the Court is incorrect in holding that Arizona may convict petitioner Eric Clark of first-degree murder for the intentional or knowing killing of a police officer when Clark was not permitted to introduce critical and reliable evidence showing he did not have that intent or knowledge.

INFANCY

At common law, children below age 7 were conclusively presumed incapable of forming criminal intent. Between 7 and 14, there was a rebuttable presumption the minor was incapable of forming intent. The prosecutor could rebut the presumption with proper evidence.

PC § 26(One) provides, "All persons are capable of committing crimes except those belonging to the following classes: One—Children under the age of 14, in the absence of clear proof that at the time of committing the act charged against them, they knew its wrongfulness." Section 26 provides a rebuttable presumption that a child under 14 years of age cannot commit a crime. The Supreme Court discussed the "infancy defense" in *People v. Cottone* (2013) 57 Cal. 4th 269, 303 P.3d 1163, 159 Cal. Rptr. 3d 385, where the court wrote:

> Penal Code section 26(One) creates a rebuttable presumption that a child under 14 is incapable of committing a crime. The prosecution may rebut Penal Code section 26(One)'s presumption of incapacity by producing clear proof that the minor appreciated the wrongfulness of the conduct when it was committed, as demonstrated by the child's age, experience, conduct, and knowledge. Clear proof in this context means clear and convincing evidence. While knowledge of wrongfulness may not be inferred from the act alone, the attendant circumstances of the crime, such as its preparation, the particular method of its commission, and its concealment may be considered. Moreover, a minor's age is a basic fact and important consideration, and, as recognized by the common law, it is only reasonable to expect that generally the older a child gets and the closer he approaches the age of 14, the more likely it is that he appreciates the wrongfulness of his acts.

Early in the 20th Century, California (and all other states) created a juvenile court, with jurisdiction over three groups of children: (1) delinquent children; (2) status offenders; and (3) abused and neglected children. Delinquency proceedings in juvenile court are civil rather than criminal. Nevertheless, the PC § 26(One) presumption that a child under fourteen is incapable of committing crime applies in juvenile court delinquency proceedings.

ENTRAPMENT

The entrapment defense is intended to discourage police misconduct. When the police entrap an innocent person into committing a crime, the entrapped individual may raise the entrapment defense to thwart prosecution.[76] Entrapment is an affirmative defense, and in California the defendant has the burden of proving entrapment by a preponderance of the evidence.

In the United States there are two approaches to entrapment, referred to as the "subjective" and the "objective" approaches. The subjective approach is used by federal courts and a majority states. The objective approach is used in California and a minority of other states. The Model Penal Code uses the objective approach.

With the subjective approach, the court asks two questions. First, was the crime induced by officers of the government? Second, was the defendant predisposed to commit the offense? The approach is "subjective" because it examines the defendant's subjective predisposition to commit the crime. With the subjective approach, evidence of the defendant's criminal history is relevant if it sheds light on predisposition. Professor Wayne R. LaFave writes, "The emphasis under the subjective approach is clearly upon the defendant's propensity to commit the offense rather than on the officer's misconduct."[77]

With the objective approach the focus is less on defendant's predisposition and more on the police conduct. Did the police create a strong likelihood that the offense would be committed by an innocent person, as opposed to someone ready and willing to break the law?

In *Sorrells v. Unites States*, the Supreme Court decided an entrapment case using the subjective approach.

SORRELLS V. UNITED STATES

Supreme Court of the United States
287 U.S. 435, 53 S.Ct. 210 (1932)

MR. CHIEF JUSTICE HUGHES delivered the opinion of the Court.

Defendant was indicted on two counts (1) for possessing and (2) for selling, on July 13, 1930, one-half gallon of whisky in violation of the National Prohibition Act (27 USCA). He pleaded not guilty. Upon the trial

---

[76] So-called "derivative entrapment" occurs when a government agent uses an unsuspecting middleman to entrap the defendant. *See United States v. Diaz-Castro* (C.A. 1st Cir. 2014) 752 F.3d 101.

[77] Wayne R. LaFave, *Criminal Law* § 9.8(b), p. 537 (5th ed. 2010) (West).

he relied upon the defense of entrapment. The court refused to sustain the defense, denying a motion to direct a verdict in favor of defendant and also refusing to submit the issue of entrapment to the jury. The court ruled that "as a matter of law" there was no entrapment. Verdict of guilty followed.

The substance of the testimony at the trial as to entrapment was as follows: For the government, one Martin, a prohibition agent, testified that having resided for a time in Haywood county, N.C., where he posed as a tourist, he visited defendant's home near Canton, on Sunday, July 13, 1930, accompanied by three residents of the county who knew the defendant well. He was introduced as a resident of Charlotte who was stopping for a time at Clyde. The witness ascertained that defendant was a veteran of the World War and a former member of the Thirtieth Division A.E.F. Witness informed defendant that he was also an ex-service man and a former member of the same Division, which was true. Witness asked defendant if he could get the witness some liquor and defendant stated that he did not have any. Later there was a second request without result. One of those present, one Jones, was also an ex-service man and a former member of the Thirtieth Division, and the conversation turned to the war experiences of the three. After this, witness asked defendant for a third time to get him some liquor, whereupon defendant left his home and after a few minutes came back with a half gallon of liquor for which the witness paid defendant $5. Martin also testified that he was "the first and only person among those present at the time who said anything about securing some liquor," and that his purpose was to prosecute the defendant for procuring and selling it. The government rested its case on Martin's testimony.

Defendant called as witnesses the three persons who had accompanied the prohibition agent. In substance, they corroborated the latter's story but with some additions. Jones, a railroad employee, testified that he had introduced the agent to the defendant "as a furniture dealer of Charlotte," because the agent had so represented himself; that witness told defendant that the agent was "an old 30th Division man" and the agent thereupon said to defendant that he "would like to get a half gallon of whisky to take back to Charlotte to a friend" of his that was in the furniture business with him, and that defendant replied that he "did not fool with whisky"; that the agent and his companions were at defendant's home "for probably an hour or an hour and a half and that during such time the agent asked the defendant three or four or probably five times to get him, the agent, some liquor." Defendant said "he would go and see if he could get a half gallon of liquor," and he returned with it after an absence of "between twenty and thirty minutes." Jones added that at that time he had never heard of defendant being in the liquor business, that he and the defendant were "two old buddies," and that he believed "one former war buddy would get liquor for another."

Another witness, the timekeeper and assistant paymaster of the Champion Fibre Company at Canton, testified that defendant was an employee of that company and had been "on his job continuously without missing a pay day since March, 1924." Witness identified the time sheet showing this employment. This witness and three others who were neighbors of the defendant and had known him for many years testified to his good character.

To rebut this testimony, the government called three witnesses who testified that the defendant had the general reputation of a rum runner. There was no evidence that the defendant had ever possessed or sold any intoxicating liquor prior to the transaction in question.

It is clear that the evidence was sufficient to warrant a finding that the act for which defendant was prosecuted was instigated by the prohibition agent, that it was the creature of his purpose, that defendant had no previous disposition to commit it but was an industrious, law-abiding citizen, and that the agent lured defendant, otherwise innocent, to its commission by repeated and persistent solicitation in which he succeeded by taking advantage of the sentiment aroused by reminiscences of their experiences as companions in arms in the World War. Such a gross abuse of authority given for the purpose of detecting and punishing crime, and not for the making of criminals, deserves the severest condemnation; but the question whether it precludes prosecution or affords a ground of defense, and, if so, upon what theory, has given rise to conflicting opinions.

It is well settled that the fact that officers or employees of the government merely afford opportunities or facilities for the commission of the offense does not defeat the prosecution. Artifice and stratagem may be employed to catch those engaged in criminal enterprises. The appropriate object of this permitted activity, frequently essential to the enforcement of the law, is to reveal the criminal design; to expose the illicit traffic, the prohibited publication, the fraudulent use of the mails, the illegal conspiracy, or other offenses, and thus to disclose the would-be violators of the law. A different question is presented when the criminal design originates with the officials of the government, and they implant in the mind of an innocent person the disposition to commit the alleged offense and induce its commission in order that they may prosecute.

The argument, from the standpoint of principle, is that the court is called upon to try the accused for a particular offense which is defined by statute and that, if the evidence shows that this offense has knowingly been committed, it matters not that its commission was induced by officers of the government in the manner and circumstances assumed. It is said that where one intentionally does an act in circumstances known to him, and the particular conduct is forbidden by the law in those circumstances, he intentionally breaks the law in the only sense in which the law considers intent. Moreover, that as the statute is designed to redress a public wrong, and not a private injury, there is no ground for holding the government estopped by the conduct of its officers from prosecuting the offender. To the suggestion of public policy the objectors answer that the Legislature, acting within its constitutional authority, is the arbiter of public policy and that, where conduct is expressly forbidden and penalized by a valid statute, the courts are not at liberty to disregard the law and to bar a prosecution for its violation because they are of the opinion that the crime has been instigated by government officials.

It is manifest that these arguments rest entirely upon the letter of the statute. They take no account of the fact that its application in the circumstances under consideration is foreign to its purpose; that such an application is so shocking to the sense of justice that it has been urged that it is the duty of the court to stop the prosecution in the interest of the government itself, to protect it from the illegal conduct of its officers and to preserve the purity of its courts. But can an application of the statute having such an effect—creating a situation so contrary to the purpose of the law and so inconsistent with its proper enforcement as to invoke such a challenge—fairly be deemed to be within its intendment?

We are unable to conclude that it was the intention of the Congress in enacting this statute that its processes of detection and enforcement should be abused by the instigation by government officials of an act on the part of persons otherwise innocent in order to lure them to its commission and to punish them. We are not forced by the letter to do violence to the spirit and purpose of the statute. This, we think, has been the underlying and controlling thought in the suggestions in judicial opinions that the government in such a case is estopped to prosecute or that the courts should bar the prosecution.

The argument is pressed that if the defense is available it will lead to the introduction of issues of a collateral character relating to the activities of the officials of the government and to the conduct and purposes of the defendant previous to the alleged offense. For the defense of entrapment is not simply that the particular act was committed at the instance of government officials. That is often the case where the proper action of these officials leads to the revelation of criminal enterprises. The predisposition and criminal design of the defendant are relevant. But the issues raised and the evidence adduced must be pertinent to the controlling question whether the defendant is a person otherwise innocent whom the government is seeking to punish for an alleged offense which is the product of the creative activity of its own officials. If that is the fact, common justice requires that the accused be permitted to prove it. The government in such a case is in no position to object to evidence of the activities of its representatives in relation to the accused, and if the defendant seeks acquittal by reason of entrapment he cannot complain of an appropriate and searching inquiry into his own conduct and predisposition as bearing upon that issue. If in consequence he suffers a disadvantage, he has brought it upon himself by reason of the nature of the defense.

We are of the opinion that upon the evidence produced in the instant case the defense of entrapment was available and that the trial court was in error in holding that as a matter of law there was no entrapment and in refusing to submit the issue to the jury.

The judgment is reversed, and the cause is remanded for further proceedings in conformity with this opinion.

Fast forward from prohibition in the 1920s, to post-9/11 America and the age of terrorism. In *United States v. Cromitie,* the Second Circuit rejected the argument that the FBI entrapped the defendant and his colleagues into a plot to bomb synagogues and fire missiles at military planes.

UNITED STATES V. CROMITIE

United States Court of Appeals, Second Circuit
727 F.3d 194 (2013)

NEWMAN, J.

This is an appeal by four defendants convicted of planning and attempting to carry out domestic terrorism offenses involving a plot to launch missiles at an Air National Guard base at Stewart Airport in Newburgh, NY, and bomb two synagogues in the Bronx. The appeal primarily presents issues concerning the extent to which a government informant may lawfully urge the commission of crimes, issues framed as claims of entrapment as a matter of law and outrageous government conduct in violation of the Due Process Clause. We reject the defendants' claims of entrapment as a matter of law, outrageous government conduct in the instigation of the offenses, and all other claims raised on appeal. We therefore affirm.

All the charged offenses resulted from an elaborate sting operation conducted by the FBI using an undercover informant. An indictment filed in June 2009, charged the four defendants with eight offenses: Count One—conspiracy to use weapons of mass destruction within the United States (18 U.S.C. § 2332a); Counts Two, Three, and Four—attempt to use weapons of mass destruction near or at the Riverdale Temple, in the Bronx, the Riverdale Jewish Center (a synagogue) in the Bronx, and the New York Air National Guard Base at Newburgh, respectively (18 U.S.C. § 2332a); Count Five—conspiracy to acquire and use anti-aircraft missiles (18 U.S.C. § 2332(g)); Count Six—attempt to acquire and use anti-aircraft missiles (18

U.S.C. § 2332(g)); Count Seven—conspiracy to kill officers and employees of the United States (18 U.S.C. §§ 1114, 1117); Count Eight—attempt to kill officers and employees of the United States (18 U.S.C. §§ 1114, 2).

A government confidential informant, Shahed Hussain, conducted an undercover investigation for several months in 2008 and 2009. Hussain is a Pakistani national who was granted asylum by the United States in the mid-1990s based on his claim of political persecution in Pakistan. In 2003, Hussain was convicted of fraud based on his misconduct as a translator working at the Motor Vehicles Bureau in Albany. To avoid being deported, Hussain agreed to cooperate with the Government's investigation of another individual. In the spring of 2007, Hussain became a paid informant of the FBI and started working in the lower Hudson Valley. As the District Court stated, Hussain's goal was to locate disaffected Muslims who might be harboring terrorist designs on the United States.

By June 2008, Hussain had been attending services at a mosque in Newburgh at the direction of the FBI. During that time, the FBI provided a house for Hussain that contained concealed video and audio recording equipment. In addition, the FBI provided Hussain with recording devices for his person and his car. Hussain presented himself at the mosque as a wealthy Pakistani businessman with knowledge of Islamic teachings. During a period of several months, Hussain cultivated a friendship with Cromitie, who subsequently recruited the other three defendants.

Cromitie, 42 years old, was an impoverished man who sustained himself by committing petty drug offenses for which he had repeatedly been caught and convicted. In addition, he worked a night shift at a local Walmart store, earning less than $14,000 per year.

On June 13, 2008, Cromitie walked up to Hussain in the parking lot of the mosque. Hussain testified that Cromitie, in an Arabic accent, introduced himself as Abdul Rahman, and claimed that his father was from Afghanistan. After a short conversation, Hussain drove Cromitie home from the mosque. On the way, Cromitie asked Hussain about violence in Afghanistan that had been reported recently on television. When Hussain asked Cromitie if he would like to travel to Afghanistan, Cromitie responded by saying he would love to. He then said, in the first indication of his proclivity to terrorism, that he wanted "to die like a shahid, a martyr" and "go to paradise," and immediately thereafter said, "I want to do something to America." As he said these words, he pointed his right index finger in the air in a gesture Hussain testified is used by "somebody in radical Islam" to mean "taking an oath in front of Allah to do take part of crime or Jihad act they want to do." During that first encounter, Hussain told Cromitie that a lot of military planes flew from what was later identified as Stewart Airport to take arms and ammunition to Afghanistan and Iraq.

Hussain met with Cromitie three more times in the summer of 2008. Hussain testified that during these meetings Cromitie said that he hated Jews and Americans and that he would kill the President of the United States "700 times because he's an antichrist." After learning of these remarks, the FBI instructed Hussain to tell Cromitie that he, Hussain, was a representative of a terrorist group in Pakistan, Jaish-e-Mohammed ("JeM"). On July 3, 2008, Hussain, following these instructions, Hussain told Cromitie he was flying to Pakistan to meet with JeM and asked Cromitie if he wanted to attend. Cromitie said he did and then volunteered that he wanted to join JeM.

Hussain recorded four conversations with Cromitie in the fall of 2008. In a conversation recorded on October 19, Cromitie said that American Muslims could do something similar to the attacks of September 11, 2001, stating: "If, if the Muslims was to want the United States down, believe me, we can do it. With the regular Muslims here, all somebody has to do is give a good fatwa to the brothers and let, make sure they understand. You, they taking down our Islamic countries. What do we do to make that stop? So, we start taking something down here. You understand what I'm saying?"

In a conversation recorded later that day, Cromitie said, "I have zero tolerance for people who disrespect Muslims."

In a conversation recorded on October 29, Cromitie said, "When the call comes, I'm gonna go, 'Allahu akbar,' and I'm gone. There's nothing no one can do. I'm gonna go all the way. There's no, no turn back." On November 14, Hussain told Cromitie that he could obtain guns and rockets.

In late November, Hussain drove Cromitie to a conference of the Muslim Alliance of North America in Philadelphia. On November 28, during the ride to the conference, Cromitie, in a recorded conversation, boasted that he had stolen three guns from Walmart, two .25 automatics and a snub nose, and had "stashed" them. Also during the ride, Cromitie indicated that he could put "a team together," and said he was "gonna try to put a plan together." Earlier that day, Cromitie for the first time expressed interest in buying "stuff" from Hussain. Hussain had previously told Cromitie that he could get "any stuff that you need," specifically guns and missiles.

On the second day of the conference, November 29, Cromitie's talk became more specific after Hussain asked Cromitie if his "team" had ever "thought about doing something here in the United States." Cromitie responded by saying that his team never considered doing that, but that he had and that he had "been wanting to do that since I was 7." Cromitie claimed that he had bombed a police station in the Bronx in 1994, but wanted to do something "a little bigger," because he had "to make some type of noise to let them know."

Hussain asked Cromitie what targets he wanted to hit in the New York area, and Cromitie said that he wanted to "hit" the George Washington Bridge. When Hussain said that bridges are too hard to hit, Cromitie replied, "Hit some small spots. This had to be a terrorist act."

Later, while Hussain and Cromitie were watching television coverage of a terrorist attack in Mumbai and the funeral of a Jew who had been killed in that attack, Cromitie said: "Look at the Jewish guy. You're not smiling no more, you fucker. I hate those bastards. I hate those motherfuckers. Those fucking Jewish bastards. I'd like to get one of those. I'd like to get a synagogue. Me. Yeah, personally."

Hussain recorded conversations with Cromitie on three occasions in December 2008. On December 5, Cromitie, after quoting a "brother" saying, " 'I think it's time we make jihad right here in America,' " said, "I agree with the brother. It makes sense to me." On December 17, when Hussain said, "Let's pick a target," Cromitie suggested "Stewart Airport."

On December 18, Hussain traveled to Pakistan and returned eight and one-half weeks later.

In a meeting with Cromitie on February 23, 2009, Hussain asked, "The synagogue, where is it in Bronx or in Brooklyn?" Cromitie replied, "There's one in the Bronx, I mean you got like, uh two or three of them in Brooklyn." The next day, Hussain bought Cromitie a camera and drove him to Stewart Airport where they conducted surveillance. While there, Cromitie took photos. Cromitie was recorded stating, "Imagine if we hit all the planes in one spot." He also told Hussain he was going to speak to another man about being a lookout and would "talk to some of the guys" and tell them they would receive $25,000 to "just look out."

Six weeks passed without any contact between Cromitie and Hussain. On April 5, 2009, Cromitie reached out to Hussain. In a recorded conversation, he told Hussain of his financial problems and said, "I have to try to make some money brother." Hussain responded, "I told you, I can make you 250,000 dollars, but you don't want it brother. What can I tell you?" At this, Cromitie answered, "Okay, come see me brother. Come see me."

On April 7, Hussain told Cromitie that JeM had already taken significant steps to support the operation, stating, "The missile was ready." Later in that conversation Cromitie said he would "take down" "a whole synagogue of men." Cromitie and Hussain then discussed the need for lookouts.

On April 10, Hussain picked Cromitie up at Cromitie's house and was introduced to a man standing in front of the house. This man, known as "Daoud," was defendant David Williams. All three men drove to the Riverdale section of the Bronx, where Cromitie photographed the Riverdale

Jewish Center and the Riverdale Temple. Later that day Cromitie took photographs of airplanes at Stewart Airport.

On April 23, the three met again. Cromitie asked at what distance could an IED (improvised explosive device) be detonated. When Hussain said 100 miles and explained, "You can sit down here, and it blows up there," Cromitie and David Williams celebrated by bumping fists. When Hussain said he would train Cromitie how to use a rocket launcher, David Williams said that he wanted to participate. The next day, the three drove to Stewart Airport. David Williams asked Cromitie for the camera and took surveillance pictures. Later, they discussed taking rooms at a nearby Marriott Hotel to hide out after the planned attacks. After Hussain outlined the attack plans, David Williams said the airport attack would be the "tricky one," compared to the synagogue attack, which would be "smooth" because the bombs would be detonated remotely from a hotel.

In less than a week, Cromitie and David Williams recruited defendants Onta Williams and Laguerre Payen. On April 25, in a recorded telephone call David Williams told Cromitie to call Hussain and "tell him I got the other brother." By April 28, when all four defendants met with Hussain, Payen had been recruited. At this meeting, when Cromitie explained that "Yahudi" means "Jews," Payen said, "Yeah you told me that," JA 4079, which permitted the jury to infer that Cromitie had recruited Payen.

Bombing two synagogues and launching Stinger surface-to-air missiles at Stewart Airport was specifically discussed at this meeting. Payen asked how long every job would take; Hussain told him ten minutes.

On May 6, Hussain drove Cromitie, David Williams, and Payen to a warehouse in Stamford, CT, where the FBI had stored three fake bombs and two fake Stinger missiles. Hussain instructed them how to launch the missiles and how to wire the detonating devices for the bombs. After one missile and the bombs were loaded into Hussain's car, the four drove to a storage facility in New Windsor, NY, where Hussain had rented storage lockers. Cromitie, David Williams, and Hussain unloaded the weapons and placed them in the lockers while Payen acted as a lookout. The group then hugged each other and shouted, "Allahu akbar, God is great." Later that night, Payen explained to Onta Williams how the missile operated. At a meeting on May 8, Cromitie told the other defendants that there were 25 thousand balls (ball bearings) in a bomb and that "once them balls go off, they go anywhere." At the end of this meeting, the defendants agreed to carry out the attacks on May 20.

On May 13, all four defendants drove with Hussain to the Riverdale section of the Bronx to conduct surveillance, specifically of the Riverdale Jewish Center. The defendants got out of the car and walked around looking for security cameras on top of nearby buildings. On May 19,

Hussain and the four defendants conducted a final surveillance of Stewart Airport, during which Onta Williams changed the locations of the lookouts for the Airport. The group returned to Hussain's house to review the plans, which were to pick up the bombs at the storage facility, drive to Riverdale to wire them, leave them in cars that the FBI had placed in front of the synagogues, drive back to Newburgh, retrieve the missiles, fire them at the military planes, and detonate the bombs using their cell phones.

On May 20, the four defendants drove with Hussain to the New Windsor storage facility, where they picked up the three bombs and drove to Riverdale. Acting according to their plan, they stopped near where the two cars had been parked by the FBI for the operation, a Pontiac directly in front of the Riverdale Temple and a Mazda directly in front of the Riverdale Jewish Center. Hussain let Onta Williams, David Williams, and Payen out to take up their positions as lookouts. Cromitie then placed one of the fake bombs in the trunk of the Pontiac and two others on the back seat of the Mazda. Moments later, FBI agents arrested all four defendants.

Cromitie presented two witnesses. The personnel manager of the Walmart store where Cromitie had worked testified that the store had stopped selling long guns before the time when Cromitie had told Hussain he had stolen guns for resale and that Cromitie stopped showing up for work in February 2009 and was subsequently fired. A neighbor of Cromitie's testified that Cromitie had sold him the camera that Hussain had purchased and had given to Cromitie for surveillance. The other defendants presented no evidence.

The jury found Cromitie and David Williams guilty on all counts and found Onta Williams and Payen guilty on all counts except Count Eight, which charged attempt to kill officers and employees of the United States. The District Court sentenced each defendant to a 25-year mandatory minimum sentence.

The defendants make three principal claims on appeal: (1) the evidence established entrapment as a matter of law; (2) the Government's conduct in persuading Cromitie and, through him, the other defendants to participate in the plan was outrageous conduct in violation of the Due Process Clause; and (3) the [third issues is not relevant for our purposes.]

A valid entrapment defense has two related elements: government inducement of the crime, and a lack of predisposition on the part of the defendant to engage in criminal conduct. Predisposition, the principal element in the defense of entrapment, focuses upon whether the defendant was an unwary innocent or, instead, an unwary criminal who readily availed himself of the opportunity to perpetrate the crime. The fact that officers or employees of the Government merely afford opportunities or facilities for the commission of the offense does not defeat the prosecution. The defendant has the burden of showing inducement, and, if inducement is shown, the prosecution has the burden of proving predisposition beyond a reasonable doubt.

We doubt that the potential terrorists who are available to be recruited by Al Qaeda or similar groups have already formed a design to bomb specific targets. Their predisposition is to have a state of mind that inclines them to inflict harm on the United States, be willing to die like a martyr, be receptive to a recruiter's presentation, whether over the course of a week or several months, of the specifics on an operational plan, and welcome an invitation to participate. The Air Force personnel at Stewart Airport and the congregants at two synagogues in the Bronx are fortunate that the person who first approached Cromitie and suggested an operational plan was only a Government agent.

Obviously any relevant evidence of what a defendant says or does before first being approached by Government agents is admissible. Not as clearly admissible is evidence of what a defendant says or does after inducement. Although as a general matter a defendant's state of mind can be inferred from his actions and statements, a broad application of that principle would undermine the entrapment defense by permitting any induced conduct to prove predisposition. To guard against that risk, the Supreme Court has required that conduct of a defendant, after contact by Government agents, offered to prove predisposition, must be independent and not the product of the attention that the Government had directed at the defendant. Of course, what a defendant says after contacted by agents is generally admissible to prove predisposition because, although some post-contact conduct might be the product of inducement, it will be a rare situation where a defendant can plausibly claim that the inducement caused him to say something that evidenced predisposition.

The defendants presented their defense of entrapment to the jury through cross-examination and summations. By its verdicts of guilty, the jury rejected the defense. On appeal, the defendants contend that entrapment was established as a matter of law, a claim we understand to mean that on the facts of this case, no reasonable jury could find predisposition beyond a reasonable doubt. We consider this claim first as to Cromitie and then as to the other defendants.

Because the conduct of government agents is the focus of the inducement component of the entrapment defense and is the entirety of a claim of outrageous government conduct, the factual predicates of the entrapment and the due process claims are somewhat related, although the applicable legal principles are distinct. In assessing the inducement component of Cromitie's entrapment claim, we will consider only the facts sufficient to show inducement, leaving the additional details of the Government's alleged misconduct for assessment of the due process claim below.

The Government initially opposes Cromitie's entrapment claim by contending that there was no inducement. In the Government's view, once Cromitie indicated in his first discussion with Hussain that he wanted to "do something to America" and thereafter evinced a willingness to act upon that desire, "any follow-up remarks by Hussain lack the specificity to constitute 'soliciting, proposing, initiating, broaching or suggesting the commission of the offense.'" Although Hussain's efforts to persuade Cromitie do not lack specificity, the Government seems to be arguing that his efforts are not relevant to inducement because Cromitie had the requisite predisposition before their initial meeting on June 13, 2008. However, in this case, Cromitie's statements on that date arguably do not make it clear whether he then had the requisite predisposition. We therefore need to consider what he said and did thereafter, but, as we discuss below, the only post-June 13 statements and actions that can be looked at to give meaning to Cromitie's June 13 statements are those that are independent of any inducement. Hussain's efforts to persuade Cromitie after June 13 are relevant to both inducement and the ultimate issue of predisposition.

In this case, Hussain's efforts to persuade Cromitie constituted inducement. As the District Court—with the benefit of hearing the recorded evidence and seeing the trial witnesses—forcefully stated, "I believe beyond a shadow of a doubt that there would have been no crime here except the government instigated it, planned it, and brought it to fruition." The record fully supports this statement. Hussain's efforts to persuade Cromitie to commit the charged offenses persisted throughout the eleven-month period from their initial meeting until the arrest. In addition to proposing specifics of the planned attacks and supplying bombs and missiles, Hussain's inducements included offers of $250,000, a barber shop at a cost of $70,000, a BMW, and an all-expense-paid, two-week vacation to Puerto Rico for Cromitie and his family. One portion of Hussain's testimony, elicited on redirect examination, is revealing:

Q. "What did the FBI tell you to do?"

A. "The FBI told me to go a little bit harder on him [Cromitie] and put some pressure on him, see where he comes out given the opportunity."

At trial, the Government disputed that Hussain had offered $250,000 to Cromitie. We set forth in detail at this point what the record reveals on this issue because whether Hussain offered Cromitie this amount of money is, or might be, pertinent to three of the defendants' claims. [The court concludes the Government did offer the $25,000.]

With respect to the three means of proving predisposition, it is clear that Cromitie had not engaged in a course of similar conduct prior to the Government's inducement, nor did he readily agree to committing the charged offenses. Thus, the issue becomes whether, prior to inducement, he had an already formed design to commit the crime or similar crimes.

On the first day that Hussain met Cromitie, Hussain quotes Cromitie as saying, "I want to do something to America." The potentially ominous meaning of these words was considerably clarified by Cromitie's immediately preceding statement that he wanted "to die like a shahid, a martyr," and the fact that, as he said them, he pointed his right index finger in the air in a gesture Hussain testified is used "by somebody in radical Islam" to "mean taking an oath in front of Allah to do take part of [sic] crime or Jihad act they want to do." The jury was entitled to think that wanting to die like a martyr, coupled with wanting to do something to America, meant a willingness to be a suicide bomber, even though Cromitie never planned to sacrifice his own life.

Fully indicating that Cromitie's initial statements to Hussain revealed a pre-existing design to commit terrorist acts against the interests of the United States are [other statements, indicated above.] These recorded statements, all of which were independent of any inducement, gave indisputable meaning to Cromitie's initial ominous, though somewhat generalized, words about wanting to "do something to America" and "die like a shahid, a martyr." The later statements also gave the jury ample basis for believing Hussain when he testified about what Cromitie had said to him during their first unrecorded conversation.

Despite moments of wavering, which do not preclude a finding of predisposition, Cromitie revealed his willingness, indeed his eagerness, to commit acts of terrorism through his own recorded statements. Two examples stand out. Referring to the initial conversation with Hussain, Cromitie recalled in a recorded conversation, "You already knew I was like that. It wasn't you who was talking to me, I talked to you about it. When we first met in the parking lot, I talked to you about it." And contemplating that "on the day of judgment" Allah would say that Hussain had enticed him, Cromitie said he would answer, "No! You [Allah] gave me my own will. I did that on my own."

From everything that Cromitie said, the jury was entitled to find that he had a pre-existing design and hence a predisposition to inflict serious harm on interests of the United States, even though Government officers afforded him the opportunity and the pseudo weapons for striking at specific targets. The fact that officers or employees of the Government merely afford opportunities or facilities for the commission of the offense does not defeat the prosecution. It is sufficient if the defendant is of a frame of mind such that once his attention is called to the criminal opportunity, his decision to commit the crime is the product of his own preference and not the product of government persuasion.

[The court rejected the entrapment arguments of the other defendants.]

As a claim distinct from their claim of entrapment as a matter of law, the defendants contend that their convictions should be reversed because the Government's conduct in persuading Cromitie, and the others through Cromitie, to commit the charged offenses was so outrageous as to violate the Due Process Clause. In Hampton v. United States, 425 U.S. 484, 96 S.Ct. 1646 (1976), the Supreme Court, by a vote of 5 to 3, ruled that, even as to a defendant predisposed to commit an offense, outrageous government conduct could invalidate a conviction. The conduct of the law enforcement officials must reach a "demonstrable level of outrageousness before it could bar conviction." We have recognized the same principle. Government involvement in a crime may in theory become so excessive that it violates due process and requires the dismissal of charges against a defendant even if the defendant was not entrapped.

Courts acknowledging the possibility of dismissal for outrageous government conduct have said little about what conduct would be considered constitutionally "outrageous." Whether investigative conduct violates a defendant's right to due process cannot depend on the degree to which the government action was responsible for inducing the defendant to break the law. Rather, the existence of a due process violation must turn on whether the governmental conduct, standing alone, is so offensive that it shocks the conscience regardless of the extent to which it led the defendant to commit his crime.

It does not suffice to show that the government created the opportunity for the offense, even if the government's ploy is elaborate and the engagement with the defendant is extensive. Feigned friendship, cash inducement, and coaching in how to commit the crime do not constitute outrageous conduct.

In asserting their claim of outrageous conduct, all four defendants focus on the Government's role in the planning of, and preparing for, the aborted attacks; Cromitie cites in addition Hussain's suggesting that he had a religious obligation to commit the crimes, exploiting professed love for Hussain, and offering him large financial benefits.

There is no doubt that Government agents planned the entire operation with respect to launching missiles to destroy airplanes at Stewart Airport. The idea of bombing synagogues appears to have originated with Cromitie, although Government agents supplied the fake bombs and instructed the defendants how to detonate them.

JACOBS, CHIEF JUDGE, concurring in part and dissenting in part:

I concur as to the affirmance of the convictions of David Williams, Onta Williams, and Laguerre Payen, and I concur in the majority's rejection of any argument premised on outrageous government misconduct, and its rejection of other defense arguments. I respectfully dissent in part because James Cromitie was entrapped as a matter of law.

In *People v. Watson* the California Supreme Court deployed the objective approach to entrapment.

PEOPLE V. WATSON

California Supreme Court
22 Cal.4th 220, 91 Cal.Rptr.2d 822, 990 P.2d 1031 (2000)

CHIN, J.

One March evening in 1997, Bakersfield police officers conducted a vehicle theft "sting" operation. They staged an arrest of a plainclothes police officer driving a black 1980 Chevrolet Monte Carlo that belonged to the police department. The arresting officers activated the emergency lights and siren of their marked patrol car and stopped the Monte Carlo. The Monte Carlo's driver drove into a parking lot and parked. While a group of spectators watched, a uniformed police officer approached the Monte Carlo, ordered the driver out, patted him down, handcuffed him, placed him in the backseat of the patrol car, and drove away, leaving the Monte Carlo behind. The police left the Monte Carlo unlocked with the keys in the ignition to make it easier to take. They wanted to "give the impression [the driver] was arrested and the vehicle was left there."

A couple of hours later, police arrested defendant after he drove the Monte Carlo from the parking lot. He told the arresting officer that his niece had informed him of the earlier apparent arrest and told him to "come and take" the car. He did just that, intending to use it to "roll," i.e., to drive it.

Defendant was charged with taking a vehicle. The court refused to instruct the jury on entrapment. The jury found defendant guilty. The Court of Appeal reversed the judgment, finding the trial court should have instructed on entrapment. We granted review.

The trial court was required to instruct the jury on the defense of entrapment if, but only if, substantial evidence supported the defense. In California, the test for entrapment focuses on the police conduct and is objective. Entrapment is established if the law enforcement conduct is likely to induce a normally law-abiding person to commit the offense. Such a person would normally resist the temptation to commit a crime presented by the simple opportunity to act unlawfully. Official conduct that does no more than offer that opportunity to the suspect—for example, a decoy program—is therefore permissible; but it is impermissible for the police or their agents to pressure the suspect by overbearing conduct such as badgering, cajoling, importuning, or other affirmative acts likely to induce a normally law-abiding person to commit the crime.

If the actions of the law enforcement agent would generate in a normally law-abiding person a motive for the crime other than ordinary criminal intent, entrapment will be established. Defendant does not rely on this principle. He does not claim his motive in taking the car was other than ordinary criminal intent. Instead, he relies on the [following] principle: affirmative police conduct that would make commission of the crime unusually attractive to a normally law-abiding person will likewise constitute entrapment. Such conduct would include, for example, a guarantee that the act is not illegal or the offense will go undetected, an offer of exorbitant consideration, or any similar enticement. Citing this principle, the Court of Appeal concluded this case warranted an entrapment instruction because the jury might have found that "the police made taking the car unusually attractive" by sending the message, "You can take this car and get away with it." We disagree. Normally, police conduct must be directed at a specific person or persons to constitute entrapment. The police must pressure the suspect by overbearing conduct. Except perhaps in extreme circumstances, the principle is limited to instances of individual, personal enticement, excluding communications made to the world at large. Merely providing people in general an opportunity to commit a crime is not an improper enticement or otherwise entrapment. The rule is clear that ruses, stings, and decoys are permissible stratagems in the enforcement of criminal law, and they become invalid only when badgering or importuning takes place to an extent and degree that is likely to induce an otherwise law-abiding person to commit a crime.

The sting operation in this case presents no evidence of entrapment, both because the police did not specifically intend it as a communication to defendant personally, and because it did not actually *guarantee* anything, but merely conveyed the idea detection was unlikely. The police did nothing more than present to the general community a tempting opportunity to take the Monte Carlo. Some persons, obviously including defendant, might have found the temptation hard to resist. But a person who steals when given the opportunity is an opportunistic thief, not a normally law-abiding person. Specifically, normally law-abiding persons do not take a car not belonging to them merely because it is unlocked with the keys in the ignition and it appears they will not be caught. Defendant presented no evidence of any personal contact whatever between police and himself; certainly he could not show that the police cajoled him, gave him any enticement or guarantee, or even knew or cared who he was.

The trial court correctly refused to instruct the second jury on entrapment. Accordingly, we reverse the judgment of the Court of Appeal and remand the matter for further proceedings consistent with our opinion.

PROBLEMS ON ENTRAPMENT

1. Officer Jones donned shabby old clothes, lay down on a public sidewalk, and pretended to be passed out drunk. Dell came along and said, "Hey dude, you alright?" Jones did not answer. Dell looked around, reached into Jones' pocket, took his wallet, and left, only to be arrested by four police officers watching the whole thing. Dell is charged with theft. Entrapment? *People v. Hanselman* (1888) 76 Cal. 460, 18 P. 425.

2. The police received a tip that Smith was engaged in drug trafficking and home invasion robberies. An undercover police officer pretending to work for a drug dealer met with Smith and asked whether she would be interested in stealing a shipment of cocaine from a rival dealer. Smith told the officer, "I'm a professional. I know what I'm doing. I always use the same crew for this type of job. We have done this many times." Smith and the officer agreed how the cocaine would be split. The officer told Smith the address of the house where the cocaine was located, how many people to expect in the house, and when to strike. The police placed a large amount of cocaine in the house. The cocaine and the house were owned by the police. The police also placed scales and packaging material in the house to make it look like it was used to package drugs. Smith and her "crew" showed up at the house at the appointed hour heavily armed. They went to the front and back doors, which were unlocked. They entered but found no one home. They loaded the cocaine into a white Chevy van and were backing out of the driveway when they were surrounded by police and arrested. Smith and her colleagues are charged with burglary and home invasion robbery. Entrapment? *People v. Smith* (2002) 99 Cal.App.4th 138, 120 Cal.Rptr.2d 831 (not published).

3. Barraza spent much of his life in prison. From his teenage years he was addicted to heroin, and he committed numerous burglaries and thefts to support his drug addiction. During his most recent stint in prison, Barraza decided to "go straight and turn my life around." He participated in drug counseling in prison, and took it seriously. Upon release from prison, Barraza got a job as a client adviser at a drug rehabilitation center. Barraza was doing well, staying clean, working, and paying his bills. Officer Smith had arrested Barraza in the past. Smith didn't believe Barraza was "playing by the rules." Smith got his fellow narcotics officer, Officer Jones, to go undercover and contact Barraza and ask Barraza to buy heroin for him. Jones posed as an addict and approached Barraza at work, asking, "Could you score me some dope? I'm really hurting." Barraza replied, "No man, I don't do that shit no more. I'm clean. Sorry. Can't help you." After this initial contact, Jones contacted Barraza eight times at work, asking him to get drugs for him. Each time Barraza declined. On the ninth request, Barraza told Jones, "Listen man, you need to quit talking to me at work. You're gonna get me fired. I don't do drugs no more, but I'll write a note for you to a friend of mine who can get you something." Barraza wrote the following note for Jones: "Saw Jones. If you have a pair of pants, let him have them. See ya soon, Barraza." (a "pair of pants" was argot for heroin). Barraza is charged with a drug offense.

Entrapment? *People v. Barraza* (1979) 23 Cal.3d 675, 153 Cal.Rptr. 459, 591 P.2d 947.

4. Reed placed an online ad stating that he was seeking a woman of any age to keep up with his sexual appetite. A sheriff's detective trained to investigate crimes against children became interested in the ad because its reference to women of any age might include children. The detective began a correspondence with Reed, representing himself as a woman named Helen Glenn, mother of Rachel and Sandi, aged 12 and 9. "Helen" wrote to Reed that she was interested in finding a man to help her girls with "special education." At first, Reed thought Helen was referring to schooling, but Helen told Reed she wanted a man to teach her daughters "the facts of life." Reed wrote back, "I spent nearly a year teaching my step-nieces the facts of life, and I taught my ex-wife since she was 13." Helen asked Reed what he could teach Rachel and Sandi, and Reed described a broad range of sex acts that "I would be proud to teach the girls." A time and place was arranged for Reed to meet Helen and the girls. Reed arrived and was arrested. Reed is charged with attempted child molestation. Entrapment? *People v. Reed* (1996) 53 Cal.App.4th 389, 61 Cal.Rptr.2d 658.

5. "Dream Girls" is a nightclub licensed to serve food and alcoholic beverages. The club provides adult entertainment. Around midnight, San Diego Police Department detective Nelson did an undercover inspection of Dream Girls. Nelson sat at a table, ordered a beer, and watched dancer Mary Gast perform two dances on stage. After Gast finished on stage, Detective Nelson approached her as she sat at the bar and requested that she perform a "couch dance" for him. Gast escorted Nelson to a couch and danced for him without violating a law that forbids dancers from exposing their breasts, buttocks, or genitals. After finishing the couch dance, Gast asked, "Would you like another?" Nelson replied, "Will there be more skin involved?" Gast performed a second dance, this time exposing her breasts and buttocks to Nelson, and rubbing her breasts against his body. Nelson paid for both dances, and gave Gast a tip. Nelson left the club. The Department of Alcoholic Beverage Control then filed a civil action against Dream Girls seeking to revoke its liquor license based on Gast's illegal couch dance. Entrapment? *Department of Alcoholic Beverage Control v. Alcoholic Beverage Control Appeals Board* (2002) 100 Cal.App.4th 1094, 122 Cal.Rptr.2d 854.

THE SO-CALLED CULTURAL DEFENSE

A person moving to this country may have grown up in a place with very different customs and laws. Behavior that is criminal in the U.S. may be legal "back home." Can a recent arrival on our shores who stands charged with crime argue that she should be acquitted because, in her culture, the conduct is legal? The short answer is no. There is no formally recognized "cultural defense." When in Rome, do as the Romans do. This is not to say, however, that culture plays no role in the criminal justice system. The following excerpt from Taryn Goldstein's law review comment provides insight.

Taryn Goldstein, (Comment) Cultural Conflicts in Court: Should the American Criminal Justice System Formally Recognize a "Cultural Defense"?, 99 *Dickinson Law Review* 141 (1994):

> On January 29, 1985, Fumiko Kimura, a 32-year-old Japanese woman, left her home and took her children on a long bus ride. She abandoned her baby stroller at the bus stop and then walked into the Santa Monica bay, carrying her two young children to their deaths. Mrs. Kimura had become despondent after she had learned of her husband's three year affair. She wanted a means to rid herself of the shame and humiliation of her husband's acts.
>
> The Japanese call it *oyako-shinju*—parent-child suicide—a tragic practice that is all too common. Although *oyako-shinju* is illegal in Japan, survivors are rarely punished due to traditional beliefs about the honor of suicide and the closeness of the parent-child bond. A mother who commits suicide without her children is seen as dooming them to the disgrace of living in an orphanage or with a single parent. She is scorned as *oni no you no hito,* a demon-like person. A woman in Mrs. Kimura's position might be pitied in Japan; the shame of having failed at her own suicide would be regarded as punishment enough.
>
> In this case, the Japanese community rushed to Mrs. Kimura's defense. Four thousand members of the Japanese community signed a petition and sent it to the Los Angeles County district attorney, asking the prosecutor to apply "modern Japanese law" to the case. However, the prosecutor, defense attorney, and presiding judge declined. Mrs. Kimura pleaded not guilty to first degree murder. After entering into a plea bargain, Mrs. Kimura was allowed to plead no contest to lesser voluntary manslaughter charges. The court then sentenced her to one year in prison and five years probation.

In her Comment, Ms. Goldstein described other disturbing cases, including *People v. Moua.* Mr. Moua emigrated to California from the mountains of Laos. He was engaged to a young woman. One day, Moua drove the woman to his cousin's house, where they had sex. The woman accused Moua of rape. In Moua's culture in Laos, there is a custom called marriage by capture. The man takes his future bride to a family member's home, ostensibly against her will. The woman knows the custom, but is expected to protest his sexual advances, while the man's role is not to take "no" for an answer. Once sex occurs, the woman cannot marry anyone else. Mr. Moua pled guilty to misdemeanor false imprisonment, and was sentenced to three months in county jail and a fine of $1,000.

In *People v. Croy* (1985), 41 Cal. 3d 1, 710 P.2d 392, 221 Cal. Rptr. 592, defendant, who was Native American, got off work on Friday, and planned to party with friends. By Sunday evening, defendant had consumed large quantities of alcohol and drugs. Along with friends, defendant got into a disagreement over money with the owner of a liquor store in the small northern California town of Yreka. Defendant had his rifle. Someone said, "I'm going to shoot the sheriff." Police arrived, and defendant and his friends drove away. A police chase ensued, during which someone fired at pursuing officers. Defendant and his friends stopped the car and split up. A gun fight broke out in which a police officer was killed. Defendant was convicted of robbery and murder, but the California Supreme Court reversed the conviction because of incorrect jury instructions. At his retrial, defendant claimed self-defense. To support his claim that defendant believed the police were out to kill him, defendant's attorney persuaded the trial judge to allow expert testimony on the long history of white oppression of Native American peoples, and how this history might impact defendant's thinking. Defendant was acquitted.

In a 1995 article, Holly Maguigan, Cultural Evidence and Male Violence: Are Feminist and Multiculturalist Reformers on a Collision Course in Criminal Courts?, 70 *N.Y.U. L. Rev.* 36 (1995) wrote:

> While both feminists and multiculturalists have advocated for inclusion of a wider variety of voices in American jurisprudence, they recently perceived themselves to be on opposite sides of a vigorously disputed issue: whether to permit criminal defendants to introduce cultural evidence. Some feminists argue that any admissibility of cultural evidence in cases involving male violence against women ultimately condones such violence. Multiculturalists, by contrast, advocate use of cultural information to counteract the injustice of applying the dominant culture's legal standards to defendants from other cultures.

Criminal law does not formally take culture into consideration. Should the answer be different when it comes to a defendant's life circumstances? What of a defendant who grew up in abject poverty, who did not finish high school, whose parents abused her, or who was discriminated against because of the color of her skin? One of the twentieth century's most respected and innovative judges, David Bazelon, opined the answer should be yes. In a dissenting opinion in *United States v. Alexander*, 471 F.2d 923 (D.C. Cir. 1972), Judge Bazelon used the phrase "rotten social background" (471 F.2d at 961) to launch an exegesis on whether systemic racial discrimination and related poverty should bare upon criminal responsibility. Judge Bazelon did not argue discrimination and poverty should completely excuse crime. Rather, he suggested that a rotten social background might, in some circumstances, provide a partial excuse. In a law review article, Judge Bazelon wrote, "In my opinion, it is simply unjust to place people in dehumanizing social conditions, to do nothing about those conditions, and then to command those who suffer, 'Behave—or Else!'" David L. Bazelon, The Morality of the Criminal Law, 49 *So. Cal. L. Rev.* 385, 401–402 (1975–1976).

Judge Bazelon's idea ignited a storm of commentary in the law reviews. See, e.g., Paul H. Robinson, Are We Responsible for Who We Are? The Challenge for Criminal Law Theory in the Defenses of Coercive Indoctrination and "Rotten Social Background," 2 *Ala. C.R. & C.L. Rev.* 53 (2011). The most stalwart critic of Judge Bazelon's idea was Stephen J. Morse. See Stephen J. Morse, The Twilight of Welfare Criminology: A Final Word, 49 *So. Cal. L. Rev.* 53 (1976). Elisabeth Winston Lambert captures the issue nicely in her article in the University of Pennsylvania Journal of Law and Social Change: "It is widely understood that poverty is a risk factor for criminal justice system involvement. Individuals living in poverty are more likely to be arrested, more likely to be convicted, and more likely to be incarcerated than individuals who are more financially secure. For many observers, this correlation is a source of deep moral unease. If a person's socioeconomic circumstances put him or her at higher risk of performing acts that our legal system labels 'crimes,' is it morally defensible to hold that person criminally responsible for those acts? Shouldn't some part of the responsibility be borne by the society that shaped the individual's circumstances in ways that made him or her unfairly prone to criminally-punishable behaviors?" Elisabeth Winston Lambert, A Way Out of the "Rotten Social Background" Stalemate: "Scarcity" and Stephen Morse's Proposed Generic Partial Excuse, 21 *U. Pa. J. L. & Soc. Change* 297 (2018).

In *People v. Romero* the California Court of Appeal grappled with a proffer of expert testimony on the culture of the urban street fighter.

PEOPLE V. ROMERO

California Court of Appeal
69 Cal.App.4th 846, 81 Cal.Rptr.2d 823 (1999)

WISEMAN, J.

In an ever-increasing trend, this murder case arises from an all-too-familiar formula: one party commits a relatively minor "infraction" which quickly escalates into street violence and then death or serious injury. Many of us can relate to this phenomenon by reflecting upon our own experience behind the wheel of a car when a driver cuts too close to your vehicle, and "road rage" sets in.

The roots of this case are planted in a simple street scene. A group of men were crossing the road when Alex Bernal sped around the corner in his vehicle, and had to quickly brake. Words were exchanged, threats were hurled, and moments later Bernal was dying with a knife wound to his heart.

What makes this case unusual is defense counsel's attempt to introduce expert testimony on the sociology of poverty, and the role of honor, paternalism, and street fighters in the Hispanic culture. Although interesting, we conclude the trial court correctly decided this evidence was irrelevant to (1) whether defendant *actually* believed he was in imminent danger of death or great bodily injury; and (2) whether such a belief was *objectively* reasonable. In the words of the trial court, we are not prepared to sanction a "reasonable street fighter standard." The judgment is affirmed.

In the late hours of August 3, and the early hours of August 4, 1995, defendant, Allen Powell, defendant's brother, Freddy Romero, Michael Madera, Jackie Fisher and Caytano Robles III (Junior), were all together at Junior's father's house in Modesto drinking alcohol. At some point they decided to walk to Diana Cantu's apartment to continue the party.

As they crossed the street near the corner of Riverside and Miller Streets, a car came speeding around the corner. The vehicle braked quickly to allow the group to cross the street. Some of the members of the group, including defendant, angrily yelled at the driver, Alex Bernal, to slow down. Bernal stated they should move out of the way, and that he was looking for somebody. He then sped up, and defendant again yelled at him to slow down.

At this point, Bernal pulled the car over and parked by the sidewalk. Defendant walked across the street toward the car shouting obscenities. Junior also approached the car on the passenger side. Bernal then pushed the driver's door open with his foot and kicked toward defendant, who was approaching him. Defendant backed off a little. As they swore at each other, Bernal said he was just looking for his daughter, Carolina, but also kept stating, "You want to fight? Come on, let's fight then." Defendant responded that he did not care that Bernal was looking for someone; he still should not have come around the corner so fast. Defendant also stated, "I'll fight, I'll fight." When Powell heard Bernal say he was looking for Carolina, he told the group that Bernal was Carolina's father, and to "settle down."

Bernal then kicked off his shoes and began kicking into the air. Freddy Romero testified that both defendant and Junior fought with Bernal. After Bernal attempted to kick defendant and Junior, defendant struck Bernal in the chest with his bare hand. Then, Junior hit Bernal with his fist. Bernal fell, and defendant started walking away. Bernal also began to walk away, however, he yelled, "I'll be back." At this point, defendant took out a knife, unfolded it, held it by the grip, and swung it twice at Bernal missing both times. After another swing, Bernal stated, "I'm bleeding, you cut me." Everyone then left.

Defendant testified that when Bernal came around the corner in the car, he yelled, "Slow down, fool." After Bernal parked and got out of his car, he and defendant began fighting. Defendant separated from the group and approached the driver because he felt he had to protect his younger brother. The fighting stopped, and defendant started to walk away. Bernal then struck him from behind. At this point defendant retrieved a knife from an unknown person, and began swinging it at Bernal to scare him away. As defendant swung the knife, Bernal was backing up. Defendant testified, "I had to stop him. From there, I didn't think of nothing else, you know." Bernal kicked at defendant a couple times, and defendant swung the knife at him. His only intention was to stop Bernal, who was kicking toward him. Defendant, however, admitted, "I can't say that I was scared." Defendant felt he had to stop Bernal from getting past him. However, he said, "I can't explain me doing what I did to him" Defendant acknowledged stabbing Bernal in the heart, but claimed he was attempting to stab Bernal in the leg. While admitting responsibility for Bernal's death, defendant maintained he never intended anyone to die.

Defendant testified he never saw Bernal with any weapons. He admitted Bernal never did or said anything to give defendant a reason to think Bernal was out to get his brother. When asked what caused him to think he had to stab Bernal to protect his brother, defendant responded: "I don't know where my brother was standing, who was doing what, where. All I know I couldn't let Bernal get there. I can't let him pass me. All I know is to stop that guy."

Defendant contends the trial court erred by ruling that the proposed testimony of Martin Sanchez Jankowski, a sociology professor, was irrelevant and inadmissible. According to defense counsel, Professor Jankowski had authored a book and numerous articles on the subject of street violence, and was an expert in Hispanic culture. We reject the claim of error and, in any event, find defendant was not prejudiced by the court's ruling.

According to defense counsel, Professor Jankowski's expertise deals with the sociology of poverty. He would testify that (1) street fighters have a special understanding of what is expected of them; (2) for a street fighter in the Hispanic culture, there is no retreat; (3) the Hispanic culture is based on honor, and honor defines a person; and (4) in this culture a person "would be responsible to take care of someone," i.e., defendant had a strong motivation to protect his younger brother. Stated differently, "He's the eldest male. He would assume a paternalistic role whether he wanted to or not. Something is expected of him."

Given the law, we conclude the testimony of Professor Jankowski was irrelevant to whether defendant actually believed he was in imminent danger of death or great bodily injury, and whether such a belief was *objectively* reasonable. We are unsure what defendant means by his reference to the sociology of poverty, and how it might affect his actual beliefs and the *objective* reasonableness of those beliefs. Similarly, even if we assume street fighters have a special understanding of what is expected of them, and that this is something with which the jurors are not acquainted, why is it relevant? Are street fighters expected to kill every person they fight with, regardless of the circumstances? If so, does this expectation replace or relax the legal requirement that before deadly force may be used a person must actually fear imminent death or great bodily injury? As noted by the trial court, "Then you're creating a separate standard for what you call street fighters." No authority or case law has been cited which supports a separate standard, and we decline to adopt one here.

In the same vein, whether a person should or should not retreat from a "street fight," has no bearing on whether that person may lawfully use deadly force. A decision not to retreat from a physical confrontation and a decision to kill are two separate acts and involve different mental exercises. The laws governing self-defense recognize these distinctions and apply different rules to these legal concepts. While defendant attempted to blur the distinctions between the laws governing self-defense, the trial court correctly did not.

The evidence regarding honor, like evidence of street fighter mentality, is not relevant to whether deadly force was warranted under the circumstances. Is there honor in killing an unarmed man, and assuming that in defendant's mind it was the honorable thing to do, how does this relate to self-defense? Clearly, the question of defendant's honor was irrelevant to whether defendant was in actual fear of death or great bodily injury, and whether his fear was objectively reasonable.

Finally, even if defendant had a strong motivation to protect his younger brother, this does not answer the question of why it was necessary to use deadly force. Self-defense and defense of another are both recognized in the law. However, as with the legal concept that one need not retreat, motive is only part of the question. Assuming defendant was justified in using force to defend himself and/or to protect his brother, the question of whether he could use deadly force was a separate issue. Any expert testimony regarding honor, tradition, street mentality, culture, paternalism, poverty or sociology simply was irrelevant.

The judgment is affirmed.

PROBLEMS

1. The X family moved to California from Asia two years ago. In their home country, honor plays a vital role in society. In their native culture it brings dishonor on a family, and especially on the male head of the family, if an unmarried daughter speaks to a man who is not her husband. Mr. X learned that his 16-year-old daughter owned a cell phone, something he had specifically forbidden her to do. Mr. X discovered his daughter using the cell phone to communicate with a teenage boy. Outraged that his daughter had dishonored him and the entire family, Mr. X killed his daughter. In Mr. X's native country, so-called honor killing is not technically legal, but it is seldom prosecuted, and has been recognized for centuries as socially acceptable in some circumstances. Should Mr. X be charged with a crime? Does he have any defenses? Can he defend based on "honor killing"? *See* John A. Cohan, Honor Killings and the Cultural Defense, 40 *California Western International Law Journal* 177 (2010).

2. Dell disciplined his 12-year-old son, Vic. Dell used electrical tape to bind Vic's hands together and then attach Vic's hands to a bed frame with Vic lying on his stomach on the bed. Vic's feet were also taped to the bed. With Vic in this position, Dell used a wooden garden stake and a short piece of garden hose with a metal nozzle on the end to hit Vic on the back several times. Dell also bit each of Vic's fingers. Vic yelled in pain. The next day, Dell again tied Vic to the bed, this time face up. A similar beating was administered. The next day at school, Vic's teacher noticed he had a black eye and cuts on his face. He was walking slowly and limping. When asked what was wrong, Vic lied to protect his father. Child protective services and the police were called. At the hospital it was determined that Vic was covered with bruises. Vic had scars that would be permanent. Vic told the doctor that in addition to the beatings described above, Dell choked and punched him to discipline him. Defendant was charged with torture and aggravated mayhem. At trial, Dell and many of his relatives testified that Dell is a good father, and that in his native Syria, it is acceptable to use physical punishment, including hitting with objects. At trial, Dell's attorney requested the judge to give the following jury instruction: "You have heard evidence that child-rearing practices and disciplinary or punishment techniques are significantly different in Syrian culture than what is acceptable in the U.S. Dell has presented evidence that may tend to explain his behavior based on cultural considerations which may have affected his perceptions and behavior at the time of the charged acts. You may take this evidence into consideration when determining Dell's intent. It is the prosecution that has the burden of proving the defendant guilty beyond a reasonable doubt. Therefore, the defendant is entitled to an acquittal if you have a reasonable doubt as to the defendant's guilt based on the cultural variance evidence presented." Should the judge give the instruction? *People v. Assad* (2010) 189 Cal.App.4th 187, 116 Cal.Rptr.3d 699.

3. Dom stabbed his wife Vicky to death. At his murder trial, Dom seeks to introduce evidence to reduce murder to heat of passion voluntary manslaughter. Dom and his wife were born and raised in Ethiopia. The couple

moved to California and worked here. The marriage deteriorated. Dom became depressed and stopped going to work. Vicky told him to leave their home and spit on him. At that point, Dom grabbed a knife and killed Vicky. He told responding police officers that his wife had betrayed him. At trial, Dom offers expert testimony on Ethiopian culture. The expert would testify that Ethiopian society is patriarchal, and that it shames and humiliates a man if his wife leaves him. The expert would state that spitting on someone is the ultimate insult. The prosecutor objects to the proposed expert testimony. Should the judge allow the expert to testify? Should the jury be instructed on voluntary heat of passion manslaughter? *In re Wendemagengehu* (2005) 2005 WL 2769014 (Cal. Ct. App. Nonpublished).

4. Nadim left his home in India to study in California. While at college he met Lori, a fellow student. They became friends and eventually lovers. Lori and Nadim discussed marriage, but nothing came of it and eventually the relationship cooled. Lori started dating another man. When Nadim learned Lori was dating someone else, Nadim asked Lori to marry him. Lori said, "No, we are too different." The next day, Nadim tried to call Lori, but she would not take his calls. The same day, Nadim bought a knife. Nadim rented a car and bought a can of pepper spray. Nadim drove to Lori's apartment and parked two blocks away. He let himself into Lori's apartment carrying the knife, the pepper spray, and a roll of tape. Two hours later, Lori came home. Nadim asked if their relationship was really over. When Lori said, "Yes," Nadim slashed Lori's throat killing her. Nadim was charged with murder. In an effort to get a jury instruction on heat of passion voluntary manslaughter, Nadim presented the testimony of a psychiatrist who would state that Nadim suffers from depression. The psychiatrist would testify that Lori's statement "we are too different" was highly insulting to Nadim, who viewed the statement as a racial insult. Lori's statement caused Nadim to fly into a blind rage. Should the judge permit the expert to testify? Should the jury be instructed on voluntary heat of passion manslaughter? *State v. Haque* (Me. 1999) 726 A.2d 205.

5. Quang was married and had three young children. Quang believed his wife was having an affair. A divorce proceeding was commenced. Quang killed his three young children by cutting their throats. Quang had nicks on his own throat. Quang told a police officer, "I cut my kids. I didn't want her to get them in the divorce. I want to die too so I can be with them." Charged with murder, Quang seeks a jury instruction on heat of passion voluntary manslaughter. Defense counsel decided to present a "cross-cultural" defense in an effort to get a jury instruction on manslaughter. The defense would present expert testimony that Quang's values and perceptions were formed as he grew up in Vietnam. Quang experienced overwhelming difficulty adjusting to life in America, and this difficulty placed him under great psychological strain. Quang was depressed by his belief that his wife was unfaithful. The expert would testify that in Vietnam, when a man's wife is unfaithful, it is a "loss of face" for the husband. The husband would return the unfaithful wife to her family. In America, however, this traditional Vietnamese "remedy" was not available to Quang. The prosecutor objects to the proposed "cross-cultural"

evidence. Should the judge allow the evidence? *Bui v. State* (Ala. Ct. App. 1997) 717 So.2d 6.

CHAPTER 10

PROPERTY CRIMES, BURGLARY, ETC.

■ ■ ■

This chapter discusses the traditional property crimes as well as burglary and an assortment of additional offenses.

As developed long ago in England, the three basic property crimes were theft, embezzlement, and false pretenses. The three are close relatives—each deals with stealing. Yet, each offense has distinct elements. In the past, the crimes had technicalities that bedeviled generations of judges, lawyers, and law students. Today, most of the technicalities are gone. Yet, the offenses retain their distinct elements.

In California as well as many other states and the Model Penal Code, the three property crimes have been consolidated into one offense called "theft." PC § 484 provides: "Every person who shall feloniously steal, take, carry, lead, or drive away the personal property of another, or who shall fraudulently appropriate property which has been entrusted to him, or who shall knowingly and designedly, by any false or fraudulent representation or pretense, defraud any other person of money, labor or real or personal property, is guilty of theft." This statute encapsulates theft, embezzlement, and false pretenses.

In *People v. Williams,* the Supreme Court provides a useful introduction to the traditional property crimes.

PEOPLE V. WILLIAMS

California Supreme Court
57 Cal. 4th 776, 161 Cal. Rptr. 3d 81 (2013)

KENNARD, J.

California statutorily defines the crime of theft by larceny as the felonious stealing, taking, carrying, leading, or driving away of the personal property of another. (§ 484(a).) That statutory definition reflects its English common law roots.

The common law defined larceny as the taking and carrying away of someone else's personal property, by trespass, with the intent to permanently deprive the owner of possession. In 1799 an English court decision introduced the concept of "larceny by trick." (Rex v. Pear (1779)

168 Eng.Rep. 208). Larceny by trick, a form of larceny, involves taking possession of another's property by fraud.

Larceny requires a trespassory taking, which is a taking without the property owner's consent. Although a trespassory taking is not immediately evident when larceny occurs by trick because of the crime's fraudulent nature, English courts held that a property owner who is fraudulently induced to transfer possession of the property to another does not do so with free and genuine consent, so the one who thus fraudulently obtains possession commits a trespass. Though the taking in larceny must be against the will of the owner or a trespass to his possession, still an actual trespass or actual violence is not necessary. Fraud may take the place of force. In cases of larceny by trick the fraud vitiates the transaction, and the owner is deemed still to retain a constructive possession of the property.

The reasoning supporting larceny by trick's inclusion within the crime of larceny—that fraud vitiates the property owner's consent to the taking—was not extended, however, to cases involving the fraudulent transfer of title. Under the common law, if title was transferred, there was no trespass and hence no larceny.

The theory was that once title to property was voluntarily transferred by its owner to another, the recipient owned the property and therefore could not be said to be trespassing upon it. Similarly, under the common law there was no trespass, and hence no larceny, when a lawful possessor of another's property misappropriated it to personal use. These subtle limitations on the common law crime of larceny spurred the British Parliament in the 18th century to create the separate statutory offenses of theft by false pretenses and embezzlement.

In 1757, the British Parliament enacted a statute prohibiting theft by false pretenses. (30 Geo. II, ch. 24 (1757).) Forty-two years later, it enacted a statute prohibiting embezzlement. (39 Geo. III, ch. 85 (1799).) Each was considered a statutory offense separate and distinct from the common law crime of larceny. Unlike larceny, the newly enacted offense of theft by false pretenses involved acquiring title over the property, not just possession. Unlike larceny, the newly enacted offense of embezzlement involved an initial, lawful possession of the victim's property, followed by its misappropriation.

Britain's 18th-century division of theft into the three separate crimes of larceny, false pretenses, and embezzlement made its way into the early criminal laws of the American states.

It was difficult at times to determine whether a defendant had acquired title to the property, or merely possession, a distinction separating theft by false pretenses from larceny by trick. It was similarly difficult at times to determine whether a defendant, clearly guilty of some theft offense, had committed embezzlement or larceny.

In the early 20th century, many state legislatures, recognizing the burdens imposed on prosecutors by the separation of the three crimes of larceny, false pretenses, and embezzlement, consolidated those offenses into a single crime, usually called "theft." The California Legislature did so in 1927, by statutory amendment. (§ 484(a)). The purpose of the consolidation was to remove the technicalities that existed in the pleading and proof of these crimes at common law.

The California Legislature's consolidation of larceny, false pretenses, and embezzlement into the single crime of theft did not change the elements of those offenses.

THEFT (LARCENY)

At common law, theft was the trespassory caption (control) and asportation (movement) of the personal property of another with the intent to steal. Today, "every person who shall feloniously steal the personal property of another is guilty of theft" (PC § 484). Theft is a specific intent crime. For purposes of theft, a leasehold is personal property.

Theft is divided into two degrees: grand theft and petty theft (PC § 486). Grand theft occurs when the value of the property stolen is greater than $950 (PC § 487). Interestingly, an individual commits grand theft when she steals "domestic fowls, avocados, olives, citrus or deciduous fruits, other fruits, vegetables, nuts, artichokes, or other farm crops" worth more than $250. Why only $250 for these farm products? It is grand theft to steal "an automobile, horse, mare, gelding, any bovine animal, any caprine animal, mule, jack, jenny, sheep, lamb, hog, sow, boar, gilt, barrow, or pig" of any value. For dog lovers, you will be interested to know that it is grand theft to steal a dog worth more than $950, and petty theft to steal a less valuable pooch.

In *People v. Davis* the Supreme Court discusses theft in the context of shoplifting.

PEOPLE V. DAVIS

California Supreme Court
19 Cal.4th 301, 79 Cal.Rptr.2d 295, 965 P.2d 1165 (1998)

MOSK, J.

We granted review to determine what crime is committed in the following circumstances: the defendant enters a store and picks up an item of merchandise displayed for sale, intending to claim that he owns it and to "return" it for cash or credit; he carries the item to a sales counter and asks the clerk for a "refund"; without the defendant's knowledge his conduct has been observed by a store security agent, who instructs the clerk to give him credit for the item; the clerk gives the defendant a credit voucher, and the agent detains him as he leaves the counter with the voucher; he is charged with theft of the item. In the case at bar the Court of Appeal held the defendant is guilty of theft by trespassory larceny. We agree, and therefore affirm the judgment of the Court of Appeal.

Defendant entered a Mervyn's department store carrying a Mervyn's shopping bag. As he entered he was placed under camera surveillance by store security agent Carol German. While German both watched and filmed, defendant went to the men's department and took a shirt displayed for sale from its hanger; he then carried the shirt through the shoe department and into the women's department on the other side of the store. There he placed the shirt on a sales counter and told cashier Heather Smith that he had "bought it for his father" but it didn't fit and he wanted to "return" it. Smith asked him if he had the receipt, but he said he did not because "it was a gift." Smith informed him that if the value of a returned item is more than $20 and there is no receipt, the store policy is not to make a cash refund but to issue a Mervyn's credit voucher. At that point Smith was interrupted by a telephone call from German; German asked her if defendant was trying to "return" the shirt, and directed her to issue a credit voucher. Smith prepared the voucher and asked defendant to sign it; he did so, but used a false name. German detained him as he walked away from the counter with the voucher.

Count 1 of the information charged defendant with the crime of petty theft, alleging that defendant did "steal, take and carry away the personal property" of Mervyn's in violation of Penal Code section 484(a). In a motion for judgment of acquittal filed after the People presented their case, defendant argued that on the facts shown he could be convicted of no more than an *attempt* to commit petty theft, and therefore sought dismissal of the petty theft charge. The court denied the motion.

The only theories of theft submitted to the jury in the instructions were theft by larceny and theft by trick and device. The jury found defendant guilty of petty theft as charged in the information.

The elements of theft by larceny are well settled: the offense is committed by every person who (1) takes possession (2) of personal property (3) owned or possessed by another, (4) by means of trespass and (5) with intent to steal the property, and (6) carries the property away. The act of taking personal property from the possession of another is always a trespass unless the owner consents to the taking freely and unconditionally or the taker has a legal right to take the property. When the consent is procured by fraud it is invalid and the resulting offense is commonly called larceny by trick and device.

The intent to steal or *animus furandi* is the intent, without a good faith claim of right, to permanently deprive the owner of possession. And if the taking has begun, the slightest movement of the property constitutes a carrying away or asportation.

Applying these rules to the facts of the case at bar, we have no doubt that defendant (1) took possession (2) of personal property—the shirt—(3) owned by Mervyn's and (4) moved it sufficiently to satisfy the asportation requirement. Defendant does not contend otherwise.

Defendant does contend, however, that the elements of trespass and intent to steal are lacking. He predicates his argument on a distinction that he draws by dividing his course of conduct into two distinct "acts." According to defendant, his first "act" was to take the shirt from the display rack and carry it to Smith's cash register. He contends that act lacked the element of intent to steal because he had no intent to permanently deprive Mervyn's *of the shirt*; he intended to have the shirt in his possession only long enough to exchange it for a "refund." His second "act," also according to defendant, was to misrepresent to Smith that he had bought the shirt at Mervyn's and to accept the credit voucher she issued. He contends that act lacked the element of trespass because the store, acting through its agent German, *consented* to the issuance of the voucher with full knowledge of how he came into possession of the shirt.

Defendant's argument misses the mark on two grounds: it focuses on the wrong issue of consent, and it views that issue in artificial isolation from the intertwined issue of intent to steal.

To begin with, the question is not whether Mervyn's consented to Smith's issuance of the voucher after defendant asked to "return" the shirt; rather, the question is whether Mervyn's consented to defendant's taking the shirt in the first instance. A self-service store like Mervyn's impliedly consents to a customer's picking up and handling an item displayed for sale and carrying it from the display area to a sales counter with the intent of purchasing it; the store manifestly does not consent, however, to a customer's removing an item from a shelf or hanger if the customer's intent in taking possession of the item is to steal it.

In these circumstances the issue of consent—and therefore trespass—depends on the issue of intent to steal. We turn to that issue. As noted earlier, the general rule is that the intent to steal required for conviction of larceny is an intent to deprive the owner *permanently* of possession of the property. For example, we have said it would not be larceny for a youth to take and hide another's bicycle to "get even" for being teased, if he intends to return it the following day. But the general rule is not inflexible: The word permanently, as used here is not to be taken literally. Our research discloses three relevant categories of cases holding that the requisite intent to steal may be found even though the defendant's primary purpose in taking the property is not to deprive the owner permanently of possession: i.e., (1) when the defendant intends to "sell" the property back to its owner, (2) when the defendant intends to claim a reward for "finding" the property, and (3) when, as here, the defendant intends to return the property to its owner for a "refund." There is thus ample authority for the *result* reached in the case at bar; the difficulty is in finding a rationale for so holding that is consistent with basic principles of the law of larceny. The cases in these three categories offer a variety of such rationales, some more relevant or more persuasive than others.

A. The "sale" cases

The classic case of the first category is *Regina v. Hall* (1848) 169 Eng.Rep. 291. The defendant, an employee of a man named Atkin who made candles from tallow, took a quantity of tallow owned by Atkin and put it on Atkin's own scales, claiming it belonged to a butcher who was offering to sell it to Atkin. The jury were instructed that if they found the defendant took Atkin's property with the intent to sell it back to him as if it belonged to another and appropriate the proceeds, he was guilty of larceny. The jury so found, and the conviction was upheld on further review.

B. The "reward" cases

The cases in the second category hold that a defendant who takes property for the purpose of claiming a reward for "finding" it has the requisite intent to permanently deprive. One line of these cases is exemplified by *Commonwealth v. Mason* (1870) 105 Mass. 163. The defendant took possession of a horse that had strayed onto his property, with the intent to conceal it until the owner offered a reward and then to return it and claim the reward, or until the owner was induced to sell it to him for less than its worth. The court affirmed a conviction of larceny on the theory that the requisite felonious intent was shown because the defendant intended to deprive the owner of "a portion of the value of the property."

C. The "refund" cases

The third category comprises a substantial number of recent cases from our sister states affirming larceny convictions on facts identical or closely similar to those of the case at bar: in each, the defendant took an item of merchandise from a store display, carried it to a sales counter, claimed to own it, and asked for a "refund" of cash or credit.

As a matter of principle, a claim of the right to "return" an item taken from a store display is no less an assertion of a right of ownership than the claim of a right to "sell" stolen property back to its owner. And an intent to return such an item to the store only if the store pays a satisfactory "refund" is no less conditional than an intent to return stolen property to its owner only if the owner pays a satisfactory reward. Just as in the latter case, it can be said in the former that the purpose to return was founded wholly on the contingency that a refund would be offered, and unless the contingency happened the conversion was complete. It follows that a defendant who takes an item from a store display with the intent to claim its ownership and restore it only on condition that the store pay him a refund must be deemed to intend to permanently deprive the store of the item within the meaning of the law of larceny.

Applying the foregoing reasoning to the facts of the case at bar, we conclude that defendant's intent to claim ownership of the shirt and to return it to Mervyn's only on condition that the store pay him a "refund" constitutes an intent to permanently deprive Mervyn's of the shirt within the meaning of the law of larceny, and hence an intent to "feloniously steal" that property within the meaning of Penal Code section 484(a). Because Mervyn's cannot be deemed to have consented to defendant's taking possession of the shirt with the intent to steal it, defendant's conduct also constituted a trespassory taking within the meaning of the law of larceny.

Affirmed.

Is it theft from the landlord when a renter fails to pay rent? Consider *People v. Bell.*

PEOPLE V. BELL

California Court of Appeal
197 Cal. App. 4th 822, 128 Cal. Rptr. 3d 588 (2011)

MALLANO, P.J.

Monique Bell used another person's name and personal identifying information to convince a lessor of an apartment that Bell was creditworthy. [Bell did not have the person's permission to use her identifying information.] Bell leased the apartment and soon was delinquent in paying rent until she was evicted. A jury convicted Bell of identity theft and related charges, including grand theft. Bell challenges the grand theft conviction, claiming that it is not supported by substantial evidence that she had the intent to permanently deprive the lessor of its property. We disagree and affirm because Bell intended to permanently deprive the lessor of a leasehold interest, at least to the extent that Bell failed to pay rent during her occupancy.

The court instructed the jury on only one legal theory with respect to the grand theft count, namely, theft by false pretenses. The instructions informed the jury that the defendant could be found guilty on that count only if the prosecution proved beyond a reasonable doubt that (1) the defendant made either a promise without intent to perform it or a false pretense or representation, (2) the defendant did so with the specific intent to defraud, (3) the victim believed and relied upon the promise or representation, which "was material in inducing the victim to part with its money or property even though the false pretense, representation or promise was not the sole cause," and (4) "the theft was accomplished in that the alleged victim parted with its money or property intending to transfer ownership thereof."

The prosecutor argued to the jury that "the theft is, it is not the property itself, obviously the apartment is still there, they don't walk away with the apartment, it is the value of the service, it is the value of the apartment during the months that they lived there without paying rent. That is a theft under false pretense because they get the apartment through false pretense, then they stop paying rent, and then the owner is out the benefit of those months' rent. That is the theft in this case."

On appeal, Bell contends that "the facts that she paid the security deposit upon renting the apartment and then paid four months' rent, indicate that her intent was to use the false identification to effect the rental, but not to permanently deprive either the owner of the property or of the identity of possession of the apartment or the rent money."

Respondent argues that Bell's false representations induced Healstone [the landlord] to allow Bell to take "possession and title to property that belonged to Healstone, namely the right to the apartment for one year pursuant to the lease which was worth around $12,000. The transfer of that property to Bell (*e.g.*, the rights under the lease), based upon Bell's fraudulent representations to Healstone that she was [the victim of the identity theft], cost Healstone approximately $4,700, based on the breach of contract, plus attorney and court costs of approximately $1,500." Respondent further argues that "Healstone transferred legal 'ownership' of the right to live in the apartment for one year pursuant to [the victim of the identity theft] based on Bell's false personation."

California's intent-to-deprive-permanently requirement for the crime of theft is flexible and not to be taken literally. The general rule is that the intent to steal required for conviction of larceny is an intent to deprive the owner permanently of possession of the property. The rule is not inflexible, however, and in certain cases the requisite intent to steal may be found even though the defendant's primary purpose in taking the property is not to deprive the owner permanently of possession, such as (1) when the defendant intends to "sell" the property back to its owner, (2) when the defendant intends to claim a reward for "finding" the property, and (3) when the defendant intends to return the property to its owner for a "refund." In each of those exceptions, although the defendant does not intend to deprive the owner permanently of possession of the property, the defendant does intend to appropriate the value of permanent possession of the property.

In *People v. Avery* (2002) 27 Cal. 4th 49, 115 Cal. Rptr. 2d 403, our Supreme Court expanded on the flexibility of the rule: "We now conclude that an intent to take the property for so extended a period as to deprive the owner of a major portion of its value or enjoyment satisfies the common law, and therefore California, intent requirement."

We conclude that the grand theft conviction is supported by substantial evidence because Bell intended to permanently deprive Healstone of a leasehold interest in real property, at least to the extent that Bell failed to pay rent during her occupancy. Bell took possession of the apartment by false pretenses and was delinquent in rent payments "right off the bat." She made partial payments, late payments, and a payment with a bad check. The jury could reasonably have concluded that she intended to deprive the owner of months of rent when she moved into the apartment under false pretenses. And because nothing in the record suggests that she intended to pay all the rent at a later time, it is evident that she intended to permanently deprive Healstone of its leasehold interest, at least to the extent of the unpaid rent.

Because a leasehold interest is by its very nature "temporary," in that the lessor will get the property back at the end of the lease, Bell argues that she did not commit theft because she never intended to keep the apartment. This ignores the obvious fact that she intended to permanently deprive Healstone of the unpaid rent.

The judgment is affirmed.

PROBLEMS ON THEFT

1. Dell was observed for several hours pushing a shopping cart around a Sears store. Eventually, Dell pushed the cart to a checkout stand. In the cart was a large cardboard box with a picture of a chandelier on it. The cashier at the check stand noticed the box was loosely taped and stated that she would have to open the box and check the contents before ringing up the sale. Dell walked away from the check stand, leaving the box with the cashier. Dell was detained by store security after the box was opened, disclosing in excess of $900 worth of store items, consisting of batteries, tools, and chain saws, but no chandelier. Theft? *People v. Khoury* (1980) 108 Cal. App. Supp. 3d 1, 166 Cal.Rptr. 705.

2. As Beth was pushing a shopping cart toward her car, Dopy grabbed a bag of groceries from the cart and ran away. Theft? *In re George B.* (1991) 228 Cal.App.3d 1088, 279 Cal.Rptr. 388.

3. Betty was sitting in a chair in a hair salon. She put her purse on the floor and put her foot against the purse to maintain contact and make sure she knew where it was. Dopy ran in, grabbed the purse, and ran away. Theft?

4. Marilyn was a long-time caregiver for an elderly woman in failing health. After the elderly woman, died, Marilyn withdrew $300,000 from the woman's bank account. Marilyn claims the money was a gift to her from the elderly woman. The prosecutor says she sole the money. If you are the prosecutor, how will you prove theft? *People v. Fenderson* (2010) 188 Cal.App.4th 625, 116 Cal.Rptr.3d 17.

5. Dell was walking down a city street when he noticed a wallet in the gutter. Dell picked up the wallet and looked inside to find $200 in cash, credit cards in the name of Ron Flemming, and a driver's license for Ron Flemming. Dell decided to keep the cash. He threw the wallet with its contents into a trash can. Theft? PC § 485 provides: "One who finds lost property under circumstances which give him or her knowledge of or means of inquiry as to the true owner, and who appropriates such property to his or her own use, or to the use of another person not entitled thereto without first making reasonable and just efforts to find the owner and to restore the property to his or her, is guilty of theft." *See People v. Moore* (1970) 4 Cal. App. 3d 668, 84 Cal. Rptr. 771.

6. Able stole a car from victim. While the stolen car was parked in front of Able's house, Baker stole the car from Able. Did Baker commit theft?

Larceny by Trick or Deception

Larceny by trick occurs when a thief obtains possession of property through lies or deception. As the Supreme Court put it in *Davis, supra*, "When the consent is procured by fraud it is invalid and the resulting offense is commonly called larceny by trick and device." Consider Sam, who intends to steal Vic's all-terrain vehicle (ATV). If Sam simply takes the ATV while Vic is distracted, this is theft. Suppose instead that Sam says to Vic, "I'd like to borrow your ATV for an hour to take a ride in the hills. Okay?" Vic says, "Sure." Sam rides off on the ATV intending to sell it. In the "borrow" scenario, Sam is guilty of larceny by trick. The essence of larceny by trick is that due to the thief's deception, the victim intends to hand over possession of property. Note that title/ownership of the ATV remains with Vic. What Vic intends is for Sam to have temporary possession, not title/ownership.

Larceny by trick is not a separate crime. It is simply a type of larceny.

Claim of Right Defense

To be guilty of theft, the accused must intend to steal. What happens when an individual takes property believing it is hers? You can't steal your own property, can you? The Court of Appeal discussed the so-called "claim of right" defense in *People v. Williams*:

PEOPLE V. WILLIAMS

California Court of Appeal
176 Cal.App.4th 1521, 98 Cal.Rptr.3d 770 (2009)

BUTZ, J.

Defendant Anthony Williams was charged with burglary (Pen.Code § 459) and robbery (§ 211). The jury convicted him of burglary, but acquitted him of the robbery.

We agree with defendant that the trial court erred in refusing a claim-of-right instruction, but find the error to be harmless. Thus, we shall affirm the judgment.

On the evening of August 27, 2007, Marlene Ayers and her three female cousins, including Johneshia Daniels, were all gathered at Daniels's apartment in Rio Linda. Around 10:00 p.m. there was a knock on the door. Marlene asked, "Who is it?" and defendant answered, "Anthony." When Marlene opened the door, she saw defendant, his brother Kendall Williams (Kendall), who was Marlene's ex-boyfriend, and Kivon Holmes. Marlene tried to shut the door, but defendant pushed it open. Defendant and Kendall entered the room, while Holmes stood in the doorway.

Kendall directed defendant to pull out his gun. Defendant reached into his waistband, pulled out a handgun and began waving it around. Addressing Marlene, defendant said, "You thought this was a game" and "Bitch, you stole my brother's car." Kendall said "Where's my shit?" and demanded that Marlene surrender the car keys and a laptop computer. Marlene directed Kendall to the car keys and told him the laptop was in the car. Kendall grabbed the keys and the men left. As he departed, defendant said, "Have a nice day." One of the three men drove away in Marlene's 1996 Aurora, which contained her laptop computer, as well as miscellaneous personal items.

Marlene testified that she and Kendall had lived together and dated intermittently until the beginning of August 2007, when they had an acrimonious break-up. She stated that she bought the Aurora from a third party, using Kendall as an intermediary. She admitted that Kendall tendered the purchase price to the seller and drove the car home, but insisted the car was purchased with her money. She acknowledged that the paperwork was still in the name of the seller, but explained that it was because neither she nor Kendall had a driver's license. She purchased the laptop at Best Buy with money received as a birthday present, although Kendall occasionally used it.

Defendant testified that the Aurora belonged to his brother Kendall and that he was present when Kendall purchased it. After Kendall and Marlene broke up, he and Holmes agreed to accompany Kendall to the apartment where Marlene was staying, in order to get the car back.

Defendant testified that he knocked on the door, and when Marlene asked who it was, he said, "Anthony." According to defendant, Marlene opened the door and "jumped back," allowing the men to enter the room unimpeded. Kendall demanded the keys to his car and his laptop. Marlene surrendered the keys and told him that his laptop was in the car. Defendant denied either owning or possessing a gun that evening, remarking "We didn't feel we needed a gun to go get our own property from some females." Defendant testified that he was the one who drove the Aurora away from Daniels's apartment.

Dierre Hudson, the registered owner of the Aurora, testified that he sold the car to Kendall. He produced a bill of sale, signed by him and Kendall. Admitting that Kendall was a friend of his, Hudson stated that he held back the pink slip because Kendall still owed him some money on the car.

Prior to trial, the prosecutor moved in limine to preclude defendant from asserting a claim-of-right defense, contending that that defense has never been extended to a defendant who aids and abets another in retrieving the other person's property. The trial court deferred ruling on the motion until it heard the evidence in the case.

Before the case went to the jury, defense counsel requested that the jury be instructed on the claim-of-right defense. The trial court refused the instruction, stating its belief that a defendant charged as an accomplice may not raise the defense with respect to recovery of any property other than his own.

Defendant was charged with both robbery and burglary in connection with the incident at Daniels's apartment. [The jury was] advised that defendant could be found guilty of burglary if he intended to enter the apartment with the intent to commit either larceny or false imprisonment.

Citing substantial evidence in support of his claim that he was simply helping his brother take back his own property, defendant argues that the trial court erred in refusing to instruct the jury on the claim-of-right defense which, if credited by the jury, would have negated the specific intent required to commit larceny and robbery. The Attorney General urges us to reject defendant's attempt to extend the claim-of-right defense to the recovery of a third party's property, pointing out that no California case has recognized such a defense, and urging that such an extension would be contrary to public policy.

An essential element of any theft crime is the specific intent to permanently deprive the owner of his or her property. A good faith belief by the defendant that the property taken is his own has long been accepted as a complete defense to theft-related crimes. Although an intent to steal may ordinarily be inferred when one person takes the property of another, particularly if he takes it by force, proof of the existence of a state of mind incompatible with an intent to steal precludes a finding of either theft or robbery. It has long been the rule in this state and generally throughout the country that a bona fide belief, even though mistakenly held, that one has a right or claim to the property negates felonious intent. A belief that the property taken belongs to the taker is sufficient to preclude felonious intent. Felonious intent exists only if the actor intends to take the property of another without believing in good faith that he has a right or claim to it.

In People v. Tufunga, 21 Cal. 4th at 950, the California Supreme Court rejected the claim-of-right defense when force is used to collect on a debt, stating that robberies perpetrated to satisfy, settle or otherwise collect on a debt, liquidated or unliquidated—as opposed to forcible takings intended to recover specific personal property in which the defendant in good faith believes he has a bona fide claim of ownership or title is unsupported by the statutory language, and contrary to sound public policy.

Defendant was tried and the jury was instructed on a theory that he *aided and abetted* his brother Kendall in stealing property that belonged to Kendall's ex-girlfriend Marlene. The evidence showed the Williams brothers acted in concert to take property by force or fear. The pivotal issue at trial was *who* was the rightful owner of the property. Thus, there is no question that, had Kendall been on trial for robbery and burglary, a claim-of-right instruction would not only have been proper, but mandatory. If the defendant relies on a claim-of-right defense or if there is substantial evidence that supports the defense and the defense is not inconsistent with the defendant's theory of the case, the trial court must instruct sua sponte on the defense.

Except for strict liability offenses, every crime has two components: (1) an act or omission, sometimes called the *actus reus*; and (2) a necessary mental state, sometimes called the *mens rea*. (Pen.Code § 20). This principle applies to aiding and abetting liability as well as direct liability. An aider and abettor must do something *and* have a certain mental state.

Defendant's guilt of robbery (and derivatively of burglary where the intent is to rob) requires not only that he commit the requisite act but also that he have the requisite specific intent. Since robbery was, at common law, simply an aggravated form of larceny, both crimes require that defendant act with the felonious intent to take property that belongs to another. The claim-of-right defense is based on the sound concept that a person who acts under a good faith belief that he is repossessing his own property lacks felonious intent to deprive another of his or her property.

To be liable as a principal on an aiding and abetting theory, the accused must act with knowledge of the criminal purpose of the perpetrator *and* with an intent or purpose either of committing, or of encouraging or facilitating commission of, the offense. Thus, when the definition of the offense includes the intent to do some act or achieve some consequence beyond the *actus reus* of the crime citation, the aider and abettor must share the specific intent of the perpetrator.

It would defy logic and common sense to hold that a defendant who absconds with goods by force under a good faith belief that he was repossessing his own property does not thereby commit robbery, but that his accomplice, who assists him in the same act and shares the same intent, may be found guilty. The latter, just as surely as the former, lacks the specific intent to deprive another of his or her property. We therefore conclude that a good faith belief by a defendant, tried as an accomplice, that he was assisting his co-principal retake the principal's property negates the "felonious intent" element of both larceny and robbery, and that a claim-of-right defense must be given where substantial evidence supports such a belief.

Defendant testified that he believed he was assisting Kendall retake Kendall's own property. There was ample evidence in the record to support a jury finding that such belief was harbored in good faith. For that reason, the trial court erred in refusing to give a modified version of [of the instruction on claim-of-right].

Affirmed.

ROBBERY

At common law, robbery was the trespassory taking and carrying away of the personal property of another with the intent to steal effectuated by force or the threat of force. PC § 211 defines robbery as "the felonious taking of personal property in the possession of another, from his person or immediate presence, and against his will, accomplished by means of force or fear." Robbery combines theft and assault. In *People v. Anderson* (2011) 51 Cal.4th 989, 125 Cal.Rptr.3d 408, 252 P.3d 968, the Supreme Court wrote, "Robbery is larceny with the aggravating circumstances that the property is taken from the person or presence of another and is accomplished by the use of force or by putting the victim in fear of injury."

Robbery requires taking of property directly from the victim, or from the victim's immediate presence. Wrestling a woman's purse away from her satisfies this requirement, as does taking property within a victim's immediate reach.

PC § 212.5 divides robbery into two degrees. First degree robbery includes robbery of the driver of a bus, cable car, light rail, or cab, robbery of a person using an automated teller machine, and robbery perpetrated in an inhabited dwelling. Other robberies are of the second degree.

PC § 211 defines robbery as the taking of property by force *or* fear. Both are not necessary. Regarding fear, the Court of Appeal, in *People v.*

Morehead (2011) 191 Cal.App.4th 765, 774–775, 119 Cal.Rptr.3d 680, wrote:

> The element of fear for purposes of robbery is satisfied when there is sufficient fear to cause the victim to comply with the unlawful demand for his property. It is not necessary that there be direct proof of fear; fear may be inferred from the circumstances in which the property is taken.
>
> If there is evidence from which fear may be inferred, the victim need not explicitly testify that he or she was afraid. Moreover, the jury may infer fear from the circumstances despite even superficially contrary testimony from the victim.
>
> The requisite fear need not be the result of an express threat or the use of a weapon. Resistance by the victim is not a required element of robbery, and the victim's fear need not be extreme to constitute robbery. All that is necessary is that the record show conduct, words, or circumstances reasonably calculated to produce fear.
>
> Intimidation of the victim equates with fear. An unlawful demand can convey an implied threat of harm for failure to comply, thus supporting an inference of the requisite fear.

Regarding force, in the typical robbery, the robber uses obvious force and/or threats to coerce the victim to part with property. For example, a robber sticks a gun in a bank teller's face and says, "Put money in the bag or I'll shoot." The use of force and fear is clear. In *People v. Anderson* (2011) 51 Cal.4th 989, 125 Cal.Rptr.3d 408, 252 P.3d 968, the Supreme Court dealt with an atypical robbery scenario. Anderson was a drug addict who broke into cars to get money for drugs. Anderson went to a large apartment complex to steal a car. The victim returned to the apartment complex from work. She parked her car in the complex's gated parking garage and went to her apartment. Anderson entered the victim's car, started the motor, and drove to the gate, only to discover that the gate would not open. Anderson decided to wait in the victim's car until someone entered the garage and then drive out while the gate was open. Meanwhile, the victim returned to the garage to discover her car was no longer in the space where she parked it. She left the garage to report the car stolen. A car entered the garage, and Anderson saw his chance to drive away in the victim's car. He was exiting the garage at a high rate of speed—25 to 30 miles an hour—when he suddenly encountered the victim standing directly in front of him. Anderson swerved to avoid her, but ran over and killed the victim. Anderson did not deny hitting the victim, but Anderson claimed it was an accident. The question was whether Anderson's crime was theft or robbery. Anderson claimed he did not rob the victim because he did not intend to use force—he claimed he hit the victim by accident. Theft, yes—robbery, no.

The Supreme Court ruled it robbery. The Court noted, "In California, the crime of robbery is a continuing offense that begins from the time of the original taking until the robber reaches a place of relative safety." From there the Court noted, "It thus is robbery when the property was peacefully acquired, but force or fear was used to carry it away." The Court described the *mens rea* of robbery as follows: "The intent required for robbery has been described as the specific intent to deprive the victim of the property permanently." The Court ruled that robbery does not require "intent to cause the victim to experience force or fear." The Court concluded that "it was robbery even if, as [Anderson] claims, he did not intend to strike [the victim], but did so accidently."

Justice Kennard concurred with the result, but questioned the Court's ruling that "robbery does not require any intent to use force."

In *People v. Mungia*, the Court of Appeal analyzed robbery.

PEOPLE V. MUNGIA

California Court of Appeal
234 Cal.App.3d 1703, 286 Cal.Rptr. 394 (1991)

TIMLIN, ACTING P. J.

Edward Mungia was charged in count 1 with robbery, a felony (Pen. Code § 211).

On December 16, 1989, Margret Hogeland, accompanied by her five-year-old daughter, went to a Kmart store in Riverside shortly after 5 o'clock in the evening. After returning a game her child had received, she left the store and walked toward her parked car, carrying her purse on a strap over her right shoulder, and holding her daughter's hand with her right hand.

Just as she passed one end of her car and let go of the child's hand, "someone came up behind me and shoved me enough to get my purse off my shoulder." Ms. Hogeland specified that she had been shoved on her right shoulder. She testified that the shove was a separate motion from the motion used to remove the purse from her shoulder. Before the purse was removed from her shoulder, she did not see or hear the person who seized it, nor did he say anything to her.

Ms. Hogeland screamed, realized there was no one else around, and gave chase. Although she was unable to retrieve her purse before the perpetrator reached a getaway car, she did manage to note his clothing and physical appearance and the description of the car. She also memorized the license number of the car and later wrote it down. Using the license plate number, the police quickly apprehended defendant and also the driver of the car.

At trial, the prosecuting attorney asked Ms. Hogeland if she had been eight months' pregnant at the time of the crime. Defendant's attorney objected on the ground of irrelevancy, and the prosecuting attorney argued that her physical condition was relevant on the issue of the force needed to establish robbery. The objection was overruled and she then stated that she had been eight months' pregnant. On cross-examination, when asked if she had fallen forward because of the push, Ms. Hogeland replied, "No, it's a good thing I didn't because I was eight months' pregnant and had toxemia." On redirect, she explained that toxemia is a condition "you get when you are pregnant, causes you to retain water and you have high blood pressure and it's dangerous for you and the baby." She also testified that she was 5 feet 4 inches tall and had weighed 180 pounds at the time of the crime.

Defendant contends that there is insufficient evidence of force or fear to establish that the crime alleged was robbery (§ 211) rather than a necessarily included lesser offense of grand theft from the person (§ 487, subd. 2).

Robbery is "the felonious taking of personal property in the possession of another, from his person or immediate presence, and against his will, accomplished by means of force or fear." It is the use of force or fear which distinguishes robbery from grand theft from the person.

Defendant acknowledges that whether there is force or fear is a factual question for the jury but contends that there must be evidence of something more than the amount of force necessary to accomplish the mere taking of the property itself. Defendant contends that in this case, "it is clear that the amount of force used was no more than that necessary to remove the property. There was no additional force, no resistance, and no threats necessary to make the offense a robbery."

However, defendant misinterprets the evidence. According to the victim, defendant first shoved her, and then, in a separate motion, snatched the purse from her shoulder. He also overstates the law, because neither resistance by the victim nor threats by the perpetrator are necessary elements of robbery.

The question then is whether Ms. Hogeland's testimony as to being shoved before the taking and as to her physical condition was sufficient evidence of force to support the implied finding by the jury that defendant used more force than necessary to accomplish the taking of her purse or, stated another way, did defendant engage in a measure of force at the time of taking to overcome the victim's resistance?

The force or fear required by section 211 is not synonymous with a physical corporeal assault. The terms "force" and "fear" as used in the definition of the crime of robbery have no technical meaning peculiar to the law and must be presumed to be within the understanding of jurors.

"Force" is a relative concept. An able-bodied and/or large person may experience a given physical act applied to her body as less forceful than would a feeble, handicapped or small person. The concept that some persons are more vulnerable, *i.e.*, more defenseless, unguarded, unprotected, accessible, assailable, or susceptible to the defendant's criminal act has been recognized by the courts and Legislature. Although we have not found any cases which explicitly hold that the victim's physical characteristics may be taken into account by the jury in determining whether the physical act applied to the victim constituted "force" within the meaning of section 211, the fact that "force" is a factual question to be determined by the jury using its own common sense leads us to conclude that the jury may properly consider such characteristics.

Here, given Ms. Hogeland's testimony that defendant shoved her, separate and apart from snatching her purse, as well as the jury's ability to view the relative size and apparent strength of defendant and Ms. Hogeland, and her further testimony that at the time of the crime she was eight months' pregnant, and thus inferably more susceptible to being shoved off-balance and less able to recover her equilibrium quickly, we cannot say that there was insufficient evidence to support the jury's implied finding, when it returned a verdict of guilty of robbery rather than grand theft from the person, that defendant used more force than necessary to accomplish the snatching of Ms. Hogeland's purse and to overcome any resistance by her.

The People also argued that there was sufficient evidence of fear to support defendant's conviction of robbery. We disagree. Although the victim need not explicitly testify that he or she was afraid in order to show the use of fear to facilitate the taking, there must be evidence from which it can be inferred that the victim was in fact afraid, and that such fear allowed the crime to be accomplished.

The evidence showed that Ms. Hogeland was not aware of defendant's approach or planned purse snatch until he had actually snatched her purse from behind. After realizing that her purse was gone and that no one was nearby, she pursued him on foot, and, failing to catch him, nonetheless bent over behind his getaway car long enough to repeat its license number to herself three times in her successful attempt to memorize it.

There is nothing in the record which indicates, or from which it can be inferred, that Ms. Hogeland's purse was taken from her through the use of fear.

Affirmed.

PROBLEMS ON ROBBERY

1. Shortly before 5:00 a.m., Dell broke into the side door of an Anaheim restaurant. Dell pried open an ATM machine in the restaurant, took cash, and

prepared to leave. As he was leaving, Dell heard someone unlocking the front door. Dell hid in the kitchen. As the restaurant manager entered the front door, the manager heard an alarm and saw the damaged ATM. The manager turned around and left the restaurant. The manager got in his car and called 911. Dell ran out the side door. From where he was parked, the manager saw Dell run out of the restaurant, jump in a car, and speed away. The manager followed Dell in his own car. After Dell had driven about 150 feet, he fired two shots at the manager. At that point the manager stopped following Dell. Of what crimes is Dell guilty? *People v. Gomez* (2008) 43 Cal.4th 249, 74 Cal.Rptr.3d 123, 179 P.3d 917.

2. Dell went to the Solano Mall in Fairfield, where he stole six bottles of perfume from a Victoria's Secret store. Dell put the perfume in a paper bag. The store manager noticed the theft and called mall security. Two security guards followed Dell as he walked away from Victoria's Secret. The guards stopped Dell and asked if they could look in the paper bag. Dell said "no," and the officers informed Dell he was being detained under citizen's arrest. Dell pulled a knife from his pocket, waived it at the guards, and ran away. The guards chased Dell and tackled him. While struggling on the ground, Dell tried to stab the guards with the knife. Of what crimes is Dell guilty? Can Dell be charged with robbery? The security guards did not own or possess the perfume. PC § 211 defines robbery as "the felonious taking of personal property in the possession of another, from his person or immediate presence, and against his will, accomplished by means of force or fear"? *People v. Bradford* (2010) 187 Cal.App.4th 1345, 115 Cal.Rptr.3d 228.

3. Luis committed three armed robberies of hotel lobby front desk clerks. Is Luis guilty of first or second degree robbery? *People v. Rosales* (2014) 222 Cal. App. 4th 1254, 166 Cal. Rptr. 3d 620.

4. Dell went to the victim's home, and knocked on the front door. When the victim came to the door, Dell forced his way inside. Holding a gun on the victim, Dell demanded the combination to a safe two miles away. Dell then called an accomplice and give her the combination. The accomplice opened the safe and made off with the contents. Robbery? Theft? Burglary? Assault? Anything else? *People v. Neely* (2009) 176 Cal. App. 4th 787, 97 Cal. Rptr. 3d 913.

FALSE PRETENSES

At common law, false pretenses was defined as a false representation of a material present or past fact which causes the victim to pass title to the victim's property to defendant. Defendant knows the representation to be false, and intends thereby to defraud the victim. The victim relied on the false representation.[1] Today, false pretenses is defined in PC § 484: "Every person who shall knowingly and designedly, by any false or

[1] The victim may rely on matters in addition to the thief's false representation, so long as the false representation played a material part in the victim's decision to part with property.

fraudulent representation or pretense, defraud any other person of money, labor or real or personal property, is guilty of theft."[2] False pretenses is a specific intent crime.

False pretenses and larceny by trick are easily confused. With both crimes the victim parts with property based on the false representation of the thief. Larceny by trick occurs when a thief who intends to steal obtains *possession* of property through lies or trickery. False pretenses occurs when a thief who intends to steal obtains *title* or *ownership* of victim's property through false representations. The difference between larceny by trick and false pretenses is the victim's intent to pass title/ownership of the property. With false pretenses, the victim intends to pass title/ownership *and* possession to the thief. With larceny by trick, the victim intends to retain title/ownership and to pass only possession.

The heart of false pretenses and larceny by trick is a false representation that causes the victim to part with property. The false representation must concern a present or past fact. What about a false promise to do something in the future? If the criminal has no intention to fulfill the promise, then the promise is a misrepresentation of a *present* fact. On the other hand, an expression of opinion that is understood to be nothing more than an opinion will not ordinarily support a prosecution for false pretenses.

The crime of false pretenses is intended to protect all citizens, including the gullible, who are easy prey for sophisticated liars. It is not a defense that the victim could have discovered the lie by conducting an investigation. The doctrine of *caveat emptor* does not apply. Mere "dealer puffery," on the other hand, will not support a prosecution for false pretenses.

People v. Ashley is instructive on the crime of false pretenses.

PEOPLE V. ASHLEY

California Supreme Court
42 Cal.2d 246, 267 P.2d 271 (1954)

TRAYNOR, J.

Defendant was convicted of four counts of grand theft under the Penal Code. He appeals from the verdicts and judgments as to each count.

The first two counts charged that defendant feloniously took $13,590 from Mrs. Maude Neal on June 19, 1948, and $4,470 from her on August 3, 1948. The remaining two counts charged that he feloniously took $3,000

---

[2] PC § 532 provides: "(a) Every person who knowingly and designedly, by any false or fraudulent representation or pretense, defrauds any other person of money, labor, or property, whether real or personal in punishable in the same manner and to the same extent as for larceny of the money or property so obtained."

from Mrs. Mattie Russ on November 19, 1948, and $4,200 from her on December 4, 1948.

Defendant was the "business manager" of "Life's Estate, Ltd.," a corporation chartered for the purpose of "introducing people."

In the latter part of 1948 Mrs. Russ, then about 70 years of age, visited the offices of Life's Estate at 1537 North La Brea Avenue in Hollywood. She was introduced to defendant, who persuaded her to join the "Life's Estate Philosophical Society." On November 18, 1948, in response to a telegraphic invitation, she returned to the La Brea offices and was offered a position as matron and hostess at a salary of $100 a month with a rent-free apartment on the property. She accepted the offer. As defendant was driving Mrs. Russ to her home in Long Beach, he went by a lot on Sunset Boulevard on which stood two sheet metal buildings. Defendant told her that "he owned that property and they also owned the La Brea property at 1537." As they drove on, defendant asked Mrs. Russ if she had any ready cash. When she told him that she had $3,000 he explained that he was building a theater on the Sunset property and needed money to proceed with the construction. He offered her interest at the rate of 6 per cent and security in the form of a first mortgage or trust deed on the La Brea property. Mrs. Russ agreed to make the loan and to go with defendant to her bank the following morning. When they arrived at the bank, defendant refused to go in with Mrs. Russ. She entered alone and secured $3,000 in currency from a safe deposit box. Defendant then took her in his automobile to a bank in Westchester, a suburb of Los Angeles. On arrival at this bank she turned the money over to defendant in reliance on his representations that she would get a first mortgage on the La Brea property and that the money would be used in the construction of a theater on the Sunset Boulevard lot, which she believed he owned. Defendant gave her a receipt for the money, which stated that she was to receive a first trust deed on the La Brea property. The money was deposited to the account of Life's Estate at the Westchester Branch of the Security-First National Bank. The corporation's books show that on that day the cash account was subject to an overdraft of $4,151.93.

After this transaction was completed, defendant took Mrs. Russ to the offices of Life's Estates and later to dinner. At dinner he told her that he needed more money to complete the theater building and asked her to make an additional loan. She said that she had a note, secured by a trust deed and a chattel mortgage, worth $4,200 that she had acquired from the sale of the home in which she had previously lived. She agreed to transfer these documents to defendant. This loan and the previous one of $3,000 were to be consolidated, and he agreed to give her a first mortgage for the full amount against the La Brea property. On November 20, 1948, defendant drove Mrs. Russ once again to her bank, which held the documents and acted as her agent for the collection of installments. Again defendant insisted that she enter the bank alone. After securing the documents, Mrs. Russ suggested that they return to the bank and have the bank's employees prepare the transfer, but defendant insisted that the necessary papers could be prepared in his office. The transfer was made that day. It was stipulated that the note secured by the trust deed and chattel mortgage was sold by defendant and the proceeds of the sale deposited to the account of Life's Estate. They were used for the operating expenses of the corporation.

On November 25, 1948, Mrs. Russ moved into an apartment at the La Brea property and undertook the duties of matron and hostess. She testified that her many requests for the promised first mortgage were unavailing and that she returned to defendant her receipt for the $3,000, when he told her that she would receive the mortgage if she did so. After frequent quarrels over the failure to deliver the mortgage and over the tasks assigned her, Mrs. Russ left the employ of Life's Estate on March 31, 1949. At this time she received a note of the corporation secured by a second trust deed on unimproved property in Nichols Canyon owned by the corporation. Mrs. Russ testified that, although this security was worthless to her, she took it because defendant had told her to "take that or nothing."

It was proved that the Sunset property was owned by the corporation and that no theater was ever built thereon. The La Brea property was owned by Dr. Louis Phillips, who had leased the property to [the corporation] for a period of five years. He had not authorized anyone to place an encumbrance on this property.

Mrs. Neal became interested in Life's Estate through a newspaper advertisement. She went to the La Brea office, where [she was] introduced to defendant. After some preliminary conversation he asked her if she owned any property. She replied that she owned $17,500 worth of war bonds. He learned that the bonds were kept in a lock-box in Mrs. Neal's home in North Carolina.

Between March and June of 1948, defendant and Mrs. Neal had a number of conversations regarding her money. She was offered a position as matron and hostess with an apartment rent-free if she would let him have all her money. He stated that he wanted her money to take up an option that he had to buy the El Patio Theater for $165,000, which he said was worth $500,000. Defendant said that he would give Mrs. Neal a note of Life's Estate and a trust deed on the theater building. She was unable to decide whether to make the loan, but offered to have her bonds mailed to her. Defendant insisted that this method was too slow and prevailed upon her to telephone her daughter to send the bonds by airmail. After receiving the bonds, Mrs. Neal went to the office of Life's Estate and talked to defendant. When she reintroduced the subject of security, he flew into a rage, saying that she talked as though she did not trust him. [Eventually, Mrs. Neal loaned the money to Defendant.]

Sometime after the events just related, defendant told Mrs. Neal that the theater building had been condemned and that the deal had fallen through. The record also discloses that Mrs. Neal consulted an attorney, but no action was taken. She had received only $649.49 in interest on her loans at the time of trial.

There is little evidence concerning the financial standing of the corporation or defendant's participation in the profits. The loans of both Mrs. Russ and Mrs. Neal were used to meet overdrafts or for the current operating expenses of the corporation.

The case went to the jury with instructions relating to larceny by trick and device and obtaining property by false pretenses. Defendant contends that the evidence is insufficient to support a conviction of either type of theft.

Although the crimes of larceny by trick and device and obtaining property by false pretenses are much alike, they are aimed at different criminal acquisitive techniques. Larceny by trick and device is the appropriation of property, the possession of which was fraudulently acquired; obtaining property by false pretenses is the fraudulent or deceitful acquisition of both title and possession. In this state, these two offenses, with other larcenous crimes, have been consolidated into the single crime of theft, but their elements have not been changed thereby. The purpose of the consolidation was to remove the technicalities that existed in the pleading and proof of these crimes at common law. Indictments and informations charging the crime of "theft" can now simply allege an "unlawful taking." Juries need no longer be concerned with the technical differences between the several types of theft, and can return a general verdict of guilty if they find that an "unlawful taking" has been proved. The elements of the several types of theft have not been changed, however, and a judgment of conviction of theft, based on a general verdict of guilty, can be sustained only if the evidence discloses the elements of one of the consolidated offenses. In the present case, it is clear from the record that each of the prosecuting witnesses intended to pass both title and possession, and that the type of theft, if any, in each case, was that of obtaining property by false pretenses.

To support a conviction of theft for obtaining property by false pretenses, it must be shown that the defendant made a false pretense or representation with intent to defraud the owner of his property, and that the owner was in fact defrauded. It is unnecessary to prove that the defendant benefited personally from the fraudulent acquisition. The false pretense or representation must have materially influenced the owner to part with his property, but the false pretense need not be the sole inducing cause.

In cases of obtaining property by false pretenses, it must be proved that any misrepresentations of fact alleged by the People were made knowingly and with intent to deceive. If such misrepresentations are made innocently or inadvertently, they can no more form the basis for a prosecution for obtaining property by false pretenses than can an innocent breach of contract. Whether the pretense is a false promise or a misrepresentation of fact, the defendant's intent must be proved in both instances by something more than mere proof of nonperformance or actual falsity.

The evidence justified the implied finding that the money had been acquired with felonious intent. The jury could reasonably conclude that defendant had deliberately set out to acquire the life savings of his victims, one a woman nearing 70 and the other a woman of little education and rural background, and both with little or no business experience. The women were won over by flattering offers of positions in the organization and false promises of security for their loans, and thereafter held in line by importunate and then menacing supplications. The lure of an ambitious theater project was held before the eyes of each, a project that was never realized. The evidence was sufficient to sustain the implied finding that defendant never intended to acquire or build such a theater, and, indeed, the financial situation revealed by the evidence made the acquisition or building of such a theater illusory. The money acquired was needed and used for the running expenses of the corporation within a short time of its receipt.

Affirmed.

EMBEZZLEMENT

Embezzlement was defined at common law as the fraudulent conversion of the personal property of another by one in lawful possession. Today, PC § 484 states: "Every person who shall fraudulently appropriate property which has been entrusted to him is guilty of theft." Similarly PC § 503 states: "Embezzlement is the fraudulent appropriation of property by a person to whom it has been intrusted." Embezzlement is a specific intent crime.

With theft and false pretenses the thief uses criminal means to obtain the victim's property. By contrast, the embezzler obtains possession lawfully and then "converts" the property, *i.e.*, steals it. Embezzlement is committed by dishonest employees,[3] bailees,[4] agents, trustees, attorneys, brokers, merchants, executors, administrators, and others entrusted with the property of another. Intent to restore the property to the owner is generally not a defense.[5]

PROBLEMS

1. Dell obtains a motel room for the night without intending to pay for it. What crime? (*See* PC § 537—Defrauding innkeepers).

2. Dell owned a 16 acre parcel of rural real property in Butte County. The land was not suitable for farming and was covered with rocks. The land was worth about $40,000. Dell sold the land to Vic, who lived in Orange County, hundreds of miles away. Vic never inspected the property. Dell told Vic the land was wonderful for farming, with rich dark soil. Vic paid Dell $1,000,000 for the land. What should Dell be charged with? Is this just dealer's puffing? *People v. Cummings* (1899) 123 Cal. 269, 55 P. 898.

3. Dell, an art dealer, bought for $100 a painting that he believed was a "very good" forgery of a Picasso. Dell then sold the fake Picasso to Mary, telling her it was a genuine Picasso. Mary paid Dell one million dollars for the painting. What crime, if any, has Dell committed?

4. Long ago at Cambridge University in England, students wore academic robes to class. Dufus was not a student at Cambridge. Dufus stole a student robe, took a bath, and put on the robe. He entered several stores asking to purchase goods on credit. He never said he was a student. The merchants assumed Dufus was a student and sold him goods on credit. What crime?

5. Dell was a construction contractor. Dell was deep in debt and could not pay his bills. To obtain cash, Dell ordered a large amount of lumber on credit from Alpine Lumbar Company. Dell told Alpine he planned to use the wood for a construction job which did not exist. When the lumber was delivered to the job site, Dell sold it for 50 cents on the dollar to his friend Zeek. Zeek hid the lumber in his warehouse. When Alpine sold the lumber to Dell on credit, Alpine retained a security interest in the lumber. What crime, if any, has Dell

[3] *See* PC § 508: "Every clerk, agent, or servant of any person who fraudulently appropriates to his own use, or secretes with fraudulent intent to appropriate to his own use, any property of another which has come into his control or care by virtue of his employment as such clerk, agent, or servant, is guilty of embezzlement."

[4] *See* PC § 505: "Every carrier or other person having under his control personal property for the purpose of transportation for hire, who fraudulently appropriates it to any use or purpose inconsistent with the safe keeping of such property and its transportation according to his trust, is guilty of embezzlement, whether he has broken the package in which such property is contained, or has otherwise separated the items thereof, or not."

[5] *See* PC § 512: "The fact that the accused intended to restore the property embezzled, is no ground of defense or mitigation of punishment, if it has not been restored before an information has been laid before a magistrate, or an indictment found by a grand jury, charging the commission of the offense." PC § 513 provides that if the embezzler restores the property timely, the judge may mitigate punishment.

See People v. Sisuphan (2010) 181 Cal.App.4th 800, 104 Cal.Rptr.3d 654.

committed? What about Zeek? *People v. Counts* (1995) 31 Cal.App.4th 785, 37 Cal.Rptr.2d 425.

6. Dell was hired by a large law firm to run the firm's information technology department. Dell informed the office manager that the firm needed to purchase licenses for its new word processing software at a cost of $37,000. Dell said he would take care of buying the licenses from the vendor. The office manager had a check made out to the vendor in the amount of $37,000 and handed the check to Dell. A few days later, Dell informed the office manager the licenses had been acquired. Dell provided fake licenses that he produced himself. Dell cashed the check and pocketed the $37,000. What crime did Dell commit? *People v. Traster* (2003) 111 Cal.App.4th 1377, 4 Cal.Rptr.3d 680.

7. Dell injured his back while working as a truck driver. As part of a workers' compensation award, Dell was awarded lifetime medical benefits from Insurance Company. Dell's chiropractor notified Insurance Company that Dell needed in-home attendant care to help him with showering, cooking, cleaning, stretching, and walking. Dell was living with his long-time partner Nancy, and Insurance Company agreed to pay Nancy to serve as Dell's in-home care attendant. Insurance Company paid Nancy $75,000 over several years. Insurance Company arranged for Dell to see an orthopedic surgeon. Dell showed up for the examination using a walker and complaining of severe, debilitating pain. The doctor agreed that Dell had an injury, but the doctor could find no reason why Dell would be in such pain. When Insurance Company received the doctor's report, it stopped paying for in-home care. Dell appealed to the state Workers' Compensation Appeals Board. While Dell's appeal was pending, the Board hired a private investigator to conduct surveillance of Dell. The investigator video recorded Dell driving a pickup truck, walking outside his house without assistance, bending over at the waist to pick things up, piloting a 26-foot commercial fishing boat, climbing ladders, using a hydraulic winch to lift baskets of fish from the boat to the dock, dragging heavy fish-laden baskets, and lifting the baskets onto tables. What crime(s) did Dell commit? Is Nancy guilty? Does it bother you that the government used a private investigator to "spy" on Dell? *People v. Webb* (1999) 74 Cal.App.4th 688, 88 Cal.Rptr.2d 259.

8. Sam is an attorney. Sam is one of a number of attorneys who accept clients from an insurance company that provides legal services for individuals. An individual pays an insurance premium to the company. When the individual needs legal services, the individual contacts one of the attorneys that contracts with the company. The attorney agrees to perform legal services for a set fee. The company referred Jane to Sam for a divorce. Sam obtained a simple divorce for Jane. Sam billed the company for the divorce work. In addition, Sam billed the company for legal services he did not perform for Jane, including a Will and a Living Trust. What crime did Sam commit? Should Sam be disciplined by the Bar? What discipline should be imposed? What if Sam did the same thing with five different clients, not just one?

9. John owned a large tract of rural land covered in trees. Robert forged a deed to John's land, conveying the land from John to Robert. Robert then recorded the deed at the county recorder of deeds office. Robert approached a lumber company, and offered to sell the company the right to harvest the trees on "his" land. The lumber company checked the title to the land at the country record's office. Because the land records indicated Robert owned the land, the company paid Robert $45,000 for the right to harvest the trees. The company harvested the trees from the land. Later, John discovered what happened, and called police. Did Robert commit a crime? What crime? *Terrell v. State* (2018) 237 So. 3d 717.

10. Charles served as general manager of a car dealership owned by Charles' father-in-law. As general manager, Charles was authorized to write checks on the corporate account. Over a three year period, Charles wrote a number of checks on the corporate account, which he used for his own purposes. The total amount was $300,000. The checks were not part of Charles' salary as general manager. Charles did not tell the bookkeeper that he was writing the checks. On the other hand, Charles did not keep it a secret. Every month, when the bookkeeper got statements from the bank, the bookkeeper listed the checks as accounts receivable from Charles. On a couple of occasions, the bookkeeper discussed the checks with Charles. Eventually, Charles' father-in-law discovered that Charles had been writing checks for his own use. Charles was fired, and the police were notified. Charles is charged with theft. Charles asks for a jury instruction that if he—Charles—believed he was authorized to write the checks, he did not commit theft. Should the instruction be given? *People v. Stewart* (1976) 16 Cal. 3d 133, 544 P.2d 1317, 127 Cal. Rptr. 117.

RECEIPT OF STOLEN PROPERTY

Receipt of stolen property is defined in PC § 496(a) as follows: "Every person who buys or receives any property that has been stolen or that has been obtained in any manner constituting theft or extortion, knowing the property to be so stolen or obtained, . . . shall be punished . . . ." Receipt of stolen property is a specific intent offense.

Brad bought a used truck from a stranger. The VIN numbers on the truck had been removed. The price was much lower than the Kelley Blue Book value, or, as Brad put it to his friend, "The price for that truck is a real steal." The seller did not have any title documents. If Brad is charged with receiving stolen property, and you are on the jury, what verdict will you return? *People v. Grant* (1968) 268 Cal. App. 2d 470, 74 Cal. Rptr. 111.

FORGERY

California Penal Code § 470 defines forgery as follows: "(a) Every person who, with the intent to defraud, knowing that he or she has no authority to do so, signs the name of another person or of a fictitious person to any of the items listed in subdivision (d) is guilty of forgery. [Subdivision

(d) is a long list of documents (*e.g.*, traveler's check, check, bond)]. (b) Every person who, with the intent to defraud, counterfeits or forges the seal or handwriting of another is guilty of forgery. (c) Every person who, with the intent to defraud, alters, corrupts, or falsified any record of any will, codicil, conveyance, or other instrument, is guilty of forgery. (d) Every person who, with the intent to defraud, falsely, makes, alters, forges, or counterfeits, utters, publishes, passes or attempts to pass, as true and genuine any [of a long list of instruments is guilty of forgery]." Fraud is the essence of forgery.

The Court of Appeal's decision in *People v. Martinez* is a good illustration of forgery.

PEOPLE V. MARTINEZ

California Court of Appeal
161 Cal. App. 4th 754, 74 Cal. Rptr. 3d 409 (2008)

RICHLI, J.

When victim Ruth Michiel ran into financial difficulties, she was afraid that two houses she owned would go into foreclosure. Defendant Paul Martinez offered to help her; at his direction, she signed a stack of documents. Later, she learned that a trust deed had been recorded against one of the houses, purportedly to secure a $25,000 debt to defendant. Michiel did not deny signing the trust deed but denied doing so knowingly.

Defendant was found guilty of forgery of Michiel's signature (Pen. Code, § 470(d)). Defendant contends that there was insufficient evidence to support his conviction for forging Michiel's signature, because there was no evidence that her signature was not genuine and no evidence that he used any affirmative misrepresentations concerning the nature of the trust deed to procure her genuine signature. We disagree; there was evidence that defendant did make affirmative misrepresentations concerning the nature of the trust deed. In any event, he could be convicted of forgery even in the absence of any such affirmative misrepresentations.

When she contacted defendant, he told her that he was going to help her, adding, "Don't worry. You won't lose the property." Michiel testified that defendant had her sign "quite a few" documents, supposedly to help her with her financial problems. Defendant's ex-girlfriend confirmed that she was present when defendant had Michiel sign "a stack of documents," supposedly so Michiel could file for bankruptcy.

In July 2001, a trust deed on the Greenwood house in favor of defendant was recorded. On the same date, a grant deed conveying the Greenwood house to defendant was also recorded. Defendant rented out the Greenwood house; he did not pass along any of the rent to Michiel.

Michiel arranged to sell the La Villa house to her stepdaughter, but they were not able to close the sale because—as they then discovered—a trust deed had also been recorded against the La Villa house. It was dated August 9, 2002, and recorded on November 20, 2002. It purported to secure a promissory note for $25,000. The beneficiaries were defendant and "Chase P.M."

Concerning this trust deed, Michiel testified:

"Q: Is that your signature?

"A: It sure looks like it.

"Q: Did you sign the document?

"A: I don't remember."

She further testified that she did not knowingly sign a trust deed in defendant's favor; she did not owe him any money and thus had no reason to sign one.

When the police interviewed defendant, he told them that the trust deed on the La Villa house "just arrived in the mail, out of the blue," from the county recorder's office. He denied having anything to do with preparing it. He admitted that Michiel did not owe him any money. He identified Chase P.M. as a defunct company that he owned. He volunteered to execute a reconveyance but never actually did.

With respect to the Greenwood house, defendant told police that Michiel had given it to him "because it was going to be foreclosed on anyway."

Defendant took the stand at trial (against his defense counsel's advice). His testimony was rambling and disjointed. [Defendant's testimony is deleted. Suffice to say, defendant probably contributed to his own conviction. If you become a defense attorney, one of the most difficult decisions you make with your client is whether the defendant should testify. If the defendant testifies, he is subject to questioning by the prosecutor, including efforts by the prosecutor to impeach defendant's credibility. If the defendant stays off the witness stand, he or she is not and witness, and cannot be impeached. In other words, if the defendant does not testify, the prosecutor can't get his or her claws into the defendant. In the final analysis, the decision to testify or not is for the defendant to make, not you. In the vast majority of cases, however, your clients will take your advice on whether or not to testify.]

There was no evidence that Michiel's signature on the La Villa trust deed was not genuine. Michiel admitted that it looked like hers. She also admitted that defendant had had her sign a number of documents. Nevertheless, a forgery conviction can be based on a document with a genuine signature. Forgery is committed when a defendant, by fraud or trickery, causes another to execute a document where the signer is unaware, by reason of such trickery, that he is executing a document of that nature.

Defendant argues that this rule applies only where the "fraud or trickery" consists of an affirmative misrepresentation regarding the nature of the document. He concedes that Michiel may have "signed the trust deed without understanding what she was signing," but he argues that he "did not make any material affirmative misrepresentations to her."

Preliminarily, even assuming defendant is correct about the law, there was sufficient evidence that he did, in fact, affirmatively misrepresent the nature of the trust deed. Michiel testified that defendant "provided [her] with a number of documents to sign to try and help [her] with [her] financial problems."

Similarly, defendant's ex-girlfriend testified:

"Q: What occurred at this meeting between Mr. Martinez and Ms. Michiel?

"A: Apparently, Ms. Michiel was having some kind of financial trouble. Paul was talking to her about how he could help her.

"Q: How did he say he could help her?

"A: He suggested she file bankruptcy, and he said he would help her file bankruptcy.

"Q: Were there a stack of documents that he had her sign?

"A: Yeah. Also, he was assisting her with the bankruptcy, so there was bankruptcy forms and things like that.

"Q: When he had her sign documents, how did he—was it just a stack of documents? Okay. I need you to sign here, here, here?

"A: Yeah.

"Q: Or was he going over these documents and explaining what—

"A: No, he would usually—there would be a stack."

In sum, there was evidence that defendant presented Michiel with a stack of documents to be signed and that he affirmatively misrepresented to her that their purpose was to help her with her financial problems and/or help her file a bankruptcy.

Separately and alternatively, however, even assuming there was no evidence that defendant affirmatively misrepresented the nature of the trust deed, he could still be found guilty of forgery. The crime of forgery is committed when a defendant, by fraud or trickery, causes another to execute a deed of trust or other document where the signer is unaware, by reason of such trickery, that he is executing a document of that nature.

Defendant relies on *People v. Looney* (2004) 125 Cal. App. 4th 242, 22 Cal. Rptr. 3d 502. There, the defendants induced Wickers, a 91-year-old man who was in a nursing home and suffering from senile dementia, to sign four documents, including a will, in their favor. One of the defendants explained to Wickers what the effect of the documents would be. The defendants were charged with four counts of forgery, but the trial court dismissed these charges. In an appeal by the People, the appellate court affirmed. It stated: "At best, the evidence here establishes the procuring of the signature of an individual whose mental competency was questionable but to whom no misrepresentations were made about the true nature of the documents signed. Defendant Burl Looney attempted to explain the true legal significance of the documents to Wickers." It concluded: "Taken to its core, the People's position is that inducing a mentally incompetent person to sign a document that has been accurately represented is committing a forgery. We do not believe that current law supports the People's theory."

In sum, then, in *Looney*, the defendants affirmatively disclosed the true nature of the documents that they were asking the alleged victim to sign. Here, of course, there was ample evidence that defendant failed to disclose the true nature of the trust deed. Thus, there was sufficient evidence to support a forgery conviction.

BURGLARY

At common law, burglary was the breaking and entering of the dwelling house of another at night with the intent to commit a felony therein.[6] There had to be a breaking. A mere trespass would not suffice. Entry through a partially or completely open door or window was not a breaking. Opening a door or window that was closed although not locked was a breaking. Many states, including California, eliminated the breaking element of burglary.[7] As for "entry," some part of defendant's body must enter the building. At common law, burglary only applied to dwellings. Today, any kind of structure will do. At common law, only nighttime entries constituted burglary. California and other states have eliminated the nighttime requirement.[8] Burglary is a specific intent crime.

A primary goal of the crime of burglary to reduce entries that pose a danger to personal safety. "Unauthorized entries present the danger that the intruder will harm the occupants in attempting to perpetrate the

---

6 *See In re H.W.* (2019) 245 Cal. Rptr. 3d 51, 436 P.3d 941, 945.

7 The California Legislature eliminated the requirement of a breaking in 1872. *People v. Colbert* (2019) 6 cal. 5th 596, 433 P.3d 536, 242 Cal. Rptr. 3d 665; *In re H.W.* (2019) 245 Cal. Rptr. 3d 51, 436 P.3d 941, 945.

Burglary of a car requires that the doors be locked. Vehicle burglary requires the defendant to in some way alter the vehicle's condition by, for example, breaking a window or illegally unlocking the vehicle.

8 The Penal Code of 1873 defined burglary as "Every person who, in the night-time, forcibly breaks and enters." Night-time was defined as the "period between sunset and sunrise."

intended crime or to escape and the danger that the occupants will in anger or panic react violently to the invasion, thereby inviting more violence. . . . The core of the crime of burglary is not theft but physical intrusion." *People v. Colbert* (2019) 6 Cal. 5th 596, 433 P.3d 536, 242 Cal. Rptr. 3d 665.

California's burglary statute provides (PC § 459): "Every person who enters any house, room, apartment, tenement, shop, warehouse, store, mill, barn, stable, outhouse, or other building, tent, vessel, floating home, railroad car, locked or sealed cargo container, trailer coach, house car, inhabited camper, vehicle when the doors are locked, aircraft, mine or any underground portion thereof, with intent to commit grand or petit larceny or any felony is guilty of burglary. As used in this chapter, 'inhabited' means currently being used for dwelling purposes, whether occupied or not."

The Court of Appeal described burglary in *People v. Sherow* (2011) 196 Cal.App.4th 1296, 128 Cal.Rptr.3d 255, "The offense of burglary is committed when a person enters a building with the intent to commit a felony." Prior to 2014, individuals were charged with burglary for entering commercial establishments, during business hours, with the intent to steal. In 2014, the People approved Proposition 47, which reclassified certain theft felonies as misdemeanors. Prop 47 altered the definition of shoplifting. Penal Code § 459.5 now reads: "(a) Notwithstanding Section 459 [defining burglary], shoplifting is defined as entering a commercial establishment with intent to commit larceny while that establishment is open during regular business hours, where the value of the property that is taken or intended to be taken does not exceed nine hundred fifty dollars ($950). Any other entry into a commercial establishment with intent to commit larceny is burglary. Shoplifting shall be punished as a misdemeanor . . . ."

In *People v. Colbert* (2019) 6 Cal. 5th 596, 433 P.3d 536, 242 Cal. Rptr. 3d 665, the Supreme Court applied the new shoplifting statute to a case in which two men entered convenience stores during business hours to commit theft. While one man distracted the clerk, the other snuck into the back office to steal. The Court ruled the new shoplifting law did not apply, and the crime was burglary. The Court wrote, "[W]e conclude that entering an interior room that is objectively identifiable as off-limits to the public with intent to steal therefrom is not punishable as shoplifting under section 459.5, but instead remains punishable as burglary."

In *People v. Glazier* (2010) 186 Cal. App. 4th 1151, 1156, 113 Cal. Rptr. 3d 108, the Court of Appeal discussed cases in which a burglar uses an instrument to gain entry: "Burglary may be committed by using an instrument to enter a building—whether that instrument is used solely to effect entry, or to accomplish the intended larceny or felony as well. The burglary-by-instrument doctrine originated in the common law, although the common law drew a puzzling distinction. An entry by instrument was sufficient for burglary only if the instrument was used to commit the target larceny or felony. Insertion of an instrument for the sole purpose of gaining entry to the building did not constitute burglary. California courts have declined to adopt" the common law approach.

Burglary is divided into two degrees. PC § 460(a) provides: "Every burglary of an inhabited dwelling house, vessel, floating home, trailer coach, or the inhabited portion of any other building, is burglary of the first degree. (b) All other kinds of burglary are of the second degree." An inhabited building need not be occupied when it is burglarized. A garage and a patio are part of an inhabited building so long as they are an integral part of the dwelling.

Burglars typically carry tools to break in. Such implements are called "burglars tools." PC § 466 provides, in part: "Every person having upon him or her in his or her possession a picklock, crowbar, keybit, screwdriver, vice grip pliers, water-pump pliers, slidehammer, slim jim, tension bar, lock pick gun, tubular lock pick, floor-safe door puller, master key, or other instrument or tool with the intent feloniously to break or enter any building is [guilty of a crime.]" Not every tool found on a person qualifies as burglar's tools. In *In re H.W.* (2019) 245 Cal. Rptr. 3d 51, 436 P.3d 941, a minor carried pliers into a store in order to remove an anti-theft tag from a pair of jeans he intended to steal. Charged with violating PC § 466, the youth argued the pliers were not burglar's tools because he did not intend to use them to break or enter the store. The Supreme Court agreed, writing that § 466 "requires a showing that the defendant intended to use the instrument or tool possessed to break or effectuate physical entry into a structure in order to commit theft or a felony within the structure."

The next three cases grapple with burglary.

PEOPLE V. DAVIS

California Supreme Court
18 Cal.4th 712, 76 Cal.Rptr.2d 770, 958 P.2d 1083 (1998)

GEORGE, C. J.

Defendant was convicted of forgery, receiving stolen property, and burglary, based upon evidence that he presented a stolen and forged check to the teller at a check-cashing business by placing the check in a chute in a walk-up window. Defendant maintains that the burglary conviction must be reversed because he did not enter the check-cashing facility. For the reasons that follow, we agree.

On May 27, 1995, defendant approached the walk-up window of a check-cashing business named the Cash Box and presented a check to the teller by placing the check in a chute in the window. The teller later described the chute as follows: "It has a handle, and it opens out like a flap. It opens out, and they put the check in. They pass the check through." The check was drawn on the account of Robert and Joan Tallman, whose names were imprinted on the check, and was payable in the amount of $274 to Mike Woody, a name defendant sometimes used. The check was signed with the name Robert Tallman.

The teller placed a small white oval sticker on the back of the check, passed the check back to defendant, and asked him to place his thumbprint on the sticker and endorse the check. Defendant placed his thumbprint on the sticker, signed the back of the check with the name Michael D. Woody, and passed the check back to the teller, using the chute.

The teller telephoned Robert Tallman, who denied having written the check. Tallman later discovered that a group of checks, including this one, had been stolen from his automobile. The teller placed Tallman on hold and telephoned the police. An officer arrived within minutes and arrested defendant, who still was waiting at the window. At the police station, the police directed defendant to give several examples of his handwriting by repeatedly signing the name "Robert Tallman."

At trial, Tallman testified that neither the signature nor any of the other writing on the check was his.

Defendant was convicted of forgery (Pen. Code § 470), burglary (§ 459), and receiving stolen property (§ 496(c)).

Under section 459, a person is guilty of burglary if he or she enters any building (or other listed structure) with the intent to commit larceny or any felony. We must determine whether the Legislature intended the term "enter," as used in the burglary statute, to encompass passing a forged check through a chute in a walk-up window of a check-cashing or similar facility.

The burglary statutes do not define the term "enter." In the present case, the Attorney General conceded at oral argument that no part of defendant's body entered the building, but it long has been established that a burglary also can be committed by using an instrument to enter a building.

The common law drew a puzzling distinction. An entry by instrument was sufficient for burglary only if the instrument was used to commit the target larceny or felony. Insertion of an instrument for the sole purpose of gaining entry to the building did not constitute burglary.

The common law drew no such distinction if any part of the defendant's body entered the building. As Rollin Perkins observes in his textbook on Criminal Law: "Where it is a part of the body itself, its insertion into the building is an entry, within the rules of burglary, whether the purpose was to complete the felonious design or merely to effect a breaking. Thus if the miscreant should open a window too small to admit his body, and should insert his hand through this opening merely for the purpose of unlocking a door, through which he intends to gain entrance to the building, he has already made an 'entry' even if he should get no farther. But where a tool or other instrument is intruded, without any part of the person being within the house, it is an entry if the insertion was for the purpose of completing the felony but not if it was merely to accomplish a breaking. If the instrument is inserted in such a manner that it is calculated not only to make a breach but also to accomplish the completion of the felonious design, this constitutes both a breach and an entry." (Perkins, Criminal Law (3d ed. 1982)). An illustrative case cited by Perkins is *Walker v. State* (1879) 63 Ala. 49, in which the defendant bored a hole through the floor of a corn crib, caught the shelled corn in a sack as it flowed through the hole, then sealed the hole using a corn cob. The entry of the bit of the auger into the corn crib was held to be a sufficient entry for purposes of burglary, because the instrument was used both to effect entry and to accomplish the larceny.

Although many jurisdictions adhere to the rule that entry by means of an instrument is sufficient for burglary only if the instrument was used to commit the intended larceny or felony, the reason for this rule is not clear, and California courts have declined to adopt it. A burglary may be committed by using an instrument to enter a building—whether that instrument is used solely to effect entry, or to accomplish the intended larceny or felony as well. But it does not necessarily follow that the placement of a forged check in the chute of a walk-up window constitutes entering the building within the meaning of the burglary statute, although that conclusion would be compelled were we to follow the decision in *People v. Ravenscroft* (1988) 198 Cal.App.3d 639, the only California authority to address an analogous question. As we shall explain, we do not find the reasoning in *Ravenscroft* persuasive.

The defendant in that case was convicted of two counts of burglary based upon his conduct of surreptitiously stealing and inserting the automated teller machine (ATM) card of his traveling companion, Barbara Ann Lewis, in two ATM's and punching in her personal identification number, which he had previously noted, on the ATM keypads in order to withdraw funds from her account.

Inserting a stolen ATM card into the designated opening in an ATM is markedly different from the types of entry traditionally covered by the burglary statute, as is passing a forged check through a chute in a walk-up window. In each situation the defendant causes an object to enter the air space of a building, but it is not apparent that the burglary statute was meant to encompass such conduct. It is important to establish reasonable limits as to what constitutes an entry by means of an instrument for purposes of the burglary statute. Otherwise the scope of the burglary statute could be expanded to absurd proportions. For example, the Attorney General asserted at oral argument that mailing a forged check from New York to a bank in California, or sliding a ransom note under a door, would constitute burglary. A person who mails a forged check to a bank or slides a ransom note under a door causes that forged check or ransom note to enter the building, but it cannot reasonably be argued that these acts constitute burglary. Under the expansive approach to the burglary statute taken by the Attorney General and reflected in the *Ravenscroft* decision, it is difficult to imagine what reasonable limit would be placed upon the scope of the burglary statute. It could be argued similarly that a defendant who, for a fraudulent purpose, accesses a bank's computer from his or her home computer via a modem has electronically entered the bank building and committed burglary.

The interest sought to be protected by the common law crime of burglary was clear. At common law, burglary was the breaking and entering of a dwelling in the nighttime. The law was intended to protect the sanctity of a person's home during the night hours when the resident was most vulnerable.

In California, as in other states, the scope of the burglary law has been greatly expanded. There is no requirement of a breaking; an entry alone is sufficient. The crime is not limited to dwellings, but includes entry into a wide variety of structures. The crime need not be committed at night.

More than a century ago, in *People v. Barry* (1892) 94 Cal. 481, this court addressed the subject of what constitutes an entry for purposes of burglary. The defendant in *Barry* entered a grocery store during business hours and attempted to commit larceny. This court, rejecting the contention that a burglary had not occurred because the defendant had entered lawfully as part of the public invited to enter the store, stated: A party who enters with the intention to commit a felony enters without an invitation. He is not one of the public invited, nor is he entitled to enter.

Inserting a stolen ATM card into an ATM, or placing a forged check in a chute in the window of a check-cashing facility, is not using an instrument to effect an entry within the meaning of the burglary statute. Neither act violates the occupant's possessory interest in the building as does using a tool to reach into a building and remove property. It is true that the intended result in each instance is larceny. But the use of a tool to enter a building, whether as a prelude to a physical entry or to remove property or commit a felony, breaches the occupant's possessory interest in the building. Inserting an ATM card or presenting a forged check does not. Such acts are no different, for purposes of the burglary statute, from mailing a forged check to a bank or check-cashing facility.

For the reasons discussed above, we conclude that defendant's placement of a forged check in the chute of the walk-up window of the check-cashing facility at issue cannot reasonably be termed an entry into the building for purposes of the burglary statute. Accordingly, the judgment of the Court of Appeal is reversed to the extent it affirms defendant's conviction for burglary, and affirmed in all other respects.

BAXTER, J.

I respectfully dissent. Defendant's act of passing a forged check through the walk-up security window of the check-cashing facility met the statutory and common law requirement of an "entry" sufficient to sustain his conviction of burglary. Defendant used the forged check as an instrumentality to trick the teller into handing him money back through a chute designed to protect this very type of particularly vulnerable business—a check-cashing facility—and its employee-occupants, from persons with criminal designs such as his. Defendant's use of the forged check served both to *breach* the security system of the business, by tricking the teller into taking the check from him through the security chute, and to gain *entry* into the premises, insofar as the check was literally used as a paper "hook" to enter the air space of the check-cashing facility and effectuate theft of cash on the spot from the business. Such was no less an act of larceny, and no less a breach of the business owner's "possessory interest" in his business premises accomplished through a burglarious entry, than if defendant had reached through an open window or entered through an unlocked door and grabbed his loot.

PEOPLE V. SALEMME

California Court of Appeal
2 Cal.App.4th 775, 3 Cal.Rptr.2d 398 (1992)

SCOTLAND, J.

This case poses the question whether defendant's alleged entry into the home of an intended victim for the purpose of selling fraudulent securities constituted burglary. Defendant contends it did not because the purpose of our state's burglary statutes is "to protect against dangers inherent in intrusion" and, on the facts of this case, "there could be no danger from the mere entry of the victim's residence for the purpose of selling fraudulent securities." The People retort that defendant committed burglary when he entered the victim's residence to commit a felony, sale of fraudulent securities, whether or not the entry presented an imminent threat of physical harm to the victim. In the People's view, California's burglary statutes (Pen. Code, §§ 459, 460) encompass an entry into a structure with the intent to commit *any* felony, not just "felonies of violence or felonies which may induce a violent response from the victim."

For reasons which follow, we conclude that a person who enters a structure enumerated in Penal Code section 459 with the intent to commit *any* felony is guilty of burglary except when he or she (1) has an unconditional possessory right to enter as the occupant of that structure or (2) is invited in by the occupant who knows of and endorses the entrant's felonious intent. Since neither condition was satisfied in this case, defendant's alleged entry constituted burglary even though the act may have posed no physical danger to the victim who had invited defendant in to purchase securities from him.

On two occasions, defendant entered the home of William Zimmerman with the intent to sell him fraudulent securities and that defendant twice succeeded in convincing Zimmerman to purchase the securities. The victim initially invested $9,900. He later spent an additional $1,100.

Defendant was charged with two counts of burglary, two counts of selling unregistered securities, and two counts of selling securities by means of misleading statements and omissions of material facts.

Penal Code section 459 provides in pertinent part: "Every person who enters any house or other building with intent to commit grand or petit larceny or *any* felony is guilty of burglary."

A century ago, our Supreme Court held that an entry into a store with the intent to commit larceny constituted burglary under section 459. *People v. Barry* (1892) 94 Cal. 481, 482–484. For 83 years, this plain meaning applied: *any* entry with the intent to commit a felony into *any* structure enumerated in section 459 constituted burglary *regardless of the circumstances of the entry*. In 1975, the Supreme Court revisited the issue of statutory interpretation of section 459 when the court was presented with the question whether a person can burglarize his or her own home. *People v. Gauze* (1975) 15 Cal.3d 709. Examining the purposes underlying common law burglary and how they may have been affected by the enactment of the Penal Code, the court concluded that the plain meaning of the statute is inconsistent with its purpose when applied to one accused of burglarizing his or her own home. The court reasoned as follows: Burglary remains *an entry which invades a possessory right in a building*. And it still must be committed by a person who has no right to be in the building.

A person has a right to be in a structure when he or she has an unconditional possessory right to enter or where the person has expressly or impliedly been invited to enter and does so for a lawful reason. A party who enters with the intention to commit larceny or a felony enters without an invitation. He is not invited, nor is he entitled to enter. Therefore, a person who enters a store with the intent to commit petty theft or a felony can be convicted of burglary even though he or she enters during regular business hours while the store is open to the general public. One who enters a structure with the intent to commit petty theft or a felony may be convicted of burglary even if he enters with consent, *provided he does not have an unconditional possessory right to enter*.

Defendant argues his alleged entry did not constitute burglary because the act posed no physical danger to the victim who had invited defendant in to negotiate the sale of securities. The primary purpose [of burglary] is to protect a possessory right in property. Thus, if there is an invasion of the occupant's possessory rights, the entry constitutes burglary regardless of whether actual or potential danger exists.

For example, the shoplifter who surreptitiously enters a store with the intent to steal commits burglary even though his or her clandestine effort to slip merchandise into a jacket does not necessarily threaten anyone's personal safety. Defendant has not distinguished the shoplifting scenario from this case and, in our view, there is no logical way to do so. As in the shoplifting cases, defendant did not have an unconditional possessory right to enter the victim's residence. Rather, he allegedly did so with the victim's uninformed consent, *i.e.*, his lack of knowledge of defendant's felonious intent. Had the victim known thereof, he could have refused admission at the threshold or ejected defendant after entry was accomplished. Consequently, defendant's alleged entry constituted burglary regardless of whether his intent to swindle the victim out of money by misleading him into buying unqualified securities posed a physical danger to the victim.

PEOPLE V. BURKETT

California Court of Appeal
220 Cal. App. 4th 572, 163 Cal. Rptr. 3d 259 (2013)

RAYE, P.J.

A jury convicted defendant Penny Lynn Burkett of first degree burglary. [The burglary occurred on May 2, 2011.] Defendant appeals, contending the jury's special finding that the burglarized dwelling was inhabited is not supported by sufficient evidence. We agree and will reduce the offense to second degree burglary.

From 2008 to April 2011 Barbara Mattos rented a home located on Michigan Avenue in West Sacramento. Her landlord was Mersa Noor. In March or April 2011 Noor gave Mattos a one-month notice to vacate with the idea she would be out of the home by May 3 or 4. Noor lived with his family on Carmel Bay Road in West Sacramento but was losing his home to foreclosure and needed to move into the Michigan Avenue home. He did not have an exact date by which he had to move out of his Carmel Bay Road home.

Mattos removed all her belongings from the Michigan Avenue home before April 30, 2011. There was nothing left inside the home. Mattos turned off all the utilities effective May 1. She had all the keys to the residence and attempted to contact Noor to return the keys to him, but she had been unsuccessful. Mattos called Noor about the burglary and returned the keys after that.

Noor testified that he did not have any keys to the Michigan Avenue residence. Noor never testified that he turned the utilities back on. He planned to move his family into the Michigan Avenue residence sometime after May 4. He had not moved anything into the home. Although he stayed a few nights after the May 2 burglary and used just a blanket, he did not move into the Michigan Avenue home until May 8 or 9.

About 2:00 p.m. on May 2, 2011, Jason Davis and Regena Langhorst, relatives of Mattos, drove by the Michigan Avenue residence on the way to Mattos's new home, located nearby. As they passed the residence, they observed defendant and Nicholas Cummings emerge from the backyard through a gate and walk along the driveway toward the street.

About 10 to 30 minutes later, Davis and Langhorst returned to the Michigan Avenue residence and discovered that it had been broken into through a kicked-in door. Finding an assortment of tools on the floor and pipes and other things amiss, they called the police. A furnace had been pulled out and sheetrock had been pulled off the garage wall. Shower handles, pipes under the bathroom sink, and a towel rack were missing. The total damage was greater than $400.

The police located defendant and Cummings within an hour and not far from the Michigan Avenue residence. Cummings had wrenches, gloves, and other tools in his backpack. He also had a small envelope with snippets of copper-colored wire. Cummings first said he and defendant rang the doorbell looking for defendant's friend "Jamie." Cummings gave the officers other stories but finally admitted entering the residence; he claimed he did not plan to steal anything. Cummings' fingerprints were found on a pipe inside the home. Defendant's fingerprints were found on the inside of the furnace closet door. Defendant often went to a recycling center with scrap metal and did so about 10:00 a.m. on May 2.

The California Penal Code demarcates two degrees of burglary. Section 459 sets forth an extensive list of buildings, vehicles, containers, and other enclosures, including "any house," and provides that any person who enters them with intent to commit grand or petit larceny or any felony is guilty of burglary. Section 460 provides that burglary of an "inhabited dwelling house" constitutes first degree burglary.

Defendant does not challenge the sufficiency of the evidence to support her conviction for burglary, for indeed she entered a house with intent to commit grand or petit larceny as prohibited in section 459. There is no dispute that the house was a dwelling house. Defendant denies, however, there is substantial evidence to support the jury's finding that the dwelling house was "inhabited," an essential element of burglary of the first degree as set forth in section 460.

The argument seems plausible at first blush, given the language of section 459 that "inhabited" means currently being used for dwelling purposes, whether occupied or not. The previous tenant had departed, leaving no items of property behind, and while the owner had plans to occupy the premises, which were vacant and without utilities, he had taken no tangible steps to do so and did not even have keys to the house because the previous tenant had yet to return them. However, in the law of burglary what seems plausible often is not, and so we will not accept the argument without closer examination, no matter its superficial appeal.

At common law a burglar was a person "that in the night breaketh and entreth into a mansion house of another, of intent to kill some reasonable creature, or to commit some other felony within the same, whether his felonious intent be executed or not." (3 Coke, Institutes of the Laws of England (1797 ed.) p. 63.) The home was hallowed at common law, so much so that burglary was punished by death.

California burglary law has never conformed perfectly to the common law, particularly in regard to the type of structure subject to burglary penalties. The concept of habitation, so critical to burglary at common law, was not central to burglary in California. All buildings were treated the same, that is, until 1923, when section 460 was amended to change the definition of first degree burglary to "burglary of an inhabited dwelling house or building committed in the night time." In 1977 section 459 was amended to add a definition for inhabited: "As used in this section, 'inhabited' means currently being used for dwelling purposes, whether occupied or not."

For burglary of the highest degree, it is the nature of the current use of the building, which is to say the use at the time of the entry rather than the design of the building, its customary use, or its current occupancy that is important. By narrowing the scope of first degree burglary to encompass only dwellings and then restricting it further to include only those dwellings that are "inhabited," the drafters intended to sweep in more burglaries of the type considered especially despicable at common law while creating a different classification, with less severe punishment, for unlawful entries into uninhabited structures.

So what then does it mean to say that a home is "currently being used for dwelling purposes?" The People recognize that more is involved than design or functionality. According to the People, the answer is multifactored, with the most important factor being the intent of the victim. The People declare: "The dispositive element is whether the person with the possessory right to the house views the house as his dwelling."

A formerly inhabited dwelling becomes uninhabited when its occupants have moved out permanently and do not intend to return to continue or to resume using the structure as a dwelling.

There is no doubt that intent can be an important factor in determining habitation. Where a tenant buys a new home and moves into it, disclaiming any plans to return to the rental home he lived in before, the rental home is no longer considered inhabited though his lease has not expired, and though his personal belongings temporarily remain in the home. The tenant's expressed intent prevails over the contrary evidence of intent presented by the continued presence of his belongings in the rental home and his continued right to possession of the home under an unexpired lease.

In the present case, none of the indicia are present except for the self-declared intent of the owner to occupy the house in the future. Only if we view the owner's reoccupation to be a continuation of his former occupation following a temporary absence can it be plausibly asserted that the house was inhabited. Here, the owner never suggested at the time he moved out of his home that he intended to return and resume occupancy. The circumstances of his return—the loss of his home in foreclosure—were unplanned and unwanted.

Whether a person inhabits a place—whether the person has made a place his or her place of residence—is a question of fact. The prosecution bears the burden of establishing beyond a reasonable doubt that someone inhabited the Michigan Avenue home. Here, there is no evidence that the burglarized residence was inhabited, that it was currently being used by someone for dwelling purposes. Under established California precedent, it is not enough to show the home was suited for use as a residence and its owner had declared his intent to move in, or that it had been recently used or would be imminently used. Nor is there evidence that its owner was merely away temporarily.

NICHOLSON, J., Dissenting.

I would affirm the first degree burglary conviction. I agree with the majority opinion's well-crafted summary of the statutory scheme and common-law underpinnings of first degree burglary under Penal Code sections 459 and 460. Nonetheless, I would reach a different conclusion in this case of first impression. I would hold that the burgled house was an inhabited dwelling because, at the time of the burglary, the owner intended to return to it as his residence.

Mersa Noor bought the house in question in 2006 or 2007 and lived in it. There can be no doubt that it was an inhabited dwelling then. In 2008, Noor moved out of the house and rented it to Barbara Mattos. There can also be no doubt that the house was an inhabited dwelling when Mattos lived in it. Then, in 2011, Noor decided to move back into the house, which required Mattos to move out. The burglary occurred after Mattos finished moving her belongings out of the house and before Noor started moving his belongings into the house. The house was not abandoned at that point; instead, it was merely in transition from the possession of a tenant back to possession of the owner.

In my view, this is akin to the vacation home scenario. The owner uses it on occasion and may even rent it to others at times, but it never loses its character as an inhabited dwelling during that process. Though it is often unoccupied, it is still inhabited.

PROBLEMS ON BURGLARY

1. Dorothy and Mary were found on the roof of a market near a vent, the cover of which had been removed and through which a rope had been lowered into the restroom of the market. The vent was large enough that a person could slide down the vent into the building. A grate on the restroom ceiling had been broken, and some tools were found lying on the broken grate, but there was nothing to suggest that these instruments were being used to accomplish the intended larceny. Burglary? Could Dorothy and Mary be charged with attempted theft? *People v. Walters* (1967) 249 Cal.App.2d 547, 57 Cal.Rptr. 484.

2. Paula and Kim were apprehended after they had succeeded in creating a small hole in the wall of an electronics store. It reasonably could be inferred that, in creating the hole in the wall, some portion of the tools had entered the building, but that the entry of these implements was not for the purpose of completing the intended larceny. Burglary? *People v. Osegueda* (1984) 163 Cal. App. 3d Supp. 25, 210 Cal.Rptr. 182.

3. Dementa attempted to pry open the front door of an apartment using a tire iron. An occupant of the apartment saw the tip of the tire iron protrude into the apartment. Burglary? *People v. Moore* (1994) 31 Cal.App.4th 489, 37 Cal.Rptr.2d 104.

4. Vic lives in a large apartment complex in Los Angeles. Vic's one bedroom apartment is on the second floor. One wall of his living room is almost completely taken up with a sliding glass door that leads to a small enclosed balcony. The balcony has a metal railing around it. There is a staircase two feet from Vic's balcony. The staircase leads to apartments on the second floor, but does not lead directly to Vic's apartment. By climbing part way up the staircase, one can easily jump from the staircase onto Vic's balcony. One day, the apartment manager observed Dell, who he had never seen before, standing on Vic's balcony looking into Vic's apartment through the closed sliding glass door. The manager said, "Hey you, what are you doing?" Dell looked surprised, and ran away. Dell is charged with burglary. You may assume that Dell intended to commit theft inside Vic's apartment. Did Dell enter Vic's dwelling? *People v. Jackson* (2010) 190 Cal.App.4th 918, 118 Cal.Rptr.3d 623.

5. Change the facts in number 4. Vic owns his own home. Vic's home has a front porch that leads to the front door. There is no gate to the porch. To enter the home, one simply steps up two steps and walks across the porch to the front door. Dell was seen standing on Vic's front porch looking into the house. A neighbor said, "Hey you, what are you doing?" Dell looked surprised, and ran away. Assume Dell intended to commit theft inside Vic's home. Did

Dell enter Vic's dwelling? *People v. Brown* (1992) 6 Cal.App.4th 1489, 8 Cal.Rptr.2d 513.

6. In the middle of the night, Dell broke into a feed store to steal. Dell made five trips in and out of the store, carrying stolen items to his truck. How many counts of burglary? *People v. Richardson* (2004) 117 Cal.App.4th 570, 11 Cal.Rptr.3d 802.

7. Dell makes his living shoplifting DVDs from stores and selling them at a pawnshop. Does Dell commit burglary or shoplifting *of the pawnshop* when he enters the pawnshop to sell stolen DVDs? You may assume the owner of the pawnshop suspects the DVDs are stolen. *People v. Sherow* (2011) 196 Cal.App.4th 1296, 128 Cal.Rptr.3d 255.

8. Dell stood in the driveway of a home, with the intent to commit larceny inside. Dell used a remote control to open the garage door. The homeowner appeared, and Dell ran away without ever setting foot inside the garage or the home. Burglary?

9. Jennifer is attempting to sell her home. Jennifer hired real estate agent Janet to sell the home. All of Jennifer's possessions are in the house. On February 6th, Janet held an open house at Jennifer's home. During the open house, from 1:00 p.m. to 4:00 p.m., Jennifer was not at home. Numerous people attended the open house, including Jeanette. Jeanette chatted with Janet for a few minutes in the kitchen, and then asked if she could look around upstairs. Janet said, "Sure." After Jeanette went upstairs, Janet got the feeling something was not right, so she went upstairs. Janet looked into the master bedroom and saw Jeanette standing over an open jewelry box, with her hand in the box. Janet said, "What are you doing?" Jeanette replied, "Oh, I just like to look at things." Janet told Jeanette to leave, which she did. After Jeanette left, Janet telephoned Jennifer and told her that Jeanette had gone through some things in the master bedroom. When Jennifer returned home after the open house, she discovered that some rings and a necklace were missing from her jewelry box. Jane owns a local pawn shop. Jeanette visited Jane's pawn shop and pawned the rings and necklace that were taken from Jennifer's home. Jeanette is charged with residential burglary. Penal Code § 460(a) states that burglary of an "inhabited dwelling house" is first degree burglary. Jeanette argues that Jennifer's house was open for sale, and thus was not a dwelling when Jeanette entered. Jeanette is also charged with commercial burglary for entering Jane's pawn shop intending to pawn stolen property. *See* Penal Code § 459. In Jeanette guilty of either or both charges? *People v. Tessman* (2014) 223 Cal. App. 4th 1293, 168 Cal. Rptr. 3d 29.

10. Juanita and Charlene needed gas for their car. Unfortunately, they had no money. They decided to go to an auto wrecking yard to steal gas out of wrecked cars in the yard. The wrecking yard was a fenced area about the size of a football field. There was a building in the middle of the yard. Once at the yard, Juanita cut the lock on the gate, and the two women entered the yard carrying empty gas cans. They used a siphoning hose to fill with gas cans. They did not enter the building; nor did they enter any of the wrecked cars. Are

Juanita and Charlene guilty of burglary? *People v. Chavez* (2012) 205 Cal. App. 4th 1274, 140 Cal. Rptr. 3d 860.

11. Randy walked into an open restaurant and took a seat in a booth. Randy ordered lunch. While eating lunch, Randy noticed the door to the business office was open. Randy decided to sneak into the office and steal any money he could find. Randy got up from his booth and walked to the office door. At the door, he looked over his shoulder to see if anyone was watching him. The coast was clear, so Randy entered the office, and, in a drawer, found $600, which he took. Randy entered the restaurant legally. He formed the intent to steal after sitting down to lunch. What, if any, crime did Randy commit? *People v. Colbert* (2019) 6 Cal. 5th 596, 433 P.3d 536, 242 Cal. Rptr. 3d 665; *People v. Young* (1884) 65 Cal. 225, 3 P. 813; *People v. Sparks* (2002) 28 Cal. 4th 71, 47 P.3d 289, 120 Cal. Rptr. 2d 508).

12. Lester broke into a school on a weekend. Once inside, he broke into five separate locked classrooms, and a locked office. How many burglaries? *People v. Elsey* (2000) 81 Cal. App. 4th 948, 97 Cal. Rptr. 2d 269.

13. Roy rented a motel room for the night. Brandon and Bernedette decided to rob Roy. Brandon knocked on the motel door. When Roy opened the door, Brandon and Bernedette forced their way in, and held Roy at knifepoint while they stole his money and car keys. Is a motel room an inhabited dwelling for purposes of first degree burglary? *People v. Villalobos* (2006) 145 Cal. App. 4th 310, 51 Cal. Rptr. 3d 678.

14. Pedro was staying as an overnight guest in his sister-in-law's home. While there, Pedro forcibly raped his 12-year-old niece. The niece was in her mother's room, getting ready to go to a party with friends. Pedro entered the room, closed and locked the door, and raped the girl. Burglary? *People v. Garcia* (2017) 17 Cal. App. 5th 211, 224 Cal. Rptr. 3d 911.

15. Carlos broke into a home in order to take a shower. He used a small amount of shampoo and soap, as well as the hot water needed for the shower. Carlos is charged with burglary. *People v. Martinez* (2002) 95 Cal. App. 4th 581, 115 Cal. Rptr. 2d 574.

16. Dell injected gasoline into the open crawlspace of his neighbor's house, and lit the gas on fire, using a torch that was 5 feet long. Burglary? *People v. Glazier* (2010) 186 Cal. App. 4th 1151, 113 Cal. Rptr. 3d 108.

17. Dom walked up to a window of victim's home. The window had a screen outside the window. Dom removed the screen with a screwdriver. At that moment, Dom heard a noise, and ran away. Dom never opened the window or entered the airspace inside the window. Burglary? *People v. Nible* (1988) 200 Cal. App. 3d 838, 247 Cal. Rptr. 396.

ARSON

At common law, arson was the malicious burning of the dwelling house of another. Today in California, arson reaches much further. PC § 451 provides: "A person is guilty of arson when he or she willfully and maliciously sets fire to or burns or causes to be burned or who aids, counsels, or procures the burning of, any structure, forest land, or property." Simple arson is a general intent offense.

In *In re V.V.* (2011) 51 Cal.4th 1020, 125 Cal.Rptr.3d 421, 252 P.3d 979, three teenage boys climbed a steep, brush-covered hillside in Pasadena. They lit a large firecracker and threw it onto the hillside. The firecracker exploded and caused a five acre brush fire. The boys did not intend to cause the fire—they just wanted to explode the firecracker. The boys were charged with arson. The Supreme Court explained that "arson requires only a general criminal intent. The arson statute does not require the intent to cause the resulting harm, but rather requires a general intent to do the act that causes the harm. A defendant may be guilty of arson if he or she acts with awareness of facts that would lead a reasonable person to realize that the direct, natural, and highly probable consequence of igniting and throwing a firecracker into dry brush would be the burning of the hillside."

Burning is an element of arson. The burned structure does not have to be destroyed or seriously damaged. The fire can impact any part of the building. With wood, burning occurs when fibers are damaged.

Question: Arson of an "inhabited structure" is punished more severely than other forms of arson. PC § 450(a) defines "structure" as "any building, or commercial or public tent, bridge, tunnel, or powerplant." Section 450(d) defines "inhabited" as "currently being used for dwelling purposes whether occupied or not. 'Inhabited structure' and 'inhabited property' do not include the real property on which an inhabited structure or an inhabited property is located."

Dell and Kathleen lived together in one of two motor homes owned by Dell and parked on a vacant lot. One of the motor homes was operable, the other was not. Inside the operable motor home, where they lived, Dell and Kathleen got into an argument while eating lunch. Dell walked out. Dell used a truck to push the inoperable motor home right next to the operable motor home, blocking the only door to the home, and trapping Kathleen inside. Dell set fire to the inoperable motor home. Kathleen escaped out a widow. The fire destroyed both motor homes. Is guilty of arson of an inhabited dwelling? *People v. Goolsby* (2014) 222 Cal. App. 4th 1323, 166 Cal. Rptr. 3d 697.

EXTORTION

PC § 518 defines extortion as "the obtaining of property from another, with his consent, or the obtaining of an official act of a public officer, induced by a wrongful use of force or fear, or under color of official right."

Tim applied for a job with a towing company. Along with his application, he left a letter in an envelope. The owner of the towing company read the letter, which provided, "It is important that we acknowledge the fact that this is not a typical situation. I was convicted of vandalizing a car with sandpaper. I intend to visit your office today at five o'clock in order to determine whether or not I am employed by your company. I will be armed with a piece of sandpaper, and we both know I will not hesitate to use it. I know how detrimental it would be to your business if the paint on a customer's car got ruined by sandpaper while the car was in your lot. I would like to avoid this at all costs." Extortion? *People v. Fisher,* 216 Cal. App. 4th 212, 156 Cal. Rptr. 3d 836 (2013).

What distinguishes extortion from theft? With extortion, the victim consents under threat to transfer property. With theft, there is not threat.

EAVESDROPPING ON OR RECORDING CONFIDENTIAL COMMUNICATIONS

PC § 632(a) provides, "Every person who, intentionally and without the consent of all parties to a confidential communication, by means of any electronic amplifying or recording device, eavesdrops upon or records the confidential communication" commits a crime.

There are exceptions to the prohibition on eavesdropping. For example, law enforcement can record communications. It is lawful to record communications to gather evidence of domestic violence.

WHITE COLLAR CRIME

What is white collar crime? A crook in a suit is a pretty good definition. Although white collar criminals use sophisticated schemes, they have the same goal as the thug on the street: Steal your money. Sophisticated criminal schemes intended to part people from their money are prosecuted as larceny, larceny by trick, false pretenses, embezzlement, and criminal fraud. California has specialized criminal statutes including identity theft. The Federal Government has statutes criminalizing wire and mail fraud.

California and federal criminal statutes focus on antitrust, deceptive trade, securities, tax offenses, and numerous additional offenses. *See* Thomas A. Papageorge & Robert C. Fellmeth, *California White Collar Crime: Criminal Sanctions and Civil Remedies* (2004) (LexisNexis).

CHAPTER 11

SENTENCING

■ ■ ■

"Let the punishment fit the crime."

"An eye for an eye."

"Don't do the crime, if you can't do the time."

"Lock 'em up and throw away the key."

"Crime doesn't pay (usually)."

"Three strikes and you're out."

These and similar idioms and colloquialisms discuss punishment, a subject that has fascinated philosophers, lawmakers, judges, and the public for centuries. What is punishment? *Black's Law Dictionary* defines punishment as "Any fine, penalty, or confinement inflicted upon a person by the authority of the law and the judgment and sentence of a court, for some crime or offense committed by him, or for his omission of a duty enjoined by law." Deirdre Golash writes, "Punishment, at its core, is the deliberate infliction of harm in response to wrongdoing."[1] In *People v. McVickers* (1992) 4 Cal. 4th 81, 84, 13 Cal. Rptr. 2d 850 (1992), the Supreme Court observed, "Commonly understood definitions of punishment are intuitive: there is little dispute that additional jail time or extra fines are punishment." The California Penal Code defines crime as an offense *plus* a punishment. (§ 15)

This chapter has four parts. The first part introduces you to the debate over the justification for punishment. The second part focuses on California sentencing law. Part three discusses the death penalty. The last part addresses cruel and unusual punishment.

PART 1. JUSTIFYING PUNISHMENT

The literature on the justification of punishment is voluminous and contentious. Four principle justifications are offered: Deterrence, retribution, incapacitation, and rehabilitation.

Deterrence: Deterrence is of two kinds, general and specific (special). General deterrence is aimed at the public at large: We obey the law not

[1] Deirdre Golash, *The Case Against Punishment* p. 1 (2005)(New York University Press).

only because it is the right thing to do, but because we realize we will be punished if we get caught. Specific deterrence is specific to the individual lawbreaker. The unpleasantness of punishment deters the criminal from doing it again.

Retribution: The philosopher H.L.A. Hart defined retribution "as the application of the pains of punishment to an offender who is morally guilty."[2] Punishment is inflicted because it is deserved. But how much punishment is deserved? This depends on the seriousness of the crime, and introduces the topic of proportionality—let the punishment fit the crime.

Incapacitation: The idea is simple: While a criminal is sitting in prison, the community is safe from further depredations at his or her hands.

Rehabilitation: Here too, the idea is simple: The goal of punishment is to teach a lesson; to reform the criminal.

These four justifications, alone and in combination, have been debated since time immemorial. Plato (427–347 B.C.) argued in his Dialogue *Gorgias* that an unjust man is "miserable," and is more miserable still "if he be not punished and does not meet with retribution." The miscreant is "less miserable if he be punished and meets with retribution at the hand of gods and men." The great religious texts grapple with the proper severity of punishment. The *Qur'an* states: "Cut off the hands of thieves, whether they are man or woman, as punishment for what they have done—a deterrent from God." (5.38). The idea of proportionality is at the heart of "an eye for an eye," found in various forms in the *Qur'an,* the *Talmud,* and the *Bible.* Thomas Hobbs (1588–1679), author of *Leviathan,* observed that punishment must be sufficient to deter would-be criminals: "For the punishment foreknown, if not great enough to deter men from the action, is an invitement to it: because when men compare the benefit of their injustice with the harm of their punishment, by necessity of nature they choose that which appeareth best for themselves." (Part II, Chapter 27). John Locke (1632–1704) argued in his second essay on government that people in "the State of Nature" are equal, and when one person in this State harms another, the measure of justice "is so much as may serve for reparation and restraint. For these two are the only reasons why one man may lawfully do harm to another, which is what we call punishment."[3] Cesare Beccaria (1738–1794) published *On Crimes and Punishments* in 1764 and wrote: "The purpose of punishment is nothing other than to dissuade the criminal from doing fresh harm to his compatriots and to keep other people from doing the same. Therefore, punishments and the method of inflicting them should be chosen that, mindful of the proportion between

---

2 H.L.A. Hart, Punishment and Responsibility: Essays in the Philosophy of Law p. 9 (1968)(Oxford University Press).

3 John Locke, *Concerning Civil Government: Second Essay* Chapter 1, Paragraphs 6 and 8.

crime and punishment, will make the most effective and lasting impression on men's minds and inflict the least torment on the body of the criminal."[4]

Two heavyweights in the debate over punishment are Jeremy Bentham (1748–1832) and Immanuel Kant (1724–1804). Bentham championed utilitarianism, and justified punishment largely on its ability to deter crime. An extended excerpt from Bentham is reproduced below. Kant rejected utilitarianism, and argued that retribution is the justification for punishment—the criminal is punished because she or he deserves it. In his *The Science of Right,* Kant wrote:

> But what is the mode and measure of punishment which public justice takes as its principle and standard? It is just the principle of equality, by which the pointer of the scale of justice is made to incline no more to the one side than the other. It may be rendered by saying that the undeserved evil which any one commit on another is to be regarded as perpetrated on himself. Hence it may be said: "If you slander another, you slander yourself; if you steal from another, you steal from yourself; if you strike another, you strike yourself; if you kill another, you kill yourself." This is the right of retaliation (jus talionis); and, properly understood, it is the only principle which in regulating a public court, as distinguished from mere private judgment, can definitely assign both the quality and the quantity of a just penalty. All other standards are wavering and uncertain; and on account of other considerations involved in them, they contain no principle conformable to the sentence of pure and strict justice.[5]

Kant rejected Bentham's utilitarian justification of punishment, writing, "The penal law is a categorical imperative; and woe to him who creeps through the serpent-windings of utilitarianism to discover some advantage that may discharge him from the justice of punishment, or even from the due measure of it."

In the Introduction to his 2011 reader on punishment—Why Punish? How Much?—Michael Tonry deepens our appreciation of the intellectual warfare between retributivists and utilitarians.

MICHAEL TONRY, WHY PUNISH? HOW MUCH?

People have been thinking about punishment for a long time. Plato pondered it. So did Aristotle and St. Thomas Aquinas. Thinking about it in our time, however, dates from the eighteenth and early nineteenth centuries when Kant and Hegel laid the foundations for modern retributivist analyses. Bentham did the same for utilitarian approaches.

---

[4] Cesare Beccaria, *On Crimes and Punishments* p. 23 (1764).

[5] Immanuel Kant, *The Science of Right*, Second Part. Public Right, paragraph 49(E).

For most of the two centuries that followed, the Kantian and Benthamite frameworks sufficed.

Kant's views are well-known albeit not free from ambiguity. Punishment is a "categorical imperative," which means that its imposition, irrespective of good or bad effects, is a moral requirement derivable from first principles. Three passages are especially well-known and frequently quoted. The first is often interpreted to forbid consequential considerations:

> Judicial punishment can never be used merely as a means to promote some other good for the criminal himself or for civil society, but instead it must in all cases be imposed on him only on the ground that he has committed a crime; for a human being can never be manipulated merely as a means to the purposes of someone else. (Kant, 1798, p. 100).

The second is often understood to require that punishments be strictly apportioned to the seriousness of the crime:

> What kind and what degree of punishment does public legal justice adopt as its principle and standard? None other than the principle of equality. (Kant, 1798, p. 101).

The third is often understood to make clear that the effects of punishment are immaterial and that the state's legal duty to enforce the categorical imperative of deserved punishment is unqualified:

> Even if a civil society were to dissolve itself by common agreement of all its members (for example, if the people inhabiting an island decided to separate and disperse themselves around the world), the last murderer remaining in prison must first be executed, so that everyone will duly receive what his actions were worth and so that the bloodguilt thereof will not be fixed on the people because they failed to insist on carrying out the punishment; for if they fail to do so, they may be regarded as accomplices in this public violation of legal justice. (Kant, 1965, p. 102).

Hegel's analysis of punishment is based on a more complex metaphysic, but shares two elements with Kant's: the idea that respect for the moral autonomy of the criminal, his capacity for making moral choices, requires that he be punished, and the idea that punishments must be apportioned to the seriousness of crimes.

Hegel offers a strikingly modern formulation:

> The universal feeling of peoples and individuals towards crime is, and always has been, that it *deserves* to be punished, and that *what the criminal has done should be done to him*. But the

> determination of *equality* has brought a major difficulty into the idea of retribution. It is very easy to portray the retributive aspect of punishment as an absurdity (theft as retribution for theft, robbery for robbery, an eye for an eye, and a tooth for a tooth, so that one can even imagine the miscreant as one-eyed or toothless); but the concept has nothing to do with this absurdity. Equality remains merely the basic measure of the criminal's *essential* deserts, but not of the specific external shape which the retribution should take. It is then, as already remarked, a matter for the understanding to seek an approximate equivalence. Retribution cannot aim to achieve specific equality. (Hegel 1991, pp.128–29; italic in original; underscoring mine).

The principle criticism of retributivism is that at base it is no more than an expression of vindictiveness or vengeance.

The object of the criminal law for Bentham was to "augment the total happiness of the community" and "to exclude as far as may be, everything that tends to subtract from that happiness: in other words, to exclude mischief" (Bentham, p. 158). The goal is sometimes expressed as achieving the "greatest good for the greatest number."

Critically, however, everyone's happiness—including that of offenders—counts: "But all punishment is mischief: all punishment is evil. Upon the principle of utility, if it is at all to be admitted, it ought only to be admitted in as far as it promises to exclude some greater evil" (Bentham, p. 158).

Penalties should be set so that the expected burden of punishment is greater than the benefits of crime. Punishments should be severer for more serious crimes than for less serious ones to provide incentives to commit the less serious.

Federal District Court Judge Jack Weinstein was one of the 20th Century's leading experts on the law of evidence. Judge Weinstein's opinion in *United States v. Blarek* offers insights into the justification of punishment.

UNITED STATES V. BLAREK

United States District Court, E.D. New York
7 F. Supp. 2d 192 (1998)

WEINSTEIN, SENIOR DISTRICT JUDGE:

Sentencing is a critical stage of a criminal prosecution. It represents an important moment in the law, a fundamental judgment determining how, where, and why the offender should be dealt with for what may be much or all of his remaining life. It is significant not only for the individual before the court, but for his family and friends, the victims of his crime, potential future victims, and society as a whole.

Four core considerations, in varying degrees and permutations, have traditionally shaped American sentencing determinations: incapacitation of the criminal, rehabilitation of the offender, deterrence of the defendant and of others, and just deserts for the crime committed.

Ascertaining priorities among these potentially conflicting notions has long been a point of contention amongst legislators, scholars, jurists, and practitioners. Somewhat oversimplifying, there are two basic camps. Retributivists contend that "just deserts" are to be imposed for a crime committed. Utilitarians, in their various manifestations, suggest that penalties need to be viewed more globally by measuring their benefits against their costs.

Implied in this debate are questions about our basic values and beliefs: Why do we impose punishment? Or is it properly to be named "punishment"? Is our purpose retributive? Is it to deter the defendant himself or others in the community from committing crimes? Is it for reform? rehabilitation? incapacitation of dangerous people? Questions like these have engaged philosophers and students of the criminal law for centuries.

In the nineteenth and most of the twentieth century American prison and punishment system reforms were designed primarily to rehabilitate the prisoner as a protection against further crime. In more recent years there has been a perception by many that attempts at rehabilitation have failed; a movement towards theoretically-based, more severe, fixed punishments, based upon the nature of the crime gained momentum. Two eighteenth and nineteenth century philosophers set the terms of the current late twentieth century debate.

1. Kant's Retributive Just Deserts Theory

Immanuel Kant, born in East Prussia in 1724, is regarded by some as "one of the most important philosophers in Western culture." Kant's anti-utilitarian thesis on criminal penalties is reflected in an oft-cited passage from his work, *The Metaphysical Elements of Justice*: "Juridical punishment can never be used merely as a means to promote some other good for the criminal himself or for civil society, but instead it must in all cases be imposed on him only on the ground that he has committed a crime; for a human being can never be manipulated merely as a means to the purposes of someone else and can never be confused with the objects of the Law of things." It follows from this position that the sole justification for criminal punishment is retribution or "jus talionis."

For Kant and his adherents, "punishment that gives an offender what he or she deserves for a past crime is a valuable end in itself and needs no further justification." "It is not inflicted because it will give an opportunity for reform, but because it is merited." Kantian "just deserts" theory, therefore, focuses almost exclusively on the past to determine the level of punishment that should be meted out to right the wrong that has already occurred as a result of the defendant's delict.

2. Bentham's Utilitarian Theory

Jeremy Bentham, an English philosopher born in 1748, advocated a far different, more prospective approach through his "Principle of Utility." For him, law in general, and criminal jurisprudence in particular, was intended to produce the "greatest happiness for the greatest number," a concept sometimes referred to as the "felicity calculus."

This is not to say that Bentham did not believe in sanctions. It was his view that punishment was sometimes essential to ensure compliance with public laws.

Unlike his contemporary, Kant, Bentham was not interested in criminal punishment as a way of avenging or canceling the theoretical wrong suffered by society through a deviation from its norms. Rather, a criminal sanction was to be utilized only when it could help ensure the greater good of society and provide a benefit to the community. Bentham's writings in *An Introduction to the Principles of Morals and Legislation* explain this theory:

> All punishment is mischief: all punishment in itself evil. Upon the principle of utility, if it ought at all to be admitted, it ought only to be admitted in as far as it promises to exclude some greater evil in the following cases punishment ought not to be inflicted.
>
> I. Where it is groundless: where there is no mischief for it to prevent: the act not being mischievous upon the whole.
>
> II. Where it must be inefficacious: where it cannot act so as to prevent the mischief.
>
> III. Where it is unprofitable, or too expensive: where the mischief it would produce would be greater than what it prevented.
>
> IV. Where it is needless: where the mischief may be prevented, or cease of itself, without it: that is, at a cheaper rate.

Under the Benthamite approach, deterring crime, as well as correction and reformation of the criminal, are primary aspirations of criminal law. While the theory of retribution would impose punishment for its own sake, the utilitarian theories of deterrence and reformation would use punishment as a means to a practical end—the end being community protection by the prevention of crime.

3. Sanctions in Strict Retributive and Utilitarian Models

Given the divergence in underlying assumptions and theory, the competing retributivist and utilitarian theories suggest opposing methods for ascertaining proper penalties. Under a Kantian model, the extent of punishment is required to neatly fit the crime. "Whoever commits a crime must be punished in accordance with his desert."

In the case of murder, some believe that just desert is clear. A taker of life must have his own life taken. Even in the case of killings, however, there are degrees of *mens rea*, and over large portions of the world capital punishment is outlawed on a variety of just deserts and utilitarian grounds.

For lesser offenses, reaching a consensus on the proper "price" for the criminal act under the Kantian approach is even more difficult.

Two main theoretical problems are presented by this just deserts approach. The degree of the earned desert—that is to say the extent or length of the appropriate punishment—is subjective.

Determining the appropriateness of sanction differs under Bentham's utilitarian approach, although it too poses challenging theoretical and practical tasks for the sentencer. Under this model, among: "the factors [to be considered] are the need to set penalties in such a way that where a person is tempted to commit one of two crimes he will commit the lesser, that the evil consequences of the crime will be minimized even if the crime is committed, that the least amount possible of punishment be used for the prevention of a given crime."

Obviously, one problem with utilizing a system based only upon this approach is that it is difficult to determine when more good than harm has been achieved. As in the case of Kantian just deserts, the felicity calculation is subject to considerable difficulty and dispute.

Given these problems, it may make sense to continue to equivocate, oscillating between these poles, tempering justice with mercy, just deserts with utility calculations, in varying pragmatic ways.

The battle over justifying punishment is far from over. Indeed, the battle will probably never end. Justifications that are in fashion at one time fall out of fashion at another. For the first six decades of the Twentieth Century, rehabilitation and utilitarianism held sway. During this period, indeterminate sentencing was the order of the day, allowing judges and parole boards broad discretion to tailor punishments to individual criminals. The 1970s witnessed widespread disenchantment with rehabilitation—"Rehabilitation doesn't work." At the same time, there was a decided move to "get tough on crime." In 1984, President Reagan famously said, "The liberal approach to coddling criminals didn't work and never will." The emphasis shifted away from rehabilitation and toward retribution and incapacitation. Along with the shift, states and the federal government replaced indeterminate sentencing with determinate sentencing based on the principles of "just deserts" and retribution. Interestingly, in the second decade of the Twenty-First Century, rehabilitation is making a comeback. The pendulum never rests.

Jeremy Bentham trained as a lawyer. He was, as the English say, "Called to the bar," although he never practiced. Bentham's *Principles of Morals and Legislation,* excerpted below, sets forth Bentham's utilitarian justification of punishment. Bentham's Chapter I defines "utility." Chapter XIII outlines circumstances where punishment should not be imposed. When punishment *is* proper, Chapter IX established the framework to determine the proper punishment.

After you read the excerpt from Bentham's *Principles of Morals and Legislation*, you will be asked to use his framework to determine the proper punishment for specified crimes. For the same crimes, you will be asked to take off your utilitarian hat and don your retributivist chapeau. Will the punishments you recommend as a utilitarian be the same as the ones you select as a retributivist?

JEREMY BENTHAM, THE PRINCIPLES OF MORALS AND LEGISLATION

Chapter I

I. Nature has placed mankind under the governance of two sovereign masters, pain and pleasure. It is for them alone to point out what we ought to do, as well as to determine what we shall do. On the one hand the standard of right and wrong on the other the chain of causes and effects, are fastened to their throne. They govern us in all we do, in all we say, in all we think: every effort we can make to throw off our subjection, will serve but to demonstrate and confirm it. In words a man may pretend to abjure their empire: but in reality he will remain subject to it all the while. The principle of utility recognizes this subjection, and assumes it for the foundation of that system, the object of which is to rear the fabric of felicity by the hands of reason and of law. Systems which attempt to question it, deal in sounds instead of sense, in caprice instead of reason, in darkness instead of light.

But enough of metaphor and declamation: it is not by such means that moral science is to be improved.

II. The principle of utility is the foundation of the present work: it will be proper therefore at the outset to give an explicit and determinate account of what is meant by it. By the principle of utility is meant that principle which approves or disapproves of every action whatsoever, according to the tendency which it appears to have to augment or diminish the happiness of the party whose interest is in question: or, what is the same thing in other words, to promote or to oppose that happiness. I say of every action whatsoever; and therefore not only of every action of a private individual, but of every measure of government.

III. By utility is meant that property in any object, whereby it tends to produce benefit advantage, pleasure, good, or happiness, (all this in the present case comes to the same thing) or (what comes again to the same thing) to prevent the happening of mischief, pain, evil, or unhappiness to the party whose interest is considered: if that party be the community in general, then the happiness of the community: if a particular individual, then the happiness of that individual.

IV. The interest of the community is one of the most general expressions that can occur in the phraseology of morals: no wonder that the meaning of it is often lost. When it has a meaning, it is this. The community is a fictitious body, composed of the individual persons who are considered as constituting as it were its members. The interest of the community then is, what?—the sum of the interests of the several members who compose it.

V. It is in vain to talk of the interest of the community, without understanding what is the interest of the individual. A thing is said to promote the interest, or to be for the interest, of an individual, when it tends to add to the sum total of his pleasures: or, what comes to the same thing, to diminish the sum total of his pains.

VI. An action then may be said to be conformable to the principle of utility, or, for shortness sake, to utility, (meaning with respect to the community at large) when the tendency it has to augment the happiness of the community is greater than any it has to diminish it.

VII. A measure of government (which is but a particular kind of action, performed by a particular person or persons) may be said to be conformable to or dictated by the principle of utility, when in like manner the tendency which it has to augment the happiness of the community is greater than any which it has to diminish it.

Chapter XIII

§ 1. General view of cases unmeet for punishment.

I. The general object which all laws have, or ought to have, in common, is to augment the total happiness of the community; and therefore, in the first place, to exclude, as far as may be, everything that tends to subtract from that happiness: in other words, to exclude mischief.

II. But all punishment is mischief: all punishment in itself is evil. Upon the principle of utility, if it ought at all to be admitted, it ought only to be admitted in as far as it promises to exclude some greater evil.

III. It is plain, therefore, that in the following cases punishment ought not to be inflicted.

1. Where it is *groundless*: where there is no mischief for it to prevent; the act not being mischievous upon the whole.

2. Where it must be *inefficacious*: where it cannot act so as to prevent the mischief.

3. Where it is *unprofitable*, or too expensive: where the mischief it would produce would be greater than what it prevented.

4. Where it is *needless*: where the mischief may be prevented, or cease of itself, without it: that is, at a cheaper rate.

§ 2. Cases in which punishment is *groundless*. These are:

IV. 1. Where there has never been any mischief: where no mischief has been produced to any body by the act in question. Of this number are those in which the act was such as might, on some occasions, be mischievous or disagreeable, but the person whose interest it concerns gave his consent to the performance of it. This consent, provided it be free, and fairly obtained, is the best proof that can be produced, that, to the person who gives it, no mischief, at least no immediate mischief, upon the whole, is done. For no man can be so good a judge as the man himself, what it is gives him pleasure or displeasure.

V. 2. Where the mischief was outweighed: although a mischief was produced by that act, yet the same act was necessary to the production of a benefit which was of greater value than the mischief.

§ 3. Cases in which punishment must be *inefficacious*. These are:

VII. 1. Where the penal provision is not established until after the act is done. Such are the cases, I. Of an ex-post-facto law; where the legislator himself appoints not a punishment till after the act is done.

VIII. 2. Where the penal provision, though established, is not conveyed to the notice of the person on whom it seems intended that it should operate.

IX. 3. Where the penal provision, though it were conveyed to a man's notice, could produce no effect on him, with respect to the preventing him from engaging in any act of the sort in question. Such is the case, (1). In extreme infancy; where a man has not yet attained that state or disposition of mind in which the prospect of evils so distant as those which are held forth by the law, has the effect of influencing his conduct. (2). In insanity; where the person, if he has attained to that disposition, has since been deprived of it through the influence of some permanent though unseen cause. (3). In intoxication; where he has been deprived of it by the transient influence of a visible cause: such as the use of wine, or opium, or other drugs, that act in this manner on the nervous system: which condition is indeed neither more nor less than a temporary insanity produced by an assignable cause.

§ 4. Cases where punishment is *unprofitable.* These are:

XIII. 1. Where, on the one hand, the nature of the offence, on the other hand, that of the punishment, are, in the ordinary state of things, such, that when compared together, the evil of the later will turn out to the greater than that of the former.

§ 5. Cases where punishment is *needless.* These are:

XVII 1. Where the purpose of putting an end to the practice may be attained as effectually at a cheaper rate: by instruction, for instance, as well as by terror: by informing the understanding; as well as by exercising an immediate influence on the will.

Chapter XIV.

I. We have seen that the general object of all laws is to prevent mischief; that is to say, when it is worth while; but that, where there are no other means of doing this than punishment, there are four cases in which it is not worth while.

II. When it is worth while, there are four subordinate designs or objects, which, in the course of his endeavours to compass, as far as may be, that one general object, a legislator, whose views are governed by the principle of utility, comes naturally to propose to himself.

III. 1. His first, most extensive, and most eligible object, is to prevent, in as far as it is possible, and worth while, all sorts of offences whatsoever: in other words, so to manage, that no offence whatsoever may be committed.

IV. 2. But if a man must needs commit an offence of some kind or other, the next object is to induce him to commit an offence less mischievous, rather than one more mischievous: in other words, to choose always the least mischievous, of two offences that will either of them suit his purpose.

V. 3. When a man has resolved upon a particular offence, the next object is to dispose him to do no more mischief than is necessary to his purpose: in other words, to do as little mischief as is consistent with the benefit he has in view.

VI. 4. The last object is, whatever the mischief be, which it is proposed to prevent, to prevent it at as cheap a rate as possible.

VII. Subservient to these four objects, or purposes, must be the rules or canons by which the proportion of punishments offences is to be governed.

VIII. Rule I. The first object, it has been seen, is to prevent, in as far as it is worth while, all sorts of offences; therefore, The value of the punishment must be less in any case than what is sufficient to outweigh that of the profit of the offence.

If it be, the offence (unless some other considerations, independent of the punishment, should intervene and operate efficaciously in the character of tutelary motives) will be sure to be committed notwithstanding: the whole lot of punishment will be thrown away: it will be altogether inefficacious.

IX. The above rule has been often objected to, on account of it seeming harshness: but this can only have happened for want of its being properly understood. The strength of the temptation, *coeteris paribus,* is as the profit of the offence: the quantum of the punishment must rise with the profit of the offence: *coeteris paribus,* it must therefore rise with the strength of the temptation.

X. Rule 2. But whether a given offence shall be prevented in a given degree by a given quantity of punishment, is never anything better than a chance; for the purchasing of which, whatever punishment is employed, is so much expended in advance. However, for the sake of giving it the better chance of outweighing the profit of the offence, The greater the mischief of the offence, the greater is the expense, which it may be worth while to be at, in the way of punishment.

XI. Rule 3. The next object is, to induce a man to choose always the least mischievous of two offences; therefore, Where two offences come in competition, the punishment for the greater offence must be sufficient to induce a man to prefer the less.

XII. Rule 4. When a man has resolved upon a particular offence, the next object is, to induce him to do no more mischief than what is necessary for his purpose: therefore, The punishment should be adjusted in such manner to each particular offence, that for every part of the mischief there may be a motive to restrain the offender from giving birth to it.

XIII. Rule 5. The last object is, whatever mischief is guarded against, to guard against it at as cheap a rate as possible: therefore, The punishment ought in no case to be more than what is necessary to bring it into conformity with the rule here given.

Exercise in Punishment: The Legislature establishes punishments for crime. For this exercise, *you* are a legislator. Employ Bentham's framework to establish the appropriate punishment for the crimes listed below. As you go about your work, consider the advice of Henry Hart in his article "The Aims of the Criminal Law": "Are comparatively severe punishments to be favored or comparatively lenient ones? Here is a question of public policy which is pre-eminently for the legislature. On this question, its cardinal aims should be its cardinal guide. Punishments should be severe enough to impress not only upon the defendant's mind, but upon the public mind, the gravity of society's condemnation of irresponsible behavior."[6] Equally good advice comes from H.L.A. Hart in his book *Punishment and Responsibility*:

> Long sentences of imprisonment might effectively stamp out car parking offenses, yet we think it wrong to employ them; not because there is for each crime a penalty "naturally" fitted to its degree of iniquity (as some Retributionists might think); not because we are convinced that the misery caused by such sentences would be greater than that caused by the offences unchecked (as a Utilitarian might argue). The guiding principle is that of proportion within a system of penalties between those imposed for different offenses where these have a distinct place in a commonsense scale of gravity. This scale itself no doubt consists of very broad judgments both of relative moral iniquity and harmfulness of different types of offense: it draws rough distinctions like that between parking offenses and homicide, or between "mercy killing" and murder for gain, but cannot cope with any precise assessment of an individual's wickedness in committing a crime (Who can?)[7]

With this guidance in mind, use Bentham's framework to set the sentences for:

Burglary.

Trespass to land.

Theft.

Robbery.

Assault.

Battery.

Rape.

---

[6] Henry M. Hart, Jr., The Aims of the Criminal Law, 23 *Law and Contemporary Problems* 401–441 (1958).

[7] H.L.A. Hart, Punishment and Responsibility: Essays in the Philosophy of Law p. 25 (1968)(Oxford University Press).

Assault with intent to commit rape.

Intent to kill murder.

Attempted murder.

Involuntary manslaughter based on criminal negligence.

Conspiracy.

Now switch gears: use retributivist reasoning to determine what punishment is deserved for each crime.

PART 2.
CALIFORNIA SENTENCING LAW

California sentencing law is complicated. If you practice in California, you will learn the details. The goal in Part 2 is to introduce the subject. Today, sentencing in California is an amalgam of determinate and indeterminate sentencing, enhancements that add years to underlying sentences, recidivist statutes, including "Three Strikes," and the death penalty.

Kara Dansky examined the history of California sentencing and divided "California's punishment history into three time periods—Statehood (1850–1916), the Indeterminate Sentencing Era (1917–1976), and the Determinate Sentencing Era (1977–present)."[8]

In 1917, the Legislature enacted the Indeterminate Sentencing Act. Judges imposed indeterminate sentences tailored to the seriousness of the crime and the attributes of the offender. A primary goal was rehabilitating offenders. The actual length of time served was decided by the Board of Prison Directors. A prisoner could earn release by proving that she or he had reformed.

There were (and are) criticisms of indeterminate sentencing. Sentences for the same offense may vary from judge to judge—one judge is "easy on crime," while the judge in the next courtroom is a "hanging judge." Indeterminate sentencing reposes tremendous discretion in judges, increasing the odds sentences will be influenced, consciously or unconsciously, by race and ethnicity. Michael Vitiello and Clark Kelso write, "Additional questions were raised concerning the lack of proportionality between the underlying crime and the term of imprisonment. For example, what if a person needs a long period of incarceration to be deterred from acts of petty theft or cured of the desire to commit such offense, while a person committing homicide does not? The system simply tolerated too much unchecked discretion: judges faced with similar offenders could and did impose wildly different sentences on the

[8] Kara Dansky, Understanding California Sentencing, 43 *U.S.F. L. Rev.* 45 (2008).

offenders. Beyond the courts, correctional authorities had unbridled discretion to determine release dates."[9]

In 1976, the Legislature abandoned indeterminate sentencing, with its emphasis on rehabilitation, and passed the Determinate Sentencing Law (DSL), with an emphasis on punishment, incapacitation, and deterrence. PC § 1170 of the 1976 law read in part: "The Legislature finds and declares that the purpose of imprisonment for crime is punishment." By 2018, the pendulum was swinging back toward rehabilitation. The Legislature amended PC § 1170 to provide: "The purpose of sentencing is public safety achieved through punishment, rehabilitation, and restorative justice."

The DSL specifies three possible sentences for most crimes. The three sentences are called triads. Not all crimes specify a triad (*e.g.*, forgery, P.C. § 473). Triads for a few crimes follow: Rape: 3, 6, or 8 years. Burglary, first degree: 2, 4, or 6 years. Grand theft: 16 months, 2, or 3 years. Extortion: 2, 3, or 7 years. Kidnapping: 3, 5, or 8 years. Robbery, first degree: 3, 6, or 9 years.

The DSL retains indeterminate sentencing for certain serious crimes. For example, kidnapping during the commission of carjacking is punished by imprisonment for life with the possibility of parole. (P.C. § 209.5(a)).

In addition to a sentence from the applicable triad, a defendant's sentence may be increased by one or more of the myriad so-called enhancements.[10] There are two types of enhancements. First, conduct enhancements related to the way the crime was committed. The list of conduct enhancements is long (more than 60)! A defendant convicted of felony arson gets a 3, 4, or 5 year enhancement if, *inter alia,* a firefighter is seriously injured fighting the fire. One of the most frequently imposed conduct enhancements is an additional 10 years for personal use of a firearm during commission of a crime.

The second type of enhancement relates to the defendant's previous criminal record. A recidivist is subject to harsher punishment. Thus, Penal Code § 667.5 provides a 3 year enhancement for a defendant convicted of a violent felony, if the defendant has served time in prison for other crimes. Indeed, the defendant gets 3 more years for *each* prior separate prison

[9] Michael Vitiello & Clark Kelso, A Proposal for a Wholesale Reform of California's Sentencing Practice and Policy, 38 *Loyola of Los Angeles Law Review* 903, 918 (2004). *See also* Michael Vitiello, Alternatives to Incarceration: Why Is California Lagging Behind?, 28 *Georgia State University Law Review* 1275 (2012); Michael Vitiello, California's Three Strikes and We're Out: Was Judicial Activism California's Best Hope? 37 *U.C. Davis Law Review* 1025 (2004).

[10] California Rules of Court, Rule 4.405(3) defines "enhancement" as "an additional term of imprisonment added to the base term." Rule 4.405(2) defines "base term" as "the determinate prison term selected from among the three possible terms prescribed by statute or the determinate prison term prescribed by law if a range of three possible terms is not prescribed."

term. For good measure, each enhancement is to be served consecutive to the base term.

California's most famous recidivist sentencing statute is the "Three Strikes" law. The name is misleading because there actually are "One," "Two," and "Three Strike" laws.[11] Penal Code § 667 is the heart of Three Strikes. Section 667(e)(1) states that if the defendant has one prior serious or violent felony conviction, the normally applicable determinate sentence, or the minimum term for an indeterminate term, shall be doubled. If the defendant has two or more prior serious or violent felony convictions, the term for the current felony is an indeterminate term of life in prison, with a minimum term calculated as the greatest of three times the normal punishment or 25 years.

The United States Supreme Court upheld California's Three Strikes law in *Ewing v. California* (2003) 538 U.S. 11, 123 S. Ct. 1179. The Court wrote:

> California's three strikes law reflects a shift in the State's sentencing policies toward incapacitating and deterring repeat offenders who threaten the public safety. The law designed was to ensure longer prison sentences and greater punishment for those who commit a felony and have been previously convicted of serious and/or violent felony offenses. On March 3, 1993, California Assemblymen Bill Jones and Jim Costa introduced Assembly Bill 971, the legislative version of what would later become the three strikes law. The Assembly Committee on Public Safety defeated the bill only weeks later. Public outrage over the defeat sparked a voter initiative to add Proposition 184, based loosely on the bill, to the ballot in the November 1994 general election.
>
> On October 1, 1993, while Proposition 184 was circulating, 12-year-old Polly Klaas was kidnapped from her home in Petaluma, California. Her admitted killer Richard Allen Davis, had a long criminal history that included two prior kidnapping convictions. Davis had served only half of his most recent sentence (16 years for kidnapping, assault, and burglary). Had Davis served his entire sentence, he would still have been in prison on the day that Polly Klaas was kidnapped.

To interrupt the Supreme Court for a moment, and to put a human face on why Three Strikes came into existence, the circumstances of Polly Klaas's kidnapping and murder are relevant. The California Supreme Court described the crime in *People v. Davis* (2009) 46 Cal. 4th 539, 552–

---

[11] *See People v. Lewis*, (2013) 222 Ca. App. 4th 108, 165 Cal. Rptr. 3d 624 ("The one strike law (§ 667.1) provides harsher sentences for sexual offenses under specified circumstances.").

558, 94 Cal. Rptr. 3d 322, where the Court affirmed the death sentence for Polly's killer:

> On Friday, October 1, 1993, Polly had a slumber party at her home with two classmates, 12-year-old Kate M. and 12-year-old Gillian P. Gillian arrived between 7:00 and 7:15 p.m. Between 8:00 and 9:00 p.m., Kate arrived with her mother. The three girls played in Polly's bedroom. Around 10:00 p.m. [Polly's mother, Nicol] told the girls not to stay up too late and to keep the noise down, as she [was] going to bed. From 10:00 to 10:30 p.m., the three girls played board games and video games.
>
> The girls decided to set up their sleeping bags. When Polly opened the bedroom door to retrieve the sleeping bags, she discovered defendant in the doorway holding a knife and a bag. Defendant said, "Don't scream or I'll slit your throats," and promised not to hurt them if they did what he said. He told the girls to lie facedown on the floor and not to look at him.
>
> All three girls lay down in a row on Polly's bedroom floor, and defendant tied their hands using a silky cloth, cords cut from Polly's Nintendo machine, and a strap from Polly's leather purse. He also gagged them with a silky cloth. He removed the cases from pillows in the bedroom and placed them over the girls' heads.
>
> Defendant told the girls that he was going to take Polly to show him where the valuables were, that he would then return Polly to Gillian and Kate, and that he would be gone after they counted to 1,000. Defendant then took Polly out of the room, promising he would not touch her. At that point, defendant had been in the bedroom for approximately 10 minutes.
>
> After a few minutes' counting, with no sign of Polly, Gillian and Kate freed themselves, went to Nichol's bedroom, and told her what had happened. After they all unsuccessfully searched for Polly around the house, Nichol called 911 around 11:00 p.m.
>
> [Defendant kidnapped Polly and drove away, only to get his car stuck on a private road. The property owner called the sheriff. Before deputies arrived, Defendant took Polly out of the car, bound and gagged, and placed her a short distance from the car. Two deputies arrived and helped Defendant free his car. Tragically, there was nothing to alert the deputies that Polly was sitting a few yards away. The deputies departed.]
>
> Defendant decided he had to kill Polly to avoid return to prison, so he strangled her with a piece of knotted cloth. He later cinched a piece of cord tight around Polly's neck "just to make sure," then dragged her to some bushes and covered her body with

a piece of plywood and chunks of wood that he found in the area. Defendant said he did not think that he had sex with Polly or that he tried to have sex with her.

Polly's badly decomposed body lay under a piece of plywood and other pieces of wood in an area covered with thorny blackberry briar, this underbrush, and debris. Her skeletonized skull lay a short distance from the rest of her body, probably a result of animal activity.

Returning to the U.S. Supreme Court's discussion of Three Strikes in *Ewing v. California*, the Supreme Court wrote:

> Polly Klaas' murder galvanized support for the three strikes initiative. Proposition 184 was on its way to becoming the fastest qualifying initiative in California history.
>
> California thus became the second State to enact a three strikes law. In November 1993, the voters of Washington State approved their own three strikes law. Between 1993 and 1995, 24 States and the Federal Government enacted three strikes laws.

In 2012, Proposition 36 was approved by popular vote. Among other things, Prop 36 limits the application of Three Strikes to cases in which the most recent conviction is for a serious or violent felony.

PART 3. CAPITAL PUNISHMENT—DEATH PENALTY

California has the death penalty for murder. California Constitution Article I, § 27 provides: "The death penalty provided under [California statutory law] shall not be deemed to be, or to constitute, the infliction of cruel or unusual punishments."

Special rules apply to jury selection in death penalty cases. In *People v. Armstrong* (2019) 6 Cal. 5th 735, 433 P.3d 987, 243 Cal. Rptr. 3d 105, the Supreme Court wrote:

> The Sixth Amendment's guarantee of an impartial jury confers on capital defendants the right to a jury not uncommonly willing to condemn a man to die. The accommodate this right, past decisions of the United States Supreme Court and this court establish that a prospective juror may be challenged for cause based upon his or her views regarding capital punishment only if those views would prevent or substantially impair the performance of the juror's duties as defined by the court's

instructions and the juror' oath. A prospective juror is properly excluded if he or she is unable to conscientiously consider all of the sentencing alternatives, including the death penalty where appropriate. . . .

Not all who oppose the death penalty are subject to removal; those who firmly believe that the death penalty is unjust may nevertheless serve as jurors in capital cases so long as they state clearly that they are willing to temporarily set side their own beliefs in deference to the rule of law. The critical issue is whether a life-leaning prospective juror—that is, one generally (but not invariably) favoring life in prison instead of the death penalty as an appropriate punishment—can set aside his or her personal views about capital punishment and follow the law as the trial judge instructs. Jurors are not required to like the law, but they are required to follow it. A jury candidate who will not, or cannot follow a statutory frame work, is not qualified to serve. Yet so long as prospective jurors can obey the court's instructions and determine whether death is appropriate based on a sincere consideration of aggravating and mitigating circumstances, they are not ineligible to serve. . . .

The state is permitted to cull from the jury pool only those who would be unable to set aside their personal views and follow the law and the court's instructions.

Linda Carter, Ellen Kreitzberg and Scott Howe discuss the arguments for and against the death penalty in their book on the subject.

LINDA E. CARTER, ELLEN S. DREITZBERT & SCOTT W. HOWE, UNDERSTANDING CAPITAL PUNISHMENT LAW

(4th ed. 2018)

§ 2.01 Major Arguments for and Against the Death Penalty

Is the death penalty a deterrent to violent crimes? Is it inherently inhumane and, if not, is it a just penalty for murder? Can the death penalty be imposed fairly? Is it cost effective? These kinds of questions about capital punishment continue to be debated in legislatures, in the press, and in the classes of our schools and universities. . . .

The American public generally continues to favor retention of the death penalty. According to a Gallup poll in October, 2016, 60% of Americans favored the death penalty for murder. . . .

The major points of contention in the ongoing debates over the death penalty can be divided into three areas. The first is whether the death penalty serves a legitimate penological purpose, and the two purposes that dominate the discussion are deterrence and retribution. The second issue is whether the system for deciding who will receive the death penalty is sufficiently accurate and nondiscriminatory to satisfy us that the process is fair. The third issue raises a pragmatic concern over the cost of pursuing a death sentence in comparison to incarcerating the defendant for life.

DEATH PENALTY PROCEDURE IN CALIFORNIA

A death penalty case is divided into two parts. In the first part—the guilt phase—the jury determines whether the defendant is guilty of first degree murder with one or more special circumstances eligible for the death penalty. If the jury convicts, the second phase is the penalty phase. In the penalty phase, the prosecution and defense present aggravating and mitigating evidence about the defendant.

In death penalty cases, special rules apply in jury selection. Prospective jurors who are unalterably opposed to the death penalty cannot apply existing law and may be excused for cause. In *People v. Blair* (2005) 36 Cal.4th 686, 742, 31 Cal.Rptr.3d 485, 115 P.3d 1145, the Supreme Court wrote: "To achieve the constitutional imperative of impartiality, the law permits a prospective juror to be challenged for cause only if his or her views in favor of or against capital punishment would prevent or substantially impair the performance of his or her duties as a juror in accordance with the court's instructions and the juror's oath."

The fact that a prospective juror is personally against the death penalty does not mean the juror cannot be impartial. Some jurors who oppose the death penalty are capable of setting aside their personal views on capital punishment and applying the law fairly. As the Supreme Court wrote in *People v. Kaurish* (1990) 52 Cal.3d 648, 699, 276 Cal.Rptr. 788, 802 P.2d 278, the law does not require "that jurors be automatically excused if they merely express personal opposition to the death penalty. The real question is whether the juror's attitude will prevent or substantially impair the performance of his duties as a juror in accordance with his instructions and his oath."

CAPITAL PUNISHMENT FOR CRIMES OTHER THAN MURDER?

In *Coker v. Georgia* (1977) 433 U.S. 584, 97 S.Ct. 2861, the U.S. Supreme Court ruled the death penalty unconstitutional for rape of an adult woman. In *Kennedy v. Louisiana* (2008) 554 U.S. 407, 128 S.Ct. 2641, the Court ruled the death penalty unconstitutional for rape of a child.

CALIFORNIA COMMISSION ON THE FAIR ADMINISTRATION OF JUSTICE

Consider the following excerpts from the majority and dissenting reports of the California Commission on the Fair Administration of Justice,

Report and Recommendations on the Administration of the Death Penalty in California (2008):

In 1978, the people of the State of California expressed their support for the death penalty and, accordingly, the death penalty is the law of this State. However, it is the law in name only, and not in realty.

We currently have a dysfunctional system. The lapse of time from sentence of death to execution averages over two decades in California. Just to keep cases moving at this snail's pace, we spend large amounts of tax payers' money each year: by conservative estimates, well over one hundred million dollars annually. The families of murder victims are cruelly deluded into believing that justice will be delivered with finality during their lifetimes. Those condemned to death in violation of law must wait years until the courts determine they are entitled to a new trial or penalty hearing. The strain placed by these cases on our justice system, in terms of the time and attention taken away from other business that the courts must conduct for our citizens, is heavy. To reduce the average lapse of time from sentence to execution by half, to the national average of 12 years, we will have to spend nearly twice what we are spending now.

The remedies which the Commission has proposed will require the new investment of at least $95 million dollars per year. We recognize that we call for this investment in the face of a budget crisis of a great magnitude for California. The Commission has examined two alternatives available to California to reduce the costs imposed by California's death penalty law. First, to reduce the number of death penalty cases in the system by narrowing the list of special circumstances that make one eligible for the death penalty, and second, to replace the death penalty with a maximum penalty of lifetime incarceration without the possibility of parole.

California law requires three separate findings before a sentence of death may be imposed. First, the fact-finder (normally a jury, unless the right to jury trial has been waived) must determine that the defendant is guilty of first-degree murder. Second, the fact-finder must determine that one or more of twenty-one separately enumerated "special circumstances" is true. Both of these findings require proof beyond a reasonable doubt during the trial. If the defendant is convicted of first-degree murder and a special circumstance is found true, a "penalty phase" trial follows, at which the fact-finder considers evidence of "any matter relevant to aggravation, mitigation, and sentence." At the conclusion of the penalty phase, the jury is instructed as follows:

> Determine which penalty is appropriate and justified by considering all the evidence and the totality of any aggravating and mitigating circumstances. Even without mitigating circumstance, you may decide that the aggravating circumstances, are not substantial enough to warrant death. To

> return a judgment of death, each of you must be persuaded that the aggravating circumstances both outweigh the mitigating circumstances and are also so substantial in comparison to the mitigating circumstances that a sentence of death is appropriate and justified.

A defendant sentenced to death in California has a right to three stages of review of the conviction and sentence: an automatic appeal directly to the California Supreme Court; a petition for a writ of habeas corpus filed in the California Supreme Court; and a federal habeas corpus petition filed in the Federal District Court.

At each of these three stages, the defendant is entitled to the appointment of counsel if he or she is indigent. All of the 670 inmates on California's death row qualify as indigents. Review of the California Supreme Court's decision of the direct appeal and the state habeas corpus petition can be sought in the United States Supreme Court by petition for a writ of *certiorari*. A Federal District Court ruling on a federal habeas corpus petition can be appealed to the United States Court of Appeals for the Ninth Circuit, and review of that Court's decision can be sought in the United States Supreme Court. A defendant can also petition the Governor for clemency prior to his or her execution.

The United States Department of Justice has tracked the elapsed time from sentence to execution for all defendants who have been executed in the United States since 1978. The average lapse of time has grown steadily throughout the United States, from an average of 4.25 years during the period of 1977 to 1983, to an average of 12.25 years in 2005. The average lapse of time between pronouncement of a judgment of death and execution in California is 17.2 years, but using an "average" number may be misleading since only thirteen have been executed.

Delay in post-conviction review is not the only dysfunction in California's death penalty law. Federal courts are granting relief in 70% of the California death judgments they review, most often because of ineffective assistance of counsel at the trial level.

The Commission has learned of no credible evidence that the State of California has ever executed an innocent person. Nonetheless, the Commission cannot conclude with confidence that the administration of the death penalty in California eliminates the risk that innocent persons might be convicted and sentenced to death. Nationally, there were 205 exonerations of defendants convicted of murder from 1989 through 2003. Seventy-four of them had been sentenced to death.

Nationally, erroneous eye-witness identifications have been identified as a factor in 80% of exonerations, and false confessions were a factor in 15%.

[One witness] told the Commission, having 21 special circumstances is "unfathomable. The problem is the front-end of the system. There are too many people eligible to receive the death penalty."

An initiative of the Constitution Project, based in Washington, D.C., established a blue-ribbon bipartisan commission of judges, prosecutors, defense lawyers, elected officials, FBI and police officials, professors and civic and religious leaders to examine the administration of the death penalty throughout the United States. The Constitution Project achieved broad consensus on two key recommendations to reserve capital punishment for the most aggravated offenses and most culpable offenders:

> Death Penalty Eligibility Should Be Limited to Five Factors:
>
> The murder of a peace officer killed in the performance of his or her official duties when done to prevent or retaliate for that performance; The murder of any person (including but not limited to inmates, staff, and visitors) occurring at a correctional facility; The murder of two or more persons regardless of whether the deaths occurred as the result of the same act or of several related or unrelated acts, as long as either (a) the deaths were the result of an intent to kill more than one person, or (b) the defendant knew the act or acts would cause death or create a strong probability of death or great bodily harm to the murdered individuals or others; The intentional murder of a person involving the infliction of torture. The murder by a person who is under investigation for, or who has been charged with or has been convicted of, a crime that would be a felony, or the murder of anyone involved in the investigation, prosecution, or defense of that crime, including, but not limited to, witnesses, jurors, judges, prosecutors, and investigators. Felony Murder Should Be Excluded as the Basis for Death Penalty Eligibility.

Dissent to California Commission on the Fair Administration of Justice Report and Recommendations on the Administration of the Death Penalty in California

We respectfully dissent from the Report and Recommendations on the Administration of the Death Penalty in California, which was issued today by the California Commission on the Fair Administration of Justice. Regrettably, we believe the majority report indirectly assaults California's death penalty by seeking to undermine public confidence in our capital punishment law and procedure.

The report discusses two "available alternatives" to increased funding: narrowing the list of special circumstances that would make a murder case eligible for the death penalty, and eliminating the death penalty altogether. The Commission purports to "make no recommendation regarding these alternatives" and claims that it merely "presents information regarding them to assure a fully informed debate." But the lengthy discussion of these proposals consists entirely of arguments in favor of these alternatives and excludes any discussion against them. A "fully informed debate" should include both sides of an issue, not just one side.

Reducing the number of special circumstances would exclude some of California's most brutal murders from death row. The report goes so far as to suggest that these changes be retroactive to killers already on death row, even though the death penalty was lawfully imposed in those cases at the time. A few examples will illustrate how reducing the number of special circumstances would exclude from the death penalty some of California's most heinous murders:

- Gregory Scott Smith is on death row for the murder of an 8-year-old boy from whom he was a teacher's aide. He had previously been mean to the victim, and on two occasions had tied him up with jump ropes. Angry that the victim had asked that Smith be fired, Smith gagged the victim with a cloth gag and duct tape, forcibly sodomized him, and strangled him. He poured fire accelerant on the body and set the body on fire, where it was discovered burning by firefighters. Smith was convicted of murder in the commission of a kidnapping, a lewd act upon a child, and an act of sodomy. None of these special circumstances would warrant the death penalty under the Commission's proposal.
- The Commission's proposal would also exclude Mitchell Sims, known as the Domino's Pizza Killer, who is on death row with all state and federal review completed. After ordering pizza to be delivered to his motel room, Sims robbed the delivery driver, tied him up, strangled him with a rope, and fully submerged him in a bathtub with a gag tied into his mouth. After killing the driver, Sims went to Domino's, robbed two other employees at gunpoint, and forced them into the cooler, suspended with nooses around their necks. When one employee warned that the delivery driver was due back, Sims took off his sweater to reveal a Domino's shirt with the driver's name tag and chuckled. "No, I don't think so." Sims was found guilty of murder with special circumstances of murder while lying in wait and during the commission of a robbery, as well as attempted murder and robbery of the other employees. These special circumstances would not warrant the death penalty under the Commission's proposal.
- Stevie Lamar Fields is also on death row, with state and federal review completed. Shortly after being released from

prison for a previous manslaughter, Fields became what the California Supreme Court described as "a one-man crime wave." Sitting in a car with a victim, he fired five shots and told the driver to keep on driving. He said that the victim was not dead and he needed to be sure she was, so he hit her in the head with a blunt object and dumped her body into an alley. He was convicted of robbery-murder with the special circumstance of murder during the commission of a robbery, as well as kidnapping for robbery and forced oral copulation of several other women. Under the Commission's proposal to limit special circumstances, Fields would escape the death penalty.

- The Commission advocates eliminating the death penalty in felony-murder cases. One such case this proposal would exclude is Vicente Benavides, who was sentenced to death for the murder of a 21 month-old girl he was babysitting. The victim died of an acute blunt force penetrating injury of the anus. The anus was expanded to seven or eight times its normal size, and multiple internal organs were injured. The victim's upper lip was torn, consistent with a hand being held over her mouth, and there was evidence of previous rib fractures. The special circumstances were felony-murder rape, felony-murder rape, and felony-murder sodomy, all of which the proposal would eliminate is bases for the death penalty.

A significant portion of the report is devoted to promising various purported benefits of eliminating the death penalty altogether, including cost savings, shorter periods of jury service, and freeing the Supreme Court to hear more cases of other types. This section makes no attempt to even mention a single argument in favor of the death penalty such as deterrence that will save lives, the community's sense of justice, or upholding the will of the People who enacted the death penalty.

PART 4.
CRUEL AND UNUSUAL PUNISHMENTS

The Eighth Amendment to the U.S. Constitution prohibits cruel and unusual punishments. Article I, § 17 of the California Constitution is similar. At their most fundamental, the cruel and unusual punishments clauses prohibit what the California Supreme Court called "barbarous" punishments like drawing and quartering, the pillory, the rack, keel hauling, and burning at the stake. *State v. McCauley & Tevis*, 15 Cal. 429, 455 (1860).

The Legislature sets the length of prison sentences. In *People v. Garcia Gomez* (2018) 30 Cal. App. 5th 493, 241 Cal. Rptr. 3d 490, the Court of Appeal noted, "The act of setting prison terms for specific crimes involves a substantive penological judgment that, as a general matter, is properly within the province of legislatures, not courts. When considering a claim that a particular sentence amounts to cruel and unusual punishment, we give substantial deference both to the Legislature's broad authority to determine the parameters for the punishments for crimes, and to the trial court's discretion in imposing specific sentences." Can a term of imprisonment be so long that it amounts to cruel and unusual punishment? The Court of Appeal addressed this issue in *People v. Meneses* (2011) 193 Cal.App.4th 1087, 123 Cal.Rptr.3d 387, where the court wrote:

> The Eighth Amendment to the United States Constitution contains a narrow proportionality principle that applies to noncapital sentences. A punishment violates the Eighth Amendment if it involves the unnecessary and wanton infliction of pain or if it is grossly out of proportion to the severity of the crime. The United States Supreme Court noted this principle is applicable only in the exceedingly rare and extreme case.
>
> A tripartite test has been established to determine whether a penalty offends the prohibition against cruel or unusual punishment. First, courts examine the nature of the offense and the offender, with particular regard to the degree of danger both present to society. Second, a comparison is made of the challenged penalty with those imposed in the same jurisdiction for more serious crimes. Third, the challenged penalty is compared with those imposed for the same offense in other jurisdictions. In undertaking this three-part analysis, we consider the totality of the circumstances surrounding the commission of the offense. A defendant has a considerable burden to show a punishment is cruel and unusual, and only in the rarest of cases could a court declare that the length of a sentence mandated by the Legislature is unconstitutionally excessive.

In *Meneses*, defendant raped his twelve-year-old cousin, causing her to become pregnant. Defendant was sentenced to 15 years to life in prison. Does this sentence violate the Eighth Amendment?

In *Graham v. Florida* (2010) 560 U.S. 48, 130 S.Ct. 2011, the Supreme Court ruled that a juvenile offender may not be sentenced to life in prison with no possibility of parole for a non-homicide crime. In *Miller v. Alabama* (2012) 567 U.S. 460, 132 S. Ct. 2455, the high Court extended this rule to juvenile murders.

INDEX

References are to Pages